CHRONOLOGY OF WORLD WAR II

Compiled by
Christopher Argyle

Exeter Books
NEW YORK

Marshall Cavendish
London & Sydney

AUTHOR'S NOTE

The Chronology of World War II is an accurate day-by-day record of events from Friday, September 1, 1939 to Sunday, September 30, 1945. The total number of entries exceeds 6,300. These are divided into eight categories – Land Campaigns; Sea War; Air War; Home Fronts; Occupied Countries; Secret War; Diplomacy; and Neutrals. Every effort has been made to check facts, statistics, ranks and designations against the latest published researches and documentation, but the reader should bear in mind that mystery and controversy still surround many famous battles and incidents. Ten key turning points in the course of the war are selected for background analysis. This complete record of events will, I hope, prove a handy and reliable work of reference for all those interested in the history of World War II.

Editor: Robin L. K. Wood
Assistant Editor: Randal Gray
Designer: Eddie Pitcher
Picture Researcher: Mark Dartford

Published and distributed by:

Marshall Cavendish Books Limited
58 Old Compton Street
London W1V 5PA

Exeter Books
A division of Bookthrift Inc.
New York, New York

IN THE UK, COMMONWEALTH AND REST OF THE WORLD, EXCEPT NORTH AMERICA

IN THE UNITED STATES OF AMERICA

ISBN: 0-85685-864-1   ISBN: 0-89673-071-9

First Printing 1980

CONTENTS

LIST OF MAPS

COUNTDOWN TO WAR
From Versailles to Poland, 1919-39

Events in Europe during the 20 years between 1919 and 1939 were overshadowed by the nightmare legacy of World War I. More than 38,000,000 people became casualties during the 'war to end all wars'. Four vast empires – Germany, Austria-Hungary, Russia and Turkey – had been utterly defeated and more or less dismembered, and ten new nations had arisen from the ruins. Even the so-called 'victorious Allies' had paid a terrible price – totalling over 5,150,000 dead and 12,830,000 wounded. Of the former, France accounted for 1,375,000 and Britain for 907,000.

During the subsequent 20 years almost every country in Europe was sooner or later convulsed by Communist or Fascist revolutions. Some countries – including Russia, Austria, Hungary, Germany and France – were stricken by largely Communist-inspired revolutionary outbursts and mutinies in their armed forces even before the end of World War I. Nowhere did they achieve any permanent success, except in Russia (then one of the most backward countries in Europe), but Communist subversion continued unabated in Germany, Hungary and Italy throughout the immediate post-war period, and Communist governments briefly held power in Munich and Budapest. During the ruthless suppression of these attempted revolutions, powerful new parties of right-wing fanatics and disaffected World War I veterans arose in Italy and Germany, with the avowed aim of overcoming the Communist menace and all other post-war social and economic problems by brute force, the suppression of all civil liberties and the persecution of Jewish shopkeepers.

'A prodigal banquet of peace and glory'

The spawning-ground of European Fascism was Italy. The Italian people had gone to war in 1915 carrying the burden of an anti-war party which had not scrupled to exploit every trick of defeatism and class strife. To keep up military morale Government leaders had promised 'a prodigal banquet of peace and glory'. But the demobilized Italian soldier, having made his sacrifice (2,197,000 casualties), felt cheated of his desserts while the stay-at-home Socialists and Communists said, 'I told you so!' The dashing of virtually all the country's cherished territorial ambitions by the Paris Peace Conference of 1919 left a very dangerous situation.

In September 1919, the flamboyant Italian poet, playwright and war hero, Gabriele D'Annunzio, led a legion of ex-servicemen into the Adriatic port of Fiume, then claimed by Yugoslavia, and expelled the French and Italian garrison. D'Annunzio established a corporative (Fascist) government in Italy's name; in November he carried out a similar coup at nearby Zara. Although the Italian Government expressed official disapproval, it waited 15 months before retaking Fiume. Meanwhile, the ecstatic Italian Press hailed D'Annunzio as 'the new Garibaldi'.

After this extraordinary precedent, another Italian ex-servicemen's leader, Benito Mussolini, found no insuperable difficulty in marching his Fascist Party on Rome in October 1922 and winning sufficient support in government, big business and military circles to have himself appointed Prime Minister by King Victor Emmanuel.

This was a tremendous boost to the morale of fledgling extreme right-wing parties all over Europe, although the attempted seizure of Munich and a planned 'March on Berlin' by four German Fascist groups (including Adolf Hitler's Nazi Party) ended ignominiously in November 1923. The increasing prosperity and international acceptance of the German Republic ruled out any renewed attempt during the mid-1920s, but the onset of the world economic Depression in 1929-30 finally gave Hitler the opportunity to connive with shifty right-wing politicians, like Brüning and von Papen, and wheedle his way into the German Chancellery. Although Fascism was held at bay during the 1920s in more developed and industrialized Europe, semi-Fascist regimes were established in Spain (1923), Poland and Lithuania (1926) and Portugal (1932). But the Depression, added to Hitler's example, combined to produce a second great explosion of European Fascism, beginning with two serious acts of political violence in 1934 and rising to a crescendo during World War II.

On the morning of July 25, 1934, a gang of Austrian Nazis, disguised as regular troops and policemen, drove up to the Vienna Chancellery of Englebert Dollfuss, forced their way into his room and shot him. They then stood and gloated for three hours as the diminutive Austrian Chancellor slowly bled to death. This Fascist rising was an ill-timed failure, partly because Mussolini threatened military intervention. But when Hitler and the Austrian Nazis made a second attempt less than four years later the Italian dictator stood by and watched.

Several months before the murder of Dollfuss, on February 6, 1934, tens of thousands of French Fascists and war veterans had attempted to storm the Chamber of Deputies in Paris, twenty of

Right: Mussolini, Europe's senior Fascist dictator, in 1927. Ten years later he was captivated by his imitator – Hitler.

KEY EVENTS OF THE INTER-WAR YEARS

1919 June 28   **Treaty of Versailles**: victorious Allies impose punitive peace terms on Germany. including loss of all colonies, cession of Alsace-Lorraine to France, West Prussia and the Corridor to Poland; Rhineland to be garrisoned by Allies for 15 years and subsequently demilitarized; massive reparations to be paid over 30 years; armaments production and development forbidden; small home defence army and navy permitted.

1920 Nov.   **League of Nations** assembles at Geneva (without USA).

1922 April 16   Rapallo Pact (Germany-Soviet Union).

Oct. 30   **March on Rome**: Mussolini appointed Prime Minister.

1923 Jan. 11   The Ruhr occupied by French and Belgians.

Nov. 8   **Munich Putsch**: Hitler captured and imprisoned.

1925 Dec. 1   Locarno Pact: Germany, France and Belgium agree to respect existing borders and refrain from use of force.

1926 Jan.   British Occupation troops leave Cologne.

Sept. 8   Germany admitted to League of Nations.

1929 Oct. 24   **'Black Thursday'** (Wall Street Crash): panic on New York Stock Exchange, leading to World Economic Depression.

1931 Sept. 18   **Mukden Incident** (Manchurian Incident) leading to Japanese occupation of Manchuria and creation of puppet 'Empire of Manchukuo'.

1933 Jan. 30   **Hitler appointed Chancellor** of National Coalition Government. Roosevelt takes office as 32nd President of USA.

Feb. 27   **Reichstag Fire**: Nazis blame Communists and suspend civil liberties.

March 27   Japan quits League of Nations.

Oct. 14   Germany quits League.

1934 Feb. 6   Fascist riots in Paris.

June 30   **'Night of the Long Knives'**: Ernst Röhm, leader of *SA* (Storm Troops), murdered by *SS* on Hitler's orders.

July 25   Chancellor Dollfuss murdered by Austrian Nazis.

Aug. 1   **Death of President Hindenburg: Hitler becomes Führer and Supreme Commander.**

1935 March 9   **Luftwaffe officially established.**

16   **Hitler reintroduces conscription.**

Sept. 15   **Nuremburg Laws**: Hitler legislates against German Jews

Oct. 3   **Italy invades Ethiopia.**

Nov. 18   Ineffective League of Nations economic sanctions against Italy.

1936 March 7   **German forces reoccupy the Rhineland.**

June 4   Popular Front Government in France.

July 16   **Spanish Civil War begins**: Germany and Italy support right-wing insurgents; USSR and International Brigades aid left-wing Government.

Oct. 25   **Rome-Berlin Axis Agreement.**

Nov. 23   German-Japanese Anti-Comintern (Communist International) Agreement.

1937 April 25   Guernica—defenceless Basque town—destroyed by German bombers.

July 7   **Marco Polo Bridge Incident**: Japanese use skirmish near Peking as pretext for invasion of China.

Nov. 6   Italy joins Anti-Comintern Pact.

Dec. 13   **Rape of Nanking**: Japanese kill 150,000 Chinese (mainly civilians) in 6 weeks.

1938 March 13   **The Anschluss**: Austria forcibly annexed to German Reich.

Sept. 29   **Munich Agreement**: Germany, Italy, France and Britain compel Czechoslavakia to cede Sudetenland to Germany.

Nov. 7   Vom Rath, German diplomat in Paris, fatally injured by Polish Jew.

Nov. 10   *Kristall Nacht* ('Night of Glass'): concerted attacks on Jewish premises throughout Germany, Austria and Sudetenland; 30,000 Jews deported to concentration camps.

1939 March 15   **Germany dismembers Czechoslovakia**; Bohemia and Moravia become German 'Protectorate'; clerical Fascist puppet regime established in Slovakia.

28   Spanish Civil War ends; Franco victorious.

31   Chamberlain announces Anglo-French guarantees to Poland.

April 26   **Britain reintroduces conscription.**

May 22   **Pact of Steel**: Germany and Italy form military/political alliance.

23   Hitler plans invasion of Poland.

Aug. 12   Anglo-French military mission begins abortive talks in Moscow.

23   **Nazi-Soviet Non-Aggression Pact** and secret agreement on partition of Eastern Europe.

24   President Roosevelt appeals to Hitler and Polish President.

25   Anglo-Polish alliance. Japan quits Anti-Comintern Pact.

31   Mussolini proposes European Conference. British Fleet mobilizes.

---

them and one policeman were killed, and more than 1,000 seriously injured. Although order was quickly restored, the shaky French Third Republic had been gravely weakened. Within a year, the right-wing French Foreign Minister, Pierre Laval, had signed a treaty with Mussolini giving tacit approval to his planned punitive expedition against Ethiopia, ostensibly to avenge the butchering of 30 Italian soldiers at Walwal on December 5, 1934. Between June and December 1935 Laval and his British opposite number, Sir Samuel Hoare, put forward four proposals for increasingly larger exchanges of territory between Italy and Ethiopia. The fourth and last was the infamous Hoare-Laval Plan of December 8, 1935. Although it caused parliamentary and public outrage in Britain and France, the policy of Appeasement soon became the main preoccupation of British and French diplomacy. This policy was doubly unfortunate since it coincided with the League of Nations' ineffective economic sanctions against Italy (November 1935).

The Italian campaign in Ethiopia lasted seven months (October 1935-May 1936). Emperor Haile Selassie appealed in vain to the League of Nations. During the Ethiopian conflict's closing stages Hitler sent his troops into the Rhineland, thereby contravening yet another clause in the Versailles Peace Treaty.

Indirect collaboration between Germany and Italy was followed later in 1936 by direct military intervention on the side of the clerical-Fascist General Franco in the Spanish Civil War. Moorish troops of Franco's grandiloquently titled 'Army of Africa' were flown across the Straits of Gibraltar in a fleet of Junkers. The insurgents, or Nationalists, also seized power in the north-west, but military revolts in Madrid, Barcelona and elsewhere were bloodily suppressed by the Communist-led workers' militia. Madrid was besieged for more than two-and-a-half years. In addition to transport aircraft Hitler provided Franco with a 6,000-man 'volunteer' air corps, the Condor Legion (equipped with deadly Messerschmitts, Heinkels and Stukas), a *Panzer* corps under Colonel von Thoma, and 30 anti-tank companies (some with the famous 88mm gun). Mussolini's contribution was even more substantial. By mid-1937 there were 50,000 Italian combat troops and 5,700 airmen in Spain; no fewer than 91 Italian warships and submarines were active, at one time or another, against the Republican (Loyalist) ships bringing large quantities of weapons from Soviet Russia. The Republican forces were also bolstered by 40,000 volunteers from 29 nations.

Fascism triumphs in Spain
Unfortunately for the Spanish Republic, Stalin stopped Soviet aid in 1938. By then he had completely lost faith in the eternally squabbling and fratricidal Republicans. The International Brigades were also withdrawn from October 1938 at the instigation of the Anglo-French inspired Non-Intervention Committee – yet another offshoot of Appeasement. Although the Republicans fought on for many months, nothing could now prevent the establishment of a new Fascist state threateningly placed between southern France and the vital British base of Gibraltar. The most important short-term strategic repercussion was the alarm produced in London, Paris, Vienna, Prague, Warsaw – and Washington – by the spectacle of Spanish towns and cities burning and crumbling under carpets of German bombs. Faced with the prospect of hundreds of thousands being killed in their own ill-defended capitals by exaggerated armadas of Heinkels and Dorniers, the British and French Premiers, Neville Chamberlain and Edouard Daladier, felt obliged to permit the Nazi occupation of Austria and the heavily-fortified German-speaking border areas of Czechoslovakia, or Sudetenland. Although the latter's hand-over at Munich in September 1938 appeared to have narrowly averted a great European war, the danger was more apparent than real. Despite their sabre-rattling and the mobilization of the British Fleet, neither Chamberlain nor Daladier had either the will or the means to go to war.

'Rape of Czechoslovakia'
In a now notorious broadcast on September 28, 1938, Chamberlain lamented: 'How horrible, fantastic, incredible it is that we should be digging trenches and trying on gas masks here because of a quarrel in a faraway country between people of whom we know nothing.' Although this so-called 'quarrel' was apparently settled two days later by the Munich Agreement the result was not 'peace in our time' – as predicted by Chamberlain – but merely a five-and-a-half month breathing-space. Filled with contempt and scorn at the gullibility of the 'nice old man' to whom he had merely given his 'autograph' at Munich, Hitler stepped up subversion and propaganda against Czechoslovakia and brazenly threatened to bomb Prague into ruins if the timid President Hacha did not accede to his demands. On March 15, 1939, Hacha signed a declaration in Berlin that 'to achieve ultimate pacification, he confidently placed the fate of the Czech people and country in the hands of the Führer of the German Reich.'
The 'Rape of Czechoslovakia' on March 15, 1939 did compel the British and French Governments to abandon Appeasement forthwith. Within two days, Chamberlain issued a public condemnation. This was followed, at the end of the same month, by an Anglo-French guarantee of assistance to Poland – evidently Hitler's next victim – 'in the event of any action which clearly threatened Polish independence, and which the Polish Government accordingly considered it vital to resist with their national forces . . . to lend the Polish Government all the support in their power'.
On April 26, in response to Mussolini's seizure of the little kingdom of Albania, Britain reintroduced conscription, as revolutionary a step in peacetime military policy as the guarantee to Poland had been in her foreign policy. Germany and Italy widened their Axis into a formal military alliance. Britain and France concluded pacts with Turkey, Greece and Rumania. Hitler, meanwhile, was busy plotting the annexation of the Polish Corridor, Danzig and the destruction of the Polish state. The Wehrmacht was publicly ordered to be ready for all eventualities by August 25.
One great question still remained. What parts were Soviet Russia and the USA going to play in the impending conflict? There was little doubt about the latter in the short term. Restrained by three self-imposed Neutrality acts, a still isolationist America was being wooed by her President to take more interest in Europe rather than the two-year-old Sino-Japanese War. There was more discussion of the policy to be followed by the Soviet Union. The so-called 'Peace Front' which Britain and France had been constructing and which now included Poland, Turkey, Greece and Rumania, could never be an effective deterrent without the Soviet Union. British and Russian diplomats engaged in continual, cordial but fruitless conferences. The Soviet Press ceased to denounce Chamberlain for his alleged betrayal of Czechslovakia and the London *Times* was unusually silent on the shortcomings of Soviet policy. Early in June William Strang, a high official at the Foreign Office and an expert in Russian affairs, went as special emissary to Moscow to initiate discussions for an Anglo-Soviet pact.

Stalin plays a double game
But for those who had eyes to see, Stalin was playing a double game. During a major speech on April 28, 1939, denouncing the German-Polish Pact of 1934 and the Anglo-German Naval Agreement of 1935, Hitler had omitted all the usual references to 'Jewish Bolshevism' and the 'sub-human monsters' inhabiting the Kremlin. On May 3, the diplomatic Anglophile Litvinov was suddenly replaced as Commissar for Foreign Affairs by the grim, provincial Molotov. Some days later a new Soviet ambassador arrived in Berlin to an exceptionally cordial reception. British and French staff officers, sent to Moscow early in August to open talks with Marshal Voroshilov, soon found themselves working against mysterious delays and obstructions. Voroshilov demanded agreement to Soviet military control of the Baltic States and there were interminable arguments over suitable military counter-measures against 'indirect aggression'. The Baltic States were averse to compromising their neutrality and preferred to negotiate separate non-aggression pacts with Germany. Poland still clung to her traditional Russophobia.
Then on August 19, 1939, Stalin announced to the Politburo his firm intention to conclude a pact with Germany. On August 21, the imminent conclusion of a Soviet-German Pact was announced in Berlin to an astonished world. Throughout the day, the British and French officers in Moscow attempted to contact Voroshilov. But when the head of the French Military Mission finally spoke to the Soviet marshal he was treated to an embarrassing lecture: 'The question of military collaboration with France has been in the air for several years, but has never been settled. Last year, when Czechoslovakia was perishing, we waited for a signal from France, but none was given. Our troops were ready . . . The French and English Governments have now dragged out the political discussions too long.' The next day, Hitler's arrogant and detestable Foreign Minister, von Ribbentrop, arrived in Moscow for the ceremonial signing of the Nazi-Soviet Non-Aggression Pact.

'Such an unnatural act'
Although at first sight the Pact appeared to be (in Churchill's words) ' such an unnatural act', it had a certain Machiavellian logic. Stalin was determined to stay out of the impending European war and leave the fighting to Germany and the democracies. This was particularly vital since the Soviet leader had recently emasculated the Red Army by purging and liquidating thousands of senior officers. Stalin believed that the democracies had always wanted to embroil him with Germany, and that they hoped to emerge dominant and unscathed from a Nazi-Soviet war of annihilation. The democracies just as firmly believed Stalin to be playing a similar game with Germany and themselves. Hitler, for his part, was not

altogether convinced by the Anglo-French guarantee to Poland, and toyed with the idea of staging another 'Munich'. But since he was determined to subjugate Poland and risk the larger war in the West, he had first to secure Stalin's neutrality – or better still, his benevolence and complicity – and thereby dispel his greatest fear – a war on two fronts. The democracies, knowing full well that another surrender to Germany would result in a final and irredeemable loss of their power and prestige, were resolved at all costs to support Poland. But they had little to offer Stalin except monotonous reassertions of the doctrine of collective security, in which he no longer had any faith, and were morally precluded from trafficking in the independence of small states in Eastern Europe.

Poland's fate is sealed
The published text of the Nazi-Soviet Pact was short and simple. The contracting parties undertook to refrain from any act of force against each other; not to support any third Power that made either of them 'an object of warlike action'; to consult on questions of common interest; and to settle any future disputes 'by the friendly exchange of views'. The Pact contained no 'escape clause' and was to be valid for ten years. In a secret codicil Germany gave the USSR carte blanche in Finland, Estonia and Latvia, but insisted that Lithuania should be in her sphere of influence. Poland was to be partitioned, Germany taking the lion's share, including Danzig, the Polish Corridor, Upper Silesia, Cracow and Warsaw, while the USSR was to reoccupy western White Russia (Byelorussia) and the western Ukraine, both having been Russian until 1920.

All this was scarcely credible to Western minds. Even the German and Russian peoples were stunned and the Japanese Government temporarily broke off negotiations for a military alliance with Germany. On August 25, Britain confirmed her earlier guarantee to Poland in a formal Anglo-Polish Alliance. Appeals to Hitler from Roosevelt and Chamberlain, a papal peace broadcast and offers of mediation from Queen Wilhelmina of the Netherlands and King Leopold III of Belgium were followed by an eleventh-hour intervention from Mussolini. The Duce, hoping to repeat his success as the 'honest broker of Munich', proposed that a five-Power conference should meet on September 5 to 'examine the clauses in the Treaty of Versailles which are at the root of the [Polish-German] trouble'. Ironically, what actually delayed the German invasion of Poland by a matter of days was Hitler's last-minute discovery that Mussolini was not going to honour his military alliance with Germany.

On August 29, Hitler demanded a Polish emissary with full powers to negotiate the cession of Danzig and the Corridor. This had an unmistakable echo of previous demands to Austria and Czechoslovakia, and the Polish Government refused. Further German proposals, in the form of an ultimatum, were prepared, but they never reached – and were never intended to reach – the Polish Government in time.

At dawn on Friday, September 1, 1939, German forces attacked Poland by land, sea and air. No declaration of war had been made, but World War II had begun.

Below: *Chamberlain waves his infamous scrap of paper on return from Munich. 'Peace in Our Time' lasted under a year.*

1939

FRIDAY, SEPTEMBER 1

GERMAN INVASION OF POLAND (code name, *Weiss:* 'White') 48 divs. (6 *Panzer*) and 1,600 aircraft invade without formal declaration of war on 3 fronts – E. Germany, E. Prussia and Slovakia. *Luftwaffe* tactical raids on Polish airfields, communications and troop concentrations; attempt to knock out Polish Air Force fails.

Air War – Strategic bombing raids on Warsaw by He 111s.

Sea War – German Navy blockades the Baltic. Training ship (old battleship), *Schleswig-Holstein,* bombards small Polish garrison at Westerplatte, near Danzig.

Diplomacy – Poland appeals for British and French intervention under terms of Mutual Assistance Treaties. Britain and France demand the withdrawal of German forces from Poland.

US Pres. Roosevelt calls for ban on indiscriminate bombing of civilians and undefended towns.

Italy dissociates herself from the conflict.

Home Front: Britain – General mobilization proclaimed (the Fleet mobilized on Aug. 31). Evacuation of 3 million women, children and invalids from cities begins (completed Sept. 3). ARP (Air Raid Precautions) introduced and the 'blackout' enforced from sunset. British Railways taken under Govt. control.

Home Front: France – General mobilization and 'state of siege' (martial law) proclaimed.

Home Front: Germany – Hitler speaks in the Reichstag, Berlin: justifies Russo-German Pact (Aug. 23), invasion of Poland, and the seizure of Danzig and the Polish Corridor; threatens the use of 'secret weapons'; names Göring and Hess as his successors.

Polish Forces

2,500,000 men in 40 divs. – only 17 divs. on frontier; 400 planes; 4 destroyers, 5 subs.

German Forces (total)

3,706,104 men (103 divs.); 3,195 tanks, over 7,000 guns; 4,093 planes inc. 1,176 bombers, 1,179 fighters, 335 *Stukas;* 2 old battleships, 2 battlecruisers, 3 pocket battleships, 8 cruisers, 22 destroyers, 56 U-boats.

Occupied Czechoslovakia – Gestapo arrest thousands of prominent Czechs and deport them to concentration camps.

Neutrals: USA – Gen. Marshall appointed US Army Chief of Staff.

SATURDAY, SEPTEMBER 2

Poland – German *Blitzkrieg* (lightning war) continues relentlessly. 18 Polish bombers attack German armour in Radom-Piotrków area, SW. of Warsaw.

Air War – *Luftwaffe* enjoys overwhelming air superiority. 6 raids on Warsaw.

RAF Advanced Air Striking Force flies to France.

Diplomacy – Hitler rejects Mussolini's offer (made Aug. 31) to mediate in German-Polish dispute and the proposed 5-power conference.

Home Front: Britain – National Service Act passed: conscription for men 19-41.

Neutrals – General mobilization in Switzerland. Scandinavian states proclaim absolute neutrality.

SUNDAY, SEPTEMBER 3

Poland – *Panzers* cross R. Warta, SW. Poland. 1st and 4th *Pz* Divs. attacked repeatedly by Polish bombers in Radom-Piotrków area. Germans capture city of Czestochowa. The Polish Corridor cut in two.

Pro-British demonstrations in Warsaw.

Diplomacy – Germany rejects Anglo-French ultimatum of Sept. 1. Final British and French Notes to Germany. Time limit set for agreement on withdrawal of German forces from Poland expires. **BRITAIN AND FRANCE DECLARE WAR ON GERMANY** at 11 a.m. and 5 p.m. respectively. **WAR DECLARED BY AUSTRALIA, NEW ZEALAND, AND BRITISH INDIA.**

Home Front: Britain – P.M. Chamberlain broadcasts to nation at 11.15 a.m.: '*You can imagine what a bitter blow it is to me that all my long struggle to win peace has failed.*' King George VI broadcasts to the peoples of the Empire. War Cabinet formed: Churchill appointed First Lord of the Admiralty. Ministry of Economic Warfare (blockade) established. First House of Commons sitting on a Sunday since 1820. First air-raid warning in London – but false alarm.

Air War – *Stukas* sink destroyer *Wicher* at Hela.

Lone RAF Blenheim aircraft photographs German Fleet in Wilhelmshaven. First of series of propaganda leaflet raids on Germany (night Sept. 3-4).

Sea War – British naval blockade of Germany announced.

First wave of U-boats begin N. Atlantic operations (27 merchant ships sunk to Oct. 3). British liner SS *Athenia* torpedoed by German submarine, *U-30,* NW. of Ireland; 112 passengers dead (inc. 28 Americans).

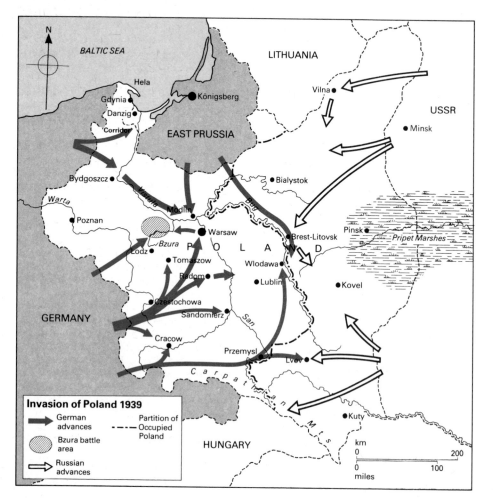

Invasion of Poland 1939

- ➤ German advances
- ⬭ Bzura battle area
- ⇨ Russian advances
- --- Partition of Occupied Poland

Neutrals – Belgium reaffirms her neutrality. King Leopold III assumes command of Belgium Army.

British Forces

897,000 men (26 divs.); 1,146 tanks, about 2,600 guns; 15 capital ships, 6 carriers, 61 cruisers, 181 destroyers, 59 subs; 1,911 planes inc. 871 bombers, 747 fighters.

French Forces

5,000,000 men (99 divs.); 2,600 tanks, about 11,000 guns; 7 capital ships, 1 carrier, 19 cruisers, 70 destroyers, 75 subs; 2,754 planes inc. 1,114 fighters, 1,002 bombers.

Above: *A London newspaper seller has the grim news of Sept. 3.*

MONDAY, SEPTEMBER 4

Poland – Me 109s destroy 11 Polish fighters and 3 bombers in battle over Lodz.

Air War – 29 RAF Blenheims and Wellingtons (7 lost) make daylight raids on German Fleet at Wilhelmshaven and Brunsbüttel (Kiel Canal). Cruiser *Emden* damaged by wreckage of shot-down Blenheim. Pocket battleship *Admiral Scheer* hit by dud bomb.

Sea War – Hitler forbids attacks on Allied passenger ships. Nazi propaganda minister Goebbels accuses Churchill of complicity in sinking of *Athenia* to create anti-German feeling in USA.
First troops of BEF (British Expeditionary Force) land from destroyers at Cherbourg.

Western Front – Skirmishing in 'No-man's Land' between Maginot Line and Siegfried Line.

Home Front: Britain – Chamberlain broadcasts to Germany, in German, explaining Britain's stand and denouncing Nazi régime.

Diplomacy – Japan not to intervene in European War.

TUESDAY, SEPTEMBER 5

Poland – Germans break through W. frontier cordon of Polish armies and cross R. Vistula. Polish High Command orders general retreat behind Vistula. Germans take Bydgoszcz at S. end of the Corridor. Bombers destroy town of Sulejow, SW. of Warsaw.

Diplomacy – Official announcement of US neutrality.

Neutrals: South Africa – Gen. Smuts replaces pro-German P.M. Hertzog.

Home Front: Britain – Ministry of Information set up.

WEDNESDAY, SEPTEMBER 6

Poland – *Panzers* take Tomaszow and Kielce, SW. of Warsaw – outflanking 2 Polish armies. Germans announce capture of Cracow. Hitler visits Gen. Guderian's XIX *Pz* Corps on NE. front.
Polish Government leaves Warsaw for Lublin.

Air War – 2 RAF Spitfires shoot down 2 Hurricanes in error ('Battle of Barking Creek').

Sea War – RN Northern Patrol formed (8 cruisers). First British E. Coast convoy sails. Germany's largest liner, *Bremen* (52,000 t) arrives at Murmansk, N. Russia, from New York.

Diplomacy – SOUTH AFRICA DECLARES WAR ON GERMANY. Spain declares her neutrality.

Home Front: France – 72-hour working week introduced in munitions industry.

THURSDAY, SEPTEMBER 7

Poland – Surrender of Westerplatte, besieged since Sept. 1. *Schleswig-Holstein* begins daily bombardment of Hela, Polish naval base.

Western Front – French Saar 'offensive' (begins night Sept. 7-8). 11 divs. advance 8 km into German territory by Sept. 12 on 32 km front, SW. and SE. of Saarbrücken, against negligible opposition.
Gen. Viscount Gort, V.C., to command BEF.

Home Front: Britain – 41 emergency bills passed through Parliament since Sept. 1.

FRIDAY, SEPTEMBER 8

Poland – Battle of Warsaw begins: 4th *Pz* Div. reaches outskirts of city, having advanced 225 km in 7 days. Garrison commander, Gen. Czuma, broadcasts defiant Order of the Day: *'We shall fight to the last ditch!'* 100,000 civilians dig trenches in city outskirts.

Air War – Situation of Polish Air Force becomes desperate. On Western Front, 5 Curtiss Hawk fighters of *l'Armée de l'Air* (French Air Force) engage 5 Me 109s (2 shot down).

Home Front: Britain – Govt. plans for 3-year war.

SATURDAY, SEPTEMBER 9

Poland – BATTLE OF THE BZURA: major Polish counter-attack across R. Bzura, W. of Warsaw, develops into largest battle in the campaign (ends Sept. 15).
4th *Pz* Div. attempts to storm Warsaw outer defences but loses 60 tanks.
Polish CinC, Marshal Smigly-Rydz, sends desperate appeal to Gen. Gamelin, French CinC, for decisive action on W. Front.

Sea War – First BEF troop convoy crosses English Channel (night).

Home Front: France – Identity Cards made obligatory.

Home Front: Germany – Göring broadcasts: scoffs at RAF leaflet raids and calls for Anglo-German peace agreement.

SUNDAY, SEPTEMBER 10

Poland – Polish general retreat to 'strong defensive positions' in SE. Poland ordered. 15 air raids on Warsaw. Germans broadcast false news bulletin, announcing the 'fall' of the capital, on same wavelength as Radio Warsaw.

Diplomacy – CANADA DECLARES WAR ON GERMANY.

Sea War – British submarine *Triton* torpedoes sister sub. *Oxley* by mistake in North Sea (only 2 survivors).

MONDAY, SEPTEMBER 11

Poland – Germans cross R. San, SE. Poland.

Diplomacy – Churchill (as 'A Naval Person') begins correspondence with Roosevelt.

Home Front: Britain – 1,330,928 people unemployed (99,236 more than in Aug.).

TUESDAY, SEPTEMBER 12

Poland – Germans rush reinforcements (inc. *Pz* units) from Warsaw front to Bzura battle area (night 12-13). Poles begin fighting withdrawal from Bzura.

Sea War: Atlantic – US Navy begins regular neutrality patrols along entire length of E. Seaboard and in Caribbean.

Diplomacy – First meeting of Allied Supreme War Council (British and French Premiers, with their top political and military advisers) takes place at Abbéville; Gen. Gamelin reveals plans to call off Saar 'Offensive'.

WEDNESDAY, SEPTEMBER 13

Poland – German infantry cross R. Vistula, S. of Warsaw. German High

GUDERIAN, Heinz Wilhelm (1888-1954)
German: *Colonel-General*

Creator of the *Panzer* divisions. Leading advocate of armoured warfare in *Wehrmacht* and, like Rommel, a personal favourite of Hitler. Led by example.

Born at Kulm, E. Germany, June 17, 1888. Attended cadet schools in Karlsruhe and Berlin, 1901-7. Commanded a wireless station on the Western Front, 1914-15. Captain, 1915. Signals officer on Western Front, 1916-17. General Staff Officer, 1917-18, on Western and Italian fronts. On staff of 'Iron Division', fighting Bolsheviks in Latvia, 1919. Held various staff and instructional posts with Motorized Troops Dept. of Defence Ministry, 1922-33. Promoted chief of staff to Armoured Troops

Command, 1934. Commander of 2nd *Panzer* Division, 1935. Promoted Maj-Gen., 1936. Commander of 16th Army Corps, Feb. 1938. Played leading role in bloodless occupation of Austria (March 1938) and the Sudetenland (Oct. 1938).

Commanded 19th *Panzer* Corps Aug. 1939-May 1940. Conspicuous successes in E. Poland, Sept. 1939. Achieved decisive armoured breakthrough against French 2nd Army at Sedan, on R. Meuse, May 1940. Handled and co-ordinated his forces – tanks, motorized inf., artillery and dive-bombers – with textbook precision. Led 'Panzer' Group Guderian' in battle of France, June 1940. Promoted Col-Gen., July 1940.

Commanded *Panzer* Grp. 2 and 2nd *Panzer* Army in W. Russia, the Ukraine and battle of Moscow, June-Dec. 1941. Relieved of duties by Hitler Dec. 1941. Recalled from the reserve March 1943 and appointed Inspector-Gen. of Armoured Troops, with sweeping powers. Hitler ignored his advice and squandered untried Tiger and Panther tanks at Kursk, July 1943.

Appointed Chief of Army Gen. Staff, July 21, 1944. Remonstrated in vain with Hitler before Ardennes offensive and warned of impending catastrophe on Russian Front (Dec. 1944). Dismissed, March 28, 1945. Captured by Americans in Austria, May 1945. Published 'Panzer Leader' (1952).

officers and men from defeated Polish 'Pomorze' and 'Poznan' Armies surrender. Germans surround Lvov, E. Poland.
Home Front: Germany – Hitler speaks at Danzig: defends Russo-German Pact.
Home Front: Britain – First broadcast of BBC radio comedy show *ITMA* (It's That Man Again), starring Tommy Handley.

WEDNESDAY, SEPTEMBER 20

Air War – RAF's first clash with *Luftwaffe*: Me 109s attack 3 Battle recce-bombers over Siegfried Line; 1 Me and 2 Battles shot down.
Home Front: Germany – US newspapers publish details of private fortunes (£7 M.) deposited by Nazi leaders in foreign banks.

THURSDAY, SEPTEMBER 21

Poland – Artillery bombardment of key points in Warsaw greatly intensified.
Neutrals: Rumania – P.M. Calinescu shot dead by fascists of the 'Iron Guard'. Assassins captured and publicly executed.
Luxemburg – Radio Luxemburg closes down.
Diplomacy – British Govt. 'Blue Book' published: pre-war diplomatic documents.
Occupied Poland – 'The Heydrich Plan': 600,000 Jews from Danzig and W. Poland to be transported to central Poland and concentrated in urban ghettoes.

FRIDAY, SEPTEMBER 22

Poland – Russo-German 'victory parade' at Brest-Litovsk. Col-Gen. von Fritsch, former German Army C in C and leading anti-Nazi, killed by sniper outside Warsaw.
Home Front: Britain – Petrol rationed.
Diplomacy – Second meeting of Allied Supreme War Council, in Sussex.

SATURDAY, SEPTEMBER 23

Poland – Germans announce capture of Lvov.
Diplomacy – Mussolini declares that the 'liquidation' of Poland presents opportunity for European peace settlement.
Home Front: Britain – Death of Austrian psychoanalyst Sigmund Freud (aged 83).
Home Front: Germany – Jews forbidden radio sets.

SUNDAY, SEPTEMBER 24

Poland – Germans isolate Modlin Fortress, N. of Warsaw. Russians enter Galician oilfields.

MONDAY, SEPTEMBER 25

Poland – Second German ultimatum to Warsaw Garrison. Mass air attack on the city: 400 bombers and *Stukas* make repeated sorties, starting huge fires.
Sea War: Atlantic – Debut of Ju 88 dive-

Command announces its intention to crush guerilla operations and sabotage by Polish civil population with indiscriminate bombing and shelling of towns. Heavy air raids on Warsaw.
Sea War – French cruiser *La Tour d'Auvergne* sunk by accidental explosion at Casablanca.
Home Front: France – War Cabinet formed; new ministries of Armaments and Blockade.

THURSDAY, SEPTEMBER 14

Poland – Fall of Gdynia (Poland's only seaport) and Brest-Litovsk, E. Poland (but Brest-Litovsk Citadel holds out).
Sea War: Atlantic – U-39 attacks RN carrier *Ark Royal* NW. of Ireland but is depth-charged by 3 destroyers and crew of 43 captured.

FRIDAY, SEPTEMBER 15

Poland – Germans surround Warsaw and occupy Galician oilfields (SE. Poland).
Sea War: Atlantic – First British trans-Atlantic convoy sails from Kingston, Jamaica.
Diplomacy – Rumanian Govt. to grant asylum to Polish civilian refugees; military personnel to be disarmed and interned.
Home Front: Germany – Germans broadcast interviews with British and NZ airmen captured during Wilhelmshaven raid (Sept.4).

SATURDAY, SEPTEMBER 16

Poland – German ultimatum to Warsaw Garrison and civil population rejected. Polish AF bombers make final sorties.

Diplomacy – USSR informs Poland that the Red Army will enter E. Poland on Sept. 17 'to protect the Ukrainian and White Russian minorities'.
Sea War: Atlantic – First U-boat attack on N. Atlantic convoy; *U-31* sinks SS *Aviemore*. 3 major escorted convoys leave Halifax (Nova Scotia) for Britain, Sept. 16, 17 and 23.
Neutrals – Armistice ends 'Nomonhan Incident' – protracted fighting between Japan and USSR on borders of Manchukuo (Manchuria) and Mongolia.

SUNDAY, SEPTEMBER 17

Poland – **SOVIET INVASION OF POLAND** against negligible defences. German Army Groups North and South link up at Wlodawa, on R. Bug, E. Poland. Brest-Litovsk Citadel captured.
Polish Government crosses into Rumania from border town of Kuty – its fifth, and last, temporary seat in the Polish provinces. All surviving Polish air crews fly to Rumania.
Sea War – **CARRIER HMS COURAGEOUS SUNK** by *U-29* W. of Ireland (514 of 1200 crew dead); British Fleet carriers withdrawn from anti-U-boat operations.

MONDAY, SEPTEMBER 18

Poland – Russian Forces now 100 km inside Poland; virtually no resistance.
Sea War: Atlantic – SS *Kensington Court* shelled and sunk by U-boat; 2 RAF Sunderland flying boats rescue 34 men.

TUESDAY, SEPTEMBER 19

Poland – Bzura Battle ends: 100,000

bomber in attack on carrier HMS *Ark Royal* and battlecruiser *Hood* (no damage). Goebbels claims destruction of the carrier. Anti-U-boat minefield laid across Straits of Dover (completed Oct. 23).
Home Front: Germany – Bread and flour rationed. Distribution of food ration cards completed.

TUESDAY, SEPTEMBER 26

Poland – Massive indiscriminate artillery bombardment of Warsaw, followed by major German infantry assault; city centre in flames. Poles recapture Mokotow Airport and 6 hastily rebuilt aircraft fly out (night, 26-27).
Home Front: France – Communist Party declared illegal.

WEDNESDAY, SEPTEMBER 27

Poland – Germans overrun outer defences of Warsaw; Garrison Commander offers to surrender (talks held in bus on city outskirts).
Air War – RAF announce total of 18 M. leaflets dropped over Germany since night of Sept. 3-4.
Western Front – Hitler tells astonished generals that he intends to attack France on Nov. 12.
Home Front: Britain – First War Budget: big increase in standard rate of income tax from 5s 6d to 7s 6d (37½p) in £1.

THURSDAY, SEPTEMBER 28

Poland – Armistice between Warsaw Garrison and German besiegers from noon.

FRIDAY, SEPTEMBER 29

Diplomacy – Russo-German 'Treaty of Frontier Regulation and Friendship' signed, partitioning Poland and defining spheres of influence. Joint Declaration issued calling for a peaceful settlement of the conflict between Germany and Britain. Soviet-Estonian Mutual Assistance Pact: Soviet forces to be based in Estonia.
Home Front: Britain – National Register taken.

SATURDAY, SEPTEMBER 30

Diplomacy – Polish Government-in-Exile and 'Cabinet of National Unity' formed in Paris under Raczkiewicz (Pres.) and Gen. Sikorski (P.M. and Minister of War).
Western Front – French forces begin stealthy retreat (night Sept. 30-Oct. 1) from German territory occupied during Saar 'Offensive' (withdrawal completed Oct. 4).
Air War – 15 Me 109s destroy flight of 5 RAF Battles over the Saar.
Sea War: Atlantic – 'Pocket-battleship' *Admiral Graf Spee* sinks SS *Clement* in S. Atlantic, capturing the crew.

SUNDAY, OCTOBER 1

Poland – German troops enter Warsaw and begin disarming the Garrison (100,000 officers and men). Surrender of Hela, last Polish stronghold.

MONDAY, OCTOBER 2

Diplomacy – Pan-American Security Zone established: USA and Latin American States forbid naval and air operations in sea areas up to 1,000 km from their coasts.
Home Front: Britain – Special tribunals begin to deal with 50,000 enemy aliens registered in London area.
Occupied Czechoslovakia – Czech National Army to be formed in France. (Franco-Czech agreement signed.)

TUESDAY, OCTOBER 3

Western Front – French withdrawal from advanced positions in German territory (Warndt Forest and Saarbrücken Salient) completed.

WEDNESDAY, OCTOBER 4

Sea War: Atlantic – *U-35* lands 28-man crew of torpedoed Greek SS *Diamantis* on Kerry coast, SW. Ireland.
Occupied Poland – Nikita Khrushchev (secretary of Ukrainian Communist Party) announces the 'Communisation' of E. Poland.

THURSDAY, OCTOBER 5

Poland – Germans 'mopping up' Polish troops still at large between R. Vistula and R. Bug. Hitler flies to Warsaw and reviews victory parade.
Sea War – 8 groups of British and French warships hunt *Admiral Graf Spee* in Atlantic and Indian Oceans. Pocket-battleship, *Deutschland*, sinks SS *Stonegate* in N. Atlantic.

Below: *The Ju 87 dive-bomber, or* Stuka, *flew 6,000 sorties over Poland.*

Diplomacy – Soviet-Latvian Mutual Assistance Pact: Soviet forces to be based in Latvia.
Home Front: France – Chamber of Deputies prorogued and 26 Communist deputies arrested.

Polish Campaign Losses
German: 10,572 dead, 30,322 wounded; 217 tanks; 285 planes. Soviet: 734 dead. Polish c. 50,000 dead, 750,000 PoWs (to Germany), 217,000 (to USSR), 105,000 escaped abroad; 333 planes.

FRIDAY, OCTOBER 6

Diplomacy – Hitler's 'Peace Plan' speech to the Reichstag: Hitler claims that the total collapse and partition of Poland has removed the necessity for war between Britain, France and Germany; Germany has no territorial claims against France; he calls for a peace conference, free trade, restoration of German colonies and arms limitation.
Poland – Last remnants of Polish Army (8,000 men) surrender to Germans at Kock, SE. of Warsaw.

SATURDAY, OCTOBER 7

Sea War – Transport of BEF to France completed – entirely without loss – under protection of British and French naval forces (161,000 troops, 24,000 vehicles and tanks and 140,000 t of supplies).

SUNDAY, OCTOBER 8

Diplomacy – Evacuation of the Baltic Germans: 50,000 German-speaking citizens of Latvia are to be 'repatriated' to the Reich (first group leaves by sea Oct. 14); similar repatriation scheme subsequently announced for Estonia (13,000 Germans) and completed Nov. 21. Finland accepts Soviet invitation to send delegation to Moscow to discuss border disputes (talks held Oct. 12-14 and Oct. 28-Nov. 8).

MONDAY, OCTOBER 9

Western Front – Hitler's 'Directive No. 6': plans and preparations to be made for an early offensive against Holland, Belgium and France. Army High Command draws up *Fall Gelb* ('Yellow Plan') (see Nov. 7, 1939 and Feb. 24, 1940).
Sea War: Atlantic – 'City of Flint' Affair: *Deutschland* captures US freighter, *City of Flint*, in N. Atlantic. Ship finally arrives back at Baltimore, Jan. 27, 1940.
China: Sino-Japanese War – Chinese victory at Changsha.

TUESDAY, OCTOBER 10

Diplomacy – Soviet-Lithuanian Mutual Assistance Pact: Soviet Forces to be based

in Lithuania; Vilna (in Soviet Zone of Poland) to be transferred to Lithuania.
Neutrals: Finland – 'Black-out' in Helsinki; voluntary evacuation of civilians begins.

WEDNESDAY, OCTOBER 11

Home Front: Britain – Clackmannan and E. Stirling by-election: Woodburn (Labour), 15,645 votes; Stewart (Pacifist), 1,060.

THURSDAY, OCTOBER 12

Western Front – BEF now fully deployed along Franco-Belgian border, between Maulde and Halluin.

FRIDAY, OCTOBER 13

Western Front – Skirmishes E. of R. Moselle. French demolish 3 Rhine bridges.

SATURDAY, OCTOBER 14

Sea War – BATTLESHIP *ROYAL OAK* SUNK in 'impregnable' anchorage of Scapa Flow, Orkney Is, by *U-47*; (833 dead). British Home Fleet subsequently retires to Loch Ewe (W. Scotland). Polish submarine *Orzel* reaches British waters after amazing escape from Baltic.
Western Front – Gen. Gamelin, French CinC, issues melodramatic Order of the Day predicting a massive German offensive 'at any moment'.
Neutrals: Finland – Military mobilization.
Secret War – Escaped Polish Intelligence team resume code-breaking operations with their highly secret replicas of the German 'Enigma' machine in France. (The Poles had supplied 1 replica each to Britain and France, July 25.)

SUNDAY, OCTOBER 15

Neutrals: Finland – Compulsory National Service introduced.

MONDAY, OCTOBER 16

Air War – 9 new Ju 88 dive-bombers in attack on warships at Rosyth, Firth of Forth. Unexploded bomb penetrates cruiser *Southampton*.
Sea War: Atlantic – French destroyer *Cyclone* sinks *U-45* in Bay of Biscay.
Western Front – Germans counter-attack in Saar region and within 48 hours expel remaining French 'covering forces'; few casualties on either side.
Poland – German High Command announces 'official' end to Polish Campaign; but some Polish regulars still hold out in remote areas.

TUESDAY, OCTOBER 17

Air War – Raid on Scapa Flow: Ju 88s cripple training battleship, HMS *Iron Duke* (W.W.I Fleet flagship).
Sea War – German destroyers lay mines by night off Humber estuary, North Sea.
Western Front – German High Command reports 'absolute quiet' on Rhine Front (1 German soldier killed by falling shrapnel from German flak!).

WEDNESDAY, OCTOBER 18

Diplomacy – Four-Power Conference at Stockholm, attended by Kings of Denmark, Norway, Sweden and President of Finland opens (ends Oct. 19).

THURSDAY, OCTOBER 19

Diplomacy – Anglo-French-Turkish Treaty of Mutual Assistance signed.

FRIDAY, OCTOBER 20

Sea War – Germany warns that neutral merchant ships joining Allied convoys will be sunk without warning.

SATURDAY, OCTOBER 21

Sea War: Atlantic – French *Force de raide* (including world's fastest destroyers) escorts large Atlantic convoy (until Oct. 30) and intercepts German SS *Sahte Fe*. RAF fighters shoot down 4 out of 9 He 115 seaplanes attacking convoy off the Humber.

SUNDAY, OCTOBER 22

Occupied Poland – 'Elections' held in Russian-held W. Ukraine and W. White Russia (Russian-occupied Poland).
Home Front: India – Congress Party declines to support the British war effort and condemns British 'imperialism'.

MONDAY, OCTOBER 23

Sea War: Atlantic – British Home Fleet escorts iron ore convoy from Narvik, Norway (arrives Oct. 31).

TUESDAY, OCTOBER 24

Diplomacy – Russo-German trade agreement: USSR to supply 1 M. tonnes of grain and fodder.
Occupied Poland – Arrival in Paris of large hoard of gold smuggled from Warsaw via Rumania and Syria.

WEDNESDAY, OCTOBER 25

Sea War – 3 U-boats despatched to Mediterranean; only *U-26* arrives and has no success.

THURSDAY, OCTOBER 26

Diplomacy – Soviet government denies Britain's right to stop Soviet merchant ships bound for Germany.

FRIDAY, OCTOBER 27

Neutrals – King Leopold in broadcast to USA declares Belgium's determination to defend its neutrality.

SATURDAY, OCTOBER 28

Diplomacy – At talks in Moscow, Russians demand strategic Finnish territory in Karelian Isthmus, Hangö naval base and ice-free port of Petsamo (Arctic) in exchange for worthless Russian territory along E. borders. Finns reject proposals (Nov. 8) and return home (Nov. 13).
Occupied Czechoslovakia – Independence Day: German police fire on demonstrators in Prague (16 casualties).

SUNDAY, OCTOBER 29

Sea War – German warships and U-boats given permission to attack passenger ships in convoys.

MONDAY, OCTOBER 30

Sea War: Atlantic – *U-56* hits battleship HMS *Nelson* W. of Orkneys but torpedoes fail to explode.

TUESDAY, OCTOBER 31

Diplomacy – Molotov, Russian P.M. and Foreign Minister, elucidates Soviet foreign policy: friendship with Germany, support for German 'peace' efforts and economic collaboration.

WEDNESDAY, NOVEMBER 1

Occupied Poland – W. Poland, from the 'Corridor', S. to Silesia, incorporated in the *Reich*. 2 new provinces *(Reichsgaue)* formed. Western Ukraine (Russian-occupied Poland) incorporated in the Ukrainian Soviet Socialist Republic.
Home Front: Germany – He 178 experimental jet aircraft displayed to senior *Luftwaffe* officers.
Neutrals: Holland – 'State of siege' proclaimed in most areas.

THURSDAY, NOVEMBER 2

Occupied Poland – Western White Russia (Russian-occupied Poland) incorporated in Byelorussian SSR.

FRIDAY, NOVEMBER 3

Diplomacy – Embargo on export of arms lifted by US Senate. Neutrality Bill amended – Britain and France now able to obtain supplies on 'cash and carry' basis. US ships forbidden to enter European 'combat zone'.

SATURDAY, NOVEMBER 4

Secret War – 'Oslo Report' – revealing

secrets of German long-range rockets and radar – sent anonymously (by anti-Nazi German scientist?) to British naval attaché in Norway.

Rear-Adm. Sinclair, head ('C') of British Secret Intelligence Service (MI6), dies of cancer. Succeeded by deputy, Col. Menzies.

SUNDAY, NOVEMBER 5

Home Front: Germany – THE ZOSSEN CONSPIRACY: Gens. von Brauchitsch (Army C in C), Halder and Beck plot to stop Hitler's planned Western Front offensive; if necessary, Brauchitsch is to arrest the *Führer* in Berlin. But, after violent argument with Hitler, Brauchitsch loses his nerve and returns to *OKH* (Army High Command) HQ at Zossen, where the conspiracy collapses.

Secret War – Col. Hans Oster of the *Abwehr* (German Military Intelligence) – one of the Zossen conspirators – warns Col. Sas, Dutch military attaché in Berlin, of impending invasion of Low Countries; Sas informs the Belgian attaché.

MONDAY, NOVEMBER 6

Western Front – 9 French Hawk fighters shoot down 4 out of 27 Me 109s over the Saar.

TUESDAY, NOVEMBER 7

Western Front – Hitler postpones offensive planned for Nov. 12 – and 13 further

postponements follow at intervals until May 9, 1940 (see also Jan. 10, 1940).

Diplomacy – Queen Wilhelmina of Holland and King Leopold of Belgium appeal for peace and offer to mediate between combatants.

WEDNESDAY, NOVEMBER 8

Home Front: Germany – BÜRGER-BRÄUKELLER BOMB INCIDENT: powerful bomb wrecks Munich beer hall (killing 8) minutes after vehement anti-British speech by Hitler, who predicts a 5-year war. Gestapo arrest hundreds of suspects. Goebbels blames the British.

Occupied Poland – Dr. Hans Frank installed as Nazi Governor-General. Consolidated plan to transport 600,000 Jews and 400,000 Poles from the incorporated territories (see Nov. 1) to Frank's *General-gouvernement* by spring 1940, (operation begins Dec. 1).

THURSDAY, NOVEMBER 9

Secret War – Venlo Incident: 2 British Intelligence officers, Major Stevens and Capt. Best, kidnapped by the Gestapo on Dutch-German border, while attempting to contact the German anti-Nazi movement (imprisoned until April 1945).

FRIDAY, NOVEMBER 10

Neutrals: Holland – Dutch reinforce border troops, cancel all Army leave and

prepare to flood 'inundation area' by opening sluice gates.

SATURDAY, NOVEMBER 11

Western Front – Slight activity by German patrols and artillery. BEF hold Armistice Day services amid the great battlefields of W.W.I.

SUNDAY, NOVEMBER 12

Diplomacy – King George VI and French Pres. Lebrun issue cautious replies to Dutch-Belgian peace appeal.

Western Front – First ENSA (Entertainments National Service Association) concert for British and French troops in France, starring Maurice Chevalier and Gracie Fields.

Neutrals – Dutch and Belgian Foreign Ministers meet at Breda, Holland.

Diplomacy – King Carol of Rumania offers to mediate; rejected Nov. 16.

MONDAY, NOVEMBER 13

Air War – Germans bomb Shetland Is.; no casualties (one rabbit killed!). Air raid warning in Paris; AA guns engage German recce aircraft.

Sea War – RN destroyer *Blanche* mined and sunk off Thames Estuary. She is the first British destroyer to be lost.

Neutrals: Holland – P.M. de Geer justifies recent defence measures and declares that the immediate danger is over.

HITLER, Adolf (1889-1945)
German: *Führer* ('Leader') *of Third Reich, Supreme Commander Armed Forces*

Megalomaniac with morbid fascination for death and destruction, and fanatical hatred of Jews and Communists. Adept liar and rabble-rousing orator; also capable of inspiring surprising degree of loyalty among subordinates. After astonishing success of his bold *Blitzkrieg* against France and believing himself to be the world's greatest military strategist, decided to invade USSR. Took personal command of Army during critical Moscow battle, Dec. 1941; insisted on right to veto all tactical decisions by field Commanders. Combined with his inflexible 'no retreat' policy, this led to disaster at Stalingrad and Kursk, in Tunisia and in 'Battle of the Bulge'. Appalling, self-imposed, strain ruined Hitler's health; became drug

addict. Spent last weeks of power closeted in Berlin *Führerbunker*, raving at 'traitorous' generals and 'Jewish Bolsheviks,' marshalling imaginary armies and ordering total 'scorched earth' policy.

Born at Braunau-am-Inn, Austria, April 20, 1889, son of a minor customs officer. Spent early years as 'starving' artist in Vienna and Munich. Served on Western Front, 1914-18, with rank of corporal; awarded Iron Cross (2nd Class); gassed and temporarily blinded Oct. 1918. Then employed as secret agent by military authorities in Munich; ordered to infiltrate German Workers' Party. Elected leader (1921) of renamed 'National Socialist German Workers' Party' (Nazi Party). Led abortive *Putsch* in Munich, Nov. 8, 1923. Imprisoned for 9 months; wrote *Mein Kampf* (My Struggle). Gained support of big industrialists from 1930 during Depression. Stood unsuccessfully against Hindenburg in presidential elections, 1932.

Appointed Chancellor, Jan. 30, 1933. All opposition parties and rivals within the govt. and Nazi movement suppressed, 1933-34: 'Night of the Long Knives', June 30, 1934. After death of Hindenburg, Aug. 2, 1934, Hitler combined duties of Chancellor and Pres., under new title of *Führer*: powers confirmed by national plebiscite, Aug. 19, 1934. Ordered creation of air force *(Luftwaffe)* Oct. 1, 1934; introduced conscription, March 1935. Legislated against Jews, Sept. 1935. Sent German Army into demilitarized Rhineland, March 1936. Assisted Franco in Spanish Civil War, July 1936. Signed Rome-Berlin Axis agreement, Oct. 1936. Annexed Austria, March 1938. Met British, French leaders and Mussolini at Munich, Sept. 1938; obtained

Sudetenland. Annexed Czechoslovakia, March 1939. Made Non-aggression Pact with Stalin, Aug. 1939. Invaded Poland, Sept. 1939.

Conquered Denmark, Norway, Luxemburg, Netherlands, Belgium and France, April 9-June 22, 1940. Visited Paris, June 1940. Planned invasion of Britain and issued 'Last Appeal to Reason', July 1940. Ordered *Luftwaffe* to bomb London in revenge for RAF attacks on Berlin, Sept. 1940. Postponed invasion of Britain. Ordered invasion of USSR, Dec. 1940. Intervened in North African campaign, Feb. 1941. Crushed Yugoslavia in 17 days. Sent airborne army to Crete, May 1941. Ordered extermination of European Jews, May 1941. Launched delayed invasion of USSR, June 22, 1941. Belatedly attacked Moscow Oct.-Dec. 1941. Prevented rout of German armies in Moscow battle (Dec. 1941) by forbidding retreat and dismissing many generals. Attempted to capture Stalingrad and Caucasus oilfields, summer 1942. Forbade encircled 6th Army to retreat from Stalingrad, Nov. 1942-Feb 1943. Launched third, and last, summer offensive in Russia, July 1943. Belatedly sent massive reinforcements to Rommel in North Africa, Nov. 1942-April 1943. Ordered destruction of London with robot missiles (V-1 and V-2), May 1944.

Rescued disgraced Mussolini, Sept. 1943. Survived assassination attempt, July 20, 1944. Launched final desperate offensive on Western Front, Dec. 1944 ('Battle of the Bulge'). Ordered 'scorched earth' policy, April 1945. Decided to remain in Berlin to the end, April 22, 1945. Married mistress, Eva Braun, April 28, 1945. Both committed suicide, April 30, 1945.

TUESDAY, NOVEMBER 14

Western Front – 'Plan D' (the 'Dyle Plan') adopted by French and British High Commands (after secret, inconclusive discussions with the Belgians): a German invasion of Belgium to be countered by an immediate Anglo-French advance to the 'Meuse-Antwerp Line', S. and E. of Brussels.

WEDNESDAY, NOVEMBER 15

Diplomacy – German Foreign Minister, von Ribbentrop, rejects Dutch-Belgian peace appeal.
Occupied Czechoslovakia – Large-scale demonstrations at funeral of Jan Opletal, a medical student mortally wounded in Prague on Oct. 28.
China – Japanese capture port of Pakhoi (since July 1937 Japanese have taken all China's seaports).
Sea War – *Admiral Graf Spee* sinks British tanker *Africa Shell* S. of Madagascar.

THURSDAY, NOVEMBER 16

Sea War – British, French and Australian warships search for *Admiral Graf Spee* in Indian Ocean and E. Indies.

FRIDAY, NOVEMBER 17

Sea War – Pocket battleship *Deutschland* (Germany) arrives at Gdynia (Baltic) after her Atlantic raiding cruise (2 ships sunk). Renamed *Lützow* by Hitler in Feb. 1940 to save face if she is sunk.
Air War – German recce aircraft flies over NW. England. Germans drop propaganda booklets over Central and SE. France. RAF photographs Wilhelmshaven naval base.
Diplomacy – Third meeting of Allied Supreme War Council in London: 'Plan D' adopted (see Nov. 14); British and French economies to be closely integrated.
Occupied Czechoslovakia – SS occupy all universities (night 16-17) and 9 student leaders are executed; 1,200 sent to concentration camp (universities closed until 1945). Czech National Committee formed by ex-Pres. Benes in Paris.

SATURDAY, NOVEMBER 18

Sea War – 4 merchant ships sunk by magnetic mines off British E. Coast; 86 killed on Dutch liner *Simon Bolivar*.
Home Front: Britain – IRA cause 4 small bomb explosions in London business premises.
Occupied Czechoslovakia – Martial law proclaimed in Prague.

SUNDAY, NOVEMBER 19

Occupied Poland – Germans erect barricades round Jewish quarter of Warsaw.

MONDAY, NOVEMBER 20

Sea War – German seaplanes begin dropping magnetic mines in British E. Coast shipping lanes (night 20-21).

TUESDAY, NOVEMBER 21

Sea War: Atlantic – German battle-cruisers *Gneisenau* and *Scharnhorst* despatched into N. Atlantic.
Mine victims off British E. Coast include new cruiser HMS *Belfast* (damaged).

WEDNESDAY, NOVEMBER 22

Sea War – RN experts defuse German magnetic mine dropped on Shoeburyness mud flats off coast of Essex. After examining its mechanism, they devise means of 'neutralising' ships' hulls.

THURSDAY, NOVEMBER 23

Sea War: Atlantic – British armed merchant-cruiser *Rawalpindi* overwhelmed by *Scharnhorst* SE. of Iceland (265 dead). *Scharnhorst* and *Gneisenau* avoid pursuit and reach port, Nov. 27.
Home Front: Britain – Bacon and butter rationed.
Occupied Poland – Polish Govt.-in-Exile established at Angers (W. France).

FRIDAY, NOVEMBER 24

Home Front: Germany – Govt. takes in trust the property and financial interests of Fritz Thyssen – the iron and steel magnate and a key supporter of Hitler in earlier years – who had fled to Switzerland in Sept. 1939.

SATURDAY, NOVEMBER 25

Sea War – Germans lay mines off SW. Sweden, inside Swedish territorial waters (Sweden protests, Nov. 27).

SUNDAY, NOVEMBER 26

Diplomacy – 'Mainila Incident': Russians accuse Finns of shelling village of Mainila, killing 4 soldiers, and demand immediate withdrawal of Finnish troops from vicinity of Leningrad.

MONDAY, NOVEMBER 27

Sea War – British Govt. orders seizure of German exports on the high seas in reprisal for magnetic mine campaign.
China – Japanese capture Nanning, important railhead in SW. China.
Neutrals – Nobel Committee of Norwegian Parliament announces cancellation of 1939 Nobel Peace Prize.

TUESDAY, NOVEMBER 28

Diplomacy – USSR renounces Soviet-Finnish Non-Aggression Pact (signed 1932). Finns inform Moscow that investigations show that Russian artillery fired the 7 shells at Mainila (Nov. 26).

WEDNESDAY, NOVEMBER 29

Diplomacy – USSR severs diplomatic relations with Finland.

THURSDAY, NOVEMBER 30

RUSSIAN INVASION OF FINLAND ('The Winter War'). 26 divs. attack on 4 fronts – Karelian Isthmus; N. of L. Ladoga; in the 'Waist'; and at Petsamo (Arctic) – supported by 900 aircraft and Baltic and Northern Fleets. Helsinki and Viipuri bombed; mass evacuation of civilians.
Field Marshal Mannerheim (aged 72) appointed 'Defender of Finland' and CinC.
Home Front: Germany – Unemployed total 120,000.

Finnish Forces
400,000 men (9 divs.); 145 planes; 2 coast defence ships, 5 subs.

Soviet Forces
600,000 men (30 divs. in 4 armies); 1,200 tanks; 696 planes divided between the 4 armies with 300 more in Estonia; 2 battleships, 1 cruiser, 9 destroyers, 16 small warships, 11 subs. deployed by the Baltic and Arctic Fleets.

FRIDAY, DECEMBER 1

Finland – Helsinki bombed (80 killed, Nov. 30-Dec.1). Finnish coalition government formed, inc. Ryti (P.M.) and Tanner (Foreign Minister).
Neutrals: Scandinavia – Widespread pro-Finnish demonstrations.

SATURDAY, DECEMBER 2

Finland – Finnish covering forces (13,000 men) on Karelian Isthmus slowly withdrawing to the 'Mannerheim Line'. Mines and traps destroy numbers of Russian tanks. Helsinki Olympic Games (planned for 1940) abandoned.
Sea War – German SS *Watussi* scuttled off South Africa, under shellfire from battle-cruiser HMS *Renown*.
Diplomacy – Finnish Govt. appeals to the League of Nations. Soviet puppet 'People's Government of the Finnish Democratic Republic' established under Finnish communist Otto Kuusinen at Terijoki on Gulf of Finland. US Govt. proposes 'moral embargo' on sale of American arms to countries guilty of 'terror' bombing from the air.
Western Front – French communiqué reports: 'A quiet day on the whole of the

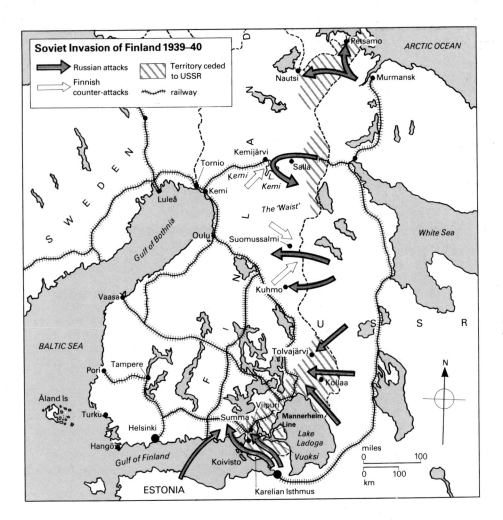

Soviet Invasion of Finland 1939–40

Russian attacks
Finnish counter-attacks
Territory ceded to USSR
railway

front . . . the air forces, on both sides, were completely inactive'.
Neutrals: Italy – Pro-Finnish demonstrations in Rome. Vatican condemns Russian aggression.

SUNDAY, DECEMBER 3

Neutrals: Sweden – Army reservists called up and minefield laid off the E. Coast.

MONDAY, DECEMBER 4

Sea War – Battleship *Nelson*, flagship of British Home Fleet, damaged by magnetic mine near Loch Ewe. RN sub. *Salmon* sinks *U-36* off Norway.
Western Front – King George arrives to inspect BEF and RAF units; he later meets Pres. Lebrun, Premier Daladier and Gen. Gamelin and sees Maginot Line (visit ends, Dec. 10).
Finland – Finns fortify Aaland Is. in Gulf of Bothnia.
Diplomacy – USSR rejects Swedish offer of mediation in Russo-Finnish conflict.

TUESDAY, DECEMBER 5

Finland – Finnish covering forces complete withdrawal to Mannerheim Line. Finnish Blenheim bombers raid Murmansk air base.

WEDNESDAY, DECEMBER 6

Finland – Russians complete series of landings on 7 islands in Gulf of Finland.
Sea War – Mines laid, by night, off British E. Coast, by German seaplanes and destroyers (which also torpedo destroyer HMS *Jersey*).

THURSDAY, DECEMBER 7

Sea War: Atlantic – Pocket-battleship, *Admiral Graf Spee*, sinks SS *Streonshalh* S. of Trinidad, her ninth and last victim. British cruiser squadron sails towards R. Plate estuary, anticipating interception. British and French submarines escort 3 N. Atlantic convoys (until Dec. 27).
Finland – Russians announce naval blockade of Finnish S. and W. coasts. Battle of Kollaa: Finns halt Russian div. N. of L. Ladoga (ends Dec. 10).

FRIDAY, DECEMBER 8

Air War – Polish squadrons to be attached to the RAF.

SATURDAY, DECEMBER 9

Western Front – Cpl. Thomas Priday of King's Shropshire Light Infantry, killed leading a patrol, is first British soldier to be killed in W.W.II.

SUNDAY, DECEMBER 10

Sea War – First Canadian troop convoy sails from Halifax, with 5 liners under heavy escort (arrives Britain, Dec. 23). Russian sub. *S-1* sinks (in error) German SS *Bolheim* in Gulf of Bothnia.

MONDAY, DECEMBER 11

Diplomacy – League of Nations urges USSR to cease hostilities in Finland within 24 hours and accept mediation (Soviet rejection on Dec. 12).
Home Front: Britain – Coventry Explosion trial: two IRA men, Barnes and Richards, sentenced to death for murdering 5 people in Coventry on Aug. 25, 1939.

TUESDAY, DECEMBER 12

Finland – Battle of Tolvaajärvi: Finns destroy two divs., N. of L. Ladoga, killing 4,000 Russians, capturing 30 guns, 60 tanks and 600 PoWs (ends Dec. 24). Battle of Kitela: Finns halt Russian 18th and 168th Divs. on N. shore of L. Ladoga; 18th Div. surrounded on Jan. 5 and 168th on Jan. 11, 1940 (q.v.).
Sea War – Liner *Bremen* arrives in Bremerhaven from Murmansk.
Air War – RAF aircraft carry out night-long 'security patrols' over Frisian Is. – bases of German minelaying seaplanes (patrols repeated at frequent intervals during winter of 1939-40).

WEDNESDAY, DECEMBER 13

Sea War: Atlantic – **BATTLE OF THE RIVER PLATE.** British cruisers *Exeter* and *Ajax* and NZ cruiser *Achilles* intercept pocket-battleship *Admiral Graf Spee* off Plate Estuary, S. America. All ships are damaged; *Exeter* retires to Falkland Is. and is replaced by cruiser *Cumberland*. *Admiral Graf Spee* (96 casualties) puts into Montevideo for emergency repairs. Pursuers wait outside Uruguayan territorial waters.
RN sub. *Salmon* damages German cruisers *Leipzig* and *Nürnberg* in Heligoland Bight (North Sea).
Finland – First shipment of French arms leaves for Finland.
Diplomacy – League of Nations adopts resolution condemning Russian aggression and calls upon all member states to assist Finland.

THURSDAY, DECEMBER 14

Finland – Russians launch new drive on Petsamo front.
Diplomacy – **LEAGUE OF NATIONS EXPELS SOVIET UNION.**
Sea War: Atlantic – German liner *Columbus* (33,000 t.) leaves Vera Cruz (Mexico) for home. She is shadowed by US warships, on neutrality patrol, and finally burned by her crew on Dec. 19, 500 km off

Cape Hatteras, to avoid capture by destroyer HMS *Hyperion*.

FRIDAY, DECEMBER 15

Finland – Battle of Suomussalmi: Finns destroy 163rd (Tula) Div. and 44th Div. (motorised) in the 'Waist'. Russian losses: 6,000-plus killed, 1,800 PoWs, 54 guns, 97 tanks, 420 vehicles and 1,170 horses (ends Jan. 5, 1940).
Western Front – P.M. Chamberlain visits the BEF.

SATURDAY, DECEMBER 16

Finland – First Battle of Summa: waves of Russian infantry and tanks, with air support, attempt to overrun the Summa sector of the Mannerheim Line. Finns repel all attacks (the heaviest on Dec. 19 and 20). Bofors anti-tank guns and special squads armed with 'Molotov cocktails' (petrol bombs) destroy 58 Russian tanks (ends Dec. 22).
Home Front: Germany – Repatriation of 51,000 'Baltic Germans' by sea from Latvia (begun Oct. 14) to the 'Incorporated Territories' of Poland completed.

SUNDAY, DECEMBER 17

Sea War: Atlantic – ADMIRAL GRAF SPEE SCUTTLED in Plate Estuary; the wreck burns for a week.

Below: Graf Spee *burns – the British bought the wreck to examine her radar.*

German aircraft bomb and strafe fishing trawlers and coasters in North Sea (repeated on Dec. 19; in all 7 boats sunk).

MONDAY, DECEMBER 18

Air War – 'Battle of the Heligoland Bight': 50 Me 109s and Me 110s destroy 12 of 22 Wellington bombers despatched on armed recce to Wilhelmshaven – 4 fighters destroyed. (RAF Bomber Cmnd. daylight raids abandoned until April 1940).
Finland – Renewed bombing of Helsinki and shelling of coastal batteries.
Sea War – Commodore Harwood – victor in R. Plate action – promoted to Rear-Adm. and knighted. 1,039 officers and men from *Admiral Graf Spee* interned in Buenos

Aires (Capt. Langsdorff commits suicide, night Dec. 19-20).

TUESDAY, DECEMBER 19

Diplomacy – Fourth meeting of Allied Supreme War Council in Paris.

WEDNESDAY, DECEMBER 20

Secret War – British expert examines radar equipment on board the wreck of *Admiral Graf Spee*.

THURSDAY, DECEMBER 21

Diplomacy – Hitler sends greetings to Stalin on his 60th birthday. French Govt. 'Yellow Book' published, equivalent to British 'Blue Book' (see Sept. 21).

FRIDAY, DECEMBER 22

Sea War – British Ministry of Economic Warfare announces that the Allied Contraband Control has detained 870,000 t. of goods destined for Germany, since Sept. 3.
Home Front: France – Chamber of Deputies votes credits of 304,000,000,000 francs for the production of armaments in 1940. P.M. Daladier announces the strengthening of the Maginot Line and the completion of new fortifications in N. France and the Jura Mts.

SATURDAY, DECEMBER 23

Finland – Finnish counterattack on Karelian Isthmus: Finns suffer 1,500 casualties and call off attack at nightfall; stalemate ensues.
Neutrals: Ireland – In Dublin, IRA gang steal Irish Army's entire reserves of small arms ammunition (1.1 M. rounds); bulk of the haul recovered during massive Army-police searches over next 11 days.

SUNDAY, DECEMBER 24

Occupied Poland – Russo-German agreement re-establishes rail links between the two occupied zones.

MONDAY, DECEMBER 25

Finland – On a cold Christmas Day

(–30°C), Helsinki, Viipuri and over 30 other Finnish towns and villages bombed or strafed, railways also attacked. Finnish fighters and AA guns destroy or damage 20 bombers.
Western Front – Hitler on 3-day visit.
Home Front: Britain – The King broadcasts a Christmas message to the Empire.

TUESDAY, DECEMBER 26

Diplomacy – USA and 20 Latin American States issue joint protest against R. Plate Battle infringement of Pan-American 'Security Zone' (rejected by Britain on Jan. 15; by Germany, Feb. 1, 1940).

WEDNESDAY, DECEMBER 27

Finland – Civilians evacuated from Viipuri.
Sea War – Defensive minefield to be laid off British E. Coast, from Moray Firth to Thames Estuary.

THURSDAY, DECEMBER 28

Finland – Russian High Command orders preparations for co-ordinated, step-by-step assault on Mannerheim Line.
Sea War: Atlantic – U-30 torpedoes battleship HMS *Barham* (slight damage)
China – Repeated Japanese bombing raids on Lanchow, vital Chinese military supply base (NW China).

FRIDAY, DECEMBER 29

Finland – 250 Finnish 'suicide squad' ski troops tear up vital Leningrad-Murmansk railway line at 3 points.

SATURDAY, DECEMBER 30

Finland – Gen. Stern, formerly in command of Russian Far Eastern Army, to direct operations N. of L. Ladoga.

SUNDAY, DECEMBER 31

Finland – Russians bomb Viipuri and other towns.
Diplomacy – Britain and France inform League of Nations that they will give all possible assistance to Finland.
Home Front: Britain – Road accident deaths (Sept.-Dec. 1939) total 4,130 (only 2,511 killed in military operations over same period). 15,626 people registered as conscientious objectors.
Home Front: Germany – Hitler's New Year Proclamation to Nazi Party: Germany's war aim is the final defeat of the British 'warmongers and war-declarers'.

> **Shipping Losses 1939**
> Allied and Neutral: 225 ships totalling 767,358 t. German: 9 U-boats.

1940

MONDAY, JANUARY 1

Finland – Finns repulse Russian probing attack in Taipale sector of Mannerheim Line.
Home Front: Britain – Royal Proclamation: 2 M. men aged 20-27 made liable for military service.
Home Front: France – Rail links with Spain reopened, after 3½-year break due to Spanish Civil War.
Neutrals: Denmark – In New Year addresses to the nation, P.M. and Foreign Minister express grave doubts about the prospects for continuance of Danish independence in 1940. *Turkey* – 32,741 die in severe floods after earthquake.

TUESDAY, JANUARY 2

Finland – Snowstorms halt fighting in Karelian Isthmus. Battle of Salla begins: Finns make unsuccessful attempts to encircle Russian 122nd Div. in the 'Waist' (ends late Jan.).

WEDNESDAY, JANUARY 3

Sea War – British warships detain American SS *Mormacsun*.
Air War – Finnish aircraft drop 3 M. pamphlets on Leningrad.
Western Front – In Vosges area, French patrols ambush 2 German detachments and take several prisoners.
Neutrals: Ireland – Eire Govt. introduces emergency legislation to intern IRA men without trial (becomes law on Feb. 9).

THURSDAY, JANUARY 4

Finland – First contingent of Norwegian volunteers leaves Oslo for Finland.
Home Front: Britain – All merchant shipping requisitioned.
Home Front: Germany – Göring appointed head of German war economy in an effort to beat the Allied blockade.
Occupied Poland – Franco-Polish military agreement: Polish Army in France to be equipped and maintained at French expense.

FRIDAY, JANUARY 5

Finland – Russian 18th. Div. encircled N. of L. Ladoga (18,000 Russians are killed or captured by Feb. 19). First contingent of Swedish volunteer troops reaches Finland.
Diplomacy – USSR accuses Norway and Sweden of pursuing 'unneutral' policy (rejected by Norway Jan. 6; by Sweden, Jan. 10).

Above: *Finnish ski-troops proved more than a match for the road-bound, poorly camouflaged Soviet invader.*

Home Front: Britain – Hore-Belisha, popular Minister of War, forced to resign by opposition of reactionary generals, led by Lord Gort. Replaced by Oliver Stanley. Lord Macmillan, Minister of Information, replaced by Sir John Reith, formerly BBC Dir.-Gen.

SATURDAY, JANUARY 6

Air War – 2 Finnish Fokkers destroy formation of 7 Ilyushin bombers over Utti, NE. of Helsinki.

SUNDAY, JANUARY 7

Finland – 400,000 Finnish civilians have now been evacuated from battle areas and large towns.
Marshal Voroshilov to command the Russian armies in Finland, with Gen. Timoshenko directing 7th and 13th Armies in Karelian Isthmus.

MONDAY, JANUARY 8

Sea War – Converted Wellington bomber, fitted with metal hoop energized to explode magnetic mines, makes first successful low-level sortie over North Sea (night Jan. 8-9).
Home Front: Britain – Food rationing begins: weekly allowance per person is 4oz (100g) of bacon or ham, 4oz butter, 12oz (350g) sugar. Ration books issued.

TUESDAY, JANUARY 9

Sea War – German patrol craft depth-charge RN subs. *Undine*, *Seahorse* and *Starfish* in Heligoland Bight (on Jan. 6, 7 and 9, respectively), British sub. ops. in Heligoland Bight temporarily abandoned. British liner *Dunbar Castle* mined and sunk off SE. England.
Home Front: Britain – P.M. Chamberlain makes first of a series of 'morale-boosting' speeches by Cabinet Ministers.

WEDNESDAY, JANUARY 10

Western Front – German Me 108 carrying Maj. Reinberger – a paratroop commander with secret documents on the planned *Gelb* Offensive in the W. – makes forced landing at Mechelen in Belgium. Reinberger makes bungled attempt to destroy documents and is captured by Belgian troops. German plans now compromised.
Diplomacy – Unofficial peace talks between Mme. Wuolijoki (Finland) and Mme. Kollontai (USSR) in Stockholm.
Sea War: Atlantic – German blockade runner *Bahia Blanca* hits iceberg and sinks NW. of Iceland. German destroyers lay mines off Newcastle and Cromer (night Jan. 10-11).

THURSDAY, JANUARY 11

Finland – Russian 168th Div. encircled N. of L. Ladoga; Finns beat off reinforcements, while Russians supply the 'pocket' by air (Russian relief column finally breaks through, March 6). New Russian drive in Salla sector ('Waist' area), toward Kemijärvi-Tornio railway (Finns counter-attack, Jan. 17-18). Swedish volunteer air group, *Flygflottilj 19,* begins operations from frozen L. Kemi, with 12 Gladiators and 4 Hart light bombers. (The Swedes shoot down 12 Russians and lose 6 aircraft, by March 13).

FRIDAY, JANUARY 12

Finland – Battle of the Taipale: Major Russian effort to break through left flank of Mannerheim Line, by crossing ice-bound R. Taipale, is defeated by hand-to-hand fighting (ends Jan. 23).

SATURDAY, JANUARY 13

Diplomacy – Franco-Spanish Trade Agreement: Spain to receive French wheat, fertilizers and manufactured goods in exchange for iron ore and other minerals.
Norway – Increased defence expenditure produces highest Govt. budget in Norwegian history.

SUNDAY, JANUARY 14

Neutrals – Russian aircraft drop bombs near Lulea, Sweden and violate Norwegian airspace; diplomatic protests in Moscow.

MONDAY, JANUARY 15

Finland – Russian heavy artillery commences 17-day preparatory bombardment of Summa sector of Mannerheim Line.
Home Front: France – Meat rationing introduced (3 'meatless' days per week).
Neutrals: Japan – Govt. of Gen. Abe resigns, following severe parliamentary criticism of its China policy; new govt. formed by Admiral Yonai.

TUESDAY, JANUARY 16

Home Front: France – 66 Communist members ejected from Chamber of Deputies.

WEDNESDAY, JANUARY 17

Finland – Finns recapture Kursu, SW. of Salla.
Secret War – Polish cryptographers in France break *Luftwaffe* Enigma key of Oct. 28. Regular decoding now possible.

THURSDAY, JANUARY 18

Home Front: Britain – 5 workmen killed in series of explosions at Waltham Abbey explosives factory.

FRIDAY, JANUARY 19

Finland – Heavy fighting continues on 3 fronts. 45°C (81°F) of frost recorded.
Sea War – Destroyer HMS *Grenville* mined and sunk off Thames Estuary.
Neutrals: USA – Death of Senator Borah, influential 'Isolationist' (aged 74).

SATURDAY, JANUARY 20

Air War – Russian bombers start big fires in Turku and Hangö.
Western Front – Hitler reduces 'alert

period' before implementation of Op. *Fall Gelb* from 4 days to 24 hours for security reasons.
Diplomacy – Churchill broadcasts appeal to neutral States to join Britain and France in resisting Nazi aggression; he compares their timid conduct with the crocodile's victims – each hoping to be eaten last (Dutch Foreign Minister rejects appeal, Jan. 25).
Home Front: Britain – London has its coldest day since 1881, with 11°C (20° F) of frost.

SUNDAY, JANUARY 21

Air War – Finnish Blenheim bombers raid Kronstadt naval base, near Leningrad. Russians bomb Oulu, NW. Finland.
Sea War: North Sea – RN destroyer *Exmouth* sunk with all hands by *U-22*.
In Pacific, *Asama Maru* Incident: Japanese liner *Asamu Maru* stopped by cruiser HMS *Gloucester* and 21 German technicians removed. Japan protests and demands return of Germans (Feb. 1); British White Paper on subject, Feb. 6; 9 Germans handed over Feb. 29.
Diplomacy – Britain rejects US protests concerning examination of mail carried aboard US merchant ships.
Vatican radio broadcasts to USA on Nazi terror campaign against Catholic clergy in Poland.
Home Front: Britain – Duke of Windsor (who, as Edward VIII, abdicated in 1936) takes leave after 5 months' tour of duty with BEF.
China – 2 former associates of Wang Ching-wei, head of Japanese-controlled 'puppet' govt. at Nanking, publish text of agreement, signed by Wang, giving Japan total political and economic dominion in China (Wang issues strenuous denial).
Neutrals – Italian liner *Orazio* catches fire off Barcelona (104 dead); French destroyers rescue survivors.

MONDAY, JANUARY 22

Finland – Finnish authorities announce formation of a Foreign Legion, inc. British volunteers.

TUESDAY, JANUARY 23

Home Front: Britain – Large number of road accidents in the 'black-out' necessitates reduction in speed limit from 30 to 20 mph.

WEDNESDAY, JANUARY 24

Finland – Fierce fighting NE. of L. Ladoga; Finns repel all attacks.

THURSDAY, JANUARY 25

Occupied Poland – 'Göring – Frank Circular': all material resources and manpower to be ruthlessly exploited for the immediate benefit of the Reich (copies of this top secret document quickly obtained by Polish Govt. in Paris and widely publicized).

FRIDAY, JANUARY 26

Home Front: France – Paul Ferdonnet, the 'Radio Traitor' – notorious for his pro-Nazi broadcasts in French from Stuttgart – is tried *in absentia* by a military tribunal (sentenced to death March 7).
Diplomacy – US-Japanese Treaty of Navigation and Commerce lapses – USA having refused to negotiate in protest against Japanese aggression in China.

SATURDAY, JANUARY 27

Home Front: Britain – Churchill (uneasy at slow increase in war production) speaks at Free Trade Hall, Manchester: *'each to our station . . . there is not a week, nor a day, nor an hour to be lost!'* Speech broadcast to the

Dominions and USA.
Home Front: South Africa – Gen. Hertzog's peace resolution in Parliament defeated by 81 votes to 59.

SUNDAY, JANUARY 28

Home Front: Britain – Director of Censorship permits newspapers belatedly to reveal details of Britain's coldest winter since 1894: R. Thames and Southampton Docks frozen; 18°C (33°F) of frost at Buxton (Derbys.).

MONDAY, JANUARY 29

Finland – Battle of Kuhmo begins: Finns encircle Russian 54th Div. at Kuhmo, in the 'Waist'. Heavy Russian air raids on Finnish ports.
Diplomacy – Russian Note to Sweden: USSR willing to negotiate peace agreement with Finnish Govt.
Sea War – In the North Sea – German aircraft attack British merchant ships (2 sunk) and 2 lightships, between Shetlands and Kent. *E. Dudgeon* lightship bombed, 7 of 8-man crew die.
Home Front: France – Premier Daladier delivers a stirring broadcast speech: *'Germany hopes to encompass our downfall by exploiting weakness at home . . .'*

TUESDAY, JANUARY 30

Sea War – Heinkel bombers again attack shipping off British coast. *U-55* attacks convoy off Land's End, sinking 2 ships; but is then damaged by sloop *Fowey* and a Sunderland flying boat and forced to scuttle.
Home Front: Germany – Hitler speaks at Berlin Sportpalast on seventh anniversary of the Nazi regime. He demands *Lebensraum* ('living space') for Germans; ridicules Chamberlain ('pious and Bible-believing'), Churchill and Daladier; and declares that, since *'they started the war, . . . they will get all the war they want!'*.

WEDNESDAY, JANUARY 31

Air War – Secret British military mission to Italy orders 300 Caproni Re2000 fighters (Germany vetoes deal in April; British attempts to obtain fighters via a Portuguese intermediary fail, June 10).
Home Front: Britain – Barlow Report on the 'Distribution of the Industrial Population' published by Royal Commission; recommends the building of 'new towns'.

THURSDAY, FEBRUARY 1

Finland – Second battle of Summa: Russian 7th Army batters key sector of Mannerheim Line near village of Summa, with waves of tanks pulling armoured infantry sledges ('Molotov Coffins') and flamethrowers; supported by 'creeping' artillery barrage and 100s of aircraft. Finns repel all attacks until Feb. 11 (ends Feb. 16).
Home Front: Britain – Admiralty takes control of merchant ship building and repairing.
Neutrals – Japan begins 5-year rearmament programme.

FRIDAY, FEBRUARY 2

Diplomacy – Balkan Entente Conference at Belgrade. Neutrals Yugoslavia, Greece, Rumania and Turkey proclaim common interests in maintenance of peace in SE. Europe and renew their pact.

SATURDAY, FEBRUARY 3

Air War – 20 Heinkels (3 lost) attack ships (2 sunk) off British E. Coast.

SUNDAY, FEBRUARY 4

Air War – Russians attack 141 targets (towns, rail junctions, harbours) over weekend Feb. 3-4, dropping approx. 6,800 bombs. Finnish casualties 193 (14 killed).

MONDAY, FEBRUARY 5

Sea War – US Maritime Commission announces that Britain and France are buying 113,000 t. of old US cargo ships.
Neutrals: Holland – CinC Gen. Reynders resigns over question of Dutch military preparedness.

Above: *Gas-mask drill was still a serious business in Britain in Feb. 1940. By Sept. 1939, 38 million masks had been issued.*

TUESDAY, FEBRUARY 6

Home Front: Britain – 4 people injured by IRA parcel bombs at Euston Station, London.

WEDNESDAY, FEBRUARY 7

Sea War: Atlantic – Irish passenger-mail ship *Munster* sunk by mine in Irish Sea.
Home Front: Britain – IRA men, Barnes and Richards, executed at Winson Green Prison, Birmingham (see Dec. 11, 1939).

THURSDAY, FEBRUARY 8

Western Front – 2 French soldiers capture German patrol in Forbach Woods (see Jan. 10, 1943).
Secret War – 'Harry Sawyer' (Sebold) arrives in New York to head German spy network in USA; his special equipment includes 'microdots'. (Sebold is a double agent, working for the FBI.)
Home Front: France – Paris police raid Soviet Press Agency and discover that it is being used as cover for pro-German propaganda agency.
Home Front: New Zealand – Centenary celebrations on anniversary of Anglo-Maori Treaty of Waitangi (foundation of New Zealand).

FRIDAY, FEBRUARY 9

Finland – Finns hold Russian attacks in Summa sector.
Neutrals: Turkey – 80 Germans technical advisers dismissed by Govt.
Sea War – German destroyers lay mines in The Wash, on British E. coast (night Feb. 9-10).

SATURDAY, FEBRUARY 10

Sea War: Atlantic – 6 German merchant ships leave Vigo, Spain to run the blockaide: Allied warships intercept 4; 1 runs aground off N. Norway and 1 (*Wangoni*) reaches Kiel.
Dutch Govt. announces decision to build 3 battlecruisers (with technical assistance from Italy) for defence of Dutch E. Indies (they are never completed).
Western Front – French communiqué reads: *Rien à signaler* ('Nothing to report').

SUNDAY, FEBRUARY 11

Finland – Russians break through Mannerheim Line in Summa sector. 123rd Div. overwhelms defending Finnish battalion. Finns launch desperate counter-attacks.
Diplomacy – Soviet-German Trade Agreement: USSR to receive latest in machinery and military equipment in exchange for wheat, cotton and oil.
Home Front: Canada – Death of Gov.-Gen. Lord Tweedsmuir (the novelist John Buchan), aged 64.

MONDAY, FEBRUARY 12

Sea War: Atlantic – *U-33* sunk in the Clyde by minesweeper HMS *Gleaner;* naval

Enigma cipher machine rotors recovered.
Finland – Finnish Cabinet decides, in principle, to make peace.
North Africa – Australian Imperial Force and detachment of NZ troops arrive at Suez.

TUESDAY, FEBRUARY 13

Sea War: Atlantic – Cruiser HMS *Dorsetshire* intercepts German blockade-runner *Wakama* (scuttled) near Rio de Janeiro (Brazil makes vigorous protest).

WEDNESDAY, FEBRUARY 14

Diplomacy – Finnish Note (circularized to many foreign govts.) accuses USSR of adopting 'illegal' methods of warfare, inc. indiscriminate bombing of unprotected towns, hospitals and railway trains and abuse of the white flag (some Russian soldiers having feigned surrender before attacking).
Home Front: Britain – IRA plants 5 bombs in Birmingham; 2 shops damaged. Govt. gives formal permission for British volunteers to serve in Finnish armed forces. Harry Tate, music-hall comedian, dies (aged 67).

THURSDAY, FEBRUARY 15

Finland – Finnish forces withdraw to second line of defences in Mannerheim Line (op. completed Feb. 17).

FRIDAY, FEBRUARY 16

Sea War: Atlantic –RESCUE FROM THE *ALTMARK:* boarding party from destroyer HMS *Cossack* rescue 299 British merchant navy personnel from German 'prison ship' *Altmark* (formerly attached to *Admiral Graf Spee*) in Joessing Fjord, SW. Norway; 7 German sailors killed. (Norway protests British violation of her neutrality, on Feb. 17, and proposes international arbitration, Feb. 25).
Diplomacy – Sweden refuses Finnish appeal for right of passage of foreign troops and direct military assistance.

SATURDAY, FEBRUARY 17

Diplomacy – Pres. Roosevelt sends Sumner Welles, Under-Secretary of State, on 'fact-finding' tour of Europe and appoints Myron C. Taylor as his 'personnal representative' to the Vatican.
Neutrals – United States Lines sells liner *President Harding* and 7 cargo ships to a Belgian concern in attempt to circumvent ban on US seaborne trade with Europe imposed by Neutrality Act.

SUNDAY, FEBRUARY 18

Sea War: Atlantic – Op. *Nordmark:* battlecruisers *Gneisenau* and *Scharnhorst* and cruiser *Admiral Hipper* make unsuc-

cessful sortie against 'HN' convoy route (Britain-Scandinavia); escorting U-boats sink 12 merchant ships and destroyer HMS *Daring.*
Western Front – German infantry detachment, with heavy mortar support, make unsuccessful raid on French outpost near R. Moselle.
China – Battle of Nanning: Japanese forced to withdraw from city after heavy fighting.

MONDAY, FEBRUARY 19

Diplomacy – King Gustav of Sweden re-affirms his determination to remain neutral in Russo-Finnish conflict: *'from the first hour I informed Finland that she unfortunately could not count on military intervention from Sweden.'*

TUESDAY, FEBRUARY 20

Finland – Finns repulse heavy attacks across frozen R. Taipale.

WEDNESDAY, FEBRUARY 21

Finland – Blizzards hamper Russian offensive in Karelian Isthmus.
Home Front: Britain – Govt. Treasury announces token defence estimates of £100 each for Army, Navy and RAF for 1940 and duration of the war (the actual figures being concealed for security reasons). Emergency measures to deal with coal shortage (severe winter) include drastic reduction of passenger train services.
Secret War – First successful test of cavity magnetron at Birmingham Univ. gives Britain unbeatable lead in development of short-wave radar.
Occupied Poland – Inspectorate of Concentration Camps reports to Himmler that Auschwitz Camp, in 'Incorporated Territories' of Poland, is suitable for use as 'quarantine centre'.

THURSDAY, FEBRUARY 22

Finland – 34th Moscow Tank Brig., encircled near Kitelaë, Ladoga Front, eats last of its packhorses (for next few days Russians survive on starvation rations plus biscuits and rusks dropped from aircraft; see Feb. 28).
Sea War – He 111s bomb 2 German destroyers by mistake off Frisian Is.; they blunder into British minefield and sink.
Home Front: Britain – IRA bomb explodes in Oxford Street, London (7 people seriously injured) – the last major incident in an IRA bombing campaign against mainland Britain, begun on Jan. 16, 1939.
Neutrals: Tibet – 6-year-old Dalai Lama, Jampel Ngawang Lobsang Yishey Tenzing Gyatso ('Tender Glory, Mighty in Speech, Excellent Intellect, Absolute Wisdom, Holding to the Doctrine, and Ocean-

Wide') enthroned at Lhasa.

FRIDAY, FEBRUARY 23

Air War – RAF leaflet recce raid on Prague (night Feb. 23-24).
Home Front: Britain – 700 officers and men of *Ajax* and *Exeter* march through cheering crowds to London's Guildhall to celebrate R. Plate victory.

SATURDAY, FEBRUARY 24

Western Front – 'MANSTEIN PLAN' ADOPTED by German Army High Command. Hitler accepts proposal by Gen. von Manstein – backed by Gens. von Rundstedt and Guderian – for drastic revision of *Fall Gelb* (limited offensive repeatedly postponed since Oct. 1939). 5 *Pz* divs. with motorized infantry and *Stukas* are to smash through weak points in the Allied line – hilly and 'impassable' Ardennes Forest – then to cross R. Meuse at Sedan and drive across N. France to the Channel, thereby cutting off main Anglo-French forces (which are to be lured into Belgium by German 6th Army). Preparations for this 'knock-out blow' are to be completed (in great secrecy) by March 7.
Home Front: Germany – Hitler boasts of his achievements in speech at Munich on 20th anniversary of founding of Nazi Party and claims: *'Germany would not have lost the last war if I had been Reichschancellor in 1918!'.*
Home Front: Britain – Chamberlain, in Birmingham, condemns Nazi war aims: *'destruction of this nation* (Britain) *and domination of the world'*, but declares his continued willingness to reach a settlement with an alternative German Govt.
Diplomacy – Conference of Scandinavian Foreign Ministers at Copenhagen (Feb. 24-25). Ministers re-assert 'absolute neutrality' of Denmark, Norway and Sweden.

SUNDAY, FEBRUARY 25

Air War – First squadron of Royal Canadian Air Force (RCAF) reaches Britain.

MONDAY, FEBRUARY 26

Finland – Finns announce evacuation of Koivisto coastal fortress, on right flank of Mannerheim Line.
Sea War: Atlantic – Liner *Queen Elizabeth* (83,700 t.) leaves Clydebank with skeleton crew on secret maiden voyage to Halifax, Nova Scotia, and New York. She is equipped with giant electric 'de-gaussing' cable, to neutralize magnetic mines.
Diplomacy – US envoy Sumner Welles, with offer of US mediation, begins series of meetings with European leaders (Mussolini, Hitler, Chamberlain, Daladier, Reynaud, the Kings of England and Italy

and the Pope); tour ends March 20.

TUESDAY, FEBRUARY 27

Finland – Finns begin to withdraw to rear positions of Mannerheim Line.

WEDNESDAY, FEBRUARY 28

Finland – Finns storm entrenched camp of starving 34th Moscow Tank Brig. near Kitelae, capturing 105 tanks, 200 trucks and field cars.
Home Front: Palestine – British Govt. limits the acquisition of Arab land by Jews.

THURSDAY, FEBRUARY 29

Finland – Battle of Viipuri begins: Russians make all-out effort to crush resistance in Karelian Isthmus by encircling city of Viipuri and reaching Viipuri-Helsinki highway (ends March 13).
Home Front: France – Paul Reynaud, Minister of Finance, broadcasts on dangers of runaway inflation (*le cycle infernal*). Govt. measures inc. a price 'freeze', stricter food rationing, petroleum rationing, revaluation of gold reserves and compulsory use of female labour.

FRIDAY, MARCH 1

Finland – Russians within 6 km of centre of Viipuri. Fierce aerial dog fights over city.

SATURDAY, MARCH 2

Finland – Russians reach S. suburbs of Viipuri. Finnish fighters foil attempted raid on Helsinki.
Air War – High-flying RAF Spitfire photographs entire Ruhr industrial region in 1 sortie.
Sea War – British liner *Domala* bombed off I. of Wight (100 killed).
Home Front: Britain – University Boat Race: Cambridge beats Oxford.

SUNDAY, MARCH 3

Finland – Hand-to-hand fighting in suburbs of Viipuri; Russians capture railway station.

MONDAY, MARCH 4

Finland – Finns repulse attacks E. and W. of Viipuri (in W. Russians attack across ice of Viipuri Bay).

TUESDAY, MARCH 5

Finland – Russians cross ice-bound Viipuri Bay but meet fierce Finnish resistance.
Air War – Russians bomb Helsinki.
Western Front – Germans capture British outpost in Maginot Line (2 killed, 16 taken prisoner); outpost later recaptured.

WEDNESDAY, MARCH 6

Diplomacy – Finnish Govt., faced with desperate military situation, sends peace delegation to Moscow.

THURSDAY, MARCH 7

Finland – Fierce fighting continues in Viipuri Bay sector.
Air War – RAF aircraft, flying from bases in France, drop Polish language leaflets over W. Poland and return via Leipzig and the Ruhr (where leaflets in German are released).
Sea War – British warships detain 13 Italian colliers with cargoes of German coal.

FRIDAY, MARCH 8

Finland – Large quantities of French arms, ammunition and aircraft (175) now *en route* to Finland.

SATURDAY, MARCH 9

Finland – Finnish communiqué admits that Russians have established bridgehead on NW. shore of Viipuri Bay but claims all other sectors of Karelian Isthmus front remain intact.
Diplomacy – Anglo-Italian compromise

Below: *A Finnish 75mm mountain howitzer engages the Russians in Karelia. Guns and ammunition were scarce.*

solution to 'Coal Ships Affair' of March 7. Colliers to be released and Italy to find alternative (overland) supply route from German coalfields.

SUNDAY, MARCH 10

Finland – Russians capture Repola (NE. of Viipuri), Karppila and Ruhela on N. shore of Viipuri Bay. Marshal Mannerheim urges Finnish Govt. to make terms with USSR.
Diplomacy – Ribbentrop has interview with Mussolini and invites him to meet with Hitler.

MONDAY, MARCH 11

Sea War – U-31 is bombed and sunk by RAF Blenheim in Schillig Roads, NW. Germany. She is subsequently raised, recommissioned, and again sunk (by destroyer HMS *Antelope*) Nov. 2, 1940, NW. of Ireland.
Sea War: Med. – French battleship *Bretagne* and cruiser *Algérie* sail from Toulon for Canada with large gold shipment (2,379 bars).
Home Front: Britain – Meat rationing begins: 1s 10d (9 pence) worth of meat per person per week.

TUESDAY, MARCH 12

Diplomacy – TREATY OF MOSCOW ends 104-day Russo-Finnish 'Winter War'. Finland loses Karelian Isthmus (inc. city of Viipuri and Vuoksi 'industrial belt'), Hangö naval base, and border areas NW of L. Ladoga, in the 'Waist' and on Arctic coast.

On the same day, French P.M. Daladier tells Chamber of Deputies that Anglo-French expeditionary force is ready to embark for Finland on receipt of formal Finnish appeal for assistance.

Sea War – British Home Fleet returns to Scapa Flow from Rosyth and Loch Ewe. AA and anti-sub. defences have been greatly strengthened.

WEDNESDAY, MARCH 13

Finland – Cease-fire on all fronts at 11 a.m. Field Marshal Mannerheim's last Order of the Day to Finnish Army: *'A severe peace [has been concluded] which cedes to Russia nearly all the battlefields we have drenched with our blood ... The deeds you have accomplished will shine for centuries in the pages of our history.'*

Soviet-Finnish War Losses
Finnish military: 24,923 dead, 43,557 wounded; 3 tanks; 61 planes; 1 armed yacht, 1 steamer. Civilian: 637 killed and 1,400 wounded in air raids; 4,500 buildings destroyed or damaged. Soviet: perhaps 200,000 dead; 750-900 planes; 1,600 tanks; over 300 guns; 1 sub.

THURSDAY, MARCH 14

Finland – Evacuation of 470,000 people from lost territories commences (completed March 26).

FRIDAY, MARCH 15

Air War – RAF aircraft drop leaflets over Warsaw (night March 15-16). A Whitley, low on fuel, lands by mistake in a field in W. Germany and crew converse with inhabitants. They take off again and escape, despite small arms fire.

Neutrals – Amnesty for fascist Iron Guard in Rumania (see Sept. 21., 1939). 800 released from prison camps after they swear oath of loyalty to King Carol.

SATURDAY, MARCH 16

Air War – German raid on Scapa Flow by 32 bombers (2 lost). Cruiser *Norfolk* damaged; 7 naval and 8 civilian casualties, inc. James Isbister, first British civilian killed by enemy air action in W.W.II.

Neutrals – Argentine Govt. deports crew of *Admiral Graf Spee* into the interior and forbids them to wear their uniforms.

SUNDAY, MARCH 17

Sea War: Atlantic – Shipping losses for week ending March 17 are 3 British, 1 French, 4 neutral, 3 German.

MONDAY, MARCH 18

Diplomacy – Mussolini meets Hitler at Brenner in Austro-Italian Alps (their first meeting since Munich, 1938). Mussolini declares readiness to join war against Britain and France 'at the decisive hour'.

TUESDAY, MARCH 19

Air War – 50 RAF bombers (1 lost) attack Sylt seaplane base, NW Germany (night March 19-20) in reprisal for Scapa raid of March 16; little damage caused.

Home Front: Britain – Chamberlain makes detailed statement in Commons on British plans and actions on Finland's behalf. 100,000-strong Anglo-French expeditionary force could not be sent due to refusal of entry by Norway and Sweden; but large quantities of arms, ammunition, equipment and aircraft (152) had been delivered or promised.

WEDNESDAY, MARCH 20

Home Front: France – **P.M. DALADIER RESIGNS,** following severe criticism of his Finland policy.

Home Front: Germany – Dr Todt appointed Min. of Armaments and War Supplies.

Sea War – German aircraft attack convoy (4 ships damaged). Goebbels boasts 9 ships totalling 42,000 t. sunk. British Admiralty describes German claims as '42,000 tons in excess of the actual facts'.

THURSDAY, MARCH 21

Home Front: France – **PAUL REYNAUD FORMS NEW GOVT.** Daladier appointed Minister of War.

Sea War – First German merchant ship (*Heddernheim*) sunk by British sub. (*Ursula*) in W.W.II, off Danish coast.

FRIDAY, MARCH 22

Air War – RAF bombers on recce/leaflet dropping ops. over the Ruhr and NW. Germany have first encounters with German night fighters. Hampden slightly damaged by Me 110.

SATURDAY, MARCH 23

Sea War – British 'Malaya Force' formed to shadow 17 German merchant ships trapped in Dutch E. Indies ports.

SUNDAY, MARCH 24

Western Front – French and German patrols active at various points.

MONDAY, MARCH 25

Home Front: Germany – British PoWs forbidden by British Govt. to broadcast for the enemy.

TUESDAY, MARCH 26

Western Front: – British 51st (Highland) Div. takes over section of French front in Saar region.

Home Front: Canada – General Election, Liberals win 178 seats, Conservatives 39, others (inc. Social Credit) 28.

Home Front: New Zealand – Michael Savage, Labour P.M., dies aged 68.

WEDNESDAY, MARCH 27

Western Front – Phoney War continues: French and German artillery exchange fire in Saar and Vosges sectors.

THURSDAY, MARCH 28

Sea War: Pacific – Russian cargo ships *Selenga* and *Vladimir Mayakovski* (carrying metallic ores to Vladivostock for trans-shipment to Germany) ordered to Hong Kong by British warships.

Diplomacy – Sixth meeting of Allied Supreme War Council, in London. Solemn signed declaration that neither Britain nor France will conclude an armistice or peace treaty, except by mutual agreement. (A similar agreement had been made early in W.W.I.) Norwegian territorial waters to be mined, thereby disrupting transport of Swedish iron ore to Germany.

FRIDAY, MARCH 29

Air War – *Capitaine* Antoine de Saint-Exupéry flies first recce sortie over W. Germany in the Bloch 174 (max. speed, 530 km/hour).

Air Marshal Portal appointed AOC, RAF Bomber Cmnd.

Sea War: Atlantic – French cruiser *Algérie* escorts 2 US ships from Halifax with cargoes of American-built warplanes.

Home Front: Britain – Prince Alexander Obolensky, famous rugby player, killed landing RAF aircraft in E. Anglia, aged 24.

SATURDAY, MARCH 30

Home Front: Britain – Sir John Gilmour, Minister of Shipping, dies aged 63.

SUNDAY, MARCH 31

Sea War – Only 1 British merchant ship – SS *Daghestan* (5,742 t.) – lost through enemy action in week ending March 31.

Home Front: Britain – A large proportion of people evacuated from cities in Sept. 1939 have now drifted back home; only 300,000 schoolchildren, out of original 1 M., remaining in country reception areas.

MONDAY, APRIL 1

Home Front: France – Govt. Decree authorizes construction of 53 warships: 2

battleships, 1 carrier, 3 cruisers, 27 destroyers and 20 subs.

China – Japanese-sponsored 'Central Govt. of China' established at Nanking, under Wang Ching-wei, a former colleague of Chiang Kai-shek (Govt. not recognized by Western Powers).

TUESDAY, APRIL 2

Air War – German aircraft raid Scapa Flow; on return flight they attack lighthouses, at Duncansby Head and Stroma I.

WEDNESDAY, APRIL 3

Air War – Sunderland flying boat disperses formation of 6 Ju 88s attacking convoy in North Sea (1 Ju 88 shot down; second makes crash-landing in Norway and crew are interned). First Spitfire lost on home defence duties – while shooting down He 111 off Yorkshire coast.

Sea War – First German Norway invasion ships sail.

Home Front: Britain – Govt. reshuffle: Adm. of the Fleet Lord Chatfield, Minister for Co-ordination of Defence, resigns; First Lord of the Admiralty, Mr Churchill, to head new committee of Service Ministers. Lord Woolton becomes Minister of Food. Gen. Sir Hugh Elles appointed National ARP Controller.

Home Front: Canada – Earl of Athlone appointed Gov-Gen. in succession to Lord Tweedsmuir (John Buchan).

THURSDAY, APRIL 4

Air War – RAF bombers attack German destroyers off Wilhelmshaven.

Sea War – Norwegian passenger ship *Mira* reaches home port after surviving numerous German air attacks during 6-day, tortuous crossing of North Sea. None of 107 passengers and crew seriously injured.

Home Front: Britain – Chamberlain tells Conservative Party meeting in London that, by not taking maximum advantage of Germany's military superiority over Britain in Sept. 1939, Hitler *'missed the bus'*. British trade with the Balkans to be fostered by new trading corporation (attempt to combat German economic penetration of the Balkans).

Home Front: Germany – Göring broadcasts to German young people: Germany will strike decisive blow against Britain and France and create the world's greatest empire; German youth must behave with decency and morality *'not only in the light of day but also in the blackout'*.

FRIDAY, APRIL 5

Sea War – First captured German merchant ship – the *Uhenfels* (renamed *Empire Ability*) – brought up R. Thames.

Diplomacy – Anglo-French note to Norway: warning of possible counter-measures against flagrant German violations of Norwegian neutrality.

SATURDAY, APRIL 6

Air War – RAF Bomber Cmnd ends its leaflet ('Nickel') raids on Germany: 65 M. leaflets and 'newspapers' dropped since Sept. 3, 1939.

SUNDAY, APRIL 7

Sea War: Atlantic – British Home Fleet leaves Scapa Flow for Norwegian Sea.

MONDAY, APRIL 8

Sea War – British destroyers lay mines in Norwegian territorial waters, SW. of Narvik (Op. Wilfred). HMS *Glowworm* becomes detached and encounters German naval force (heavy cruiser *Admiral Hipper* and 4 destroyers) heading for Trondheim. *Glowworm* rams *Hipper* and sinks.

Diplomacy – Norway protests against British minelaying ops.

Air War – First operational sorties by German Fw 200C 4-engine maritime-recce bombers over North Sea.

TUESDAY, APRIL 9

Norway – **GERMAN INVASION OF NORWAY** (Op. *Weserübung Nord*: 'Weser Crossing North') – 6 regts; 1 parachute bn.; 1,000 aircraft; 2 battlecruisers, 1 pocket-

Below: *Until Sept. 1940 ships in convoys were seldom attacked by U-boats.*

battleship, 7 cruisers, 14 destroyers, 30 U-boats. Germans land at Oslo, Kristiansand, Stavanger, Bergen, Trondheim and Narvik. Norwegian coastal batteries sink cruiser *Blücher* in Oslo Fjord (1,600 killed). Airborne troops seize Fornebu Airport (Oslo) and Stavanger-Sola airfield. German destroyers sink Norwegian armoured ships *Eidsvold* and *Norge* at Narvik and land troops; Norwegian garrison betrayed by its CO, Col. Sundlo. King Haakon escapes German trap at Oslo. Vidkun Quisling proclaims himself head of Norwegian Govt. and says *'I shall be called the big traitor'.*

Norwegian Forces
6 divs. (mobilizing); 4 coast batteries; 80 planes; 4 coast defence ships, 1 mine-layer, 6 torpedo boats, 9 subs.

Denmark – **GERMAN INVASION OF DENMARK** (Op. *Weserübung Sud*: 'Weser Crossing South') – 2 divs; 1 brig. grp. and 1 bn. airborne troops; 60 aircraft; 2 old battleships, light warships and auxiliaries. Germans land at Copenhagen, Aalborg Airfield, Esbjerg and other towns and seize Jutland-Funen Bridge. Danish troops offer some resistance in S. Jutland and Royal Guard makes brief stand at Amalienborg Palace, Copenhagen. Me 110s strafe Vaerlose Airfield, HQ of Danish AF – destroying many planes (1 Danish fighter destroyed in combat). He 111s drop leaflets over Copenhagen. No resistance from Danish Navy.

Sea War – British Home Fleet approaches Bergen, but is forced to withdraw by German land-based bombers (47 Ju 88s and 41 He 111s). Battleship *Rodney* and 3 cruisers damaged; destroyer *Gurkha* sunk (4 Ju 88s shot down). Battlecruisers exchange fire SW. of Narvik: *Renown* and *Gneisenau* both slightly damaged. 19 British subs. commence intensive ops. in Norwegian Sea, Skagerrak, Kattegat and North Sea; *Truant* cripples cruiser *Karlsruhe* in Skagerrak. (German torpedo boat sinks the hulk.)

Diplomacy – German 'Memoranda' to Denmark and Norway: both countries to be given German 'protection' for the duration of the war. Britain promises all possible military aid to Norway.

Home Front: Britain – Death of Mrs Patrick Campbell, actress; aged 75.

Danish Forces
15,450 men (2 brigs.); 100 planes; 2 coast defence ships, 9 patrol boats, 9 subs.

Danish Campaign Losses
Danish: 13 dead, 23 wounded; 9 planes.
German: 20 dead, 65 wounded.

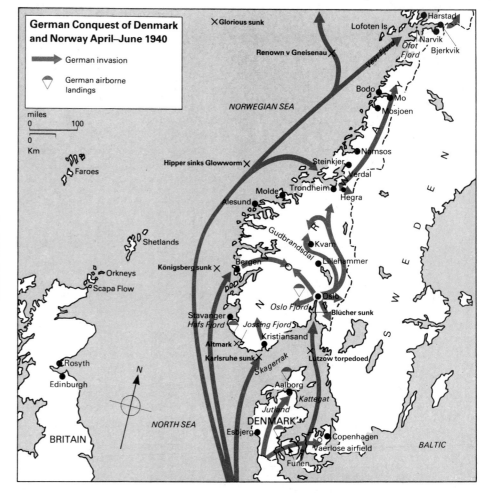

German Conquest of Denmark and Norway April–June 1940
→ German invasion
▽ German airborne landings

miles 0 — 100
Km 0 —

Glorious sunk
Lofoten Is
Harstad
Narvik
Bjerkvik
Ofot Fjord
Vest Fjord
Renown v Gneisenau
NORWEGIAN SEA
Bodo
Mo
Mosjoen
Namsos
Hipper sinks Glowworm
Steinkjer
Verdal
Molde
Trondheim
Hegra
Alesund
Gudbrandsdal
Kvam
Bergen
Lillehammer
Königsberg sunk
Oslo Fjord
Oslo
Blücher sunk
Stavanger / Hafs Fjord
Jossing Fjord
Altmark
Kristiansand
Karlsruhe sunk
Lutzow torpedoed
Skagerrak
Faroes
Shetlands
Orkneys
Scapa Flow
Aalborg
Kattegat
Jutland
DENMARK
Copenhagen
Vaerlose airfield
Esbjerg
Funen
BALTIC
Rosyth
Edinburgh
N
NORTH SEA
BRITAIN
SWEDEN

WEDNESDAY, APRIL 10

Sea War – **FIRST BATTLE OF NARVIK.** 5 British destroyers engage 10 German destroyers and shore batteries in Ofot Fjord, W. of Narvik. *Hardy, Hunter* (British), *Wilhelm Heidkamp* and *Anton Schmitt* (German) lost. Capt. Warburton-Lee and Commodore Bonte (OC German Destroyers) killed. 8 German merchant ships and ammunition carrier *Rauenfels,* also sunk. British sub. *Thistle* sunk by *U-4* off Stavanger.

Air War – 15 Blackburn Skua dive-bombers of British Fleet Air Arm sink cruiser

Below: *The London* Daily Sketch *cartoon of April 10.*

Königsberg at Bergen, first major warship to be sunk by dive-bombing. German aircraft (4 lost) raid Scapa Flow.
Neutrals: Iceland – Icelandic Parliament (the *Althing*) severs constitutional links with Denmark and declares that Icelandic Govt. will conduct its own affairs.

THURSDAY, APRIL 11

Norway – Gen. Ruge appointed CinC. Norwegian Army, in place of Maj-Gen. Laake.
Air War – 6 Wellingtons (1 lost) attack Stavanger-Sola airfield (first British daylight raid on continental target).
Sea War – British sub. *Spearfish* cripples pocket-battleship *Lützow*, S. of Oslo (night April 10-11).

FRIDAY, APRIL 12

Air War – 90 RAF bombers, despatched to Stavanger area to attack *Gneisenau* and *Scharnhorst*, fail to make contact.
Diplomacy – Danish Gov. of Faeroe Is. agrees to accept British protection (troops land April 13).

SATURDAY, APRIL 13

Sea War – SECOND BATTLE OF NARVIK. Battleship HMS *Warspite* and 9 destroyers attack 8 German destroyers – which are all sunk or disabled (and then scuttled by their crews, which escape ashore). 3 British destroyers damaged. *Warspite*'s Swordfish spotter plane bombs *U-64*. Adm. Whitworth decides to occupy Narvik, but quickly reverses his decision.
Air War – 15 Hampdens drop parachute mines off Danish coast (night April 13-14), first British aerial mining.

SUNDAY, APRIL 14

Norway – British North Western Expeditionary Force begins landing at Harstad (near Narvik) and Namsos (N. of Trondheim). Gen. von Falkenhorst, Cdr. of German Forces in Norway, threatens draconian measures against civilian resistors.
Air War – RAF bombs Stavanger-Sola airfield and seaplanes in Hafrs Fjord. Norwegian Fokker biplanes bomb Ju 52 seaplane transports on L. Harting.

MONDAY, APRIL 15

Norway – Siege of Hegra: Norwegian detachment holds antiquated Hegra Fortress, E. of Trondheim, against strong German ground and air forces for 3 weeks (ends May 5).
King Haakon issues proclamation appealing for all Norwegians to do their utmost *'to save the freedom and independence of our beloved country'.* He denounces the Blitzkrieg *'by a nation with which we always maintained friendly relations'.*

Western Front – Anglo-French 'Plan D' (*see* Nov. 14, 1939) amended to include drive by French mechanized 7th Army (Gen. Giraud) into S. Holland.
Sea War – *U-49* sunk off Harstad by destroyers *Brazen* and *Fearless* (a chart is recovered showing U-boat dispositions).
Air War – 15 RAF Bomber Cmnd Blenheims attack Stavanger-Sola. Fleet Air Arm bombers raid shipping at Bergen.
Occupied Denmark – Demobilization of Danish Army in progress.
Occupied Norway – Quisling puppet govt. resigns in Oslo and is replaced by 'Administrative Council' of Norwegian bureaucrats and lawyers.
Home Front: Britain – 972,695 people unemployed; 148,518 less than in March 1940 and the lowest monthly total since 1920.

TUESDAY, APRIL 16

Sea War – *U-1* sunk by British sub. *Porpoise*, off Stavanger.
Diplomacy – Norwegian White Paper on German invasion: listing 13 demands made by German Minister in Oslo (April 9), several hours after commencement of German invasion.

WEDNESDAY, APRIL 17

Norway – British troops land at Andalsnes (Op. Sickle). German troops isolated at Narvik ordered to 'hold out as long as possible'.
Air War – RAF bomb Trondheim-Vaernes airfield.
Sea War – British cruiser *Suffolk* bombards Stavanger-Sola airfield and seaplane base (heavy damage). Cruiser pursued by Ju 88s and seriously damaged.

THURSDAY, APRIL 18

Norway – British base established at Molde; troops land at nearby Alesund. Op. Hammer cancelled – British plan (Churchill and Adm. Keyes) for direct assault on Trondheim by British Home Fleet and landing of 4,500 troops.
Diplomacy – Norwegian Govt. declares war on Germany.

FRIDAY, APRIL 19

Norway – British brig., advancing S. from Namsos, reaches Verdal, 80 km from Trondheim. French troops (*Chasseurs Alpins*) land at Namsos. British brig. joins Norwegians at Lillehammer. German troops, landed from 2 destroyers, outflank British 146th Inf. Brig. near Steinkjer (Trondheim Fjord) and force it to withdraw.
Air War – Destruction of Namsos: German bombers make repeated raids on this Allied base in central Norway until May 13; town and harbour completely destroyed; civilian population evacuated.

SATURDAY, APRIL 20

Air War – German bombers (3 lost) attack British naval units off Norway.

SUNDAY, APRIL 21

Air War – RAF bombers (1 lost) raid Aalborg airfield (N. Denmark) and Stavanger-Sola.

MONDAY, APRIL 22

Air War – French reconnaissance aircraft reach Prague (night April 22-23).

TUESDAY, APRIL 23

Air War – German bombers raid Scapa Flow (night April 22-23).
Home Front: Australia – P.M. Menzies threatens to re-open coal mines by force if miners do not end their 6-week strike (strike settled by arbitration May 15).
Home Front: Britain – Second War Budget presented by Chancellor of the Exchequer, Sir John Simon: income tax raised to 7s 6d in the £; higher duties on beer, spirits and tobacco; increased postal charges; planned introduction of a new 'Purchase Tax'.

WEDNESDAY, APRIL 24

Sea War – British battleship *Warspite* and 3 cruisers bombard Narvik, planned landing of troops from cruiser *Vindictive* is cancelled. 3 French destroyers engage German patrol boats in the Skagerrak (night April 23-24) and repel air attacks.

THURSDAY, APRIL 25

Sea War – British armed trawlers *Bradman*, *Hammond* and *Larwood* sunk by German aircraft off Andalsnes (they are subsequently raised and operated as German patrol boats *Friese*, *Salier* and *Franke*).

FRIDAY, APRIL 26

Norway – Norwegians and British halt German advance along Gudbrandsdal Valley at Kvam. Norwegian CinC Gen. Ruge issues optimistic Order of the Day: *'now the time of retreat has come to an end . . . Stand fast . . . and the victory will be ours!'*

SATURDAY, APRIL 27

Diplomacy – Germany officially at war with Norway. Ribbentrop attempts to justify German invasion of Norway by describing vast, carefully prepared, Anglo-French-Norwegian 'conspiracy' (he does not mention Germany's actions in Denmark).
Home Front: Britain – Men aged 26 registered for military service.

Occupied Norway – Terboven appointed *Reichskommissar* for Norway (formerly *Gauleiter* of Essen).

SUNDAY, APRIL 28

Sea War: Atlantic – Liner *Queen Mary* (81,200 t.) arrives at Cape Town after record-breaking 12-day voyage from New York.

MONDAY, APRIL 29

Norway – British troops land at Bodo. Cruiser HMS *Glasgow* transports King Haakon, Crown Prince Olav and Norwegian Govt. from Molde to Tromso. Norwegian Govt. issues declaration condemning German 'terrorism' – members of the Govt. having personally witnessed such acts of violence against unarmed and innocent Norwegian civilians.
Sea War – *U-50* sunk by HM destroyers *Amazon* and *Witherington* off Shetlands. British submarine *Unity* rammed and sunk by SS *Atle Jarl* off the Tyne.
Air War – Empire Air Training Scheme: Training of pilots and air crews begins at schools in Canada, Australia and New Zealand.

TUESDAY, APRIL 30

Norway – British commence evacuation of Andalsnes, Molde and Ålesund (completed night May 1-2). German columns from Oslo and Trondheim link up in central Norway. Hitler issues congratulatory Order of the Day.
Air War – He 111, carrying magnetic mine, is damaged by AA fire and crashes in Clacton-on-Sea, Essex; 4-man crew, 2 civilians killed; 156 people injured; 50 houses wrecked.

WEDNESDAY, MAY 1

Norway – British troops evacuated from Ålesund. Germans counter-attack near Narvik (and on May 2); attack repulsed. German forces link up between Oslo and Bergen. Surrender of 4,000 Norwegian troops, trapped at Lillehammer.
Western Front – Hitler orders *Gelb* ('Yellow') offensive against Low Countries and France to commence May 5.
Home Front: Germany – Krupp armament works at Essen designated a 'National Socialist model plant' for its outstanding services to the Third Reich.

THURSDAY, MAY 2

Norway – Evacuation of Namsos: British and French troops leave ruined town night May 2-3. *Stukas* attack May 3, sinking French destroyers *Afridi* and *Bison*. British troops land at Mosjoen.
Sea War: Med. – Chamberlain announces that powerful Anglo-French fleet is *en route* to Alexandria.

FRIDAY, MAY 3

Norway – Surrender of Norwegian forces in Trondheim area.
Western Front – Hitler postpones *Gelb* offensive from May 5 to May 6 (further postponements on May 4, 5, 7 and 8). Gen. Huntziger, CO French 2nd Army, orders demolition of anti-tank obstacles (built without his sanction) on two main roads from Ardennes forest.
Secret War – Col. Oster of the *Abwehr* tells Col. Sas, Dutch military attaché in Berlin, that Germany will attack Low Countries soon (probably May 8).
Air War – RAF bomb Ry (Denmark), Fornebu and Stavanger airfields.

SATURDAY, MAY 4

Sea War – Polish destroyer *Grom* bombed and sunk off Narvik.
Norway – British troops land at Mo, S. of Narvik.
Secret War – Papal Nuncio warns King Leopold of Belgium that German attack is imminent.

SUNDAY, MAY 5

Norway – French Foreign Legionnaires and Polish troops land at Harstad and Tromso.
Secret War – *Kapitan* Hermann Goertz, of the *Abwehr*, lands by parachute near Dublin. He subsequently establishes contact with Irish Army officers and the IRA (Goertz detained by Irish authorities in Nov. 1941).

MONDAY, MAY 6

Norway – Norwegians fight back in Roeros-Stoeren sector (E. central Norway).
Norwegian gold reserve (£33 M.) safe in London.
Secret War – The Pope tells Princess Marie-José, wife of Italian Crown Prince, that Germany is about to attack Low Countries. The Princess informs her brother, King Leopold.

TUESDAY, MAY 7

Home Front: Britain – 'NORWAY DEBATE' begins in House of Commons; Chamberlain defends Conservative Govt's. strategy. He comes under fierce attack from Adm. Keyes and L. S. Amery (Cons): *'In the name of God, go!'*
Secret War – French pilot returning from leaflet raid on Düsseldorf (night May 7-8) reports seeing German motorized column 96 km long heading W. for the Ardennes.

WEDNESDAY, MAY 8

Home Front: Britain – 'Norway Debate' concluded: severe criticism of Chamberlain by Lloyd George (*'The P.M. . . . has appealed*

for sacrifice . . . he should sacrifice the Seals of Office!'*). Final Vote: Govt. 281, Opposition 200 (33 Conservatives vote with Opposition). Chamberlain decides to resign.
Western Front – Hitler postpones *Gelb* offensive from May 9 to May 10.
Secret War – Belgian Embassy in Berlin warns Brussels that German Foreign Office is preparing ultimatum to Belgium and that OKW (German High Command) has just given the order for the invasion.

THURSDAY, MAY 9

Western Front – At noon Hitler orders *Gelb* offensive to begin at 5.35 a.m. May 10. At 9 a.m. code word *'Danzig'* transmitted to German commanders on W. Front. Hitler leaves Berlin in special train for his forward HQ near Münstereifel on Belgian border.
Home Front: France – CABINET CRISIS. Reynaud denounces CinC Gen. Gamelin for his failure to defeat German invasion of Norway and demands appointment of new CinC. Minister of Defence Daladier defends Gamelin; Reynaud offers to resign but swears his colleagues to secrecy.
Sea War – Cruiser *Birmingham* and 7 destroyers attacked in Skagerrak by 4 'E-boats' ('S'-class MTBs): *S31* hits *Kelly* (Commanded by Lord Mountbatten), which has to be towed to Newcastle. French sub. *Doris* sunk by *U-9* off Holland.
Air War – German aircraft drop 100 mines off Dutch and Belgian ports (night 9-10).
Secret War – Col. Oster tells Col. Sas that German attack in the W. will begin at dawn May 10. French *Deuxième Bureau* reports no signs of 'abnormal German movements' beyond frontiers of Holland and Belgium.

FRIDAY, MAY 10

Western Front – GERMANS INVADE HOLLAND, BELGIUM AND LUXEMBURG without warning (Op. *Gelb*) employing 77 divs. (10 *Pz*, 2 airborne) and 3,500 aircraft. Three *Pz* corps – Guderian's XIX, Reinhardt's XLI and Hoth's XX – strike through the Ardennes in S. Belgium and Luxemburg, towards R. Meuse. Belgian forces withdraw from the

> **Dutch Forces**
> 270,000 men (11 divs.); 126 planes; 72 warships and subs. (many in E. Indies).

> **Belgian Forces**
> 650,000 men (22 divs.); 42 tanks; 179 planes; 1 sloop.

Ardennes behind R. Meuse, except for 2 infantry comps. (*Chasseurs Ardennais*),

which delay 1st *Pz* Div. (Guderian's corps) with road blocks. Anglo-French Army Group 1 (includes BEF), 32 divs., crosses into Belgium ('Dyle Plan'). Gen. Gamelin, Allied CinC, issues Order of the Day: *'Germany has engaged in war to the death against us . . .* [have] *courage, energy, confidence.'* Hitler issues Order of the Day: *'Soldiers of the West Front! The battle which is beginning today will decide the fate of the German nation for the next thousand years.'* Dutch Army carries out pre-arranged flooding of 'inundation areas' in E. Holland.

Dutch foil attempted abduction (by German paratroops) of Queen Wilhelmina. Op. Royal Marine begins: 1,700 mines laid in R. Rhine by May 17.

Air War – Luftwaffe raid airfields and towns in Holland, Belgium and N. France at dawn. German airborne forces invade Holland and Belgium, seizing key airfields and bridges; gliders land storm troops at Fort Eben-Emael (Belgium). Dutch liners *Statendam* (28,300 t) and *Veendam* (15,500 t) bombed and sunk at Rotterdam. Dutch air forces and RAF destroy many Junkers transport aircraft over Holland. RAF Battle bombers make low-level attacks on *Pzs* advancing through Luxemburg (16 of 32 shot down; remainder damaged). German aircraft bomb Freiburg (Germany) by mistake; 57 killed (Goebbels blames the French). 9 Belgian Fairey Fox biplanes intercept group of Me 109s; 1 Me shot down, 3 Foxes shot down and 6 damaged. RAF bombs lines of communication E. of S. Dutch-German border (night May 10-11).

Sea War – British destroyers, minesweepers and Marines sent to coast of Holland. German troopship mined S. of Oslo. British troops land in Iceland. British and French troops land in Dutch W. Indies; Dutch seize 26 German merchant ships in E. and W. Indies.

Norway – British troops evacuated from Mosjoen, S. of Narvik.

Diplomacy – German 'Memoranda' to Brussels and The Hague justifying invasion. Belgian and Dutch Govts. appeal to Britain and France. Queen Wilhelmina makes 'flaming protest' against unprovoked German aggression. Luxemburg Govt. flees to France. British and French Govts. warn Germany against carrying out air raids on civilian targets.

Home Front: Britain – CHAMBER-

LAIN RESIGNS. CHURCHILL BECOMES PRIME MINISTER and forms Coalition Govt.

Home Front: France – Temporary reconciliation between P.M. Reynaud and the CinC, Gen. Gamelin.

SATURDAY, MAY 11

Western Front – Guderian's *Pz* Corps disperses French horse cavalry and light mechanized forces in the Ardennes and 2 of his 3 *Pz* divs. reach R. Semoy, 16 km N. of Sedan. Belgian troops fall back from Albert Canal towards R. Dyle (night May 11-12). French 7th Army reaches Breda, SW. Holland, after rapid advance through Belgium.

Air War – French Sud-Est LeO-451 fast medium bombers attack German motorized columns invading Belgium. 7 out of 8 RAF Battles shot down while attacking German columns in Luxemburg. Do 17s wipe out No. 114 Sqn. RAF, destroying 30 Blenheims. Belgian Battles make suicidal attacks on captured bridges over Albert Canal. 36 RAF Whitleys and Hampdens (3 lost) bomb communications in München-Gladbach area.

Diplomacy – Japanese Foreign Minister, Arita, warns the warring powers, USA and Italy, that Japan will not tolerate any change in *status quo* in Dutch E. Indies.

Home Front: Britain – Govt. appoint-

ments: Attlee, Lord Privy Seal; Alexander, First Lord of Admiralty; Eden, Sec. for War; Sinclair, Sec. for Air.

SUNDAY, MAY 12

Western Front – French light mechanized units withdraw and all the bridges over R. Meuse are blown up, except those at Mézières, where French 'fortress' troops continue to hold both banks. Advance guards of three *Pz* corps reach the Meuse later in the day along 130 km front, from Dinant to Sedan, having advanced 120 km in 3 days. French 7th Army comes under severe pressure from 9th *Pz* Div. and *Stukas* and is forced to retreat from Breda and Tilburg to Antwerp.

Norway – French Foreign Legion (2 bns.) land at Bjerkvik, near Narvik.

Air War – 5 Battles flown by volunteers make suicidal attack on Vroenhoven and Veldwezelt bridges over Albert Canal, Belgium; all 5 shot down by flak; Veldwezelt bridge damaged.

Home Front: Britain – 3,000 enemy aliens and 11,000 non-enemy aliens interned. Kingsley Wood, Chancellor of Exchequer; Anderson, Home Sec.; Morrison, Min. of Supply.

Neutrals: Spain – Gen. Franco issues Note affirming Spain's continued adherence to the policy of 'strict neutrality', decreed on Sept. 5, 1939.

CHURCHILL, Winston Leonard Spencer (1874-1965)
British: *Prime Minister, First Lord of the Treasury, Minister of Defence, Leader of the House of Commons*

Greatest British war leader since the Elder Pitt. Renowned for his masterful morale-boosting broadcast speeches in 1940-41, his extensive wartime travels to confer with other Allied leaders, and his remarkable relationship with Pres. Roosevelt. Deeply involved in every aspect of the war, from grand strategy to the tactics of Commando ops. and technicalities of secret weapons. Nobel prize-winning author and gifted artist.

Born at Blenheim Palace, Oxfordshire; descendant of great Duke of Marlborough. Son of Lord Randolph Churchill (1849-95), brilliant but wayward Conservative politician, and Jenny Jerome, witty and vivacious American. Educated at Harrow and Sandhurst. Commissioned in 4th Hussars, 1895. In battle of Omdurman, 1898. War correspondent in South Africa, 1900; captured by Boers, but made daring escape. Conservative M.P. for Oldham, 1900. Joined Liberal Party, 1905. Under-sec. for the Colonies, 1905-8; Pres. Board of Trade, 1908-10, Home Secretary 1910-11.

Popular, and generally successful, First Lord of the Admiralty, 1911-15, but resigned following severe criticism of Navy's role in Dardanelles débâcle, 1915. Lt-Col. of 6th Royal Scots Fusiliers on Western Front, 1915-16. Min. of Munitions, 1917; Min. of War, 1918-21; Min. of Air, 1919-21. Sec. of State for the Colonies, 1921-22. Defeated in three parliamentary by-elections, 1922-24. Elected 'Constitutionalist' (Conservative) M.P. for Epping, 1924 (held seat until 1945). Chancellor of the Exchequer, 1924-29. Out of office, 1929-39, because of disagreements over India, rearmament and Appeasement. Condemned Munich Agreement of Sept. 1938.

Appointed First Lord of the Admiralty by Chamberlain on Sept. 3, 1939; continually urged more aggressive war strategy on Cabinet. Appointed P.M. of National Coalition Govt., May 10, 1940. Faced daunting series of crises and heart-rending decisions, 1940-42, including: retention of RAF Fighter Cmnd. for home defence in face of desperate French cries for help, May 1940; withdrawal from France of BEF at Dunkirk, May 1940; destruction of French Fleet at Oran, July 1940; sanctioning of area bombing raids on German cities, Dec. 1940 onwards; giving of support to Stalin, after June 1941; sending of HMS *Prince of Wales* and *Repulse* to Singapore, Nov. 1941; Dieppe raid, Aug. 1942; and many others. Effected closest personal contact with Roosevelt; signed Atlantic Charter, Aug. 1941. Travelled the world to confer with Stalin, Roosevelt, de Gaulle and Chiang Kai-shek; attended Yalta (Feb. 1945), Potsdam (July 1945) conferences.

P.M. of 'Caretaker' Govt. May 23 – July 26, 1945. Decisively defeated by Labour Party under wartime deputy P.M., Attlee, in July 1945 General Elections. Returned to power, 1951-55. Resigned April 5, 1955. Made hon. US citizen, 1963. Died Jan. 24, 1965, aged 90. State funeral; buried in churchyard at Woodstock, near Blenheim Palace.

His many books include 'The Second World War' (published 1948-54).

which burn for days. 30,000 people feared dead (revised total: 980); 78,000 homeless.

WEDNESDAY, MAY 15

Western Front – Hoth's *Pzs* defeat French 1st Armoured Div. W. of Dinant; latter loses 125 of its 175 tanks. By nightfall, shattered French 9th Army is in full retreat W. of Meuse and its CO, Gen. Corap, is replaced by Gen. Giraud. German 6th Army launches major attack on Anglo-French front in Belgium ('Dyle Line'), but is bloodily repulsed.
FORMAL CAPITULATION OF DUTCH ARMY (isolated Dutch and French forces hold out in Zeeland, Walcheren and Beveland until May 17).

Dutch Campaign Losses
Dutch military: 2,890 dead, 6,889 wounded. Civilian: 2,500 dead. German *c.* 3,500; over 162 planes.

Occupied Holland – First issue of a Dutch 'underground' news sheet – *Geuzenactie*. Dutch resistance groups subsequently publish approx. 1,000 clandestine newspapers, news sheets and pamphlets.
Sea War – British destroyers *Valentine* (sunk) and *Winchester* (badly damaged) bombed in Scheldt Estuary.
Air War – RAF BOMBER COMMAND BEGINS STRATEGIC AIR OFFENSIVE AGAINST GERMANY: 99 aircraft (1 lost) sent to attack oil installations and marshalling yards in the Ruhr; targets only slightly damaged (night May 15-16). Germans announce that they consider city of Brussels a legitimate military target. Radio Brussels bombed.
Home Front: France – **PANIC IN PARIS** on reports of German breakthrough at Sedan. Many thousands of civilians leave city; Govt. depts. burn secret files; Premier Reynaud telephones Churchill: *'We are beaten; we have lost the battle!'*

THURSDAY, MAY 16

Western Front – By nightfall Guderian's leading tanks are 89 km W. of Sedan. Anglo-French-Belgian armies commence withdrawal from Dyle Line to Scheldt Line, W. of Brussels. Belgian Govt. moves to Ostend.
Air War – 26 LeO-451s (4 lost) with fighter escort bomb *Pzs* refuelling at Montcornet. RAF's Advanced Air Striking Force withdraws from bases S. of the Meuse to Troyes area E. of Paris.
Diplomacy – Churchill flies to Paris to consult with Reynaud, Daladier and Gen. Gamelin.
Neutrals: USA – Roosevelt sets US aircraft industry a production target of 50,000 warplanes a year.

MONDAY, MAY 13

Western Front – **BATTLE OF THE MEUSE:** *Pz* corps of Guderian, Hoth and Reinhardt, with strong air support, establish bridgeheads over R. Meuse at Sedan, Monthermé and Dinant, destroying French 9th Army and opening 80-km gap in the Allied line (ends May 17).
Battle of Tirlemont: French 2nd and 3rd Light Mechanized Divs. engage XVI *Pz* Corps (3rd and 6th *Pz* Divs.) NE. of Namur – after fierce all-day struggle, French retreat; both sides lose many tanks.
Air War – First unit of Dewoitine D-520 fighters (French equivalent of Spitfire) in action – over Meuse front – destroying 4 German aircraft without loss.
Home Front: Britain – Churchill presents new War Cabinet in House of Commons: *'I have nothing to offer but blood, toil, tears and sweat.'* New Govt.'s policy is to wage war and its aim victory. Bevin, Min. of Labour.
Home Front: Canada – Dr Manion resigns leadership of defeated Cons. Party.

TUESDAY, MAY 14

Western Front – Guderian's 1st *Pz* Div. crosses the Meuse at Sedan. 150 British and French bombers (inc. obsolete Battles and Amiot 143s) make suicidal daylight attacks on German pontoon bridges at Sedan; Me 109s, flak and small-arms fire destroy 45 RAF and 5 French bombers; bridges undamaged. French tank-infantry counter-attack in Sedan sector fails. Gen. Touchon appointed to command French reserves, earmarked to plug the gap developing between 9th and 2nd French armies W. of Sedan. Rotterdam Garrison surrenders. Dutch Army CinC, Gen. Winkelman, broadcasts Cease Fire call.
Home Front: Britain – Lord Beaverbrook appointed 'Minister of Aircraft Production'. War Office **APPEALS FOR 'LOCAL DEFENCE VOLUNTEERS'**, aged 17 to 65, to combat possible German parachute landings. Eden, Secretary for War, broadcasts personal appeal. (*See* July 23; 'Home Guard'.)
Air War – **DESTRUCTION OF ROTTERDAM:** In attempt to crush stubborn Dutch resistance – and bring tentative ceasefire negotiations to a speedy conclusion – 100 He 111s are despatched to bomb the city centre. Dutch garrison then offers to surrender, but 60 bombers cannot be recalled and start huge fires among fats and margarine stores,

FRIDAY, MAY 17

Western Front – Germans enter Brussels. Col. de Gaulle's 4th Armoured Div. counter-attacks Guderian's XIX *Pz* Corps at Montcornet, but is repulsed. Gen. von Kleist reprimands Guderian for the 'excessive' speed and extent of his advance! Guderian immediately resigns; he is persuaded to reverse his decision later in evening by List and Rundstedt. XVI and XXXIX *Pz* Corps detached from 6th Army in Belgium and sent S. to Meuse sector.
Air War – German bombers destroy Middelburg on Walcheren (Holland).
Sea War – Cruiser HMS *Effingham* hits uncharted rocks off Bodo and capsizes (finally scuttled, May 21). German aircraft commence minelaying ops. outside French Channel ports, from Le Havre to Dunkirk (night May 17-18). Venezuelan Navy seizes 2 German merchant ships at Maracaibo to prevent them leaving and causing diplomatic incidents.

SATURDAY, MAY 18

Western Front – Guderian's *Pzs* reach Péronne, on R. Somme; Hoth's *Pzs* reach Cambrai (scene of first British tank attack in 1917). Germans capture Antwerp.
Sea War – Heavy bomb penetrates battleship *Resolution* during Ju 88 raids over Narvik area.

Air War – Germans raid Dieppe (night May 18-19).
Home Front: France – Cabinet reshuffle. P.M. Reynaud takes over Defence Ministry; Daladier becomes Foreign Minister; Marshal Pétain returns from Madrid to become Vice-Premier; Mandel to Ministry of the Interior.

SUNDAY, MAY 19

Western Front – **GAMELIN DISMISSED. WEYGAND MADE ALLIED CINC.** De Gaulle's tanks make second counter-attack on Guderian's Corps, in Laon-Montcornet sector; some French tanks threaten Guderian's HQ and he summons assistance from 10th *Pz* Div., but *Stukas* halt French advance before they arrive. Gen Giraud, CO of French 9th Army, captured by German *Pz* Unit. Germans capture St Quentin.
Sea War: Atlantic – *U-37* sinks 9 merchant ships off NW. Spain (May 19-June 2).
Air War – Sensational reports of 100,000 people killed in Rotterdam raid (May 14). RAF bomb oil installations in NW. Germany.
Neutrals: Sweden – Home Defence Corps (Home Guard) to be formed. Petrol rationing introduced.

Below: SS *motorcycle troops in Aire-sur-la Lys, closing in on Dunkirk.*

MONDAY, MAY 20

Western Front – Guderian's 1st and 2nd *Pz* Divs. race to the Channel Coast, despite gallant but ineffectual resistance by troops from British 12th and 23rd (Territorial) divs. 1st *Pz* captures Amiens at midday and 2nd reaches Abbéville and Noyelles, at mouth of R. Somme, in the evening, after advancing 386 km in 11 days. Germans capture Laon, near Paris.
Air War – RAF attack *Pzs* in Arras-Cambrai sector; carry out night raid on Rotterdam oil storage tanks; and attack German communications at Givet, Dinant and Charleville.
Secret War – Tyler Kent, cipher clerk in US Embassy, London, detained by British police and charged with copying hundreds of confidential documents over 5-year period (some had been passed on to Nazi sympathizers and thence to Italian Embassy, London).

TUESDAY, MAY 21

Western Front – British and French armour counter-attack Rommel's 7th *Pz* Div. at Arras; after initial success attacks fail and end May 23. Germans besiege Maubeuge on R. Sambre, W. of Dinant. Anglo-French Army commanders, Weygand, Billotte and Gort, confer at Ypres; while returning to his HQ, Billotte is injured in car accident (he never regains

consciousness and dies May 23). Gen. Blanchard, CO of French 1st Army, assumes command of Anglo-French Army Group 1.

Belgian Govt. moves to Bruges.

Air War – Intensive RAF daylight ops. over battle fronts in S. Belgium and N. France. Nights raids on road and rail targets in Namur, Dinant and Aachen and troop concentrations at Arras (night May 21-22).

Sea War – French destroyer *L'Adroit* bombed and sunk off Dunkirk.

Home Front: France – Premier Reynaud tells Senate: *'France cannot die! . . . if I were told tomorrow that only a miracle could save France, I should reply, "I believe in miracles because I believe in France!" '*

WEDNESDAY, MAY 22

Western Front – Guderian's *Pz* Corps strikes N. from Abbéville towards Boulogne, Calais and Dunkirk.

Sea War – French destroyers give covering fire to Anglo-French forces in Boulogne.

Air War – RAF bomb German communications and dumps on R. Meuse near Namur and N. of R. Aisne. Attempted raid on Leipzig power station (night May 22-23).

Home Front: Britain – Emergency Powers Defence Act passed through Parliament.

Secret War – British Govt. Code and Cipher School breaks *Luftwaffe* 'Enigma' cipher for May 20. *Luftwaffe* 'Enigma' now read almost daily for rest of war.

THURSDAY, MAY 23

Western Front – Germans cross R. Scheidt at Oudenarde. BEF in Belgium put on half-rations following loss of supply depots.

Sea War – 6 British destroyers evacuate 4,400 troops from Boulogne, under heavy fire. French destroyers *Jaguar* and *Orage* sunk.

Air War – 18 Latécoère seaplanes dive-bomb bridges and road junctions between Boulogne and the Somme. Me 109s shoot down 3.

Home Front: Britain – Sir Oswald Mosley, leader of British Union of Fascists, and Capt. Ramsay, president of Right Club and Conservative M.P. for Peebles, arrested. 76 IRA men arrested in N. Ireland.

FRIDAY, MAY 24

Western Front – German infantry storm old Citadel, Boulogne. Guderian seals off Calais 'pocket'. **HITLER AND RUNDSTEDT HALT PANZERS** at Gravelines, SW. of Dunkirk. French fortress of Maubeuge surrenders, after destruction of many reinforced concrete works by heavy artillery and demolition charges. Fall of Ghent and Tournai.

Sea War – British cruisers and destroyers give supporting fire in Calais sector. French destroyer *Chacal* bombed and sunk off Boulogne.

Air War – Scattered raids over Yorkshire, E. Anglia and Essex (night May 24-25); 8 people injured at Middlesbrough – first civilian casualties in air-raid on England. RAF bomb Cologne marshalling yards (night May 24-25).

Secret War – British Govt. Code and Cypher School begins regular transmissions of de-coded German 'Enigma' messages to GHQ, BEF and RAF HQ in France.

SATURDAY, MAY 25

Western Front – BEF despatch 2 divs. to block the gap between Menin and Ypres. Germans capture 5,000 British and French troops at Boulogne. British garrison repels assault on Calais Citadel and rejects surrender call. French recapture part of Amiens.

Sea War – Cruisers *Arethusa* and *Galatea*, 6 British destroyers and Polish destroyer *Bzura* give covering fire to small British garrison besieged in Calais Citadel; destroyer *Wessex* bombed and sunk. German aircraft drop mines off English S. Coast ports (night May 25-26).

Diplomacy – Belgian P.M. Pierlot and Foreign Minister Spaak in London.

Home Front: Britain – Munitions factories now working round the clock.

Secret War – Highly secret documents discovered in captured German staff car reveal German plan to attack gap between Menin and Ypres with 2 corps.

SUNDAY, MAY 26

Sea War – **DUNKIRK EVACUATION** (Op. Dynamo) begins. Zeebrugge harbour sabotaged by Royal Navy; 4 block ships sunk.

Air War – Spitfires destroy 6 Me 109s and 6 Ju 87s over Dunkirk. *Stukas* pound British forces in Calais Citadel. Berlin falsely claims Calais has fallen. RAF bomb railway targets in Rhineland (night May 26-27).

Western Front – German ground and air forces crush stubborn British resistance in Calais Citadel. Hitler orders Rundstedt to resume advance by *'armoured groups and infantry divisions in direction Tournai . . . Dunkirk'.* German 6th Army launches powerful assault on Belgians holding Allied left flank. BEF send reinforcements. French and Belgians withstand violent German attacks between Courtrai and Valenciennes. French recapture several bridgeheads over the Somme E. of Amiens.

Home Front: Britain – Gen. Sir Edmund Ironside appointed CinC Home Forces; Gen. Sir John Dill appointed CIGS. Day of National Prayer.

Secret War – Adm. Schniewind, Chief of German Naval War Staff, predicts: *'Evacuation of [BEF] troops without equipment . . . is conceivable by means of large numbers of smaller vessels . . . even from the open coast.'*

MONDAY, MAY 27

Sea War: Atlantic – U-boat sinks Argentine SS *Uruguay* off Cape Finisterre (Argentina protests June 1 and later forbids its merchant ships to enter European waters).

Western Front – Guderian is permitted, by his superiors, to continue the advance from R. Aa towards Dunkirk, employing motorized infantry (tanks to be held in reserve). Franco-British counter-attacks against German 38th Corps holding Abbéville bridgehead S. of the Somme; these attacks gravely threaten Germans May 29 but finally fail May 30.

LE PARADIS MASSACRE: 90 captured British soldiers from 2nd Bn. Royal Norfolk Regt. shot by detachment of *SS Totenkopf* Div. in meadow near hamlet of Le Paradis, Pas-de-Calais.

Norway – French Foreign Legion, with light tanks, cross Rombaks Fjord and advance along iron-ore railway to Narvik (night May 27-28). Polish Brigade close in from the W.

TUESDAY, MAY 28

Sea War – 17,800 troops evacuated from Dunkirk; destroyer *Windsor* damaged by bombs; small steamer sunk by German MTB *S-34*.

Western Front – **UNCONDITIONAL SURRENDER OF BELGIAN ARMY:** cease fire at 4 a.m. except in isolated

Above: *British troops on Dunkirk beach take pot shots at the* Luftwaffe.

French recapture part of Abbéville.
Air War – Twenty LeO-451s (9 lost) attack Amiens and Abbéville, Douglas DB-7 bombers make low-level attacks on German columns near St Quentin.
China – Japanese High Command in China announces its intention to bomb Chiang Kai-shek's capital of Chungking daily 'until the spirit of Chinese resistance is broken'.
Neutrals: USA – Roosevelt sends $1,000 M. supplementary emergency defence budget to Congress.

SATURDAY, JUNE 1

Sea War – 64,400 troops evacuated from Dunkirk. Destroyers *Keith* (flagship), *Basilisk* and *Havant*, French destroyer *Foudroyant* and large transport *Scotia* bombed and sunk. 5 destroyers damaged by bombing. Evacuation by day has to be abandoned.
Air War – Germans bomb Lyons-Marseilles railway; British liner *Orford* (20,000 t) sunk at Marseilles.

SUNDAY, JUNE 2

Sea War – 26,200 troops evacuated from Dunkirk; destroyers *Malcolm* and *Sabre* damaged (night June 2-3).
Air War – Further German raids on Lyons and Rhône Valley region (97 civilian casualties, June 1 and 2). Single Gladiator biplane, flown by Pilot Officer Jacobsen of 263 Sqn. RAF, shoots down 6 German bombers (4 He 111, 2 Ju 88) near Narvik (Jacobsen killed June 8).
Diplomacy – Anti-British crowds, demanding return of Gibraltar, mark arrival in Madrid of Sir Samuel Hoare, new British Ambassador to Spain.

MONDAY, JUNE 3

Sea War – Last evacuation ships leave Dunkirk (night June 3-4).

> **Dunkirk Evacuation**
> Total evacuated: 338,226 men inc. about 120,000 French and Belgians; 861 ships and many private craft employed; 243 sunk. Aircraft losses: Luftwaffe: over 130, RAF: 106 (87 pilots dead or PoWs).

Air War – Heavy raid on Paris (Op. *Paula*): 200 German bombers (20 lost) attempt to destroy aircraft factories and airfields near capital; 254 people killed in suburbs. French lose 33 fighters.

TUESDAY, JUNE 4

Western Front – Germans capture Dunkirk, taking 40,000 French prisoners (rearguard plus many stragglers), and great quantities of abandoned British equipment, inc. 2,472 guns, 84,427 vehicles

sectors (all resistance ends May 29). Elimination of the Belgians opens 32 km gap on left flank of BEF-French 'pocket'; this is closed after fierce fighting in Nieuport area between ad hoc British forces (armoured cars of 12th Lancers, 'infantrymen' of Royal Engineers and Royal Artillery) and German 256th Div. French 1st Army (6 divs.) surrounded by 7 German divs. near Lille.

> **Belgian Campaign Losses**
> Belgian: 7,550 killed, 15,850 wounded. German casualties not known.

Norway – **NARVIK CAPTURED** by French Foreign Legion and Norwegians.
Air War – LeO-451 bombers, escorted by Hurricanes, attack bridges in Aubigny area.
Belgium – Belgian P.M. Pierlot broadcasts from Paris: he declares that Belgians are 'dumbfounded' by King Leopold's capitulation and that, since the King acted against Govt. advice, 'henceforth he has no power to govern', and the Belgian Cabinet will take over all his powers.

WEDNESDAY, MAY 29

Sea War – 47,300 troops evacuated from Dunkirk. Destroyers *Wakeful*, *Grenade* and *Grafton* sunk (latter by *U-62*). 6 British and 1 French destroyer damaged by bombing;

Mackay and *Montrose* collide and run aground. 8 auxiliary ships and 7 merchant ships bombed and sunk.
Norway – British troops evacuated from Bodo.
Western Front – Germans occupy Ostend, Ypres and Lille.
Air War – 2 elite units of Ju 88 bombers join assault on Dunkirk. Sqn. of RAF Defiant 2-seat fighters claim 37 'kills' over Dunkirk (actual total: 14).
Occupied Holland – Dr Seyss-Inquart takes office as *Reichskommissar* for Holland.

THURSDAY, MAY 30

Sea War – 53,800 troops evacuated from Dunkirk. French destroyer *Bourrasque* sunk by artillery fire and mine damage; 3 British destroyers damaged by bombing. 3 large transports sunk.

FRIDAY, MAY 31

Sea War – 68,000 troops evacuated from Dunkirk. French destroyers *Sirocco* and *Cyclone* torpedoed by German MTBs; 6 British destroyers damaged by bombing.
Western Front – French 1st Army surrenders in Lille sector after 4-day siege. BEF withdraw from Belgian sector of Dunkirk 'pocket' (night May 31-June 1).

and motorcycles and 657,566t. of ammunition and stores.

Air War – French Govt. threatens reprisals for Paris raid (June 3); French bombers attack Munich and Frankfurt (night June 4-5).

Home Front: Britain – Churchill tells House of Commons that a week earlier he had anticipated *'the greatest military disaster in our history';* but the Dunkirk Evacuation had transformed the situation. *'We shall defend our island whatever the cost may be, we shall fight on the beaches . . . we shall never surrender. . . .'*

WEDNESDAY, JUNE 5

France – **BATTLE OF FRANCE BEGINS.** Op. *Rot* (Red): 119 German divs. (10 *Pz*) against 65 French divs. (3 armoured, 3 mechanized cavalry), and 1 British div. German Army Group B (50 divs.) attacks on the Somme. (Army Groups A and C in state of readiness.) French defend fortified villages and road blocks tenaciously (Weygand Line). By nightfall Rommel's 7th *Pz* Div. is 13 km S. of Somme.

Air War – Hauptmann Mölders, leading German fighter 'ace', shot down in his Me 109 near Compiègne and taken prisoner. 30 German bombers attack airfields near British E. Coast; little damage. RAF bomb railways in Rhineland (night June 5-6), similar raid on night June 6-7.

Home Fronts: France – Cabinet changes: P.M. Reynaud takes personal responsibility for Foreign Affairs; Gen. de Gaulle becomes Under-Secretary for Defence, ex-P.M. Daladier leaves Govt. (at the insistence of Pétain and of Reynaud's domineering mistress, Countess de Portès).

THURSDAY, JUNE 6

France – Despite strong French resistance, Rommel breaks through W. of Amiens and advances 32 km.

Air War – 21 LeO-451 bombers (11 lost) attack German spearheads at Chaulnes, W. of St Quentin, and engage Me 109s and Me 110s.

Sea War: Atlantic – Armed merchant cruiser *Carinthia* (20,300 t) sunk by *U-46* W. of Ireland.

Diplomacy – Sir Stafford Cripps appointed British Ambassador in Moscow (the post has been vacant since Jan. 1940).

FRIDAY, JUNE 7

France – Rommel advances 48 km to Forges-les-Eaux, N. of Rouen.

Air War – French Naval Air Force attempts token bombing raid on Berlin: converted *Centre* NC223 4-engined mailplane makes 13½-hour flight, Bordeaux–Channel–North Sea–Baltic Sea–Berlin(?)–Paris. Crew claim to have attacked Berlin,

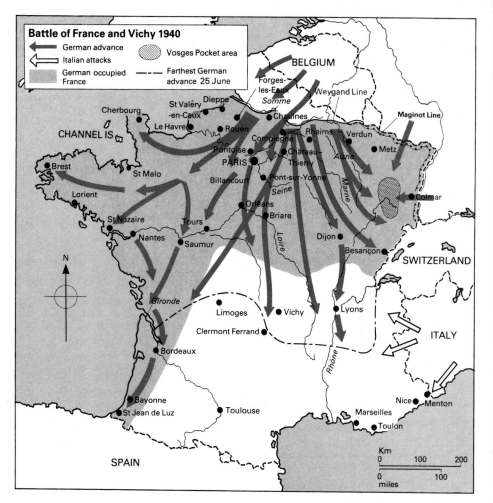

Battle of France and Vichy 1940

→ German advance (German advance arrow)
⇨ Italian attacks
▓ German occupied France
▨ Vosges Pocket area
- - - Farthest German advance 25 June

BELGIUM · Forges-les-Eaux · Weygand Line · Somme · Maginot Line · Cherbourg · St Valéry-en-Caux · Dieppe · Chaulnes · Rheims · Verdun · Le Havre · Rouen · Compiègne · Metz · CHANNEL IS · Pontoise · Château-Thierry · PARIS · Aisne · Brest · St Malo · Billancourt · Pont-sur-Yonne · Seine · Colmar · Lorient · Orléans · Briare · Marne · St Nazaire · Tours · Dijon · Nantes · Saumur · Besançon · Loire · SWITZERLAND · Gironde · Limoges · Vichy · Lyons · Clermont Ferrand · ITALY · Bordeaux · Rhône · Bayonne · Nice · Menton · St Jean de Luz · Toulouse · Marseilles · Toulon · SPAIN

N

Km 0 100 200
miles 0 100

but bombs apparently fall in open country (night June 7-8).

Home Front: Britain – Late Capt. Warburton-Lee awarded first V.C. of W.W.II (*see* April 10).

Sea War – First successful landings by Hurricanes on a British carrier, when evacuated from Norway by HMS *Glorious*.

SATURDAY, JUNE 8

France – Rommel advances 72 km and reaches R. Seine.

Norway – Evacuation of 24,000 Allied troops from Narvik and Harstad completed: 4-5,000 men evacuated per night since June 3-4. Port installations at Narvik rendered useless. King Haakon and Norwegian Govt. leave Tromso for England on British cruiser *Devonshire*.

Sea War – Carrier *Glorious* and escorting destroyers *Acasta* and *Ardent* sunk in desperate battle with *Gneisenau* and *Scharnhorst* SW. of Narvik. *Acasta* scores damaging torpedo hit on *Scharnhorst*. Casualties: British, 1,515; German, 48. German Adm. Marschall is dismissed for putting *Scharnhorst* at risk and failing to carry out planned attack on Harstad (Op. *Juno*).

Air War – Capt. Wuillame, of *Groupe de Chasse* (Fighter Group) I/2, flying a Morane, claims 3 Me 109s in only 15 secs. over Somme sector.

SUNDAY, JUNE 9

France – German Army Group A (45 divs.) attacks on the Aisne. 5th *Pz* Div. captures Rouen.

Norway – **GERMAN-NORWEGIAN ARMISTICE:** Gen. Dietl receives surrender of Gen. Ruge at Narvik.

Norwegian Campaign Losses
British: 1,869 dead and wounded; 100 planes; 19 warships. French/Polish: 533. Norwegian: 1,335. German: 3,692 dead or missing, 1,604 wounded; 242 planes; 19 warships.

MONDAY, JUNE 10

Diplomacy – **ITALY DECLARES WAR ON BRITAIN AND FRANCE.** Hostilities to begin at midnight. **CANADA DECLARES WAR ON ITALY.** French

Italian Forces
1,633,000 men (73 divs.); 1,600 tanks, 7,365 guns; 3,296 planes inc. 1,332 bombers, 1,160 fighters (1,796 operational); 6 battleships, 21 cruisers, 59 destroyers, 63 torpedo boats, 68 MTBs, 114 subs.

Govt. leaves Paris for Tours, on R. Loire.

France – Rommel drives French IX Corps and British 51st Highland Div. towards coast, N. of Le Havre. Manstein's 38th Inf. Corps crosses the Seine.

Sea War: Med. – 6 British subs leave Malta for ops. off Italian harbours and naval bases. Italian destroyers and torpedo boats sink *Odin, Grampus* and *Orpheus* (June 13, 16 and 27, resp.).

Neutrals: USA – Roosevelt speaks at Univ. of Virginia: *'On this tenth day of June 1940 the hand that held the dagger has struck it in the back of its neighbor.'*

Home Front: Britain – Duff Cooper, Minister of Information, condemns Mussolini: '[he] *has declared war upon the Allies with whom Italy fought in the last Great War and who . . . saved Italy from destruction.'*

TUESDAY, JUNE 11

Western Front – German vanguards approach Pontoise, thereby threatening Paris from the NW.

Sea War: Med. – British Med. Fleet and French cruiser sqn. sweep E. Med. and Aegean for Italian shipping. British cruisers bombard Tobruk and cruiser *Calypso* is sunk S. of Crete by Italian sub.

Air War – First RAF bombing raids on Italian airfields in Libya and E. Africa cause great damage (3 British aircraft lost). 2 Italian raids on Malta; 35 civilians, 6 British soldiers killed. 36 Whitleys (1 lost) bomb Turin and Genoa (night June 11-12) after refuelling stop in Channel Is. French authorities at Marseilles prevent Wellingtons from taking off to bomb targets in N. Italy by blocking runway with trucks (they fear Italian 'reprisal' raids).

Diplomacy – **AUSTRALIA, NEW ZEALAND AND SOUTH AFRICA DECLARE WAR ON ITALY.**

Home Front: Britain – Attlee, Lord Privy Seal, denounces Mussolini's declaration of war, comparing him with 'the jackal' which scents the possibility of getting some scraps from another beast's kill!

WEDNESDAY, JUNE 12

France – Rommel captures remnants of French IX Corps and British 51st Highland Div. at St. Valéry-en-Caux, near Le Havre. Germans reach the Marne and cross at Château-Thierry. Fall of Rheims.

North Africa – British capture 62 Italians in skirmish on Egyptian border.

Diplomacy – Egypt breaks off diplomatic relations with Italy. Turkey breaks off commercial relations with Italy. Britain and France sign non-aggression treaties with Thailand. Thai-Japanese Treaty of Friendship (to run for 5 years).

China – Japanese capture Ichang, vital port and air base on R. Yangtse, E. of Chungking.

Home Front: Italy – Vatican newspaper

Osservatore Romano, banned for publishing British and French war Communiqués (ban lifted June 13, when editors agree not to publish war news).

THURSDAY, JUNE 13

France – Paris declared an 'open city'; all French forces withdraw S. of the capital. Oil stores in suburbs set on fire. Germans reach N. outskirts in evening. Germans capture Le Havre.

Diplomacy – Final meeting of Allied Supreme War Council: Reynaud tells Churchill that France must make separate peace; Churchill suggests 'last ditch' appeal to Roosevelt.

Sea War – *Ark Royal* launches 15 Skua dive-bombers (8 lost) to attack *Scharnhorst* at Trondheim; 1 direct hit (unexploded bomb). French cruisers and destroyers, with air cover, bombard Genoa area in Italy (night June 13-14). Armed merchant cruiser *Scotstoun* (17,000 t) sunk by *U-25* off Ireland. German disguised raider *Orion* lays mines off Auckland, New Zealand.

Home Front: Britain – 120,000 schoolchildren to be evacuated from London.

Home Front: Germany – Hitler gives interview to American journalist Carl von Wiegand: he had no desire to smash British Empire but would 'destroy those who are destroying that Empire'. US aid to Britain would not affect the outcome of the war.

China – Japanese bombers make devastating fire raid on city of Chungking.

Neutrals: Spain – Franco prepares for closer collaboration with Germany and Italy by announcing new policy of 'non-belligerency'.

Air War – Italian bombers attack Toulon naval base, S. France.

Below: *A German soldier pitches his stick grenade into a bunker on the Maginot Line.*

FRIDAY, JUNE 14

France – **GERMAN FORCES ENTER PARIS.** Gen. von Bock, CO Army Group B, reviews victory parades in Place de la Concorde and at Arc de Triomphe. Germans capture intact Renault tank factory at Billancourt and Schneider-Creusot armament works. Only 700,000 people remain in city out of pop. of 5 M. German Army Group C (24 divs.) attacks Maginot Line and prepares to cross the Rhine. Churchill orders immediate evacuation of all remaining British troops. French Govt. leaves Tours for Bordeaux.

China – Japanese High Cmnd. advises British, American, Russian and German Embassies to evacuate their nationals from Chungking to places of safety.

Neutrals: Spain – Spanish Moroccan troops occupy 'International Zone' of Tangiers (N. Africa).

Diplomacy – French P.M. Reynaud sends desperate appeal for help to Pres. Roosevelt: if America does not declare war on Germany within a short time France is doomed.

Soviet Ultimatum to Lithuania.

Sea War: Med. – 3 Italian destroyers shell Sollum, Egypt.

Secret War – French and Polish 'Enigma' codebreakers leave Paris. They fly from Toulouse to Algiers, June 24.

SATURDAY, JUNE 15

France – Germans capture Verdun. German 7th Army (Army Group C) crosses Rhine opposite Colmar. French Army GHQ moves S. from Briare, on the Loire, to Vichy.

Sea War – Evacuation of British and Allied troops from NW. France (Op. Cycle) begins: 30,600 British troops begin to leave Cherbourg.

Diplomacy – Roosevelt replies to

Reynaud's appeal of June 14: USA will continue to give France all possible material help and moral support, but is unable to make any direct military commitment.
Neutrals: Baltic States – Soviet forces enter Lithuania.
Air War – Italian aircraft raid targets in S. France and Corsica.

SUNDAY, JUNE 16

France – Guderian captures Besançon.
Home Front: France – Reynaud Cabinet resigns; **PETAIN FORMS NEW GOVT.** Gen. Weygand, Min. of Defence. British Ambassador presents Draft Declaration of 'Act of Union' between Britain and France; French rejection.

PETAIN, Henri Philippe (1856-1951)
French: *Marshal and Chief of the French State*

Pétain is one of the most controversial figures in French history. He played many parts in his long life – the indomitable 'Saviour of Verdun' in 1916; champion of the ordinary French soldier; 'Grand Old Man' of Vichy; puppet of diehard French fascists; and finally the pathetic, senile prisoner of a windswept Atlantic isle.
    Born April 24, 1856. Attended St. Cyr military school, 1876-78; instructor at *École de Guerre* (under Foch); promoted to Colonel, 1912; corps commander, 1914-15; commanded an army, 1915. Took command at Verdun, Feb. 1916, and repulsed repeated German onslaughts until Dec. Appointed COGS, April 1917; CinC, May 1917; dealt with Communist-inspired mutinies with masterly skill. Created Marshal of France Nov. 1918; appointed Vice-Pres. of Supreme War Council, 1920; Inspector-Gen. of the Army, 1922; advocated purely defensive strategy. Crushed protracted Riff rebellion in Morocco, 1925-26.
    Associated with Fascist politicians, 1934-38. Ambassador to Spain, March 1939; recalled at the height of the French collapse, May 1940; succeeded Reynaud as P.M., June 16, 1940 and immediately sought armistice with Germany and Italy.
    Chief of French State, July 10, 1940, with Napoleonic powers. Established new capital at Vichy and called for a 'National Revolution' based on 'Work, Family and Fatherland'. Dismissed P.M. Laval, Feb. 1941, but forced to reinstate him under German pressure, April 1942. Grew weaker, personally and politically.
    Arrested by the Germans, Aug. 20, 1944; deported to Belfort (NE. France), then to Sigmaringen (SE. Germany). Voluntarily returned to France, April 1945; sentenced to death by High Court of Justice (14 votes to 13); commuted to life imprisonment by de Gaulle; banished to Ile d'Yeu (Bay of Biscay).

Sea War – 32,500 British and Allied troops and RAF personnel evacuated from Brest; 21,500 Canadian troops evacuated from St Malo (June 16-17). British cargo liner *Wellington Star* (13,200 t) sunk by *U-101* in Bay of Biscay. Evacuation of British and Allied troops from Biscay ports (Op. Ariel) begins: 57,000 troops leave Nantes and St Nazaire. Italian submarine *Galilei* sinks Norwegian tanker *James Stove* (8,200 t) in Indian Ocean.
Diplomacy – Soviet ultimatums to Estonia and Latvia.
Secret War – British SS *Broompark* leaves the Gironde (W. France) carrying 26 containers of 'heavy water', previously obtained from Norway by Joliot-Curie, the atomic physicist.

MONDAY, JUNE 17

Diplomacy – Pétain requests Germany's and Italy's armistice terms via Spanish Ambassador and the Vatican; he broadcasts to French Army and people: '. . . *it is necessary to stop the fighting.*'
Sea War – Evacuation ship *Lancastria* (16,243 t) bombed and sunk at St Nazaire: only 2,477 rescued out of 5,000 British, French and Belgians aboard (inc. civilians). Italian submarine *Provana* rammed and sunk by French sloop *La Curieuse* off Oran.
France – Rommel races towards Cherbourg, covering 241 km in the day.
Home Front: Britain – Churchill broadcasts: '*We have become the sole champions now in arms to defend the world cause.*'
Neutrals: Baltic States – Soviet forces occupy Estonia and Latvia. Left-wing govt. formed in Lithuania.

Neutrals: USA – British Purchasing Commission takes over all outstanding French arms contracts and offers to purchase as much war material as US can produce.

TUESDAY, JUNE 18

France – Rommel captures Cherbourg; 5th *Pz* Div. captures Brest. All large French towns to be surrendered without resistance. Civil administrators and military forces to await arrival of Germans. Gen. Legentilhomme, French CO in Somaliland, declares for de Gaulle.
Air War – 70 German bombers raid E. England; 11 killed at Cambridge (night June 18-19). Similar raids on most nights to end of month. Total German losses over England, June 5-30: 11 bombers. Evacuation of last RAF sqns. from France completed.
Sea War: Atlantic – All French and Allied shipping evacuated from Brest and naval installations and harbour works destroyed. New French battleship *Richelieu* leaves Brest for Dakar (arrives June 23). Uncompleted battleship *Jean Bart* towed out of St Nazaire; fuelled under German air attack and sails under half-power for Casablanca (night June 18-19; arrives 22). 30,600 British and Allied troops evacuated from Cherbourg; French battleship *Courbet* gives covering fire. French troopship *Champlain* (28,100 t) crippled by mine (finally sunk by *U-65,* June 21) in Bay of Biscay.
Sea War: Pacific – British liner *Niagara* (13,400 t), carrying £2.25 M. of gold, mined and sunk off Auckland, New Zealand (gold salvaged from record depth of 135m in 7 weeks).
France – De Gaulle broadcasts from London.
Home Front: Britain – Churchill declares in Commons: '*Let us so bear ourselves that if the British Commonwealth and Empire lasts for a thousand years men will say, "This was their finest hour!"*'
Diplomacy – Hitler and Mussolini meet in Munich.

WEDNESDAY, JUNE 19

Western Front – Germans capture Brest naval base, and begin crossing R. Loire on broad front. Cadets of Saumur Cavalry School under Col. Michon prevent German 1st Cavalry Div. (motorized) from crossing Loire.
Air War – Italian aircraft raid Bizerta. Germans bomb Bordeaux: 63 killed, 180 injured (night June 19-20).
Sea War – 19,000 Polish and British troops evacuated from Bayonne and St Jean-de-Luz, near Franco-Spanish border (op. completed June 25).
Home Front: Britain – Children's Overseas Reception Board established to send 20,000 schoolchildren to the Dominions for the duration of the war.

THURSDAY, JUNE 20

France – Germans capture Lyons. Saumur Cadets forced to surrender when ammunition supplies for their training weapons run out (200 cadets killed, June 19-20).
Italian offensive on the Riviera (extended along entire Franco-Italian frontier to Mt Blanc, June 21).
Sea War – *Gneisenau* torpedoed off Trondheim by British sub. *Clyde.*
Home Front: Britain – Entire output of Thompson sub-machine guns (300 t per week) to be delivered from US manufacturers in weekly shipments.
Home Front: France – Pétain broadcasts: he describes the defeat of France as 'inevitable' and compares the 185 British, American and Italian divs. supporting the French Army in May 1918 with the 10 British divs. of May 1940.

Diplomacy – French authorities in Indo-China bow to Japanese threat and halve transit of arms to China via Haiphong.

FRIDAY, JUNE 21

Diplomacy – Hitler attends Franco-German armistice negotiations in Forest of Compiègne.

Air War – 50 German aircraft make scattered night raids over many parts of England, guided by radio beams.

Secret War – Specially equipped RAF Anson aircraft detects radio beam transmitted from Germany in direction of Rolls-Royce works, Derby. Counter-measures are quickly devised against this system (German code name *Knickebein*, or 'bent leg').

Sea War: Atlantic – 2 U-boats disappear: *U-122* (June 21) and *U-102* (June 30) missing off N. Channel (Irish Sea); possibly sunk by mines. 2 'Special Service Vessels' (decoy ships) sunk by U-boats, W. of Ireland: *Prunella* (June 21) and *Williamette Valley* (June 29).

Neutrals: Rumania – King Carol forms 'National Party' inc. members of Iron Guard (Jews excluded from membership).

Neutrals: USA – Death of Col. Thompson, inventor of the 'Tommy Gun' (a sophisticated submachine gun), aged 80.

SATURDAY, JUNE 22

France – **ARMISTICE BETWEEN FRANCE AND GERMANY** signed at Compiègne by Gen. Keitel (Germany) and Gen. Huntziger (France). Signing ceremony takes place in Marshal Foch's old railway carriage, previously used for signature of Armistice, Nov. 11, 1918. Armistice terms: Germany to occupy two-thirds of Metropolitan France inc. entire Channel and Atlantic coastlines; all major industrial areas; Alsace-Lorraine and Paris. French armed forces to be disarmed and demobilized, with exception of token defence forces; French Fleet to be disarmed and demobilized under German and Italian supervision; France to pay costs of German army of occupation. French PoWs to remain in Germany until signature of peace treaty. 3 French armies (400,000 men) surrender in Vosges pocket, W. of Maginot Line. Germans occupy Lorient.

Air War – Italian SM81 3-engined bombers raid Alexandria; 25 casualties (night June 22-23).

Sea War: Atlantic – *U-46* attacks British Force H as it battles against hurricane-force winds *en route* from Scapa to Gibraltar; *Ark Royal* probably hit, but torpedoes fail to explode.

Neutrals: Baltic States – Left-Wing Govts. formed in Estonia and Latvia.

SUNDAY, JUNE 23

France – Italians occupy Riviera resort of Menton described by Italian commentators as a 'strongly fortified town'!

Sea War – Uncompleted French destroyer *Lansquenet* escapes from Gironde Estuary, W. France, under German artillery fire (arrives Casablanca June 27). Italian submarine *Galvani* sinks sloop *Pathan* (Royal Indian Navy) off Bombay; Italian submarine *Torricelli* sunk in gun battle with 3 British destroyers and a sloop off Perim (Persian Gulf); destroyer *Khartoum* also sunk.

France – Gen. de Gaulle forms French National Committee in London. Hitler makes sight-seeing tour of Paris.

Secret War – First unsuccessful British Commando raid on Boulogne.

Home Front: France – Laval appointed Vice-Premier and Minister of State.

Air War – French bombers raid Palermo (Sicily).

Neutrals: Egypt – Coalition Govt. of Aly Pasha Maher falls. The Wafdist (Nationalist) Party leader Nahas Pasha refuses to form new govt. New weak Coalition Govt. formed under Hassan Pasha Sabry (June 28).

MONDAY, JUNE 24

Diplomacy – **FRANCO-ITALIAN ARMISTICE** signed at Villa Inchesa, near Rome, by Gen. Huntziger and Marshal Badoglio. Armistice Terms: demilitarized zones to be established along Franco-Italian border and between French and Italian territories in N. and E. Africa. French troops to be evacuated within 10 days. French naval and air bases in Mediterranean to be demilitarized within 15 days.

Sea War – Italian submarine *Galvani* sunk by British sloop *Falmouth* in Persian Gulf, on basis of secret documents recovered from captured Italian submarine *Galilei*. (*See* June 19).

TUESDAY, JUNE 25

France – Cease-fire on all fronts from 12.35 a.m. (BST). Italians have made virtually no progress in their offensive except at Menton, on French Riviera.

Sea War – Ops. Cycle and Ariel completed: 214,000 British and Allied troops evacuated from NW. and W. France since June 15.

Home Front: France – Day of national mourning. Flags flown at half-mast.

Home Front: Germany – Armistice celebrations: Hitler issues proclamation announcing 'the end of the war in the West' and 'the most glorious victory of all time!' Flags to be flown throughout the *Reich* for 10 days and church bells to be rung for 7 days.

Neutrals: Switzerland – Pres. Pilet-Golaz makes controversial broadcast: he expresses 'relief' at the 'end of the war in Europe' and suggests the replacement of Swiss democracy by an authoritarian system.

Battle of France Losses
Totals (May 10–June 25) – French: 84,000 –92,000 dead, 200,000-250,000 wounded, 1,900,000 PoWs, 892 planes. British: 3,475 dead, 15,850 wounded, 48,804 missing/PoWs; 400 tanks, 2,472 guns. German: 27,074 dead, 111,034 wounded, 18,384 missing/PoWs; 534 planes. Italian: 631 dead, 2,631 wounded, 2,151 sick, 4,494 missing/PoWs.

WEDNESDAY, JUNE 26

Diplomacy – French Ambassador in London (M. Corbin) resigns. Soviet ultimatum to Rumania demanding immediate hand-over of Bessarabia and N. Bukovina districts.

THURSDAY, JUNE 27

Sea War – Britain announces general blockade of European Coastline from Bay of Biscay to N. Cape of Norway. British destroyers and Sunderland flying boats sink 4 Italian submarines and damage 3 more in E. Med. (June 27-29).

FRIDAY, JUNE 28

Air War – Marshal Italo Balbo, celebrated Italian aviator, Minister for Air and Gov.-Gen. of Libya, killed during air battle over Tobruk; his SM79 aircraft accidentally shot down by *Italian* flak.

Germans bomb and strafe Jersey and Guernsey (33 killed, 40 injured).

Sea War – Canadian destroyer *Fraser* and British cruiser *Calcutta* collide in Gironde Estuary; *Fraser* sunk. Italian destroyer *Espero* sunk in gallant action with 5 cruisers while carrying supplies to Tobruk.

Neutrals: Rumania – Rumanian Govt. submits to Soviet ultimatum of June 26. Soviet paratroops and armoured forces enter Bessarabia and N. Bukovina; several major clashes between Soviet and Rumanian troops (occupation completed July 1).

Occupied France – Former French P.M. Reynaud injured in car accident near Bordeaux; his mistress, Countess de Portès, is killed.

THE FALL OF FRANCE

On Armistice Day, November 11, 1918, France was indisputably the strongest military power in the world. After more than four years of heroic, triumphant struggle, she and her allies had humbled and disarmed her deadly foe, Imperial Germany. How was it then that, little more than 20 years later, the French armed forces were humiliatingly defeated in only six weeks by an 'upstart' German army and air force which had only been in existence for five years?

Viewed in the cold light of history, the arrogance, obstinacy and short-sightedness of the French generals is quite unbelievable. For example, only days before Guderian's *Panzer* Corps poured through the Ardennes Forest, General Huntziger, commander of the French 2nd Army, ordered the removal of all anti-tank obstacles from the roads in this area, on the grounds that their existence was contrary to standing orders. More incredible still is Marshal Pétain's contemptuous dismissal of the value of armoured vehicles and aircraft in a major European war.

Inevitably, the senility of the French General Staff, combined with a weak government – the legacy of the almost continuous series of political crises in France from February 1934 until the very eve of Hitler's Blitzkrieg – had drastic effects on the rearmament morale and effectiveness of the armed forces. Even as early as 1931, the world economic Depression had seriously interfered with the completion of the legendary Maginot Line. The extension of the Line to the Channel coast was vetoed because of the cost and the government's reluctance to bar the Franco-Belgian border.

Pétain's influence stifled the creation of a French armoured corps capable of dealing with Hitler's *Panzer* divisions. Eight 'mechanized cavalry divisions' were formed between 1934 and 1940, but these were not true armoured divisions. In 1937, an 'all-tank' *Division Cuirassé de Réserve* (DCR) was authorized but the division existed only on paper until September 1939. Three additional divisions – including de Gaulle's 4th DCR – were training feverishly when Hitler struck on May 10, 1940.

The awesome strength of the Maginot Line actually completed, together with the greater numbers, thicker armour and heavier guns of the French tanks, tended to obscure the true state of affairs until it was too late. However, when it came to the French Air Force *(Armée de l'Air)*, no such self-deception was possible. The French aircaft industry had been thrown into confusion by nationalization during 1936-37 and production figures did not recover until spring 1940. At the outbreak of war, France found herself with too few modern fighters and an obsolete bomber force restricted to flying at night.

The nationalized French aircraft industry made a spectacular recovery between January and June 1940. Aircraft were turned out faster than the *Armée de l'Air* could collect them, install guns and radio sets or train crews to fly them; the 'French Spitfire', Émile Dewoitine's sleek D.520, was being produced at the rate of *one an hour* by June. Even bomber production rose sharply, with the ironic result that the French Air Force had more aircraft on strength at the end of the 1940 campaign than it had at the beginning.

The repercussions of the Fall of France were incalculable and lasted far beyond the end of World War II. In the short-term, it seemed to confirm Adolf Hitler's once-ridiculed boast that the German people were destined to rule from the Atlantic Ocean to the Urals. As for Britain, reasoned Hitler, it could surely only be a matter of weeks before she acknowledged the 'hopelessness' of her military position and agree to compromise – leaving Germany a free hand in Eastern Europe in return for a Vichy-like 'independence' and the retention of the British Empire.

In the unlikely event that Britain would choose to fight on, Germany could threaten or actually launch an invasion or, alternatively, enforce a crippling blockade from the newly-occupied submarine and air bases dotted along the entire western European coastline from Norway to the Bay of Biscay. This double threat to Britain's survival brought about an horrific sequel to the Fall of France when, 11 days after the Armistice ceremony, Churchill ordered the Royal Navy to destroy a powerful French naval squadron off the North African coast to prevent it falling into German hands. When this 'outrage' was followed in September 1940 by a British-Free French attack on the naval base of Dakar, French

West Africa, the collaborationist Vichy Government ordered reprisals against Gibraltar and British shipping and came within an ace of actually declaring war. Thus only three months after the Fall of France the former close allies had become bitter enemies. Meanwhile, some 10,000 km away in Indochina, forgotten French colonial garrisons were fighting hopeless rearguard actions against the Japanese, who had been quick to take advantage of France's domestic calamities.

In the long-term, the Fall of France meant that World War II was certain to be a protracted struggle. Despite the exertions of de Gaulle's Free French, France's only real hope of liberation depended on a fundamental change in Germany's fortunes, such as the intervention of the USA or the USSR. The involvement of both great powers gave new heart to growing Resistance Movements inside occupied France. In the longer-term, the entry of the USA raised hopes of a Second Front and ultimate liberation.

Below left: The serene progress of the Blitzkrieg *across Northern France. Well spread-out infantry squads accompany Panzer IIs (20mm gun) and Czech-made Panzer 35(t)s (37mm gun) of 6th Panzer Div. An eighth of German tanks invading the West in 1940 were Czech made, equipping three out of 10 Panzer divs.*

Below right: A defender of the Maginot Line emerges from his bunker to surrender. When finally attacked, the much reduced garrisons were the last French troops to yield.

East Africa – Battle of Moyale: Powerful Italian forces attack small British garrison (King's African Rifles) on Kenya-Ethiopia border. Garrison counter-attacks July 2; heavy Italian bombardment July 9; garrison withdraws July 14.

Home Front: Britain – Channel Is. demilitarized and 26,700 civilians evacuated.

SATURDAY, JUNE 29

Diplomacy – German Govt. 'White Book' published containing details of Allied plans to 'invade' Low Countries.

SUNDAY, JUNE 30

Occupied Channel Is. – Germans land in Channel Is. – the only British territory occupied in W.W.II.

France – Franco-German-Italian Armistice Commission in session at Wiesbaden. Surrender of 220,000 French troops cut off in underground fortresses of Maginot Line.

Sea War: Atlantic – British cargo liner *Avelona Star* (13,400 t) sunk by *U-43*.

MONDAY, JULY 1

Air War – Hull and Wick (NE. Scotland) bombed in daylight; 12 killed, 22 injured. 12 Hampdens bomb Kiel naval base; Guy Gibson drops 2,000 lb. bomb near *Scharnhorst*, cruiser *Prinz Eugen* hit by 2 small bombs (night July 1-2).

Vichy France – French Govt. moves from Bordeaux to Vichy.

Occupied Channel Is. – German occupation completed.

Neutrals: Rumania – Rumania renounces Anglo-French guarantee of her territorial integrity. Hungary alleges frontier violations by Rumanian troops; several civilians killed. Both countries mass troops along borders.

Diplomacy – Britain warns that she will not countenance Axis occupation of Syria.

Neutrals: Japan – Sugar and matches rationed.

TUESDAY, JULY 2

Sea War – British liner *Arandora Star* (15,501 t), carrying 1,500 Italian and German internees and PoWs to Canada, sunk by *U-47* W. of Ireland. Panic-stricken passengers fight for places in lifeboats (670 dead). (*See* Dec. 20, 1940.)
Hitler makes first tentative plans for seaborne invasion of England.

Occupied Poland – Gen. Sikorski issues Order of the Day to Polish Forces in Britain: '*We shall continue to fight with an iron will until victory is won.*'

WEDNESDAY, JULY 3

Sea War – **THE MERS-EL-KEBIR AFFAIR** (Op. Catapult): British 'Force H' opens fire on French naval sqn. in Mers-el-Kebir naval base, Algeria, after failure of prolonged negotiations and refusal of Adm. Gensoul to join British Fleet. French battleship *Bretagne* sunk (977 killed); battlecruiser *Dunkerque* damaged (210 killed); battlecruiser *Strasbourg* escapes to Toulon, under air attack.

Sea War – British forces seize 59 major French warships in British harbours, inc. battleships *Courbet* and *Paris* and giant sub. *Surcouf*, fighting aboard *Surcouf* and destroyer *Mistral* (some casualties).

Occupied Holland – Gen. Winkelman, former Dutch CinC., arrested and taken to Germany for 'hindering' the demobilization of the Dutch Army.

THURSDAY, JULY 4

Sea War – *Stukas* and German MTBs attack convoy, S. of Portland, sinking 5 merchant ships and auxiliary AA ship *Foyle Bank*.

Air War – Italians raid Malta and Alexandria.

East Africa – Italian forces, supported by aircraft and armour, occupy frontier outposts of Kassala and Galabat (Anglo-Egyptian Sudan).

Neutrals: Rumania – New Cabinet under Gigurtu ('a personal friend of Field-Marshal Göring'), including 2 leaders of the previously outlawed Iron Guard: Manoilesca (Foreign Minister) and Sima ('Minister for Arts'!). 22 British oil technicians expelled.

FRIDAY, JULY 5

Sea War: Atlantic – Destroyer *Whirlwind* sunk by *U-34* SW. of Ireland. Vichy French warships and submarines capture 3 British merchant ships in reprisal for Mers-el-Kébir attack. *U-30* enters new U-boat base at Lorient.

Air War – RAF daylight raids on shipping off Dutch coast and Waalhaven airfield; night raids on Kiel and Wilhelmshaven. Vichy French aircraft make unsuccessful 'reprisal raid' on shipping at Gibraltar.

Diplomacy – Vichy France breaks off relations with Britain. Swedish-German Railways Agreement: Germany obtains permission to utilize Swedish railways for the transport of war supplies and troops 'on leave' to and from Norway (vigorous British and Norwegian protests, July 8 and 17).

SATURDAY, JULY 6

Sea War – French battlecruiser *Dunkerque* crippled at Mers-el-Kébir by Swordfish torpedo-bombers from *Ark Royal*.
5 British submarines sunk off Norway (July 6-Aug. 2) – *Shark*, *Salmon*, *Thames*, *Narwhal* and *Spearfish*. British submarine ops. in the area temporarily suspended.

Home Front: Germany – Hitler returns to Berlin in triumph after 8 weeks 'in the field'.

SUNDAY, JULY 7

Sea War: Med. – French naval sqn. at Alexandria interned and demobilized by amicable agreement between British and French adms. (it includes battleship *Lorraine* and 4 cruisers).
Italy waives article of June 24 Armistice which ordered demilitarization of French naval bases.

Sea War: Atlantic – British naval forces disable battleship *Richelieu* at Dakar, following French rejection of ultimatum: motor launch drops depth charges under battleship's stern and 6 Swordfish aircraft from carrier *Hermes* score 1 torpedo hit.

Air War – 11 Italian SM-81 bombers (2 lost) raid Alexandria (night July 7-8).

MONDAY, JULY 8

Sea War: Med. – Destroyer *Escort* torpedoed by Italian submarine *Guglielmo Marconi* in W. Mediterranean (she founders while in tow).

Sea War: Atlantic – 2 destroyers and 2 torpedo boats – bought by Sweden from Italy and detained by British forces in Faeroe Is. – are bombed in error by British aircraft (damaged ships reach Sweden July 10).

Home Front: Britain – 9 BEF divs., rescued from Dunkirk, have now been reorganized. Tea rationing begins (2 oz. per person per week).

TUESDAY, JULY 9

Sea War: Med. – Naval action off Calabria ('Battle of Punta Stilo'): British Mediterranean Fleet attempts to cut off Italian Fleet from its Taranto base, but Italians escape at high speed covered by smoke screen; battleship *Giulio Cesare* and cruiser *Bolzano* damaged (98 casualties). Repeated attacks by Italian land-based aircraft damage cruiser *Gloucester* (and narrowly miss Italian warships). Italian bombers also make heavy attacks on British Force 'H', attempting to reach battle area from the W. Mussolini issues Order of the Day to Italian Fleet: '*You have obtained our first naval victory . . .*'.

Sea War – German disguised raider *Komet* leaves Bergen for the Pacific, via NE. Passage (assisted by Russian ice-breakers).

Air War – 12 Blenheims (7 lost, 5 damaged) raid Stavanger airfield.

Home Front: Britain – £1,000 M. Vote of Credit for war expenditure approved by House of Commons.

WEDNESDAY, JULY 10

Air War – **BATTLE OF BRITAIN (DAY 1).** Widespread raids – 25 Do 17s, escorted by Messerschmitts, attack convoy near Dover (1 ship sunk); 60 Ju 88s bomb ports of Falmouth and Swansea and Pembrey Royal Ordnance Factory, S. Wales (30

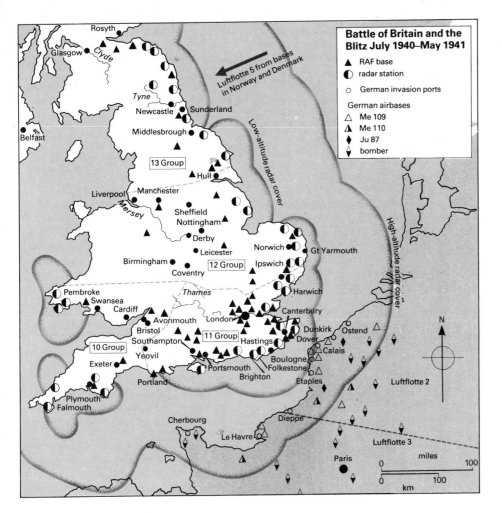

Battle of Britain and the Blitz July 1940–May 1941
▲ RAF base
◐ radar station
○ German invasion ports
German airbases
△ Me 109
▲ Me 110
◆ Ju 87
▽ bomber

HITLER ORDERS PREPARATION FOR SEABORNE INVASION OF ENGLAND

(Op. *Seelöwe*: 'Sea Lion'), to be completed by mid-Aug., inc. the reduction of the 'English Air Force' so that it is incapable of delivering 'any significant attack' during the crossing.
Neutrals: Japan – Cabinet resigns.

WEDNESDAY, JULY 17

Diplomacy – Britain agrees (under severe Japanese diplomatic pressure) to close the 'Burma Road' – a vital supply route for Chiang Kai-shek's armies – for 3 months.

THURSDAY, JULY 18

Air War – Germans attack shipping off S. England. RAF daylight raids on invasion barges at Rotterdam and St Omer airfield (3 aircraft lost). RAF Bomber Command night raids on Krupp's armament works at Essen, in the Ruhr; targets at Bremen and Hamm marshalling yards (1 aircraft lost). Coastal Command bomb Emden naval base.
Neutrals: Japan – New Cabinet formed: Prince Konoye, P.M.; Matsuoka, Foreign Minister.

FRIDAY, JULY 19

Air War – Me 109s overwhelm sqn. of Defiant 2-seat fighters (6 lost, 1 damaged) S. of Folkestone. 4 Do 17s bomb Rolls-Royce engine factory at Glasgow.
Diplomacy – **HITLER'S 'LAST APPEAL TO REASON'**: in speech in *Reichstag*, Berlin, says Britain has no sensible alternative but to reach peace agreement; (Britain rejects, July 22).
Home Front: Germany – The *Führer* creates 19 new Field-Marshals.
Sea War: Med. – Battle of Cape Spada: Italian cruisers *Bartolomeo Colleoni* and *Giovanni delle Bande Nere* (world's fastest cruisers) intercepted off Crete by Australian cruiser *Sydney* and 5 destroyers; *Colleoni* sunk, *Sydney* damaged.
Neutrals: USA – 'Two-Ocean Navy' Bill signed by Pres. Roosevelt: warships totalling 1,325,000 t and 15,000 naval aircaft authorized.

SATURDAY, JULY 20

Air War – Göring orders creation of 1st specialized night-fighter wing – *Nachtjagdgeschwader* 1 (NJG 1) – under *Oberst* Josef Kammhuber. Me 110 night fighter achieves first 'kill' of W.W.II (a Whitley over NW. Germany).
Sea War: Med. – 2 Italian destroyers and cargo ship torpedoed by FAA Swordfish biplanes near Tobruk.

SUNDAY, JULY 21

Diplomacy – Rumania cedes S. Dobrudja area to Bulgaria. National assemblies in

---

killed); Martlesham airfield, near Ipswich, bombed. Losses (in combat or following combat damage): German, 11; British, 1.
First Free Czech fighter sqn. (No. 310) formed in Britain.
Sea War: Atlantic – British minefield, Orkneys-Iceland-Greenland completed. Five U-boats leave new base at Bergen, Norway.
Vichy France – French National Assembly at Vichy gives full powers to Pétain by 569 votes to 80, with 17 abstentions.

THURSDAY, JULY 11

Vichy France – Pres. Lebrun resigns; Pétain proclaims himself 'Head of the French State', abolishes Republican Constitution of 1875, and dismisses Senate and Chamber of Deputies.
Home Front: Britain – Beaverbrook Minister of Aircraft Production, appeals for aluminium pots and pans, 'to build Spitfires' (vast quantities are collected but the value of the campaign is negligible).

FRIDAY, JULY 12

Air War – Hurricanes destroy 4 bombers attacking convoy off Suffolk coast. Night raids on Aberdeen (60 casualties) and Cardiff.

Neutrals: USSR – Kuusinen, former head of the short-lived 'Terijoki Govt.' (*see* Dec. 2, 1939), appointed President of Karelo-Finnish Soviet Republic, in territory gained from Finland, March 13, 1940.

SATURDAY, JULY 13

Air War – First Free Polish fighter sqn. (No. 302) formed in Britain, with Hurricanes.

SUNDAY, JULY 14

Home Front: France – Day of National Mourning.
Occupied France – Gen. de Gaulle attends Bastille Day ceremonies in London.

MONDAY, JULY 15

Air War – Hurricanes beat off 15 Dorniers attacking convoy in English Channel. Hidden by low cloud, Ju 88s hit targets in SW. Britain, inc. 2 airfields and railway in Avonmouth.

TUESDAY, JULY 16

Air War – RAF raid airfields in N. France.
Sea War – Cruiser *Glasgow* and destroyer *Imogen* collide off NW. Scotland; latter sunk.

Baltic States vote for union with USSR.
Home Front: Britain – Lt.-Gen. Sir Alan Brooke appointed CinC Home Forces.

MONDAY, JULY 22

Air War – First 'kill' by RAF night fighter equipped with AI (Airborne Interception) radar: Do 17 shot down S. of Brighton by Blenheim.

TUESDAY, JULY 23

Home Front: Britain – Local Defence Volunteers renamed 'Home Guard': 1,300,000 men have volunteered since May 14; recruiting officially terminated. Third War Budget: income tax raised to 8s 6d. in £, 1d on pint of beer. New Purchase Tax retitled 'Merchant Sales Tax' (title later dropped).
Neutrals: Hungary – Pro-Nazi demonstrations in Budapest.
Occupied Czechoslavakia – Provisional Czechoslovak Govt. established in London by members of former 'Czechoslovak National Committee', with Benes (President) and Masaryk (Foreign Minister). Britain recognizes new Govt.
East Africa – Gen. Legentilhomme – Free French – commander in French Somaliland, replaced by pro-Vichy Gen. Germain. French troops abandon vital Jirre pass, July 27 – thereby exposing British Somaliland to Italian invasion.

WEDNESDAY, JULY 24

Sea War → Repatriation steamer *Meknès* carrying 1,277 French sailors to Marseilles, sunk by German MTB *S-27* off Portland (383 dead).
Neutrals: Rumania – Rumanian Govt. takes over Astra-Romana Oil Co. (Shell).

THURSDAY, JULY 25

Sea War – Stukas and German MTBs launch series of attacks (repeated July 26) on Convoy CW.8: 8 coasters sunk, 5 coasters and destroyers *Boreas* and *Brilliant* damaged.
Neutrals: Switzerland – Gen. Guisan, the CinC, addresses all Army officers on the Rütli Meadow – the birthplace of Swiss independence in 1307 – and exhorts them to be ready, at a moment's notice, to defend Swiss independence and liberties.

FRIDAY, JULY 26

Air War – RAF daylight raid on Dortmund power station.
Diplomacy – M. Avenol resigns as Secretary-Gen. of League of Nations.

SATURDAY, JULY 27

Air War – 50 *Stukas* attack Convoy 'Bacon' in English Channel. Destroyer *Codrington* sunk at Dover and destroyer *Wren* off Aldeburgh (Suffolk).
Sea War – Following loss of HMS *Codrington*, all British destroyers are temporarily withdrawn from Dover.

SUNDAY, JULY 28

Air War – Battle of Britain (Day 19): air battle over Straits of Dover. 'Sailor' Malan wounds Mölders – German fighter 'ace' – who crash-lands his Me 109.
Sea War: Atlantic – 3 Italian subs begin ops. in Azores-Madeira area, sinking 2 ships. British armed merchant cruiser *Alcantara* (22,200 t) fights German disguised raider *Thor* off Brazil; *Alcantara* hit in engine room (9 casualties) and forced to put into Rio.
Diplomacy – Act of Havana: USA and 20 Latin American Republics in conference at Havana agree to take immediate action if any European colony in the Americas is threatened with aggression. (*See* Sept. 27, 1940.)

MONDAY, JULY 29

Air War – *Stukas* with heavy Me 109 escort raid Dover. Destroyer *Delight* bombed and sunk off Portland. Losses: German, 11; British, 3. British Air Ministry announces that German air-sea rescue machines (Heinkel seaplanes) behaving suspiciously will be shot down despite their Red Cross markings – 4 already destroyed.
Vichy France – Vichy Govt. establishes Supreme Court to try former leaders of French Third Republic on 'war-guilt' charges. (*See* Feb. 20, 1942.)

TUESDAY, JULY 30

Air War – German bombers attack shipping between Thames Estuary and Harwich.

WEDNESDAY, JULY 31

Air War – Battle of Britain: In attacks on convoys during July, 18 small steamers and 4 destroyers are sunk. Aircraft losses: German, 139; British, 52.

THURSDAY, AUGUST 1

Air War – Norwich bombed. Leaflets dropped over S. England, giving text of Hitler's 'Last Appeal to Reason' speech of July 19.
Sea War – Hitler sets provisional date for Op. Sealion – Sept. 15. Italian destroyer *Vivaldi* rams submarine *Oswald* and captures crew.
Neutrals: Japan – Govt. declares its intention of establishing a 'New Order' in 'Greater East Asia'.
Neutrals: Switzerland – Gen. Guisan, the CinC, declares in a broadcast that the Army will *defend the passage of the Alps to the end'* and uphold the country's strict neutrality.

FRIDAY, AUGUST 2

Sea War: Med. – Op. Hurry: Force H approaches Sardinia and Swordfish aircraft from *Ark Royal* attack Cagliari; 8 Italian subs sent in vain pursuit.

SATURDAY, AUGUST 3

East Africa – Italians invade British Somaliland: Camel Corps fights delaying actions.

SUNDAY, AUGUST 4

Sea War: Atlantic – Force H leaves Gibraltar for home waters to counter German invasion threat.

MONDAY, AUGUST 5

Neutrals: USA – Roosevelt proposes legislation to combat 'fifth column' activities, following exhaustive enquiries by J. Edgar Hoover and FBI.

TUESDAY, AUGUST 6

Sea War: Med. – Italians lay extensive minefields in Sicilian Channel in which 2 British destroyers are sunk: *Hostile* (Aug. 23, 1940) and *Gallant* (Jan. 10, 1941).

Below: *Spitfire pilots 'scramble'. The Battle of Britain began in earnest on Aug. 13, 1940 – 'Eagle Day'.*

WEDNESDAY, AUGUST 7

East Africa – Last reinforcements (2nd Bn. Black Watch) reach British Somaliland.

THURSDAY, AUGUST 8

Air War – Battle of Britain (Day 30): Large formations of *Stukas,* with heavy fighter escort, make 3 separate attacks on 18-ship convoy in English Channel – following attack of German MTBs (1 lost), which sink 3 ships. *Stukas* sink 2 ships and damage 7 more. German reconnaissance aircraft active over S. England. Losses: German, 31; British, 19. RAF raids on Schiphol and Valkenburg airfields, Holland (1 aircraft lost); night raids on Hamburg docks, marshalling yards at Hamm and Soest and power station at Cologne (1 aircraft lost). RAF and Italian fighter biplanes engaged over Western Desert (Libya). 7 Italian and 2 British (Gladiators) shot down.
Home Front: India – Lord Linlithgow, Viceroy of India, offers nationalist leaders immediate, but limited constitutional reform – with full examination of independence issue after the war.

FRIDAY, AUGUST 9

Air War – Sunderland shipyard bombed (raider shot down). Widespread night raids over Britain. RAF raid Guernsey airfield.

SATURDAY, AUGUST 10

Air War – First flight of Macchi-Castoldi C. 202 powered by imported Daimler-Benz engine – designed to replace obsolete fighters of Italian *Regia Aeronautica* (enters service in Libya, Nov. 1941).
Sea War: Atlantic – British armed merchant cruiser *Transylvania* (16,900 t) sunk by *U-56* N. of Ireland.
Home Front: Germany – Baldur von Schirach, leader of Hitler Youth since 1933, appointed *Gauleiter* of Vienna. Artur Axmann becomes Youth leader.

SUNDAY, AUGUST 11

Air War – Battle of Britain (Day 33): While German fighters stage diversions over Dover, Ju 88s and He 111s bomb Portland and Weymouth. Me 110s of élite fighter-bomber unit *Erpr. Gr. 210* attack convoy off Harwich. Losses: German, 35; British, 30.
Sea War: Atlantic – Troopship *Mohamed Ali el-Kebir* (formerly Egyptian liner) sunk by U-boat; 120 dead.
East Africa – Battle of the Tug Argan Gap: Small British force holds mtn. pass for 5 days against repeated attacks by strong Italian forces, supported by aircraft (British withdraw Aug. 15-16).

MONDAY, AUGUST 12

Air War – Heavy German raids on shipping

off English S. Coast, radar stations (inc. Ventnor), and airfields. Losses: German, 32; British, 21. 5 Hampdens (2 lost) attack heavily defended Dortmund-Ems Canal with delayed-action bombs; Flt.-Lt. Learoyd, V.C., secures vital hit, which stops passage of invasion craft for 10 days (night Aug. 12-13).

TUESDAY, AUGUST 13

Air War – ADLER TAG ('EAGLE DAY'): Launching of great *Luftwaffe* offensive planned to destroy RAF Fighter Cmnd. in 4 days begins amid confusion. Göring postpones morning raids at last minute, but 70 unescorted Dorniers bomb Eastchurch airfield (Thames Estuary). Ju 88s sent to Farnborough fail to find target. Afternoon raid more successful, but Spitfire sqn. destroys 9 *Stukas* over Hants. Ju 88s start fires in Southampton Docks. Germans lose 42 aircraft, RAF 13 fighters. Elite German night-bomber group *K.Gr.100* (He 111s) bomb Spitfire 'shadow factory' at Castle Bromwich and Shorts' bomber factory at Belfast.
Home Front: Australia – Two Cabinet Ministers and COGS killed in air crash near Canberra.
Secret War – Parachutist Scare: German aircraft drop parachutes over S. England and S. Scotland (Aug. 13 and 14), which carry bogus 'ops. orders', intended to create impression that invasion has begun.

WEDNESDAY, AUGUST 14

Air War – Battle of Britain (Day 36): Widespread small raids on airfields and railway lines. Me 109s strafe Dover balloon barrage; E. Goodwin lightship bombed. Losses: German, 19, British, 4.
Sea War – Evacuation of Berbera (capital of British Somaliland) begins: British and Australian warships take 5,700 troops, 1,500 civilians and sick to Aden and bombard advancing Italian forces who occupy the town on Aug. 19.

THURSDAY, AUGUST 15

Air War – Battle of Britain (Day 37): **GÖRING EMPLOYS THREE 'AIR FLEETS'** *(Luftflotten* 2, 3 and 5) **IN MASSED DAYLIGHT RAIDS** on airfields from Portsmouth to Tyne. RAF defeat attacks by *Luftflotte* 5 from Scandinavian bases, but Ju 88s destroy 10 Whitleys at Driffield (Yorks). Elite fighter-bomber group *Erpr.Gr.210* attacks Croydon Airport (62 killed), but loses 6 Me 110s and its CO. Göring forbids further attacks on British radar stations. Losses: German, 76; British, 50.
Sea War: Med. – The *Helle* Incident: Greek cruiser *Helle* sinks in mysterious circumstances off Tinos I., while crew are attending Mass. Fragments indicate that

torpedoes are of Italian manufacture. Italy denies responsibility (Aug. 16), but later admits 'mistake' may have occurred. HM subs. *Pandora* and *Proteus* carry essential supplies to Malta.

FRIDAY, AUGUST 16

Air War – *Stukas* (7 lost) wreck Tangmere Airfield (Hants); 7 other airfields bombed.
Secret War – *Luftwaffe* Command Staff estimate that RAF now have only 300 fighters (actual total is 700).

SATURDAY, AUGUST 17

Sea War: Med. – *Warspite*, *Malaya* and *Ramillies* bombard Bardia and Fort Capuzzo, Libya. Italian bombers (12 lost) attack bombardment force, Aug. 18.
Diplomacy – Germany announces 'total blockade' of British Isles; in reply to the 'British hunger blockade against German women and children'. All ships – Allied and neutral – in British waters are to be sunk on sight.
Home Front: West Indies – Duke of Windsor sworn in as Governor of Bahamas.

SUNDAY, AUGUST 18

Air War – Heavy raids on RAF bases and other targets in S. and SE. England: 19 *Stukas* lost; 8 of 50 escorting Me 109s also destroyed at cost of 4 Hurricanes and 2 Spitfires. Losses: German, 62; British, 34.
Diplomacy – Joint US-Canadian Defense Board established, to include both military and civilian members.

MONDAY, AUGUST 19

Air War – Battle of Britain (Day 41): *Luftwaffe* ops. hampered by bad weather (cloud and rain), Aug. 19-23. Light raids on airfields, shipping and coastal targets. Ju 88s set fire to oil storage depot near

Pembroke Dock, S. Wales (Aug. 19). Losses: German, 24; British, 9. *Stukas* withdrawn from the Battle (57 lost since Aug. 8). RAF raid Kiel, Zschornewitz power station near Leipzig and 30 airfields; 2½-hour air-raid alarm in Berlin (no bombs).
East Africa – Italians occupy Berbera, capital of British Somaliland. British casualties since Aug. 3, 250; Italian casualties, 2,050.

TUESDAY, AUGUST 20

Sea War: Med. – Italian Navy to carry out 'total blockade' of Gibraltar, Malta, Suez and other British possessions.
Sea War: Pacific – German disguised raider *Orion* sinks SS *Turakina* (8,700 t) after 2½-hour battle in Tasman Sea. (*See* Dec. 21, 1940.)
Home Front: Britain – Churchill praises RAF Fighter Command (the 'Few').
China – Heavy Japanese bombing raid on Chungking; many thousands made homeless.

WEDNESDAY, AUGUST 21

Secret War – Trotsky, exiled Russian Revolutionary leader and founder of Red Army, assassinated by NKVD agent in Mexico City; aged 61.

THURSDAY, AUGUST 22

Sea War – German super-heavy artillery bombards convoy for 80 mins (no hits).

Above left: *The true Aug. 15 losses were Luftwaffe 76, RAF 50.* Below: *A doomed Dornier 17, shot down on Aug. 18.*

Fire switched to Dover town in evening; British 14-inch gun replies (first of many cross-Channel 'duels').

FRIDAY, AUGUST 23

Sea War – He 115 seaplanes torpedo 2 cargo ships and damage third in Moray Firth.

SATURDAY, AUGUST 24

Air War – Heavy raids on airfields in SE. England: Manston evacuated; N. Weald and Hornchurch also hard hit. Residential areas of Portsmouth and Ramsgate bombed. Losses: German, 30; British, 23. German bomber crews, ordered to attack Shorts' aircraft factory at Rochester (Kent) and Thameshaven oil tanks, are confused by British radio counter-measures and bomb central London and the E. End, starting numerous fires (night Aug. 24-25).

SUNDAY, AUGUST 25

Air War – Battle of Britain (Day 47): air battle over Portland-Portsmouth area. 19 German aircraft destroyed for loss of 8 RAF fighters; Warmwell airfield bombed. 150 night raiders over Britain: main target Birmingham. **FIRST RAF NIGHT RAID ON BERLIN:** 81 bombers despatched, but many fail to find target; slight damage in city centre and suburbs. Raids on other targets inc. Cologne, Hamm and Boulogne. Total losses: 5 aircraft.
China – Token British garrisons withdrawn from Shanghai and Tientsin (latter had been blockaded by Japanese since 1939).

MONDAY, AUGUST 26

Air War – Battle of Britain (Day 48). Attempted raids on airfields round London, inc. Debden (heavy damage), and Portsmouth area. Losses: German, 31; British, 27. Night raids on Birmingham, Coventry and Plymouth.
Sea War – He 115s and Ju 88s sink 1 large cargo ship and cripple second off Fraserburgh, Scotland.
German disguised raider *Pinguin* sinks or captures 5 merchant ships in Indian Ocean (Aug. 26-Sept. 10).

TUESDAY, AUGUST 27

Sea War – Hitler modifies Op. Sea Lion invasion plan: landings to be made on 'narrow front', Eastbourne-Folkestone, in preference to earlier 'broad front' proposal. RAF Coastal Command begins anti-U-boat patrols from Iceland, using Fairey Battle aircraft.
Occupied France – Free French forces take over Duala in Cameroons (Aug. 27) and Brazzaville, French Congo (Aug. 28).

Left: *A British coastal convoy under fire from German cross-Channel guns for the first time, Aug. 22.*

WEDNESDAY, SEPTEMBER 4

Air War – Me 110 fighter-bombers (6 lost) make devastating low-level raid on Vickers' factory at Brooklands (Surrey) killing 88, injuring 600 and halting production of Wellington bombers for 4 days. Other raiders attack airfields and Dover balloon barrage.
Sea War – German MTBs sink 5 ships in convoy off Gt. Yarmouth, North Sea.
Home Front: Germany – Hitler speaks in Berlin – threatening to invade Britain and raze British cities to the ground by bombing.
Neutrals: Rumania – Gen. Antonescu given full powers by King Carol.

THURSDAY, SEPTEMBER 5

Air War – Germans raid Biggin Hill and Detling airfields; Ju 88s and He 111s fire oil storage tanks at Thameshaven (these burn for many days); Maidstone bombed. Night raids on Liverpool and Manchester. *Oberleutnant* von Werra captured when he force-lands Me 109 in Kent; von Werra is later only German PoW to escape (from Canada) and return to Germany.
Sea War – Op. *Walter*. German minelayers active in Straits of Dover (night Sept. 5-6).

FRIDAY, SEPTEMBER 6

Air War – Battle of Britain (Day 59): airfield attacks continue; Hawker factory at Weybridge bombed.
Home Front: Britain – King and Queen visit RAF Fighter Command HQ at Bentley Priory, Stanmore (Middx.).
Sea War: Atlantic – *U-47* is guided to Convoy SC.2 by *U-65* and sinks 3 ships (night 6-7). *U-47* sinks fourth ship following night – outwitting escorts equipped with 'Asdic' by attacking on the surface.
Neutrals: Rumania – King Carol abdicates following fascist riots in Bucharest and leaves the country with his mistress, Magda Lupescu. Prince Michael ascends the throne for second time (his wayward father having renounced the succession in 1925 but returned in 1930).
Vichy France — Gen. Weygand quits Govt.; to command Vichy forces in N. Africa.
Secret War – Two German agents – Caroli and Schmidt – land by parachute in Oxon. (Sept. 6 and 10); Caroli arrested almost immediately.

SATURDAY, SEPTEMBER 7

Air War – 'BATTLE OF LONDON' BEGINS. Göring launches massive daylight 'reprisal' raid, in answer to RAF attacks on Berlin, with 1,000 aircraft (inc. 350 bombers). Heavy HE bombs and

WEDNESDAY, AUGUST 28

Air War – Battle of Britain (Day 50): German bombers raid Eastchurch and Rochford airfields and Messerschmitts carry out sweeps over SE. England. A second Defiant sqn. (*see* July 19) is virtually destroyed by Me 109s. First attempt to carry out major night raid on a British city – Liverpool – completely misfires: 160 bombers, inc. 4-engined Focke-Wulfs, scatter their bombs far and wide. Similar attempts on Aug. 29-30 and Aug. 30-31 also fail. (*See* Aug. 31.) RAF night raid on Berlin: 10 killed, 28 injured.
Sea War: Atlantic – Armed merchant cruiser *Dunvegan Castle* (15,000 t) sunk by *U-46* W. of Ireland.

THURSDAY, AUGUST 29

Air War – Battle of Britain (Day 51): 720 Messerschmitts carry out sweeps over Kent but fail to provoke large-scale fighter-v-fighter combats (RAF fighters are being conserved for attacks on bomber formations).

FRIDAY, AUGUST 30

Air War – Battle of Britain (Day 52): devastating attacks on Biggin Hill airfield; Detling airfield also damaged. Vauxhall works at Luton bombed (50 killed). Losses: German, 24; British, 20. RAF night raid on Berlin.
Diplomacy – The 'Vienna Award': Hitler imposes settlement of territorial dispute between Hungary and Rumania, under which the former is to receive N. Transylvania.

SUNDAY, AUGUST 31

Air War – German raids on Biggin Hill, Debden, Hornchurch and Eastchurch airfields and Croydon Airport. Losses: German, 38; British, 34. 140 bombers raid Liverpool and Merseyside (night Aug. 31-Sept. 1): Battleship *Prince of Wales* damaged; 160 small fires in central Liverpool. 109 casualties (23 killed). Germans lose 7 bombers in the consecutive night raids on Liverpool. Fourth RAF night raid on Berlin.
Sea War – British destroyer flotilla runs on to German minefield near the Texel (night Aug. 31-Sept. 1): *Esk* and *Ivanhoe* sink, *Express* seriously damaged.

SUNDAY, SEPTEMBER 1

Air War – Battle of Britain (Day 54): four major attacks on fighter airfields in the SE.; Biggin Hill again badly damaged. First RAF raid on Munich – targets are BMW works and railway sidings; Fiat works, Turin, also attacked.
Sea War – Italian submarine command ('BETASOM') established at Bordeaux.

MONDAY, SEPTEMBER 2

Air War – Heavy raids on airfields: serious damage at Detling and Eastchurch (bomb dump explodes). Surprise low-level attack on Biggin Hill. Fighter-bomber unit *Erpr. Grp. 210* suffers heavy losses (8 Me 110s). Small-scale night raids on Birmingham, Liverpool and Cardiff. Mines dropped in Thames Estuary (similar ops. on 6 other nights in Sept. 1940).

TUESDAY, SEPTEMBER 3

Air War – RAF night raid on Berlin (first of 9 raids in Sept.).
Sea War – Hitler postpones launching of Op. Sea Lion from Sept. 15 to Sept. 21. US forces to occupy naval and air bases in Bahamas, Bermuda, British Guiana, Jamaica, St Lucia, Trinidad and Newfoundland on 99-year lease; Britain to receive in exchange 50 old destroyers.
Home Front: Germany – Unemployed total 32,000.

clusters of incendiaries start huge fires in Docks (15 ships seriously damaged) and Silvertown (E. End); also at Woolwich Arsenal, Thameshaven and Tilbury. RAF are temporarily confused by new German tactics, but destroy 30 raiders after the bombing (28 RAF fighters lost). **THE 'BLITZ':** 247 bombers (2 lost) take part in 7-hour. raid on London (night Sept. 7-8), dropping 352 t of bombs. Civilian casualties (afternoon Sept. 7-dawn Sept. 8): 448 killed, 1,600 seriously injured.

Home Front: Britain – GHQ Home Forces sends code-word 'Cromwell' ('invasion imminent') to Southern and Eastern Cmnds. and London-area commanders at 8 p.m. Church bells rung and Home Guard put on action stations. Air Ministry issues similar warning to all RAF Commands.

Home Front: Germany – Göring broadcasts: '*For the first time the* Luftwaffe *has struck at the heart of the enemy.*'

SUNDAY, SEPTEMBER 8

Air War – Small-scale raids on airfields in SE. England and Dover. 9½-hour night raid on London by 170 bombers: 12 large fires, all railway lines to S. Coast blocked; casualties: 412 killed, 747 injured.

Sea War – Op. *Hannelore:* German torpedo boats lay mines in Straits of Dover.

Secret War – Vichy French agents in London report that Free French expeditionary force is at sea *en route* for one of France's African colonies. (*See* Sept. 23.)

Home Front: Germany – Deputy *Führer* Rudolf Hess asks Prof. Haushofer: 'Is there nobody in Britain willing to make peace?'

MONDAY, SEPTEMBER 9

Air War – RAF foils series of intended raids on London, Thameshaven, Tilbury and aircraft factories. Losses: German, 23; British, 20. Bombs jettisoned at many points from Canterbury to Chelsea and Kingston. *Luftwaffe* Command staff divides London into 2 target areas: 'A', E. End and Docks; 'B', W. London, including power station and 'provision installations'. Daylight raids to be carried out by *Luftflotte 2* and night raids by *Luftflotte 3*. Night raids on London by 190 aircraft; Somerset House hit. 370 killed, 1,400 injured.

Air War – Italian bombers (4 lost) raid Tel-Aviv (Palestine) killing 111; leaflets dropped on Jaffa promise freedom for Palestinian Arabs.

Neutrals: USA – US Navy orders 7 battleships, 12 aircraft carriers and 191 other warships.

TUESDAY, SEPTEMBER 10

Air War – Little daylight activity; 'hit-and-run' raiders attack airfields and Portsmouth Dockyards. 148 night raiders sent to London, but massive AA barrage

GÖRING, Hermann Wilhelm (1893-1946) German: *Reichsmarschall, CinC Luftwaffe*

Most colourful and approachable figure in the Nazi hierarchy. Fighter 'ace' in World War I. Played important part in rise to power of Nazi Party and creation of new German Air Force *(Luftwaffe)*. Later his monstrous arrogance, vanity, taste for luxurious living and addiction to morphine combined with his lack of specialized knowledge in vital aspects of military aviation eventually resulted in total humilia-

tion and disgrace. Committed suicide, 1946.

Born at Rosenheim, near Munich. Commissioned as Lt. in Bavarian Army, 1912. Fought on Western Front, Aug.-Oct. 1914. Transferred to Army Air Service as observer. Flew fighters, 1915-18. Achieved 22 aerial victories; awarded *Ordre Pour le Mérite* ('Blue Max'), May 1918. Took command of *JG1* (von Richthofen's 'Flying Circus'), July 1918.

Civil aviation ventures in Germany and Sweden, 1919-23. Joined Nazi Party; founded *SA* (Storm Troops). Badly wounded in November 1923 Munich *Putsch*. Fled to Sweden; became addicted to morphine. Returned to Germany under general amnesty, 1927. Elected to Reichstag as Nazi deputy, 1928. Min. for Air, 1933. Stage-managed burning of Reichstag building (Feb. 1933) and carried out bloody reprisals against Communists. CinC *Luftwaffe*, 1935; Field Marshal, 1938; *Reichsmarschall* (unique distinction), 1940.

As Director of Four-year Economic Plan, he mobilized Germany for war under slogan: 'Guns before butter'. Head of War Economy from 1940. Directed brutal exploitation of conquered areas in USSR from June 1941. Unable either to halt massive Allied bombing raids on Germany from summer 1943 onwards or to launch effective reprisals. Had become little more than a cypher when he staged abortive coup in order to save himself by negotiating with Western Allies. Stripped of all offices and condemned to degradation and death, *in absentia*, by Hitler, April 23, 1945.

Captured by Americans, May 1945. Sentenced to death at Nuremberg for crimes against humanity, Oct. 2, 1946, but cheated hangman by taking cyanide smuggled into cell, 13 days later.

from 199 guns forces many of them to turn away and jettison bombs over suburbs. Buckingham Palace damaged by delayed-action bomb. Casualties: 180 killed, 280 injured.

Sea War – Following bombing of 66,000 t of shipping in Port of London since Sept. 7, all ocean-going ships are banned from London until Jan. 1941.

Sea War: Med. – Italian Expeditionary Corps transported from Brindisi to Albania in readiness for invasion of Greece.

Home Front: Germany – Number of *Panzer* divisions to be doubled from 10 to 20 for planned May 1941 invasion of USSR.

WEDNESDAY, SEPTEMBER 11

Air War – Dover suffers its worst attack of the war.

Sea War – Vichy French sqn. (3 cruisers and 3 destroyers) makes high-speed dash in daylight through Straits of Gibraltar, eludes British Force H and reaches Dakar, French W. Africa (night Sept. 14-15).

Home Front: Britain – Lord Mayor of London opens Air Raid Relief Fund: £5 M. received by Oct. 5.

THURSDAY, SEPTEMBER 12

Air War – RAF Bomber Command attacks Hamm marshalling yards for sixtieth time (night Sept. 12-13).

Occupied Poland – 500,000 Warsaw Jews to be confined in walled ghetto.

Vichy France – 5 French schoolboys discover 10,000-year-old wall paintings of animals and hunters in Lascaux Cave (Dordogne).

FRIDAY, SEPTEMBER 13

North Africa – ITALIAN INVASION OF EGYPT: 10th Army occupies Sollum.

Air War – 5 bombs dropped on Buckingham Palace by daylight raider.

Sea War: Atlantic – *Hood, Nelson* and *Rodney* leave Scapa Flow for Rosyth to counter threatened German invasion.

Home Front: Germany – Govt. to subsidize voluntary evacuation of children from Berlin to safer areas.

China – Debut of Japan's Mitsubishi Zero fighter: 13 Zeros escort bomber formation to Chungking and shoot down all defending fighters (20-plus); 4 Zeros damaged.

SATURDAY, SEPTEMBER 14

Air War – Bombs dropped on Kingston, Wimbledon, Brighton, Eastbourne, Ipswich and in NW. England. These relatively successful daylight raids in cloudy weather encourage Göring to believe that Fighter Command is weakening. Losses: German, 8; British, 13. Bomber Command sinks many invasion barges in ports between Boulogne and Antwerp.

Sea War – Hitler postpones final decision on Op. Sea Lion until Sept. 17.

SUNDAY, SEPTEMBER 15

Air War – 'BATTLE OF BRITAIN SUNDAY': 2 major raids on London smashed by RAF, which claims 185 'kills'; Germans actually lose 53 aircraft, plus 16 damaged. 26 British fighters shot down; 13 pilots killed. Bombs scattered widely across London; Buckingham Palace hit. Unsuccessful diversionary raids on Southampton and Portland. Heavy night raids on London by 180 aircraft (1 lost). 1,000-kg delayed-action bomb removed from deep crater near St Paul's Cathedral and exploded on Hackney Marshes. RAF night raids on Berlin and invasion barges at Antwerp.
Neutrals: Rumania – Antonescu establishes dictatorial régime; all political parties – except Iron Guard – are banned.

MONDAY, SEPTEMBER 16

Air War – Minor daylight raids on SE. England (bad weather). Night raids on London by 150 aircraft; damage in W. End. Göring orders fresh attacks on RAF Fighter Command – which he still hopes to crush within 4-5 days; aircraft factories also earmarked for attack. Small formations of fast bombers to be closely escorted by large numbers of Me 109s.
Sea War: Med. – RN carrier raid on Benghazi: Swordfish aircraft from *Illustrious* torpedo 1 Italian destroyer and 2 cargo ships and sink second destroyer with mine (night Sept. 16-17).
Neutrals: USA – Conscription Bill signed by Roosevelt.

TUESDAY, SEPTEMBER 17

Air War – Large formations of Me 109s carry out sweeps over Kent. Germans lose 8 aircraft; RAF, 5 fighters. Night raiders (total 268) destroy 3 large dept. stores in Oxford Street, London. 1 Ju 88 shot down. Glasgow bombed – factories hit and cruiser *Sussex* badly damaged on the Clyde.
RAF night raids on Channel ports: 26 invasion barges and 500-t ammunition dump destroyed at Dunkirk.
Sea War – HITLER ORDERS INDEFINITE POSTPONEMENT OF OP. SEA LION – the proposed invasion of England.
German disguised raider *Atlantis* sinks Free French liner *Commissaire Ramel* (10,000 t) in Indian Ocean. *City of Benares* Affair: *U-48* sinks liner carrying 102 children to Canada under the CORB scheme (Children's Overseas Reception Board). 77 children and 248 crew dead. Activities of CORB suspended Oct. 2.

WEDNESDAY, SEPTEMBER 18

North Africa – Italian 10th Army halts near Sidi Barrani, Egypt (captured Sept. 16), and remains inactive for next 3 months because of 'supply difficulties' – despite its overwhelming numerical superiority over defending British and Australian forces.

THURSDAY, SEPTEMBER 19

Sea War – Hitler orders dispersal of invasion fleet to reduce losses from British bombing raids.
Home Front: Britain – Waterloo railway station reopened (bombed Sept. 7).
Home Front: Rhodesia – Fiftieth anniversary of the founding of Southern Rhodesia.

FRIDAY, SEPTEMBER 20

Sea War: Atlantic – First successful U-boat 'Wolf-pack' op.: 3 of the 'ace' commanders – Schepke (*U-100*), Prien (*U-47*) and Kretschmer (*U–99*) – scatter Convoy HX.72 in NW. Approaches and sink 12 ships totalling 77,900 t. (Sept. 20-22).
Diplomacy – Japanese ultimatum to Vichy authorities in French Indo-China, demanding air bases, use of Haiphong harbour and freedom to transport troops to China via Indo-China. (Vichy French agree Sept. 22.)

SATURDAY, SEPTEMBER 21

Air War – RAF bomb Sidi Barrani.
Sea War – German invasion fleet in Channel ports now totals 155 steamers, 1,277 barges, 471 tugs and 1,161 motor boats.
U-100 sinks 7 ships of convoy HX. 72 in 4 hours; 12 out of 41 ships lost.
Home Front: Australia – General Election (results announced Oct. 11): United Australia Party, 24 seats; Country Party (allied with UAP), 14 seats; Labour, 32; Non-Communist Labour, 4. The P.M. Robert Menzies increases his personal majority eightfold, despite having 5 opponents.

SUNDAY, SEPTEMBER 22

Neutrals: Egypt – Saadist Party ministers withdraw from Coalition Govt. in protest against P.M.'s failure to declare war on Italy.

MONDAY, SEPTEMBER 23

Air War – German fighter sweeps over SE. England: 10 Me 109s, 2 Spitfires and 6 Hurricanes shot down. Night raids on London by 261 aircraft. 119 RAF bombers sent to Berlin.
Sea War: Atlantic – DAKAR EXPEDITION (*Op. Menace*): Unsuccessful British-Free French attempt to occupy Dakar, Vichy stronghold in W. Africa. Vichy battleship *Richelieu* (partially repaired following July 7, 1940, incident, q.v.), shore batteries and submarines hold off 3 British battleships, 4 cruisers and carrier *Ark Royal*. *Barham*, *Resolution* and cruiser *Cumberland* damaged; 1 Vichy destroyer and 2 submarines sunk. Total French casualties, 563.
Home Front: Britain – George Cross and George Medal instituted for civilian bravery.
Indo-China – Vichy French garrison at Da Nang, C. Vietnam, offers fierce resistance to Japanese occupation forces.

TUESDAY, SEPTEMBER 24

Air War – Vichy French bombers make ineffectual 'reprisal' raids on Gibraltar (Sept. 24 and 25).

WEDNESDAY, SEPTEMBER 25

Air War – Bristol Aeroplane Company's factory at Filton bombed.
Portal becomes RAF Chief of Air Staff.
Occupied Norway – Quisling 'Govt.' formed in Norway.
Secret War – US Signals Intelligence first reads Japanese *Purple* code.

THURSDAY, SEPTEMBER 26

Air War – Supermarine factory at Southampton bombed: Spitfire production halted. Night raids on London and Liverpool (fires in Docks area).

FRIDAY, SEPTEMBER 27

Air War – Fighter-bomber raid on London followed by major raid (300 bombers and fighters) on the capital and 80-plane attack on Bristol. Only 200 raiders penetrate to central London. Aircraft losses: German, 55; British, 28. Night raids on London by 163 aircraft. Number of Londoners sheltering in 'Underground' stations reaches record total of 177,000.
Diplomacy – TRIPARTITE PACT: Germany, Italy and Japan make 10-year military, political and economic alliance in Berlin.
Convention of Havana – whereby the Pan American State appoint themselves joint trustees of any European colony or colonies in the Americas which are threatened by Axis Powers. (*See* July 28, 1940.)
Sea War – Veteran British sub. H.49 (built 1919) returns after successful patrol off Frisian Is. (2 convoys attacked). She is sunk by German patrol boats in same area, Oct. 18.

SATURDAY, SEPTEMBER 28

Home Front: Britain – 'Mother and Child' evacuation scheme: 489,000 leave London by Oct. 17.

SUNDAY, SEPTEMBER 29

Air War – Hurricanes intercept formation of Heinkels over Irish Sea: each side loses 3 aircraft.

THE BATTLE OF BRITAIN AND THE BLITZ

'Thus our youngest weapon has been baptized and tempered in the flames. Now the winged host reaches out to the sea; we are ready for battle. Forward against the British Lion, for the first decisive blow . . . .

Do you hear the password?
Forward at the enemy!
Do you hear the password?
Forward at the enemy!
Onward! Onward! Bombs on England!
Bombs, bombs, bombs on England!'

***Luftwaffe** marching song (Bomben Auf England), circa* **September 1940**

Four great inventions – the internal combustion engine, aeroplane, machine gun and radio – all developed around the turn of the twentieth century, had reached a relatively advanced stage of development by 1939. Consequently World War II was pre-eminently a war of machines. Nowhere was this more true than in the air; great armies were decimated or put to flight and heavily-armoured tanks destroyed by low-flying dive-bombers and fighter-bombers; not even the biggest battleship or most elusive submarine was safe from air attack; and great cities could be devastated by fire in a single night by huge formations of bombers.

However, in July 1940, when the German *Luftwaffe* stood poised to attack the British Royal Air Force from its recently-acquired Channel and North Sea bases, the concept of air power was barely out of its infancy. No full-scale set-piece battle, fought entirely in the air between roughly equal opponents, had taken place before the so-called 'Battle of Britain' (Churchill's phrase) began over Southern England and South Wales on July 10, 1940. During the next 15 weeks almost every aspect of the philosophy and mechanics of air power and military aircraft design was put to the test. Unfortunately for Hitler and his corpulent air force commander, *Reichsmarschall* Göring, the *Luftwaffe* was found to be lacking, both in terms of leadership and tactics and of its equipment – short-range Me 109 fighters and Ju 87 *Stukas* (dive-bombers), ponderous twin-engined Me 110 'destroyers' *(Zerstörern)* and poorly-armed long-range medium bombers – none of which had been designed for the operations which characterized the end of the 'Battle' and the

Below: *The RAF fighter partnership that won the Battle of Britain. The Spitfire (foreground) could master the Me 109 while the Hurricane decimated bomber formations.*

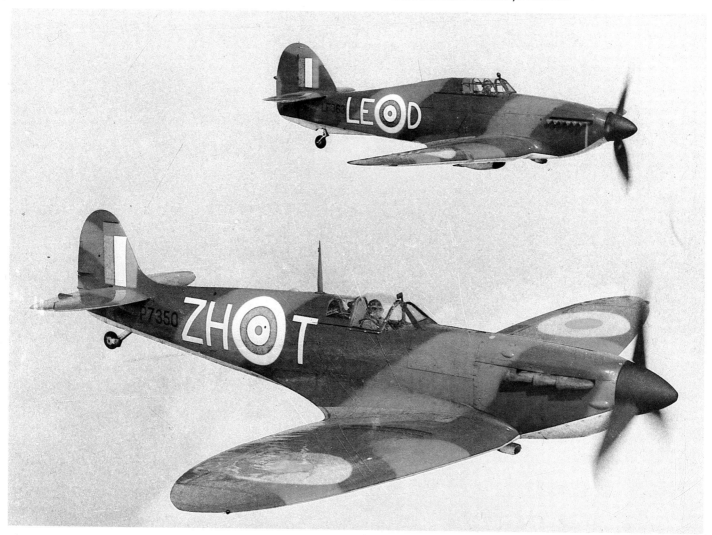

Above: *The morning after the night before, Coventry city centre on Nov. 15, 1940. The* Luftwaffe *was never able to sustain or surpass the effectiveness of this one raid.*

accompanying night 'Blitz'. The results of the secret 'electronic war' were equally unfortunate from the German viewpoint. The radio 'beams' directed towards British cities form ground stations on the French coast were invariably detected and 'jammed' by the RAF, whereas the latter's own radar stations gave invaluable early-warning of German bomber formations. The Hurricane and Spitfire squadrons were thus deployed to maximum advantage, eliminating wasteful 'standing patrols' over the English coast. The RAF also profited from information gleaned from deciphered *Luftwaffe* 'Enigma' messages.

Frustrated by RAF Fighter Command, Hitler indefinitely postponed his projected invasion of Britain (Operation Sea Lion) and Göring resorted to improvization and terror tactics. By day from early October, swarms of Messerschmitts, many equipped as make-shift fighter-bombers, swept high over the Straits of Dover on hit-and-run raids which, although highly inconvenient and exhausting for the defenders, had no ultimate effect. By night the *Luftwaffe* engaged in repeated indiscriminate 'reprisal' raids on London and other British cities in reply to the early RAF raids on Berlin.

Although the defences of British cities were still rudimentary, the *Luftwaffe* failed to exploit this golden opportunity. One reason was its lack of four-engined heavy bombers – comparable with the later British Lancaster – but far more important was the misuse of the available 700 medium bombers. Instead of delivering a limited number of devastating attacks on carefully selected targets (such as aircraft factories or power stations) Göring ordered long processions of bombers to scatter bombs across wide areas of London in the course of all-night raids 10 or more hours in duration. Such tactics meant that the ARP personnel and fireman could deal with

individual incidents, and were seldom in danger of being overwhelmed as often happened during the short, sharp, RAF saturation raids on German cities from July 1943. Equally underwhelmed was civilian morale, which the conventional wisdom of the 1930s believed incapable of withstanding prolonged aerial bombing. From mid-November 1940, Göring dissipated his efforts even further by sending his night bombers to 15 cities and ports in addition to London.

Though bad weather and muddy French airfields seriously hampered the Blitz during the winter and caused heavy German aircraft losses, the onslaught against Britain was resumed with a vengeance in March 1941 – Glasgow and Clydeside, Plymouth, Belfast, Liverpool and London came in for a series of raids noticeably more concentrated and accurate than previous efforts. Many feared that this onslaught was the preliminary to the long-feared invasion of Britain. But we now know that it was merely an elaborate diversion to conceal Hitler's preparations for the invasion of Russia. During the entire Blitz – September 1940-May 1941), more than 40,000 British civilians were killed (half of them in London), 46,000 seriously injured and well over 1,000,000 houses destroyed or damaged; approximately 2,500 German airmen died in the wrecks of some 600 bombers. In all since July 1940, the *Luftwaffe* had lost roughly 2,400 aircraft but had failed either to gain air superiority – the vital pre-condition for a successful German invasion – or to terrorize the British people into submission.

MONDAY, SEPTEMBER 30

Air War – Battle of Britain (Day 82): Five attempted raids on London. Aircraft from first and second raids jettison bombs over Hastings and Bexhill. 30 Ju 88s from fourth raid reach W. suburbs of London, causing some casualties. 40 Heinkels (4 lost) escorted by Me 110s, sent to Westland Aircraft Factory, Yeovil, but miss target and bomb Sherborne (Dorset); 5 Hurricanes shot down. Aircraft losses: German, 47; British, 20. Night raids on London by 218 aircraft: bombs fall mainly on suburbs. Other targets include Liverpool (some fires). RAF night raids on Berlin, invasion ports, airfields and numerous other objectives in Germany and Occupied territory (5 aircraft lost).
Secret War – Op. *Hummer* ('Lobster'): 3 German agents put ashore from seaplane on coast of Banff, Scotland. All captured; 2 executed. The third, double-agent Vera von Schalburg, disappears.
Home Front: Britain – 50 London firemen killed and 501 injured during Sept.

TUESDAY, OCTOBER 1

Air War – Battle of Britain (Day 83): Fighter-bomber raids on SE. England. German 2-engined bombers (except few fast Ju 88s) withdrawn from daylight ops. and replaced by makeshift conversions of Me 109 and Me 110. These carry out frequent high-altitude raids – some penetrating to London – until mid-Dec. 1940. German aircraft drop 700 mines off British E. Coast in Oct. 9 RAF night raids on Berlin in Oct., despite bad weather over W. Europe.
Sea War: Med. – Cruisers *Gloucester* and *Liverpool* land 1,200 British troop reinforcements on Malta.
Diplomacy – Finnish-German arms agreement: Germany receives sole rights to Finnish nickel exports.

WEDNESDAY, OCTOBER 2

Air War – Numerous raids over SE. England by high-flying Me 109 fighter-bombers. Spitfires break up most attacks, but a few bombs fall on SE. London. Fleeing Mes jettison bombs over Kent and Sussex seaside towns.

THURSDAY, OCTOBER 3

Home Front: Britain – Chamberlain resigns as Lord President of the Council. Herbert Morrison becomes Home Secretary; Reith, Minister of Works.

FRIDAY, OCTOBER 4

Air War – Night raids on London and SE. England by 130 aircraft. German aircrews raiding London are now frequently accompanied by Italian AF observers, who make their presence known by dropping trinkets and medallions bearing propaganda slogans.
Diplomacy – Hitler and Mussolini meet at Brenner Pass.

SATURDAY, OCTOBER 5

Air War – German fighter-bombers, attempting to reach London and SE. airfields, jettison bombs over Hastings.

SUNDAY, OCTOBER 6

Air War – Brief lull in night Blitz on London due to bad weather: few HE bombs dropped near the capital.
Sea War: Med. – Italian sub. *Gemma* accidently sunk by sister craft *Tricheco*.

MONDAY, OCTOBER 7

Air War – Night raids on London by 179 aircraft; Liverpool and Swansea bombed. RAF night raid on Berlin: 42 bombers despatched; 33(?) attack target.
Neutrals: Rumania – German forces occupy Ploesti oilfields.

TUESDAY, OCTOBER 8

Air War – Battle of Britain (Day 90): Hurricane flown by Sgt. Frantisek, leading Czech fighter 'ace' (17 victories), missing in combat over Sussex.
Diplomacy – Churchill announces re-opening of Burma Road.

WEDNESDAY, OCTOBER 9

Home Front: Britain – Churchill elected Leader of Conservative Party, in succession to Chamberlain.

THURSDAY, OCTOBER 10

Sea War – Battleship *Revenge* bombards Cherbourg docks (night Oct. 10-11).
Home Front: Britain – Myra Hess gives her daily piano recital in National Gallery, London, on anniversary of first recital in Oct. 1939.

FRIDAY, OCTOBER 11

Sea War – HMS *Ajax* routs force of 7 Italian destroyers and torpedo boats S. of Sicily – sinking 2 and damaging a third (latter sunk later by cruiser *York*). German torpedo boats sink 2 Free French anti-submarine vessels off I. of Wight (night Oct. 11-12).

SATURDAY, OCTOBER 12

Sea War – Hitler postpones Op. Sea Lion until Spring 1941.
Neutrals: Argentina – J. M. Fangio (World Motor Racing Champion, 1951-57) wins the longest ever motor race: 9,447 km Buenos Aires-Lima-Buenos Aires in 109 hours 36 mins., driving a Chevrolet.

SUNDAY, OCTOBER 13

Sea War – Engagement off S. Norway between British destroyers and German flotilla; 2 of latter sunk (night Oct. 13-14).
China – Nationalist Chinese artillery, secretly transported deep behind Japanese lines, shells Ichang Airfield – key base for enemy raids on Chungking.

MONDAY, OCTOBER 14

Air War – RAF raid Berlin. Night raids on London by 240 aircraft.

TUESDAY, OCTOBER 15

Air War – 400 German bombers raid London by moonlight, dropping 530 t of HE, starting 900 major fires and seriously disrupting road and rail communications; Oxford St. blocked; BBC Broadcasting House hit. 400 killed, 900 injured (600 trapped in Balham Underground Station). RAF night raid on Kiel (repeated Oct. 16-17): 5 aircraft lost on second raid.
Sea War: Med. – British sub *Rainbow* and Italian sub *Enrico Toti* (damaged previously and unable to submerge) fight gun battle off Calabria; *Rainbow* sunk.
Neutrals: USA – 16 M. men register for military service.

WEDNESDAY, OCTOBER 16

Sea War: Atlantic – Four U-boats operating off N. Channel (Oct. 5-16) sink 4 merchant ships and damage 3 other vessels, inc. armed merchant cruiser *Cheshire*.

THURSDAY, OCTOBER 17

Air War – Messerschmitt fighter bombers raid London: bomb destroys all signalling equipment at Waterloo Stn.
Sea War – German destroyers and torpedo boats carry out offensive sweep towards Land's End, but retire when engaged by British cruiser and several destroyers.
Home Front: Britain – London Transport appeal to provincial bus companies for replacement vehicles after air-raid losses.

FRIDAY, OCTOBER 18

Air War – RAF and S. African AF raid targets in Italian E. Africa.
Indo-China – Japanese bomb Burma Road.

SATURDAY, OCTOBER 19

Sea War – Destroyer *Venetia* mined and sunk in Thames Estuary.

SUNDAY, OCTOBER 20

Air War – RAF night raids on Berlin, Milan and Turin. Italian aircraft drop bombs near

Cairo. Italian bomber formation flies 4,506 km from Dodecanese Is. to Eritrea via Bahrein, making abortive attack on oil installations.
Sea War – Italian destroyers make unsuccessful night attack on large British convoy in Red Sea: *Francesco Nullo* beached, and later sunk by Blenheim bombers.

MONDAY, OCTOBER 21

Home Front: Britain – Churchill broadcasts to France, in French; he pours scorn on the threatened invasion of Britain: '*We are waiting. . . . So are the fishes!*' and warns that Hitler ('*this monstrous abortion of hatred and defeat*') is plotting the total subjugation of France.
Purchase Tax introduced.
Sea War: Med. – Italian Navy forms new command – '*Maritrafalba*' – to escort vital convoys from Brindisi and Bari to Albania, in readiness for impending invasion of Greece.

TUESDAY, OCTOBER 22

Air War – S. African AF planes attack Birikau, Italian E. Africa, for the fifth time.

Below: *The West Front of St. Paul's Cathedral in the City of London, lit by searchlights during the Blitz.*

Shortest night raid on London since onset of Blitz: large dept. store wrecked.

WEDNESDAY, OCTOBER 23

Diplomacy – Hitler and Gen. Franco meet at Hendaye on French-Spanish border.
Sea War: Atlantic – Pocket battleship *Admiral Scheer* sails from Gotenhafen.

THURSDAY, OCTOBER 24

Air War – RAF night raids on Berlin and Hamburg: first raids to inflict significant civilian casualties.
Diplomacy – Hitler meets Pétain and discusses Franco-German collaboration.
Home Front: Britain – First of 2,000 provincial buses appear on London routes.

FRIDAY, OCTOBER 25

Air War – Formations of high-flying Me 109s make several attempts to reach London, but few penetrate RAF fighter screen: heavy casualties when loaded tramcars are bombed. He 111s make surprise dusk raid on Montrose airfield (Scotland); heavy damage. Night raids on London by 150 aircraft. Italian expeditionary air corps (*Corpo Aereo Italiano*) in action for first time: 16 Fiat bombers (3 lost) despatched from Belgian bases to Harwich (little damage).

SATURDAY, OCTOBER 26

Sea War: Atlantic – Liner *Empress of Britain* (42,300 t) bombed, strafed and set on fire by Focke-Wulf Condor, 241 km W. of Donegal; she is taken in tow. 3 U-boats sent in pursuit; *U-32* sinks liner Oct. 28.

SUNDAY, OCTOBER 27

Neutrals: USA – New York World's Fair closes after 2 seasons (first opened April. 1939).

MONDAY, OCTOBER 28

Balkans – ITALIAN INVASION OF GREECE. Italians attack at 3 points on Albanian-Greek frontier – Adriatic coast, Pindus Mts., and Macedonia – employing 27 divs., 380 aircraft, supported on seaward flank by naval forces.

> **Greek Forces**
> 430,000 men (16 divs.); 126 planes; 1 old cruiser, 10 destroyers, 13 torpedo boats, 2 MTBs, 6 subs.

Gen. Papagos appointed Greek CinC.
Diplomacy – Italian ultimatum to Greece, demanding right of passage for Italian forces to unspecified 'strategic points', by 6 a.m. Greek P.M. Metaxas rejects ultimatum. Italian forces begin invasion at 5.30 a.m. Britain promises all possible aid to Greece.
Vichy France – Laval becomes Vichy Foreign Minister.
Air War – Italians bomb Patras (100 killed).

TUESDAY, OCTOBER 29

Home Front: Britain – Gen. Legentilhomme joins Gen. de Gaulle in London.

WEDNESDAY, OCTOBER 30

Sea War: Atlantic – *U-32* sunk while attacking convoy by destroyers *Harvester* and *Highlander*. Destroyer *Sturdy* wrecked in Hebrides.

THURSDAY, OCTOBER 31

Air War – BATTLE OF BRITAIN ENDS (Day 114): *Luftwaffe* loses 116 fighter-bombers and escort fighters during raids on London and SE. England in Oct. 1940. RAF loses 190 fighters.

Raids on Coventry (Aug. 18-Oct. 31): 198 t of bombs dropped in 17 raids; 176 killed, 229 seriously injured.
Balkans – British forces land on Crete.

Battle of Britain Losses
Since July 10. Luftwaffe: 1,733 planes, 3,893 men; RAF: 828 planes, 1,007 men.

FRIDAY, NOVEMBER 1

Air War – *Stukas* attack convoy off Thames Estuary. 8 RAF raids on Berlin in Nov. (heavy casualties in first raid – Nov. 1-2). Italians bomb Salonika (59 killed), Piraeus, Larissa, Corfu, Corinth and Candia (Crete). Greeks bomb Italian HQ at Koritsa (Albania).
Balkans – Italians reach R. Kalamas, near Adriatic coast.
Sea War: Atlantic – 9 Italian subs now operating from Bordeaux.

SATURDAY, NOVEMBER 2

Air War — Italians bomb Salonika (Nov. 2 and 3).

SUNDAY, NOVEMBER 3

Sea War: Atlantic – *U-99* torpedoes 2 British armed merchant cruisers: *Laurentic* (18,700 t) and *Patroclus* (11,300 t).
Air War – Bad weather halts night 'Blitz' on London: for only second time since Sept. 7-8. Some raiders over NE. England and E. Scotland. RAF bomb Kiel.
Balkans – In Pindus Mts. Greeks defeat 3rd Alpini Div.

MONDAY, NOVEMBER 4

Air War – Sneak raiders active over S. and E. England and London; second strafing attack on London streets in 2 days. 150 night bombers over London. RAF night raids on Channel ports; Italian ports of Bari and Brindisi bombed by aircraft from Crete.
Neutrals: Spain – Spanish administration established in former International Zone of Tangier.

TUESDAY, NOVEMBER 5

Sea War: Atlantic – *Admiral Scheer* attacks large eastbound convoy, escorted

---

by armed merchant cruiser *Jervis Bay*. Latter sunk after gallant resistance which saves convoy from complete destruction. *Scheer* sinks 5 ships; tanker *San Demetrio* badly damaged and abandoned (crew later reboard her). Eastbound convoys from Halifax to Britain are cancelled until Nov. 17.
USA – **PRESIDENTIAL ELECTIONS:** Roosevelt (Democratic), 27,241,939; Willkie (Republican), 22,237,226. Roosevelt carries 39 States and is re-elected for record third term. 5 'fringe' candidates (inc. Socialist, Norman Thomas) together receive insignificant total of votes.

Air War – Italians bomb Yugoslav border town of Monastir.

WEDNESDAY, NOVEMBER 6

Air War – Daylight raid on Southampton; 190 aircraft raid London by night. RAF raid Italian airfields in Albania.
Sea War – 7 German torpedo boats carry out offensive sweep towards E. Coast of Scotland (night Nov. 6-7); op. abandoned when *T.6* sinks on mine.
Home Front: Britain – Home Guard officers to be commissioned.
Home Front: S. Africa – Gen. Hertzog resigns leadership of Nationalist Party.

THURSDAY, NOVEMBER 7

Air War – Night raid on Essen by 50 aircraft. RAF make surprise low-level attack on Valona air base, Albania.

CUNNINGHAM, Andrew Browne (1883-1963)
British: *Admiral of the Fleet, Viscount Cunningham of Hyndhope*

As CinC Med. Fleet, Cunningham waged masterly campaign against fast, modern, Italian fleet, foiling every attempt to interfere with vital Allied convoys on Gibraltar-Malta-Alexandria route. Won two great victories over Italians – at Taranto (1940) and Cape Matapan (1941) – sinking or crippling 3 battleships and 3 heavy cruisers without losing single one of his own ships.
Son of Professor D. J. Cunningham and brother of Sir Alan Gordon Cunningham, commander of British 8th Army. Entered Royal Navy, 1898. Served in World War I. Rear-Admiral, 1932; Vice-Admiral, 1937. CinC Med. Fleet, 1939-42. Naval CinC of Expeditionary Force to North Africa, Nov. 1942. Admiral of the Fleet and CinC of Allied Naval Forces in Med., 1943. First Sea Lord and Chief of Naval Staff, 1943-46. Created baron, 1945; Viscount Cunningham of Hyndhope, 1946. Published memoirs, 'A Sailor's Odyssey' (1951).

Vichy France – Free French troops of Foreign Legion land near Libreville, French Equatorial Africa.

FRIDAY, NOVEMBER 8

Air War – *Stukas* attack shipping in Straits of Dover and Thames Estuary, sinking 1 ship. Hurricane sqn. drives off the raiders. RAF bomb Munich.
Sea War – British SS *Cambridge* and American SS *City of Rayville* sink on minefield laid in Bass Str., S. of Australia by German raider *Passat* (Nov. 7-8). Port of Melbourne temporarily closed.

SATURDAY, NOVEMBER 9

Home Front: Britain – Death of Neville Chamberlain, aged 71. (Funeral in Westminster Abbey, Nov. 14.)
Sea War – Liner *Empress of Japan* (26,000 t) attacked in Atlantic by a Focke-Wulf Condor (she reaches port). German aircraft now laying acoustic mines (actuated by noise from ships' propellors) along British S. and W. coasts (countermeasures involve the use of modified pneumatic drills!).
Neutrals: Rumania – Earthquake rocks Bucharest and Ploesti oilfields; 400 dead.

SUNDAY, NOVEMBER 10

Air War – RAF bomb Danzig, Dresden, Krupp's Works, Essen and many other targets in Germany, Occupied territory and Italy (night Nov. 10-11) despite severe storms and icing (5 aircraft lost). 170 night raiders over London.
East Africa – British recapture Gallabat in Sudan.

MONDAY, NOVEMBER 11

Sea War: Med. – THE TARANTO RAID (Op. Judgement): 21 Swordfish biplanes (2

lost) from carrier *Illustrious* carry out surprise torpedo/bomb attack on Italian Fleet in Taranto naval base. 3 battleships hit – *Conte di Cavour* sunk, *Caio Duilio* and new *Littorio* damaged (night Nov. 11-12). Italian Fleet subsequently leaves Taranto for Naples and Genoa. Cruisers *Ajax*, *Orion* and *Sydney* destroy Italian convoy in Strait of Otranto; 4 transports sunk (night Nov. 11-12).

Air War – 2 large formations of fighter-bombers attempt to reach London; a few aircraft drop bombs in 3 London districts. *Stukas* make unsuccessful raid on convoy off Kent. 50-strong Italian formation defeated off Suffolk coast by 2 Hurricane sqns. British losses, nil; Italian losses, 6. Short night raid on London (20 aircraft). RAF night raids on Italian supply ports of Valona and Durazzo (Albania).

Neutrals: USA – First Jeep delivered to US Army.

TUESDAY, NOVEMBER 12

Diplomacy – Molotov, Russian Foreign Minister, begins 3-day official visit to Berlin to discuss closer collaboration with Axis Powers. He is forced to take shelter during RAF night raid.

Secret War – British Air Intelligence learn from captured German pilot that a 'colossal raid' on Coventry or Birmingham by 'every bomber in the *Luftwaffe*', will take place by moonlight between Nov. 15 and 20. However, other information suggests target will be London.

WEDNESDAY, NOVEMBER 13

Air War – RAF night raid on Berlin and Taranto naval base.

THURSDAY, NOVEMBER 14

Air War – **COVENTRY BLITZ** (Op. *Mondlicht Sonate:* 'Moonlight Sonata'): 440 aircraft (2 lost) led by He 111 'pathfinders'. City centre and Cathedral largely destroyed and 12 important aircraft component factories shut down. Casualties: 568 killed, 863 seriously injured. (17 other provincial cities and ports receive total of 81 heavy raids, Nov. 17-18, 1940 to May 16-17, 1941.) Op. Cold Water: RAF attempt (with little success) to pre-empt the 'colossal raid' predicted by British Intelligence by bombing enemy bases, scrambling 121 night fighters and jamming radio transmissions. Spitfire sqn. routs 30 *Stukas* over Dover.

Balkans – **MAJOR GREEK COUNTER-OFFENSIVE** in Epirus and Macedonia leads to first Axis land defeat.

Neutrals: Liechtenstein – Blackout enforced because of danger of air raids.

FRIDAY, NOVEMBER 15

Air War – Heavy night raids on London (350 aircraft).

SATURDAY, NOVEMBER 16

Sea War – Three German cargo ships leave Tampico (Mexico), but fail to break through the British blockade: *Phrygia* scuttled; *Idarwald* and *Rhein* return to Tampico.

SUNDAY, NOVEMBER 17

Air War – Heavy night raids on Southampton by 150 aircraft. RAF's Army Co-operation Cmnd. established. Night raids on Gelsenkirchen (Ruhr) oil plant.

MONDAY, NOVEMBER 18

Balkans – All invading Italian forces have now been driven back over R. Kalamas.

TUESDAY, NOVEMBER 19

Air War – Heavy night raid on Birmingham by 350 aircraft; second raid, by 116 aircraft, on following night is unsuccessful; third raid (200 aircraft), Nov. 22-23, again causes serious damage, and numerous fires. Germans lose total of 5 aircraft. Casualties: 900 killed, 2,000 injured. Birmingham Cathedral damaged.

Neutrals: Switzerland – Pro-Nazi 'Swiss National Movement' banned.

WEDNESDAY, NOVEMBER 20

Air War – Air Marshal Boyd, RAF, captured by Italians when his plane makes forced landing in Sicily.

Diplomacy – Hungary signs Tripartite Pact. (*See* Sept. 27, 1940.)

Below: *Coventry's 14th century cathedral after the devastating Luftwaffe raid of Nov. 14-15.*

THURSDAY, NOVEMBER 21

Secret War – Dies Committee Report on German espionage and 'fifth Column' activity in Britain published.

FRIDAY, NOVEMBER 22

Balkans – Greeks capture Koritsa – important town in SE. Albania.

Diplomacy – Willington Trade Mission arrives in Rio de Janeiro to promote British interests.

SATURDAY, NOVEMBER 23

Air War – Heavy night raids on Southampton by 120 aircraft: numerous fires; liner *Llandovery Castle* (10,600 t) badly damaged.

Diplomacy – Rumania signs Tripartite Pact. (*See* Sept. 27, 1940). US appoints Adm. Leahy Ambassador in Vichy.

SUNDAY, NOVEMBER 24

Air War – Heavy night raid on Bristol by 130 aircraft (3 lost).

Sea War – German destroyers carry out 2 sorties off Plymouth (nights Nov. 24-25 and 28-29): 4 coasters sunk and British destroyer *Javelin* damaged by torpedo.

Diplomacy – Slovakia joins Tripartite Pact.

Home Front: Britain – Death of Lord Craigavon, P.M. of N. Ireland since 1921, aged 69. Succeeded by J. M. Andrews.

MONDAY, NOVEMBER 25

Air War – Slight German air activity over SE. England, but prototype De Havilland Mosquito makes uninterrupted maiden flight from Hatfield. RAF night raids on Kiel and Wilhelmshaven.

Sea War: Med. – SS *Patria* blown up and sunk at Haifa by Zionist terrorist organization *Irgun Zvai Leumi* to prevent its use as deportation vessel for Palestinian Jews.

TUESDAY, NOVEMBER 26

Air War — Heavy RAF raid on Cologne (repeated following night).

Home Front: Britain – Death of Lord Rothermere (Harold Northcliffe), founder of 'Sunday Pictorial' and former Air Minister, aged 72 (at Bermuda).

WEDNESDAY, NOVEMBER 27

Air War – Jean Chiappe, newly appointed High Commissioner in Syria and Lebanon and a former pro-Fascist Chief of Police in Paris, killed when the aircraft taking him to Beirut is accidentally shot down during Battle of Spartivento (q.v.). Aged 62.

Occupied Rumania – Iron Guard killer-squads 'execute' veteran ex-P.M. and noted scholar Prof. Jorga and over 60 other Rumanian anti-Fascists.

Sea War: Med. – Action off Sardinia ('Battle of Cape Spartivento'): Italian fleet attempts to disrupt major British convoy movements (Op. Collar.) British cruiser *Berwick* damaged in running fight. Italian battleship *Vittorio. Veneto* escapes undamaged despite torpedo-bomber attacks.

THURSDAY, NOVEMBER 28

Air War – Heavy night raid on Liverpool by 300 aircraft: parachute mine explosion kills 164, injures 96. Spitfires intercept Me 109 formation off I. of Wight: Flt.-Lt. Dundas shoots down leading German ace Maj. Wick (56 victories), but is killed himself seconds later.

FRIDAY, NOVEMBER 29

Air War – Heavy night raid on London and Home Counties by 330 aircraft.
Occupied France – Gen. de Gaulle broadcasts to France: Free French Forces now number 35,000 trained troops and 1,000 airmen.

SATURDAY, NOVEMBER 30

Air War — First of 2 consecutive night raids on Southampton – by 128 and 123 bombers, respectively – serious damage in city centre and suburbs. Total casualties: 370.
Balkans – Greeks capture Progradets in SE. Albania, after 7-day battle.
Home Front: Greece – Civilian air raid casualties since Oct. 28: 604 killed, 1,070 injured.
Diplomacy – Treaty between Japan and puppet Central Govt. of China.

SUNDAY, DECEMBER 1

Sea War – Armed merchant cruiser *Forfar* (16,400 t) sunk by *U-99* W. of Ireland. Free Norwegian liner *Oslofjord* (18,700 t) and a British tanker mined and sunk off the Tyne in North Sea.
Home Front: Italy – Rationing of flour, rice, spaghetti and macaroni.

MONDAY, DECEMBER 2

Air War: Britain – Bristol raided by 120 aircraft (night Dec. 1-2): serious damage in residential areas.
Sea War: Atlantic – Adm. Tovey succeeds Adm. Forbes as CinC British Home Fleet.

TUESDAY, DECEMBER 3

Sea War: Med. – British cruiser *Glasgow* damaged by Italian torpedo-bombers in Suda Bay, Crete.

WEDNESDAY, DECEMBER 4

Balkans – Greeks capture Premeti, SW. Albania. Italians abandon important

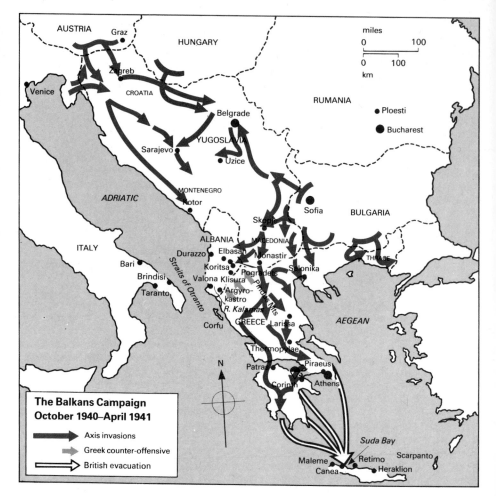

The Balkans Campaign
October 1940–April 1941
→ Axis invasions
→ Greek counter-offensive
→ British evacuation

supply base of Argyrokastro, SW. Albania, and nearby port of Santi Quaranta.

THURSDAY, DECEMBER 5

Sea War: Atlantic – German disguised raider *Thor* damages British armed merchant cruiser *Carnarvon Castle* (20,000 t) off Rio de Janeiro.

FRIDAY, DECEMBER 6

Balkans – In Pindus Mts. Greeks advance towards Klisura. In Macedonian sector Greeks advance along valleys towards Elbasan. Marshal Badoglio, Duke of Addis Ababa, and Chief of Gen. Staff, relieved 'at his own request'.

SATURDAY, DECEMBER 7

Air War – No raids on Britain, either by day or night – first such 24-hour period since Aug. 7. RAF night raid on Düsseldorf (repeated Dec. 8-9).

SUNDAY, DECEMBER 8

Air War: Britain – Fire raid on London by 413 aircraft (2 lost): In 14-hour onslaught bombs are scattered over many metropolitan and suburban districts and between London and S. and E. Coasts, but all fires quickly controlled. 7 hospitals and 4 churches hit. Total bomb-load: 115,000 1-kg (2.2-lb) incendiaries and 387 t HE.
RAF attack many Italian airfields and landing-grounds in Libya (night Dec. 8-9).
Home Front: Italy – Three admirals dismissed, inc. Cavagnari, Chief of Naval Staff.

MONDAY, DECEMBER 9

North Africa – **FIRST BRITISH OFFENSIVE IN WESTERN DESERT** (Op. Compass): 2 divs. attack 10 Italian divs. (10th Army), in their fortified camps S. of Sidi Barrani (Egypt).
Sea War: Med. – Four special task forces of British Med. Fleet formed to bombard Italian positions and communications along Egypt-Libya coast. Adm. Iachino, former Naval Attaché in London, appointed CinC of Italian Fleet.
Home Front: Britain – 705,279 people unemployed.

TUESDAY, DECEMBER 10

Air War – *Luftwaffe* ordered to transfer *Fliegerkorps X* to S. Italy.
Home Front: Germany – Hitler condemns British aristocracy and 'financial magnates' in speech to Berlin munitions workers, and predicts: *there will be no defeat of Germany, either by military or economic means, or by time.'*

WEDNESDAY, DECEMBER 11

North Africa – British capture Sidi Barrani.
Air War – Heavy night raid on Birmingham by 270 aircraft: 6 churches, 11 schools, several hundred houses damaged.

THURSDAY, DECEMBER 12

Air War: Britain – 336 bombers sent to Sheffield (night Dec. 12-13): many streets blocked by debris and wrecked tramcars. Follow-up raid by 94 planes 3 nights later.
Diplomacy – Death of Lord Lothian, British Ambassador to USA, aged 58. Yugoslav-Hungarian 'Friendship Pact' signed.

FRIDAY, DECEMBER 13

Sea War – Cruiser *Coventry* damaged by Italian sub *Neghelli* off coast of Libya.

SATURDAY, DECEMBER 14

Air War – RAF night raid on Naples: cruiser *Pola* damaged.
Vichy France – Pétain dismisses Foreign Minister Laval and appoints Flandin. (German Ambassador subsequently intercedes on Laval's behalf.)
Neutrals: Irish Republic – IRA internees set fire to Curragh Camp near Dublin and fight with troops and *Garda* (police); 4 injured (1 IRA man shot dead in further clashes next day).

SUNDAY, DECEMBER 15

Air War – RAF night raids on Berlin and Naples (Italian cruiser damaged).
Occupied France – Coffin of Napoleon II (1811-1832), transported from Vienna to Paris on Hitler's orders, is reburied in Les Invalides.

MONDAY, DECEMBER 16

Air War – First 'area bombing' raid on German city: 134 RAF aircraft sent to Mannheim (night Dec. 16-17). Large fires started on both banks of Rhine. Other targets include Speyer-am-Rhein and Heilbronn, but Basle (Switzerland) accidentally bombed: 4 killed. (*See* Feb. 18, 1941.)

TUESDAY, DECEMBER 17

North Africa – British capture Sollum and Fort Capuzzo. 20,000 captured Italians to be sent to India and interned at Ahmednagar, Ramgarh and Deolali.
Sea War – British destroyer *Acheron* mined and sunk off I. of Wight.

WEDNESDAY, DECEMBER 18

Sea War: Med. – British submarine *Triton* sunk by Italian torpedo boat in Straits of Otranto. Battleships *Warspite* and *Valiant* bombard Valona, Italian-held port in Albania (night Dec. 18-19). Italian cruisers and destroyers bombard Greek positions on Albanian coast.
Home Front: Britain – 10,969 evacuees have now arrived from Gibraltar.
Home Front: Germany – HITLER ORDERS PREPARATIONS FOR INVASION OF RUSSIA (Op. *Barbarossa*) with deadline of May 15, 1941. Soviet Army to be encircled and destroyed in W. Russia by *Pz* columns with powerful air support. Final objective: line Archangel-Urals-R. Volga.

THURSDAY, DECEMBER 19

Neutrals: Finland – Pres. Kallio dies of heart failure on the day of his retirement; aged 67.

FRIDAY, DECEMBER 20

Air War: Britain – First of 2 consecutive heavy night raids on Liverpool.
Home Front: Britain – Committee of Enquiry into *Arandora Star* disaster (*see* July 2, 1940) publishes its findings. Main criticism concerns the indiscriminate deportation of both Fascist and anti-Fascist Italians on the liner.

SATURDAY, DECEMBER 21

Sea War: Pacific – German disguised raiders *Komet* and *Orion* land 496 survivors (inc. 70 women and 7 children) from 10 British and Allied merchant ships – sunk since Aug. – on Emirau I. (New Guinea). Survivors subsequently rescued by Royal Australian Navy.
Air War – RAF night raid on Porto Marghera docks and oil installations, near Venice.
Neutrals: USA – Death of writer F. Scott Fitzgerald, in Hollywood; aged 44.

SUNDAY, DECEMBER 22

Air War: Britain – First of 2 consecutive heavy night raids on Manchester.

MONDAY, DECEMBER 23

Home Front: Britain – Eden becomes Foreign Secretary; Lord Halifax goes to Washington Embassy.

TUESDAY, DECEMBER 24

Sea War: Med. – Greek sub *Papanicolis* sinks Italian transport off Albania.

WEDNESDAY, DECEMBER 25

Air War – Italian aircraft raid Corfu for twenty-third time (15 killed).
Sea War: Atlantic – *Admiral Hipper* attacks large British troop convoy W. of C. Finisterre, damaging 2 ships and escorting cruiser *Berwick*.

THURSDAY, DECEMBER 26

Air War – RAF daylight raids on airfields in Brittany; night raid on Bordeaux.

FRIDAY, DECEMBER 27

Air War: Britain – Night raids on London by 100 aircraft.

SATURDAY, DECEMBER 28

Secret War – The Gelsenkirchen Report: RAF PR of Ruhr synthetic oil plant, flown Dec. 24, shows it not destroyed.

SUNDAY, DECEMBER 29

Air War: Britain – 'SECOND GREAT FIRE OF LONDON': 136 aircraft drop 30,000 incendiaries – great conflagration in 'City' area; Guildhall and 8 Wren churches gutted.
Neutrals: USA – Roosevelt declares in a radio 'fireside chat' broadcast: *'We must be the great arsenal of democracy.'*

MONDAY, DECEMBER 30

Home Front: Britain – Royal Engineers and Pioneers dynamite fire-gutted buildings in City of London.

TUESDAY, DECEMBER 31

Air War – RAF daylight raids on Cologne, Rotterdam (oil supplies), Ijmuiden (docks) and bridge over Rhine near Emmerich. Valona (Albania) and Assab (Italian E. Africa) also bombed by RAF.
Home Front: Britain – 'Fire-watchers' to be stationed in all factories, shops and offices in attempt to combat increasingly serious threat from incendiary bombs.

Shipping Losses 1940
Allied and Neutral: 1,059 ships totalling 4,055,706 t. Axis: 22 U-boats, 20 Italian subs.

WEDNESDAY, JANUARY 1

Air War: Europe – 95 RAF bombers raid Bremen (night Jan. 1-2).

THURSDAY, JANUARY 2

Air War: Britain – 100 German bombers raid Cardiff (night Jan. 2-3); many fires started. Llandaff Cathedral badly damaged.

FRIDAY, JANUARY 3

Balkans – Italians launch unsuccessful counter-offensive in Albania.
Air War: Britain – Night raids on Bristol by 170 aircraft: 8,000 t. of grain destroyed.
Vichy France – Foreign Min. Baudouin resigns from Vichy Cabinet.

SATURDAY, JANUARY 4

North Africa – The Murzuk Raid: small force of Tuareg and Tibesti tribesmen under Free French officers cross 485 km of desert from Chad to Murzuk Oasis, S. Libya, and destroy Italian air base.
Air War: Europe – RAF night raids on Brest naval base.

SUNDAY, JANUARY 5

North Africa – British capture Bardia; 45,000 PoWs, 130 tanks taken.
Home Front: Britain – Amy Johnson, famous long-distance flier, dies in crash over Thames Estuary while working for the Air Transport Auxiliary.

MONDAY, JANUARY 6

Neutrals: USA – Roosevelt's 'Four Freedoms' Speech to Congress: '*We look forward to a world founded on four essential human freedoms . . . freedom of speech . . . of worship . . . freedom from want . . . freedom from fear . . .*'

TUESDAY, JANUARY 7

Air War/Sea War: Atlantic – Condor 4-engined reconnaissance bombers, based near Bordeaux, transferred to operational command of Adm. Dönitz. British corvette *Anemone* sinks large Italian sub. *Nani* NW. of Ireland.

WEDNESDAY, JANUARY 8

Neutrals: USA – $17.5 billion Defense Budget announced.
Home Front: Britain – Death of Lord

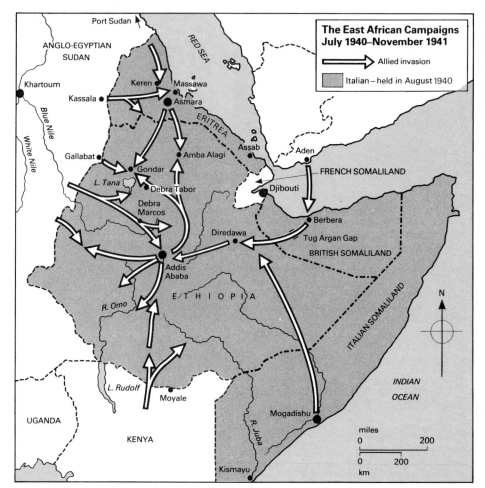

The East African Campaigns July 1940–November 1941
→ Allied invasion
▨ Italian – held in August 1940

Baden-Powell, World Chief Scout, Founder of Scout movement and Boer War hero, at Nyeri, Kenya, aged 84.
Air War – RAF night raid on Naples: battleship *Giulio Cesare* damaged (she has to be moved to La Spezia).

THURSDAY, JANUARY 9

Diplomacy – Harry Hopkins, Roosevelt's personal representative, arrives in London (leaves Feb. 16).
Home Front: Britain – Air Training Corps to be formed.

FRIDAY, JANUARY 10

Sea War: Med. – Stukas score 6 hits on carrier *Illustrious* escorting convoy W. of Malta (*see* Jan. 16). Cruiser *Southampton* crippled (abandoned Jan. 11).
Air War: Europe – First large-scale RAF daylight raid over France since June 1940. 100 fighters escort Blenheim bombers in sweep over Pas de Calais – airfields and cross-Channel gun positions attacked. Night raids on Brest and Palermo (Sicily). Total aircraft losses, German, 3; British, nil.
Air War: Britain – 150 aircraft (6 lost) drop 50,000 incendiaries on Portsmouth, starting 28 large fires (night Jan. 10-11).
Diplomacy – Soviet-German agreement on population exchanges in Baltic States.

SATURDAY, JANUARY 11

Sea War – Stukas cripple cruiser HMS *Southampton* near Malta. German and Italian submarines and Condor aircraft carry out first successful combined ops. (Jan. 11-Feb. 4): U-boats sink 13, Italian submarines sink 5, Condors sink 15 ships.

SUNDAY, JANUARY 12

Sea War: Atlantic – 21-ship troop convoy leaves Britain for N. Africa.
Air War: Europe – RAF night raids on oil installations at Regensburg and Porto Marghera near Venice; leaflets dropped over Padua.

MONDAY, JANUARY 13

Air War – RAF bombs Lorient U-boat base (night Jan. 13-14). German night bombers shower incendiaries over Plymouth.
Neutrals: Switzerland – Death of James Joyce, author of *Ulysses* and *Finnegan's Wake,* in Zürich, aged 58.

TUESDAY, JANUARY 14

Sea War – German disguised raider *Pinguin* captures a Norwegian whaling fleet – 3 factory ships and 11 whale catchers in Antarctic. Skeleton crews are put on

board and the ships reach French ports in March 1941.
Air War – RAF night raids on Benghazi and Assab (Eritrea).

WEDNESDAY, JANUARY 15

East Africa – Emperor Haile Selassie returns to Ethiopia (night Jan. 15-16).
Air War: Europe – 76 RAF bombers raid Wilhelmshaven (night Jan. 15-16).

THURSDAY, JANUARY 16

Air War – *Stukas* escorted by Italian fighters raid Malta, inflicting further damage on carrier *Illustrious* and damaging cruiser *Perth*. (*Illustrious* again damaged by bombing Jan. 19).

FRIDAY, JANUARY 17

Sea War – Battle of Koh-Chang in China Sea: Vichy French sqn. defeats Thai Navy, sinking 3 ships.

SATURDAY, JANUARY 18

Vichy France – Pétain and Laval reconcile their differences.

SUNDAY, JANUARY 19

East Africa – British recapture Kassala (Sudan): start of Eritrea campaign.
Neutrals: China – Nationalist Chinese disband Communist New 4th Army in Yangtse Valley following serious outbreak of fighting.

MONDAY, JANUARY 20

Air War – British, S. African and Rhodesian aircraft raid power stn. at Massawa and other targets in E. Africa.
Neutrals: USA – Roosevelt inaugurated.

TUESDAY, JANUARY 21

Neutrals: Rumania – Ultra-fascist Iron Guard attempts to overthrow Rumanian military dictator, Gen. Antonescu, and conducts simultaneous pogrom against the Jews (approx. 1,000 killed); many are butchered in Bucharest animal slaughter-house. Rising finally crushed Jan. 24 and ringleader (Sima) flees to Germany.

WEDNESDAY, JANUARY 22

North Africa – BRITISH CAPTURE TOBRUK.
Sea War: Atlantic – 'Op. Berlin': *Gneisenau* and *Scharnhorst* leave Kiel in Baltic to attack Atlantic convoys (*see* Feb. 22).

THURSDAY, JANUARY 23

Sea War – After emergency repairs carrier *Illustrious* leaves Malta for Alexandria

(then goes to Norfolk Navy Yard, USA). 5 Norwegian merchant ships – interned at Gothenburg, Sweden, since April 1940 – elude German minefields and the *Gneisenau* and *Scharnhorst* and rendezvous with British Home Fleet in Skagerrak.

FRIDAY, JANUARY 24

Diplomacy – Lord Halifax, new British Ambassador to USA, arrives aboard new battleship *King George V*.

SATURDAY, JANUARY 25

Balkans – Many cases of frostbite are reported on both sides in wild mtn. battle areas of S. Albania. Italians also suffering with typhoid.

SUNDAY, JANUARY 26

East Africa – British capture Biscia in Eritrea.
Diplomacy – Wendell Willkie, defeated US presidential candidate, visits London.

MONDAY, JANUARY 27

Sea War: Med. – British sub. *Upholder* operates against Italian convoy route, Trapani (Sicily)-Tripoli.

TUESDAY, JANUARY 28

Sea War: Med. – British sub. *Rorqual* lays mines off Adriatic coast port of Ancona.

WEDNESDAY, JANUARY 29

East Africa – S. Africans invade Italian Somaliland.
Air War – He 111s drop mines by night in Suez Canal (repeated Feb. 18-19 and 22-23).
Home Front: Greece – Death of Gen. Metaxas, President since 1936, aged 70. Successor is Alexander Koryzis, former minister and bank governor.

THURSDAY, JANUARY 30

North Africa – British capture Derna.
Air War: Britain – German 'hit and run' raiders attack London in cloudy weather. Me 109s strafe Dover balloon barrage.

FRIDAY, JANUARY 31

Air War: Britain – 3 London hospitals damaged by 'hit and run' raiders.
Diplomacy – Vichy French authorities in Indo-China sign armistice with Thailand aboard Japanese warship off Bangkok, ending desultory border war.

SATURDAY, FEBRUARY 1

Home Front: South Africa – Serious riots in Johannesburg between off-duty soldiers

and members of fascist *Ossewabrandwag* ('Ox-wagon Guard'): 140 injured.
East Africa – British capture Agordat (Eritrea).

SUNDAY, FEBRUARY 2

Sea War: Med. – Swordfish from *Ark Royal* make unsuccessful attack on Tirso Dam (Sardinia).

MONDAY, FEBRUARY 3

East Africa – Battle of Keren: Italians surprise British by holding this mtn. stronghold for 8 weeks. (Italians retreat March 27, *q.v.*)

TUESDAY, FEBRUARY 4

North Africa – British 7th Armoured Div. launches outflanking movement across desert SE. of Benghazi.

WEDNESDAY, FEBRUARY 5

North Africa – BATTLE OF BEDA FOMM: encircled Italian forces make desperate efforts to escape from British 7th Armoured Div. and Australian infantry, S. of Benghazi, but are completely defeated. Italians lose 20,000 men, 216 guns, 112 tanks and 1,500 trucks.

THURSDAY, FEBRUARY 6

Diplomacy – J. G. Winant to succeed Joseph Kennedy as US Ambassador in London.

FRIDAY, FEBRUARY 7

North Africa – BRITISH CAPTURE BENGHAZI. Italians surrender to Wavell's forces. Free French under Leclerc with air

---

North African Campaign Losses
Since Dec. 9, 1940. Italian: 133,295 PoWs; 400 tanks, 850 guns. British, Australian, Indian: 555 dead and missing, 1,373 wounded; about 10 tanks.

---

support besiege Kufra Oasis, important Italian garrison town and air base in S. Libya.

Above: *Italian troops surrender to one of Wavell's 'Thirty Thousand'.*

SATURDAY, FEBRUARY 8

Home Front: Britain – Lord Moyne appointed Colonial Sec.; Ernest Brown, Min. of Health.

SUNDAY, FEBRUARY 9

North Africa – Wavell's forces reach El Agheila 265 km SW. of Benghazi.
Sea War: Med. – Bombardment of Genoa: HMS *Renown*, *Malaya* and *Sheffield* fire 300 t. of shells, inflicting heavy damage on merchant shipping and the city, with many casualties. Italian Fleet and shore batteries taken by surprise and further confused by thick mist and mis-identification of Vichy French convoy.
Sea War: Atlantic – Focke-Wulf Condors sink 5 ships in large convoy off Azores.
Home Front: Britain – Churchill tells Americans in a broadcast speech: *'Give us the tools and we will finish the job'.*
Vichy France – Vichy Foreign Min. Flandin resigns; Adm. **DARLAN APPOINTED VICE-PREMIER.**

MONDAY, FEBRUARY 10

Air War: Europe – 189 RAF bombers raid Hanover (night Feb. 10-11). Stirling 4-engined bombers on first op.: 3 aircraft of No. 7 Sqn. attack oil tanks at Rotterdam (night Feb. 10-11). Op. Colossus: British paratroops, dropped from Malta-based Whitleys, destroy Tragino Aqueduct, S. Italy.
Sea War – 8 Italian and 2 German merchant ships leave Kismayau (Italian Somaliland) in attempt to reach Diego Suarez (Madagascar): only 2 Italians succeed.

TUESDAY, FEBRUARY 11

Neutrals: USA – Wendell Willkie urges rapid increase in US aid to Britain.
Sea War – British destroyers bombard Ostend docks.

WEDNESDAY, FEBRUARY 12

Sea War: Atlantic — *Admiral Hipper* sinks 7 ships from convoy off Azores.
Diplomacy – Gen. Franco meets Mussolini at Bordighera, on Italian Riviera.

THURSDAY, FEBRUARY 13

Diplomacy – Gen. Franco meets Pétain at Montpellier.
Sea War – Op. Composition: Albacore biplanes from British carrier *Formidable* raid shipping at Massawa (Italian E. Africa).

FRIDAY, FEBRUARY 14

North Africa – Advanced elements of German *Afrika Korps* arrive at Tripoli.
Diplomacy – Britain severs diplomatic relations with Rumania.

SATURDAY, FEBRUARY 15

Neutrals: USA – Roosevelt sends James B. Conant, Pres. of Harvard Univ., to Britain to exchange views on war technology.
Air War – Home-based RAF aircraft drop leaflets over Cracow and Katowice, S. Poland (night Feb. 15-16).

SUNDAY, FEBRUARY 16

Air War – S. African aircraft dive-bomb Italian positions on E. bank of R. Juba, in S. Italian Somaliland.

MONDAY, FEBRUARY 17

Diplomacy – Japan offers its services as mediator to end all current wars and blames Britain and USA for prolongation of European War.

TUESDAY, FEBRUARY 18

Diplomacy – Amicable settlement of Anglo-Swiss dispute over alleged British bombing raids on Basle and Zurich in Dec. 1940.

WEDNESDAY, FEBRUARY 19

Air War: Britain – First of 3 consecutive night raids on Swansea.

CHIANG KAI-SHEK (1887-1975)
Chinese: *Generalissimo and President*

Supreme Allied Commander in China. A remarkable soldier in his youth. Defied Japanese invaders, 1937-45. Despite massive US aid during and after the war, his regime fell to the Communist forces under Mao Tse-tung and was forced to retreat to Formosa (Taiwan) in 1949.

Born and educated in Chekiang province. At Paoting Military Academy, 1906. At Preparatory Military Academy, Tokyo, 1907-9. Served in Japanese 13th Field Artillery Regt., 1909-11. Fought in 1911 Chinese Revolution.

Elected to central executive committee of Kuomintang (Nationalist) Party; appointed CinC of 'Northern Punitive Expedition', 1927. Defeated great warlord, Wu Pei-fu, and captured Peking, 1927-28. Appointed Generalissimo and chairman of State Council in Nationalist Govt. at Nanking, 1928. Resigned all posts, following rebellion in S. China, 1931.

Recalled by desperate govt. to repel Japanese attack on Shanghai, 1932. Defeated Communist rebellion in Fukien province. Compelled 100,000 Communists under Mao to make tortuous retreat, 10,000 km from SE. to NW. China ('Long March'); 92,000 Communists killed. Rejected demand by Japanese for him to accept their 'special position' in N. China. Made pact with Mao, July 5, 1937, two days before Japanese attack near Peking. Delayed Japanese advance for 3 months at Shanghai, Sept.-Nov., 1937. Withdrew to Hankow (Dec. 1937) and Chungking (Oct. 1938). Remained in Chungking despite savage Japanese air raids, 1939-41.

Dispersed Communist 4th Route Army, Jan. 1941, thus breaking July 1937 pact. Diverted precious US arms deliveries – sent at great cost, over the 'Hump' (Himalayas) – for purposes of blockading Mao's forces, 1942-45. Compelled Roosevelt to recall Stilwell, Oct. 1944. Prestige and military hold on S. China gravely weakened by great Japanese offensive, April 1944-Jan. 1945. Ordered cautious counter-attacks against retreating Japanese, summer 1945. Received surrender of all Japanese forces in China, Sept. 1945.

Defeated in renewed civil war with Communists, 1946-49. Died on Formosa April 5, 1975.

THURSDAY, FEBRUARY 20

East Africa – British cross R. Juba.

FRIDAY, FEBRUARY 21

Home Front: Canada – Sir Frederick Banting, discoverer of insulin treatment for diabetics and Nobel Prize winner, killed in air crash whilst flying to England; aged 49
Home Front: Italy – 50 per cent cut in rations of olive oil, cooking fats and butter.

SATURDAY, FEBRUARY 22

Sea War: Atlantic – *Gneisenau* and *Scharnhorst* scatter convoy E. of Newfoundland and sink 5 ships.
Air War – *Stukas* cripple British monitor *Terror* in Benghazi harbour (she sinks, in tow, Feb. 23).

SUNDAY, FEBRUARY 23

Home Front: Italy – Mussolini speaks at Fascist rally in Adriano Theatre, Rome: *'We shall fight to the last drop of our blood'.* He attempts to minimize disastrous Italian campaigns in Greece and N. Africa. He lists 10 reasons why Britain cannot win the war, promises *'victory and peace with justice'.*

MONDAY, FEBRUARY 24

North Africa – First skirmish between British and *Africa Korps* patrols on coast road W. of El Agheila.
Vichy France – Adm. Darlan forms Cabinet.
Air War – RAF raid on Brest: Manchester 2-engined bombers participate for first time. (These aircraft withdrawn in June 1942 because of repeated engine failures.)

TUESDAY, FEBRUARY 25

East Africa – Nigerian troops under British command occupy Mogadishu, capital of Italian Somaliland, after whirlwind advance of 355 km in 2 days.
Sea War – Italian fast cruiser *Armando Diaz* sunk by British sub. *Upright* in Med. Escort destroyer *Exmoor* sunk by German MTB off Lowestoft.

WEDNESDAY, FEBRUARY 26

Air War – 60 German bombers and *Stukas* (7 lost) with fighter escort, raid airfields on Malta, destroying or damaging 13 Wellingtons and 3 Hurricanes.

THURSDAY, FEBRUARY 27

Sea War – Italian armed merchant raider *Ramb I* (3,700 t.) catches fire and blows up during engagement with RNZN cruiser *Leander* off the Maldives.
Diplomacy – Italy sends Spain bill for

7,500 M. lire for military aid during Spanish Civil War.

FRIDAY, FEBRUARY 28

Air War – Blenheims and single-engined Wellesleys bomb Asmara (Eritrea).
Neutrals: Spain – Death of ex-King Alfonso XIII in Rome, aged 54.
Neutrals: USA – US Treasury completes secret shipment of gold reserves from New York City to Fort Knox (Kentucky).

The Blitz Feb. 1941
British civilian casualties: 789 dead, 1,068 seriously wounded.

SATURDAY, MARCH 1

Air War: Europe – 100 RAF bombers raid Cologne (night March 1-2).
Diplomacy – BULGARIA JOINS THE AXIS. German troops enter Sofia.
Home Front: Greece – Earthquake at Larissa: 10,000 homeless.
Occupied Holland – German authorities fine city of Amsterdam 15 M. guilders for popular anti-German demonstrations.
North Africa – Free French under Leclerc capture Kufra Oasis – Italian air base and garrison in S. Libya – after 22-day siege.

SUNDAY, MARCH 2

Air War – BOAC begin regular, clandestine, night flights between N. Scotland and Stockholm, using modified Whitley bombers, carrying agents, diplomats, Swedish ball-bearings and electrical equipment, etc.

MONDAY, MARCH 3

Air War – Italians bomb earthquake-stricken town of Larissa. RAF Hurricanes destroy 5 Cant bombers (probably returning from Larissa) over Corfu.
Diplomacy – USSR denounces Bulgarian signature of Axis Pact.

TUESDAY, MARCH 4

Occupied Norway – British-Norwegian raid on Lofoten Is. (Op. Claymore): British commandos and Norwegian marines destroy 6 fish-oil plants (connected with explosives production), capture nos. of Germans and quislings, liberate 300 Norwegian patriots and distribute cigarettes and confectionery to local inhabitants. British destroyers sink 6 merchant ships. Casualties (killed): Allied, nil; German, 7.

WEDNESDAY, MARCH 5

Sea War: Med. – Op. Lustre: 58,000 British troops convoyed from Alexandria to Greece (March 5-April 2). Italian subs. carry out

repeated, but unsuccessful, patrols along convoy routes.
Diplomacy – Britain severs diplomatic relations with Bulgaria.
Göring sees Rumanian dictator, Gen. Antonescu, in Vienna about securing Rumanian participation in Op. *Barbarossa.*
Secret War – Italian soldiers captured by Greeks in Albania report that 1,500 *Alpini* troops have recently been drowned when transport *Liguria* was torpedoed and that Allied bombing raids have caused heavy casualties and great confusion behind Italian lines.

THURSDAY, MARCH 6

Balkans – Greeks launch successful counter-attacks in central sector of Albanian front, capturing several vital mtn. crags and taking 1,000 Italian prisoners. RAF and Greek aircraft fly in close support.
Home Front: Britain – Industrial dispute leads to strike at John Brown's Shipyard, Clydeside.
Neutrals: USA – Death of John Gutzon Borglum, sculptor of the Mt. Rushmore Monument (gigantic rock-hewn busts of 5 presidents), aged 70.

FRIDAY, MARCH 7

Sea War: Atlantic – U-boat 'ace' Cdr. Günther Prien, the 'Bull of Scapa Flow', dies; his *U-47* is sunk by HMS *Wolverine* while attacking Convoy OB.293.
Home Front: Britain – Admiralty to control labour in shipyards.

SATURDAY, MARCH 8

Air War: Britain – Night raids on London: Café de Paris hit (34 killed, 60 injured).

SUNDAY, MARCH 9

Balkans – Major Italian counter-offensive (spring offensive) launched in Albania. Greeks repel all attacks and inflict heavy casualties on Giulia Div., but are weakened themselves (offensive ends March 25).

MONDAY, MARCH 10

Air War: Britain – Heavy night raid on Portsmouth (repeated March 10-11).
Air War: Europe – Halifax 4-engined bombers attack Le Havre (night March 10-11).
Occupied France – Pétain appeals to USA for food.

TUESDAY, MARCH 11

Diplomacy – ROOSEVELT SIGNS LEASE-LEND BILL. USA now able to supply all Britain's arms requirements.
Diplomacy – Thai-Vichy French Frontier Agreement signed aboard Japanese

Above: *An* Afrika Korps *half-track by the fort at El Agheila, taken on March 24.*

warship in Gulf of Siam (following serious border clashes in Jan.).
Secret War – Bomb explodes in luggage of Mr. Rendel, late British Minister to Bulgaria, at Istanbul hotel: Rendel unhurt, but 4 others killed.

WEDNESDAY, MARCH 12

Air War: Europe – RAF raid on Berlin: first of 10 heavy raids during 1941.
Halifax 4-engined bombers participate in night raid on Hamburg.
Home Front: Britain – Churchill describes Lease-Lend Act as a 'new Magna Carta'.

THURSDAY, MARCH 13

Air War: Britain – Devastating night raids on Glasgow and Clydeside (March 13-14 and 14-15); 35,000 homeless in Clydebank (total pop. 47,000). 460 killed, 750 seriously injured.
Home Front: Britain – Death of Tom Mann, Trade Union leader, aged 84.

FRIDAY, MARCH 14

Air War: Britain – Night raids on Glasgow and Sheffield.

SATURDAY, MARCH 15

Sea War: Atlantic – U-105 and U-106 hound Convoy SL.68 for a week off W. Africa, sinking 7 ships and damaging battleship *Malaya*.

SUNDAY, MARCH 16

Sea War: Atlantic – 2 U-boat 'aces' Kretschmer (*U-99*) and Schepke (*U-100*) lost while attacking Convoy HX.112. *U-100* rammed by HMS *Vanoc*; *U-99* depth-charged by HMS *Walker*. Kretschmer captured – his total score is 266,629 t. of Allied shipping.
Home Front: Germany – Hitler predicts that Germany will win the war during 1941, in speech in Berlin. Liner *Bremen*

catches fire at Bremerhaven.
East Africa – Indian troops make success-ful sea-borne landing at Berbera.

MONDAY, MARCH 17

East Africa – Italians launch unsuccessful counter-attack in Eritrea.
Home Front: Britain – Jam and marmalade rationed: 8 oz. (225 g) per person per month.

TUESDAY, MARCH 18

East Africa – Ethiopian 'Patriot' tribes-men attempt to surround Italian garrison at Debra Marcos.
Diplomacy – British Foreign Minister, Eden, meets his Turkish counterpart in Cyprus for talks.

WEDNESDAY, MARCH 19

Air War: Britain – Heaviest night raid on London since Dec. 1940.

THURSDAY, MARCH 20

Air War – RAF and S. African AF bomb Italian positions around Keren (Eritrea).

FRIDAY, MARCH 21

North Africa – Italian garrison of Jarabub, S. Libya, surrenders to British and Australians after 15-week siege.
Neutrals: USA – New York bus strike ends after 11 days.

SATURDAY, MARCH 22

Sea War: Atlantic – *Gneisenau* and *Scharnhorst* return to Brest having sunk 22 ships totalling 116,000 t. ('Op. *Berlin*').
Vichy France – Britain gives its per-mission for emergency supplies of American flour to be shipped to Vichy France.
Balkans – Roberto Farinacci, member of Italian Fascist Grand Council and editor of newspaper *Regime Fascista*, reported killed in action.
Neutrals: USA – Grand Coulee Dam

operational 2 years ahead of schedule – world's largest source of electric power.

SUNDAY, MARCH 23

Air War – *Stukas* with fighter escort carry out major raid on Malta: 13 *Stukas* shot down (2 RAF fighters lost), but British decide on immediate withdrawal of all bombers and flying boats.

MONDAY, MARCH 24

North Africa – **ROMMEL OPENS OFFENSIVE** in the Western Desert and captures El Agheila.
Sea War: Med. – British sub. *Rorqual* lays mines W. of Sicily which sink 2 merchant ships and a torpedo boat; third merchant ship and Italian sub. torpedoed (March 28 and 31).

TUESDAY, MARCH 25

North Africa – Marshal Graziani, CinC Italian Armies in Libya and Chief of General Staff, retires at his own request.
Diplomacy – **YUGOSLAVIA SIGNS TRIPARTITE PACT** in Vienna, allying herself with the Axis Powers.

WEDNESDAY, MARCH 26

Sea War: Med. – Italian one-man explosive motorboats (*barchini esplosivi*), launched from destroyers, cripple British cruiser *York* and sink Norwegian tanker in Suda Bay, Crete (*York* bombed May 20 and abandoned May 22).
Home Front: Britain – Meat ration re-duced to 6 oz. (170 g) per person per week.

THURSDAY, MARCH 27

East Africa – Battle of Keren ends: Casualties – British, 536 killed, 3,229 wounded; Italian, approx. 3,000 killed, 4,500 wounded.
Yugoslavia – **BLOODLESS COUP D'ÉTAT IN BELGRADE:** pro-Axis P.M. Tsvetkovich and Foreign Minister Cincar-Markovich arrested; Air Force CinC, Gen. Simovic, forms all-Party anti-Nazi Govt. Regent Prince Paul resigns and 17-year-old Prince Peter proclaimed King Peter II.
Home Front: Germany – Hitler issues directive on Yugoslavia, which is to be '*beaten down as quickly as possible ... Belgrade will be destroyed from the air.*' At the same time Salonika and E. Greece are to be occupied (Op. *Marita*). Op. *Barbarossa* postponed for 'up to 4 weeks' (from mid-May to mid-June).
Secret War – British Signals Intelligence intercepts radio traffic suggesting that major Italian naval op. is in progress.

FRIDAY, MARCH 28

Sea War – **BATTLE OF MATAPAN:**

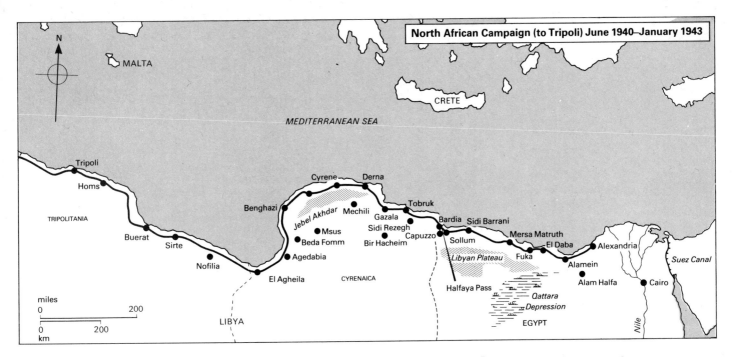

North African Campaign (to Tripoli) June 1940–January 1943

Italian Fleet is attacked by British torpedo-bombers while returning from unsuccessful sortie into Aegean Sea. Battleship *Vittorio Veneto* and cruiser *Pola* both hit; former escapes but latter crippled. Cruisers *Fiume* and *Zara* attempt to cover *Pola*, but all 3 destroyed by 3 British battleships (night March 28-29). Italian casualties: 3,000 killed.

SATURDAY, MARCH 29

East Africa – S. Africans occupy Diredawa, third city of Ethiopia, with important railway repair shops.

SUNDAY, MARCH 30

Air War/Sea War – 'Blockade of Brest': 109 RAF bombers attack *Gneisenau* and *Scharnhorst* (night March 30-31) in first of 63 raids on the battlecruisers by bombers and torpedo planes during 1941.
Neutrals: USA – 65 Axis ships seized in US ports.
Neutrals: Yugoslavia – All German and Italian nationals have now left Belgrade.
Secret War – Churchill learns that, following Yugoslav signature of Axis Pact, 3 *Pz* divs. have been railed from Rumania to S. Poland – indicating firm intention to invade USSR – then returned to Balkans after Yugoslav revolution – indicating punitive expedition against Belgrade.

MONDAY, MARCH 31

North Africa – Rommel breaks through British defences at Mersa Brega, near El Agheila. British withdraw, abandoning 50 armoured cars and 30 light tanks.
Sea War: Med. – British cruiser *Bonaventure* sunk by Italian submarine *Ambra* off Sollum.
Air War: Europe – 4,000-lb (1,800 kg) bomb ('Cookie') first used against a

German target (Emden, night March 31-April 1).
Neutrals: USA – 875 Italian and German seamen arrested on charges of sabotage. 400,000 coal miners on strike. Police use tear gas to disperse 3,000 union pickets at factory near Milwaukee.

TUESDAY, APRIL 1

Sea War – Tankers *San Conrado* and *Hidlefjord* bombed and sunk by He 111s in Bristol channel.
East Africa – British capture Asmara (Eritrea).
Neutrals: Iraq – Raschid Ali and clique of pro-German officers ('Brethren of the Golden Square') seize power.
Neutrals: Japan – Rationing of rice begins in Tokyo and other cities.
Diplomacy – New Yugoslav P.M., Gen. Simovic, refuses to meet Eden (in Athens) for fear of antagonizing Hitler.

WEDNESDAY, APRIL 2

North Africa – Rommel reaches Agedabia on road to Benghazi and sends 2 other columns across desert towards Derna and Tobruk.
Sea War – 5 Italian destroyers leave Massawa to attack Port Sudan. Next day *Daniele Manin* and *Nazario Sauro* are bombed and sunk by British aircraft. A third destroyer turns back and 2 others scuttle.
Air War – Blenheims attack shipping off Dutch coast.
Maiden flight of He 280 – world's first experimental jet fighter – at Rostock, Germany.
Neutrals: USA – 4 killed in clashes between striking coal miners and non-union miners at Harlan, Kentucky.
Neutrals: Hungary – Hungarian P.M. Count Pal Teleki discovers that Gen.

Werth, COGS, has made secret arrangements for entry of German forces into Hungary. He denounces Werth as a traitor and commits suicide, after receiving warning from British Govt. that Hungarian intervention in Yugoslavia will result in British declaration of war. His successor is Bardossy, formerly Foreign Minister.

THURSDAY, APRIL 3

Diplomacy – Britain breaks off diplomatic relations with Hungary. German diplomats leave Belgrade.

FRIDAY, APRIL 4

North Africa – Rommel captures Benghazi.
Sea War: Atlantic – Disguised German raider *Thor* sinks armed merchant cruiser *Voltaire* (13,300 t.).
Diplomacy – Japanese Foreign Minister, Matsuoka, and Hitler discuss possibility of Japanese attack on Singapore and prospect of war with USA.

SATURDAY, APRIL 5

North Africa – Rommel captures Barce, E. of Benghazi.
East Africa – S. African and Commonwealth troops capture Addis Ababa, capital of Italian E. Africa.
Diplomacy – Yugoslav-Soviet Friendship and Non-Aggression Pact.
Home Front: Britain – Death of Sir Nigel Gresley, designer of the Flying Scotsman

---

Yugoslav Forces
640,000 (28 divs.); 50 tanks; 284 planes; 1 old cruiser, 4 destroyers, 6 torpedo boats, 10 MTBs, 4 subs.

express and the record-setting 126 mph (200km/hour) 'Mallard' Pacific locomotive, aged 64.

SUNDAY, APRIL 6

Balkans – **GERMAN INVASION OF YUGOSLAVIA AND GREECE.** Germans employ 15 divs. (5 *Panzer*) and 800 aircraft. Yugoslav Govt. flees from Belgrade to Uzice.

Air War: Europe – **LUFTWAFFE DESTROYS BELGRADE** (Op. *Bestrafung*: 'Punishment') and raids Yugoslav air bases. German bombers and *Stukas* fly 500 sorties against undefended Yugoslav capital, starting huge fires, destroying many public buildings and hospitals and Royal Palace; fleeing civilians strafed (raids repeated April 7-8). Approx. 17,000 killed, April 6-8.
British munition ship *Clan Fraser* explodes during German raid on Piraeus (night April 6-7) wrecking harbour, sinking 13 other ships and inflicting heavy casualties. RAF Beaufort torpedo-bomber hits *Gneisenau* at Brest. Wellingtons bomb Sofia (Bulgaria).

North Africa – Rommel captures Mechili, S. of Derna.

Sea War: Atlantic – Armed merchant cruiser *Comorin* (15,400 t.) destroyed by fire (accidental).

Diplomacy – US Secretary of State, Cordell Hull, describes German invasion of Balkans as 'barbarous'.

MONDAY, APRIL 7

North Africa – Rommel captures Derna and 2 British Gens. (Neame and O'Connor).

Balkans – Germans capture Skopje, S. Yugoslavia.

Home Front: Britain – Govt. Budget for 1941-42: income tax increased by 1s 6d to 10s in the £.

Air War: Europe – Heavy RAF night raid on Kiel shipyards.

TUESDAY, APRIL 8

East Africa – British and Free French capture port of Massawa.

Air War: Britain – Second 'Blitz' on Coventry. 230 aircraft drop 330 t. of bombs, inflicting heavy civilian casualties.

Neutrals: USA – Earle W. Graser, hero of radio series 'The Lone Ranger', killed in motor accident.

WEDNESDAY, APRIL 9

Balkans – Germans enter Salonika.

Diplomacy – Yugoslav Govt. issues protest 'to all civilized nations' against indiscriminate German bombing of Belgrade. This *'open and undefended city was bombed without a declaration of war. . . . Never . . . were such cruelties committed, even by the most primitive invaders'.*

Air War: Europe – RAF night raid on

ROMMEL, Erwin (Johannes Eugen) (1891-1944)
German: *Field Marshal;* **'The Desert Fox'**

Master tactician of the German Army; idolized by German public and much respected by his adversaries. Achieved spectacular success in North Africa but was cheated of final victory by Hitler's miserly allocations of troops, equipment and fuel supplies.

Born at Heidenheim near Ulm. Joined army, 1910; served with 124th Inf. Regt., 1910-15; twice wounded on Western Front; won Iron Cross 1st Class, Jan. 29, 1915: crawled through 100-metre belt of barbed wire to capture four heavily-defended French blockhouses. Served with *Württembergische Gebirgsbataillon* (Württemberg Mountain Battalion) Oct. 1915-Jan 1918 in Rumania (wounded) and N. Italy. Awarded *Ordre Pour le Mérite* ('Blue Max'). Various staff posts,

Jan.-Dec. 1918. Held training posts, 1919-38. Published *Infanterie Greift An (Infantry on the Attack)*, a manual of infantry tactics. Commanded Hitler's personal bodyguard, Oct. 1938-Feb. 1940. Led 7th ('Ghost') *Panzer* Div., Feb. 1940-Feb. 1941; made daring thrust over R. Meuse, routing French forces. Defeated British at Arras and St. Valéry.

Took *Deutsches Afrika Korps* to Tripoli, Feb. 1941. Soon confirmed that desert was ideal theatre for his daring unorthodox tactics. Escaped attempted assassination by British Commandos, Nov. 1941. Twice besieged Tobruk. Appointed *Oberkommando der Panzer Armee Afrika,* Jan. 1942. Field Marshal from June 1942. Advanced to El Alamein July 1942; defeated and forced to begin long retreat to Tunisia, Oct.-Nov. 1942. Won last victory at Kasserine, Feb. 1943. Cdr. Army Grp. B in N. Italy, July-Nov. 1943. Inspected Atlantic Wall from Denmark to Spain, Nov.-Dec. 1943, and devised anti-invasion measures. Cdr. of 15th and 7th Armies (Army Grp. B) from Holland to R. Loire, Feb.-July 1944. Secretly encouraged anti-Hitler army conspirators, July 1944, but severely wounded by low-flying British fighters in Normandy, July 17, 1944, three days before attempt on Hitler's life. Came under suspicion while recuperating at home and resolved to commit suicide to save wife Lucie-Maria and son Manfred from possible reprisals. Drove away with *SS* guard, Oct. 14, 1944, and took cyanide poison. Goebbels announced Rommel died nobly from wounds received in July. Göring represented Hitler at state funeral.

His remarkable war 'Papers' were edited and published by Capt. Sir Basil Liddell Hart (1953).

Berlin: State Opera House gutted by fire. (Hitler furious!)

THURSDAY, APRIL 10

Balkans – Germans capture Zagreb (Croatia) and Monastir (S. Yugoslavia). Pavelich and Kvaternik, leaders of Croat terrorist organization, the *Ustachi*, proclaim the separation of Croatia from kingdom of Yugoslavia.

Occupied Denmark – Greenland (Danish possession) to receive US protection.

FRIDAY, APRIL 11

Balkans – Italian and Hungarian forces invade Yugoslavia.

SATURDAY, APRIL 12

North Africa – Rommel captures Bardia.

Balkans – Germans enter Belgrade.

SUNDAY, APRIL 13

North Africa – **FIRST SIEGE OF TOBRUK** begins: Australian 9th Div. (Gen. Morshead) repels Rommel's *Pzs* (April 14, 17, 19 and 24). German and Italian aircraft carry out 437 raids April-July, dropping 350 t. of bombs. Germans also carry out long-range artillery barrages.

Sea War: Atlantic – Armed merchant cruiser *Rajputana* (16,400 t.) sunk by *U-108* in Denmark Str.

Diplomacy – **RUSSO-JAPANESE NON-AGGRESSION PACT** (for 5 years) signed in Moscow.

MONDAY, APRIL 14

Diplomacy – King Farouk of Egypt sends secret message to Hitler, via Egyptian Minister in Iran, expressing hope that Germany will *'soon liberate Egypt from the British yoke'.*

TUESDAY, APRIL 15

North Africa – Rommel's *Afrika Korps* drives into Egypt, capturing Sollum and moving through Halfaya Pass.

Air War: Britain – Heavy night raid on Belfast, N. Ireland (180 aircraft): 500 killed, 400 seriously injured; shipyards badly damaged. Dublin Fire Brigade renders assistance.

Air War: Europe – RAF night raid on Kiel (210 killed).

Neutrals: USA – Vought-Sikorsky VS-300 helicopter completes 1 hour 5 min. endurance flight at Stratford, Connecticut, piloted by Igor Sikorsky. 4 men killed, 20 wounded in gun battle between striking coal miners and mining company officials near Middlesboro, Kentucky.

WEDNESDAY, APRIL 16

Air War: Britain – Massive night raids on London: approx. 300 bombers (6 lost)

make 2-3 sorties each (total sorties 685), dropping over 1000 t. of bombs and mines, causing widespread damage and many fires. (Reprisal for RAF raid on Berlin, April 9.)

Sea War: Med. – Italian convoy of 5 transports with 3 destroyers annihilated by 4 British destroyers off C. Bon (Tunisia); HMS *Mohawk* lost.

Balkans – Germans capture Sarajevo.

THURSDAY, APRIL 17

Balkans – YUGOSLAV ARMY CAPITULATES. Gens. Bodi (Yugoslav) and Weichs (German) sign armistice in Belgrade. King Peter escapes from Kotor in RAF Sunderland flying boat.

Yugoslav Campaign Losses
Yugoslav military: 343,712 PoWs. Civilian: 17,000 dead, 20,000 wounded in Belgrade alone. German: 151 dead, 15 missing, 392 wounded.

Air War: Europe – 118 RAF bombers, inc. Stirlings, raid Berlin (night April 17-18), minor raids on Cologne and Rotterdam. 8 bombers lost.

Air War: Britain – Night raid on Portsmouth.

Neutrals: USA – Car production to be cut by 1,000,000 from Aug. 1, 1941.

Sea War: Atlantic – Disguised German raider *Atlantis* sinks Egyptian liner *Zamzam* (8,300 t.) and captures 312 passengers, inc. 138 Americans.

FRIDAY, APRIL 18

Home Front: Greece – Pres. Koryzis commits suicide; King George assumes temporary leadership of the Govt. Martial law declared in Athens.

Air War – First flight of Me 262 fighter, powered by Junkers piston engine (the specified pair of jet engines cannot be installed until Nov., *see* Nov. 25, 1941).

SATURDAY, APRIL 19

Air War: Britain – Massive night raids on London: 712 sorties; 1,180 t. bombs; 2 aircraft lost. Total casualties (April 16-17 and 19-20): 2,300 killed, 3,000 seriously injured; 150,000 houses damaged.

SUNDAY, APRIL 20

Balkans – GREEK ARMY IN ALBANIA SURRENDERS to SS Div. *Leibstandarte Adolf Hitler.*

Home Front: India – Nearly 400 casualties in rioting between Sikhs and Moslems at Ahmedabad, Bombay (April 18-20).

Air War – 90 German aircraft raid Athens: small force of Hurricanes (7 lost) shoot down 15. Sqn. Ldr. Pattle, top-scoring RAF fighter pilot of W.W.II (41 victories) killed.

Sea War: Med. – Bombardment of Tripoli: British battleships *Warspite, Valiant, Barham* and cruiser *Gloucester* fire 530 t. of shells, damaging 7 ships and setting fire to oil installations (night April 20-21). *Valiant* damaged by mine while returning to Alexandria.

Diplomacy – US-Canadian agreement on joint production of war materials for Britain.

MONDAY, APRIL 21

Air War: Britain – PLYMOUTH BLITZ: 5 devastating night raids, April 21-22 to April 29-30 by total of 640 bombers (17 lost). Few public buildings or houses escape damage; 750 killed, 30,000 homeless.

Air War – German bombers and *Stukas* sink old Greek battleship *Kilkis*, 10 other warships and 43 merchant ships in Greek coastal waters (April 21-24).

Home Front: Greece – New Govt. formed under Tsouderos, former Governor of Bank of Greece.

Above: *A Greek captain urges on his men as they shift a field gun in Epirus.*

TUESDAY, APRIL 22

Balkans – GREEK ARMY IN THRACE CAPITULATES. British forces begin to fall back.

Greek Campaign Losses: 1
Greek: 15,700 dead and missing, 218,000 PoWs. Italian: 13,755 dead, 50,874 wounded, 25,065 missing.

Diplomacy – Soviet protest to Germany over violations of Soviet air space by high-altitude reconnaissance aircraft – 80 such incidents having taken place, March 27-April 18.

WEDNESDAY, APRIL 23

Neutrals: USA – Charles Lindbergh addresses 30,000 people attending 'America First' rally in New York: he condemns Britain for having *'encouraged the smaller nations of Europe to fight against hopeless odds',* and warns that the British are attempting to drag the USA into the *'fiasco of this war'.*

THURSDAY, APRIL 24

Sea War: Med. – Evacuation of British and Commonwealth troops from Greece (Op. Demon): 51,000 troops transported to Crete and Egypt (April 24-29). German aircraft sink destroyers *Diamond* and *Wryneck* and 4 transports.

Diplomacy – Hitler and Hungarian leader Adm. Horthy confer and dine in the *Führer's* train near Graz (Austria): Horthy lavishes praise on the *Führer*, but Hitler refuses to be drawn into promising major territorial concessions in return for Hungarian participation in Op. *Barbarossa.*

Balkans – Germans penetrate Pass of Thermopylae.

FRIDAY, APRIL 25

North Africa – Rommel captures vital Halfaya Pass, on Egypt-Libya border.

Sea War: Atlantic – Roosevelt announces that 'neutrality patrols' by US Navy are to be vastly extended.

SATURDAY, APRIL 26

Air War – German paratroops capture Corinth.

SUNDAY, APRIL 27

Balkans – Germans enter Athens.

MONDAY, APRIL 28

Air War – Malta bombed.
Neutrals: USA – Lindbergh resigns his commission as Col. in USAAC Reserve, following severe condemnation of his April 23 speech by Roosevelt. Month-long coal miners' strike ends – men to receive extra $1 a day.

TUESDAY, APRIL 29

Middle East – Iraqi forces surround British base at Habbaniyah and sabotage oil pipelines.

WEDNESDAY, APRIL 30

Air War: Europe – RAF attack shipping off Dutch coast. Heavy night raid on Kiel; light raid on Berlin.

Greek Campaign Losses: 2
British: 900 dead, 1,200 wounded, 1,612 missing, 9,000 PoWs; 209 planes.
German: 1,518 dead, 3,360 wounded.

North Africa – German and Italian forces make renewed efforts to capture Tobruk; sizeable salient driven into SW. corner of perimeter by May 4.

THURSDAY, MAY 1

Air War: Britain – First of 8 consecutive night raids on Liverpool: 1,450 killed, 1,100 seriously injured, 76,000 homeless. 33 ships sunk or damaged; docks badly damaged (*see* May 3).
Home Front: Britain – Lord Brabazon appointed Minister of Aircraft Production. Ministry of War Transport established, amalgamating former ministries of Shipping and Transport.
Neutrals: USA – Defense bonds on sale.

FRIDAY, MAY 2

Middle East – Iraqi artillery shells Habbaniyah base.
Sea War: Med. – British destroyer *Jersey* mined and sunk in entrance to Valletta Harbour, Malta.
Home Front: Germany – 'Oldenburg Plan': German Economic Staff formed to plan large-scale economic exploitation of conquered Russian territories reports: '. . . *many millions of people will starve to death in Russia if we take out of the country the things necessary for us'*.

SATURDAY, MAY 3

Air War: Britain – Night raids on Liverpool by nearly 300 aircraft; munition ship *Malakand*, carrying 1,000 t. HE bombs, explodes in Huskisson Dock.

Below: *The crew of a Luftwaffe 37mm flak gun in newly conquered Athens.*

East Africa – Battle of Amba Alagi (ends May 19): Italian forces make their last important stand in mtns. of N. Ethiopia, prisoners inc. the Italian Viceroy, Amadeo, Duke of Aosta.
Middle East – British repel Iraqi attacks on Basra. Motley force of RAF, inc. trainers, take off under artillery fire to bomb Iraqis besieging Habbaniyah.
Secret War – Radio equipment recovered from 3 Heinkels shot down during Liverpool raid enables RAF to jam new *Y-Gerät* blind-bombing system.

SUNDAY, MAY 4

Home Front: Germany – Hitler speaks to members of Reichstag in Kroll Opera House, Berlin: he claims that by withdrawing troops from N. Africa to Greece, Churchill has made the *'biggest strategic mistake in history'*. German casualties in Balkans campaign were only 1,151 killed and 3,892 wounded. He predicts that National Socialist Germany will survive for 1,000 years.

MONDAY, MAY 5

East Africa – Emperor Haile Selassie returns to Addis Ababa.
Sea War: Med. – 'Tobruk Ferry': first of many night supply missions by British and Australian destroyers from Alexandria.

TUESDAY, MAY 6

Middle East – British raise Iraqi siege of Habbaniyah.

WEDNESDAY, MAY 7

North Africa – Exchanges of artillery fire along Tobruk front.

Air War: Britain – First of 2 consecutive night raids on Hull: 40,000 homeless, food stores and marine engineering works hit.
Sea War – German weather ship *München* sunk in Arctic by British destroyers.
Home Front: Britain – Churchill wins Parliamentary vote of confidence by 447 votes to 3.

THURSDAY, MAY 8

Sea War – German disguised raider *Pinguin* sunk by HMS *Cornwall* off the Seychelles.
Air War – British radio counter-measures and decoy fires (code-named 'Starfish') foil attempted night 'Blitz' on Rolls-Royce works at Derby; many bombs are wasted on Peak District, Nottingham and agricultural Vale of Belvoir. Waddington (Lincs.) airfield and village bombed. RAF night raids on Germany by 359 aircraft: main targets, Hamburg and Bremen.

FRIDAY, MAY 9

Diplomacy – USSR withdraws diplomatic recognition of Yugoslav Govt.-in-Exile.
Sea War: Atlantic – *U-110*, commanded by the 'ace' Lt.-Cdr. Lemp, depth-charged by British corvette *Aubretia*. Crew abandon ship and destroyer HMS *Bulldog* takes in tow (*U-110* sinks May 11). Naval *Enigma* cipher machine captured.

SATURDAY, MAY 10

Air War: Britain – **MASSIVE NIGHT RAID ON LONDON** (climax of 'Blitz'): 507 German bomber sorties (8 aircraft lost); 795 t. bombs dropped, 2,200 serious fires from Hammersmith to Romford, hundreds of streets blocked; rail traffic virtually halted; House of Commons and Westminster Abbey badly damaged.
Air War: Europe – Heavy RAF night raid on Hamburg (5 aircraft lost).
Diplomacy – **HESS FLIES TO BRITAIN.** Rudolf Hess, the Deputy *Führer* of Germany, makes unauthorized solo flight in Me 110 fighter from Augsburg (S. Germany) to Petersfield near Glasgow, to arrange 'peace talks'. He parachutes from his damaged plane and is taken into custody (night May 10-11). Hess is detained for the duration of the war.

Home Front: Britain – War Cup Final (soccer): Arsenal and Preston N. End draw 1-1 at Wembley (Preston win replay at Blackburn, May 31, by 2 goals to 1).

SUNDAY, MAY 11

Balkans – Germans complete occupation of Aegean Is.

MONDAY, MAY 12

Sea War: Med. – Op. Tiger: 240 tanks delivered to Alexandria.
Home Front: Britain – Charles, Earl of Suffolk and Berks., a volunteer bomb-disposal officer, is killed attempting to defuse delayed-action bomb in London: aged 35.
Home Front: Germany – Official statement on the Hess Affair: Deputy *Führer* suffering from 'hallucinations and a mental disease'.

TUESDAY, MAY 13

Home Front: Germany – Martin Bormann appointed Nazi Party Chancellor.
Sea War: Atlantic – Armed merchant cruiser *Salopian* (10,500 t.) sunk by *U-98* SE. of Greenland.
Sea War: Med. – British sub. *Undaunted* sunk by Italian torpedo boat *Pleiadi* off Tripoli.
Air War – RAF receive confirmation that German aircraft are operating over Iraq.

WEDNESDAY, MAY 14

Air War – *Luftwaffe* switches attacks from British shipping off Crete to airfields on the island.

THURSDAY, MAY 15

North Africa – First British Offensive against *Afrika Korps* (Op. Brevity): Halfaya Pass and Sollum recaptured.
Air War – British Govt. authorizes counter-measures against German aircraft refuelling on Syrian airfields en route to Iraq.
Home Front: Britain – First British jet aircraft – Gloster E.28/39 Pioneer – tested at Cranwell, Lincs.
Neutrals: USA – US coastguards board every French merchant ship in American ports, inc. liner *Normandie*. Battleship *Washington* (launched June 1940) joins the fleet 5 months ahead of schedule.
Occupied Channel Is. – Mrs. Sybil Hathaway, Dame of Sark (Channel Is.), deported to German concentration camp as reprisal for anti-Nazi activities on Guernsey.

FRIDAY, MAY 16

Air War – German fighter-bombers raid SE. England. **NIGHT 'BLITZ' ON BRITISH CITIES ENDS** with raid by 111 aircraft on Birmingham and W. Midlands; RAF airfields also bombed (3 German aircraft lost). (*See* May 31, 1941.)
RAF night raid on Cologne (fires on both banks of Rhine); targets in France and Holland also raided (2 aircraft lost). He 111s bomb Habbaniyah causing serious damage.
Neutrals: Bolivia – Govt. takes over German-owned airline *Lloyd Aero Boliviano*.
North Africa – Rommel receives orders from Berlin to concentrate *Afrika Korps* against British at Sollum, leaving Italians to guard Tobruk siege ring.
Occupied Denmark – Icelandic Parliament (*Althing*) issues formal declaration of independence from Denmark. Regent is appointed on June 17.

SATURDAY, MAY 17

Diplomacy – USSR concludes agreement with Raschid Ali régime in Iraq.

SUNDAY, MAY 18

Sea War – Op. *Rheinübung* ('Rhine Crossing'): Battleship *Bismarck* and cruiser *Prinz Eugen* leave Gdynia (Baltic) to attack Atlantic convoys.
Occupied Yugoslavia – Croat delegation arrives in Rome to offer Crown to Duke of Spoleto: he is subsequently proclaimed King Tomislav II of Croatia, but returns to Italy after a short visit to his new 'kingdom' (relinquishes throne in 1943).

MONDAY, MAY 19

Neutrals: USA — Mayor La Guardia appointed head of Office of Civilian Defense.

TUESDAY, MAY 20

Air War – **GERMAN AIRBORNE INVASION OF CRETE** (Op. *Merkur*: 'Mercury'): 490 Ju 52 transports take off from primitive strips near Athens, towing 100 DFS gliders and land 6,000 paratroops and airborne infantry on and around Maleme airfield; bombers pound New Zealand troop positions at Maleme.
Sea War – 4 Italian subs. arrive at Bordeaux on Bay of Biscay (May 7-20) from Massawa (Red Sea), which they had left in early March.

WEDNESDAY, MAY 21

Air War – German airborne troops storm 'Hill 107', overlooking Maleme airfield (Crete). 80 Junkers crash-land on shell-swept airfield, bringing regt. of mtn. troops.
Sea War: Med. – British 'Force D' (3 cruisers and 4 destroyers) scatters seaborne invasion fleet N. of Crete, destroying 10 converted fishing boats (night May 21-22).
Sea War: Atlantic – American cargo ship *Robin Moor* sunk by *U-69* (crew spend 2½ weeks in open boats before rescue).

THURSDAY, MAY 22

Air War – Ju 52s land reinforcements at Maleme.
Sea War: Med. – German bombers, fighter-bombers and *Stukas* carry out violent attack on British Med. Fleet in Cretan waters; cruiser *Gloucester* sunk (693 killed), cruiser *Fiji* crippled and abandoned, destroyer *Greyhound* sunk, battleship *Warspite* damaged. 3 British destroyers shell German airborne forces on Maleme airfield, night May 22-23. *Decoy* and *Hero* evacuate King George of Greece and his staff from the island.
Air War – Kesselring, CO *Luftflotte 2*, moves into his new HQ at Poznan, Poland; this signifies the completion of large-scale transfer of German air forces from W. to 'Russian Front'.

FRIDAY, MAY 23

Sea War: Med. – Destroyers *Kashmir* and *Kelly* (Lord Louis Mountbatten) sunk by *Stukas* off Crete. Me 109 fighter-bombers destroy 5 British MTBs in Suda Bay.
Home Front: Britain – Death of Lord Austin, motor pioneer; aged 74.

SATURDAY, MAY 24

Sea War: Atlantic – HMS *Hood* sunk by *Bismarck* in Denmark Strait, E. of

Greenland – only 3 survivors out of 1,419. *Prince of Wales* damaged by *Bismarck* and *Prinz Eugen; Bismarck* slightly damaged but begins losing fuel oil. *Prinz Eugen* is detached for independent ops., night May 24-25.

Sea War: Med. – Sub. *Upholder* attacks Italian convoy E. of Sicily, sinking troopship *Conte Rosso* (17,900 t.); 800 drown.

Air War – Col.-Gen. Grauert, senior *Luftwaffe* commander, reported missing in action over England.

SUNDAY, MAY 25

Sea War: Atlantic – Lagos and Takoradi harbours mined by *U-69* (nights May 25-26 and 26-27).

Diplomacy – Adm. Raeder, C-in-C. German Navy, warns that sending of US supply convoys to Britain will be regarded as a *'plain act of war'.*

MONDAY, MAY 26

Sea War: Atlantic – Swordfish torpedo-bombers score 2 hits on *Bismarck,* disabling her steering-gear; the battleship's AA gunners are confused by the slow-flying biplanes. 5 destroyers harass *Bismarck* during night May 26-27.

Sea War: Med. – British carrier *Formidable* launches air strike against *Stuka* base on Scarpunto I., E. of Crete. Later *Formidable* and escorting destroyers are bombed by *Stukas;* carrier badly damaged.

Crete – German airborne troops take Canea, capital of Crete.

Neutrals: Irish Republic – P.M. De Valera cautions Churchill against introduction of conscription in N. Ireland (Churchill concedes May 27).

Neutrals: USA – Air raid black-out test in Newark, New Jersey.

TUESDAY, MAY 27

Sea War: Atlantic – BISMARCK SUNK. Damaged German flagship fights hopeless battle against *King George V* and *Rodney* and is finally torpedoed and sunk by cruiser *Dorsetshire,* with loss of 2,200 lives.

North Africa – Rommel recaptures Halfaya Pass.

Home Front: Britain – Churchill declares, in broadcast, that American aid will help Britain to pass through *'long, stern, scowling valley of war, to victory'.*

Home Front: Germany – Walther Hewel, liaison officer at Hitler's HQ, notes in diary: '*Bismarck sunk .... Führer melancholy beyond words'.*

Neutrals: USA – Roosevelt proclaims national emergency; to place country on war footing.

WEDNESDAY, MAY 28

Sea War: Atlantic – German bombers attack 2 British destroyers W. of Ireland: *Mashona* sunk, *Maori* damaged.

Sea War: Med. – Evacuation of British and Commonwealth forces from Crete begins: 17,000 evacuated up to night May 31-June 1.

THURSDAY, MAY 29

Sea War: Med. – British destroyers *Imperial* and *Hereward* lost to air attack while evacuating troops from Crete.

FRIDAY, MAY 30

Middle East – Fall of the Raschid Ali régime in Iraq: the usurper flees to Iran.

SATURDAY, MAY 31

Air War – Dublin bombed in error by German aircraft under orders to attack Bristol and Liverpool: 28 killed, 87 seriously injured.

> **The Blitz**
> British civilian losses Sept. 1940–May 1941: 39,678 dead, 46,119 injured.

Middle East – Armistice signed between British and Iraqi Army.

Neutrals: Thailand – Death of ex-King Prajadhipok, son of Chulalongkorn, at Virginia Water, England, aged 47.

SUNDAY, JUNE 1

Sea War: Med. – Ju 88s sink AA cruiser *Calcutta* N. of Alexandria. British naval losses in 'Battle of Crete': sunk – 3 cruisers, 6 destroyers; damaged – 3 battleships, 1 carrier, 6 cruisers, 7 destroyers. 15,000 Commonwealth and Greek troops evacuated to Egypt.

> **Crete Campaign Losses**
> Allied (exc. Greek): 1,742 dead, 1,737 wounded, 11,835 PoWs; 3 cruisers, 6 destroyers (2,011 dead and wounded); 46 planes. German: 3,985 dead or missing, 2,131 wounded; 220 planes.

Home Front: Britain – Rationing of clothing and footwear introduced with points system – adult mackintosh (raincoat): 16 points; woman's petticoat: 4

points; and pair of stockings: 2 points. Each person to be allotted 66 points per year.

Air War – Air Vice-Marshal Tedder appointed AOCinC RAF Middle East.

Air War: Britain – 110 night raiders over Britain: main target, Manchester.

MONDAY, JUNE 2

Diplomacy – Hitler and Mussolini confer at Brenner Pass.

Vichy France – Census of Jews ordered.

TUESDAY, JUNE 3

Sea War: Med. – Italian transport explodes during attack by RAF Martin Maryland bombers off Tunisian coast: explosion wrecks second Italian ship and destroys 1 bomber.

Air War – RAF bomb and strafe oil installations at Beirut (Lebanon).

East Africa – British regain control of Debarech, near Gondar (Ethiopia), after Italians have twice recaptured the town.

WEDNESDAY, JUNE 4

Home Front: Germany – Death of ex-Kaiser Wilhelm II, aged 82 (at Doorn, Holland).

Air War: 170 killed, 200 injured in night raid on Alexandria.

THURSDAY, JUNE 5

Sea War: Med. – British sub. *Taku* sinks 3 Italian ships in gun battle off Libya.

Neutrals: China – Air raid on Chungking: 700 Chinese entombed and suffocated in tunnel shelter.

FRIDAY, JUNE 6

East Africa – Commonwealth forces cross R. Omo, capturing 2,000 Italians and 14 guns.

SATURDAY, JUNE 7

Air War – 230 killed in night raid on Alexandria (evacuation of 40,000 people commences, June 8).

SUNDAY, JUNE 8

Middle East – INVASION OF SYRIA AND LEBANON by British Commonwealth and Free French forces at 3 points.

Diplomacy – Free French promise full independence to Syria and Lebanon.

MONDAY, JUNE 9

Middle East – Allied forces occupy Tyre and cross R. Litani (Lebanon).

Sea War: Med. – Vichy destroyers *Guépard* and *Valmy* bombard Australian troops advancing along coast of Lebanon, but are driven off by 4 British destroyers (2 damaged).

TUESDAY, JUNE 10

Home Front: Britain – House of Commons debate the Crete debacle. Hore-Belisha declares: *'For the first time in history an island has been captured by an airborne attack.'* He asks why all the mistakes made in Norway have been repeated in Crete. Churchill defends the decision to fight in Crete and declares it will pay future dividends.

Neutrals: Bolivia – All tungsten mined over next 3 years to be sold to USA, following rejection of Japanese counter-bid.

East Africa – Op. Chronometer: Indian troops landed from British warships capture port of Assab.

WEDNESDAY, JUNE 11

Air War: Britain – Widespread German night raids over England; leaflets dropped over rural areas in E. Anglia threatening starvation as a result of German victory in Battle of the Atlantic.

Air War: Europe – RAF begins series of 20 consecutive night raids on the Ruhr, the Rhineland, Hamburg and Bremen.

Diplomacy – Trade negotiations between Japan and Netherlands E. Indies are broken off, because Dutch are unwilling to consider exorbitant Japanese demands for raw materials.

THURSDAY, JUNE 12

Home Front: Germany – Berlin civil defence authority warns population to take immediate shelter in air raids owing to danger posed by heavy HE bombs and mines, which have caused *'a great number of bomb victims'.*

Sea War: Atlantic – Pocket-battleship *Lützow* torpedoed by RAF Beaufort aircraft off S. Norway: she has to limp back to Kiel and is out of action until Jan. 1942.

Diplomacy – Allied and 'Free' European representatives, meeting in London, pledge mutual assistance until victory is won. Churchill declares that every trace of Hitlerism will be *'blasted from the surface of the Earth',* and that the RAF *'will continue to teach the German homeland that war is not all loot and triumph'.*

FRIDAY, JUNE 13

Sea War – Ferry steamer *St Patrick* sunk by German aircraft in Irish Sea off Fishguard (23 killed).

Air War: Britain – Attempted night raid on Chatham naval base completely misfires: bombs scattered widely over S. and E. England and 7 aircraft shot down.

SATURDAY, JUNE 14

North Africa – Op. Battleaxe begins: British attempt to raise siege of Tobruk

achieves initial success (at cost of many tanks), but Rommel counter-attacks (June 17) and op. is abandoned.

Air War: Europe – First of month-long series of daylight fighter 'sweeps' by RAF Fighter Cmnd. over Channel and N. France.

Air Chief Marshal Sir Philip Joubert becomes AOCinC RAF Coastal Cmnd. Malta receives 43 Hurricanes from *Ark Royal.*

Neutrals: USA Roosevelt orders immediate freezing of assets of Axis and occupied countries (except Japan).

Diplomacy – Croatia signs Tripartite (Axis) Pact.

Home Front: Germany – Hitler informs his senior generals that during the forthcoming attack on Russia, prisoners of war do not have to be treated according to the Articles of the Hague Convention since the USSR has not signed the latter. Soviet Commissars are *'not to be considered PoWs'* (i.e., they are to be summarily executed).

SUNDAY, JUNE 15

Middle East – Allied forces capture Sidon.

Air War – Catalina flying-boat routs 4 German aircraft off Gibraltar (1 crashing in Portugal).

MONDAY, JUNE 16

Neutrals: USA – Roosevelt orders closing of all German consulates by July 15.

Sea War: Med. – Vichy destroyer *Chevalier Paul,* carrying ammunition to Syria, sunk by British torpedo-bombers.

TUESDAY, JUNE 17

Middle East – Fierce fighting at Kuneitra (Syria), which twice changes hands.

Above: *Victim of Operation Battleaxe. One of the 64 Matilda tanks lost by 4th Armoured Brigade, June 14-17.*

WEDNESDAY, JUNE 18

Diplomacy – German-Turkish non-aggression pact.

Secret War – British radar development, under Watson-Watt, is revealed in the Press as 'Detection of Enemy Aircraft by Ether Waves'.

Neutrals: USA – Joe Louis defends World Heavyweight Boxing title, knocking out Billy Conn in 13th round.

THURSDAY, JUNE 19

Sea War: Med. – Tobruk Ferry: Australian and British destroyers and sloops (11 vessels) carry out frequent night supply/troop transport missions from Alexandria and Mersa Matruh to Tobruk (June 19-20 to July 11-12): Axis aircraft sink sloop *Auckland* and destroyers *Waterhen* and *Defender.*

FRIDAY, JUNE 20

Neutrals: Finland – General mobilization.

Neutrals: USA – Maj.-Gen. H. H. 'Hap' Arnold appointed Chief of Army Air Forces. Roosevelt describes torpedoing of SS *Robin Moor* (May 21) as an act of 'piracy'.

SATURDAY, JUNE 21

Middle East – Free French occupy Damascus.

North Africa – Auchinleck succeeds Wavell as British CinC Middle East. Wavell appointed CinC India.

Occupied Yugoslavia – King Peter and

Yugoslav P.M., Gen. Simovic, arrive in London.

Neutrals: USSR – 1,500,000 children to be evacuated from large cities.

German Forces

Forces committed to *Barbarossa*, inc. those held in reserve: 3,200,000 men (151 divs.); 3,350 tanks, 7,184 guns; 1,945 planes. Also 18 Finnish, 14 Rumanian, 2 Hungarian divs. [German forces committed elsewhere: 600,000 men (61 divs.); 600 tanks; 1,300 planes.]

SUNDAY, JUNE 22

Russian Front – **GERMAN INVASION OF RUSSIA** ('Op. *Barbarossa*') along 2,900 km front from Baltic to Black Sea. 3 Army Groups, comprising 120 divs. (inc. 17 *Pz* and 12 motorized) with 3,200 tanks; 1,945 aircraft; miscellaneous naval units (inc. minelayers and 5 U-boats).

Soviet Forces

2,500,000 men (132 divs., inc. 34 armoured); 20,000 tanks; 7,700 planes. [Forces not in W. inc. 2,200,000 men; 3,500-4,000 planes.]

Air War – Devastating German air strikes on 66 Russian airfields along entire front: 1,800 planes destroyed – 1,500 on the ground, 300 in air combat; Germans lose 35 aircraft. Russian bombers attack Constanta, Rumania (first of 38 raids, June 22-30).

Diplomacy – Germany declares war on USSR. **ITALY AND RUMANIA DECLARE WAR ON USSR.** Churchill pledges British material and moral support for USSR.

Sea War: Atlantic – *U-48* returns to Kiel after her twelfth and last war cruise. Total sinkings: 54 merchant ships of 322,000 t. and sloop *Dundee*.

Home Front: USSR – General mobilization; martial law proclaimed.

MONDAY, JUNE 23

Russian Front – Germans cross R. Bug, E. Poland.

Diplomacy – Puppet state of Slovakia declares war on USSR.

TUESDAY, JUNE 24

Russian Front – Germans take Kaunas and Vilna in Lithuania.

Diplomacy – Hungary breaks off diplomatic relations with USSR.

WEDNESDAY, JUNE 25

Neutrals: Sweden – Swedish Govt. grants permission for a German div. to be

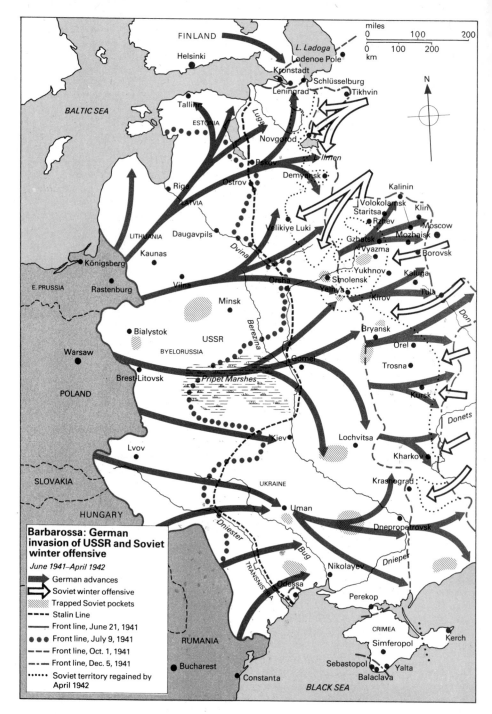

Barbarossa: German invasion of USSR and Soviet winter offensive

June 1941–April 1942

- German advances
- Soviet winter offensive
- Trapped Soviet pockets
- ‑ ‑ ‑ Stalin Line
- ——— Front line, June 21, 1941
- ●●● Front line, July 9, 1941
- – – Front line, Oct. 1, 1941
- –·–·– Front line, Dec. 5, 1941
- ⋯⋯ Soviet territory regained by April 1942

transported by train from Norway to Finland.

Air War: Europe – Blenheims, under heavy fighter escort, bomb Hazebrouck marshalling yards, N. France – blowing up munitions train and bridge. Russians bomb Helsinki and 5 other Finnish towns.

THURSDAY, JUNE 26

Russian Front – *Pzs* reach R. Dvina and Daugavpils. Siege of Hangö: Russian garrison holds out in naval base, W. of Helsinki, until evacuated, Dec. 1941. Italian expeditionary force to be sent to Russia.

Sea War – Russian destroyers shell Constanta (munition train explodes); *Moskva* mined and sunk.

Air War – Germans bomb Leningrad; Russians attack Bucharest. Kassa Incident: 2 aircraft bomb Hungarian border town of Kassa, killing 20 and injuring 41. Hungary blames USSR, but raid probably fabricated by *Luftwaffe*.

Diplomacy – **FINLAND DECLARES WAR ON USSR.**

Home Front: Germany – P. G. Wodehouse, the author, broadcasts a 'non-political' talk from Berlin (Wodehouse had been captured at Le Touquet in 1940).

FRIDAY, JUNE 27

Sea War – German blockade runner *Regensburg* reaches Bordeaux after hazardous voyage from Dairen (Port Arthur), Manchuria.

Diplomacy – HUNGARY DECLARES WAR ON USSR. British military mission arrives in Moscow.
Air War – Hurricanes disperse formation of Italian Macchi fighters off Malta, shooting down 6. First flight of Douglas B-19 – world's largest bomber – at Santa Monica (USA).

SATURDAY, JUNE 28

Air War – Ju 88s drop 1,800-kg (3,970-lb) 'block-buster' bombs on besieged fortress of Brest-Litovsk (in former Russian-occupied Poland). Garrison surrenders, June 29.
Russian Front – Germans capture Minsk.

SUNDAY, JUNE 29

Russian Front – Op. *Silberfuchs* ('Silver Fox'): German ski troops (*Gebirgskorps*) led by 'Dietl of Narvik', begin advance from N. Finland towards Murmansk (3 successive attacks all fail and Dietl's troops dig in along R. Litsa in Sept.).
Home Front: USSR – Stalin takes over Defence Ministry from Marshal Voroshilov and forms 5-man Council of Defence – Stalin, Molotov, Voroshilov, Malenkov and Beria (Chief of NKVD: the Soviet secret police and intelligence Commissariat).
Home Front: Britain – Lord Beaverbrook appointed Minister of Supply.
Neutrals: USA – Death of Paderewski, Polish statesman and musician, in New York, aged 80.

MONDAY, JUNE 30

Air War – Élite German fighter wing JG 51 shoots down 100 Russian bombers attacking Guderian's *Panzers* E. of Minsk. The CO, Mölders, personally destroys 5 bombers. First air raid alert in Moscow (false alarm). RAF daylight raids on Bremen and Kiel; Halifax bombers participate in the Kiel raid.
Russian Front – Germans complete encirclement of large Russian forces in Bialystok 'pocket'.
Sea War: Med. – Sub. *Torbay* sinks 2 merchant ships, 6 sailing vessels and Italian sub. *Jantina* (June 30-July 5).
Diplomacy – Vichy France breaks off diplomatic relations with USSR.

TUESDAY, JULY 1

Russian Front – Guderian's *Pzs* cross R. Berezina. *Pzs* of Army Grp. N. cross the Dvina and advance towards Pskov; Riga occupied.

WEDNESDAY, JULY 2

Air War: Europe – Blenheims, with strong escort (inc. American-volunteer 'Eagle Sqn.'), bomb airfield and rail junction near Lille.

THURSDAY, JULY 3

Middle East – Allied forces capture Palmyra (Syria).
East Africa – Commonwealth forces capture Debra Tabor (Ethiopia).
Home Front: USSR – STALIN'S 'SCORCHED EARTH' POLICY BROADCAST. *'We must not leave . . . a single kilogram of grain or a single litre of petrol to the enemy'.* Guerrilla tactics are to be employed: *'It is necessary to create in invaded areas conditions unbearable to the enemy'.* All workers must defend Russia *'in our patriotic war against German Fascism'.*

FRIDAY, JULY 4

Russian Front – Germans capture Ostrov, S. of Pskov.
Air War: Europe – 11 Blenheims carry out daylight raid on Bremen factory targets at roof-top height.

SATURDAY, JULY 5

Air War: Europe – RAF night raids on Munster (railway targets) and Bielefeld (power stn.); heavy civilian casualties.

SUNDAY, JULY 6

Neutrals: Ecuador/Peru – Border War: Peru ousts Ecuadorian forces from 2 disputed areas and recaptures Matapalo I. (occupied by Ecuador in 1938); Peruvian aircraft and paratroops in action. US, Argentinian and Brazilian mediators arrange cease-fire, July 26. (*See* Oct. 2, 1941.)

MONDAY, JULY 7

Sea War: Atlantic – US Marines land in Iceland, from powerful naval task force, to relieve British garrison.

Below: *One of Guderian's* Panzer *divisions in the early days of* Barbarossa.

Occupied Greece – King George and Greek Royal Family arrive in S. Africa.

TUESDAY, JULY 8

Air War – First daylight op. by RAF 4-engined Fortress I bombers (B-17C Flying Fortresses) against Wilhelms-haven.
Diplomacy – Soviet Military Mission arrives in London.
Neutrals: China – After being damaged repeatedly in previous Japanese air raids on Chungking, the British Embassy is completely destroyed.
Occupied Yugoslavia – Italo-German agreement on territorial dismemberment of Yugoslavia. Italy annexes Dalmatian coast; Hungary annexes Dráva 'triangle'; Croatia 'independent' state; Serbia under German military administration. Bulgaria receives part of Macedonia.

WEDNESDAY, JULY 9

Russian Front – Germans capture Vitebsk.
Air War – RAF night raids on railways at Aachen (W. Germany) and Naples.
Secret War – Merchant seaman George Armstrong, first British traitor to be executed in W.W.II, hanged after offering services to German Consul in USA.

THURSDAY, JULY 10

Neutrals: USA – Roosevelt asks Congress for additional defence expenditure of $4,770 M. US Navy warns that entrance to San Francisco harbour has been mined.

FRIDAY, JULY 11

Russian Front – *Pzs* cross R. Dnieper. Army Grp. S. beats off major Soviet counter-attack and threatens city of Kiev. 3 new Soviet front-line commanders: Voroshilov in N., Timoshenko in centre and Budënny in S.

HITLER INVADES RUSSIA

One of the most fascinating questions about World War II is: if Nazi Germany had invaded the Soviet Union on the day originally earmarked by Hitler (May 15, 1941), instead of more than five weeks later, would the Red Army and the Communist system have collapsed?

Many have argued strongly that the five-week delay imposed on Operation *Barbarossa* by Hitler's sadistic desire to punish the defiant Yugoslavs and Greeks (April/May 1941) made all the difference between success and failure on the Russian Front. However, in our opinion, arguments about a few weeks lost here or there in 1941 are not nearly so important as whether the Germans should have invaded Russia at all in 1941! Back in September 1939, the bulk of Hitler's new *Wehrmacht,* including all 14 armoured or mechanized divisions and half the *Luftwaffe's* combat planes, had been thrown against Poland. The entire campaign was over in four weeks. Eight days before attacking Poland, Hitler had concluded a so-called 'Non-Aggression Pact' with Stalin whereby the Red Army was to occupy eastern Poland. This world-shaking *volte-face* ran counter to the German leader's anti-Communist stand since the days of *Mein Kampf* (1923) when he had written that Germany's destiny lay in conquering the vast *Lebensraum* (living space) of European Russia. It would surely have been entirely possible for Hitler to have overlooked this 'thieves' charter' and to have simply continued driving eastwards.

The main argument for Hitler's cautious, step-by-step strategy in Eastern Europe, is that, since France and Britain had declared war, Germany had to avoid repeating the 1914-18 'Two-Front War'. However this reasoning does not stand up to careful re-examination. In complete contrast with August 1914, neither the French nor the British Government had willingly gone to war with Germany in September 1939. The French High Command was entirely wedded to the concept of static defence – as exemplified by the Maginot Line. And there was no more than a token British force of four divisions (rising to ten by March 1940) on the Western Front. Franco-British reluctance to attack Germany was doubly reinforced by greatly exaggerated fears of the *Luftwaffe's* large force of fast medium bombers and Me 109 fighters.

By June 1940, Stalin had alarmed Hitler by invading Finland and the Baltic States and by moving to within striking distance of the valuable Rumanian oilfields by taking Bessarabia (Rumania). Hitler could simply have stood still in the West while he crushed Soviet Russia in a rapid campaign. European Russia under Nazi control would provide all Germany's requirements of oil, minerals, wheat

Left: *Two* Panzer *IVs lead three Czech-made* Panzer *38(t)s into Russia. To double the* Panzer *divs. for* Barbarossa *when tank production was inadequate meant reducing divisional tank strength from 218 to 160.*

Above: *German transport feels the heat of a Russian summer. Neither railways nor motor vehicles from Occupied Europe could replace the invader's horse-drawn transport.*

and slave labour and make a nonsense of the British Royal Navy's blockade, upon which so many Allied hopes were pinned.

Given the actual course of events, could Hitler have still succeeded in destroying the 'Soviet Colossus' in the five months between June 22, 1941 and the appalling Russian winter? Surprisingly the answer is still probably, 'Yes'. An essential pre-condition was a sensible, logical, plan of attack. Ideally this would have involved two powerful armoured striking forces driving along the northern and southern edges of the impassable Pripet Marshes, through Minsk and Smolensk and on to Moscow (heart of the Soviet political and military system), with a powerful secondary group to trap the Soviet armies between Moscow and Kiev and light flanking forces south of Leningrad. Such was the plan of Major-General Marcks, a senior OKH (Army High Command) staff officer, as early as August 5, 1940. But Marcks' excellent scheme underwent two major revisions: General Halder, OKH Chief of Staff, decided to give equal priority to the capture of both Moscow and Leningrad and later Hitler made Moscow a secondary objective, to be attempted *after the capture of Leningrad.*

These basic flaws in German strategy, added to faulty intelligence work, terrifying supply problems and the lack of suitable tanks and

long-range bombers, go a long way towards explaining the subsequent German débâcle in Russia, but the war on the Eastern Front was more than just a straightforward exercise in strategy, tactics and military technology. Hitler saw the war against Russian as an ideological struggle against a race of 'sub-human' Slavs (fit only for exploitation or extermination) who were governed by 'Bolshevik criminals'. In effect, he ruled out any possibility of the collapse of the Soviet system through internal pressures. Even so, during the initial advances into the Baltic States and the Ukraine, the native populations often welcomed the enemy as 'liberators' and thousands of young men volunteered to fight side-by-side with the *Wehrmacht.* But when German soldiers were quickly followed by *SS* murder squads the mood quickly changed. Thus in spite of the innumerable crimes committed against the peasants, old Party comrades and even the most senior Red Army officers by Stalin, the Russian leader was able, thanks to Hitler's even more blatant atrocities, to appeal successfully to the passionate, in-born, patriotism of the people of 'Mother Russia'. Allied to Stalin's 'Scorched Earth' policy, the release of divisions from the Far East thanks to the Russo-Japanese Non-Aggression Pact of April 13, 1941, and technical suprises such as the superlative T-34 tank and Katyusha rocket launcher, these factors make up the Russian (as opposed to German) reasons for Barbarossa's failure.

Instead of conquering the Soviet Union as far east as the Ural Mountains by the end of the 1941 campaigning season, Hitler and the German nation found themselves enmeshed in a fight for survival. Some 21,000,000 Russians and 7,000,000 Germans, together with 500,000 Rumanians, Italians, Hungarians, Bulgarians, Finns and Spaniards, perished in this apocalyptic struggle between Fascism and Communism.

Sea War: Med. – Destroyer *HMS Defender* bombed by German aircraft during supply mission from Alexandria to Tobruk (night July 11-12).
Air War – German night raid on Port Said and Ismailia.
Secret War – William J. Donovan appointed US 'Co-ordinator of Defense Information' in Washington.

SATURDAY, JULY 12

Diplomacy – **ANGLO-SOVIET MUTUAL ASSISTANCE PACT** – inc. declaration that neither UK nor USSR will make a separate peace agreement with the Axis.

SUNDAY, JULY 13

Sea War – Russian naval forces (destroyers and MTBs) and bombers make determined efforts to destroy German convoy off coast of Latvia, only sink 1 ship.
Air War – Germans bomb Kiev; Russians attack Ploesti (Rumania).

MONDAY, JULY 14

Russian Front – Germans reach R. Luga.
Middle East – **CONVENTION OF ACRE ENDS SYRIAN CAMPAIGN.**
Air War – Ju 88s bomb troopship *Georgic* off Crete.

TUESDAY, JULY 15

Russian Front – **BATTLE OF SMOLENSK:** Germans encircle 300,000 Russians in Smolensk-Orsha pocket.

WEDNESDAY, JULY 16

Sea War – Battleship *Oktyabrskaya Revolutsiya* and cruiser *Kirov,* with air support, bombard German-held port of Riga (Baltic).
Air War: Europe – Blenheim bombers (4 lost) carry out devastating low-altitude raid on shipping at Rotterdam: 12 ships hit, inc. former Dutch liner *Baloeran.*
Russian Front – Stalin's son, Lt. Jacob Dzhugashvili, captured by Germans.

THURSDAY, JULY 17

Neutrals: Spain – Gen. Franco makes speech condemning US refusal to sell urgently needed supplies of wheat to Spain and declaring that the *Wehrmacht* is fighting a 'crusade' in Russia.

FRIDAY, JULY 18

Diplomacy – **RUSSO-CZECH AGREEMENT:** Czech Govt. in London and Govt. of USSR to exchange ambassadors: Czech Army to be formed in USSR. British Govt. gives full recognition to Czech Govt. in London and appoints ambassador.

Neutrals: Japan – Cabinet reshuffle: strongly pro-Axis Foreign Minister, Matsuoka, dropped.

SATURDAY, JULY 19

Neutrals: Bolivia – State of siege declared following discovery of pro-Axis conspiracy. German Minister Herr Wendler declared *persona non grata.*
Diplomacy – German-Swiss Trade Agreement.
Home Front: Britain – Govt. appointments: Brendan Bracken, Minister of Information; R. A. Butler, President of Board of Education; Lord Hankey, Paymaster-Gen.; Duncan Sandys, Financial Secretary to War Office.
Occupied Europe – 'Col. Britton' initiates the 'V for Victory' campaign in midnight broadcast on the BBC: he calls on all the oppressed peoples of Europe to join resistance movements, and declares: *'In a few minutes there will be millions of new "Vs" on walls and doors and pavements all over Europe."*

SUNDAY, JULY 20

Home Front: USSR – Stalin becomes People's Commissar for Defence.

MONDAY, JULY 21

Air War – **MOSCOW 'BLITZ'** commences with raid by 127 aircraft (night July 21-22), led by He 111 pathfinders of *K. Gr. 100* and *K. Gr. 26*. 110 t. of bombs dropped, but strong AA defences prevent concentrated attack and inflict losses. 2 further large-scale attacks in July are followed by 73 minor raids July-Dec. 1941. Muscovites shelter in newly completed underground railway stations (British ARP experts give advice).
Home Front: Britain – 'Churchill' tank now in mass-production.
Sea War: Med. – Op. Substance: Force H and powerful sqn. from British Home Fleet escort 7-ship convoy from Gibraltar to Malta (arriving July 24). Italian bombers hit cruiser *Manchester* and 2 destroyers, July 23 (HMS *Fearless* lost); Italian MTBs torpedo cargo ship, July 24.

TUESDAY, JULY 22

Russian Front – German spearheads halt for rest and recuperation near L. Ilmen, S. of Leningrad.
Sea War: Atlantic – *Scharnhorst* transferred from Brest to La Pallice (bombed there, July 23).
Home Front: India – All-India Defence Council to be established.

WEDNESDAY, JULY 23

Indo-China – Vichy French permit Japanese to establish naval and air bases in S. Indo-China.

THURSDAY, JULY 24

Air War: Europe – 149 RAF bombers attack Brest, Cherbourg and La Pallice (where *Scharnhorst* is damaged).

FRIDAY, JULY 25

Sea War: Med. – Attempted night raid on shipping in Grand Harbour, Malta, by Italian explosive boats and 'human torpedoes'.

SATURDAY, JULY 26

Occupied France – Marx Dormoy, former Minister of Interior and outspoken critic of Vichy Govt., killed by terrorist bomb; aged 51.
Diplomacy – All Japanese assets in USA and UK frozen.

SUNDAY, JULY 27

Air War: Britain – Night raid on London by 50 aircraft (4 lost).

MONDAY, JULY 28

Air War – RAF destroy 36 aircraft during raids on airfields in Sicily. Gen. Federigi, CO Italian *Regia Aeronautica* in Central Mediterranean, reported killed in action over Malta.
Diplomacy – Oil exports from Neths. E. Indies banned by Dutch authorities.
Indo-China – 40,000 Japanese troops begin landing in S. Vietnam.

TUESDAY, JULY 29

Home Front: Germany – Gen. Ludwig von Schroeder, former head of civil defence and president of 13,000,000-strong 'Air Raid Protection League', dies of injuries received in air crash near Belgrade.
Diplomacy – Vichy-Japanese Agreement on surrender of bases in S. Vietnam.

WEDNESDAY, JULY 30

Sea War – British carriers *Victorious* and *Furious* raid Petsamo (Finland) and Kirkenes (Norway): 13 of 29 aircraft from *Victorious* are shot down over Kirkenes.
Secret War – 17 Japanese 'fishing boats', each equipped with radio transmitters and cameras and carrying a reserve officer of the Imperial Japanese Navy, detained off Hawaii.
Neutrals: China – Japanese bomb Chungking; US gunboat *Tutuila* hit.
Diplomacy – Polish-Soviet Agreement signed in London. Harry Hopkins in Moscow to discuss US aid.

THURSDAY, JULY 31

Neutrals: USA – Roosevelt establishes Economic Defense Board, under Vice-President Wallace.

STALIN (Joseph Vissarionovich Djugashvili) (1879-1953)
Russian: *Chairman of the Council of People's Commissars and Generalissimo*

Soviet dictator who became a vital figure-head and source of inspiration during W.W.II to his suffering people, despite his bloody record in the 1930s, his direct responsibility for Soviet unpreparedness for war and his often harmful interference in military matters. The Soviet Red Army somehow survived catastrophic losses to launch the great series of counter-offensives which eventually destroyed the Third Reich. Stalin also proved to be a surprisingly astute and successful diplomatist at the wartime Allied conferences.

Born in Georgia, the son of a shoemaker. Educated for the priesthood but expelled from seminary for carrying on Marxist propaganda. Joined Social Democratic Party, 1898. Exiled to Siberia five times, 1903-12, but escaped on each occasion and resumed revolutionary activities. Edited *Pravda* and directed Bolshevik group in the *Duma* (Tsarist parliament) during 1913. Exiled to Siberia, 1913-17. Adopted the name *Stalin* – 'steel'. Member of Communist Party's political bureau, March 1917; sat on committee which organized October 1917 Revolution. Appointed Commissar for Nationalities by Lenin. Defended Tsaritsyn during the Civil War of 1918-22 (city renamed Stalingrad in his honour, 1928). Gen. Sec. of Communist Party, 1922. Ousted Trotsky and achieved supreme power, 1927. Directed first 'Five-year Plan' to accelerate modernization of industry and agriculture, 1928. Forced peasants onto collective farms; all who resisted being executed or exiled. Purged the Party and Armed Forces of 'traitors' and 'spies'; officer corps decimated and entire Red Army severely weakened – a key factor in the massive Soviet defeats, 1941-42.

Attempted to appease Hitler, Aug. 1939-June 1941, and to grab buffer territories in E. Europe. Embarrassed by disastrous 'Winter War' against Finland, 1939-40. Appointed Chairman of Council of People's Commissars, 1941. Appealed for a 'holy war' to defend 'Mother Russia' against Nazi invaders. Marshal of Soviet Union, 1943. Met Churchill and Roosevelt at Teheran (1943), Yalta and Potsdam (1945). Generalissimo of Soviet Union, 1945. Ordered testing of first Soviet atomic bomb, 1949. Died March 6, 1953.

Home Front: Germany – **THE 'FINAL SOLUTION' ORDER.** Göring, on Hitler's instructions, orders Heydrich to make *'all necessary preparations ... for bringing about the complete solution of the Jewish question'.*

FRIDAY, AUGUST 1

Diplomacy – Britain breaks off diplomatic relations with Finland.

SATURDAY, AUGUST 2

Neutrals: USA – Rayon rationed (imported mainly from Japan).

Below: *German infantry watch the handiwork of a* Panzer IV *on the Russian Front. The tank is loaded down with spare gear.*

SUNDAY, AUGUST 3

Russian Front – Germans trap large Russian force in Uman 'pocket'.
Sea War: Atlantic – Focke-Wulf Condor shot down in mid-ocean by Hurricane catapulted from converted SS *Maplin* ('Catafighters' destroy 4 more Condors during later ops.).

MONDAY, AUGUST 4

Air War – S. Africans bomb Gondar – last Italian stronghold in E. Africa (Aug. 4, 5 and 6).

TUESDAY, AUGUST 5

Russian Front – Guderian liquidates Smolensk-Orsha 'pocket'. **SIEGE OF ODESSA** by Rumanian-German forces begins (ends Oct. 16). Rumanians suffer heavy casualties.

WEDNESDAY, AUGUST 6

Russian Front – Special *communiqué* issued by German High Command claims that *Wehrmacht* has inflicted *'annihilating blows unique in history'*; 895,000 prisoners taken, 10,388 guns, 13,146 tanks and 9,082 aircraft captured or destroyed.
Occupied Poland – Gen. Anders appointed CinC of Polish Army to be formed in USSR.
Diplomacy – Eden announces that British Govt. have complained to Iranian Govt. about thousands of German 'tourists' in Iran; Japan has also been advised not to interfere in Thailand.

THURSDAY, AUGUST 7

Air War: Europe – RAF carries out repeated sweeps over N. France: 10 fighters lost, 7 Me 109s shot down. Douglas Bader's aircraft collides with a Messerschmitt; he parachutes to safety (losing 1 of his artificial legs).
First Russian raid on Berlin: 4-engined Petlyakov and 2-engined Ilyushin bombers operate by night from islands in the Baltic; a few bombs fall in suburbs of Berlin. German radio blames RAF, but later confirms that attackers were Russian (further minor raids in Aug.).
Home Front: Italy – Bruno Mussolini, second son of the *Duce*, killed testing experimental bomber near Pisa; aged 25.

FRIDAY, AUGUST 8

Occupied USSR – Marshal Timoshenko issues proclamation to all Russians in enemy-occupied areas, urging them to join partisan detachments, carry out Stalin's 'scorched-earth' policy and *'wreak merciless vengeance on the enemy .... for the death of your children ...'*.
Neutrals: China – 40 Japanese air raids on Chungking (Aug. 8-13).

SATURDAY, AUGUST 9

Sea War – German destroyers make sortie to Kola Inlet (Aug. 9-10), sinking Russian patrol ship, but withdraw under heavy air and artillery bombardment.

SUNDAY, AUGUST 10

Diplomacy – Britain and USSR pledge themselves to assist Turkey if she is attacked.

MONDAY, AUGUST 11

Air War – British torpedo-bombers sink Italian hospital ship *California* at Syracuse (Sicily).

TUESDAY, AUGUST 12

Russian Front – HITLER POST-PONES DIRECT ADVANCE ON MOSCOW in favour of massive onslaught against Kiev. Guderian pushes S. towards Gomel. Germans resume advance on Leningrad.

Nikolayev Bridge destroyed by Hungarian bombers, trapping 60,000 Soviet troops.

Diplomacy – ATLANTIC CHARTER SIGNED after series of meetings aboard HMS *Prince of Wales* and USS *Augusta,* in Placentia Bay, Newfoundland. Churchill and Roosevelt issue joint statement of their war and peace aims.

Sea War: Med. – British fast minelayers *Abdiel* and *Latona* bring 6,000 fresh troops to Tobruk and evacuate 5,000 Australians (Aug. 12-13 to 18-19). Similar ops. in Sept. and Oct.

Neutrals: USA – Bill extending period of military service from 12 to 30 months passed by House of Representatives by 203 votes to 202.

Air War: Europe – RAF daylight raid on Cologne: 54 Blenheims (12 lost) bomb Knapsack and Quadrath power stations; fighter escort over E. England-Antwerp sections of flight path. Night raids on Berlin, Cologne and 9 other German cities, airfields and shipping (13 bombers lost).

Vichy France – Admiral Darlan appointed Vichy Minister of National Defence, with wide powers. Pétain bans all political activities and declares, in a broadcast: *'In 1917 I put an end to the [French Army] mutinies. In 1940 I put an end to the rout. Today I wish to save you from yourselves.'*

WEDNESDAY, AUGUST 13

Occupied Poland – USSR releases 'all' Polish POWs taken in Sept. 1939 (*see* April 12, 1943).

THURSDAY, AUGUST 14

Sea War – Russian transport *Sibir,* carrying 2,500 wounded from Tallinn (Estonia) to Kronstadt (Leningrad), sunk by German bombers. Russians evacuate Nikolayev dockyard and destroy un-completed battleship *Sovetskaya Ukraina.*

FRIDAY, AUGUST 15

Diplomacy – POLISH-SOVIET MILITARY AGREEMENT signed in Moscow.

SATURDAY, AUGUST 16

Sea War: Atlantic – 8 German and 3 Italian subs. make repeated, but unsuccessful, attempts to attack Convoy HG.69 NW. of Gibraltar (Aug. 9-16).

SUNDAY, AUGUST 17

Diplomacy – Churchill visits Iceland.

RUNDSTEDT, (Karl Rudolf) Gerd von (1875-1953)
German: *Field Marshal*

The ablest of the German generals in World War II, in the opinion of Eisenhower.

Born into noble Prussian family at Aschersleben, E. Germany. Served in Alsace and Poland during World War I and assisted in reorganization of Turkish general staff. Held important staff posts in *Reichswehr* (army of German republic) and played part in secret rearmament. Retired in 1938 as senior field commander in *Wehrmacht.*

Commanded army groups in Polish, French and Russian campaign. His Army Group 'A' played major role in great breakthrough at Sedan, May 1940. Promoted Field Marshal, July 19, 1940. His Army Group South achieved equally spectacular successes in Russia, June-Nov. 1941. but dismissed after successful Russian counter-attacks.

Appointed CinC in Occupied France, 1942. Quarrelled with Rommel over plans to defeat impending Allied invasion of France, winter 1943-44. Recalled from duty in France, July 1944, but reinstated in Sept., as one of a few generals Hitler felt able to trust after July 1944 Army Bomb Plot.

Rundstedt's name is often linked with the Dec. 1944 Ardennes offensive ('Battle of the Bulge'), but he subsequently denied any responsibility for this fiasco. Replaced by Kesselring, March 1945. Captured by American forces, May 1, 1945. War crime charges dropped by Allies, 1949, owing to Rundstedt's poor health. Died Feb. 24, 1953.

MONDAY, AUGUST 18

Home Front: Britain – National Fire Service formed: 1,400 local fire brigades, amalgamated into 33 'fire forces'.

TUESDAY, AUGUST 19

Sea War: Atlantic – British expedition to Spitzbergen (Aug. 19-Sept. 3): Norwegian and Russian mining communities evacuated and coal mines destroyed.

WEDNESDAY, AUGUST 20

Russian Front – Marshal Voroshilov calls on citizens of Leningrad to defend their city to the death.

THURSDAY, AUGUST 21

Sea War: Atlantic – FIRST TRIAL CONVOY TO N. RUSSIA (code name 'Dervish') leaves Reykjavik, with 7 ships and arrives Archangel Aug. 31.

FRIDAY, AUGUST 22

Occupied France – German authorities in Paris threaten to shoot hostages if attacks on German troops continue (20,000 troops comb city for suspects).

SATURDAY, AUGUST 23

Vichy France – Pétain empowers Vichy courts to impose death penalty for 'terrorist' offences (3 men guillotined, Aug. 28).

SUNDAY, AUGUST 24

Sea War: Med. – Op. Mincemeat (I): HMS *Manxman* (disguised as large French destroyer) lays 140 mines off Livorno (Italy), while Swordfish from *Ark Royal* operate over Sardinia.

Diplomacy – Churchill warns Japan to desist from further aggression.

MONDAY, AUGUST 25

Russian Front – Germans capture Dnepropetrovsk, S. of Kiev; Guderian advances on latter city from the N. Germans capture Novgorod.

Middle East – ANGLO-RUSSIAN OCCUPATION OF IRAN begins.

Sea War – Op. Countenance: British forces land at Abadan, Khorramshahr and Bandar Shapur; naval forces sink 2 Iranian gunboats and capture 7 Axis merchant ships.

Diplomacy – Mussolini confers with Hitler at Rastenburg (E. Prussia) at HQ known as *Wolfsschanze* ('Wolf's Lair') – 2 leaders then tour the Ukraine. Mussolini confesses to Hitler that he cannot rely on loyalty of Italian Army.

TUESDAY, AUGUST 26

Diplomacy – Japan protests to USSR about passage of American war supplies through Vladivostok.

WEDNESDAY, AUGUST 27

Russian Front – Retreating Soviet forces sabotage great Zaporozhe Dam (Dnepropetrovsk Dam) over R. Dnieper. Germans capture Tallinn, capital of Estonia. Besieged Russian garrison of Hangö repels determined Finnish attacks by land and sea.

Air War – Russians bomb Königsberg (night Aug. 27-28).

Sea War: Atlantic – U-570 captured by Royal Navy, S. of Iceland following damage sustained from depth charges dropped by RAF Hudson. (Recommissioned as HM sub *Graph*, Sept. 19, 1941; wrecked March 20, 1944.)

Vichy France – Vichy leaders Laval and

Déat shot and wounded at Versailles; gunman arrested (*see* Oct. 5, 1941).

THURSDAY, AUGUST 28

Home Front: Australia – P. M. Menzies resigns; Fadden takes over.

FRIDAY, AUGUST 29

Russian Front – Finns recapture Viipuri.
Middle East – Cease fire in Iran.

SATURDAY, AUGUST 30

Russian Front – Russians launch unsuccessful counter-offensive against Guderian's *Pzs* N. of Kiev (ends Sept. 2).
Occupied Yugoslavia – Serbian puppet govt. formed, under Gen. Nedic.

SUNDAY, AUGUST 31

Middle East – British and Russian forces meet at Kazvin (Iran).

MONDAY, SEPTEMBER 1

Russian Front – Leningrad comes under long-range artillery fire.

TUESDAY, SEPTEMBER 2

Home Front: Italy – Fascist newspaper *Il Popolo d'Italia* reports that Hitler and Mussolini propose to unify Continent and foster *'harmonious co-operation of all European peoples'.*

WEDNESDAY, SEPTEMBER 3

Russian Front – Russians counter-attack in Smolensk sector.

THURSDAY, SEPTEMBER 4

Air War – Russian night raid on Berlin (1 aircraft lost): 30 killed, 72 injured.
Sea War: Atlantic – Greer Incident: US destroyer *Greer* attacked by *U-652* off Iceland; she replies with depth charges.

FRIDAY, SEPTEMBER 5

Air War – RAF Flying Fortresses attack *Admiral Scheer* in Oslo Fjord (further abortive raid Sept. 8).

SATURDAY, SEPTEMBER 6

Russian Front – Germans capture Schlüsselburg, 40 km E. of Leningrad, at junction of R. Neva and L. Ladoga.
Home Front: Hungary – Gen. Werth, Chief of Gen. Staff, resigns due to 'ill health'; succeeded by Gen. Szombathelyi (See April 2, 1941).

SUNDAY, SEPTEMBER 7

Sea War – Russian battleship *Marat* – trapped at Leningrad – bombards German forces attempting to encircle city. Bombardment supplemented by sister ship *Oktyabrskaya Revolutsiya*, Sept. 8.
Sea War: Atlantic – German gunnery training ship *Bremse* – employed as troopship escort – sunk near North Cape by British cruisers *Aurora* and *Nigeria*.

MONDAY, SEPTEMBER 8

Russian Front – **SIEGE OF LENINGRAD** (Day 1): *Pzs* of German Army Grp. N. reach shore of L. Ladoga, E. of the city; Finns control Karelian Isthmus to the N. and W. Finns capture Lodenoe Pole, on Leningrad-Murmansk railway. City's central food store destroyed in air raid.
Russians recapture Yelna, near Smolensk.
Air War: Europe – RAF night raid on Kassel, centre of German locomotive and armoured vehicle production.
Home Front: USSR – 600,000 Volga Germans to be deported to Siberia.
Sea War – Russian subs. commence regular supply missions to besieged garrison of Hangö (3 lost, Sept.-Nov.).

Below: *German heavy artillery passes a T26 tank in Aug. By then the Red Army had lost over 5,000 tanks.*

TUESDAY, SEPTEMBER 9

Russian Front – Siege of Leningrad: Finns halt on N. outskirts of Leningrad (Finnish CinC having refused German demands to assist in the final assault).
Air War – Stirlings and Halifaxes raid Turin (night Sept. 9-10).

WEDNESDAY, SEPTEMBER 10

Sea War: Pacific – New Zealand naval forces renamed 'Royal New Zealand Navy'.

THURSDAY, SEPTEMBER 11

Russian Front – Siege of Leningrad: General Zhukov replaces Voroshilov as Leningrad Defence Commander – he immediately rouses the dispirited garrison to greater efforts and organizes the erection of many new strong points and barricades.
Sea War – Roosevelt orders USN to 'shoot on sight' in US-protected waters.
Occupied Belgium – King Leopold III of Belgium marries Mlle. Marie Lilian Baels (his first wife, Queen Astrid, having died in 1935). Mlle Baels refuses title of Queen and is to be known as Princess de Réthy.

FRIDAY, SEPTEMBER 12

Russian Front – Russians withdraw from Chernigov, key town mid-way between Kiev and Gomel.
First snow reported on E. Front.

SATURDAY, SEPTEMBER 13

Neutrals: Japan – Japanese Combined Fleet completes rigorous 4-day exercise in N. Pacific.

SUNDAY, SEPTEMBER 14

Secret War – 3 German minesweepers sabotaged in Helsinki dockyard.

MONDAY, SEPTEMBER 15

Russian Front – **BATTLE OF KIEV**: *Pz* spearheads of Guderian (Army Grp. Centre) and Kleist (Army Grp. S.) meet at Lochvitsa, E. of Kiev, completing the encirclement of 4 Russian armies, 600,000 prisoners taken by Sept. 27.

TUESDAY, SEPTEMBER 16

Russian Front – Siege of Leningrad: transfer of *Pz* divs. from Army Grp. N. to Army Grp. Centre begins. Hitler declares that city must vanish from the earth's surface and is to be 'bombarded to pieces' by artillery and the *Luftwaffe*.
Neutrals: Iran – Abdication of Shah Reza Pahlevi Khan; succeeded by his son 21-year-old Shah Mohammed Reza Khan (rules 1941-1979).

WEDNESDAY, SEPTEMBER 17

Middle East – Russians enter Teheran (withdraw Sept. 19).
Air War – RAF Hurricane wing in action over NW. Russia.
Sea War: Atlantic – US Navy takes over HX and ON convoys escort duties between Newfoundland and Iceland.

THURSDAY, SEPTEMBER 18

Russian Front – Siege of Leningrad: German artillery fire seriously damages Russian battleship *Petropavlovsk* in Kronstadt Harbour.
Sea War: Med. – Italian troopships *Neptunia* and *Oceania* (both 19,500 t.) sunk in central Med. by HM sub. *Upholder* (384 drowned).

FRIDAY, SEPTEMBER 19

Russian Front – Germans capture Kiev: retreating Russians have carried out many demolitions and planted innumerable mines and time-bombs.
Occupied Yugoslavia – Tito meets Chetnik resistance leader Mihailovic.

SATURDAY, SEPTEMBER 20

Sea War: Med. – Italian 'human torpedo', launched from sub. *Sciré,* sinks a naval tanker at Gibraltar.

SUNDAY, SEPTEMBER 21

Air War – Siege of Leningrad: 60 *Stukas* make repeated attacks on Russian Baltic Fleet in Kronstadt Harbour, near Leningrad (Sept. 21-24): battleship *Marat* sunk, battleship *Oktyabrskaya Revolutsiya* hit by 6 bombs and 2 cruisers damaged. RAF Mosquito flies first (recce) op.

MONDAY, SEPTEMBER 22

Occupied Greece – King George of Greece arrives in London.

TUESDAY, SEPTEMBER 23

Occupied France – De Gaulle forms Free French National Committee. German authorities in Paris announce that any French male assisting or hiding a British airman will be shot; French females guilty of similar offences are to be sent to a concentration camp in Germany.

WEDNESDAY, SEPTEMBER 24

Russian Front – Marshal Budënny re-groups Russian forces to defend city of Kharkov.

THURSDAY, SEPTEMBER 25

Air War – German parachute troops dropped over the Crimea.

FRIDAY, SEPTEMBER 26

Home Front: Britain – Wrekin (Shropshire) by-election: Colegate (Conservative) wins with 9,946 votes, but Pemberton-Billing ('Bomb Berlin' candidate) gets 7,121 votes.

SATURDAY, SEPTEMBER 27

Air War: Europe – Blenheims, escorted by Spitfires, bomb Amiens rail junction; 21 German and 13 British fighters shot down. Debut of Focke-Wulf FW 190.
Sea War: Med. – HMS *Nelson* damaged by Italian aircraft torpedo S. of Sardinia.

SUNDAY, SEPTEMBER 28

Occupied Czechoslovakia – Heydrich, Himmler's deputy, appointed *Reichsprotektor* of Bohemia and Moravia.

MONDAY, SEPTEMBER 29

Sea War: Atlantic – British convoy PQ.1 leaves Reykjavik for Archangel with war supplies for Russia (arrives without incident, Oct. 11).
Air War: Europe – RAF night raids on Stettin and Hamburg.
Russian Front – Germans enter Donets Basin (Donbas) industrial region, source of over 60 per cent of USSR coal output.
Occupied Czechoslovakia – Gen. Elias, puppet P.M. of Bohemia-Moravia 'Protectorate' arrested by Heydrich and deported to Berlin (sentenced to death Oct. 1, but later reprieved).
Diplomacy – Three-Power Conference in Moscow: (Sept. 29-Oct 1) Beaverbrook (GB) and Harriman (USA) arrange for massive deliveries of war supplies to Russia.

TUESDAY, SEPTEMBER 30

Russian Front – Siege of Leningrad: 200 artillery bombardments and 23 air raids on city in Sept.; 4,409 killed.

Russian Front – OP. TAIFUN ('Typhoon'): Guderian's 2nd *Pz* Army spearheads major offensive by Army Grp. Centre, aimed at capture of Moscow before the winter (2nd, 4th and 9th German armies attack, Oct. 2.).
Occupied USSR – **BABI YAR MASSACRES.** 33,771 Jews killed by *SS* and Ukrainians outside Kiev (Sept. 29-30).

WEDNESDAY, OCTOBER 1

Russian Front – Finns capture Petrozavodsk, on Leningrad-Murmansk railway.
Home Front: USSR – Deportation of N. Caucasus Germans to Kazakstan begins.

THURSDAY, OCTOBER 2

Russian Front – Op. *Taifun:* main German armies committed to drive on Moscow. Hitler issues Order of the Day: *'Today is the beginning of the last decisive battle of the year'.*
Home Front: Germany – Me 163 V1 rocket-propelled research aircraft achieves speed of 1,000 km/hour in level flight over Peenemünde (a fighter version is developed later and enters limited service in 1944).
Neutrals: Ecuador/Peru – Border agreement: 15-km 'neutral' zone established, to be patrolled by Ecuadorian police.

FRIDAY, OCTOBER 3

Home Front: Germany – Hitler claims in Berlin speech that: *'this enemy [Russia] has already been broken and will never rise again!'* Goebbels announces that 1,500,000 children and 150,000 mothers have been evacuated from cities to safer areas.
Occupied Czechoslovakia – Mayor Klapka of Prague executed for alleged anti-Nazi activities.

Below: Panzers *reap their Oct. harvest of Soviet prisoners. The Vyazma-Bryansk victories dwarfed any in history.*

SATURDAY, OCTOBER 4

Air War – RAF night raid on Benghazi.

SUNDAY, OCTOBER 5

Air War – RAF night raid on Tripoli.
Occupied France – Germans blow up 6 Paris synagogues. Pétain commutes death sentence on Paul Collette, would-be assassin of Laval and Déat.

MONDAY, OCTOBER 6

Russian Front – **BATTLE OF BRYANSK**: Guderian's *Pzs* capture Bryansk SW. of Moscow and link up with 2nd Army (Oct. 9). 2 Russian armies encircled (ends Oct. 19).
Air War – RAF night raid on port of Piraeus (Greece).
Home Front: Australia – Curtin (Labour) forms Govt.

TUESDAY, OCTOBER 7

Russian Front – **BATTLE OF VYAZMA**: *Pzs* break through 'Vyazma Defence Line'. 6 Russian armies encircled (ends Oct. 14).
Home Fronts: Britain/Germany – Proposed exchange of badly wounded POWs comes to nought.
China – Chinese recapture Ichang, E. of Chungking.

WEDNESDAY, OCTOBER 8

Russian Front – Germans capture Orel, SW. of Moscow.

THURSDAY, OCTOBER 9

Neutrals: Panama – President Arias overthrown in bloodless coup.

FRIDAY, OCTOBER 10

Sea War – Rumanian minelayer *Regele Carol I* sinks in Russian minefield.

SATURDAY, OCTOBER 11

Home Front: USSR – Mass evacuation of women and children from Moscow; thousands of workers and students dig anti-tank ditches in outskirts.

SUNDAY, OCTOBER 12

Sea War – German MTBs sink 2 ships in convoy off Cromer, England.

MONDAY, OCTOBER 13

Sea War – Russian sub. *Shch-323* attacks German cruiser *Köln* and 7 merchant ships in Baltic (Oct. 13-Nov. 5), but sinks only 1 of the latter.
Germans occupy Dagö I.
Air War – Germans bomb railways in Moscow sector.

TOJO, Hideki (1884-1948)
Japanese: *Prime Minister and Chief of General Staff; Lamasori* **('The Razor')**

Most hated and feared Japanese leader of W.W.II. Archetypal image of a Japanese general – short, balding domed head; steel-rimmed spectacles and sinister, leering countenance.
Son of Gen. Eikyo Tojo, a hero of Russo-Japanese war. Entered Imperial Guards, 1908. Adjutant to War Min. 1916. Military Attaché in Germany, 1919; various staff appointments; headed *Kempei-tai* (secret police) of Kwantung Army in Manchuria, 1935. COS Kwantung Army, 1937. Vice-Min. of War and Inspector-Gen. of Army Aviation, 1938. Unofficial leader by 1940 of war party in Japanese Army bent on sabotaging all proposals of civilian P.M., Prince Fumimaro Konoye, aimed at achieving compromise peace with Chiang Kai-shek and improving US-Japanese relations.
Appointed Min. of War by Konoye, July 1940. Succeeded Konoye as P.M., Oct. 18, 1941. Took Japan into war against USA and British Empire, Dec. 1941.
Boasted of his victories in speech to Japanese Diet (Parliament), May 1942, but military reverses led him to assume dictatorial powers, Feb. 1943. Toured conquered territories, spring 1943, to enlist native support in war effort. Appointed himself Min. of Commerce and Industry and Munitions Min., Oct./Nov. 1943. Failure to prevent US forces capturing Saipan I. (June-July 1944) and air raids on cities of S. Japan compelled Tojo to resign, July 18, 1944. Placed on Army Reserve officers list.
Attempted suicide to avoid arrest by US Occupation troops, Sept. 11, 1945. Admitted full responsibility for starting Pacific War, but denied committing war crimes, during 400-day trial before International Military Tribunal at Tokyo, 1947-48. Hanged Dec. 23, 1948.

Occupied Holland – Gen. Berenschot, commander of Dutch E. Indies Army, killed in air crash; aged 54.

TUESDAY, OCTOBER 14

Russian Front – Germans capture Mozhaysk, W. of Moscow.

WEDNESDAY, OCTOBER 15

Russian Front – Germans take Kalinin, 160 km NW. of Moscow.
Occupied USSR – SS mobile extermination squad, *Einsatzgruppe A*, reports that it has shot 125,000 Jews and 5,000 Russians.

THURSDAY, OCTOBER 16

Home Front: USSR – 'MOSCOW PANIC'. Soviet Govt. and the Diplomatic Corps leave for Kuibyshev on the Volga (Stalin remains in the capital).
Vichy France – Pétain imprisons Reynaud, Daladier, Blum, Mandel (the Jewish ex-Minister of the Interior) and Gen. Gamelin.
Neutrals: Japan – P.M. Prince Konoye resigns after Cabinet divides over negotiations with USA.
Secret War – Richard Sorge, Soviet master spy on close terms with German embassy in Tokyo, arrested by Japanese authorities; hanged Nov. 7, 1944.

FRIDAY, OCTOBER 17

Home Front: India – Arrangements completed to transport Moslem pilgrims to Mecca, despite war-time transportation problems.

SATURDAY, OCTOBER 18

Russian Front – Snow, slush and deep mud hamper German drive towards Moscow.
Neutrals: Japan – **GEN. TOJO FORMS CABINET.** Togo, Foreign Minister.
Occupied Rumania – Rumania incorporates captured Russian territory between R. Dniester and R. Bug as 'Transnistria'.

SUNDAY, OCTOBER 19

Russian Front – Germans capture Tagonrog (Donets Basin).
Home Front: USSR – 'State of siege' declared in Moscow.
Neutrals: Afghanistan – All Axis nationals (200 Germans and Italians) to be expelled.

MONDAY, OCTOBER 20

Sea War: Med. – Italian torpedo boats *Aldebaran* and *Altair* sink off Athens in minefield laid by sub. *Rorqual* (night Oct. 20-21).

Vyazma-Bryansk Battle Losses
Soviet: 70-80 divs. destroyed, yielding 673,000 PoWs (dead and wounded unknown); 5,142 guns and 1,242 tanks captured or destroyed. German: perhaps 50,000 dead and wounded.

TUESDAY, OCTOBER 21

Russian Front – Zhukov takes command of Moscow garrison.

WEDNESDAY, OCTOBER 22

Diplomacy – Rumania denounces 'Vienna Award' of Aug. 1940 and re-opens old rift with Hungary over Transylvania.
Sea War: Atlantic – British naval tanker *Darkdale* sunk by *U-68* off St Helena.
Occupied Rumania – Rumanian CO at Odessa, Gen. Glugoscianu, and 50 of his staff killed by delayed-action bomb left by retreating Russians.

THURSDAY, OCTOBER 23

Sea War: Atlantic – Destroyer HMS *Cossack* torpedoed by *U-563* (she founders, under tow, Oct. 26).
Occupied Rumania – In reprisals for assassination of Rumanian Gen. at Odessa, 19,000 Jews are rounded up and shot in city and further 40,000 taken to collective farm and massacred.

FRIDAY, OCTOBER 24

Russian Front – **GERMANS CAPTURE KHARKOV** (E. Ukraine). Stalin appoints Zhukov to command N. half of front; Timoshenko to direct ops. in the S.

SATURDAY, OCTOBER 25

Sea War: Med. – British fast cruiser-minelayer *Latona* sunk by *Stukas* off Bardia (night Oct. 25-26).
Diplomacy – Roosevelt and Churchill condemn recent German reprisals in France – 100 hostages shot at Bordeaux and Nantes following assassination of 2 German officers.

SUNDAY, OCTOBER 26

Russian Front – Germans break through Perekop Isthmus into the Crimea.

MONDAY, OCTOBER 27

Neutrals: USA – Roosevelt's Navy Day Speech: he denounces attacks on US shipping and reveals Nazi plot in Latin America.

TUESDAY, OCTOBER 28

Russian Front – Germans reach Volokolamsk, NW. of Moscow.

WEDNESDAY, OCTOBER 29

Russian Front – Germans invade Crimea.

THURSDAY, OCTOBER 30

Russian Front – **SIEGE OF SEBASTOPOL** begins with great on-slaught by German 11th Army and Rumanian forces on outer defence line (Oct. 30-Nov. 21). Russian Black Sea Fleet and 21,000 Marines repel many attacks,

but Germans capture Balaclava Hills. (*See* Dec.17.)

FRIDAY, OCTOBER 31

Russian Front – Siege of Leningrad: electricity supplies greatly reduced; many factories have closed down; no electric light for domestic consumers. Germans capture Simferopol (Crimea).
Sea War: Atlantic – **REUBEN JAMES INCIDENT.** *U-552* sinks US destroyer *Reuben James* (part of US escort group accompanying British convoy); 95 killed.
Home Front: Britain – 41 killed in fire at Huddersfield clothing factory.

SATURDAY, NOVEMBER 1

Russian Front – Germans capture Tula, S. of Moscow.

SUNDAY, NOVEMBER 2

Russian Front – Germans capture Kursk.

MONDAY, NOVEMBER 3

Occupied USSR – *Einsatzgruppe C* reports to Himmler that it has shot 75,000 Jews in Russia.

TUESDAY, NOVEMBER 4

Neutrals: USA – La Guardia elected to serve as Mayor of New York for third consecutive term.

WEDNESDAY, NOVEMBER 5

Diplomacy – Japan sends veteran diplomat, Saburo Kurusu, to Washington on 'peace mission'.

THURSDAY, NOVEMBER 6

Diplomacy – $1,000 M. American loan to USSR, under provisions of Lend-Lease Act.
Home Front: USSR – **STALIN'S CALL TO DEFEND 'MOTHER RUSSIA'**; demands a 'Second Front' in W. Europe and predicts 'inevitable doom' for Hitler.

FRIDAY, NOVEMBER 7

Air War – 300 RAF bombers (37 lost) carry

out night raids on Berlin, Cologne and Mannheim (many aircraft lost through severe weather conditions).
Home Front: USSR – Stalin reviews military parade in Moscow and predicts fall of Nazi Germany within 12 months.

SATURDAY, NOVEMBER 8

Home Front: Germany – In speech at Munich, Hitler describes USSR as '*this Mongol State*' and Stalin as a '*second Genghis Khan*'. Red Army can never recover from losses totalling 10 M. men, claims the *Führer*.

SUNDAY, NOVEMBER 9

Russian Front – Siege of Leningrad (Day 63): Germans capture Tikhvin, E. of city, and sever vital rail link. Germans capture Yalta (Crimea).
Sea War: Med. – Large Italian convoy destroyed in Central Med. by British 'Force K' (cruisers *Aurora* and *Penelope*, destroyers *Lance* and *Lively*).

MONDAY, NOVEMBER 10

Diplomacy: Churchill says in speech that Britain and USA will form common front in event of blatant Japanese aggression against latter.

TUESDAY, NOVEMBER 11

Diplomacy – Finland rejects American advice to cease hostilities.

WEDNESDAY, NOVEMBER 12

Sea War: Med. – 34 of 37 Hurricanes flown off *Ark Royal* and *Argus* land in Malta (Op. Perpetual).
Vichy France – Huntziger, former Vichy Minister of War, killed in air crash near Nîmes; aged 61.

THURSDAY, NOVEMBER 13

Sea War: Med. – **HMS ARK ROYAL TORPEDOED** by *U-81*: despite all efforts to save her she sinks, Nov. 14, only 40 km E. of Gibraltar.
Russian Front – Germans and Rumanians make unsuccessful attempt to take Sebastopol by storm.

FRIDAY, NOVEMBER 14

Neutrals: USA – Token contingents of US Marines to be withdrawn from Peking, Tientsin and Shanghai.
Air War – Italian torpedo planes sink 2 British transports off Tunisia.

SATURDAY, NOVEMBER 15

Sea War – *U-752* torpedoes 2 Russian ships in White Sea.
Russian Front – Germans, under von Bock, resume direct advance on Moscow.

SUNDAY, NOVEMBER 16

Russian Front – Germans take Kerch (Crimea).

MONDAY, NOVEMBER 17

North Africa – The Keyes Raid: British commandos, led by Lt.-Col. Keyes, V.C., attack Rommel's HQ at Beda Littoria, W. of Tobruk at night (Nov. 17-18). But Rommel is at Gazala; Keyes killed; only 2 commandos escape.
Home Front: Germany – Col.-Gen. Ernst Udet, Director-Gen. of *Luftwaffe* Equipment and W.W.I fighter 'ace', commits suicide in despair at ever-increasing losses in Russia and the failure of his bomber development programme, aged 45. (Göring conceals true facts of his death, and announces that Udet has been killed testing a new warplane.) F. M. Milch takes over.
Occupied USSR – Alfred Rosenberg, author of the Nazi 'bible', *The Myth of the Twentieth Century,* appointed Minister for Occupied Eastern Territories.

TUESDAY, NOVEMBER 18

North Africa – OP. CRUSADER. British 8th Army launch successful counter-offensive in Western Desert. Rommel smashes S. African 5th Brig., then retreats (Nov. 23-24), relieving pressure on Tobruk.
Sea War – The 'sailor-poet' Lt. Aleksei Lebedev (aged 29) lost aboard Russian sub. *L-2* (mined and sunk of S. Finland).

WEDNESDAY, NOVEMBER 19

Sea War – Battle off Shark Bay (W. Australia) between disguised raider *Kormoran* and cruiser *Sydney,* both ships crippled – *Sydney* drifts away, enveloped in flames, and disappears over horizon (550 killed).

THURSDAY, NOVEMBER 20

Russian Front – Siege of Leningrad (Day 74): personal food ration cut for fifth time since early Sept.
Diplomacy – Japanese negotiators in Washington present ultimatum.

Above: *Polish troops were among 14,000 men replacing the Australians in Tobruk by Oct. 26 after a 7-week exchange.*

FRIDAY, NOVEMBER 21

Sea War: Med. – 2 Italian cruisers torpedoed: *Trieste* by British sub. *Utmost* and *Luigi di Savoia Duca Degli Abruzzi* by Malta-based aircraft.

SATURDAY, NOVEMBER 22

Sea War: Atlantic – German disguised raider *Atlantis* intercepted by cruiser HMS *Devonshire* off Ascension I. and scuttled by her crew. *Atlantis* has been at sea for 622 days, sinking 22 merchant ships totalling 146,000 t.
Russian Front – Germans capture Rostov-on-Don (recaptured by Russians, Nov. 28).
Home Front: Germany – Gen. Mölders, fighter 'ace' (115 victories), killed in air accident near Breslau (Silesia); aged 30.

SUNDAY, NOVEMBER 23

Home Front: Britain – Death of P. C. Wren, author of 'Beau Geste', aged 56.

MONDAY, NOVEMBER 24

Sea War: Atlantic – Cruiser HMS *Dunedin* sunk by *U-124* off Pernambuco (300 killed).
Russian Front – Germans capture Solnechaya Gora, 48 km NW. of Moscow.

TUESDAY, NOVEMBER 25

Sea War: Med. – Battleship *Barham* sunk by *U-331* off Bardia (862 killed in magazine explosion).
Sea War: Pacific – US Navy orders all merchant ship masters to travel in convoys.
Air War – First prototype Me 262 fighter fails to take off with 2 experimental jet engines and 1 piston engine. (*See* July 18, 1942.)

WEDNESDAY, NOVEMBER 26

Russian Front – Germans capture Klin 85 km NW. of Moscow.
Sea War: Pacific – Japanese 'Carrier Striking Force' leaves secret anchorage in N. Japan and heads for N. Pacific, in order to approach Pearl Harbor from unexpected direction.
Diplomacy – US ultimatum to Japanese negotiators in Washington.

THURSDAY, NOVEMBER 27

Russian Front – German offensive stalls only 30 km from Moscow.
East Africa – 20,000 Italians surrender at Gondar: liberation of Ethiopia completed.

FRIDAY, NOVEMBER 28

North Africa – Gen. von Ravenstein, GOC 21st *Pz* Div., captured when Bren gunner shoots up his staff car.

SATURDAY, NOVEMBER 29

North Africa – Rommel counter-attacks; heavy fighting develops between Tobruk and Sidi Rezegh.

SUNDAY, NOVEMBER 30

Occupied USSR – *Obergruppenführer* Prutzmann and *Einsatzkommando 2* kill 10,600 Jews and Communists in Riga.
Russian Front – Hitler vetoes withdrawal from Rostov. Rundstedt resigns; replaced as cdr. of Army Grp. South by Reichenau.

MONDAY, DECEMBER 1

Russian Front – German 4th Army with Guderian's and Hoepner's *Pz* Armies make final attempt to envelop and capture Moscow.

Sea War – Adm. Sir Tom Phillips appointed CinC British Eastern Fleet.

TUESDAY, DECEMBER 2

Russian Front – German inf. detachment reaches Khimki tram station, 19 km from centre of Moscow, but is repulsed by Russian 'home guards' (*Opolchenie*).

Sea War – 'Force Z' – battleship *Prince of Wales*, battlecruiser *Repulse* and 4 destroyers – arrive at Singapore (planned inclusion of carrier *Indomitable* is impossible because of accidental damage).

WEDNESDAY, DECEMBER 3

Sea War – Transport *J. Stalin* (7,500 t.), evacuating Russian troops besieged at Hangö since June, wrecked by 4 mines, approx. 2,000 killed; wreck later captured by Germans.

THURSDAY, DECEMBER 4

Occupied Poland – Gen. Sikorski, P.M. of Polish Govt.-in-Exile, broadcasts to Russian people from Moscow.

FRIDAY, DECEMBER 5

Russian Front – SURPRISE RUSSIAN COUNTER-OFFENSIVE IN MOSCOW SECTOR. 4 armies attack N. of city. Coincidentally, Guderian has already decided to withdraw his 2nd *Pz* Army, which is ravaged by heavy casualties, frostbite and mechanical breakdowns.

Sea War – Japanese invasion fleet leaves S. China for Thailand and Malaya.

SATURDAY, DECEMBER 6

Russian Front – Russian counter-offensive in Moscow sector gathers momentum: 10 armies now engaged on 322-km front, inc. many Siberian units and thousands of T-34 tanks. Siege of Leningrad (Day 90): 'Road of Life' – 322-km track over ice-covered L. Ladoga – used by first supply truck (each vehicle can only cover 32 km a day). Finns capture Medvezhegorsk, on Leningrad-Murmansk railway.

Diplomacy – Roosevelt makes personal appeal for peace to Emperor Hirohito of Japan.

Britain declares war on Finland, Hungary and Rumania.

SUNDAY, DECEMBER 7

Sea War: Pacific – JAPAN ATTACKS PEARL HARBOR. 350 bombers torpedo planes and Zero fighters in 2 waves from 6 carriers attack US Pacific Fleet and air bases in Hawaii. Battleship *Arizona* explodes, battleships *California,*

ROOSEVELT, Franklin Delano (1882-1945) American: *President and CinC*

'FDR' died in the hour of victory like his great predecessor, Abraham Lincoln. Restored US economy and morale after the Depression. Skilfully outmanoeuvred powerful Isolationists and directed greatest mobilization of manpower and industrial capacity ever harnessed in war. Fought and won four great election campaigns – a unique feat – despite crippling illness. Reputation somewhat tarnished by his alleged appeasement of Stalin at Yalta Conference, Feb. 1945.

Born at Hyde Park, New York. Educated at Harvard and in Europe. Practised law, 1907-10. Democratic senator, 1910-13. Assistant Sec. of the Navy, 1913-21. Unsuccessful candidate for vice-presidency, 1920. Stricken with poliomyelitis (infantile paralysis) and confined to wheelchair or crutches for life. Gov. of New York State,

1929-33. Defeated Hoover in 1932 Pres. Election by promising American people a 'New Deal'; escaped assassination in Florida. In 1933-38 introduced many economic, financial and social reforms with the aid of a 'Brains Trust'. Won 1936 election on the record of the 'New Deal'. Attempted to dissuade Germany, Italy, Japan and USSR from committing acts of aggression and imposed 'moral embargo' on arms sales. Carried out 'Good Neighbour' policy in Latin America. Attempted to mediate in the Czech and Polish crises of 1938-39. Although officially neutral in the European war, pursued equivocal policy Sept. 1939-Dec. 1941, supplying arms to the Allies, initially on a 'cash and carry' basis and then under 'Lend-Lease'. Used similarly ingenious procedure (lottery system) when introducing conscription Sept. 1940.

Ordered creation of two-ocean navy capable of engaging both Germany and Japan and building of 50,000 warplanes a year. Broke long-standing precedent by standing for third term as pres., Nov. 1940. Prepared for inevitable collision with Germany during Sept. 1940-Nov. 1941. Attempted to avert Japanese threat through negotiation and economic sanctions. Rallied universal support by his 'Day of Infamy' speech, Dec. 1941 after surprise attack on Pearl Harbor.

Following declaration of war by Germany, Dec. 11 1941, gave first priority to defeat of Hitler. Advised against early Allied invasion of France and planned assault on North Africa. Took part in six war-time conferences; gravely ill and exhausted by end of Yalta Conference, returned home via Britain, March 1945. Died suddenly of cerebral haemorrhage, April 12, 1945, at Warm Springs, Georgia.

Nevada, Oklahoma, West Virginia sink; *Maryland, Pennsylvania* and *Tennessee* damaged. 10 other warships sunk or seriously damaged. 188 US aircraft destroyed. Casualties – American: 2,403 killed, 1,178 wounded – Japanese: 55 killed (29 aircraft lost). Midget submarine attacks on Pearl Harbor fail completely: 5 midgets sunk ('mother' submarine *I-70* sunk Dec. 10).

Japanese land at Singora and Patani (Thailand) and Kota Bharu (Malaya).

United States Forces
1,643,477 men (34 divs.) – 31,000 in Philippines; limited numbers of tanks; *c.* 2,846 planes; 17 battleships (9 in Pacific), 6 carriers (3 Pac.), 37 cruisers (24 Pac.), 171 destroyers (80 Pac.), 114 subs. (56 Pac.).

Japanese Forces
1,400,000 men (51 divs.) – 1,000,000 (40 divs.) in China, Korea and Manchuria; 2,400 planes, 1,540 for the Pacific; 10 battleships, 11 aircraft carriers, 41 cruisers, 129 destroyers, 67 subs.

Diplomacy – JAPAN DECLARES WAR ON USA AND BRITISH COMMONWEALTH.

MONDAY, DECEMBER 8

North Africa – SIEGE OF TOBRUK RAISED.

Sea War: Med – Tobruk Ferry: British Med. Fleet has delivered 32,667 troops and 34,000 t. of supplies; 34,115 troops, 7,516 wounded and 7,097 POWs evacuated (April 13-Dec. 8, 1941). Losses: 1 cruiser/minelayer, 2 destroyers and 24 other vessels.

China – Battle of Hong Kong: Japanese 38 Inf. Div., supported by heavy artillery and aircraft, attacks 12,000-strong British-Canadian-Indian garrison.

Philippines – Japanese land on Batan I., S. of Formosa.

Air War – Japanese destroy 100 aircraft in raids on Philippines.

TUESDAY, DECEMBER 9

Russian Front – Siege of Leningrad: Russians restore railway supply line.

Diplomacy – Nationalist China declares war on Japan (an unofficial 'state of war' had existed since 1937), Germany and Italy.

WEDNESDAY, DECEMBER 10

Sea War – *PRINCE OF WALES* AND *REPULSE* SUNK 322 KM NE. OF SINGAPORE by 88 Japanese bombers and torpedo planes (4 lost) operating from bases near Saigon. British casualties: 730 killed, inc. Adm. Phillips.
Sea War: Pacific – JAPANESE LAND IN N. PHILIPPINES. Japanese capture Guam I. (USA) and Tarawa and Makin I. (GB).

THURSDAY, DECEMBER 11

Sea War: Pacific – Defence of Wake Island: small garrison of US Marines, with coastal battery and 12 fighters, repulses Japanese invasion force, sinking destroyer and damaging cruiser. Japanese bombers and carrier planes make repeated raids and second invasion attempt (Dec. 23-24) finally crushes all resistance. US Pacific Fleet races towards Wake but is too late to intervene.
Diplomacy – GERMANY AND ITALY DECLARE WAR ON USA. USA declares war on Germany and Italy.

FRIDAY, DECEMBER 12

Diplomacy – Rumania declares war on USA.

SATURDAY, DECEMBER 13

Sea War: Med. – Italian fast cruisers *Alberico da Barbiano* and *Alberto di Giussano*, loaded with petrol drums for Italian forces in N. Africa, sunk by 3 British destroyers and Dutch destroyer *Isaac Sweers* S. of Sicily (900 killed).
Russian Front – STALIN ORDERS GENERAL OFFENSIVE.
China – Japanese cross from Kowloon to Hong Kong I. (night Dec. 13-14).
Diplomacy – Bulgaria declares war on Britain and USA. Hungary declares war on USA.

SUNDAY, DECEMBER 14

Sea War: Med. – Battleship *Vittorio Veneto* torpedoed by British sub. *Urge* off Straits of Messina.

MONDAY, DECEMBER 15

Sea War: Med. – Cruiser *Galatea* sunk by *U-557* N. of Alexandria.

TUESDAY, DECEMBER 16

Sea War – Dutch sub. *O.16* torpedoes 4 Japanese transports in Gulf of Siam (*O.16* later destroyed in British minefield off Singapore). Japanese land in N. Borneo: Dutch and British set fire to oilfield.

WEDNESDAY, DECEMBER 17

Russian Front – Siege of Sebastopol: second German-Rumanian attack (Dec. 17-31) forces garrison back to final lines of defences 8 km N. of city.
HITLER ISSUES 'HALT ORDER'. All German troops on E. Front *'are to be forced to put up a fanatical resistance in their lines'*, even when out-flanked and cut off by Russians. Such resistance will give time for transport of reinforcements from Germany and the W.

THURSDAY, DECEMBER 18

Sea War: Med. – Severe British naval losses (night Dec. 18-19): 'Force K' runs into minefield off Tripoli – cruiser *Neptune* and destroyer *Kandahar* sink (1 survivor on *Neptune*); 2 other cruisers damaged, 3 'human torpedo' crews penetrate Alexandria Harbour and sink *Queen Elizabeth* and *Valiant* (they are subsequently raised and repaired).
China – Japanese land on Hong Kong I. (night Dec. 18-19).

FRIDAY, DECEMBER 19

Malaya – British evacuate Penang I. and Georgetown harbour.
Philippines – Japanese land at Davao on Mindanao.
Home Front: Germany – Hitler dismisses Army CinC, von Brauchitsch, and takes personal command of military ops.
Sea War: Atlantic – 2 Focke-Wulf Condors shot down by Grumman Martlet fighters from escort carrier HMS *Audacity*.

SATURDAY, DECEMBER 20

Home Front: Germany – Goebbels appeals for donations of clothing for troops fighting in deep snow and sub-zero temperatures on Russian Front.
Russian Front – Hitler orders German Army to copy Stalin's 'scorched earth' tactics.

SUNDAY, DECEMBER 21

Sea War: Atlantic – HMS *Audacity* sunk by *U-751* (night Dec. 21-22).
Sea War – Russian warships transport 10,000 reinforcements to Sebastopol and shell German positions (Dec. 21-27).

MONDAY, DECEMBER 22

Philippines – Japanese land in Lingayen Gulf and Lamon Bay and advance towards Manila from N. and S.
Diplomacy – FIRST WASHINGTON CONFERENCE. Churchill, Beaverbrook and chiefs of 3 services meet their US counterparts.

TUESDAY, DECEMBER 23

Philippines – US-Filipino forces begin withdrawal into Bataan Peninsula. Manila declared an 'open city'.

WEDNESDAY, DECEMBER 24

Philippines – Japanese land on Jolo I. (occupied Dec. 25).
Vichy France – Free French Forces land on tiny island colonies of St Pierre and Miquelon, off Newfoundland.

THURSDAY, DECEMBER 25

North Africa – 8TH ARMY CAPTURES BENGHAZI.
Russian Front – Guderian dismissed by Hitler for refusing to obey 'Halt Order'.
China – FALL OF HONG KONG.

FRIDAY, DECEMBER 26

Sea War – Russian landings on Kerch Peninsula, to assist garrison of Sebastopol (Dec. 26-30). British naval commando raid on Lofoten Is. (Norwegian Sea).

SATURDAY, DECEMBER 27

Sea War – Op. Archery: British naval forces and commandos again attack Lofoten Is., cruiser *Kenya* damaged by German shore battery.

SUNDAY, DECEMBER 28

Air War – JAPANESE BOMB MANILA. They refute 'arbitrary and unilateral' US announcement declaring Philippine capital an 'open city'.

MONDAY, DECEMBER 29

Malaya – Japanese capture Ipoh and advance towards Kuantan on E. Coast.

TUESDAY, DECEMBER 30

Russian Front – Russians recapture Kaluga, SW. of Moscow.
Home Front: India – Gandhi resigns leadership of Congress Party when it decides to support British war effort.

Shipping Losses 1941
Allied and Neutral: 1,299 ships totalling 4,398,031 t. Axis: 35 U-boats, 18 Italian subs., 3 Japanese subs.

WEDNESDAY, DECEMBER 31

Philippines – US-Filipino forces form new defence line N. of Bataan Peninsula.
Russian Front – Siege of Leningrad (Day 115): 52,000 people die of starvation and lack of medical treatment in Dec.

AMERICA ENTERS THE WAR

Japan's attack on Pearl Harbor shattered the illusion of US neutrality that had characterized the war up to December 7, 1941 – Roosevelt's 'date that will live in infamy'. Within days, the industrial might and military potential of the strongest nation on earth was lined up against not only Japan, but also Germany and Italy. And Japan's intended decisive blow proved to be only a short-term set-back.

Despite the progressive deterioration of diplomatic and commercial relations between the USA and Japan, most objective observers believed that Japan's leaders saw no necessity to go to war with America while the mineral-rich British, French and Dutch possessions in the Far East lay more or less at their mercy and while the German invasion of the USSR offered similar opportunities for aggrandisement in eastern Siberia and the Soviet Far East. They reckoned, however, without the boundless arrogance, political naiveté and sheer stupidity of the military clique, headed by General Tojo, which had gained absolute control of the Japanese Government in October 1941. Nor had they taken into account the professional vanity of the Japanese naval CinC.

Admiral Yamamoto had strongly advocated the development of the aircraft carrier for many years. By November 1941, he was able to deploy six fast carriers, accommodating more than 350 high-performance aircraft, many of them armed with 'Taranto-type' torpedoes (designed to run in shallow water) or with armour-piercing bombs. Equally impressive were the Zero escort fighters – the first carrier-based fighters in the world capable of out-performing their land-based opponents.

Yet, in spite of apparently wholehearted enthusiasm for these new weapons, Yamamoto remained a conventionalist at heart. He failed to seek out and destroy the three US Pacific Fleet carriers absent from Pearl Harbor that day. Well-satisfied with the sinking of five battleships and the destruction of 188 planes, Yamamoto remained convinced that when it came to the final decisive battle on the open sea between the 'remnants' of the US Pacific Fleet and the Japanese Combined Fleet that his own flagship – the super-battleship *Yamato* – and her ten smaller sisters would decide the day. Yamamoto clung stubbornly to his secret passion for the 'mighty dreadnought' and six months later these ill-founded and contradictory notions were to contribute significantly to the shattering defeat of the Japanese Combined Fleet in the battle of Midway.

Since the Japanese had deliberately chosen to attack a key base of one of the world's greatest powers, they would have been prudent to have inflicted the maximum possible damage. At the very least, before withdrawing, the Japanese carrier force should have launched a third wave of planes, targeted on still untouched installations and supplies including the slowly accumulated, almost irreplaceable fuel reserves. Yamamoto's attack on Pearl – for all its disastrous short-term effects – was merely a glorified raid. When it was over, the Japanese fleet stole away into the vast empty reaches of the North Pacific, as swiftly as they had come.

One question cannot be left unanswered. Did Yamamoto really need to attack Pearl Harbor at all on that fateful Sunday? Should he instead have played a waiting game? Many experts have agreed that if the Japanese had proceeded with the rest of their complex offensive strategy – including the invasion of the American-held Philippines – then the US Pacific Fleet would have been forced to leave Pearl Harbor and make the long voyage to the Western Pacific to face virtually in *Japanese home waters,* the assembled might of the Japanese Combined Fleet. There, the Japanese would have been able also to use their large force of long-range land-based bombers to repeat the devastating tactics first employed against HMS *Prince of Wales* and *Repulse*.

Not only were Tojo and Yamamoto guilty of ordering an inconclusive ill-timed attack, they also displayed an astonishing lack of political awareness. By this single 'infamous, cowardly' act, the Japanese leaders had transformed a reluctant, disunited, political opponent into a single-minded, mortal foe, bent on obtaining vengeance by all conceivable military means.

Hitler's declaration of war on December 11 was also a turning point. Between September 1939 and December 1941, the ever-increasing American material and moral support for the embattled British, and the unavoidable involvement of the US Navy in Hitler's indiscriminate U-boat campaign, suggested that sooner or later America would be at war with Germany. Roosevelt himself had long been committed to the fight against Hitler, but Congress and public opinion had not. There was considerable sentiment in the US to consider the Pacific war as 'our war' and the European war as 'their war', and to concentrate efforts against Japan.

Instead, under Roosevelt's leadership, America committed herself to a 'Germany first' policy that was to determine the conduct and outcome of the war. In 1940, America – the great arsenal of democracy – produced only limited quantities of military equipment; three years later her output exceeded that of Germany, Italy and Japan combined. By 1945, 15 million Americans had served in the armed forces.

Above right: *An early US war poster puts the industrial worker on a par with the fighting man.*

Below left: *The battleship USS* Arizona *sinks on Dec. 7.*

Below right: *The destroyers USS* Cassin *and* Downes *sunk in dry dock in front of the Pacific Fleet flagship, the battleship* Pennsylvania, *and the cruiser* Helena *(behind crane).*

GIVE 'EM

BOTH BARRELS

1942

THURSDAY, JANUARY 1

Russian Front – Russians recapture Staritsa (48 km NE. of Rzhev), which has been destroyed by the Germans.
East Indies – Japanese land on Labuan I.
Home Front: Britain – 58 miners killed in explosion in colliery in Burslem (Staffs.).
Neutrals: USA – Ban on sale of new private passenger cars and trucks, to conserve steel.
Diplomacy – **UNITED NATIONS DECLARATION SIGNED** in Washington: 26 nations pledge themselves not to make separate peace agreement and to commit all their resources in struggle against the Axis.
Occupied France – Pétain broadcasts request for relaxation in severity of German occupation policies.

FRIDAY, JANUARY 2

Russian Front – Russians recapture Maloyaroslavets 129 km SW. of Moscow, defeating 3 German divs. On Kerch Pen. Russians capture (Dec. 28-Jan. 2) 48 guns and over 1,000 motorcycles.
Philippines – Japanese occupy Manila and Cavite naval base.
North Africa – British and S. Africans capture Bardia.
Air War: Europe – First of 11 RAF night raids on German battlecruisers in Brest during Jan.

SATURDAY, JANUARY 3

East Indies – ABDA (American-British-Dutch-Australian) Command formed under Wavell.
Sea War – 'Port T' – secret British naval base hacked out of virgin jungle and swamp on Addu Atoll (Maldive Is.) in only 3 months despite appalling problems of climate and terrain – becomes operational. First convoy of troopships, escorted by cruiser *Emerald*, arrives.

SUNDAY, JANUARY 4

Sea War – Russian cruiser *Krasny Kavkaz* badly damaged by *Stukas* in Black Sea.
Sea War: Pacific – 3 US submarines operate off E. coast of Japan (Jan. 4-18).
Air War: Europe – Wellingtons bomb Castel Vetrano airfield, Sicily (night 4-5).

MONDAY, JANUARY 5

Russian Front – **STALIN ORDERS 'GENERAL OFFENSIVE'** in address to

Stavka (GHQ of Soviet High Command). Offensive to be on 4 fronts: Leningrad, Moscow, Ukraine and Crimea. Zhukov urges that all efforts be concentrated on crushing the disorganized German Army Grp. Centre, W. of Moscow, and that to attack on all fronts is overambitious – Stalin refuses to alter his plans. Russians recapture Kirichi rail junction on Leningrad front and announce recapture of 572 populated localities on Central (Moscow) front. Booty includes 462 guns, 86 tanks and armoured cars, 202,000 shells, 75,210 mines, 3,091 field cars, 9 railway trains and 1,235 t. of food (Jan. 1-5). Siege of Sebastopol: garrison counter-attack N. of city while Black Sea Fleet lands reinforcements.
Malaya – Japanese land on W. coast of Malaya.
Sea War – Battleship *Parizhskaya Kommuna* shells German positions on Crimean coast (repeated Jan. 12 and 15-16).
Sea War: Med. – Large Italian convoy reaches Tripoli. *Upholder* sinks Italian sub. *Ammiraglio St. Bon*, carrying petrol to N. Africa.
Occupied France – Dismembered body of Yves Paringaux, head of anti-terrorist activities at Vichy Ministry of the Interior, found on railway line at Melun. Vichy blames 'Communists'.

Below: *Japanese troops watch Manila burn from their landing craft.*

TUESDAY, JANUARY 6

Russian Front – Siege of Leningrad: Russians recapture Hogland I., Gulf of Finland after crossing ice. Spanish volunteer 'Blue Div.', fighting on Leningrad front, have now suffered heavy casualties, inc. many frostbite victims.
Home Front: USA – 60,000 aircraft and 8 M. t. of merchant shipping are to be built in 1942; 125,000 planes and 10 M. t. of shipping in 1943, declares Roosevelt in State of the Union Message to Congress.
Home Front: Britain – Lord Woolton, Minister of Food, declares that, thanks to the success of the Govt.'s food policy, the British people are 'fighting fit'. Black marketeers had caused problems, but some of those responsible were 'having a diet at Wormwood Scrubs'. Emergency feeding arrangements now include 1,170 'British Restaurants'.

WEDNESDAY, JANUARY 7

Russian Front – Russians advancing N. and S. of Mozhaisk. On the S. flank they recapture Meshchovsk.
China – Japanese admit defeat by Nationalist Chinese in battle of Changsha.

THURSDAY, JANUARY 8

Russian Front – S. of Mozhaisk, Russians recapture Mosalsk Vetchino and Serpeysk;

N. of Mozhaisk, Zhukov's forces have recaptured 51 villages in 2 days but German garrison at Mozhaisk continues obstinate resistance.

Neutrals: Iraq – Raschid Ali sentenced to death *in absentia* by court-marshal in Baghdad.

Sea War – 45 Japanese troop transports arrive at Patani and Singora (Thailand). Japanese land at Jesselton (N. Borneo).

FRIDAY, JANUARY 9

Russian Front – 3 Russian 'Fronts' (grps. of armies) make deep penetration W. and SW. of Moscow (Germans stage recovery and stabilize front in late Jan.). 'Battle of the Valdai Hills': during 12 days of bitter fighting (Jan. 9-21) Russians make 113-km-deep break-through between Smolensk and L. Ilmen, capturing 9 towns. By Jan. 22 Russians seriously threaten Velikie Luki, a vital rail junction.

Philippines – Japanese attempt to break through US-Filipino line across Bataan Pen.: fierce fighting until end of Feb.

Sea War – Destroyer *Vimiera* mined and sunk in Thames Estuary.

Home Front: USA – Joe Louis knocks out Buddy Baer in first round of World Heavyweight Boxing Championship.

SATURDAY, JANUARY 10

East Indies – Japanese land on Tarakan I. (night Jan. 10-11): Dutch Martin bombers make repeated attacks on invasion fleet. Wavell arrives in Java, activates ABDA.

Air War: Europe – RAF night raid on Emden (repeated on 6 nights during Jan.).

Sea War – Russian sub. *M-175* sunk by *U-584* in the Arctic.

Home Front: Germany – Berlin Radio reports that German troops are defending their positions on Russian Front in a 'wall of blood'.

SUNDAY, JANUARY 11

Russian Front – Russians recapture Liudinovo, SW. of Kaluga, Tikhonovo Pustyn railway junction, NW. of Kaluga and Popovka in Donets Basin (Ukraine). Number of coal mines in the Donets are back in production. Battle of Mozhaisk: Russians oust Germans from stronghold W. of Moscow (ends Jan. 19).

Malaya – Japanese take Kuala Lumpur.

Air War – Japanese paratroops land at Menado (Celebes).

Sea War: Atlantic – Op. *Paukenschlag* ('Drumbeat'): 5 U-boats commence ops. off American E. Coast – 20 ships sunk Jan. 11-Feb. 7.

Sea War: Pacific – US carrier *Saratoga* damaged by sub. *I-6* off Hawaii.

MONDAY, JANUARY 12

Diplomacy – Japan declares war on Netherlands E. Indies.

US-Mexican Joint Defence Commission established.

Occupied Yugoslavia – Gen. Simovic resigns as P.M. of Yugoslav Govt.-in-Exile; succeeded by Prof. Yovanovic. Gen. Mihailovic, leader of *Chetniks* (Serbian partisans) appointed Minister of National Defence and CinC of all Yugoslav resistance forces.

Home Front: USA – National War Labor Board established, with wide-ranging powers to settle industrial disputes.

Sea War: Med. – *U-374* sunk by British sub. *Unbeaten* off Catania (Sicily).

TUESDAY, JANUARY 13

Russian Front – Russians now in complete control of railway from Maloyaroslavets S. to Kaluga. Russians recapture Kirov, SE. of Smolensk, and Dorokhovo, near Mozhaisk.

Malaya – Japanese capture Port Swettenham.

Diplomacy – Allied Conference at St. James's Palace, London, pledges action against 'War Criminals'.

Home Front: USA – War Production Board to be headed by Donald M. Nelson.

WEDNESDAY, JANUARY 14

Russian Front – Russian armoured spearheads only 13 km from Kharkov. Russians recapture Medya W. of Maloyaroslavets.

Sea War: Atlantic – U-boat 'ace' Lt.-Cdr. Lüth, of *U-43*, attacks Convoy ON. 55 during severe storm and sinks 3 ships.

THURSDAY, JANUARY 15

Russian Front – Russians recapture Selijarovo NW. of Rzhev.

Diplomacy – Pan-American Conference (Jan. 15-23): Argentina objects to American proposal that all relations with Axis Powers be ended. Amicable settlement of Peru-Ecuador border dispute.

Home Front: Britain – Death of F.M. the Duke of Connaught, third son of Queen Victoria and former Gov.-Gen. of Canada (1911-16); aged 91.

FRIDAY, JANUARY 16

Diplomacy – Cripps replaced by Kerr as British Ambassador in Moscow.

Home Front: USA – Movie star Carole Lombard killed in air crash on Table Mtn. near Las Vegas. She was returning from 'War Bond' fund-raising rally in Indianapolis; aged 41.

Home Front: USSR – Russian High Command publishes contents of document found at Klin, NW. of Moscow and signed by F.M. von Reichenau, GOC German 6th Army, instructing German troops to be 'merciless' with the civil population. Reichenau himself killed in plane crash on way to hospital after heart attack.

SATURDAY, JANUARY 17

North Africa – Halfaya Pass recaptured by British: 5,000 Axis prisoners.

Sea War: Pacific – Sub. *I-60* sunk near Krakatoa I. by British destroyer *Jupiter*.

Sea War – First U-boat attack on an Arctic convoy: destroyer *Matabele* and 1 merchant ship sunk.

Sea War: Med. – British destroyer *Gurkha II* torpedoed by *U-133; Isaac Sweers* (Dutch) tows her out of burning oil and rescues crew.

Air War – American Volunteer Group led by Gen. Chennault claims to have destroyed 90 Japanese planes over SW. China and Burma since Dec. 7, 1941. 3 US fighters and pilots lost.

SUNDAY, JANUARY 18

Russian Front – On Central Front, advancing Russians within 97 km of Smolensk. Heavy fighting in suburbs of Orel, S. of Kaluga. Timoshenko commences general offensive on Ukrainian front, advancing to within 97 km of R. Dnieper and Dnieprostroy, vital German supply base. Maj.-Gen. Gretchko (postwar Marshal and Minister of Defence) particularly distinguishes himself.

Air War: Europe – Russian parachute brig. and airborne regt. land behind German lines S. of Vyazma (Jan. 18-24).

MONDAY, JANUARY 19

Russian Front – Fall of Mozhaisk (night 19-20). Russian Guards and tank units capture town after house-to-house fighting. Germans retreating W. towards Vyazma, harried at Borodino by Russian cavalry, ski troops and Ilyushin *Shturmovik* aircraft. Germans recapture Feodosia. 57°F of frost on Leningrad front.

Sea War: Atlantic – Canadian SS *Lady Hawkins* sunk by U-boat with heavy loss of life.

TUESDAY, JANUARY 20

Sea War: 2 Japanese subs. shell Midway I. Japanese carrier planes bomb Rabaul (New Britain). Minelaying sub. *I-124* sunk off Darwin by USS *Edsall* and Australian warships. 'China Force' (3 cruisers, 6 destroyers and 2 sloops) formed to escort Allied convoys between Singapore and E. Indies.

Home Front: Germany – **WANNSEE CONFERENCE (BERLIN):** Heydrich outlines Hitler's plans for *'Final Solution'* of Jewish 'Problem' – all European and British Jews to be deported to E. Europe, to either die from forced labour or be liquidated.

Russian Front – Russians recapture Toropetz, NE. of Velikie Luki.

Burma – **JAPANESE INVADE BURMA.**

WEDNESDAY, JANUARY 21

Air War: Pacific – Hurricanes destroy 8 Japanese bombers over Singapore. 120 Japanese aircraft attack Rabaul: 7 Australian Wirraway army co-op aircraft intercept *Zeros,* destroy 3 and badly damage 2 others.

Nakajima fighters shoot down 5 Hurricanes over Singapore.

THURSDAY, JANUARY 22

North Africa – Rommel captures Agedabia.

Russian Front – Russians recapture Uvarovo, 32 km W. of Mozhaisk.

Siege of Leningrad: Mass evacuation of civilians via the 'ice road' across L. Ladoga; 440,000 taken out, Jan. 22-April 15, 1942.

Home Front: Britain – Death of W. R. Sickert, painter and noted eccentric, at Bath; aged 82.

FRIDAY, JANUARY 23

Sea War: Pacific – Japanese land at Rabaul (New Britain): small Australian garrison overwhelmed after gallant stand.

Sea War: Atlantic – Spanish SS *Navemar* sunk by Italian sub. *Barbarigo* off Azores.

Sea War: Pacific – Battle of Makassar Strait: Dutch Martin bombers, sub. *K-XVIII* and 4 US destroyers attack Japanese fleet off blazing oil fields of Balikpapan (Borneo), sinking 4 transports; *K-XVIII* damaged (Jan. 23-24).

Russian Front – Russians break through N. of Smolensk.

Malaya – Japanese within 97 km of Singapore.

SATURDAY, JANUARY 24

Sea War – Japanese land at Balikpapan and Kendari (Celebes).

Air War – RAAF bombs Rabaul (night Jan. 24-25). Dutch bombers and American B-17s attack shipping at Balikpapan (repeated Jan.25, Feb. 1 and 2).

Russian Front – Russians recapture Barvenkovo, SE. of Kharkov.

SUNDAY, JANUARY 25

Russian Front – Zhukov attempts to storm fortified town of Gzhatsk, W. of Mozhaisk, but, as he had predicted, his weakened forces are inadequate for the task demanded of them.

Sea War – Japanese carriers *Hiryu* and *Soryu* launch air strikes against Amboina I. naval base, Neths. E. Indies.

Diplomacy – Thailand declares war on Britain and USA. Peru and Uruguay break off relations with Axis Powers.

MONDAY, JANUARY 26

Sea War: Atlantic – First American troop convoy reaches N. Ireland. (Op. Magnet.)

Sea War – 68 British aircraft (13 lost) attack Japanese troop convoy off E. coast of Malaya. In night Jan. 26-27 destroyers *Thanet* (British) and *Vampire* (Australian) attack; *Thanet* sunk by Japanese warships.

TUESDAY, JANUARY 27

Russian Front – Russians recapture Lozovaya, railway junction and supply base, S. of Kharkov.

Sea War – 6 American subs. carry supplies to Corregidor I. (op. continues until May 6).

Air War – Japanese bomb Bandjermasin airfield (S. Borneo), hitting 9 Dutch bombers. RN carrier *Indomitable* flies off 48 Hurricanes for Java's defence.

WEDNESDAY, JANUARY 28

Air War – 8th USAAF formed in Georgia.

Russian Front – Russian successes in Ukraine.

Diplomacy – Brazil breaks off diplomatic relations with Axis Powers.

Home Front: S. Africa – Numerous bomb explosions disrupt electricity supplies to gold mines in the Rand (extremists plant 2 bombs in Johannesburg, Feb. 1).

THURSDAY, JANUARY 29

North Africa – Rommel recaptures Benghazi.

Home Front: Britain – Churchill wins Parliamentary Vote of Confidence, 464-1. First broadcast of 'Desert Island Discs' – BBC's longest-running record programme.

Sea War: Atlantic – US Coast Guard cutter *Alexander Hamilton* (2,000 t.) sunk by *U-132,* off Reykjavik.

FRIDAY, JANUARY 30

Malaya – British and Commonwealth forces withdraw to Singapore I. and blow up 1-km-long Causeway across Johore Str.

Diplomacy – Govt. of Irish Republic protests against landing of US troops in N. Ireland – which represents a 'Violation' of Eire's neutrality and recognition of the 'Quisling' régime in Ulster.

SATURDAY, JANUARY 31

Sea War – Japanese land on Amboina I.

Burma – Japanese capture port of Moulmein.

Russian Front – Siege of Leningrad: total number of deaths from starvation, typhus, dysentery, heart failure, etc., in Jan.-Feb. 1942 is more than 200,000. There is an outbreak of cannibalism.

SUNDAY, FEBRUARY 1

Sea War: Pacific – US carriers *Enterprise* and *Yorktown* and cruisers *Northampton* and *Salt Lake City* attack Gilbert and Marshall Is.

Home Front: Japan – Clothing rationing commences.

Air War: Britain – RAF Regt. formed for local defence of UK airfields.

Air War: Pacific – Japanese commence series of day and night raids on Rangoon.

Occupied Norway – Quisling Govt. established in Norway.

Vichy France – King Koadio Adiomani of Bonduku in Ivory Coast (Vichy Africa) now in Gold Coast with several thousand of his subjects preparatory to joining Free French Movement.

Home Front: USA – Death of Marion Sayle ('Voice of Experience') Taylor, author and lecturer; aged 52.

MONDAY, FEBRUARY 2

East Indies – Japanese overcome resistance of Dutch-Australian forces on Amboina I.

Secret War – British Naval Staff reports that *Gneisenau* and *Scharnhorst* will probably attempt to leave Brest and pass up Channel through Strs. of Dover. (*See* Feb. 11.)

Neutrals: Egypt – Cabinet resigns after petty dispute with King Farouk over his pro-Axis sympathies.

TUESDAY, FEBRUARY 3

Russian Front – Russians recapture Lozovaya in Barvenkovo Salient, SW. of Kharkov.

Air War: Pacific – Japanese bomb Port Moresby (New Guinea) and Surabaya naval base (Java) (31 killed and 139 injured).

Home Front: Britain – Sir Arnold Bax appointed Master of the King's Musick.

WEDNESDAY, FEBRUARY 4

Malaya – Japanese demand unconditional surrender of Singapore. Wavell declares that large Allied reinforcements are on the way.

Sea War – US cruiser *Marblehead* severely damaged by Japanese bombers.

Home Front: Britain – Beaverbrook appointed Minister for Production.

Home Front: Italy – Göring completes 8-day visit to Italy which includes talks with Mussolini and the King and a 3-day tour of *Luftwaffe* bases in Sicily.

Air War: Pacific – Last British flying boat leaves Singapore.

THURSDAY, FEBRUARY 5

Sea War – Troopship *Empress of Asia* (16,400 t.) sunk by Japanese bombers off Singapore.

Diplomacy – USA DECLARES WAR ON THAILAND.

Home Front: USSR – Pres. Kalinin predicts in broadcast that the hour is near when all the occupied Republics of Russia will return to the Soviet Union.

Air War: Europe –RAF drop 1.4 M. copies of 2 American leaflets, describing gigantic US arms programme, over 8 French cities and towns.

FRIDAY, FEBRUARY 6

North Africa – Rommel's offensive grinds to a halt W. of Gazala.
Philippines – Emilio Aguinaldo, Filipino nationalist leader, broadcasts appeal to embattled US-Filipino forces on Bataan to surrender.
Sea War: Atlantic – British corvette *Genista* shoots down Focke-Wulf Condor.
Neutrals: Egypt – Nahas Pasha, leader of nationalist, anti-British, Wafd Party, forms new Govt. (Parliament dissolved, Feb. 7).
Air War: Europe – RAF night raids on German battlecruisers at Brest (repeated Feb. 10-11 and 11-12).
Secret War – Bomb hidden in mail steamer baggage explodes on quayside at Tangier (Spanish Morocco) killing 14 (6 British) and injuring 39. Spanish Press blames 'British Secret Service'.
Diplomacy – Exiled Iraqi leader, Raschid Ali, and the anti-British Grand Mufti of Jerusalem, Sayed Emin el Husseini, arrive in Rome from Berlin.

SATURDAY, FEBRUARY 7

Russian Front – Fierce fighting in suburbs of Rzhev, 209 km NW. of Moscow. In Ukraine, Timoshenko recaptures Trosna, SW. of Orel and Krasnograd, SW. of Kharkov. Heavy fighting on Leningrad front.
Malaya – Japanese artillery bombardment of Singapore I.
Air War: Pacific – Japanese bomb Palembang, destroying 34 British aircraft.
Neutrals: Spain – Anti-British riots in Tangier (Consulate wrecked); martial law declared next day.

SUNDAY, FEBRUARY 8

Philippines – Bataan garrison finally annihilates remnants of 2 Japanese bns. which had landed on rugged W. coast of the pen. in late Jan. Casualties (killed): Japanese, 900; Americans and Filipinos, 500. Roosevelt rejects proposal that Philippines should be declared an independent neutral state.
Malaya – Japanese land on Singapore I. (night Feb. 8-9) and capture Tengah airfield.
Home Front: Germany – Todt, Minister of Armaments and Munitions, killed in air crash at Rastenburg, E. Prussia; aged 50. Succeeded by Prof. Albert Speer.
Sea War – Japanese land at Makassar (Celebes).
Sea War: Pacific – Japanese occupy Gasmata, New Britain.
Air War: Pacific – Japanese bomb Surabaya (51 killed, 54 injured).

YAMASHITA, Tomoyuki (1888-1946)
Japanese: *Lieutenant-General;* 'Tiger of Malaya'

Most talented and inventive Japanese general of W.W.II. Conquered Malaya in less than two months by employing lightly-armed and equipped infantry, trained to infiltrate through jungle and mangrove swamps. Despite being outnumbered more than 3-to-1, compelled 85,000-strong garrison of Singapore to capitulate within 7 days. Waged brilliant guerrilla campaign against lavishly-equipped US forces in Philippines, Oct. 1944-Aug. 1945.

Began military career as intelligence officer. Played key role in suppressing 'February Mutiny' of fanatical, right-wing officers (1936). Chief of Staff in N. China, 1938. Inspector-gen. of Army aviation, 1940. Led Japanese military delegation to Germany, spring 1941, to meet Hitler and study *Blitzkrieg* victories. Directed training of Japanese expeditionary forces before invasion of Malaya, Philippines and Dutch E. Indies.

Fell into disfavour despite his spectactular victory at Singapore; sent to cmnd. Army grp. on Russian-Manchurian border. Recalled Sept. 1944 to cmnd. Army grp. in Philippines. Arrived 9 days before US invasion of Leyte. His prudent ultra-defensive strategy aroused fierce opposition in Imperial GHQ and Yamashita was forced to divert precious reserves to futile defence of Leyte (Oct.-Dec. 1944).

Surrendered at Baguio, N. Luzon, Sept. 3, 1945. Tried by military court in Manila, Oct.-Dec. 1945 for alleged complicity in massacres committed by Japanese forces in Philippines. Despite weak prosecution case, found guilty and sentenced to death, Dec. 7, 1945. Execution delayed by appeal to US Supreme Court. Yamashita hanged, Feb. 23. 1946.

MONDAY, FEBRUARY 9

Burma – Japanese cross R. Salween.
Air War – Japanese raid airfields near Batavia, capital of Dutch E. Indies.
Home Front: USA – Troopship *Lafayette* (83,000 t.) – ex-French liner *Normandie* – catches fire in New York Harbor. She capsizes, Feb. 10.
Home Front: Britain – Soap rationed: 4 oz (113 g) household or 2 oz (56 g) toilet per person per month.
Home Front: Canada – 4 by-elections: 'Anti-Conscription' candidates heavily defeated.
Diplomacy – Chiang Kai-shek visits Delhi.

TUESDAY, FEBRUARY 10

Sea War: Atlantic – Churchill offers to transfer immediately to US Navy 34 anti-sub. vessels and trained crews (first arrives New York early March).
Air War – Last RAF fighters withdrawn from Singapore to Sumatra.
Diplomacy – Pacific War Council (GB, Australia, NZ and Netherlands) meets in London.
Home Front: USSR – Only 702 of 30,000 Jews in Dnepropetrovsk (Ukraine) have escaped repeated *SS* massacres.

WEDNESDAY, FEBRUARY 11

Occupied Dutch WI – Dutch W. Indian Is. of Aruba and Curaçao occupied by US.
Air War: Europe – 'Blockade of Brest' ends: since March 1941 RAF has flown 3,299 sorties (43 aircraft lost) and dropped 4,000 t. bombs. RAF night raid on Mannheim (repeated Feb. 14-15).
Sea War: Pacific – V.-Adm. Helfrich (R.

Neths. N.) succeeds Adm. Hart (USN) as Allied Supreme Naval Cdr.
Sea War – **THE CHANNEL DASH** (Op. Cerberus): *Gneisenau, Scharnhorst* and *Prinz Eugen* leave Brest (night Feb. 11-12) under heavy escort and with massive air cover. Planned British counter-measures (Op. Fuller) involving cross-Channel guns, MTBs, destroyers and heavy torpedo planes fail abysmally (42 British aircraft lost). Swordfish sqn. (Lt.-Cdr. Esmonde, V.C.) wiped out in suicidal torpedo attack. *Gneisenau* and *Scharnhorst* are both damaged by mines, but arrive in Elbe Estuary and Wilhelmshaven, resp.

THURSDAY, FEBRUARY 12

Sea War: Pacific – 'Anzac Squadron' formed at Suva (Fiji) – cruisers *Australia, Chicago* (American), *Achilles* and *Leander* plus 2 US destroyers.
Diplomacy – Franco and Portuguese dictator Salazar, meet at Seville.

Air War – Destroyer *Maori* bombed and sunk at Malta.
Home Front: USA – Death of Grant Wood, artist noted for his depiction of Mid-Western farm folk, e.g., 'American Gothic'; aged 49.

FRIDAY, FEBRUARY 13

Russian Front – Russians re-enter Byelorussia (White Russia).
Malaya – Japanese cut off water supply to Singapore.
Sea War – Japanese bombers and subs. sink or damage many ships carrying military personnel and refugees from Singapore.
Home Front: Germany – Quisling and Terboven, *Reichskommissar* in Norway, visit Hitler.

SATURDAY, FEBRUARY 14

Air War – Japanese paratroops land at Palembang (Sumatra): Dutch destroy 1 oil refinery, but the second and airfield are captured.
Home Front: Soviet Union – Universal conscription for labour service.

SUNDAY, FEBRUARY 15

Malaya – FALL OF SINGAPORE. Gen. Percival surrenders unconditionally to Gen. Yamashita. 80,000 PoWs taken.

Malayan Campaign Losses
Japanese: 3,507 dead, 6,150 wounded. Allied: 138,708 (130,000 PoWs); *c.* 740 guns, over 2,500 machine-guns, 65,000 small arms, *c.* 200 armoured cars, *c.* 1,000 rail engines and trucks; 10 light planes.

Burma – Commonwealth forces withdraw to R. Bilin.
East Indies – Japanese seaborne reinforcements land at Palembang.
Sea War: Atlantic – Brazilian ships *Buarque* and *Olinda* sunk by U-boats off American E. coast (Feb. 15 and 18).
Home Front: Britain – Mrs Churchill's Red Cross Fund for Russia reaches £1.5 M.

MONDAY, FEBRUARY 16

Sea War – Op. *Neuland*: 2 U-boats make simultaneous attacks on oil installations and tankers at Curaçao and Aruba. 7 tankers torpedoed (3 sunk).
Home Front: Australia – P.M. Curtin declares that fall of Singapore is 'Australia's Dunkirk' and the prelude to 'Battle of Australia' (he orders 'total mobilization' Feb. 17).

TUESDAY, FEBRUARY 17

Home Front: Britain – Commons debate on escape of German battlecruisers from

Brest. Churchill announces setting up of commission of inquiry under Mr Justice Bucknill.
Occupied Singapore – Japanese rename Singapore, *Shonan* ('Light of the South').
Sea War: Pacific – Japanese sub. *I-25* launches diminutive Yokosuka seaplane for recce flight over Sydney (similar flights over Melbourne, Hobart and Wellington, Feb. 26-March 8).

WEDNESDAY, FEBRUARY 18

Air War: Pacific – RAF and RAAF units withdrawn from Sumatra to Java.
Sea War – Free French sub. *Surcouf*

Below: *Lt-Gen. Percival (right) leads his surrender party to Yamashita's HQ at Bukit Timah, Singapore on Feb. 15.*

(world's largest) sunk in collision with US merchantman.

THURSDAY, FEBRUARY 19

Sea War: Pacific – THE DARWIN RAID. Japanese Carrier Force and land-based bombers make devastating strikes on Port Darwin, sinking or damaging 16 ships and panicking civilian population (172 killed, 349 injured aboard ships); heavy civilian casualties.
Sea War – Japanese land on Bali. Battle of Lombok Strait (night Feb. 19-20): 2 Dutch-American sqns. have several fierce engagements with Japanese naval units E. of Bali – Dutch cruiser *Tromp* damaged and a destroyer sunk; 1 Japanese destroyer badly damaged.
U-161 attacks shipping in Port of Spain (Trinidad). British troopships are temporarily diverted elsewhere for refuelling.
Home Front: Britain – Govt. reshuffle: Attlee, Deputy P.M. and Dominions Sec.; Cripps, Lord Privy Seal; Beaverbrook leaves Govt.

FRIDAY, FEBRUARY 20

Russian Front – German frostbite casualties now total 112,627, inc. 14,357 requiring amputation.
East Indies – Japanese land on Timor I., N. of Australia (occupation completed Feb. 24).
Air War – Demiansk Airlift: force of Ju 52s (increasing from 40 in Feb. to 300 in May) maintains trapped German 16th Army in Demiansk 'Cauldron', N. of Smolensk, losing 262 aircraft.
Wildcat fighter flown by Lt. 'Butch' O'Hare, of USS *Lexington*, shoots down 5 Mitsubishi G4M bombers in ten mins near Gilbert Is.
Vichy France – THE RIOM WAR GUILT TRIAL. Vichy French Supreme Court, sitting at Riom, near Clermont-Ferrand, examines ex-P.M.s Daladier and Blum, Gen. Gamelin and others on charges of being 'responsible for the defeat of France'. Accused later deported to Germany and Court dissolved, June 13, 1942.
Sea War – Italian sub. group *Da Vinci* (4 boats) sinks 14 merchantmen (Feb. 20-March 24) in the Caribbean.

SATURDAY, FEBRUARY 21

Diplomacy – Salazar makes 'energetic protest' against Japanese occupation of Portuguese Timor.
Neutrals: Uruguay – Pres. Baldomir foils attempted coup.
Burma – British begin withdrawal over R. Sittang (night Feb. 21-22).
Home Front: USA – Pacific coast declared 'strategic defense area'.

SUNDAY, FEBRUARY 22

Air War: Europe – Air Marshal Harris becomes AOCinC RAF Bomber Cmnd.

Home Front: Britain – Col. Llewellin appointed Minister of Aircraft Production; Grigg becomes Sec. for War. Dr William Temple nominated Archbishop of Canterbury and Primate of all England.
Sea War – Japanese subs. sink 11 ships S. of Java (Feb. 22-March 1).

MONDAY, FEBRUARY 23

Diplomacy – Mutual Aid Agreement between UK, USA, Australia and New Zealand.
Sea War: Pacific – Japanese sub. *I-17* shells oil installations near Santa Barbara, California (night Feb. 23-24).
Sea War – *Prinz Eugen* torpedoed off Trondheim by British sub. *Trident*.
Russian Front – Russians recapture Dorogobuzh, E. of Smolensk. Russians reach R. Dnieper in strength.
Philippines – Roosevelt orders Gen. MacArthur to leave Bataan for Australia. Gen. Wainwright takes command. MacArthur appointed CinC Allied Forces in Australia.
Home Front: Germany – Death of Prof. August von Parseval, aeronautical engineer and inventor of the Parseval 'kite balloon' used on Western Front in W.W.I.; aged 81.
Home Front: Brazil – Stefan Zweig exiled Austrian author and his wife commit suicide at Petropolis; (Stefan) aged 60.

TUESDAY, FEBRUARY 24

Sea War: Pacific – WAKE ISLAND RAID. US carrier *Enterprise* launches air strike against Wake I. (similar attack on nearby Marcus I., March 4).
Air War: Pacific – Japanese paratroops land on Kupang airfield, Timor.
Sea War: Atlantic – US destroyer *Truxton* and naval transport *Pollux* reported

wrecked in gale off St Lawrence R. (189 missing).
Sea War – *Struma* Affair: Russian sub. *Shch-213* sinks decrepit Bulgarian SS *Struma* carrying 764 Rumanian Jews (only 1 survivor). Turkish authorities had earlier forced vessel's crew to put to sea because none of the passengers had visas.
Diplomacy – Von Papen, German Ambassador in Turkey, narrowly escapes death in assassination attempt. Vichy France reaffirms her neutrality following US protest against incidental aid given to German *Afrika Korps*.
Occupied Norway – Norwegian bishops resign their offices in collective protest against Nazi-Quisling oppression.
Occupied Holland – Death of L. E. Bisser, Pres. of Netherlands High Court of Justice until removed by Germans in 1940; active in Jewish welfare work; aged 70.

WEDNESDAY, FEBRUARY 25

Burma – Retreating British use 'scorched earth' tactics in Rangoon, inc. setting fire to oil installations.
Air War: Europe – RAF night raid on Kiel (repeated next 2 nights).
Home Front: USA – Air raid scare in Los Angeles: heavy AA barrage. Sec. of War Stimson announces that *'15 commercial planes operated by enemy agents'* have flown over city – false alarm; no bombs dropped.

THURSDAY, FEBRUARY 26

Air War: Europe – RAF cripples *Gneisenau* at Kiel: a complete rebuilding is planned, but never implemented.
Home Front: USA – All 3,000 Japanese-American residents of Terminal I. in Los Angeles harbour ordered to leave within 3 days.

FRIDAY, FEBRUARY 27

Sea War – BATTLE OF JAVA SEA (Feb. 27-March 1): Allied fleet, under Dutch Adm. Doorman, makes repeated but largely ineffectual attempts to repulse 2 Japanese invasion fleets approaching Java from E. and W. Cruisers *De Ruyter*, *Java*, *Houston*, *Perth* and *Exeter* and destroyers *Kortenaer*, *Electra*, *Jupiter*, *Encounter* and *Pope* are sunk. Japanese lose 2 transports, 1 cruiser and 6 destroyers are damaged.
Air War – Japanese bombers make devastating incendiary raid on Toungoo (Burma Road); 400 killed.
Secret War – The Bruneval Raid (Op. Biting): British paratroops destroy radar station near Le Havre and escape by sea with vital components (night Feb. 27-28).
Home Front: Germany – Orders given for the building of 5 crematoria at Auschwitz, capable of 'processing' 12,000 gas chamber victims per day.

SATURDAY, FEBRUARY 28

Burma – Japanese cut road N. of Rangoon.
Sea War: Atlantic – U-boats sink 69 ships (mainly tankers) off American E. Coast and in Caribbean during Feb.
Home Front: USA – Rear Adm. Kimmel and Lt.-Gen. Short – US Navy and Army CinCs in Hawaii on Dec. 7, 1941 – to face court-martial for 'dereliction of duty', after the war.
Diplomacy – Subhas Chandra Bose, renegade ex-president of Indian Congress Party, makes anti-British broadcast speech from Berlin (repeated March 11). (*See* April 26, 1943.)
Home Front: Germany – Dr Mansfeld appointed Reich Labour Controller with overall responsibility for the exploitation of foreign workers and PoWs in the armaments industry and agriculture.
Home Front: Australia – Gen. Bennett escapes from Singapore to Australia.

SUNDAY, MARCH 1

Russian Front – Russians counter-attack in the Crimea.
Sea War – HMS *Exeter* sunk by Japanese cruisers and destroyers S. of Borneo. US destroyer *Pope* crippled by dive bombers and sunk by gunfire.
2 Japanese task forces (inc. 4 carriers and 2 fast battleships) under Adms. Nagumo and Kondo wreak havoc among Allied shipping around Java. 9 warships and 10 merchant ships sunk and 3 merchant ships captured (March 1-7). Ships sunk include 3 destroyers – USS *Edsall*, *Pillsbury* and HMS *Stronghold* – and naval tanker *Pecos* (carrying survivors from USS *Langley*).
Air War – Severe raids on Malta. RAF night raid on shipping at Tripoli.
Home Front: USA – Death of Cornelius Vanderbilt III, multi-millionaire railway magnate, inventor and soldier; aged 68.

HARRIS, Sir Arthur Travers (1892-)
British: *Marshal of the Royal Air Force*;
'Bomber', 'Bert' or 'Butcher'

Controversial mastermind of RAF Bomber Cmnd. saturation bombing raids on German cities, 1942-45. His basic contention – often forcefully expressed – that Germany could be defeated by air power alone, was never confirmed by actual results, despite great damage inflicted on Berlin and massive civilian death-toll in Hamburg and Dresden. Constantly repeated night raids also involved heavy British losses, totalling 8,000 planes, 47,293 officers and men. Strict disciplinarian.

Born in Cheltenham. Went to Rhodesia shortly before W.W.I; became successful tobacco planter. Served in 1st Rhodesian Regt., 1914-15. Joined Royal Flying Corps 1915; commanded Sopwith Camel fighter sqn. on Western Front, 1917. Big game hunter between the wars.

Air Commodore, 1937; Air Vice-Marshal, 1938; Commander No. 5 Group Bomber Cmnd., 1939-40; Deputy Chief of Air Staff, 1940-41; head of RAF delegation at Washington, June 1941-Feb. 1942. AOCinC Bomber Cmnd. Feb. 1942-Sept 1945. Went into complete retirement at war's end.

MONDAY, MARCH 2

Air War: Europe – Wellingtons destroy munition ship *Cuma* at Palermo (night March 2-3) – 13 other ships damaged by the blast.
Home Front: Australia – All civilians now liable for compulsory war service.
Home Front: USA – 112,000 Japanese-Americans to be deported from Pacific Coast to inland 'assembly centres'.

TUESDAY, MARCH 3

Air War: Europe – Renault works at Billancourt (Paris) severely damaged in RAF night raid: some casualties among 3,000-strong French workforce. Lancasters in combat debut: dropping mines in Heligoland Bight.
Air War – RAF night raid on Benghazi. RAAF bomb airfields and shipping at Gasmata, New Britain. Japanese bomb Port Moresby, New Guinea. 60 Japanese aircraft (5 lost) raid Banduang, Java (102 casualties). Japanese bomb Wyndham and Broome (NW. Australia). Flying boats – refuelled by subs. – make unsuccessful night raid on Pearl Harbor.
East Africa – Duke of Aosta, chivalrous former CinC of Italian forces in E. Africa, dies from tuberculosis at Nairobi; aged 43.
Diplomacy – USA purchases large quantities of rubber from Brazil to help make up shortfall in supplies resulting from Japanese occupation of Malaya (similar agreements concluded in April-Aug. with Peru, Nicaragua, Colombia, Bolivia and British Honduras).

WEDNESDAY, MARCH 4

East Indies – Lt.-Gen. Hein ter Poorten appointed CinC Allied Land Forces and Rear Adm. van Stavern CinC Allied Naval Forces.
Home Front: Britain –Jowett appointed Paymaster Gen.; Maxwell Fyfe, Solicitor-Gen.
Home Front: USA – 20 killed in explosion at ordnance works in Burlington, Iowa.
Air War – 394 raids on Malta, by day and night, over previous 2 months.

THURSDAY, MARCH 5

East Indies – Dutch evacuate Batavia, which becomes 'open city'.
Burma – Alexander appointed GOC.
Russian Front – Russians recapture Yukhnov, E. of Smolensk.
Air War: Britain – A few bombs dropped over I. of Wight and Dorset – Germans claim to have 'blown up an ammunition dump near Portsmouth'.
Air War – Night raid on Moscow.
Home Front: Britain – Conscription extended to men aged 41-45.
Home Front: USSR – First performance of Shostakovich's 7th ('Leningrad') Symphony, at Kuibyshev.

FRIDAY, MARCH 6

East Indies – Japanese occupy Batavia.
Sea War – *Tirpitz* leaves Trondheim for unsuccessful sortie against Convoy QP. 8 (ends March 9).
Air War: Pacific – RAAF bombs Kupang airfield, Timor.
Home Front: USA – Death of Tom Mooney, union leader and revolutionary, sentenced to death in 1916 for the San Francisco bomb outrage but reprieved and imprisoned for 22 years. He dies in hospital; aged 60.

SATURDAY, MARCH 7

Air War – First sqn. of Spitfires lands in Malta after taking off from carriers *Argus* and *Eagle* S. of Majorca (10 similar ops. late March-end Oct. 1942).

SUNDAY, MARCH 8

Air War: Europe – RAF daylight raid on Matford truck works at Poissy, near Paris. RAF night raid on Essen: 'Gee' radar navigation equipment tested.
Burma – **FALL OF RANGOON.**
New Guinea – Japanese land at Lae and Salamaua.
Home Front: Cuba – Death of J. R. Capablanca, diplomat, and world chess champion, 1921-27, in New York; aged 53.

MONDAY, MARCH 9

East Indies – **CAPITULATION OF DUTCH AND ALLIED FORCES ON JAVA.** Japanese take 60,000 prisoners including Gen. ter Poorten.
Burma – Battle of Taukkyan: Japanese block line of retreat of British forces 32 km N. of Rangoon; they defend formidable road block for 24 hours against tanks and infantry. British CinC Lt.-Gen. Alexander in danger of capture. British force trapped at Pegu, NE. of Rangoon, fights its way out and rejoins Gen. Alexander.
Air War: Europe – RAF bombs Essen and Hamborn (Duisburg).

TUESDAY, MARCH 10

Sea War: Pacific – US carrier planes strike Japanese shipping at Lae and Salamaua. Japanese land at Buka (Bougainville), Solomon Is.
China – Lt.-Gen. 'Vinegar Joe' Stilwell, US Army, appointed COS by Chiang Kai-shek.
Home Front: Hungary – Kallay succeeds Bardossy as P.M.
Home Front: Britain – Eden reports to House of Commons on Japanese outrages following capture of Hong Kong (Dec. 25, 1941) including massacre of hospital staff and patients.

WEDNESDAY, MARCH 11

Sea War: Med. – Cruiser *Naiad* (Adm. Vian) sunk by *U-565*.
Home Front: Britain – Max. penalty for black-marketeering increased to 14 years' penal servitude.

STILWELL, Joseph Whitaker (1883-1946) American: *General*; 'Vinegar Joe'

Hard-bitten, hard-swearing, American gen. of the old school. As Commander of US forces in China-Burma-India theatre and COS to Chiang Kai-shek, made commendable efforts to transform fossilized Chinese Nationalist Army into modern fighting machine. However, Stilwell was out of his depth in the Chinese hotbed of diplomatic intrigue, political double-dealing and massive corruption, and was ignominiously recalled to USA.
Born at Polatka, Florida. Graduated from West Point, 1904. Served in France during W.W.I. US military attaché to China, 1935-38. Lt.-Gen., Feb. 1942. COS to Chiang Kai-shek, Feb.-March 1942. Commanded Chinese 5th and 6th Armies protecting Burma Road, March-May 1942; forced to retreat into India. US commander, SE. Asia (deputy to Mountbatten), 1943-44; Gen., Aug. 1944. Relieved of command of CBI theatre of war, Oct 28, 1944, and recalled to Washington. Commanding gen., US 10th Army on Okinawa, June 22, 1945. Accepted surrender of 105,000 Japanese troops in Ryukyu Is.

THURSDAY, MARCH 12

Philippines – MacArthur with family and staff leaves Corregidor for Australia aboard PT boat; they are flown from S. Philippines to Australia in B-17, March 16.
East Indies – Japanese land at Sabang, N. Sumatra.
Sea War – German auxiliary minelayer *Doggerbank* lays mines off Cape Town (night March 12-13); repeated April 16.
Home Front: Britain – Death of Sir William Bragg, scientist and Nobel Prize-winner; aged 79.
Lyttelton appointed Minister of Production.
Home Front: Germany – Death of Robert Bosch, industrialist and inventor; aged 80.

FRIDAY, MARCH 13

Sea War: Atlantic – Chilean SS *Tolten* torpedoed and sunk off American E. coast (27 killed, 2 survivors).
Occupied Greece – SS *Rabmanso* leaves Haifa (Palestine) for Piraeus (Greece) with emergency supplies of grain.

SATURDAY, MARCH 14

Sea War: Med. – 3 Italian subs. sunk by British subs. *Unbeaten, Ultimatum* and *Upholder* (March 14-18).
Sea War – German MTBs lay mines and engage British light naval forces in North Sea: 2 E-boats lost; British destroyer *Vortigern* sunk (night March 14-15).
Air War – RAF night raid on Rhodes, some bombs dropped in error on Milas (Turkey), 113 km to the E.
Home Front: Germany – Hitler orders terror attacks (*Terrorangriffe*) against British provincial towns.
Home Front: Australia – Substantial numbers of US troops have now arrived.
Home Front: China – Maj.-Gen. Dennys, British military adviser to Chiang Kai-shek, killed in air crash near Chungking.

SUNDAY, MARCH 15

Sea War: Med. – Cruisers *Dido* and *Euryalus,* with 6 destroyers, bombard harbour of Rhodes (night March 15-16).
Home Front: USA – Death of Rachel Field, author of 'All This and Heaven Too'; aged 47.
Home Front: Norway – Grp. of Norwegian patriots seize Oslo-Bergen SS *Galtesund* and sail her to British port, arriving March 17.

MONDAY, MARCH 16

Home Front: USA – Death of Francis Du Pont, research chemist and industrialist; aged 68.

TUESDAY, MARCH 17

Home Front: Australia – MacArthur appointed Supreme Cdr. of Allied Forces in SW. Pacific. MacArthur promises (in Adelaide, March 20) *'I shall return'* to Philippines. Maj.-Gen. Wainwright to command all US-Filipino forces in Philippines.

WEDNESDAY, MARCH 18

Home Front: Britain – Adm. Lord Mountbatten appointed Chief of Combined Ops.

THURSDAY, MARCH 19

Burma – Gen. Slim arrives to take over command of British and Commonwealth forces.
Stilwell to command Chinese 5th and 6th Armies.
Home Front: Rumania – Michel Antonescu, Vice-Premier, makes vehement anti-Hungarian speech in Bucharest, concerning disputed province of Transylvania.

FRIDAY, MARCH 20

Sea War: Med. – U-652 sinks British destroyers *Heythrop* and *Jaguar* N. of Sollum (Egypt) (on March 20 and 26 resp.).
Home Front: Japan – Japanese Navy Minister, Adm. Shimada, announces that Japan will no longer observe the recognized rules of naval warfare, since Allied forces in the Pacific are waging *'extreme warfare, based on retaliation and hatred'.*

SATURDAY, MARCH 21

Air War – Heavy raids on Malta.
Home Front: Britain – London 'Warship Week' (March 21-28): business community and public raise £146 M. (1,178 local Warship Weeks held 1941-1942, raising total of £546 M. The earlier 'War Weapons Weeks' had raised £451.5 M.).

SUNDAY, MARCH 22

Philippines – Japanese demand surrender of Bataan garrison.
Sea War: Med. – BATTLE OF SIRTE. Italian battleship *Littorio* intercepts Alexandria-Malta convoy MW. 10, but is denied crushing victory by Adm. Vian's skilful deployment of his cruisers and destroyers and by rough seas, which hamper accurate gunnery. Cruiser *Cleopatra* and destroyers *Havock* and *Kingston* badly damaged. During night March 22-23, destroyers *Lanciere* and *Scirocco* sink in a storm; many other ships (British and Italian) damaged. Convoy heavily bombed off Malta, March 23: transport *Breconshire* capsizes. Only 5,000 t. out of original 25,000 t. of supplies unloaded.
Home Front: India – Cripps arrives at Karachi, *en route* for New Delhi, to discuss constitutional problems with Moslem League and Congress party leaders.

MONDAY, MARCH 23

Air War: Britain – Night raid on Dover.
Air War: Pacific – Japanese bomb Port Moresby and Wyndham (N. Australia). RAAF attack Dilli airfield, Timor.
Sea War – Japanese land at Port Blair, Andaman Is.

TUESDAY, MARCH 24

Sea War: Med. – Destroyer *Southwold* mined and sunk off Malta.
Air War – Maj. John Van Kuren Newkirk ('Scarsdale Jack') top fighter 'ace' (25 victories) of the AVG ('Flying Tigers') killed during sweep over Chiang Mai airfield, Thailand; aged 28.
British Army Air Corps formed.
Occupied Poland – Gen. Sikorski visits Roosevelt in Washington.
Neutrals: Egypt – General Election: Wafdists (Nationalists) win overwhelming victory.

WEDNESDAY, MARCH 25

Air War – Japanese aircraft destroy large number of RAF and AVG fighters at Magwe (Burma).
Sea War Atlantic – Italian sub. *Pietro Calvi* sinks 5 ships off NE. coast of Brazil (March 25-April 12).
Home Front: Britain – Grantham by-election: Kendall (Indep. 'Production for Victory' Candidate), 11,758; Air Chief Marshal Longmore (Cons.), 11,391. First seat lost by Govt. since by-election 'truce' began in Sept. 1939 (in numerous cases, Cons., Lab. or Lib. candidates have been returned unopposed).

THURSDAY, MARCH 26

Sea War: Atlantic – American 'Q-ship' *Atik* (disguised anti U-boat hunter) sunk in fierce gun duel with the *U-123*.
Air War: Europe – RAF daylight raid on Le Havre.
Home Front: USA – Accidental explosion of 21 t. of gelignite at Pennsylvania quarry kills 31.
Home Front: Germany – Fritz Sauckel appointed 'General Commissioner for the Employment of Labour'.

FRIDAY, MARCH 27

Sea War – ST NAZAIRE RAID (Op. Chariot): HMS *Campbeltown* (ex-USS *Buchanan*) deliberately rams dock gates at St Nazaire, under murderous German fire, while commandos destroy dock machinery. 5 t.-HE charge in *Campbeltown*'s bows explodes later, killing many German naval personnel.
Sea War – Adm. Somerville appointed CinC British Eastern Fleet.
Home Front: Japan – Kammon Tunnel opened – 2-km-long rail link for coal trains from Kyusha I. to cities of Honshu I.

SATURDAY, MARCH 28

Air War: Europe – The Lübeck Raid: 190 RAF bombers attack historic Baltic coastal town, which is largely destroyed by fire (night March 28-29). Hitler orders reprisals against historic British cities (April 14). RAF daylight raid on Ostend.

Sea War: Atlantic – Battle of Convoy PQ. 13: after being scattered by storms, convoy and escort are harried by German bombers, torpedo planes, 6 U-boats and 3 destroyers (March 28-31): 5 merchant ships sunk. Cruiser *Trinidad* cripples destroyer *Z-26* with gunfire, but is then hit by 1 of her own torpedoes, which circles back, causing serious damage. (*See* May 14.)

SUNDAY, MARCH 29

Home Front: India – British Govt. publishes its constitutional proposals for India – Dominion status after war; Britain to defend sub-continent until then. (Congress Party objects April 2.)

MONDAY, MARCH 30

Air War: Europe – 33 Halifaxes (5 lost) attack *Tirpitz* near Trondheim.

Russian Front – Only 8 of the 162 German divs. are at full strength at conclusion of great Russian counter-offensive. The 16 *Pz* divs. have grand total of only 140 serviceable tanks.

Russian Front Losses
Since June 22, 1941. German: 295,000 dead or missing, 823,000 wounded. (Oct. 1–March 15): over 3,000 tanks, over 2,800 guns, over 2,000 planes. Soviet: over 3,500,000 PoWs, perhaps 4,000,000 dead and wounded; up to 18,000 planes; 14,287 tanks, 25,212 guns.

TUESDAY, MARCH 31

Philippines – Filipino detachments make surprise raids on Japanese supply dumps on Mindanao I. (March 31 and April 1) and burn down 45 warehouses.

WEDNESDAY, APRIL 1

Air War – Improved Ju 87D *Stuka* makes its debut during 11-day 'blitz' on shipping at Malta (Spitfires and AA destroy 13 *Stukas*). Warships sunk or damaged beyond repair inc. destroyers *Gallant*,

Kingston and Lance, subs. *P.36, Pandora* and *Glavkos* (Greek) and naval tanker *Plumleaf*; and cruiser *Penelope* damaged. British sub. ops. from Malta temporarily suspended in mid-April.

Air War: Europe – First of 14 RAF raids on Le Havre in April (11 by night, 3 by day).

Sea War: Med. – Fast cruiser *Giovanni delle Bande Nere* sunk by HM sub. *Urge* off Stromboli (*Urge* lost April 28). 11 Norwegian merchant ships – trapped at Gothenburg since April 1940 – attempt to run the German blockade and reach English ports: 2 get through on April 5; 6 sunk or scuttled; 3 return to Gothenburg.

Home Front: Germany – Speer, Minister for Armaments, creates new system for allocation of raw materials by 'Central Committees', 'Special Committees' and 'Industrial Rings'.

THURSDAY, APRIL 2

Air War: Britain – Night raid on Weymouth: 2 hospitals hit, heavy casualties.

FRIDAY, APRIL 3

Philippines – Japanese forces, with strong air support, launch final offensive against American-Filipino line in Bataan.

Air War: Europe – German bombers destroy 2 ships from Convoy PQ. 13, at Murmansk.

Gen. Quaade, *Luftwaffe* spokesman, admits that the *Luftwaffe* has been unable to neutralize Malta because of its 'tremendously strong' AA defences and subterranean storerooms – *'but you cannot expect the Luftwaffe to sink the island with bombs'.*

Occupied Norway – Bishop Berggrav of Oslo forcibly prevented from preaching in his cathedral and placed under house arrest. (*See* April 10.)

SATURDAY, APRIL 4

Air War: Europe – Op. *Eisstoss* ('Ice Strike'): *Stukas,* Ju 88s and He 111s attack Russian Baltic Fleet in Leningrad. Battleships *Oktyabskaya Revolutsiya* and *Petropavlovsk* and cruisers *Maksim Gorski* and *Kirov* badly damaged.

Air War: Pacific – Destruction of Mandalay: Japanese bombers start huge fires in bazaar quarter of city, crowded with natives; trainload of RAF bombs explode. Approx. 2,000 killed.

SUNDAY, APRIL 5

Sea War – JAPANESE CARRIER STRIKE ON COLOMBO, CEYLON. 91 bombers and dive-bombers cripple AMC *Hector* and destroyer *Tenedos* in harbour, while 36 *Zeros* (7 lost) defeat 42 Hurricanes and Fulmars (19 lost). Later; 53 Aichi dive-bombers overwhelm cruisers *Cornwall* and *Dorsetshire,* off Colombo.

Sea War: Med. – Destroyer *Havock* runs aground on Tunisian coast (later torpedoed by Italian submarine).

Russian Front – Hitler issues 'Führer Directive' No. 41: *'German and Axis forces are to capture oilfields of Caucasus and Leningrad, by series of complex, consecutive ops. – priority being given to former objective. German forces W. of Moscow to remain on the defensive.'*

MONDAY, APRIL 6

Sea War – Three sqns. of Japanese cruisers and destroyers ravage Allied shipping in Bay of Bengal – sinking 16 vessels. Planes from carrier *Ryujo* sink 3 more and also bomb small Indian ports of Cocanada and Vizagapatam.

Air War – Night raid on Alexandria (132 casualties).

Home Front: Germany – Bread, meat and fat (i.e., margarine) rations cut, inc. quantities allowed to heavy industrial workers and infants.

Diplomacy – Italian liners *Saturnia* and *Vulcania* arrive at Gibraltar *en route* for Somaliland, where they are to repatriate 11,000 Italian colonists. 2 other passenger ships sent later in month (return Italy, July 1942).

TUESDAY, APRIL 7

Occupied Holland – Adm. Helfrich appointed CinC of all Dutch forces in Far East and SW. Pacific.

Diplomacy – Exchange of wounded British and Italian PoWs at Smyrna (Turkey): 60 British and 344 Italian. 4 similar exhanges take place (last June 2, 1943).

WEDNESDAY, APRIL 8

Air War: China – First experimental flight by US transport plane over 'The Hump' – mtn. barrier between India and China (regular service established April 22).

Secret War – German agents land in Iceland from *U-252* (sunk night April 13-14).

THURSDAY, APRIL 9

Sea War – Japanese Carrier Force raids Trincomalee naval base (Ceylon): dive-bombers sink British carrier *Hermes,* Australian destroyer *Vampire,* a corvette and 2 tankers. 9 Blenheims (5 lost) make suicidal bombing raid on Japanese carriers. British Eastern Fleet retires to Bombay and Kilindini (Kenya).

Philippines – CAPITULATION OF AMERICAN/FILIPINO ARMY IN BATAAN PENINSULA. I. fortress of Corregidor still defies Japanese. 35,000 troops and 25,000 civilians fall into Japanese hands. Largest surrender in US history.

Home Front: USA – Cut back in petrol deliveries to 17 states.

FRIDAY, APRIL 10

East Indies – Japanese land on Billiton I. and seize tin mines.
Home Front: India – Congress Party and Moslem League reject Sir Stafford Cripps' proposals on the independence issue.
Occupied Norway – Bishop Berggrav sent to Bredvedt Concentration Camp, near Oslo (Quisling threatens him with execution).

SATURDAY, APRIL 11

Home Front: India – British Govt.'s constitutional proposals withdrawn, following their outright rejection by Congress Party. Stafford Cripps broadcasts to Indian people.
Occupied Bulgaria – Bulgarian Cabinet resigns in protest over German demands for Bulgaria's direct participation in Russian Campaign. P.M. Filov forms new Cabinet.

SUNDAY, APRIL 12

Air War: Pacific – 12 Japanese raids on Corregidor and Manila Bay forts.

MONDAY, APRIL 13

Air War: Pacific – 'The Royce Raid': special sqn. of 3 B-17s and 10 B-25s (1 lost) led by Brig.-Gen. Royce, flies from N. Australia to secret strip in S. Philippines, bombs Japanese-held airfields and harbours (inc. Manila) and returns to Australia (April 16) with 44 US and Filipino officers and civilians.
Sea War: Med – U-boats lay mines off Famagusta (Cyprus), Beirut, Haifa and Port Said (April 13-16).

TUESDAY, APRIL 14

Sea War: Med. – Lt.-Cdr. Wanklyn, British sub. 'ace', lost when *Upholder* is depth-charged off Tripoli by Italian torpedo boat *Pegaso*.
Sea War: Atlantic – Destroyer *Roper* sinks *U-85* off C. Hatteras – first major success for US anti-sub. forces.
Home Front: Britain – Budget: Purchase Tax doubled to 66⅔% on clothing, carpets and many other items; 6½d-7½d on 10 cigarettes.
Home Front: USSR – War Loan subscription of 10 billion roubles opened: workers urged to subscribe 4 weeks' wages (Loan over-subscribed by April 23).

WEDNESDAY, APRIL 15

Occupied France – French Resistance carries out grenade attack on German HQ building in Arras.

Above: *B-25s on board USS* Hornet *prior to the Doolittle Raid on Tokyo.*

THURSDAY, APRIL 16

Home Front: Malta – **GEORGE CROSS AWARDED TO MALTA** in recognition of untold heroism of entire civilian and military population during countless enemy raids. (*See* Sept. 13, 1942.)
Occupied France – F.M. von Rundstedt put in charge of the 'Atlantic Wall'.
Sea War: Med. – Sub. *Marcantonio Colonna* laid up at Genoa (scrapped 1943); 2 sister ships consigned to harbour service.

FRIDAY, APRIL 17

Occupied France – Gen. Henri Giraud, ex-CO French 9th Army, escapes from Konigstein Castle, near Dresden, by climbing down 46-m-long 'home-made' rope. He disguises himself as a commercial traveller and reaches Switzerland by circuitous train journeys (assisted by Free French agents), April 21. Hitler offers reward of 100,000 marks for his recapture. This is 63-year-old Giraud's second escape from captivity in Germany – during W.W.I he had reached England disguised as tram-conductor.
Burma – Retreating British set fire to Yenangyaung oilfields.
Air War: Europe – The Augsburg Raid: 12 RAF Lancasters (7 lost, 5 damaged) despatched to diesel engine factory in Bavaria; 8 reach target at roof-top height and drop 17 bombs. First ATS fatal casualty: Pte. Nora Caveney (aged 18) killed at AA battery during night raid on Southampton.
Diplomacy – Adm. Leahy, US Ambassador to Vichy, recalled for 'consultations'.

SATURDAY, APRIL 18

Air War: Pacific – **DOOLITTLE RAID.** 16 US Army AF B-25 Mitchell bombers, commanded by Lt.-Col. 'Jimmy' Doolittle, operating from carrier *Hornet*, make surprise daylight raid on Tokyo, Yokosuka naval base, Nagoya, Osaka and Kobe, and crash-land in E. China.
Air War: Europe – Heavy daylight raid on Malta.
Occupied France – Laval forms new Cabinet at Vichy, with himself as 'Chief of Govt.', Minister of Home and Foreign Affairs; Darlan becomes Supreme Commander of Armed Forces.
Russian Front – Siege of Leningrad: von Leeb, commanding German forces, relieved of duty.

SUNDAY, APRIL 19

Sea War – *U-130* shells Curaçao oil refinery.

MONDAY, APRIL 20

Sea War: Atlantic – Major reorganization of Allied convoy system: first of 11 new 'escort groups' commences regular patrols between 'WESTOMP' ('Western Ocean Meeting Point'), off Newfoundland, and 'EASTOMP', off Londonderry.
Occupied France – French Fascist leader Jacques Doriot survives assassination attempt at Rennes. Laval broadcasts on France's 'place' in the 'New Order'.
Home Front: USA – Roosevelt orders US Navy to take over 4 New York plants of inefficient Brewster Aeronautical Corp. (Brewster subsequently produce 735 Corsair fighters, but management problems persist and the works finally close July 1944.)

TUESDAY, APRIL 21

Occupied France – 20 French hostages executed at St Nazaire for alleged complicity with British during Op. Chariot.

WEDNESDAY, APRIL 22

Sea War – Maj. Lord Lovat and commandos raid Boulogne; Naval forces cripple 2 armed trawlers.

THURSDAY, APRIL 23

Air War: Britain – Baedeker Raids: *Luftwaffe* commences series of night reprisal raids on English cathedral cities (*see* March 28), allegedly selected from Baedeker Guidebook – Exeter, Bath, Norwich, York and Canterbury – 400 killed, Bath (April 25-26 and 26-27); station hit at York (April 28-29), Exeter (May 3-4) and Canterbury (May 31-June 1). Germans lose 40 aircraft.

Air War: Europe – First of 4 devastating RAF night raids on Rostock (April 23 to 26): 100,000 civilians (many panic-stricken) evacuated; Heinkel works badly hit.

Malta raid casualties: 1,031 killed, 1,245 seriously injured since June 1940.

Diplomacy – S. Africa breaks off diplomatic relations with Vichy.

Sea War: Atlantic – First 'milch cow' U-boat *U-459* refuels 14 other U-boats at secret rendezvous 805 km NE. of Bermuda (April 23-May 5).

FRIDAY, APRIL 24

Air War: Europe – Op. *Götz von Berlichingen*: cruiser *Kirov* receives further damage from *Luftwaffe* at Leningrad.

Home Front: Canada – Death of Lucy Maud Montgomery, author of 'Anne of Green Gables'; aged 67.

Secret War – Germans smash 'Autogiro' – SOE Spy Circuit in Paris (4 agents court-marshalled Dec. 1942 and sent to Colditz).

SATURDAY, APRIL 25

Air War – Heavy raid on Leningrad. Free French Bretagne bomber sqn. attacks Italian outposts in S. Libya.

SUNDAY, APRIL 26

Home Front: Germany – Reichstag rubber stamps Hitler's assumption of total dictatorial powers.

MONDAY, APRIL 27

Home Front: Canada – Conscription Plebiscite: voters in 8 provinces approve introduction of conscription for service overseas, but in Quebec there is 71% majority against. (*See* July 29, 1942.)

Home Front: Japan – HONKEIKO

COLLIERY DISASTER. World's worst ever mining disaster. Accidental gas/dust explosion at Japanese-operated mine in Manchuria kills 1,527 (mainly Chinese conscripts).

Air War: Europe – Halifaxes and Lancasters attack *Tirpitz* in Trondheim Fjord (nights April 27-28 and 28-29). 77 sorties, 7 aircraft lost. No hits.

TUESDAY, APRIL 28

Air War – Night raid on Alexandria (102 killed, 111 injured).

Japanese incendiary raid on Lashio, at S. end of Burma Road.

Home Front: USA – Office of Price Administration freezes prices of all essential items affecting cost of living.

WEDNESDAY, APRIL 29

Burma – JAPANESE CUT BURMA ROAD by seizing town of Lashio.

Philippines – Japanese 240-mm howitzers pound Corregidor.

Occupied Belgium – 250 killed in explosion at chemical works in Tessenderloo, Belgium.

Home Front: Britain – Rugby and Wallasey by-elections; Independent candidates win both seats.

Home Front: USA – Upper stories of New York skyscrapers blacked out and neon signs in Times Square dimmed (ARP measures).

Diplomacy – Hitler and Mussolini confer near Salzburg (April 29 and 30).

THURSDAY, APRIL 30

Sea War: Arctic – Cruiser *Edinburgh* torpedoed by *U-456*. Next day she is further damaged by 3 German destroyers (1 lost): *Edinburgh* sunk by RN.

Home Front: USSR – Stalin declares that USSR has no territorial ambitions and its sole aim is to liberate occupied Russian territory.

Sea War: Atlantic – Secret meteorological station established on Tristan da Cunha by SAAF and RN.

Air War: Pacific – Gen. H. H. George, USAAF, killed in air crash. During

Philippines Campaign, George's 'bamboo fleet' of 4 antiquated planes flew vital supplies from S. Philippines to Bataan. Aged 49.

FRIDAY, MAY 1

Russian Front – Siege of Sebastopol: May Day celebrations and demonstrations held despite German air raids and artillery fire. Siege of Leningrad: 448,694 civilians evacuated by boat across L. Ladoga, May-Nov. 1942.

Sea War: Atlantic – Destroyer *Punjabi* sunk in collision with battleship *King George V;* latter damaged by exploding depth charges.

Sea War: Med. – 2 U-boats sunk, while attempting to disrupt 'Tobruk Ferry' (May 1 and 2).

Home Front: USSR – Stalin's Order of the Day calling for total effort to achieve victory in 1942. Workers at Stalin Metal Plant at Kuznetsk and Kirov Tank Works pledge themselves to achieve unprecedented production targets. The example is followed throughout USSR ('Socialist Emulation Campaign').

SATURDAY, MAY 2

Burma – FALL OF MANDALAY.

Philippines – Japanese 240-mm AP shell blows up powder magazine on Corregidor, hurling super-heavy mortars into the air. 3,600 shells fall on I. in 5 hours.

SUNDAY, MAY 3

Air War: Europe – 'Baedeker' Raid on Exeter: 90 aircraft (7 lost) start conflagration in city centre. Cathedral and 9 churches wrecked; firemen and ARP personnel machine-gunned in bright moonlight. 2 He 111s, taking off from N. French airfield shot down by Sqn.-Ldr. Maclachlan, one-armed fighter pilot. RAF night raids on Hamburg, St Nazaire U-boat base and Kristiansand airfield (Norway). 5 bombers lost.

Occupied Denmark – Death of Thorvald

Below: *US prisoners pass their captors on Corregidor, May 7.*

NIMITZ, Chester William (1885-1966)
American: *Fleet Admiral*

One of America's greatest naval heroes. After surprise promotion to command Pacific Fleet at moment of supreme crisis, Dec. 1941, he displayed immense moral courage and professional expertise. Used the three existing carriers to strike telling blows at isolated Japanese island bases (Jan.-March 1942). Oversaw great victory in Coral Sea (May 1942) and decisive battle of Midway (June 1942). Organized relentless series of offensives which drove Japanese Fleet from the seas by late Oct. 1944.

Graduated from Annapolis Naval Academy, 1905. Served on China station, 1905-09. Commands in sub. service, 1909-19. Various surface ship commands and staff appointments, 1919-39. Chief, Bureau of Navigation, 1939-41, with rank of Rear-Adm.

Promoted over heads of 28 more senior officers to succeed Adm. Kimmel as CinC of Pacific Fleet, Dec. 17, 1941. Assumed command at Pearl Harbor, Dec. 31, 1941. CinC Pacific Ocean Areas, April 1942, with authority over all forces in theatre, except SW. Pacific. Transferred HQ to Guam after recapture, Aug. 1944. Fleet Admiral Nov. 1944. Signed Japanese surrender document for USA aboard flagship *Missouri*, Sept. 2, 1945.

Publications include, 'Sea Power' (1960) and 'The Great Sea War' (1961).

Stauning P.M. of Denmark, 1929-42; aged 68.

MONDAY, MAY 4

Sea War: Pacific – **BATTLE OF THE CORAL SEA** (May 4-8): first carrier-*versus*-carrier naval battle (opposing surface ships never exchange fire). Carriers *Lexington* and *Shoho* sunk; *Shokaku* seriously damaged. Japanese decide to abandon imminent landings at Port Moresby, New Guinea.
Burma – Japanese capture Akyab I.
Air War – German night raid on I. of Wight (repeated May 24-25 and June 3-4).

TUESDAY, MAY 5

Sea War: – Op. Ironclad: British forces land near Diego Suarez, Madagascar. Carriers *Illustrious* and *Indomitable* provide air cover – Vichy AMC and sub. sunk. British corvette *Auricula* mined.
Philippines – Japanese storm troops cross narrow strait from Bataan Peninsula to Corregidor and establish beachhead in the face of desperate US-Filipino resistance (night May 5-6).

WEDNESDAY, MAY 6

Burma – Stilwell's Chinese recapture Maymo.
Philippines – **FALL OF CORREGIDOR** and US forts in Manila Bay: Japanese take 12,495 prisoners, inc. Gens. Wainwright and King.

Philippines Campaign Losses
US and Filipino: 140,000. Japanese: 4,000.

Madagascar – Royal Marine Commandos, landed from destroyer *Anthony*, break stubborn resistance by Vichy troops at Diego Suarez.
Sea War – American sub. *Skipjack* sinks 3 Japanese ships during May in China Sea. Vichy gunboat *D'Entrecasteaux* crippled by bombing off Diego Suarez.

THURSDAY, MAY 7

Sea War – 24 Russian subs. (4 lost) carry out 77 supply missions to Sebastopol and evacuate wounded (May 7-July 2).
Vichy subs. *Le Heros* and *Monge* sunk off Diego Suarez.
Madagascar – Vichy French surrender Diego Suarez.
Home Front: Germany – State Armaments Council (*Rüstungsrat*) formed under Speer with Milch, 3 generals, 1 admiral and 8 representatives of the armaments industry.
Diplomacy – Peruvian Trade Agreement: Pres. Prado visits Washington. Expresses whole-hearted support for Pres. Roosevelt's policies and profound admiration for heroic efforts of the British people.

FRIDAY, MAY 8

Sea War – Japanese liner *Taiyo Maru* (14,000 t.) sunk by American sub. off Hong Kong. 780 oil industry experts and technicians, travelling to E. Indies to reactivate oilfields, are drowned.
Occupied Philippines – Pres. Quezon arrives in San Francisco.
Home Front: Britain – Sinclair, Sec. for Air, declares at Birmingham that the RAF does not wish to destroy historic German cities but *'we must and will destroy the enemy's means of making war – his defences, factories . . . wherever they may be found . . . a terrible summer is in prospect for the German Air Force. By day and night,* *in the air and on the ground they will be exposed to unrelenting attacks . . .'*.

SATURDAY, MAY 9

Russian Front – **BATTLE OF KHARKOV.** The front line sways back and forth in E. Ukraine throughout May and June, before Germans finally regain the initiative.

SUNDAY, MAY 10

Home Front: Britain – Churchill warns Germany in broadcast that Britain will retaliate if poison gas is used on Russian Front (unknown to British, *SS* killer squads have already used carbon monoxide gas vans to kill Soviet Jews).

MONDAY, MAY 11

Sea War: Med. – British destroyers *Lively*, *Kipling* and *Jackal* bombed by Ju 88s W. of Alexandria. Sister ship *Jervis* rescues 630 survivors.

TUESDAY, MAY 12

Russian Front – Russian 'South-West Front' (Army Grp.) launches counter-offensive from Barvenkovo Salient, S. of Kharkov.
Air War: – RAF Kittyhawks and Beaufighters attack formation of 16 Ju 52 troop-carriers off N. African coast: 9 shot down, 2 badly damaged.
Burma – Early monsoon breaks.

WEDNESDAY, MAY 13

Sea War – British MTBs sink torpedo boats *Iltis* and *Seeadler* (200 killed) escorting disguised raider *Stier* from Rotterdam to Bordeaux; MTB 220 lost.
Mexican tanker *Portrero dell Llano* sunk by U-boat off Miami; 13 killed (Mexico demands compensation May 15). Japanese liner *Nagasaki Maru* sinks on Japanese mine off Nagasaki; 39 killed (Capt. rescued but he commits *hara-kiri*).

THURSDAY, MAY 14

Sea War: Med. – Sub. *Turbulent* makes repeated attacks on heavily escorted Italian convoys making for Benghazi (May 14-29); sinking 3 merchant ships and destroyer *Emanuele Pessagno*.
Sea War: Atlantic – First major convoy op. along US E. Coast – from Hampton Roads (Virginia) to Key West (Florida).
Damaged cruiser *Trinidad* leaves Murmansk for Scapa Flow under heavy escort. Dive-bombed by Ju 88s and set on fire (scuttled, May 15).
Secret War – American experts – who have broken Japanese naval code – learn that Adm. Yamamoto plans complex op. to destroy US Pacific Fleet in Central Pacific. (*See* June 4, 1942.)

FRIDAY, MAY 15

Burma – Retreating British forces cross Indian border.
Air War: Europe – Rocket-powered fighter (Berezniak-Isnaev BI-1) flight-tested in USSR. *Stukas* attack shipping at Murmansk (repeated June 1 and 24).
China – Japanese forces in E. China launch punitive campaign in Chekiang province: 100 families massacred on suspicion of harbouring 'Doolittle's Raiders'; several thousand houses destroyed.
Home Front: USA – Petrol rationing introduced in 17 E. States and Washington DC.
Vichy France – 3 Vichy French warships – carrier *Béarn* and 2 cruisers – immobilized at Martinique at insistence of US Govt.

SATURDAY, MAY 16

Russian Front – GERMANS CAPTURE KERCH – dashing Russian hopes that siege of Sebastopol can be lifted.
Air War – RAF bombs Akyab (Burma).
Home Front: USA – Mrs Hobby appointed Director of Women's Auxiliary Army Corps.

SUNDAY, MAY 17

Russian Front – German counter-offensive against Barvenkovo Salient, which quickly forces Russians to abandon thrusts towards Kharkov and the Donbas (May 19).
Sea War: Pacific – US subs. *Tautog* and *Triton* sink Japanese subs. *I-28* and *I-164*, off Truk and Kagoshima, resp.
Home Front: India – Moslem fanatics (Hurs) derail Punjab Mail Train near Karachi, killing 25 passengers and injuring 140. 4 days later Hurs stop a bus at Mirpukhas and slaughter 13 passengers. (*See* June 1, 1942.)
Secret War – Op. *Kremlin:* German High Command makes unsuccessful attempt to mislead Red Army Intelligence into believing that the *Wehrmacht* is about to launch a major drive to capture Moscow.

MONDAY, MAY 18

Sea War: Med. – Adm. Harwood appointed CinC; Adm. Cunningham to head naval delegation to Washington.
Diplomacy – Malik appointed Soviet Ambassador in Tokyo.

TUESDAY, MAY 19

Air War – Doolittle awarded Congressional Medal of Honor for leading Tokyo Raid, April 18, 1942.
Air War – UN Air Training Conference in Ottawa, May 19-22 (enlarged Empire Air Training Scheme signed at Ottawa, June 5, 1942)

WEDNESDAY, MAY 20

Home Front: Germany – Göring exhorts munitions workers and farmers to 'rally and cling together. Like the front [line soldiers] welded together by blood, so must you be welded together by work.'
Sea War – Mexican tanker *Faja de Oro* sunk by U-boat off Florida.

Burma Campaign Losses
British, Indian and Burmese: 13,463 dead, wounded and missing of the 47,000 involved. Chinese: unknown; 95,000 involved. Japanese: 4,597 dead and wounded; 75,000 involved.

THURSDAY, MAY 21

Philippines – Japanese land in Leyte Gulf.
Air War – Op. *Herkules* – planned German airborne invasion of Malta – postponed indefinitely.
Diplomacy – Japan agrees to request by International Red Cross for representative to visit British PoWs.

FRIDAY, MAY 22

Air War – Lt.-Col. Kato, Japanese AAF fighter 'ace' (58 victories) disappears in his Nakajima fighter over Bay of Bengal.
Diplomacy – Mexico declares war on Germany, Italy and Japan (as from June 1).

SATURDAY, MAY 23

Russian Front – *Pz* spearheads trap 2 Russian armies in Barvenkovo Salient (Germans take 241,000 PoWs by May 31).
Home Front: USA – Grumman Hellcat naval fighter – designed to outclass Mitsubishi Zero – ordered into production 1 month ahead of prototype's first flight (production begins in Oct. while the Long I. assembly plant is still under construction!).

SUNDAY, MAY 24

Burma – Stilwell arrives Delhi after 20 days' trek through Burma-Assam jungle.

MONDAY, MAY 25

Sea War – Japanese repair ship *Asahi* (old battleship) sunk by American sub. *Salmon* in S. China Sea.
Home Front: Australia – 'Australia First' conspiracy: 3 men and a woman arrested at Perth for plotting to set up Fascist Govt.; to negotiate peace with Japan, assassinate politicians, Communists and Catholic priests and sterilize the Jews (2 men sentenced to imprisonment June 29).

TUESDAY, MAY 26

North Africa – Op. *Theseus.* Rommel attacks Gazala Line.

Diplomacy – Anglo-Soviet '20-year' Mutual Assistance Treaty.
Pastor Dietrich Bonhoeffer has secret 'peace talks' with Bishop of Chichester in Stockholm (May 26-31).
Sea War: Pacific – Japanese Combined Fleet sets out for Midway Op. (May 26-28).

WEDNESDAY, MAY 27

Occupied Czechoslovakia – 'HANGMAN' HEYDRICH ASSASSINATED. Deputy 'Protector' of Bohemia-Moravia and head of the SD ambushed while driving near Prague by 2 Free Czech agents (he is critically wounded by grenade and dies June 3); aged 38.
North Africa – Defence of Bir Hakeim: Free French Brig. under Koenig defies Rommel May 27-June 10 and rejects 3 surrender ultimatums. *Stukas* pound the French, who have to be supplied by air. Koenig obeys superior orders and withdraws night June 10-11.
China – Chinese evacuate Kinhwa after fierce fighting and severe Japanese bombing.
Sea War: Pacific – Damaged carrier *Yorktown* arrives Pearl Harbor for emergency repairs (completed in 48 hours).
Sea War: Arctic – 7 He 111s and 111 Ju 88s sink 5 ships of Convoy PQ.16.
Home Front: Japan – P.M. Tojo claims, in speech to Imperial Diet (Parliament), that Japan stands on the verge of 'ultimate victory'. Australia lies defenceless and must 'reconsider her attitude . . . or suffer the consequences. Japan will never sheathe the sword of righteousness until the influence of the Anglo-American Powers . . . has been completely uprooted.'
Home Front: South Africa – 50% reduction in size of postage stamps announced, in order to save paper.

THURSDAY, MAY 28

Air War – RAF pounds Rommel's *Pzs* as they attempt to pass through narrow gaps in British minefields.
Sea War: Pacific – 2 US task forces leave Pearl Harbor to intercept Japanese armada off Midway I.; they include 3 carriers, but no battleships (the Japanese have 4 carriers and 9 battleships).

FRIDAY, MAY 29

Diplomacy – Molotov, Soviet Foreign Minister in Washington (until June 4).
Home Front: USA – Death of John Barrymore, actor and movie star; aged 60.

SATURDAY, MAY 30

Russian Front – Special announcement from Hitler's HQ claims the great battle round Kharkov is ended and that the German and Axis forces have transformed their defence against strong enemy into a proud victory of annihilation and that the

Luftwaffe has driven the enemy out of the air.

Air War: Europe – **FIRST 'THOUSAND BOMBER' RAID ON COLOGNE** (Op. Millenium): 1,046 RAF bombers (inc. 101 with Polish crews and 367 bomber/trainers) – 40 lost – drop 1,455 t. of bombs. 600 acres of built-up area devastated by fire; 18,472 houses and buildings destroyed, 40,000 buildings damaged, 368 industrial plants hit and railway repair shops destroyed. Casualties: 486 killed, 5,027 injured, 59,100 homeless. Prior to this historic raid, Air Marshal Harris sends Message to all Bomber Cmnd. stations: *"Press home your attack . . . . with the utmost determination . . . . if you individually succeed the most shattering and devastating blow will have been delivered against the very vitals of the enemy. Let him have it – right on the chin!"* 50 RAF aircraft (2 lost) carry out diversionary raids on airfields in Germany and occupied territory.

Sea War – Japanese midget subs. torpedo battleship *Ramillies* and a tanker in Diego Suarez harbour, Madagascar (night May 30-31).

SUNDAY, MAY 31

Burma – 400,000 refugees have crossed Burma-India frontier since Dec. 1941.

Air War: Europe – Mosquitoes fly their first bombing sorties against German city (Cologne).

Home Front: Britain – Air raid casualties April-May, 1942: 1,337 killed, 1,423 injured.

Sea War: Pacific – Japanese midget subs. penetrate Sydney Harbour: old SS *Kuttabul* sunk (21 killed).

MONDAY, JUNE 1

Air War: Europe – 'THOUSAND BOMBER' RAID ON ESSEN AND THE RUHR. 950 aircraft (31 lost) are sent, but cloud hampers bombing.

Sea War: Pacific – Seaplane launched from sub. *I-26* reconnoitres Seattle.

Home Front: India – Martial law declared in Sind following repeated outrages by the Hurs; aircraft and paratroops have to be employed; 2,000 Hurs captured June-July; 69 hanged.

Home Front: Germany – Himmler takes control of ARP (*Luftschutz*).

Russian Front – Siege of Sebastopol: German super-heavy mortars and world's largest artillery piece – 80-cm *Dora* – bombard fortifications. German aircraft fly up to 18 bombing sorties per day.

Diplomacy – Burmese Govt. to be re-established at Simla (India).

TUESDAY, JUNE 2

N. Africa – Rommel destroys 150th Brigade.

WEDNESDAY, JUNE 3

Sea War: Pacific – Japanese carrier planes raid Dutch Harbor, Aleutian Is.

Air War: Britain – Night raid on Poole.

THURSDAY, JUNE 4

Sea War: Pacific – **BATTLE OF MIDWAY** (June 4-6): Japanese Combined Fleet attempts to lure US Pacific Fleet into trap off Midway Atoll (NW. of Hawaii), but complex battle plan completely misfires. Dauntless dive-bombers cripple carriers *Akagi*, *Kaga*, *Soryu* and *Hiryu* and 2 cruisers; Americans lose carrier *Yorktown*, 1 destroyer and 179 aircraft.

FRIDAY, JUNE 5

North Africa – 8th Army engages Rommel.

Diplomacy – USA declares war on Bulgaria, Hungary and Rumania.

Sea War – Japanese subs. active in Mozambique Channel.

Home Front: USA – Roosevelt condemns use of 'poisonous and noxious gases' by Japanese forces in China and warns Japan that if such actions continue the USA will retaliate 'in kind'.

SATURDAY, JUNE 6

Sea War: Atlantic – Disguised raider *Stier* sinks Panamanian tanker *Stanvac Calcutta* (10,200 t.).

Home Front: Britain – Undetected German bomb (probably dropped May 1941) explodes near Elephant and Castle, London: 20 killed, 59 injured.

Air War – Hurricane 'tank-busters' in action over Libya for first time.

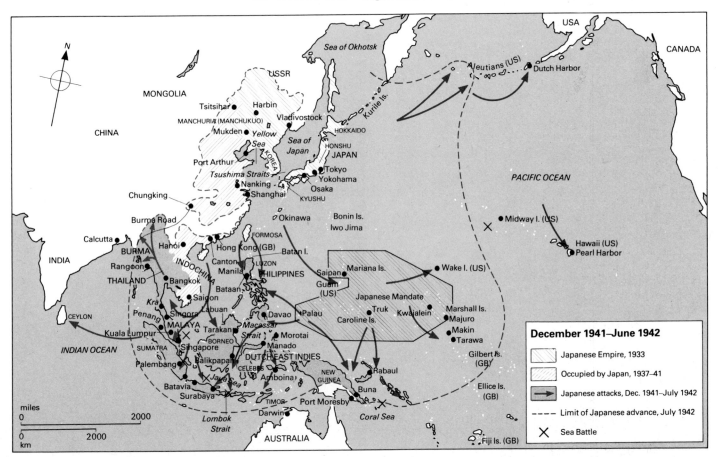

December 1941–June 1942

▨ Japanese Empire, 1933

▨ Occupied by Japan, 1937–41

➤ Japanese attacks, Dec. 1941–July 1942

--- Limit of Japanese advance, July 1942

✕ Sea Battle

MIDWAY......
THE DECISIVE NAVAL BATTLE

In only six months the Japanese overran all the British, Dutch and American colonies in the Far East. Japanese fleets blazed a fiery trail of destruction across two oceans, from Hawaii to Ceylon. And yet Japan's leaders knew that their war could not be considered as won until the remnants of the US Pacific Fleet had been forced to give battle and annihilated.

Even so, the one man in Japan with prime responsibility for arranging such a decisive confrontation – Admiral Yamamoto – did not issue final orders on the subject until May 5, 1942. This extraordinary delay had resulted from the Japanese Naval CinC's decision to disperse the precious fleet of six aircraft carriers – his most deadly striking force – for secondary operations in the Central Pacific, South China Sea, Indian Ocean, South-West Pacific and Coral Sea. As a result, he was unable to reassemble the carrier striking force – less *Shokaku* and *Zuikaku,* which were non-operational after the battle of the Coral Sea (May 7-8) – until the last week of May 1942. Although the absence of these two big ships was offset by the availability of five other carriers (the new *Junyo* and four older, light carriers) Yamamoto unwisely chose to employ two of these in a diversionary attack on the Aleutian Islands and relegate others to second-line escort duties, while the four veteran carriers bore the brunt of the real fighting in the area of Midway Atoll.

These faulty tactical dispositions exemplify the fatal flaws which ran right through Yamamoto's entire, excessively complex, plan for the 'decisive battle' of Midway. According to his American opposite-number, Admiral Nimitz, 'Even with the most complete warning, [US signals experts had broken the secret Japanese naval code] it is inconceivable that the three United States carriers could by any combination of luck and skill have defeated and turned back the 8 carriers, 11 battleships and immense number of supporting vessels . . . had the Japanese fleet been concentrated.

As it was, June 3 [1942]... found the Japanese surface ships in no fewer than ten groups scattered all over the North and Central Pacific... when the crisis developed Yamamoto found his force were too widely separated for mutual support. He found, after a vain attempt, that he could not bring the scattered groups together in time to retrieve the situation.'*

Perhaps the real truth is that, when it came to the crunch, not only Admiral Yamamoto, but also the Imperial Japanese Navy were unprepared and ill-equipped to wage modern naval warfare on the grand scale. For, quite apart from their grave shortcomings in the field of strategy, the Japanese also made serious tactical mistakes at Midway. Although no fewer than 29 large 'cruiser' submarines had been allocated to the operation, these craft failed completely in their prime task of informing Yamamoto that the Pacific Fleet had left Pearl Harbor. This calamity was all the more deplorable and inexplicable since the Japanese submarine-building programme had been geared, since 1918, to the

Below left: B5N 'Kate' Japanese torpedo-bombers from Hiryu attack USS Yorktown on the afternoon of June 4, 1942. She suffered two torpedo and three earlier bomb hits, being finished off by the Japanese sub. I-168 on June 7.

Below right: US Douglas SBD Dauntless dive-bombers over a victim on the morning of June 4. Three Japanese carriers were crippled in five minutes by 55 Dauntlesses.

proposition that the true *forte* of this type of war vessel was scouting (reconnaissance) for the main battle fleet.

The four carriers of Admiral Nagumo's 1st Mobile Force – the most vital ships in Yamamoto's armada – were inadequately escorted. Unlike the US Navy who were quick to learn that battleships were invaluable as heavy floating anti-aircraft batteries operating in close concert with a carrier force, Yamamoto dispersed his powerful force of battleships even before the main battle of Midway had begun. The weak AA defences of the carriers were especially significant because these ships had not been constructed with armoured flight decks – as fitted in British carriers – and there was no such thing as early-warning radar in the Japanese Navy.

As a result of all these and numerous other errors of judgement, the Americans were able to sink all four Japanese carriers which attacked Midway on June 4, 1942. Some 3,500 Japanese sailors and airmen were killed or drowned compared with only 307 Americans; 280 first-line Japanese aircraft were lost as against 179 American. However, the bulk of the latter were obsolete Douglas Devastator torpedo planes, a type which was soon to be completely supplanted aboard US carriers by the formidable new Grumman Avenger. Although the damaged US carrier *Yorktown* was sunk by a Japanese submarine after the main battle, Midway was a decisive material and moral victory for the Americans, and the end of Japan's career of conquest in the Pacific.

*The Great Sea War, Chester W. Nimitz.

SUNDAY, JUNE 7

Russian Front – Siege of Sebastopol: Manstein's 11th Army attempts to storm Russian defences, but initially makes little progress.
Sea War: Pacific – Japanese land at Attu and Kiska Is., in American-owned Aleutian archipelago.

MONDAY, JUNE 8

Home Front: Germany – State Funeral of Heydrich in Berlin: Himmler eulogizes his former deputy and promises vengeance.

TUESDAY, JUNE 9

Russian Front – Renewed German offensive in Kharkov sector.

WEDNESDAY, JUNE 10

Russian Front – 1st *Pz* Army and Paulus' 6th Army drive Russians back on broad front E. of Kharkov, capturing Volchansk and Kupyansk and reaching R. Oskol (June 10-26).
Sea War – Russian supply convoy destroyed by Ju 88s while unloading at Sebastopol.
Occupied Czechoslovakia – **DESTRUCTION OF LIDICE.** *SS* depopulate and totally destroy village of Lidice, near Prague (some of the inhabitants are suspected of helping assassins of Heydrich). 173 men and boys shot, 198 women and 98 children deported to concentration camp.

Home Front: Britain – Death of Stanley Lupino, actor and comedian; aged 48.

THURSDAY, JUNE 11

Sea War: Atlantic – U-boats lay mines off Boston (Mass.), Delaware and Chesapeake Bay during June.

Diplomacy – Soviet-Canadian agreement to reopen diplomatic relations.

FRIDAY, JUNE 12

Sea War: Med. – Double convoy op. (Harpoon and Vigorous): British convoys attempt to reach Malta from Gibraltar (Harpoon) and Alexandria (Vigorous): German and Italian aircraft and warships, subs. and mines take a heavy toll (6 merchant ships sunk and 2 damaged, 6 warships sunk and 9 damaged) and Alexandria convoy turns back; Convoy Harpoon reaches Malta. Italian cruiser *Trento* torpedoed and sunk by Beaufort aircraft and sub. *Umbra;* battleship *Littorio* hit by a bomb and torpedo.
Air War: Europe – American Liberators bomb Ploesti and Constanta (Rumania). 4 planes crash-land in Turkey (crews interned). Single RAF Beaufighter drops *tricolor* flag over Arc de Triomphe and strafes *Gestapo* HQ, Paris.

SATURDAY, JUNE 13

North Africa – 8th Army loses 138 tanks before noon; only 75 tanks operational by dusk.
Secret War – British discover that US Military Attaché in Cairo is sending messages which are being intercepted by the Germans and read to Rommel.

SUNDAY, JUNE 14

Sea War – *Roma* – newest and last Italian battleship – completed at Trieste (she joins the Fleet Nov. 1942).

Above: *Three of Lidice's destroyers pose beside the buildings they have blown up, never since repaired.*

Secret War – Op. Pastorius: 2 U-boats each land a 4-man team of saboteurs on US Eastern Seaboard – at Long I. (June 14) and near Jacksonville, Florida (June

17). All are subsequently captured before they can commence ops. 6 executed.

MONDAY, JUNE 15

Sea War: Atlantic – *U-552* sinks 5 ships from Convoy HG.84.
Home Front: Britain – Unemployment now below 100,000.

TUESDAY, JUNE 16

Sea War: Med. – Cruiser *Hermione* sunk by *U-205* S. of Crete.

WEDNESDAY, JUNE 17

North Africa – 8th Army withdraws E. of Tobruk.
Sea War – Destroyer *Wild Swan* shoots down 6 of 12 German bombers. She is crippled and finally sinks after colliding with a Spanish trawler.
Secret War – Kornilov and Pavlov (2 NKVD agents) sentenced to 20 years' imprisonment at Ankara for attempted assassination of von Papen. *(See* Feb. 24, 1942.)
Diplomacy – Churchill makes 27-hour non-stop flight from Stranraer (Scotland) to Washington to confer with Roosevelt.

THURSDAY, JUNE 18

Russian Front – Siege of Sebastopol: German 11th Army, reinforced by elements of 17th Army, breaks through defences and reaches North Bay.
Neutrals: Turkey – Rail links between Turkey and Central Europe (severed April 1941) re-opened.

FRIDAY, JUNE 19

Occupied Czechoslovakia – Gen. Elias, ex-P.M. of 'puppet' régime in Bohemia-Moravia Protectorate, executed by firing squad (Elias had been arrested by Heydrich, Sept. 1941, and condemned to death, Oct. 1941). Aged 52.

SATURDAY, JUNE 20

Sea War: Atlantic – Last of 8 grps. of U-boats despatched to American E. Coast since Jan. 1942 fail to find 'worthwhile targets' (i.e., ships sailing independently, without adequate escort). 2 U-boats are sunk and, on July 19, remainder are ordered away.
Sea War: Pacific – Sub. *I-26* shells Govt. telegraph station on Vancouver I. (no damage).

SUNDAY, JUNE 21

North Africa – **FALL OF TOBRUK.** Germans take 32,000 prisoners, several hundred guns and 100 tanks. Rommel pursues 8th Army to Mersa Matruh (June 21-26).

Gazala and Tobruk Losses

British: 15,000 dead and wounded, 45,000 PoWs; 1,000 tanks, 400 guns. German: 3,360 dead and wounded. Italian: c. 3,000 dead and wounded.

Air War: Britain – Night raid on Southampton.

MONDAY, JUNE 22

Diplomacy – Litvinov, Soviet Ambassador to USA, demands immediate launching of a 'Second Front', during speech in New York.
Russian Front – Rumanian casualties in 12 months: 157,572.

TUESDAY, JUNE 23

Russian Front – Siege of Sebastopol: Russians withdraw from N. shore of North Bay.
Air War – Heavy bombers of US 10th AAF ordered from India to Egypt to support British 8th Army.
Secret War – RAF captures Focke-Wulf FW 190 – latest German piston-engined fighter – which the pilot lands by mistake at Pembrey, S. Wales.

WEDNESDAY, JUNE 24

Air War: Britain – First of 4 attempted night raids on Birmingham during 1942 – only 2 (July 27-28 and 29-30) find the target.
Occupied Yugoslavia – In Yugoslavia 2 major offensives by German, Italian and 'puppet' troops (Jan. – June 1942) force Tito's Partisans to retreat 241 km from Serbia into Croatia.

THURSDAY, JUNE 25

Air War: Europe – 'THOUSAND-BOMBER' RAID ON BREMEN. 1,006 aircraft despatched (49 lost) inc. 272 bomber/trainers and 102 Coastal Cmmd. machines. First successful test of 'Gee' 'blind-bombing' equipment against major target. Focke-Wulf works badly damaged and 27 acres of business district destroyed.
North Africa – Auchinleck sacks Ritchie and takes personal command of 8th Army.
Home Front: USA – Maj.-Gen. Eisenhower appointed Cdr. of US Forces in Europe.

FRIDAY, JUNE 26

Sea War: Atlantic – Germany announces 'blockade' of American E. Coast.
North Africa – 8th Army carries out 'panic' retreat from Mersa Matruh – unaware that Rommel's forces are virtually exhausted.
Home Front: Germany – Rommel promoted to Field Marshal.

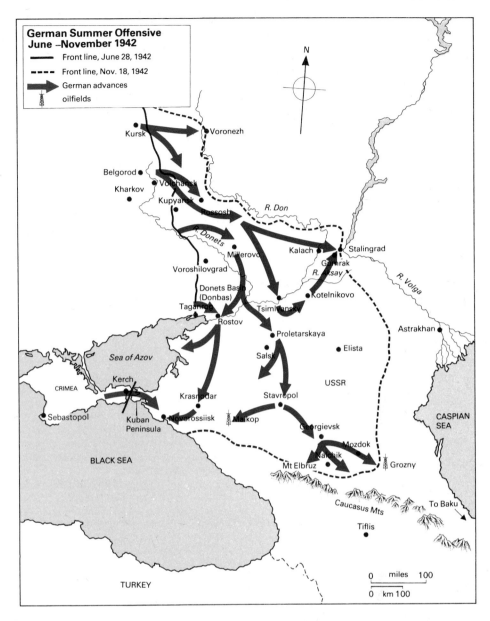

German Summer Offensive June –November 1942
— Front line, June 28, 1942
--- Front line, Nov. 18, 1942
➤ German advances
oilfields

SATURDAY, JUNE 27

Sea War – Russian destroyer *Tashkent* evacuates 2,300 wounded and civilians from Sebastopol: she is bombed repeatedly *en route* to Novorossisk, but transfers her passengers and reaches port before sinking.
Air War: Britain – Night raid on Weston-super-Mare (repeated June 28-29): serious fire damage.
Neutrals: Argentina – Pres. Ortiz resigns because of failing eyesight. Succeeded by Dr Castillo.

SUNDAY, JUNE 28

Russian Front – Siege of Sebastopol: Germans establish bridgehead on S. shore of North Bay, directly threatening Sebastopol city (night June 28-29). **AXIS SUMMER OFFENSIVE** (Op. *Blau:* 'Blue') begins on S. front, with 100 divs. (50 German, 9 Italian, 27 Rumanian, 13 Hungarian and 1 Slovak) supported by

1,500 aircraft. Russians have 120 divs. German 2nd Army and 4th *Pz* Army drive E. from Kursk towards Voronezh.

MONDAY, JUNE 29

North Africa – Rommel takes Mersa Matruh and 6,000 PoWs.
Air War – Mussolini flies to Derna (Libya), in aircraft marked with Red Crosses to lead expected Axis 'victory parade' through Cairo.

TUESDAY, JUNE 30

Air War – Siege of Sebastopol: Germans break into the city. Attempted evacuation of garrison begins.
Russian Front – Col.-Gen. von Küchler, German commander on Leningrad Front, promoted to Field-Marshal.
North Africa – Rommel reaches El Alamein.
Sea War – **EVACUATION OF SEBASTOPOL.** Russian subs. and small

naval craft take off small numbers of troops (June 30-July 3), but larger vessels are unable to approach owing to severity of German-Italian air/sea blockade.

Returning from successful cruise in Gulf of Mexico (12 ships sunk) *U-158* is sunk off Bermuda by US Martin Mariner flying boat.

Sea War: Med. – Sub. depot ship *Medway* sunk off Port Said by *U-372*.

WEDNESDAY, JULY 1

North Africa – **FIRST BATTLE OF EL ALAMEIN.** Rommel reaches El Alamein, having advanced 644 km in 36 days, and immediately attempts to push on towards Alexandria. Gen. Auchinleck calls for 'supreme effort' from 8th Army.

Air War: China – American bombers raid Hankow – main Japanese supply base in China.

Neutrals: Sweden – Athletics: Gundar Haegg sets new world mile record of 4 min. 6.2 sec., beating Wooderson's 1937 mark by 1.4 sec. (Haegg achieves time of 4 min. 1.4 sec., July 17, 1945.)

Diplomacy – Finland establishes diplomatic relations with the Vatican.

Home Front: Britain – Wardlaw Milne moves vote of censure against Churchill in the Commons for mismanagement of the war effort. (Churchill wins the vote 476-25, July 2.)

Occupied Poland – US-Polish Lease-Lend Agreement.

Occupied France – Death of Leon Daudet, French satirical writer and editor of Royalist anti-Semitic newspaper *Action Française;* aged 74.

THURSDAY, JULY 2

Russian Front – Germans bomb Russian warships at Novorossisk.

Diplomacy – Wheat Agreement between GB, USA, Argentina, Australia and Canada.

FRIDAY, JULY 3

Russian Front – **SIEGE OF SEBASTOPOL ENDS.**

Diplomacy – Axis Powers promise Egypt complete independence and national sovereignty.

SATURDAY, JULY 4

Sea War: Arctic – **DESTRUCTION OF CONVOY PQ. 17.** Following damaging attacks by German torpedo planes and U-boats and threatening movements by *Tirpitz, Admiral Scheer* and *Lützow*, Convoy is ordered to scatter and all escorting warships are withdrawn. 24 ships sunk by bombers, torpedo planes and U-boats, July 5-10. 13 ships reach N. Russian harbours by July 28. German losses: 5 aircraft.

Sea War: Pacific – AVG 'Flying Tigers'

Above: *Scots Guards and a Matilda tank attack at Alamein, July 4.*

incorporated in USAAF and redesignated 'China Air Task Force' – few survivors of original complement of P-40 fighters, supplemented by 1 grp. of B-24s and 2 sqns. of B-25s. *(See* March 10, 1943.)

North Africa – Stubborn resistance by 8th Army and ceaseless Allied air raids compel Rommel to abandon his assault on the Alamein 'Line'.

SUNDAY, JULY 5

Russian Front – Germans reach R. Don, near Voronezh.

Sea War: Pacific – 4 Japanese destroyers torpedoed by US submarines off Aleutian Is: *Arare* and *Nenohi* sunk; *Kasumi* and *Shiranuhi* damaged.

MONDAY, JULY 6

Sea War: Atlantic – *U-132* attacks convoy in Gulf of St Lawrence and sinks 3 ships.

Air War: Britain – Incendiary raid on Middlesbrough (night July 6-7).

TUESDAY, JULY 7

Russian Front – Germans capture Voronezh on R. Don, NW. of Stalingrad.

Sea War – Russian marines attempt to seize Someri I. in Gulf of Finland, but are routed by Finnish naval and air forces (July 9).

WEDNESDAY, JULY 8

Occupied Greece – Death of Marshal Franchet d'Esperey, hero of the Salonika Campaign, where he crushed the German-Bulgarian forces in 10 days (Sept. 1918). Aged 86.

THURSDAY, JULY 9

Sea War – German MTBs sink a tanker

and 4 coasters in English Channel.

Occupied Holland – Anne Frank and family (Dutch Jews) go into hiding in the Prinsengacacht, a large building in centre of Amsterdam. Here they remain for next 2 years until betrayed to Gestapo. Anne Frank dies in Buchenwald, Feb. 1945 (Dr Frank survives and publishes his daughter's diary after the war).

FRIDAY, JULY 10

Sea War – *U-160* and *U-66* commence successful ops. around Trinidad (15 ships sunk in 2 months).

SATURDAY, JULY 11

Air War: Europe – Lancasters bomb Schichau U-boat yards at Danzig in thunderstorm (longest daylight raid to date); several aircraft stray over W. Sweden and Swedish fighters are scrambled.

Sea War: Med. – S. African armed whalers *Protea* and *Southern Maid* sink Italian sub. *Ondina* off Beirut.

SUNDAY, JULY 12

Russian Front – 'Stalingrad Front' army grp. established to defend city.

Home Front: USA – Stern Park Gardens, near Joliet (Illinois), renamed 'Lidice' in honour of the martyred Czech village.

MONDAY, JULY 13

Sea War: Pacific – 3 Japanese subs. operate off Sydney (5 ships sunk in July-Aug.).

Secret War – Roosevelt creates Office of Strategic Services (OSS) to replace COI; names Donovan as Director.

TUESDAY, JULY 14

Occupied France – Free French movement is renamed *La France Combattante*.

MANSTEIN, Fritz Erich von (1887-1973)
German: *Field Marshal*

Probably greatest German strategist of W.W.II. His brilliant plan for *Panzer* breakthrough in N. France was followed by great successes as field commander in Russian Campaign, especially in the Caucasus and Battle of Kharkov.

Born in Berlin, of Polish ancestry. Christened Lewinski; adopted by von Manstein family. Served briefly in W.W.I, before going to War Academy. Various staff posts, 1917-18. Major, 1927; Col., 1933. Head of Ops. Dept. of Gen. Staff, 1935. Deputy Chief of Gen. Staff, with rank of Maj-Gen., 1937. Fell into official disfavour due to unorthodox, outspoken views on strategic questions.

COS to CinC East, Aug. 1939. Similar position in Rundstedt's Army Group A, Oct. 1939. Demoted to command of 38th Inf. Corps, Feb. 1940. Led this corps with conspicuous success, during French campaign. Gen. of Inf., June 1940. Named as cdr. of 56th Motorized Corps for invasion of Russia. Subsequently held high commands on Russian Front. Captured Sebastopol after bloody siege, July 1942. Made strenuous but unavailing efforts to save 6th Army, trapped at Stalingrad. Skilfully extricated outnumbered German right wing (Army Grp. A) from the Caucasus. Then staged surprise counter-attack at Kharkov, which temporarily stabilized the front. Imprisoned for alleged war crimes against Russian PoWs and Jews, 1946-53. War memoirs, 'Lost Victories' (1959).

Home Front: India – Congress Party Working Committee calls for ending of British rule and campaign of 'civil disobedience'.

WEDNESDAY, JULY 15

Air War – 200 Spitfires carry out offensive sweep over N. France. Wing Cdr. 'Paddy' Finucane – 21-year-old 'ace' (32 victories) – shot down and killed by machine gun fire near Le Touquet.
Neutrals: Argentina – Death of ex-President Ortiz; aged 55.
Sea War – Op. EON 18: Russian destroyer sqn. transferred from Vladivostok to Kola Inlet, via Bering Str. (July 15-Oct. 14).
Home Front: Brazil – Petrol rationing introduced.

THURSDAY, JULY 16

Sea War: Med. – Turkish tanker *Antares* torpedoed by Italian sub. *Alagi* and beached on Lebanon coast.

FRIDAY, JULY 17

Russian Front – Germans capture Voroshilovgrad, chief town of Donets coalfield.

SATURDAY, JULY 18

Air War: Europe – Lancasters fly daylight mission to the Ruhr and bomb Duisburg.
Home Front: Germany – First flight of Me 262 V3, prototype jet fighter, at Leipheim, near Ulm.

SUNDAY, JULY 19

Air War: Europe – Capt. Antonio Lavat, cdr. of *Esquadra Azul* ('Blue Sqn.') – Spanish volunteer fighter unit in Russia – killed in action.

MONDAY, JULY 20

Air War: Europe – Russians bomb airfields in N. Norway. 200 Spitfires strafe 'targets of opportunity' over N. France (1 aircraft collides with a tree).

TUESDAY, JULY 21

New Guinea – Japanese land at Buna, N. of Port Moresby: which they plan to capture by advancing over Owen Stanley Mtns.

WEDNESDAY, JULY 22

Home Front: India – Ban on Communist Party lifted.

THURSDAY, JULY 23

Russian Front – Hitler orders simultaneous operations against Stalingrad and the Caucasus, thereby compromising the chances of capturing either objective. Hoth's 4th Pz Army ordered to abandon its direct advance on Stalingrad (thereby depriving 6th Army of vital support) and push S. to assist Kleist's 1st Pz Army to cross R. Don. Hitler dismisses Bock, CinC Army Grp. B. on Don front.

FRIDAY, JULY 24

Sea War: Atlantic – Adm. Dönitz, broadcasting from Berlin, describes the ever-increasing threat to his sub. ops. from British and American warships and aircraft, which are *'always on the heels of our U-boats'*.
Occupied Yugoslavia – US-Yugoslav Lease-Lend Agreement.

SATURDAY, JULY 25

Russian Front – Kleist's *Pzs* begin crossing R. Don.
North Africa – British and American Chiefs of Staff decide to carry out Op. Torch (formerly 'Super-Gymnast') – seaborne invasion of Vichy French N. Africa. led by Gen. Eisenhower – thereby opening a 'Second Front' in Africa. (*See* Nov. 8, 1942.)

SUNDAY, JULY 26

Air War: Europe – RAF Bomber Cmnd. drops 175,000 IBs on Hamburg.
Russian 8th Air Army and 4-engined Pe-8s of the ADD ('Long-range Bombing Force') carry out round-the-clock ops. in support of hard-pressed 62nd Army, SW. of Stalingrad.
Home Front: Britain – Chocolates and confectionary rationed.

MONDAY, JULY 27

Air War: Britain – 30 German raiders, operating singly in cloudy weather over many parts of England, bomb 2 airfields, 4 factories and 4 railway junctions (50 people killed). Night raid on Birmingham.

TUESDAY, JULY 28

Home Front: Britain – Death of Sir Matthew Flinders Petrie, archaeologist; aged 89.

WEDNESDAY, JULY 29

Russian Front – Hoth's *Pzs* capture Tsimlyanskaya, on R. Don, SW. of Stalingrad. Farther S. Kleist's *Pzs* capture Proletarskaya.
New Guinea – Japanese advancing on Port Moresby take Kokoda, 80 km S. of Buna.
Air War – RAF night raid on Saarbrücken (9 bombers lost).
Home Front: Canada – National Resources Mobilization Act amended by Parliament to permit introduction of conscription for overseas service – despite strong opposition from French-Canadian Liberals.
Diplomacy – London Combined Production and Resources Board established under Lyttleton, British Minister of Production, and Harriman, US Lease-Lend representative.

THURSDAY, JULY 30

Air War: Britain – New type of incendiary bomb used in night raids on W. Midlands (damage in Wolverhampton).
Air War: China – American P-40s repulse series of Japanese raids on Hengyang air base, SW. China (July 30-31)
China – Chinese recapture Tsingtien.

FRIDAY, JULY 31

Russian Front – Germans cross R. Don on wide front.

Air War: Europe – 630 RAF bombers (inc. 211 bomber/trainers) make concentrated 50-min. night raid on Düsseldorf; light raids on airfields in Low Countries and rail targets in France (30 bombers and 1 fighter 'intruder' lost).

Sea War: Atlantic – *U-754* sunk by RCAF plane off Nova Scotia. Carrier *Essex* launched at Newport News, Virginia.

SATURDAY, AUGUST 1

Sea War – Op. Stab: British Eastern Fleet carries out protracted manoeuvres in Bay of Bengal in attempt to divert Japanese naval forces from SW. Pacific before Op. Watchtower. (*See* Aug. 8.)

SUNDAY, AUGUST 2

Home Front: India – Mahatma Gandhi warns that Indian people will welcome Japanese invasion unless British grant full independence.

MONDAY, AUGUST 3

Air War: Europe – Russian naval planes attack *Luftwaffe* bomber base near Sea of Azov.

TUESDAY, AUGUST 4

Home Front: Britain – House of Commons passes Bill transferring jurisdiction over offences committed by American servicemen from British civil courts to US military tribunals.

WEDNESDAY, AUGUST 5

North Africa – Churchill visits 8th Army; decides to replace Auchinleck.

Russian Front – Heavy fighting in Rzhev sector (Central Front).

THURSDAY, AUGUST 6

Diplomacy – British Govt. formally denounces Munich Agreement of Sept. 1938. Queen Wilhelmina of Holland addresses joint session of US Congress.

FRIDAY, AUGUST 7

Solomons – Op. Watchtower: **US MARINES LAND ON GUADAL-CANAL** and Tulagi. On the former the few Japanese construction troops and Korean labourers flee into the jungle. Small Japanese garrison on Tulagi annihilated after fierce fighting. Marines rename half-completed airfield on Guadalcanal 'Henderson Field', after a hero of Battle of Midway.

North Africa – Gen. Gott, 8th Army CinC designate, killed when plane shot down.

SATURDAY, AUGUST 8

Russian Front – Germans reach Maikop oilfield (Caucasus), which has been destroyed.

Sea War: Pacific – **BATTLE OF SAVO** (night Aug. 8-9): Japanese cruisers destroy 4 cruisers – USS *Astoria*, *Quincey* and *Vincennes* and HMAS *Canberra* – off Savo I., near Guadalcanal. Japanese cruisers *Chokai* and *Kinugasa* damaged. During return journey Japanese sqn. loses cruiser *Kako* (sunk by US sub. *S-44*).

SUNDAY, AUGUST 9

Sea War: Pacific – Following Savo I. debacle, all US transports and escorting warships have to be temporarily withdrawn from Guadalcanal area.

Air War – US bombers raid Haiphong (Indo-China).

Home Front: India – Mahatma Gandhi and Nehru arrested for leading Civil Disobedience Campaign. Widespread outbreaks of sabotage and bloody riots (721 killed, 1,219 injured).

MONDAY, AUGUST 10

Sea War: Med. – **OP. PEDESTAL.** 14-ship British convoy leaves Gibraltar for Malta under heavy escort – only 4 transports and burning tanker *Ohio* reach Malta, Aug. 13-15. From Aug. 11-14 they are battered by Axis aircraft, subs. and MTBs. Ships sunk: carrier *Eagle*, cruisers *Cairo* and *Manchester*, destroyer *Foresight* and 7 merchant vessels. Ships badly damaged: carrier *Indomitable*, 2 cruisers, 1 destroyer and 7 merchant vessels. 2 Italian subs. rammed and sunk by British destroyers.

Air War: Britain – Night raid on Colchester and E. Anglia: direct hit on mental hospital (heavy casualties).

Russian Front – Paulus' 6th Army reaches outskirts of Stalingrad; Hoth's *Pzs* drive towards city from SW.

TUESDAY, AUGUST 11

Air War: Europe – Destructive RAF night raid on Mainz (repeated Aug. 12-13); Cathedral destroyed.

Sea War: Med. – Carrier *Eagle* sunk by *U-73* N. of Algiers (260 killed).

Sea War – Japanese Combined Fleet leaves home waters for Truk (Caroline Is.) to counter US landings on Guadalcanal.

WEDNESDAY, AUGUST 12

Diplomacy – First Moscow Conference: Churchill informs Stalin that there can be no 'Second Front' in Europe until 1943 and reveals details of Op. Torch. (*See* July 25, 1942.)

THURSDAY, AUGUST 13

Sea War: Med. – Powerful force of Italian cruisers and destroyers departs Naples to strike battered Convoy 'Pedestal', but turns back when the promised close air cover fails to appear. Cruisers *Bolzano* and *Muzio Attendolo* are then torpedoed by British sub. *Unbroken*, off Lipari Is.

North Africa – Montgomery takes command of 8th Army.

FRIDAY, AUGUST 14

Sea War: Med. – 74 German and Italian aircraft, 2 subs. and an MTB make unsuccessful attacks on British cruiser-

ALEXANDER, Harold Rupert Leofric George (1891-1969)
British: *Field Marshal, Viscount Alexander of Tunis and Errigal;* 'Alex'

CinC of Allied armies in North Africa and Italy, 1942-45. Twice, in Tunisia and N. Italy, he brought about the capitulation in the open field of an entire Axis army group. His charm, tact, modest simplicity and sheer professionalism made Alexander a living legend.

Son of 4th Earl of Caledon. Educated at Harrow and Sandhurst. Received commission in Irish Guards. Outstanding young British officer of his generation in W.W.I ; twice wounded. Led brigade of Baltic German volunteers to free Latvia from Communist rule, 1919-20. Served on NW. Frontier of India, 1935.

Assumed command of 1st Corps, BEF, at Dunkirk, May 1940; organized final stages of Evacuation and left on one of last destroyers. GOCinC Southern Command, 1940-42. GOC Burma, March-July 1942: conducted masterly retreat, fighting numerous delaying actions against previously triumphant Japanese. Narrowly escaped capture near Rangoon, March 1942. CinC Middle East, Aug. 1942, in overall command of Montgomery's 8th Army. Deputy to Eisenhower, Jan. 1943, in command of Allied forces in Tunisia. Deputy CinC of Med. Combined Ops, May 1943. SAC, Med. Theatre, 1944-45.

Field Marshal, Viscount and Knight of the Garter, 1946. Last British-born Gov-Gen. of Canada, 1946-52. Min. of Defence in Churchill's last administration, 1952-54. Published 'Battle of Tunis' (1957); 'The Alexander Memoirs, 1940-1945' (1962).

destroyer escort force returning to Gibraltar from Op. Pedestal.

SATURDAY, AUGUST 15

Air War: Europe – Pathfinder Force established within RAF Bomber Cmnd. under Air Cdre. Bennett. (First op. against Flensburg shipyards, night Aug. 18-19.)

SUNDAY, AUGUST 16

Sea War – Op. *Wunderland* (Aug. 16-30): *Admiral Scheer* penetrates into Kara Sea (Arctic) to attack Russian shipping.
Secret War – The Makin Raid: US Marines (Carlson's Raiders) land from subs. on Makin I. (Gilberts grp.) in unsuccessful attempt to divert Japanese attention from ops. on Guadalcanal. In addition, 9 marines are captured and beheaded and the Japanese begin conversion of nearby Tarawa I. into well-nigh impregnable fortress. (*See* Nov. 20, 1943.)

MONDAY, AUGUST 17

Air War: Europe – FIRST 'ALL-AMERICAN' BOMBING RAID OVER EUROPE IN W.W.II. 12 B-17s of 8th AAF, led by Brig.-Gen. Eaker in 'Yankee Doodle', attack Rouen marshalling yards; 4 Spitfire sqns. fly as escort.

TUESDAY, AUGUST 18

North Africa – Gen. Alexander appointed CinC Middle East, in place of Auchinleck; Lt.-Gen. Montgomery replaces Ritchie as GOC 8th Army – special announcement.

WEDNESDAY, AUGUST 19

Russian Front – Paulus and Hoth attempt to storm Stalingrad. Siege of Leningrad: Garrison establishes small bridgeheads on German-held left bank of R. Neva. (*See* Aug. 24.)
Sea War/Air War – DIEPPE RAID (Op. Jubilee): 6,100 Canadian troops and British Commandos with 30 tanks carry out trial invasion, but are pinned down on the beaches and are unable to capture any important objectives. The secondary aim of the op. – to force the Luftwaffe in the W. into a decisive battle and destroy its 500 bombers and fighters – is only partially successful. 60 RAF fighter sqns. claim 91 destroyed and 44 probably destroyed (but Germans admit only 48 destroyed and 24 damaged). Destroyer *Berkeley* crippled by

---

Dieppe Raid Losses
British and Canadian: 4,340 inc. 1,179 dead, 2,190 PoWs; 30 tanks; 1 destroyer, 33 small craft; 100 planes. German: 591 inc. 311 dead and missing; 1 sub-chaser; 48 planes.

German fighter-bomber and finally scuttled; 33 landing craft lost.

THURSDAY, AUGUST 20

Air War – Sqn.-Ldr. Stephen Horthy, Vice-Regent of Hungary, killed in action over S. Russian Front; aged 38.
US Wildcat fighters and Dauntless dive-bombers flown into Henderson Field.

FRIDAY, AUGUST 21

Russian Front – Germans plant Swastika flag on Mt. Elbruz in the Caucasus.
Solomons – BATTLE OF TENARU RIVER. Marines annihilate first contingent of Japanese reinforcements on Guadalcanal.
Sea War: Pacific – 5 merchant ships and 2 fishing boats sunk off N. Japan by US sub. *Guardfish*.

SATURDAY, AUGUST 22

Russian Front – Pzs make narrow breach in Russian line at Vertyachi, N. of Stalingrad.
Home Front: USA – Death of Michael Fokine, Russian choreographer and ballet master, in New York; aged 61.
Home Front: Britain – Sir A. Sinclair, Sec. of State for Air, speaks at Swansea about work of RAF Bomber Cmnd.: as the German people 'gaze at their homes' they should remember all the cities destroyed by Hitler's bombers and thank the *Führer*.
Diplomacy – BRAZIL DECLARES WAR ON GERMANY AND ITALY.

SUNDAY, AUGUST 23

Russian Front – Pzs reach right bank of R. Volga, N. of Stalingrad.
Sea War: Pacific – Japanese occupy Nauru I. and Ocean I. (Aug. 26.)
Air War – STALINGRAD 'TERROR' RAID. 600 German bombers, *Stukas* and

Ju 52 bomber/transports attack city throughout night Aug. 23-24 (many crews make up to 3 sorties). Incendiaries start vast conflagrations. Approx. 40,000 killed; many thousands more flee across the Volga to shelter in caves and sewers.

MONDAY, AUGUST 24

Air War – Stripped-down Spitfire destroys Ju 86R high-altitude reconnaissance aircraft over Suez Canal.
Sea War: Pacific – BATTLE OF THE EASTERN SOLOMONS. Japanese make fruitless attempt to land reinforcements on Guadalcanal under protection of their Combined Fleet. Carrier *Ryujo* sunk; US carrier *Enterprise* damaged.
Russian Front – Siege of Leningrad: Red Army attempts to raise the siege by so-called Op. Sinyavino. Troops of Volkhov Front push W. to outskirts of Sinyavino, but are unable to link up with Leningrad Front forces attempting to extend Neva bridgeheads during Sept.

TUESDAY, AUGUST 25

Russian Front – Stalingrad Communist Party Committee proclaims state of siege: *'We shall never surrender the city of our birth; every house of every street is to be transformed into an impregnable fortress.'* Germans reach Mozdok, 80 km from main Caucasus oilfields.
Home Front: Britain – HRH the Duke of Kent killed in air crash near Wick; aged 39. (Rear gunner of Sunderland flying boat is the only survivor.)

WEDNESDAY, AUGUST 26

New Guinea – Japanese land at Milne Bay, SE. of Port Moresby.

Below: *The Dieppe Raid fiasco: a landing craft, and its Churchill tanks that never got inland.*

GUADALCANAL......
FIRST STEP TO TOKYO

On the morning of August 7, 1942, more than 15,000 United States Marines landed on the Japanese-held islands of Guadalcanal, Tulagi, Gavutu and Tanambogo in the British Solomons group. This was the first offensive undertaken by the Allies in the South-West Pacific and the start of the bloody series of amphibious assaults in the face of suicidal Japanese resistance.

Since their attack on Pearl Harbor, the Japanese had enjoyed a series of triumphs, broken only by naval defeats in the Coral Sea and at Midway. Despite these reverses, the presence of Japanese bases at Rabaul, on New Britain Island and along the coast of New Guinea, and further south, in the Solomons, still posed a major threat to Australia and remaining Allied strongholds in the South Pacific (such as Port Moresby, New Caledonia, Fiji and Samoa). Since June 1942, the Japanese had been constructing a bomber base on Guadalcanal, with the aim of carrying out devastating attacks on Allied seaborne communications.

The Allied naval victories in the Coral Sea and off Midway had paved the way for a limited offensive to check decisively the Japanese 'island-hopping' campaign in the South-West Pacific. Racing against time, a powerful US-Australian task force moved

through the Coral Sea in early August 1942 to attack and seize the Japanese-built airfield on Guadalcanal before it was stocked with planes. Bad weather hid the Allied task force and the weak Japanese garrison were taken completely by surprise. The Americans speedily occupied the airfield (which was named 'Henderson Field' in memory of a hero of the battle of Midway). However, the 250-strong Japanese garrison of nearby Tulagi island fought to the death for three days (only three being taken prisoner).

Japanese headquarters at Rabaul, meanwhile, had reacted to the American landings by despatching air strikes and a powerful force of heavy cruisers to Guadalcanal. The latter surprised and overwhelmed three American cruisers and the Australian *Canberra* early on August 9, and slaughtered nearly 1,300 officers

and men. Although no one could have guessed at the time, this savage battle was merely the first act in an incredible six-month-long campaign which was to transform the waters around Guadalcanal and the jungle-shrouded ridges of the island itself into one vast graveyard.

More than 30,000 Japanese died, including at least 9,000 suffering from horrible diseases or starvation. Twenty-four Japanese warships and 16 troopships, grossing 100,000 tonnes were sunk; 1,000 aircraft were shot down or failed to return to base. Allied casualties were lighter: 7,100 dead, including 5,000 sailors and 1,592 ground troops. However, 15,000 more were wounded or incapacitated by disease. Thirty-one Allied ships were sunk.

Although these horrific casualty figures are impressive enough in themselves, the most important effects of the Guadalcanal campaign were strategic. It confirmed and underlined the slim advantage which the Americans had gained at Midway. It safe-

Below left: A US Marine fighting patrol sets out at sunset on Guadalcanal, Aug. 1942. Terrain and climate were as much enemies as the Japanese. A day's rainfall might amount to 20 cm and rivers could rise over 2 m in two hours. Malaria casualties in November alone came to 3,200.

Below right: A Dauntless dive-bomber flies over a Marine position at 'Hell's Corner'. The US 'Cactus Air Force' of up to 100 planes was based on Henderson Field.

guarded the sea-lanes to Australia and provided a major air base and advanced staging post for the reconquest of the entire South-West Pacific area. Above all it shattered the Japanese Army's overweening confidence in its own invincibility and widened the already appreciable gulf of mutual distrust between the Japanese armed services. The Navy were quick to point out – with some justification – that all the potential advantage accruing from its costly victories and often suicidal convoy operations had been squandered by the inept Army commanders on Guadalcanal.

After the final evacuation of the tattered Japanese garrison in February 1943, Guadalcanal assumed a vital new role as a forward base supporting the northward advance of Allied forces towards New Britain Island. This was part of 'Operation Cartwheel' – a multi-pronged advance, through the Solomons, along the New Guinea coast and nearby islands, aimed at neutralizing Rabaul, where more than 100,000 Japanese sheltered in a labyrinth of caves and bunkers, sandwiched between two major airfields and the great harbour. For this purpose Henderson Field was expanded from a primitive front-line airstrip into a vast all-weather airfield complex.

On April 18, 1943, a squadron of P-38 fighters took off from Henderson Field to intercept and destroy an aircraft carrying Admiral Yamamoto, CinC of the Japanese Combined Fleet, as it prepared to land at Buin, 480 km to the north. It could truthfully be claimed that this successful operation alone more than repaid all the sacrifices made by the Americans and Australians in the six-month-long Guadalcanal campaign.

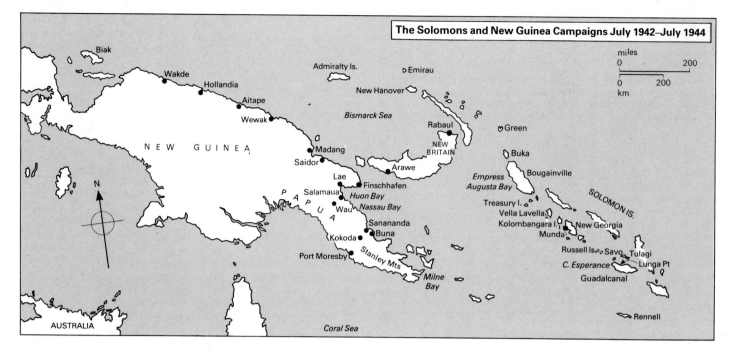

The Solomons and New Guinea Campaigns July 1942–July 1944

Air War: Europe – Russian night raids on Berlin, Aug. 26-27 and 28-29 (4-engined bombers used in latter op.).
Home Front: Britain – Govt. lifts ban on publication of *Daily Worker,* Communist Party newspaper.

THURSDAY, AUGUST 27

Air War: Europe – Night raid on Helsinki by 60 Russian bombers.
Sea War – Canadian corvette *Oakville* rams repeatedly and sinks *U-94* in Windward Passage (Cuba-Haiti).
Occupied France – Hitler orders release of 800 French PoWs as reward for 'exemplary conduct' of civil population during Allied raid on Dieppe.

FRIDAY, AUGUST 28

Air War – Single bomb dropped by high-altitude Ju 86P kills 48 and injures 26 in centre of Bristol.
RAF night raids on Nuremburg and Saarbrücken (30 aircraft lost).
Sea War: Pacific – Seaplane, launched from sub. *I-25,* drops incendiaries over Oregon forest (night Aug. 28-29; repeated Sept. 9-10).

SATURDAY, AUGUST 29

Air War: Europe – Russian night raids on Berlin and Königsberg.

SUNDAY, AUGUST 30

North Africa – **BATTLE OF ALAM HALFA** (Aug. 30-Sept. 4): Rommel attempts to outflank El Alamein 'Line', but his *Pzs* are starved of fuel and harassed repeatedly from the air. (New Zealand troops counter-attack Sept. 3-4.) Rommel issues Order of the Day: '. . . *reinforced by new divisions we will launch a new attack in*

order finally to destroy the enemy'.
Occupied Luxemburg – Grand Duchy of Luxemburg annexed to German *Reich.*

MONDAY, AUGUST 31

Sea War: Pacific – Carrier *Saratoga* torpedoed by *I-26* in Solomons.

Above: *A US Marine Corps M2 light tank on Guadalcanal in Aug.*

Secret War – Gestapo smash *Rote Kapelle* ('Red Orchestra') – major Soviet spy ring inside the Reich; many arrests during Aug.
Home Front: Britain – Royal Ulster Constabulary seize 2 large caches of sub-MGs and ammunition and make 90 arrests in Belfast (Aug. 31-Sept. 5), following discovery of IRA plan to attack British and American troops in N. Ireland.

TUESDAY, SEPTEMBER 1

Sea War: Atlantic – USN and RAF Catalinas defeat all attacks on Convoy SC. 97 by U-boat grp. *Vorwärts* ('Onward'): *U-756* sunk.
Home Front: Japan – Resignation of Foreign Minister Togo – only civilian in the Cabinet.

Air War: Europe – RAF night raid on Saarbrücken.

WEDNESDAY, SEPTEMBER 2

Home Front: Germany – German High Command threatens to put all British prisoners captured at Dieppe in chains, as a reprisal for alleged ill-treatment of German PoWs in Britain.
Air War – FW 200 Condor shot down over Iceland by US fighters. RAF drops 8,000-lb. bombs on Karlsruhe.

THURSDAY, SEPTEMBER 3

Home Front: Australia – 'Austerity Campaign': new restrictions on entertainments and sports; increased taxes on alcoholic drinks and tobacco.
Neutrals: Spain – Pro-Axis Foreign Minister Súñer replaced by more moderate Gen. Gomez-Jordana.
Diplomacy – Reciprocal Lease-Lend Agreement between USA, UK, Australia, NZ and Free French.

FRIDAY, SEPTEMBER 4

Russian Front – Fierce fighting on outskirts of Stalingrad (Sept. 4-13): Germans reach Volga S. of city, thereby cutting off Russian 62nd Army.
Air War: Europe – RAF night raid on Bremen: many 4,000-lb. bombs dropped. Russian night bombers (1 lost) raid Budapest, Vienna, Breslau and Königsberg. Damage and casualties at Budapest necessitates immediate introduction of 'black-out'.
Air War: Britain – 'Hit and run' raiders bomb and strafe Torquay (1 shot down on beach). At night, leaflets containing photographs of Dieppe Raid dropped on English S. coast.
Secret War – First accurate details of per-

formance of Mitsubishi Zero fighter are distributed to US air forces in Pacific. These are based on examination and testing of a crashed Zero (lost June 3, 1942) recovered almost intact from bog on one of the Aleutian Is.

SATURDAY, SEPTEMBER 5

Sea War: Pacific – JAPANESE EVACUATE MILNE BAY (New Guinea). Japanese fast destroyers land reinforcements and essential supplies on Guadalcanal (night 5-6). US Navy and Marines soon nickname this almost nightly service the 'Tokyo Express'.
Home Front: Britain – IRA ambush RUC patrol in Co. Tyrone (2 killed, 1 wounded).

SUNDAY, SEPTEMBER 6

Air War: Britain – Debut of Me 210 fighter-bomber: 2 shot down by RAF Typhoons over N. Yorks. Coast. Night raid on Sunderland.
Air War: Europe – B-17s attack Rouen marshalling yards. RAF night raid on Duisburg.
Home Front: Britain – British and German cross-Channel guns exchange fire for an hour.

MONDAY, SEPTEMBER 7

Diplomacy – Italy declares war on Brazil.

TUESDAY, SEPTEMBER 8

Sea War – British MGBs engage German coastal convoys off Cherbourg and in Strs. of Dover (German shore batteries open fire at Cherbourg).
Home Front: USA – Roosevelt declares in one of his broadcast 'Fireside Chats': *This is the toughest war of all time.'* But, he adds, Americans are tough enough to meet this unprecedented challenge and the decision has already been taken to launch a great offensive (i.e., Op. Torch).

WEDNESDAY, SEPTEMBER 9

Air War: Europe – 'Whirlibombers' (Whirlwind 2-engined fighter-bombers) sink 2 German armed trawlers near Alderney I.
Occupied France – Germans introduce military conscription in Alsace-Lorraine.

THURSDAY, SEPTEMBER 10

Air War: Europe – 476 RAF bombers (inc. 174 bomber/trainers) make second concentrated 50-min. night raid on Düsseldorf (31 bombers lost).
Sea War – British MTBs and MGBs attack strongly escorted convoy off the Dutch I. of Texel (night Sept. 10-11), damaging 2 ships; *MGB 335* lost.
Madagascar – After 4-month stalemate British and S. Africans take steps to occupy

entire I. British 29th Brig. lands at Majunga (W. coast), while S. Africans advance S., overland from Diego Suarez, towards the capital, Tananarive.

FRIDAY, SEPTEMBER 11

New Guinea – Japanese advance on Port Moresby halted at Ioribaiwa, 51 km N.
Home Front: USA – 12 workers killed and 35 injured when plane crashes in flames on Curtiss-Wright aircraft factory, Buffalo (New York).

SATURDAY, SEPTEMBER 12

Russian Front – Gen. Chuikov appointed GOC Russian 62nd Army at Stalingrad.
Sea War: Atlantic – LACONIA INCIDENT. Liner *Laconia*, carrying 1,800 Italian PoWs, sunk by *U-156* off Ascension I. Attempts by U-boats to rescue survivors are interrrupted by US Liberator bomber. Dönitz calls off the rescue op. and forbids similar humanitarian gestures ('Laconia Order' of Sept. 17, 1942). However, Vichy French warships subsequently rescue bulk of ship's passengers and crew.
Home Front: Britain – Horse Racing: Gordon Richards wins St Leger at Newmarket, riding 'Sun Chariot'.

SUNDAY, SEPTEMBER 13

Russian Front – 'FINAL' GERMAN OFFENSIVE AT STALINGRAD. Savage hand-to-hand fighting continues in city until Nov. 18.
Solomons – BATTLE OF BLOODY RIDGE. Japanese reinforcements attempt to storm Henderson Field; they are repulsed with severe casualties.
Home Front: Malta – The Governor, Lord Gort, presents George Cross (awarded to entire population in April) to Chief Justice at ceremony in bomb-battered Palace Square, Valletta.

Sea War – German ops. against Convoy PQ. 18 (Sept. 13-18): 10 ships are sunk by aircraft and 3 by U-boats, but Sea Hurricanes shoot down 7 raiders (20 German aircraft lost *in toto*); 3 U-boats sunk.
Air War: Europe – 100th RAF raid on Bremen (19 4-engined bombers lost).

MONDAY, SEPTEMBER 14

North Africa – Op. Agreement: combined op. against Tobruk by seaborne and land-based commandos fails disastrously. *Stukas* sink AA cruiser *Coventry*, German flak battery disables destroyer *Sikh* and Italian Macchi fighter-bombers sink *Zulu* and 3 MTBs. Damaged *MTB 314* captured and redesignated *RA.10* (sunk by British aircraft April 1943). 579 commandos and naval personnel taken prisoner.

TUESDAY, SEPTEMBER 15

Russian Front – Rodimtsev Div. ordered to 'clear' Germans from Mamai Hill and railway station in Stalingrad city centre (latter changes hands several times).

Below: *A German MG34 team, well armed with grenades, fires across Stalingrad's wooden roof tops.*

Sea War: Pacific – US carrier *Wasp* sunk by *I-19*, S. of Guadalcanal; battleship *North Carolina* damaged by torpedo.

WEDNESDAY, SEPTEMBER 16

Russian Front – In Stalingrad, Rodimtsev Div. recaptures Mamai Hill, but suffers appalling casualties (fighting continues on and around Hill until Jan. 1943).
Air War – 3 American-volunteer 'Eagle Sqns.' to be transferred from RAF to USAAF.
Madagascar – Vichy Governor-Gen. requests armistice terms.

THURSDAY, SEPTEMBER 17

Madagascar – Vichy Governor-Gen. Annet rejects British armistice terms.
Home Front: USA – Roosevelt begins 15-day nationwide inspection tour of military bases, shipyards and aircraft plants, inc. vast new Ford heavy bomber assembly plant at Willow Run, Detroit.
Occupied Norway – Quisling reintroduces capital punishment in Norway.

FRIDAY, SEPTEMBER 18

Sea War – Op. Jane: British brig. lands at Tamatave, on E. coast of Madagascar.

SATURDAY, SEPTEMBER 19

Air War: Europe – 30 Finnish bombers despatched to Lavansaari I. (Gulf of Finland): many aircraft lose their way in thick fog and crash-land.

SUNDAY, SEPTEMBER 20

Air War – Tobruk raided by Allied bombers for seventh time in 8 nights.

MONDAY, SEPTEMBER 21

Burma – British begin first land counter-offensive against Japanese, in the Arakan (area along Bay of Bengal coast).

TUESDAY, SEPTEMBER 22

Russian Front – Germans take Stalingrad grain silo after a week's fighting.
Madagascar – E. African Brig. and artillery break through well-defended road block at Mahitsy, a few miles W. of Tananarive.
Air War – US and British bombers raid Benghazi.

WEDNESDAY, SEPTEMBER 23

New Guinea – Australians counter-attack at Ioribaiwa, N. of Port Moresby.
Air War – US 12th AAF established to support US ground forces during Op. Torch.
Sea War: Atlantic – 2 U-boat packs make repeated, but largely unsuccessful, attempts to destroy fast Convoy RB. 1 off Newfoundland – which is wrongly believed to contain large troopships: 3 vessels and escorting destroyer *Veteran* sunk, Sept. 25-26.
Sea War: Pacific – Australian destroyer *Voyager* lost off Timor while attempting to land reinforcements for Australian-Dutch 'Sparrow Force', which is waging guerrilla campaign behind Japanese lines.
Home Front: USA – First 'Liberty Ship' – prefabricated, mass-produced merchant ship – launched *10 days* after keel had been laid; at Portland, Oregon.
Secret War – Ultra discovers that Rommel has left N. Africa on sick leave.

THURSDAY, SEPTEMBER 24

Air War: Britain – FW 190 fighter-bombers raid 3 SE. England coastal towns.

FRIDAY, SEPTEMBER 25

Air War – Mosquitoes attack *Gestapo* HQ in Oslo.
Night raid on Penzance (Cornwall).
US bombers raid airfield near Hanoi.
Home Front: New Zealand – Waikato Miners' Strike ends.

SATURDAY, SEPTEMBER 26

Russian Front – Germans reach right bank of Volga in centre of Stalingrad.
Air War: Europe – RAF high-altitude fighter sweep over France has to be abandoned due to severe icing (11 aircraft lost).
Diplomacy – Wendell Willkie, speaking in Moscow, calls for launching of 'Second Front' without delay, 'next year may be too late'.
Home Front: Britain – Death of Prebendary Carlile, founder of the Church Army, known as the 'Archbishop of the Gutter'. Aged 95.

SUNDAY, SEPTEMBER 27

Sea War: Atlantic – 'Liberty Ship' *Stephen Hopkins* (1 x 4-in. gun) fights epic engagement with disguised raider *Stier* (6 x 5.9-in. guns, 2 TT): both sink. German crew rescued by SS *Tannenfels*, but Americans make 31-day voyage to Brazil (15 survivors out of 57).
Home Front: Germany – Halder, COGS, replaced by Zeitzler.

MONDAY, SEPTEMBER 28

Sea War – *Hipper* and 4 destroyers return from minelaying sortie to Novaya Zemlya (Op. *Zarin*: 'Czarina').

TUESDAY, SEPTEMBER 29

Sea War – S. African troops land at Tuléar, in S. Madagascar.
Air War: Britain – School bombed at Petworth, Sussex: 31 children and 2 teachers killed; 28 children injured.
Secret War – Richard Sorge, Soviet master spy, sentenced to death by Tokyo Criminal Court.

WEDNESDAY, SEPTEMBER 30

Air War – Hptm. Marseille, top fighter 'ace' in N. Africa – 151 victories (plus 7 over English Channel) – killed baling out of Me 109 with faulty engine. Aged 22.
Home Front: Germany – Hitler speaks at Berlin *Sportspalast*: describes Britain's leaders as 'military idiots'. (!)
Home Front: New Zealand – Cabinet Split: 6 National Party members withdraw.

Below: *German troops and a* Panzer III *near the Stalingrad grain silo, Oct 5.*

Secret War – British liaison mission contacts Greek Resistance.

THURSDAY, OCTOBER 1

Sea War – *Lisbon Maru*, carrying 1,816 British and Canadian PoWs and 2,000 Japanese troops from Hong Kong to Japan, torpedoed by US sub. *Grouper*. Guards batten down hatches to prevent PoWs from leaving crippled vessel, while crew and troops are taken off. Ship sinks Oct. 2 (840 PoWs lost).

FRIDAY, OCTOBER 2

Air War – Maiden flight of Bell XP-59 Airacomet, the first Allied jet fighter (2 Whittle-type engines), from Muroc Dry Lake, California.
Sea War: Atlantic – Cruiser *Curacoa* rammed and cut in two by *Queen Mary* (carrying 15,000 American troops) off Donegal; 338 killed. *U-512* sunk by Douglas B-18 bomber off Devil's I.

SATURDAY, OCTOBER 3

Home Front: Germany – First successful launching of *A4* rocket (forerunner of *V-2*) from Peenemünde.

SUNDAY, OCTOBER 4

Sea War – British Commando raid on Sark (Channel Is.).

MONDAY, OCTOBER 5

Home Front: Britain – RAF aircraft crashes in village of Somersham (Hunts.): 6 cottages wrecked, 10 people killed.

TUESDAY, OCTOBER 6

Sea War: Atlantic – Cdr. of Italian sub. *Barbarigo* reports that he has sunk

American battleship of Idaho Class off W. Africa (in previous May, Cdr. Grozzi had 'sunk' a US battleship off Brazil): in actual fact the 'battleships' are a corvette and a merchant ship resp. (*Barbarigo* lost, June 1943.)
Air War: Europe – RAF night raid on Osnabrück.

WEDNESDAY, OCTOBER 7

Sea War – U-boat 'wolf pack' *Eisbär* ('Polar Bear') sinks 28 ships off S. and E. Africa (Oct. 7-Nov. 3). *U-179* sunk by British destroyer *Active*.

THURSDAY, OCTOBER 8

New Guinea – Japanese rearguard makes a stand at Templeton's Crossing (they retreat Oct. 29).

FRIDAY, OCTOBER 9

Air War – Allied warplanes (12 lost) make round-the-clock attacks on landing grounds in El Daba area of N. Africa; defending fighters routed.

SATURDAY, OCTOBER 10

Diplomacy – Argentina and Chile protest about 'offensive' remarks about Axis espionage ops. in their resp. countries, made by US Sec. of State, Sumner Welles.

SUNDAY, OCTOBER 11

Sea War – **BATTLE OF CAPE ESPERANCE.** US cruiser-destroyer force surprises Japanese sqn. NW. of Guadalcanal and sinks cruiser *Furutaka* (night Oct. 11-12).
Air War – Axis air forces launch final major air offensive against Malta – but Spitfires

inflict heavy losses. From Oct. 16 Ju 88 bombers are restricted to night ops. – all daylight bomber raids abandoned, Oct. 17. (*See* Nov. 8, 1942.)

MONDAY, OCTOBER 12

Home Front: USA – 600,000 Italian-Americans no longer to be classified as 'enemy aliens'.

TUESDAY, OCTOBER 13

Solomons – Japanese heavy artillery and bombers pound Henderson Field.
Sea War – German disguised raider *Komet* attempts to break out into Atlantic from Le Havre, under heavy escort (night Oct. 13-14), but is sunk with all hands by British *MTB 326*.
Sea War: Pacific – Japanese fast battleships *Hiyei* and *Kirishima* bombard Henderson Field (night Oct. 13-14).

WEDNESDAY, OCTOBER 14

Sea War: Atlantic – Nova Scotia-Newfoundland ferry steamer *Caribou* sunk by U-boat (137 killed).
Sea War: Pacific – Japanese cruisers bombard Henderson Field (repeated Oct. 15-16) while Japanese reinforcements land on Guadalcanal.
Russian Front – At Stalingrad Germans launch a second 'final' offensive, preceded by ferocious artillery/mortar barrage and deadly accurate *Stuka* raids. Ruined Tractor Factory overrun, but Siberian regt. holds 'Red October' works in city centre against 117 separate attacks (inc. 23 in 1 day). Offensive ends in late Oct.

Below: *German runners cross the ruins of the Red October tractor plant in Nov. after it had changed hands many times.*

THURSDAY, OCTOBER 15

Sea War – Norwegian sub. *Uredd* sinks German transport *Libau* in Norwegian Sea.

FRIDAY, OCTOBER 16

Home Front: India – Cyclone kills approx. 40,000 in Bengal.

SATURDAY, OCTOBER 17

Air War: Europe – 94 Lancasters (1 lost) attack Schneider armaments and locomotive works at Le Creusot, SE. of Paris, at dusk.

SUNDAY, OCTOBER 18

Home Front: Germany – Hitler orders all captured British Commandos to be summarily executed.
Pacific – Vice-Adm. Halsey replaces Vice-Adm. Ghormley as CinC S. Pacific.

MONDAY, OCTOBER 19

China – 30 additional Chinese divs. to be armed and equipped by USA.
Madagascar – King's African Rifles encircle and capture 800 Vichy troops, with artillery and MT, near Ivato (KAR casualties, nil).

TUESDAY, OCTOBER 20

Air War – Fighter-bomber raids on Malta. Italian 4-engined night raiders intercepted by RAF fighters over Gibraltar and forced to jettison bombs over Spanish territory, causing damage and casualties.

WEDNESDAY, OCTOBER 21

Air War: Europe – RAF Mustangs strafe barges on Dortmund-Ems Canal. 8th AF B-17s raid Lorient U-boat base.

THURSDAY, OCTOBER 22

Air War: Europe – RAF launches series of **DEVASTATING RAIDS ON THE TURIN-MILAN-GENOA 'TRIANGLE'** (Italian equivalent of the Ruhr) with night attack by 100 Lancasters on Genoa. 6 heavy night raids on Genoa and 7 on Turin by year's end. Both industrial production and civilian morale affected.
Russian Front – Siege of Leningrad: Germans make unsuccessful assault on Suho I. in L. Ladoga.
Secret War – Lt.-Gen. Mark Clark lands on N. African coast from British sub. *Seraph* and contacts pro-Allied French Officers (night Oct. 22-23).

FRIDAY, OCTOBER 23

North Africa – **SECOND BATTLE OF EL ALAMEIN.** Montgomery launches all-out offensive against Axis line in Western Desert – preceded by greatest artillery barrage (900 guns) yet employed in the Campaign.

Masterly camouflage operations organized by Lt.-Col. Barkas (involving use of many dummy tanks, trucks and dumps) to convince Rommel that attack will take place farther south. First phase of Battle ends Nov. 1.

Gen. Stumme CinC *PAA*, killed; Gen. von Thoma takes command until return of Rommel.

Second Alamein Forces
8th Army: 195,000 men (11 divs.); 1,029 tanks (252 Shermans), 2,311 guns; 750 planes. Axis *Panzerarmee Afrika*: 104,000 (13 divs.), 489 tanks, 1,219 guns; 675 planes.

Above: *Two of the six British Churchill tanks at Alamein.*

Solomons – Japanese make desperate efforts to capture Henderson Field, but their 3-pronged 4-day offensive is unco-ordinated and US Marines defeat each attack in turn. Elite Japanese 2nd Div. annihilated.

Sea War: Atlantic – Cruiser *Phoebe* damaged by *U-161* off Congo Estuary.

Home Front: Italy – King Victor Emmanuel and Queen Elena visit Genoa – still burning from previous night's bombing.

SATURDAY, OCTOBER 24

Air War: Europe – DAYLIGHT RAID ON MILAN by 88 Lancasters (3 lost), flying unescorted at low altitude: great damage to railway targets; many fires. Follow-up night raid by Stirlings, Halifaxes and Wellingtons (5 lost).

RAF night intruders attack 12 trains in N. France.

Sea War: Atlantic – British sub. *Unique* disappears W. of Gibraltar.

SUNDAY, OCTOBER 25

North Africa – Germans suffer heavy losses. Rommel returns (arrives Oct. 26).

MONDAY, OCTOBER 26

Sea War: Pacific – BATTLE OF SANTA CRUZ ISLANDS. Japanese carriers approach Guadalcanal in anticipation of the capture of Henderson Field and sink US carrier *Hornet;* Japanese cruiser *Yura* lost.

Air War: Pacific – US bombers raid Hong Kong power station and airfield at Canton.

TUESDAY, OCTOBER 27

Air War – Allied fighters rout large force of *Stukas*, attempting to bomb British forward positions W. of Alamein.

WEDNESDAY, OCTOBER 28

Air War – Allied bombers break up attempted *Pz* counter-attacks at Alamein. Greek aircraft raid Italian positions.

THURSDAY, OCTOBER 29

Madagascar – E. Africans capture 440 Vichy troops at Alakamisy and occupy Fianarantsoa, 418 km S. of Tananarive.

Home Front: USA – 'Alaska Highway' opened, running 2,689 km from Dawson Creek (BC) to Fairbanks (begun March 1941).

FRIDAY, OCTOBER 30

Sea War: Atlantic – Transport *President Doumer* (11,900 t.) sunk by *U-604* off NW. Africa.

SATURDAY, OCTOBER 31

Air War: Britain – German fighter-bomber raid on Canterbury: 68 *Jabos*, escorted by 68 fighters (3 lost), approach target, but balloon barrage hampers bombing. Night raid on same target (7 aircraft lost).

SUNDAY, NOVEMBER 1

Solomons – US Marines launch counter-offensive on Guadalcanal.

Home Front: Brazil – Currency changes: *Cruzeiro* of 100 *Centavos* replaces the *Milreis* of 1,000 *Reis*.

MONDAY, NOVEMBER 2

North Africa - ALLIED VICTORY AT EL ALAMEIN. Phase 2 of Battle – Op. Supercharge: 8th Army compels Axis army to withdraw from Alamein Line and

pursues it to Tobruk (Nov. 13), Benghazi (Nov. 20) and El Agheila (Nov. 24, *q.v.*). Two sqns. of armed cars and carriers of Royal Dragoon Gds. carry out 4-day raid behind Rommel's lines – destroying 200 vehicles, cutting telephone lines and capturing several hundred Italians – at cost of 3 killed and 12 wounded. Rommel orders *PAA* to retreat from El Alamein (Hitler countermands order Nov. 3).

Sea War: Atlantic – *U-518* sinks 2 iron-ore ships in Conception Bay, Newfoundland.

Air War – Eastern Air Command, RAF, formed at Gibraltar to support British 1st Army during Op. Torch.

TUESDAY, NOVEMBER 3

North Africa – Montgomery breaks through Rommel's scratch defences W. of El Alamein.

Solomons – Japanese reinforcements land E. and W. of Henderson Field (night Nov. 3-4).

WEDNESDAY, NOVEMBER 4

Air War – Allied bombers and fighter-bombers wreak havoc among hordes of German and Italian vehicles and infantry retreating westwards from Alamein. After a single (abortive) *Stuka* raid, the Axis air forces remain inactive on their bomb-cratered airstrips.

Second Alamein Losses
8th Army: 13,560 inc. 2,350 dead, 2,260 missing; 500 tanks, 110 guns; 97 planes. Axis: 25,000 dead and wounded, 30,000 PoWs (10,724 German); 320 tanks; 1,000 guns; 84 planes.

Secret War – British Merchant Seaman Duncan Scott-Ford, who admitted taking £18 from a Nazi agent in Lisbon, Portugal, hanged at Wandsworth Prison, London, after secret Old Bailey trial under 1940 Treachery Act.

THURSDAY, NOVEMBER 5

North Africa – Rommel attempts to make a stand at Fuka, 113 km W. of El Alamein, but once again his lines are broken.
Madagascar – **FINAL SURRENDER OF VICHY FORCES IN MADAGASCAR.** Gen. Guillemet and Governor-Gen. Annet accept Allied terms.
Home Front: USA – Death of George M. Cohan, song writer ('Over There', etc.); aged 63.

FRIDAY, NOVEMBER 6

North Africa – Heavy rain slows down 8th Army mechanized columns and gives Rommel brief respite.

SATURDAY, NOVEMBER 7

Sea War: Med. – U-boats and Italian subs. attack Allied Task Forces engaged in Op. Torch (Nov. 7-15): 7 transports sunk and 3 damaged; destroyers *Martin* and *Isaac Sweers* (Dutch) sunk. 5 U-boats and 1 Italian submarine lost.
Secret War – Gen. Giraud picked up from S. France by sub. *Seraph*, which transfers him to Gibraltar-bound flying boat.

SUNDAY, NOVEMBER 8

Sea War: Med. – **OP. TORCH LANDINGS IN NORTH AFRICA.** 3 powerful Allied Task Forces, inc. US battleships *Massachusetts* and *Texas* and 5 carriers, land 34,300 troops near Casablanca, 39,000 US troops near Oran and 33,000 British and US troops near Algiers. Vichy French naval forces offer fierce resistance and make repeated sorties against the Task Forces, losing 1 cruiser *Primauguet*, 10 destroyers and 13 submarines. At Casablanca, *Massachusetts* exchanges heavy fire with partially operational battleship *Jean Bart* and powerful shore battery. British sloops *Walney* and *Hartland* and destroyers *Broke* and *Malcolm,* sent into Oran and Algiers harbours in attempted parleys, come under murderous fire – only *Malcolm* escapes. New Italian fast cruiser *Attilio Regolo* damaged by sub. *Unruffled,* W. of Sicily.
Home Front: Germany – Hitler announces fall of Stalingrad ('except for some very small parts').
Air War – *Luftwaffe* lands advance elements of German expeditionary force at El Aouina Airport, Tunis. *Luftwaffe* losses in Malta raids, Jan. 1-Nov 8, 1942: 172 bombers and 99 fighters. German bombers and torpedo planes hit 5 transports, carrier *Argus* and monitor *Roberts* off N. Africa (Nov. 8-14).

MONDAY, NOVEMBER 9

North Africa – Cease-fire in French N. Africa arranged by Adm. Darlan and Lt.-Gen. Mark Clark. Gen. Giraud arrives in Algeria to rally support for the Allies. Rommel commences rapid retreat from Sidi Barrani to El Agheila (1,014 km by the coastal road). Vichy France breaks off diplomatic relations with USA. USA and Canada break off relations with Vichy. Pétain dismisses Darlan and assumes command of Vichy forces.
Sea War: Atlantic – Adm. Sir Max Horton appointed CinC Western Approaches (anti-U-boat war).

TUESDAY, NOVEMBER 10

Home Front: Britain – Churchill describes 8th Army's 'glorious and decisive victory' over Rommel in speech at London's Mansion House.
Secret War – Swiss Joint Federal Assembly rejects appeals against death sentences imposed on 3 Swiss soldiers (Zürcher, Feer and Schrämli) convicted of passing details of Switzerland's alpine defences to foreign Powers.

WEDNESDAY, NOVEMBER 11

Russian Front – At Stalingrad, Germans make another attempt to eliminate Russian bridgehead on R. bank in city centre. Squads of assault engineers crawl through sewers and tunnels while tanks attempt to traverse shattered rubble-clogged streets. Unparalleled ferocity continues for 4 days and nights, but the few German squads that reach the Volga are cut off and annihilated.
Vichy France – Op. Anton: **GERMAN AND ITALIAN FORCES OCCUPY VICHY FRANCE;** Italians seize Corsica.
Diplomacy – Germany announces that she will respect Spanish neutrality, despite developments in S. France (but Hitler has previously ordered contingency planning for the occupation of Spain).
Sea War – RIN minesweeper *Bengal* and armed tanker *Ondina* rout 2 heavily armed Japanese merchant raiders SW. of Cocos Is. – *Hokoku Maru* sinks; *Aikoku Maru* retires, after inflicting serious damage on *Ondina*. *Bengal* escorts *Ondina* to Fremantle.
Sea War: Med. – Troopship *Viceroy of India* (19,600 t.) sunk by *U-407* off N. African coast.
Sea War: Atlantic – All available U-boats (25) withdrawn from N. Atlantic and formed into 2 grps.: *Schlagetot* ('Bully') and *Westwall* off Morocco and Gibraltar for ops. against Allied Task Forces engaged in Op. Torch: 10 transports sunk, 1 transport and 1 tanker damaged, 1 carrier and depot ship sunk (1 U-boat sunk and 8 damaged).

THURSDAY, NOVEMBER 12

Air War – British paratroops dropped on Bône airfield, Algeria, by US C-47s – narrowly forestalling a planned German paratroop drop. US 9th AAF formed in N. Africa.
Sea War: Pacific – **FIRST BATTLE OF GUADALCANAL.** In chaotic night action, US cruiser-destroyer sqn. intercepts and turns back Japanese battleships *Hiyei* and *Kirishima*, thereby saving Henderson Field from devastating bombardment. *Hiyei* crippled (sunk Nov. 13 by torpedo planes and a B-17). US cruiser *Atlanta* sunk.

MONTGOMERY, Bernard Law (1887-1976)
British: *Field-Marshal, Viscount Montgomery of Alamein;* 'Monty'

Great commander of British 8th Army during decisive final phases of North African Campaign, Oct. 1942-May 1943. Renowned for ability to inspire confidence in his troops and painstaking, logical approach to strategic, tactical and logistical problems. Much criticized for bitter dispute with Eisenhower concerning theoretical choice between 'broad-front' and 'narrow-front' advance to Berlin, (autumn 1944).

Born at Kennington, London, son of Right Rev. H. H. Montgomery, Bishop of Tasmania. Educated at St. Paul's School and Sandhurst. Entered Warwickshire Regt., as 2nd Lt., 1908. Served in France, World War I (mentioned in despatches). Maj-Gen., 1938; commanded 3rd Div., BEF Aug. 1939-June 1940, taking part in Dunkirk evacuation. GOCinC SE. Command, 1941-42. Commanded 8th Army in North Africa, Sicily and Italy, Aug. 1942-Dec. 1943. CinC of Allied Armies for the Invasion of Europe from Dec. 1943. CinC 21st Army Grp. (France-Belgium), Aug 30, 1944; Field Marshal, Aug. 31, 1944.

1st and 9th US Armies temporarily transferred to his command during 'Battle of the Bulge' (Dec. 20, 1944). Led 21st Army Grp. across the Rhine to the Elbe, March-April 1945. Received surrender of all German forces in NW. Europe at ceremony on Lüneburg Heath, W. Germany, May 4, 1945.

CinC British Army on the Rhine (BAOR), and member of Allied Control Commission in Germany, 1945-46. Chief of Imperial General Staff, 1946-48. Created viscount, 1946. Deputy supreme commander, SHAPE, 1951-58. Writings include: 'Ten Chapters' (1946); 'Forward to Victory' (1946); 'Normandy to the Baltic' (1947); 'El Alamein to the River Sangro' (1948); 'Memoirs' (1958); 'History of Warfare' (1968).

ALAMEIN......
VICTORY IN THE DESERT

The moon was almost full on the evening of Friday, October 23, 1942. After a warm day, the desert was now cold and silent, save the occasional burst of machine gun fire. Then, at 9.35 pm it began. The night sky was lit up by the leaping flashes of 900 guns in an incessant bombardment of the kind rarely heard since World War I. The second battle of El Alamein was under way.

The famous Alamein Barrage heralded the beginning of the end of Rommel's German-Italian *Panzer Armee Afrika,* which had led the British such a merry dance around the North African desert, ever since its modest beginnings as the *Afrika Korps,* back in March 1941. However, Rommel's tactical victories had been cancelled out by chronic, perennial shortages of vital weapons and equipment and dangerously exposed supply lines. The fortuitous capture of all the British trucks, fuel and food dumps at Tobruk on

June 21, 1942 tempted Rommel to pursue the fast-retreating 8th Army deep into Egypt. But he was well aware that, if this desperate final effort failed, the entire Desert War campaign was as good as lost.

There now followed more than a month of chaotic, desperate fighting for possession of El Alamein, near the coast, and Alam Halfa Ridge, further to the south-east. Alamein presented Rommel with a battlefield unlike any other in which he had

perfected his mobile approach to war in the Western Desert. It is located in a gap of just 60 km (40 miles) between the coast and the impassable salt marshes of the Qattara Depression. Although Rommel once again defeated or skilfully side-stepped every armoured counter-attack – destroying 118 British tanks at a cost of only 3 German on one day alone – he failed to break through. Virtually neglected by the depleted Axis air forces in North Africa, and under constant Allied air attacks, Rommel's forces were eventually compelled in early September to beat a hasty retreat to high ground west of Alamein.

An oppressive six-week lull fell over the desert battlefield. Neither side welcomed the stalemate, but Rommel had fallen ill and his forces were too weakened to either advance further or even fall back to Tobruk. But while the Axis troops dug themselves in and laid hundreds of thousands of mines, the British, under their new commanders, Alexander and Montgomery, took advantage of the quiet spell to assemble fresh troops, supported by masses of new Sherman tanks, field guns and tactical warplanes. With these Montgomery intended to tear great gaps in Rommel's defences and destroy his army piece-by-piece, during ten days of continuous fighting. Even though Montgomery's cautious tactics – and heavy

rain – enabled the ever-elusive 'Desert Fox' to escape from the inferno of Alamein, he soon found himself trapped between the advancing 8th Army and the Anglo-American armies which landed in Morocco and Algeria on November 8, 1942 in Operation Torch.

Montgomery's victory at El Alamein marked the turning point in the Desert War. When the North African campaign ended in Tunisia seven months later, Germany and Italy had lost almost one million soldiers killed or taken prisoner. Victory at El Alamein also gave the British people their first clear-cut success in over three years of war. In a speech at London's Mansion House on November 10, 1942 Churchill sounded a note of cautious optimism: 'This is not the end. It is not even the beginning of the end. But it is, perhaps, the end of the beginning.' Years later, Churchill was still elated: 'Before Alamein we never had a victory; after Alamein we never had a defeat.'

Below: *The crew of an* Afrika Korps Panzer *III surrender to British infantry on the sixth day of Second Alamein. The battle left Rommel with 12 tanks fit to fight against 8th Army's 800-plus.*

FRIDAY, NOVEMBER 13

Diplomacy – Darlan recognized by Allies as French head of state.
Air War – Strong formations of RAF Eastern Air Cmnd. land at Bône (and on Nov. 14); *Luftwaffe* carry out heavy counter-raids.

SATURDAY, NOVEMBER 14

Sea War: Pacific – 7 of 11 Japanese transports, carrying reinforcements to Guadalcanal, sunk by US planes from carrier *Enterprise* and Henderson Field. **SECOND BATTLE OF GUADALCANAL.** Battleship-*v*-battleship action; *Washington* sinks *Kirishima*; *South Dakota* damaged.
Sea War: Med. – British occupy Bône harbour (first tanker arrives Nov. 17).

SUNDAY, NOVEMBER 15

North Africa – British enter Tunisia.
Sea War: Atlantic – Escort carrier *Avenger* sunk by *U-155* W. of Gibraltar.
Sea War: Pacific – 4 remaining Japanese troopships beached on Guadalcanal, where they are destroyed by US planes and artillery.
Air War: Europe – Hampdens of RNZAF attack shipping off Norwegian coast.
Home Front: Britain – Church bells rung throughout Britain (for first time since June 1940) to celebrate victory of 8th Army at El Alamein. BBC broadcasts sound of bells worldwide. 'Civil Defence Day': the King inspects parade of 1,500 in London.

MONDAY, NOVEMBER 16

New Guinea – Americans and Australians begin assault on fortress of Buna.
Air War – US bombers raid Bangkok.

TUESDAY, NOVEMBER 17

Air War – British paratroopers land at Souk-el-Arba airfield, commandeer French MT and leave at top speed for Bizerta.

WEDNESDAY, NOVEMBER 18

North Africa – 8th Army captures Cyrene. British 1st Army (actually only amounting to 1 div.) advancing in 3 columns and along coast road and mtn. roads towards Bizerta and Tunis.

THURSDAY, NOVEMBER 19

Russian Front – **ZHUKOV LAUNCHES SURPRISE COUNTER-OFFENSIVE AT STALINGRAD** (Op. Uranus) employing 3 fronts, totalling 10 armies and 1 tank army (900 tanks) supported by 13,500 guns and mortars and Katyusha rocket launchers and 1,100 aircraft, along a 402-km front. By Nov. 23, the Russian armoured spearheads have smashed through weak Rumanian armies N. and S. of Stalingrad and linked up at Kalach, encircling German 6th Army. Red Army Order of the Day: 'The hour of stern and righteous reckoning with the foul enemy, the German Fascists, has struck ... we must make the enemy's black blood flow in rivers.'
North Africa – British paratroops advancing from Souk-el-Arba encounter Germans at Sidi Nsir, SW. of Bizerta.

FRIDAY, NOVEMBER 20

North Africa – Benghazi captured by 8th Army.
Home Front: Hungary – Death of Count Leopold von Berchtold, notorious Austro-Hungarian Foreign Minister at the outbreak of W.W.I; aged 79.

Above: *A German 75mm infantry gun crew in Stalingrad's outskirts.*

SATURDAY, NOVEMBER 21

Air War – B-17s and P-38s raid Tunis Airport. RAF bombers hit fuel dump on Mingaladon airfield, Burma.

SUNDAY, NOVEMBER 22

Air War: Europe – Stirlings bomb Stuttgart (night Nov. 22-23).
Russian Front – Siege of Leningrad: German heavy artillery continues to bombard city.
Home Front: Britain – Sir Stafford Cripps becomes Minister of Aircraft Production.

MONDAY, NOVEMBER 23

Russian Front – Siege of Leningrad: German heavy artillery and bombers in action before dawn. 50,000 shells hit the

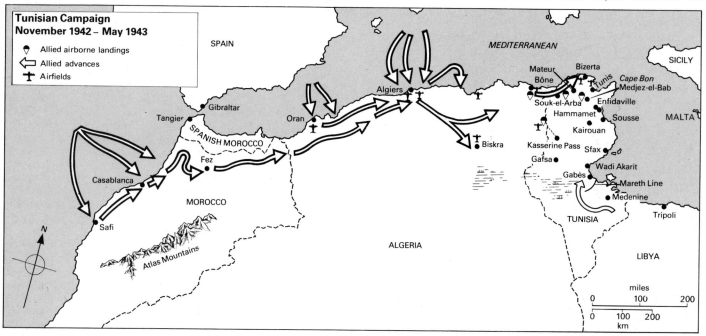

Tunisian Campaign November 1942 – May 1943

- Allied airborne landings
- Allied advances
- Airfields

city during 1942; shelling takes place on 254 days.

North Africa – Rommel evacuates Agedabia.

Air War – American aircraft dive-bomb bridge at Hankow and hit Canton airfield; RAF Wellingtons bomb Meiktila airfield (Burma), starting large fires. Japanese night raid on Kweilin – US air base in SW. China.

Occupied France – Dakar – vital base in French W. Africa – comes under Allied control following decision of Governor-Gen. Boisson to abandon his former allegiance to Vichy.

TUESDAY, NOVEMBER 24

Air War – RAF raids airfields at Gabes, Bizerta and Tunis.

WEDNESDAY, NOVEMBER 25

Air War: Europe – STALINGRAD AIRLIFT (Nov. 25, 1942-Feb. 2, 1943): *Luftwaffe* transport units (joined by bomber units, from Nov. 30) attempt to fulfil Göring's verbal promise to Hitler that encircled 6th Army can be entirely supplied by air. Total number of planes involved rises from 320 in Nov. to 500 in early Dec. and 850 in late Dec. Deliveries promised: 500 t. per day; actual daily average, 100 t. Losses: 489 aircraft (inc. 266 Ju-52s and 165 He 111s).

THURSDAY, NOVEMBER 26

North Africa – British capture Medjez-el-Bab, SW. of Tunis.

Air War – US bombers attack Bangkok oil refinery.

FRIDAY, NOVEMBER 27

Air War – Heavy RAF raid on Tripoli. US B-25s and P-40s hit docks and shipping at Canton and rout defending Japanese fighters.

Sea War: Med. – SCUTTLING OF FRENCH FLEET. German plan to capture fleet intact at Toulon is foiled by Adm. de Laborde, who orders all crews to destroy their ships. 2nd *SS Pz* Div.

races belatedly to the naval base, while German aircraft drop mines and flares.

Ships sunk inc. battle cruisers *Dunkerque* and *Strasbourg*, battleship *Provence*, cruisers *Algérie, Colbert, Dupleix, Foch, La Galissonnière, Marseillaise* and *Jean de Vienne*. 30 destroyers, 16 subs. and seaplane carrier *Commandant Teste* (Italian Navy subsequently salvages and repairs 5 destroyers), 4 subs. escape – *Iris* to internment in Spain and 3 others to N. Africa.

SATURDAY, NOVEMBER 28

Air War – RAF drop 8,000-lb bombs on Turin (night Nov. 28-29). US bombers hit port facilities and power station at Tripoli.

Home Front: USA – At least 493 people killed in accidental fire and subsequent panic at Cocoanut Grove night club, Boston (Massachusetts).

Vichy France – Vichy forces demobbed.

SUNDAY, NOVEMBER 29

North Africa – Battle of Tebourba-Djedeida: British armoured 'Blade Force', supported by American tanks, makes costly efforts to storm German hilltop strongholds near Tunis. Local German air superiority is decisive. British paratroops land near Oudna airfield S. of Tunis: they launch 2 attacks in spite of German tanks and armd. cars and sabotage airfield, then beat a fighting retreat to the Tunis road.

Home Front: Britain – Churchill broadcasts on war situation. He describes the 'measureless calamities' brought upon Italy by 'the Hyena' (Mussolini) – all for the sake of 'a brief promenade, by German permission, along the (French) Riviera and a flying visit to Corsica'.

Home Front: USA – Coffee rationing introduced.

MONDAY, NOVEMBER 30

North Africa – British 36th Brig., advancing towards Bizerta, held up by German paratroops on Djebel Azzag (Green Hill) and Djebel Agred (Bald Hill).

Sea War: Pacific – German naval tanker *Uckermark* (ex-*Altmark*: see Feb. 16, 1940) sunk by accidental explosion at Yokohoma. The blast also destroys disguised raider *Thor*. BATTLE OF TASSAFARONGA: US cruiser force attempts to destroy the 'Tokyo Express' – 8 destroyers carrying rice to Guadalcanal – but is ignominiously routed. 4 US cruisers torpedoed; 1 Japanese destroyer sunk.

TUESDAY, DECEMBER 1

New Guinea – Australians capture Gona.

Sea War: Med. – Italian convoy destroyed off Tunis by British Force Q (3 cruisers, 2 destroyers). Destroyer *Quentin* later sunk by Italian torpedo planes.

Diplomacy – Ethiopia declares war on Germany, Italy and Japan.

Home Front: Britain – 'Beveridge Report' (Social Insurance and Allied Services) published: lays framework for post-war National Health Service and Social Security system. Report is a bestseller (635,000 copies sold).

Sidney Silverman M.P. claims that 2 M. Jews have been killed by the Nazis up to Sept. 30, 1942.

Air War – Gen. Eaker takes over command of 8th USAAF from Gen. Spaatz who takes over 12th AF in N. Africa.

WEDNESDAY, DECEMBER 2

Home Front: USA – FIRST CONTROLLED NUCLEAR CHAIN-REACTION initiated by Prof. Enrico Fermi in makeshift laboratory under Univ. of Chicago football stadium.

Home Front: Italy – Mussolini breaks 18-month silence to refute Churchill's broadcast of Nov. 29.

THURSDAY, DECEMBER 3

North Africa – Germans counter-attack in Tebourba sector.

FRIDAY, DECEMBER 4

Air War: Europe – Liberators of 9th USAAF bomb Naples: fast cruiser *Muzio Attendolo* sunk, 2 other Italian cruisers and 4 destroyers damaged; railway installations hit. Casualties: 159 killed, 358 injured.

Sea War: Med. – 3 Italian battleships subsequently leave Naples for La Spezia (N. Italy).

Air War – 9 Bisley (Blenheim Mk. V) light bombers, led by Wing-Cdr. Malcolm, V.C., attack Chouigui landing ground (Tunisia): 50 Me 109s annihilate the unescorted bombers. Thereafter all RAF bombing ops. over Tunisia are carried out at night.

SATURDAY, DECEMBER 5

Home Front: USSR – Huge new blast furnace lit at Magnitogorsk (Urals).

Sea War: Pacific – US Navy Dept. Report on Pearl Harbor Raid (Dec. 7, 1941) and salvage ops.: *Arizona*, the only battleship totally beyond repair; *Oklahoma* is still half-submerged, keel up; *Maryland, Pennsylvania* and *Tennessee* and cruisers *Helena, Honolulu* and *Raleigh* repaired and returned to service; 50% of machinery of sunken destroyers *Cassin* and *Downes* salvaged; heavily damaged destroyer *Shaw* repaired and recommissioned. Naval and Marine Corps casualties: 2,117 killed, 960 missing (i.e., bodies still not recovered); 876 wounded. US Army casualties: 226 killed, 396 wounded.

SUNDAY, DECEMBER 6

North Africa – BATTLE OF MEDJEZ-EL-BAB (Dec. 6-9): 2 German *Pz* columns attempt to retake Medjez, 56 km SW. of Tunis in torrential rain; Grant tanks and Allied fighters halt 1 column, and second is smashed by artillery in outskirts of town. US armd. force, Combat Cmnd. B, is cut off and attempts to escape across Borj Toun Bridge, only to lose most of its vehicles in deep mud.

Air War: Europe – Low-level daylight raid by 78 RAF Mosquitoes, Bostons and Venturas (12 lost) on Philips radio works at Eindhoven. US B-17s attack Lille locomotive works. 500 RAF, USAAF, and Allied fighters fly escort and diversionary sorties. RAF night raids on Karlsruhe and Pforzheim, SW. Germany (4 bombers lost).

Home Front: USA – Claude R. Wichard appointed War Food Administrator.

MONDAY, DECEMBER 7

Air War – Japanese aircraft make 3 attacks on US and Australian field hospitals in Buna-Gona area of New Guinea (Nov. 28, Dec. 2 and 7): 36 fatal casualties.

Solomons – US 155-mm howitzers pound Japanese positions from dawn to dusk ('Hate Shoot' to commemorate Pearl Harbor anniversary).

Sea War: Atlantic – Liner *Ceramic* (18,700 t.) sunk by U-515: stormy weather prevents launching of lifeboats (500-plus lost; 1 survivor).

TUESDAY, DECEMBER 8

Sea War: Pacific – US sub. *Halibut* sinks 4 ships in Japanese home waters during Dec.

Sea War – Russian sub. *D-5* sinks Turkish sailing ship *Koçiboglu*.

WEDNESDAY, DECEMBER 9

Solomons – Maj.-Gen. Vandergrift, US Marines, hands over Guadalcanal to Maj.-Gen. Patch, US Army.

Air War: Europe – RAF night bombers shower 'block-busters' and incendiaries over Turin for second night in succession: huge fires light up alpine peaks many km to the N.

THURSDAY, DECEMBER 10

Home Front: Britain – British and German guns exchange fire across Strs. of Dover for 90 min.

Air War: Europe – German, Italian and Hungarian aircraft bomb marshalling yards and depots NW. and SE. of Stalingrad.

FRIDAY, DECEMBER 11

Sea War – 'Cockleshell Heroes' Raid: 5 canoes, each manned by 2 British Commandos, are launched from sub. *Tuna* (Dec. 7). 3 lost, but 2 survivors travel 146

km up Gironde R. to Bordeaux, where 4 merchant ships, a tanker and a naval auxiliary are disabled with limpet mines. (6 captured Commandos later executed by Germans.)

SATURDAY, DECEMBER 12

Russian Front – Op. *Wintersturm* ('Winter Storm'): 13 German divs., under Manstein and Hoth, attempt to punch a corridor from Kotelnikovo to Stalingrad, through which 6th Army can withdraw. R. Aksay is reached and crossed, but the attack grinds to a halt at R. Myshkova (Dec. 18)

Sea War: Med. – 4 ships disabled by Italian 'human torpedoes' and frogmen at Algiers.

SUNDAY, DECEMBER 13

North Africa – Rommel retreats from El Agheila as 8th Army resumes advance.

Occupied Holland – Anton Mussert, leader of Dutch Nazi Party (NSB), appointed 'Leader of Netherlands People' by Hitler.

Occupied France – Laval says '*without equivocation . . . I want Germany's victory*'.

MONDAY, DECEMBER 14

New Guinea – Japanese reinforcements land near Buna.

North Africa – Rommel skilfully evades 8th Army trap at El Agheila (Dec. 14-18).

Diplomacy – Franco-British Agreement on Madagascar: Gen. Legentilhomme appointed High Commissioner.

Home Front: Japan – Newspapers *Nichi Nichi* of Tokyo and *Mainichi* of Osaka merge as *Mainichi Shimbun*.

TUESDAY, DECEMBER 15

Air War – RAF and USAAF batter retreating German columns W. of El Agheila throughout the day, against negligible *Luftwaffe* opposition; huge 'traffic jam' at 'Marble Arch' (monument erected by Mussolini).

WEDNESDAY, DECEMBER 16

Russian Front – Op. Saturn: Russians smash Italian 8th Army along R. Don,

Below: *Desert-worn 8th Army Stuart light tanks pass along Benghazi's waterfront in pursuit of Rommel.*

NW. of Stalingrad (Dec. 16-18).
New Guinea – Australian inf. and tanks land in Oro Bay, near Buna.
Air War: Britain – Hit-and-run raiders (2 lost) attack 20 towns and villages in S. Britain, under cover of low cloud; 2 aircraft machine-gun a train (7 killed).
Home Front: USA – 'Whipple's Comet' discovered by Dr Whipple of Harvard Univ. Observatory (visible to the naked eye from Great Britain in Jan. 1943).

THURSDAY, DECEMBER 17

Home Front: Britain – Foreign Minister Eden announces that the Germans '*are now carrying into effect Hitler's oft-repeated intention to exterminate the Jewish people in Europe*'.
New Guinea – Americans and Australians launch final assault on Buna.

FRIDAY, DECEMBER 18

Russian Front – Hoth makes repeated attempts to force the R. Myshkova, 40 km SW. of Stalingrad (Dec. 18-23), but without success.
Air War: Europe – 74 Pe-2s and 10 Shturmoviks, escorted by 28 Yak fighters,

carry out devastating attack on Hoth's *Pzs* at Karpovka, near Stalingrad.
Sea War: Pacific – Cruiser *Tenryu* sunk by US sub. *Albacore* in Madang Harbour, New Guinea.

SATURDAY, DECEMBER 19

North Africa – Maj.-Gen. Dan Pienaar, GOC S. African Div. in Libya and leader of victorious S. African troops during E. African Campaign, killed while flying home – his aircraft crashing in L. Victoria (E. Africa). Aged 49.

SUNDAY, DECEMBER 20

Air War: Europe – US B-17s and B-24s (6 lost), escorted by 300 Allied fighters, bomb aircraft repair depot at Rommilliessur-Seine, and shoot down 21 German fighters. RAF night raid on Duisburg (11 aircraft lost).
Air War – First of 5 Japanese night raids on Calcutta in Dec.

MONDAY, DECEMBER 21

New Guinea – Stuart tanks penetrate strongly held Japanese perimeter at Buna.

TUESDAY, DECEMBER 22

Air War: Europe – RAF fighters, fighterbombers and Boston light bombers make day and night attacks on rail communications in W. Germany, Holland, N. and NW. France.
Home Front: Britain – Announced that Roll of Honour of British war dead is to be deposited in Westminster Abbey, London.

WEDNESDAY, DECEMBER 23

Air War: Europe – RAF Bostons and Venturas bomb St Malo and Den Helder.

THURSDAY, DECEMBER 24

North Africa – Adm. Darlan assassinated by French fanatic in Algiers. French authorities apprehend the assassin and execute him (Dec. 26).
Russian Front – Russians throw back Hoth's 'relief force' from R. Myshkova to R. Aksay (Dec. 24) and Kotelnikovo (Dec. 29)
North Africa – Brig. of Guards capture 'Long-stop Hill' (Djebel Ahmera) near Medjez: severe German counter-attacks force them to withdraw, Dec. 27.
Air War: Pacific – Hawaii-based B-24s of 7th AF start big fires on Wake I.

FRIDAY, DECEMBER 25

Russian Front – Russians recapture 2 towns near Nalchik and reopen 'Ossetian Military Highway'.
North Africa – 8th Army captures Sirte.

SATURDAY, DECEMBER 26

North Africa – Giraud appointed High Commissioner in French N. Africa.
Air War – US 10th AAF bombers raid Lashio (Burma Road) and Bangkok (night Dec. 26-27).

SUNDAY, DECEMBER 27

Air War: Pacific – Japanese parachute supplies to half-starved expeditionary forces on Guadalcanal.

MONDAY, DECEMBER 28

North Africa – De Gaulle welcomes Giraud's appointment (*see* Dec. 26) and appeals for French Unity. French Somaliland joins Free French cause.
Russian Front – Hitler orders Army Grp. A to withdraw from dangerously exposed salient in the Caucasus.

TUESDAY, DECEMBER 29

Russian Front – Kotelnikovo, 153 km SW. of Stalingrad, recaptured by Russians after house-to-house fighting.

WEDNESDAY, DECEMBER 30

Air War: Europe – B-17s and B-24s bomb Lorient U-boat base. Night raid on Casablanca by Focke-Wulf Condors from Bordeaux.
Home Front: Britain – Harold Macmillan M.P. made Minister Resident N. Africa.

THURSDAY, DECEMBER 31

Sea War – 107 ships attacked by U-boats in 'Gulf Sea Frontier' area during 1942 – 25 sunk off New Orleans and 25 off Florida; 882 casualties. (Only 4 ships attacked in 1943.)
Sea War: Atlantic – BATTLE OF THE BARENTS SEA (Op. *Regenbogen*: 'Rainbow'): *Lützow* and *Admiral Hipper* make repeated, bungled, attempts to destroy Convoy JW. 51B – after which *Lützow* is to break out into Atlantic (Op. *Morgenröte*: 'Aurora'). Resourceful tactics by British destroyers and cruisers plus extraordinary vacillation of German commanders results in fiasco. 2 British destroyers lost, but convoy escapes intact and Germans retire ignominiously to Norway (1 destroyer lost). Hitler is beside himself with fury and orders immediate scrapping of battle fleet.
Diplomacy – International Red Cross is now spending £375,000 per month on food parcels for PoWs.

Shipping Losses 1942
Allied and Neutral: 1,570 ships totalling 7,915,737 t. Axis: 86 U-boats, 22 Italian subs., 16 Japanese subs.

1943

FRIDAY, JANUARY 1

Russian Front – Velikie Luki rail junction, on Central Front, stormed by Russians; German garrison annihilated. Russians drive towards Rostov and take the offensive in the Caucasus. Elista, capital of Kalmuck SSR, recaptured.
Sea War: Atlantic – German blockade-runner *Rhakotis* sunk by HMS *Scylla* off C. Finisterre. Hitler orders all big warships to be laid up.
Air War – US bombers raid 3 airfields on Crete (night Jan. 1-2).

SATURDAY, JANUARY 2

Russian Front – Germans withdrawing from Caucasus.
New Guinea – BUNA CAPTURED by Allied forces: many underground bunkers destroyed one by one by tanks and explosive charges.
Air War – *Stukas*, FW 190 fighter-bombers and He 111 torpedo planes make frequent sorties against Allied shipping in and around Bône, Bougie and Algiers during Jan.: 4 ships sunk; cruiser *Ajax*, destroyer and AA ship damaged. First Allied daylight raid on Crete (main target, Suda Bay).

SUNDAY, JANUARY 3

Sea War: Med. – British 'human torpedoes' ('Chariots') penetrate Palermo harbour; cruiser *Ulpio Traiano* and a tanker severely damaged. U-boats torpedo 7 out of 9 tankers in Convoy TM.1 (Trinidad-Mediterranean), Jan. 3-10.
Russian Front – Mozdok (Caucasus) recaptured by Russians.
Air War: Pacific – B-17s bomb Rabaul.

MONDAY, JANUARY 4

Sea War: Pacific – TF 67 (3 US cruisers and 2 destroyers) carries out night bombardment of Munda Airfield, Solomons.
Solomons – Japanese Imperial GHQ orders evacuation of 17th Army from Guadalcanal.

TUESDAY, JANUARY 5

Air War – B-17s and B-24s make low-level attack on shipping at Rabaul (New Guinea).
North Africa – US 5th Army formed in Tunisia under Lt.-Gen. Mark W. Clark. 8th Army reach Buerat, 97 km W. of Sirte. British storm 'Green Hill' (Tunisia) but are driven off by heavy MG fire.

WEDNESDAY, JANUARY 6

Air War/Sea War: Pacific – BATTLE OF HUON GULF (Jan. 6-9): all available Allied bombers and fighters in SW. Pacific make round-the-clock attacks on Japanese troop convoy, making for Lae (New Guinea); 3 transport and approx. 80 Japanese aircraft destroyed. Allied losses, light.
North Africa – Free French, advancing N. from Chad, capture Oum-el-Arameb (S. Libya) after heavy fighting.

THURSDAY, JANUARY 7

Air War: Europe – US 9th AF bombs Palermo harbour (308 civilian casualties).
Occupied France – Gen. Legentilhomme begins duties as High Commissioner for Madagascar.

FRIDAY, JANUARY 8

Russian Front – Stalingrad: Paulus rejects Rokossovsky's surrender ultimatum.
Sea War: Med. – British Force K (2 cruisers, 4 destroyers) harries last convoys between S. Italy and Tripoli, sinking 14 ships of all sizes (nights between Jan. 8-9 and 20-21).

SATURDAY, JANUARY 9

Diplomacy – Puppet 'Central Govt. of China' declares war on Britain and USA.
Air War – Flt.-Lt. Richard Hilary, author of 'The Last Enemy', killed on active service; aged 23. Maiden flight of Lockheed C-69 military transport (forerunner of Constellation airliner).

Below: *Soviet recapture of Mozdok: a German defender surrenders, Jan. 3.*

SUNDAY, JANUARY 10

Russian Front – Stalingrad: Red Army launches Op. Ring – series of co-ordinated attacks from NW. and S. (by Don Front), and from the E. (by Stalingrad Front). By Jan. 15, German 6th Army is split into several grps. or 'pockets'.
Sea War: Pacific – Giant US sub. *Argonaut* lost off New Guinea.
Occupied France – *Milice Nationale* (secret police force) created in Vichy France headed by Joseph Darnand, one of the heroes of Forbach Wood Incident. (*See* Feb. 8, 1940.)

MONDAY, JANUARY 11

Russian Front – Russians retake Georgievsk, Mineralniye, Vody and 6 other towns in Caucasus.
Home Front: USA – $100 billion defence Budget.
Diplomacy – Britain and USA formally relinquish their 'extra-territorial' rights in Peking, Tientsin and Chinese 'Treaty Ports' (all presently under Japanese occupation).
Air War – US daylight raid on Naples.

TUESDAY, JANUARY 12

Air War: Europe – B-17s wreck buildings and aircraft on Castel Benito airfield, near Tripoli, while escorting P-38s rout 20 defending Me 109s.
North Africa – Montgomery sends 'Personal Message' to men of 8th Army, calling for supreme effort to drive Italians from Tripoli – their last African stronghold: *'Our families and friends . . . . will be thrilled when they hear we have captured that place.'*
Leclerc's Free French now in complete control of S. Libya (Fezzan).

WEDNESDAY, JANUARY 13

Russian Front – Fourth Battle of Kharkov: Russians drive 2 large salients into German lines W. of R. Don, capturing Kursk and Kharkov, but Manstein counter-attacks and recaptures Kharkov (Jan. 13-March 26).
North Africa – Germans move out of Pont du Fahs, S. of Medjez and capture 'Two Tree Hill'.
Air War: Europe – First of eight RAF night raids in Jan. on the Ruhr.

THURSDAY, JANUARY 14

Russian Front – Stalingrad: Russians capture Pitomnik airfield – vital base for German airlift.
Air War – 3 Japanese bombers shot down in 4 min. by RAF Beaufighter night fighter over Calcutta.
Air War: Europe – First of 5 heavy RAF night raids on Lorient.
Diplomacy – **CASABLANCA CONFERENCE** (Jan. 14-25): Churchill and Roosevelt demand 'Unconditional' surrender of Germany, Italy and Japan. Defeat of U-boats to receive top priority; Sicily to be invaded during 1943. De Gaulle and Giraud attend.

FRIDAY, JANUARY 15

Solomons – Final US ground offensive begins on Guadalcanal.
North Africa – 8th Army push W. from Buerat.
Sea War: Med. – 'Inshore Squadron' of British Med. Fleet delivers supplies to 8th Army, advancing along N. African coast (Jan.-Feb.). Cruiser *Dragon* transferred from RN to Polish Navy (name not changed).
Home Front: Britain – Hugh McAteer and 3 other IRA 'officers' escape from Crumlin Rd. Prison, Belfast (McAteer recaptured Sept. 1943).

SATURDAY, JANUARY 16

North Africa – 8th Army and Free French, advancing from S. Libya, join forces.
Air War: Europe – First RAF raids on Berlin since Nov. 1941 (nights Jan. 16-17 and 17-18): first raid takes defences by surprise (1 plane lost), but 22 lost in second. 'Marker Bombs' (Target Indicators) tested; Daimler-Benz engine works badly hit, but many bombs wasted on suburbs.
Air War: Pacific – B-17s carry out night raid on shipping at Rabaul.
Diplomacy – Iraq declares war on Germany, Italy and Japan.

SUNDAY, JANUARY 17

Russian Front – German High Command belatedly admits loss of Velikie Luki (*see* Jan. 1, 1943) after repeated counter-attacks have failed to take the town. Russians capture Millerovo, near Voronezh.
Burma – Commonwealth forces occupy Kyauktaw (Arakan).
Air War: Britain – *Luftwaffe* 'reprisal' raid on London (night Jan. 17-18): 118 aircraft (6 lost) attack in 2 waves. Bombs fall mainly on outskirts; Greenwich power station hit.

MONDAY, JANUARY 18

Russian Front – **SIEGE OF LENINGRAD:** after week-long battle, **GERMAN ENCIRCLEMENT PARTIALLY BROKEN** by recapture of Schüsselburg and Sinyavino and link-up of Leningrad and Volkhov Fronts E. of city. Rail communications are subsequently restored, but trains are shelled repeatedly in this 'Corridor of Death'.
North Africa – Germans and Italians, supported by *Pzs*, attempt to capture Bou Arada Hill and Robaa Hills, near Medjez.

TUESDAY, JANUARY 19

Sea War: Pacific – 'Cactus Striking Force' (4 American destroyers) commence regular bombardment of Japanese positions on Guadalcanal.
New Guinea – Australians destroy Japanese remnants in Sanananda village (750 killed) – thereby ending Papuan fighting.

New Guinea Campaign Losses
Since Nov. 1942. Japanese: 9,390 dead. Allies: 3,095 dead, 5,451 wounded; over 200 die of typhus.

Solomons – US forces launch final offensive on Guadalcanal: Mt. Austen ('Strongpoint Gifu') captured.
North Africa – 8th Army occupies Homs. *Pzs* launch diversionary attack through Ousseltia Valley, but are held by French Foreign Legion and tanks of Combat Command B.
Occupied Holland – Birth of Princess Margriet in Ottawa – third child of Princess Juliana and Prince Bernhard of the Netherlands.
Russian Front – Russians have now captured 27,600 Hungarians, 22,000 Italians and 2,500 Germans in Voronezh sector.

WEDNESDAY, JANUARY 20

Air War: Britain – Daylight fighter-bomber raid on London: 28 fighter-bombers (3 lost) and 50 escort fighters (6 lost) carry out devastating surprise attack. 22 bombs on target, 39 children and 5 teachers killed at Lewisham school; Surrey Docks hit. Typhoons intercept raiders as they withdraw.
Diplomacy – Chile breaks off diplomatic relations with Germany, Italy and Japan.

THURSDAY, JANUARY 21

Russian Front – Stalingrad: Russians capture Gumrak airfield. This is a virtual death-blow to the German airlift. From now on all supplies must be dropped by parachute.

FRIDAY, JANUARY 22

Russian Front – Salsk rail junction, SW. of Stalingrad, stormed by Russian armour.
Sea War: Med. – Force K bombards Rommel's retreating forces E. of Tripoli.

SATURDAY, JANUARY 23

North Africa – **8TH ARMY CAPTURES TRIPOLI.**
Sea War: Pacific – Cruisers *Nashville* and *Helena*, 'Cactus Striking Force' and planes from *Saratoga* batter Vila airfield on Kolombangara I. (Solomons).

Below: *The first British tank (a Valentine) to enter Tripoli is played in by a Gordon Highlanders piper.*

SUNDAY, JANUARY 24

Russian Front – Stalingrad: Hitler wires Paulus: *'Surrender is forbidden ... 6 [th] Army will hold their positions to the last man and the last round ...'*.
Sea War – Destroyers *Mendip* and *Windsor* drive off 16 German MTBs attempting to attack convoy off Lowestoft.

MONDAY, JANUARY 25

Russian Front – Stalin issues Order of the Day: in 2 months Red Army has routed 102 enemy divs. and advanced 402 km. *Forward to the rout of the German invader and their expulsion from ... our Motherland.'*

TUESDAY, JANUARY 26

Russian Front – Russians retake Voronezh.
Secret War – Franciscus Johannes Winter, 40-year-old Belgian, executed at Wandsworth, London. He is the thirteenth spy executed in Britain since Sept. 1939.
Home Front: Britain – War expenditure now running at £14 M. per day.

WEDNESDAY, JANUARY 27

Russian Front – Stalingrad: Russians begin final assault on 2 large German 'pockets' in ruined city.
North Africa – Churchill arrives in Cairo for talks with Alexander.
Air War: Europe – First US bombing raid on Germany in W.W.II: 58 8th AF B-17s attack Wilhelmshaven. Mosquitoes knock out Burmeister and Wain diesel engine works at Copenhagen. Lancasters and Halifaxes raid Düsseldorf by night.

THURSDAY, JANUARY 28

Air War: Europe – 2 Belgian fighter pilots of RAF drop Belgian flags over centre of Brussels.

FRIDAY, JANUARY 29

Sea War: Pacific – Giant Japanese submarine *I-1* sunk in engagement with NZ armed trawlers *Kiwi* and *Moa* off Guadalcanal. 3 US cruisers hit by Japanese torpedo planes near Guadalcanal (*Chicago* sunk, Jan. 30).
Home Front: Germany – Dr Ernst Kaltenbrunner, *SS* Group Leader and Lt.-Gen. of Police, appointed Heydrich's successor as head of *SD (Gestapo)*. Sex murderer Bruno Lüdke claims his last victim – the 85th (?) since 1928. Lüdke subsequently arrested and given fatal injection (April 8, 1944).
New Guinea – Australians airlift 800 troops to Wau, S. of Lae, where small Australian garrison faces overwhelmingly superior Japanese forces.

SATURDAY, JANUARY 30

Russian Front – Maikop (Caucasus) recaptured by Russians.
North Africa – Germans expel French from Faid Pass, S. Tunisia.
Air War: Europe – FIRST ALLIED DAYLIGHT BOMBING RAIDS ON BERLIN. 6 RAF Mosquitoes (1 lost) attack in 2 waves – timed to interrupt broadcasts by Göring and Goebbels on tenth anniversary of Nazi régime. H2S radar bombing equipment tested over Hamburg.
Home Front: Germany – Göring broadcasts (1 hour late): *'if Germany collapsed ... the Soviet would sweep through Europe.'* Every German must be prepared to give his life *'so that his race may live'*.
Diplomacy – The Adana Conference: Churchill and Alanbrooke confer with Turkish leaders (Jan. 30-31) and promise direct military assistance if Turkey is forced into war.

SUNDAY, JANUARY 31

Russian Front – Stalingrad: Paulus surrenders at Univermag dept. store; capitulation of German forces in S. pocket.
Air War – Liberators bomb Messina: many hits on ferry terminal (Strs. of Messina) and heavy casualties, inc. Archbishop of Reggio.
Sea War: Atlantic – Karl Dönitz succeeds Adm. Raeder as CinC German Navy, with rank of Grand-Adm.
Home Front: Italy – Marshal Cavallero, COGS, replaced by Gen. Ambrosio.

MONDAY, FEBRUARY 1

Sea War: Pacific – Op. *KE*: Japanese destroyers secretly evacuate 11,700 men of 17th Army from Guadalcanal by night (Feb. 1-2 to 7-8); US 'Cactus Striking Force' heavily bombed while attempting to intervene.
Sea War: Med. – Cruiser-minelayer *Welshman* sunk by *U-617* off Crete. *U-118* lays minefield in Strs. of Gibraltar (4 ships sunk, 3 damaged).
New Guinea – Japanese withdrawing from Wau.

TUESDAY, FEBRUARY 2

Russian Front – BATTLE OF STALINGRAD ENDS. 40,000 Germans surrender in N. 'Pocket'. Gen. Rokossovsky takes the salute at the victory parade.

> **Stalingrad Campaign Losses**
> Since Aug. 23, 1942. German: 110,500 dead, *c.* 50,000 wounded, 107,500 PoWs. Soviet: 750,000 plus 250,000 civilians.

WEDNESDAY, FEBRUARY 3

Russian Front – 3 Hungarian gens. captured at Voronezh.

THURSDAY, FEBRUARY 4

North Africa – 8th Army enters Tunisia.
Air War – RAF Liberators bomb Rangoon docks. RAF night bombers start huge fires in and around Turin and hit nearby naval

Above: *A Degtyarev light machine-gun covers advancing Soviet infantry in the ruins of Stalingrad.*

base of La Spezia and Lorient U-boat base.
Sea War – Russian Black Sea Fleet lands troops and marines near Novorossisk (these are overwhelmed by Feb. 6). Convoy Pamphlet: 30,000 battle-weary Australian troops leave Suez for home aboard *Queen Mary* and 4 other liners.
Sea War: Atlantic – Op. Gondola: first in lengthy series of RAF and USAAF ops. against U-boats in Bay of Biscay. Total number of U-boats sunk Feb.-June, 1943, 12. 'Leigh Lights' (immensely powerful searchlights) used with great success.
Home Front: Germany – 3 days of 'national mourning' ordered to commemorate the 'Stalingrad Disaster'; all theatres, cinemas and night clubs closed.

FRIDAY, FEBRUARY 5

Air War: Pacific – Heavy incendiary raid by US bombers on Rabaul airfields.
Sea War – Second Russian landing op. near Novorossisk: 17,000 troops put ashore by Feb. 9.

SATURDAY, FEBRUARY 6

Air War: Pacific – 26 of 70 Japanese planes shot down by 37 Allied fighters over Wau.

SUNDAY, FEBRUARY 7

Sea War: Atlantic – 6 ships of strongly escorted Convoy SC. 118 sunk by *U-402*.

MONDAY, FEBRUARY 8

Russian Front – Kursk recaptured by Russians.

Home Front: Germany – Himmler orders special precautions to be taken at concentration camps, to prevent mass escapes in the event of air raids – inc. sub-division of each camp into blocks, each containing 4,000 prisioners, which are to be surrounded by minefields, electrically charged barbed wire, searchlights and dogs trained to kill on sight.

TUESDAY, FEBRUARY 9

Sea War: Med. – First of 7 troop convoys leave S. Italy with powerful reinforcements for Axis forces in Tunisia (Feb. 9 – March 22): Malta-based RAF aircraft sink 10 ships; specially laid minefields and British subs. also score numerous successes (3 subs. lost).

Guadalcanal Campaign Losses
Japanese: 24,000 dead; 1 aircraft carrier, 2 battleships, 4 cruisers, 11 destroyers, 6 subs., 16 transports. US: 1,600 dead (troops), 4,709 wounded; 2 aircraft carriers, 8 cruisers, 17 destroyers, 6 MTBs, 4 transports.

WEDNESDAY, FEBRUARY 10

Sea War – Norwegian sub. *Urred* disappears off Bodo.
RAF 'Whirlibombers' hit German disguised raider *Coronel* as she attempts to break out into the Atlantic. *Coronel* puts into Boulogne.

THURSDAY, FEBRUARY 11

Air War: Europe – First of 3 heavy RAF night raids on Wilhelmshaven during Feb.

FRIDAY, FEBRUARY 12

Russian Front – Russians recapture Krasnodar (Kuban).

SATURDAY, FEBRUARY 13

Air War: Europe – RAF night raid on Lorient U-boat base (1,000 t. bombs).

SUNDAY, FEBRUARY 14

Russian Front – Rostov recaptured by Red Army.
North Africa – **BATTLE OF KASSERINE PASS** (Feb. 14-25): Rommel launches surprise counter-offensive (Op. *Frühlingswind*: 'Spring Wind'): *Pzs* supported by *Stukas* throw inexperienced Americans into confusion. Germans reach Kasserine Pass, Feb. 20, but are soon forced back. Allied casualties: 10,000; German casualties, 2,000.
Burma – **FIRST 'CHINDIT' OP.** behind Japanese lines, led by Brig.-Gen. Orde Wingate (begins night Feb. 14-15). Force of 3,000 begins 6-week op.

MONDAY, FEBRUARY 15

Air War: Europe – Allied bombers raid Dunkirk harbour. RAF night intruders damage 11 locomotives in N. France.

TUESDAY, FEBRUARY 16

Russian Front – Kharkov recaptured by Red Army.
Home Front: Germany – The Munich Students' 'Revolt': *Gauleiter* Geisler of Bavaria harangues assembled university students and taunts them with insults and obscenities. Meeting ends in pandemonium as students overpower *SS* guards and police and take to the streets. Widespread outbreaks of sabotage, etc., in Munich and sympathetic student demonstrations in Vienna, Mannheim, Stuttgart, Frankfurt and the Ruhr.

WEDNESDAY, FEBRUARY 17

Sea War – 15 German MTBs lay mines off Gt. Yarmouth and Lowestoft: *S. 71* rammed and sunk by destroyer *Garth* (night Feb. 17-18).

THURSDAY, FEBRUARY 18

Home Front: Germany – Hans and Sophie Scholl, leaders of Munich Student's Revolt and authors of anti-Nazi 'White Rose Letters', tried by People's Court and executed Feb. 21.
Goebbels calls upon German people to wage 'Total War' in histrionic speech at Berlin Sportpalast.
Home Front: USA – B-29 Superfortress 4-engined bomber catches fire during test flight and crashes into a Seattle factory. 31 killed, inc. 'Eddie' Allen, Boeing's chief test pilot.

FRIDAY, FEBRUARY 19

Russian Front – Russians capture Oboyan, on Kursk-Kharkov railway.
Air War: Europe – RAF Army Co-op. Cmnd. planes bomb electrical transformer stations in Loire Valley.

SATURDAY, FEBRUARY 20

Russian Front – Manstein's *Pzs* counter-attack in Pavlograd Sector.
North Africa – 8th Army takes Medenine, E. Tunisia.

SUNDAY, FEBRUARY 21

Sea War: Pacific – Op. Cleanslate: Americans land on Russell I., N. of Guadalcanal.

MONDAY, FEBRUARY 22

Sea War: Atlantic – US Navy reveals 850 Americans killed or missing when U-boats sank 2 passenger-cargo ships.

STALINGRAD......
THE REAL TURNING POINT

Few armies in history have been more decisively defeated than was the German 6th Army at Stalingrad. This unparalleled military catastrophe marked the definitive end of Hitler's Blitzkrieg and the beginning of the end of the Third Reich. In five months of the most savage fighting of World War II, more than 323,000 Germans lost their lives; fewer than 5,000 of the 91,000 PoWs returned to Germany after the war.

But like the ignominious retreat of Napoleon's *Grande Armée* from Moscow in 1812, Hitler's catastrophic Stalingrad campaign also involved the decimation of large contingents from many satellite or allied nations, including 450,000 Italians, Rumanians and Hungarians killed and over 400,000 others captured. Even these staggering figures were exceeded by the million or more Russian casualties, including at least 750,000 Red Army soldiers killed, wounded or missing.

By the morning of January 26, 1943, the encircled German 6th Army had been cut in two. Five days later its once arrogant and foppish commander, Field-Marshal Friedrich Paulus – by now reduced to a ragged, shambling, broken man – tamely surrendered to the Russians. By February 2, 1943, the last pocket of German resistance in the ruined city, was finally crushed.

Marshal Chuikov, one of the Red Army's best generals and commander of the 62nd (Siberian) Army which bore the brunt of the fighting in Stalingrad, has described the battle as *'the fundamental turning-point of World War II . . . the Russian soldier, having retreated hundreds of kilometres to the Volga, suddenly became invincible'.*

He also takes Montgomery and other British experts to task for venturing to suggest that El Alamein was THE turning point of World War II '. . . as though the sands of Africa were more important to Hitler than the oil, coal, metals and grain of Russia. But Hitler was not as stupid as Montgomery paints him, and the

number of troops sent by Hitler in one direction alone – to the Volga – was some ten times more than he had in Africa . . . the facts show that the turning point in the war came not in Africa but on the Volga (at Stalingrad) . . .' *(The Beginning of the Road, Vasili I. Chuikov.)*

Moreover, thanks to the united efforts of the whole Soviet people, 'mobilized by the Communist Party and its Central Committee', the Red Army was able to bring about a crucial change in the progress of World War II. The immediate consequences of this change of fortune were the slow, but inexorable advance of the Soviet forces from Stalingrad to Hitler's Bunker in Berlin. But in the longer term it was to lead to the transformation of Eastern Europe into a bloc of satellite states and the brutal division of Germany itself into two separate republics.

Below: *German infantry and 75mm assault guns advance through the shell of Stalingrad in October 1942.*

Above right: *That same month German wounded are loaded into a Junkers 52 transport. Göring misread the earlier Demiansk airlift (Feb. 19-May 18) when 600 planes maintained 90,000 troops with 273 tonnes of supplies daily; Stalingrad was to get an average of 90 tonnes for 250,000 men.*

Below right: *Soviet infantry clamber through the ruins.*

TUESDAY, FEBRUARY 23

Sea War: Atlantic – U-boat grp. *Rochen* ('Castles') torpedoes 7 tankers from Convoy UC.1 (Feb. 23-24). Acoustic homing torpedoes used.

Home Front: USSR – Stalin issues Order of the Day to Red Army on its 25th Anniversary: '*For 20 months the Red Army has been waging an heroic struggle without parallel in history against the German Fascist hordes. It has become the terror of the Fascist armies.*'

WEDNESDAY, FEBRUARY 24

North Africa – Allied planes harry German forces withdrawing through Kasserine Pass; Italian rearguards destroyed, many being captured.

THURSDAY, FEBRUARY 25

Sea War: Atlantic – Five-day battle of Convoy ON. 166 ends, 15 out of 49 ships sunk; *U-606* lost.

Home Front: New Zealand – Japanese PoWs stage mass break-out attempt (48 Japanese and 1 guard killed).

FRIDAY, FEBRUARY 26

Sea War – German MTBs attack convoy in Lyme Bay (S. England).

North Africa – Op. *Ochsenkopf* ('Oxhead'): Germans launch multi-pronged counter-offensive and attempt to encircle Medjez.

SATURDAY, FEBRUARY 27

Russian Front – Russians recapture Pavlograd SW. of Kharkov near R. Dnieper. *Pzs* reach banks of the Donets S. of Kharkov.

North Africa – Battle of Hunt's Gap: (Feb. 27-March 2) *Kampfgruppe Lang* ('battle grp.' inc. Tiger tanks and *Pz Grens.*) attempts to drive W. through Sidi Nsir valley but is defeated by lone British inf. brig.

SUNDAY, FEBRUARY 28

Air War: Europe – 1,000 t. bombs dropped on St Nazaire U-boat base by 400 RAF night bombers.

Home Front: Germany – GUDERIAN APPOINTED 'INSPECTOR-GEN. OF ARMOURED TROOPS', responsible directly to Hitler and with wide-ranging powers to re-equip, re-train and re-vitalize the decimated *Pz* force and '*make that arm of the Service into a decisive weapon for winning the war*'.

Secret War – NORSK HYDRO RAID. 9 Norwegian paratroopers, led by Lt. Haugen, blow up 286 heavy water cells thereby depriving Nazis of raw materials for atomic weapon research (Haugen escapes to Sweden).

MONDAY, MARCH 1

Russian Front – Russians recapture Demiansk.

Air War: Europe – First of 3 RAF night raids on Berlin in March.

Occupied France – Lens-Béthune railway line closed following derailment of 40 wagons by French Resistance Grp. 'Farmer'.

TUESDAY, MARCH 2

Sea War: Pacific – BATTLE OF THE BISMARCK SEA (March 2-5): Allied bombers and MTBs shatter big Japanese troop convoy off Lae (New Guinea). 8 transports and 4 destroyers sunk; 6,000 Japanese killed. 6 Allied planes lost.

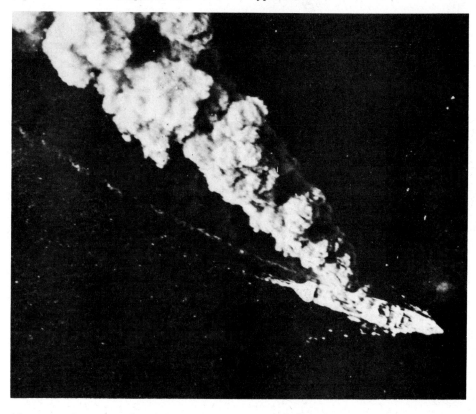

Above: *A sinking armed Japanese merchantman burns in the Bismarck Sea.*

Russian Front – *Pzs* destroy Russian 3rd Tank Army near Kharkov (March 2-4). Mussolini issues Order of the Day announcing repatriation of Italian Expeditionary Force (*Corpo Spedizionario Italiano*) '*to rest and have their ranks refilled*'.

Air War – Spitfires intercept Japanese bombers over Darwin, taking raiders by surprise (6 out of 15 shot down).

WEDNESDAY, MARCH 3

Russian Front – Rzhev – German stronghold W. of Moscow – stormed by Russian forces. Russians now control long stretches of Moscow-Riga railway.

Air War: Europe – Mosquitoes bomb

Knaben molybdenum mines, Norway (vital to German steel industry). RAF night raid on Hamburg. 117 German night raiders (6 lost) despatched to London: only 126 bombs on target. AA rockets supplement regular barrage but cause panic at Bethnal Green tube station, where 400 people pile up on the steps (173 suffocate, 62 injured).

Home Front: Britain — Death of Capt. FitzRoy, Speaker of the House of Commons; age 73.

THURSDAY, MARCH 4

Sea War — Unsuccessful night sortie by German MTBs off Gt. Yarmouth: *S.70* mined and sunk; *S.75* sunk by Spitfires and Typhoons.

FRIDAY, MARCH 5

Sea War: Atlantic – *U-130* sinks 4 ships from Convoy XK. 1.

Air War: Europe – BATTLE OF THE RUHR OPENS with devastating raid on Krupps Works at Essen by 367 RAF night bombers (14 lost) led by Mosquito pathfinders, guided by 'Oboe' equipment (26 raids on targets in and near the Ruhr, March 5-6 to June 28-29, 1943).

Home Front: Finland – Coalition Govt. formed.

SATURDAY, MARCH 6

Sea War: Atlantic – BIGGEST CONVOY BATTLE OF THE WAR. U-boat 'wolf-pack' attacks convoys SC. 121, HX. 228, SC. 122, HX. 229 (March 6-20) sinking 21 ships totalling 140,842 t. 4 U-boats destroyed.

Cdre. Birnie of SC. 121 lost with his ship.
North Africa – **BATTLE OF MÉDENINE:** in his last battle in Africa, Rommel attacks 8th Army but is defeated with heavy losses from antitank guns.

SUNDAY, MARCH 7

Russian Front – Germans retreating towards Vyazma.
Sea War – Night engagement near 'Sunk' Lightship between German MTBs and British MGBs: 2 German boats collide (1 sunk by shellfire).

MONDAY, MARCH 8

Sea War – U-510 torpedoes 8 ships in Convoy BT. 6 off French Guiana (March 8-9).
Sea War: Med. – HMS *Lightning* sunk by German MTB S.55.
Diplomacy – Adm. Standley, US Ambassador in Moscow, embarrasses Soviet Govt by denouncing the secrecy surrounding delivery of US Lease-Lend supplies.

TUESDAY, MARCH 9

Russian Front – Russians withdraw from Krasnodar (Donets Basin) and Barvenkovo.
North Africa – Von Arnim succeeds Rommel in Tunisia; Rommel leaves Africa.
Air War: Europe – Night raid on Munich (500 t. bombs); Nymphenburg Castle damaged.
Sea War – 3 trapped German merchant ships scuttled at Marmagao (Portuguese India) by British commandos of the Calcutta Light Horse in SOE operation to stop radioing of shipping movements to U-boats in the Indian Ocean. Not made public till 1978.

WEDNESDAY, MARCH 10

Air War: China – 14th AF formed under Maj.-Gen. Claire Chennault and incorporating his 'China Air Task Force', formerly known as 'Flying Tigers'.
Sea War: Atlantic – Blockade runner *Karin* scuttled when US Navy intercept.
Home Front: Britain – Death of Laurence Binyon, poet ('To the Fallen'); aged 73.
Home Front: USA – House of Representatives votes to continue Lease-Lend programme (Senate concurs March 11).

THURSDAY, MARCH 11

Air War: Britain – Fighter-bomber raid on Hastings. 50-plane night raid on Newcastle (similar op. night March 12-13).
Sea War: Atlantic – HMS *Harvester* rams U-444; the 2 vessels are locked together for 10 mins. U-444 then crawls away but is again rammed and sunk by Free French corvette *Aconit*. On March 12 *Harvester* is sunk by U-432, but *Aconit* again destroys attacker.

FRIDAY, MARCH 12

Russian Front – Russians occupy Vyazma (no resistance).
Air War: Britain – FW 190 fighter-bombers raid London.
Sea War – Murmansk Convoys abandoned for the summer by British Admiralty following alarming reports that *Scharnhorst* has joined *Tirpitz* and *Lützow* in N. Norway.
Diplomacy – Eden confers on Pacific War situation in Washington.

SATURDAY, MARCH 13

Russian Front – Hitler issues preliminary orders for Op. *Zitadelle* ('Citadel') – the attempted elimination of the Kursk Salient. *(See* July 5, 1943.)
Secret War – Time-bomb placed in Hitler's personal aircraft at Smolensk, by *Wehrmacht* conspirators, fails to explode.
China – Chinese counter-attack in Yangtze Valley.

SUNDAY, MARCH 14

North Africa – Cardinal Spellman, Archbishop of New York and Military Vicar of US Army and Navy, broadcasts to US Forces from Algiers; describes American troops as 'modern crusaders' who will be 'the sacred instruments of our cause'.

MONDAY, MARCH 15

Russian Front – Kharkov recaptured by Germans.
Air War: Europe – Russians bomb German pontoon bridges over R. Don.
Air War: Pacific – Australian and Dutch bombers drive off Japanese convoy approaching Aru Is. (E. Indies).
Sea War: Pacific – British MTBs sink 2 transports in convoy off Terschelling. US 7th Fleet formed in SW. Pacific
Sea War: Atlantic – Troop transport *Empress of Canada* (21,500 t.) sunk by Italian sub. *Leonardo da Vinci*.
Diplomacy – Finnish-German trade agreement.

TUESDAY, MARCH 16

Sea War: Pacific – 'Cactus Striking Force' shells Vila.
Sea War: Atlantic – U-600 hits 3 ships with single salvo of 'pattern-running' torpedoes (*FAT*).

WEDNESDAY, MARCH 17

Burma – Japanese launch counter-attack against British and Indian forces advancing along Arakan coast.

THURSDAY, MARCH 18

Russian Front – Pzs reach Belgorod on R. Donets, NE. of Kharkov.

Air War: Britain – 2 unsuccessful night raids on Norwich (March 18-19 and 28-29). Further raid in Oct. equally unsuccessful.
Air War: Europe – B-17s and B-24s attack Vegesack U-boat building yard near Bremen; fierce fighter opposition.
Diplomacy – Provisional Govt. in Lebanon under Dr Ayoub Tabet.

FRIDAY, MARCH 19

Air War – German aircraft employ 'circling torpedoes' against Allied shipping in Tripoli harbour.
Home Front: USA – Frank Nitti, notorious gangster and close associate of Al Capone, commits suicide.
Occupied France – Pro-Vichy Governor of French Guiana resigns.

SATURDAY, MARCH 20

North Africa – **BATTLE OF MARETH:** (March 20-28). 8th Army attack Axis forces holding the 'African Maginot Line', along Tunisia-Libya border. NZ Corps makes flanking attack.

SUNDAY, MARCH 21

Russian Front – Germans recapture Belgorod, NE. of Kharkov. Spring thaw slows down operations.
Sea War – US sub. *Herring* sinks U-163 in Bay of Biscay.
Home Front: Britain – After tunnelling for 5 months 21 IRA men escape from Londonderry Jail; 15 reach Eire and are interned.

MONDAY, MARCH 22

Air War – Hurricanes smash *Pz* counter-attack near Mareth Line with their 40-mm AP cannon, while simultaneously driving off German fighters with MG fire. Mosquito fighters shoot down 2 Ju 88s over Bay of Biscay. Nearly 300 night bombers attack St Nazaire.
Sea War – 10 US sub. chasers transferred to Cuban Navy.

TUESDAY, MARCH 23

North Africa – Germans counter-attack at Mareth; 8th Army withdraws.
Sea War: Med. – Troopship *Windsor Castle* sunk by He 111 torpedo planes off Algeria.
Occupied Denmark – General Elections. National Coalition (anti-Nazi), 143 seats; Danish Nazi Party, 3 seats; Peasant Party (pro-Nazi), 2 seats.

WEDNESDAY, MARCH 24

Air War: Britain – Fighter-bomber raid on Ashford. 8 night raiders shot down over N. England and S. Scotland.
Sea War: Med. – Sub. *Thunderbolt* (ex-*Thetis*) sunk by Italian corvette.

THURSDAY, MARCH 25

Sea War: Atlantic – 2 U-boats sunk by RAF Fortress bomber (March 25 and 27).
Sea War: Med. – Repatriated survivors of British naval vessels *Sikh*, *Oswald*, *Tempest*, *Cachalot* and *P.32* arrive at Alexandria.

FRIDAY, MARCH 26

Sea War: Pacific – Battle of the Kommandorsky Islands: Japanese Adm. Hosogaya bungles rare opportunity to destroy outnumbered US cruiser-destroyer force in daylight, during 3½-hour pursuit off Siberian coast. US destroyers make suicidal torpedo attack to save disabled cruiser *Salt Lake City* (Hosogaya dismissed on returning home).
Russian Front – Spring thaw halts fighting around Kharkov.
Occupied France – Laval reshuffles Vichy Cabinet and takes wider powers.

SATURDAY, MARCH 27

North Africa – US 34th Inf. Div. makes unsuccessful assault on Fondouk Pass (Tunisia).
Sea War – Escort carrier *Dasher* lost in Clyde Estuary following accidental petrol explosion and fire.

SUNDAY, MARCH 28

North Africa – 8th Army captures Mareth; Axis forces abandon Mareth Line.
Home Front: Italy – German munition ship catches fire and explodes in Naples harbour (heavy casualties).

MONDAY, MARCH 29

Burma – British and Indian forces withdraw on Arakan front.
North Africa – 8th Army captures Gabès (Tunisia).
Sea War – 3 Russian subs. attack 2 German convoys off Norway; 1 steamer sunk.

TUESDAY, MARCH 30

Sea War: Atlantic – Crew of German blockade-runner *Regensburg* immolate themselves when intercepted by HMS *Glasgow* in Denmark Str. (6 survivors).

WEDNESDAY, MARCH 31

Sea War: Pacific – 9 Japanese ships sunk by US sub. *Wahoo* during Mar.
Air War – 29-year-old Maj.-Gen. Peltz, *Stuka* 'ace' and tactician, appointed *Angriffsführer England* ('Attack Leader England') in attempt to revitalize the flagging *Luftwaffe* offensive against the UK.
Diplomacy – King Boris of Bulgaria confers with Hitler.

THURSDAY, APRIL 1

Sea War: Atlantic – Italian blockade-runner *Pietro Orseolo* attacked off Spain by Beaufort and Beaufighter torpedo planes, but escorting German destroyers shoot down 5. Later US sub. *Shad* hits Italian ship.

FRIDAY, APRIL 2

Air War: Pacific – US planes bomb Kiska (8 raids) and Attu.

SATURDAY, APRIL 3

Air War: Britain – FW 190 fighter-bombers raid Eastbourne and strafe streets crowded with shoppers.
Air War – Spitfires, flown by American pilots, destroy *Stuka* sqn. over Tunisia.

SUNDAY, APRIL 4

Air War – 1,300 t. bombs dropped on Kiel during RAF night raid. German aircraft drop mines in Thames Estuary.

MONDAY, APRIL 5

Home Front: Germany – Bonhoeffer arrested and Col. Oster dismissed from *Abwehr*.
Air War – P-38 Lightnings shoot down 14 Ju 52 transports off Tunisian coast.

TUESDAY, APRIL 6

North Africa – **BATTLE OF WADI AKARIT.** 8th Army breaks through Axis line S. of Sfax, but fails to exploit initial success.
Occupied Russia – Soviet Commission reports on Nazi atrocities against Russian soldiers, civilians and Jews in Rzhev-Gzhatsk-Vyazma 'triangle' and names 23 of the perpetrators.

WEDNESDAY, APRIL 7

Sea War: Med. – Sub. *Rorqual* and mine-layer *Abdiel* lay minefields off Tunisia to hamper Axis troop convoys.
Air War: Pacific – Op. I: massive Japanese air strike against Allied shipping off Guadalcanal. US destroyer *Aaron Ward*, HMNZS *Moa* and tanker sunk; second tanker and transport damaged. Similar raids off New Guinea (2 transports sunk).
Diplomacy – Bolivia declares war on Germany, Italy and Japan.
Litvinov arrives in Havana to become first Soviet Minister to Cuba. Hitler and Mussolini confer; Dönitz in attendance.
North Africa – British 9th Brig. attacks Fondouk Pass.
Home Front: Britain – Publication of Keynes' Plan for international banking agreement.
Home Front: USA – Sec. of Treasury

Morgenthau's Plan for stabilization of international finance published by Office of War Information.

THURSDAY, APRIL 8

Burma – Gen. Kawabe succeeds Gen. Iida as Japanese CinC.
Home Front: USA – Roosevelt freezes wages and sets price ceiling for essential commodities.

FRIDAY, APRIL 9

North Africa – British 26th Armd. Brig. drives through Fondouk Pass to Kairouan.

SATURDAY, APRIL 10

North Africa – 8th Army captures Tunisian port of Sfax.
Air War – P-38s and B-25s scatter 2 large formations of German and Italian transport aircraft over Sicilian Channel (20? shot down). 84 Liberators attack La Maddalena naval base (Sardinia): cruiser *Trieste* sunk, cruiser *Gorizia* severely damaged.

SUNDAY, APRIL 11

North Africa – British 1st Army enters Kairouan, third city of Tunisia. Patrols from 1st and 8th Armies link up W. of Kairouan.
Sea War – 2 U-boats lay mines off Casablanca.

MONDAY, APRIL 12

North Africa – 8th Army occupies Sousse, N. of Sfax.
Occupied Poland – **KATYN MASSACRES.** German News Agency reports discovery of mass graves of 10,000 Polish officers in Katyn Forest, near Smolensk; claims they were murdered in 1940 by the Soviet Secret Police.

TUESDAY, APRIL 13

Air War – US bombers raid Kiska (Aleutian Is.) round the clock.
Sea War – Norwegian/British destroyer *Eskdale* sunk by German MTBs off The Lizard (night April 13-14).

WEDNESDAY, APRIL 14

North Africa – Allied forces compress Axis perimeter in Tunisia from 3 sides.
Air War: Britain – Night raid on Chelmsford: prison set on fire; ball-bearing factory hit.
Air War: Europe – Russians bomb Königsberg and Danzig.

THURSDAY, APRIL 15

Russian Front – Hitler signs operational order for Op. *Zitadelle* ('Citadel') – a 'decisive' spring offensive against the Kursk Salient – to begin May 3 (postponed to May 9 on April 29).

Sea War: Atlantic – British sub. *P.615* sunk by *U.123*.

Air War – ACM Tedder's new 'Mediterranean Air Command' includes following formations; Middle East Cmnd., NW. African Air Forces (inc. Free French), RAF Malta, Strategic AF, Tactical AF, Coastal AF, (Western) Desert AF, 12th US Air Support Cmnd.

FRIDAY, APRIL 16

Sea War: Med. – British destroyer *Pakenham* abandoned following engagement with Italian torpedo boats *Cassiopaea* and *Cigno* (sunk) off Sicily.

Occupied France – Vichy announces evacuation of children and non-essential civilians from Channel Ports.

Air War: Britain – **FIRST NIGHT RAID BY GERMAN FIGHTER-BOMBERS.** 30 FW 190s sent to London but only 2 bombs on target. 4 confused pilots mistake W. Malling airfield (Kent) for their home base; 1 crashes, 3 captured on landing.

Air War: Europe – 240 RAF aircraft drop heavy bomb load near lunatic asylum at Dobrany, Czechoslovakia – mistaken for Skoda works at Pilsen. Mannheim bombed.

Home Front: Italy – Sicily and Sardinia declared to be operational areas.

SATURDAY, APRIL 17

Occupied Poland – Polish Govt. demands Red Cross investigation of Katyn 'Massacre'; request withdrawn April 30 under British and Soviet diplomatic pressure.

Air War – 115 B-17s (16 lost) attack Focke-Wulf aircraft works at Bremen; 10 German fighters shot down. RAF night bombers start big fires at Catania (Sicily). Germans bomb Algiers (16 nuns killed in convent).

Diplomacy – In attempt to curry favour with the Pope and with Spain, Hitler appoints 2 'old school' diplomats – von Weizsäcker and Dieckhoff – as Ambassadors in the Vatican and Madrid, resp.

SUNDAY, APRIL 18

Air War – 59 Ju 52 troop transports and 10 escort fighters shot down by P-40s of US 9th AAF off C. Bon (6 P-40s and 3 escorting Spitfires lost).

Diplomacy – Soviet Govt. alleges that German allegations of Soviet responsibility for Katyn massacre is Gestapo 'frame-up'.

Turco-German Trade Agreement signed.

Air War: Pacific – **DEATH OF ADM. YAMAMOTO,** CinC Japanese Combined Fleet killed during flying visit to bases in SW. Pacific. Lightning fighters from

Henderson Field intercept Adm.'s plane over Bougainville I. Adm. Koga appointed CinC.

MONDAY, APRIL 19

North Africa – 8th Army attacks Enfidaville Line in moonlight, protected by creeping barrage.

Diplomacy – Hitler and Quisling confer.

Occupied Poland – **BATTLE OF WARSAW GHETTO.** Following deportation of 310,000 Jews in 1942-43, *SS* move to destroy remaining 63,000, but 'Jewish War Organization' (ZOB), Irgun and a few Polish supporters totalling 1,500 fight for 27 days from dugouts, cellars and sewers. Over 7,000 Jews killed, 7,000 captured Jews shot, 22,000 sent to concentration

Above: SS troops burn the Warsaw Ghetto to flush out the inmates.

camps and 20,000 to labour camps. *SS* casualties: 16 killed, 85 wounded.

Diplomacy – Conference on refugees in Bermuda (ends April 29)

TUESDAY, APRIL 20

North Africa – 8th Army attacks Axis positions at Enfidaville, N. of Sousse.

Air War: Europe – RAF night raids on Berlin and port of Stettin. First 'nuisance' raid on the capital by 11 Mosquitoes (1 lost). Russians bomb Tilsit (E. Prussia).

Home Front: Japan – Shigemitsu appointed Foreign Minister (replacing Tani).

YAMAMOTO, Isoroku (1884-1943)
Japanese: *Admiral, CinC Japanese Combined Fleet*

Director of Japanese strategy from Pearl Harbor Attack (Dec. 1941) to Guadalcanal campaign (Aug. 1942-Feb. 1943). Most venerated senior officer in Imperial Japanese Navy. Although a gambler by nature, he unaccountably failed to exploit a priceless opportunity to completely destroy vital American installations and oil supplies at Pearl Harbor. Strategy during decisive battle of Midway, when he failed to concentrate huge Japanese fleet and annihilate small American naval force, has also been severely criticized. Said to have boasted that he would

'dictate peace to the US in the White House at Washington'. His violent death was severe blow to Japanese morale.

Graduated from Etajima Naval Academy, 1904. Ensign aboard armoured cruiser *Nisshin* during Russo-Japanese War (1904-5). Wounded in great battle of Tsushima (May 1905); knocked unconcious, hit in leg and left hand (losing two fingers). Studied potentialities of aircraft in naval warfare and prophesied (1915) that most important warship of the future would be the aircraft carrier. Naval attaché in Japanese embassy, Washington, 1925. Japanese delegate at London Naval Conference, 1934-35.

CinC of the fleet, 1939. Planned devastating surprise air attack on Pearl Harbor, main base of US Pacific Fleet, after studying Royal Navy's successful operation against Italian battle fleet at Taranto. Sent his aircraft carriers to the East Indies, Australian waters, Indian Ocean and Central Pacific (Feb.-June 1942). His immense self-confidence temporarily shaken by Midway disaster, but made valiant and repeated efforts to recapture initiative during Guadalcanal campaign.

While personally directing series of massive air strikes against Allied shipping in SW. Pacific his secret itinerary was deciphered by American code-breakers. Yamamoto's plane shot down, 500 km N. of Guadalcanal, despite strong escort, April 18, 1943. Admiral's body discovered on Bougainville I., still strapped into seat and holding ceremonial sword. Remains cremated and returned to Tokyo aboard battleship *Musashi* for state funeral, attended by several million people.

Home Front: Mexico – Roosevelt and Pres. Camachio confer at Monterey.

WEDNESDAY, APRIL 21

Home Front: USA – Roosevelt condemns beheading of US airmen captured by Japanese during 'Doolittle Raid'.
Air War: Britain – Night raid on Aberdeen: direct hit on air raid shelter causes heavy casualties.

THURSDAY, APRIL 22

Air War – 16 giant Me 323 transports shot down over Gulf of Tunis by RAF and SAAF Spitfires and Kittyhawks.
North Africa – 1st Army attacks at Bou Arada, S. of Tunis.
Occupied Poland – Warsaw Ghetto: *SS* destroy fortified factory buildings with point-blank artillery fire and explosives.

FRIDAY, APRIL 23

North Africa – After secret redeployment of 193 km behind Tunisian front, US 2nd Corps captures several wooded heights near Mateur and holds them against fierce counter-attacks; Lt.-Gen. McNair, US Army, severely wounded.

SATURDAY, APRIL 24

Sea War: Med. – British sub. *Sahib* sunk off Stromboli by Italian corvette *Gabbiano* and German bomber.
Home Front: Germany – Death of Lt.-Gen. Kurt von Hammerstein-Equart, former COGS and leading anti-Nazi conspirator; aged 64.
Home Front: Britain – IRA leaders, McAteer and Steele, commandeer Broadway Cinema, Belfast, and make propaganda speeches; then escape (Lord Haw-Haw later broadcasts this news).

SUNDAY, APRIL 25

Air War: Europe – US bombers raid Bari airfield, S. Italy.

MONDAY, APRIL 26

North Africa – British 1st Army captures 'Longstop Hill' and Djebel Bou Aoukaz.
Air War: Europe – 557 RAF bombers despatched to Duisburg, but vast majority miss target.
Sea War – *U-180* meets *I-29* near Mauritius and transfers Subhas Chandra Bose, pro-Axis Indian nationalist *en route* from Berlin to Penang (Malaya).
Diplomacy – USSR breaks off diplomatic relations with Polish Govt.-in-exile, following latter's request for Red Cross inquiry into Katyn Massacres.
Home Front: India – Pres. Roosevelt's personal representative complains that Viceroy has refused him permission to see imprisoned Gandhi. Moslem League Con-

ference demands creation of 'Pakistan' as only means of preventing bloodshed.

TUESDAY, APRIL 27

North Africa – Americans storm 'Sugar Loaf Hill' (Jebel Azag), near Mateur. *Pzs* expel British from Sidi Abdallah.

WEDNESDAY, APRIL 28

North Africa – *Pzs* attack Djebel Bou Aoukaz; British forced to retreat, April 30.
Air War: Europe – Major RAF mine-laying op. in Baltic and N. Sea (23 aircraft lost). Albacore biplanes make night attack on convoy off Boulogne.

THURSDAY, APRIL 29

North Africa – British recapture Sidi Abdallah.
Home Front: Germany – Hitler receives Laval: last of 5 meetings with satellite and quisling leaders in April.
Occupied Poland – German sponsored 11-man 'International Medical Commission' dissects 8 Polish corpses at Katyn and reports that Russians committed massacre in spring 1940, using *German* small arms.

FRIDAY, APRIL 30

Sea War: Atlantic – RN and RCN form 'Support Groups' for anti-U-boat ops. *U-515* sinks 7 ships from Convoy TS. 37 (April 30 – May 1).
Sea War: Med. – 3 Italian destroyers bombed off Tunis. During April Axis convoys transport 2,800 troops, 18,690 t. supplies, 26 guns and 46 tanks to Tunisia despite incessant Allied naval and air countermeasures.
Air War: Europe – 55th RAF raid on

Essen (71 aircraft lost in 4 major raids, March-April 1943).
Home Front: Britain – Death of Beatrice Webb (Lady Passfield), champion of Socialism; aged 85.
Secret War – OP. MINCEMEAT (II): Civilian corpse, dressed as 'Maj. Martin, RM', and carrying false top-secret orders for planned Allied invasions of Sardinia (Op. Brimstone) and Greece (Op. Husky), deposited in sea off Huelva, Spain. Body recovered and documents made known to Germans, who immediately send reinforcements to 'threatened' areas.

SATURDAY, MAY 1

North Africa – US heavy artillery begins 3-day bombardment of Mateur, W. of Tunis.
Home Front: Britain – Dover shelled for 75 mins.
Sea War: Med. – Italian and German vessels lay minefields off W. Coast of Greece, Sicily and Sardinia – 3,156, 1,036 and 4,248 mines resp. (May 1 – July 20).

SUNDAY, MAY 2

Air War: Europe – Mosquitoes bomb Thionville railway workshops. 68 Dorniers (5 lost) lay mines off estuaries of Thames and Humber in 3 night missions during May.
Sea War – German liner/transport *Gneisenau* sunk by RAF mine in Baltic.

MONDAY, MAY 3

North Africa – Americans and French capture Mateur.

Below: *8th USAAF B-24 Liberator 'Lucky Luke' is 'bombed up' for its 28th mission from Hardwick, England, April.*

Sea War – Carrier *Ark Royal* (II) laid down at Birkenhead (launched 1950).
Air War – Lt.-Gen. Andrews, Commanding Gen. US Forces ETO; killed in air crash over Iceland; aged 59.

TUESDAY, MAY 4

Russian Front – Hitler postpones launching of Op. *Zitadelle* ('Citadel') from May 9 to mid-June.
China – Japanese advance S. of R. Yangtze.
Air War: Europe – P-47s escort B-17s during raid on automobile factory in Antwerp.

WEDNESDAY, MAY 5

North Africa – British inf. recapture Djebel Bou Aoukaz, S. of Tunis.
Air War: Europe – Germans accuse RAF Bomber Cmnd. of dropping explosive pencils and fountain-pens, 'with the intention of killing German children'.

THURSDAY, MAY 6

North Africa – **FINAL BRITISH OFFENSIVE IN TUNISIA.** 1st Army, reinforced with 7th Armd. and 4th Indian divs. from 8th Army, smashes through Medjerda Valley defences, in Medjez-el-Bab sector; Axis forces stunned by 600-gun preparatory barrage and ceaseless daylight bombing raids.
New Guinea – Australians capture Mubo.
Air War: Europe – Russian bombers raid German troop concentrations and railways in Novgorod and Bryansk-Orel areas and the Ukraine (repeated May 7); fierce air battles.

FRIDAY, MAY 7

North Africa – British occupy Tunis. Americans take Bizerta.
Air War: Britain – Fighter-bomber raid on Great Yarmouth: there are 4 day and 1 night raids on Yarmouth and Lowestoft in 1943.
Sea War: Med. – British destroyers of Force K and Force Q blockade C. Bon to prevent an Axis 'Dunkirk'-style evacuation from Tunisia.
Sea War – Russian subs., supported by aircraft and minesweepers, make unsuccessful attempts to break through German-Finnish blockade in Baltic.
Home Front: Canada – House of Commons vote to contribute additional $1 billion towards the war effort.

SATURDAY, MAY 8

Sea War: Pacific – 3 Japanese destroyers sunk by mines in central Solomons.
North Africa – Allies capture Tebourba and Djedeida. French occupy Zaghouan (S. Tunisia).
Occupied Poland – Mordechai Anielewicz,

25-year-old cdr. of Jewish fighters in Warsaw, and 80 others blown up and killed by *SS* in Mila St. HQ.

SUNDAY, MAY 9

Secret War – *Luftwaffe* defectors land Ju 88R night-fighter at Aberdeen.

MONDAY, MAY 10

North Africa – British 6th Armd. Div. races across base of C. Bon to outskirts of Hammamet, trapping German forces.

TUESDAY, MAY 11

Sea War: Pacific – Op. Landcrab: Americans land on Attu (Aleutian Is.): Japanese garrison withdraws to strong defensive positions and fights to the death; US troops gravely hampered by appalling weather and bad terrain.
Sea War: Atlantic – 3 U-boats sunk during attacks on Convoy HX. 237 (May 11-13). Destroyer *Hesperus* and *U-223* fight dramatic but inconclusive battle with guns, torpedoes and depth-charges. *U-223* escapes despite ramming. First of 5 Italian subs. leaves Bordeaux on transport mission to Sumatra and Singapore (2 lost).
Air War: Britain – FW 190 fighter-bombers attack Gt. Yarmouth: 26 killed in ATS hostel.

WEDNESDAY, MAY 12

North Africa – **END OF ALL ORGANIZED AXIS RESISTANCE IN TUNISIA.** Col.-Gen. von Arnim surrenders to British forces. 150,000 (approx.) Axis troops captured since April.

Tunisian Campaign Losses
Axis: 250,000 PoWs (100,000 German); 890 planes since April 22. French: 19,439. US: 18,221. British: 38,360; 155 planes.

Occupied Poland – Szmul Zygielbojm; leader of Polish Jews and hero of Siege of Warsaw, commits suicide in London, aged 48 (his wife and children having been murdered by Nazis).
Air War: Europe – 20 hectares of central Duisburg destroyed by RAF bombers; 4 Thyssen plants damaged.
Diplomacy – **SECOND WASHINGTON CONFERENCE** (May 12-25): Churchill presses for invasion of Italy, but Roosevelt and US Chiefs of Staff demur; every effort to be made to persuade Turkey to join Allies. Ceaseless pressure to be made against Japan.

THURSDAY, MAY 13

North Africa – Surrender of Marshal Messe, cdr. of Italian 1st Army.

Air War: Europe – RAF night raids on Bochum (Ruhr), Berlin and attempted raid on Skoda Works at Pilsen.
Home Front: USA – Pres. Beneš (Czech leader) addresses Congress.

FRIDAY, MAY 14

Sea War: Pacific – Australian hospital ship *Centaur* sunk off Brisbane by Japanese sub. *I-177*: 268 killed.
Air War: Europe – 125 US bombers attack Kiel: 3 U-boats sunk.

SATURDAY, MAY 15

Air War: Britain – Night raid on Sunderland.
Sea War – Cuban sub.-chaser *CS.13* and a US aircraft sink *U-176* off Havana.
Diplomacy – USSR dissolves the Comintern (Communist International established in 1919).
Occupied Tunisia – Pro-Axis Bey of Tunis deposed.
Occupied Yugoslavia – Fifth Axis Offensive against Tito's Partisans (May 15-June 15): Germans, Bulgarians and Croats participate, supported by *Luftwaffe*.

SUNDAY, MAY 16

North Africa – Gen. Alexander informs Churchill: *'Sir, it is my duty to report that the Tunisian Campaign is over.'*
Air War: Europe – **THE 'DAMBUSTERS' RAID** (Op. Chastise): 19 Lancasters (8 lost) breach Möhne and Eder Dams in the Ruhr, using 'bouncing bombs'. Wing-Cdr. Guy Gibson leads specially formed No. 617 Sqn., RAF.

Air War: Britain – Thousands of leaflets containing names of 412 British ships claimed as sunk since June 1941, dropped over NE. England.
Sea War: Atlantic – 4 U-boat wolf-packs attack 5 convoys (May 16-23) but sink only 1 ship (9 U-boats lost; 4 damaged).
Occupied Holland – Germans confiscate all wireless sets in Holland.
Occupied Poland – Only 8 buildings left standing in Warsaw Ghetto; *SS* dynamite Tlomacki Synagogue.

MONDAY, MAY 17

Air War: Europe – **IJMUIDEN RAID.** Formation of 10 Marauders annihilated by

flak and Me 109s during low-level raid on power station. 8th AF then successfully transfers this type to medium-altitude missions with strong fighter escort.
Air War: Britain – Night raid on Cardiff by 89 aircraft (6 lost).
Neutrals: Spain – Disastrous fire at El Ferrol naval base: 3 cruisers and 2 destroyers seriously damaged.

TUESDAY, MAY 18

China – Japanese launch offensive in Middle Yangtze area.
Diplomacy – United Nations Food Conference.

WEDNESDAY, MAY 19

Air War – Me 109s intercept US formations bombing airfields on Sicily and Sardinia, but are driven off with loss.

THURSDAY, MAY 20

Sea War: Atlantic – US 10th Fleet formed for anti-U-boat ops.
China – Chinese counter-attack in Middle Yangtze front.
Air War – Warhawks destroy 7 giant Me 323s near Decimomannu airfield (Sardinia).

FRIDAY, MAY 21

Sea War: Med – In ops. off French Riviera, British sub. *Sickle* sinks *U-303* and 'torpedoes' Monte Carlo Casino – 2 torpedoes miss their intended targets, run up the beach and explode below the famous gaming establishment. French sqn. – interned in Alexandria since July 1940 – joins the Allies. Vichy alleges that crews have been 'starved into submission'.(!)

Below: *The revolutionary twin-turbojet Messerschmitt 262 fighter that Hitler saw as the 'Blitz bomber'.*

Air War – FW 190 fighter-bombers raid Malta.

SATURDAY, MAY 22

Air War – Adolf Galland, fighter 'ace' and 'General of Fighters', test-flies Me 262 jet fighter. He reports to *Luftwaffe* QMG Milch that if mass production of the jet is begun immediately, Germany can regain air superiority.

SUNDAY, MAY 23

Sea War: Atlantic – 21 German MTBs begin intensive minelaying operations along English S. Coast (to 12 June). *U-752* damaged by rocket-firing Swordfish biplane and later scuttled.
Air War: Britain – Fighter-bomber raids on Bournemouth and Hastings; night raid on Sunderland. Total sorties: 99 (5 aircraft lost).
Air War: Europe – RAF drop 2,000 t. bombs on Dortmund (night May 23-24).
Home Front: Canada – Death of William Aberhart, 'Social Credit' Premier of Alberta, 1935-42; aged 64.

MONDAY, MAY 24

Sea War: Atlantic – DÖNITZ SUSPENDS U-BOAT OPS. AGAINST CONVOYS (56 U-boats lost April – May, 1943). 'Flak-trap' U-boat *U-441* shoots down Sunderland in Bay of Biscay. U-boats in this area frequently proceed in grps. on the surface and fight off Allied aircraft with gunfire.

TUESDAY, MAY 25

Home Front: USA – Death of Edsel Ford, Pres. of Ford Motor Co., aged 49.

WEDNESDAY, MAY 26

Sea War: Pacific – Japanese subs. begin evacuation of Kiska I. garrison.
Home Front: Canada – Meat rationed.
Home Front: USA – Pres. Barclay of Liberia arrives in Washington.
Occupied Yugoslavia – Fifth Axis offensive against Tito's Partisans: 120,000 Germans, Italians, Bulgarians and *Chetniks* (turncoat partisans) trap 16,000 Partisans in Montenegro, but they fight their way out in June (8,000 killed). Germans deport all civilians from the area.

THURSDAY, MAY 27

Air War: Europe – Mosquitoes bomb Carl Zeiss works at Jena, at roof-top height, despite balloon barrage and flak.
Occupied Yugoslavia – British military mission parachutes into Yugoslavia and joins Tito's partisans.
Home Front: Britain – Death of Arthur Mee, author of children's books and editor of 'Children's Newspaper'; aged 67.
Diplomacy – Pope appoints Mgr. Godfrey Papal Chargé d'Affaires to Polish Govt.

FRIDAY, MAY 28

Air War: Europe – 100 B-17s attack oil refinery and shipping at Leghorn (Livorno). P-40s and Marauders hit 4 Sicilian airfields despite 'terrific flak'.
Home Front: USA – Office of War Mobilization established to co-ordinate production.

SATURDAY, MAY 29

Air War: Europe – Wuppertal Raid: 719 RAF bombers (33 lost) despatched; approx. 475 find target, dropping 1,900 t. Huge fires kill 2,450 and halt industrial production. Local flak taken by surprise.
China – Chinese recapture Yuyangkwan, E. of Ichang.

SUNDAY, MAY 30

Sea War: Pacific – End of organized Japanese resistance on Attu. 2,622 Japanese and 549 Americans killed.
Air War: Europe – FW 190 fighter-bombers raid Torquay: church hit (20 children and 5 adults killed).
Diplomacy – De Gaulle and Churchill meet in Algiers.

MONDAY, MAY 31

Air War: Europe – B-17s destroy many grounded planes on Foggia airfield.
Air War: Pacific – B-24s bomb Lae. Lone B-17 routs Japanese fighter sqn. over Finschhafen (3 crew wounded).
Occupied France – De Gaulle and Giraud confer in Algiers and attempt to resolve Free French leadership struggle.
Home Front: Germany – Speer's Armaments Ministry assumes responsibility for naval armaments.

TUESDAY, JUNE 1

Air War – Allied air and naval forces commence round-the-clock bombardment of Pantellaria I., Italian naval base. (*see* June 11.) Large formations of Russian bombers make frequent night raids on railway junctions – esp. Smolensk, Orsha, Bryansk and Orel – and airfields behind the Front, throughout June.
Secret War – Ju 88C long-range fighters shoot down Dutch airliner over Bay of Biscay; following false report from agents in Lisbon that Churchill is aboard. No survivors: among 17 dead is film actor Leslie Howard (aged 50).
Sea War – Surfaced U-boats begin crossing Bay of Biscay in grps. of 2-5 and attempt to fight off attacking planes with concentrated flak.

WEDNESDAY, JUNE 2

Air War: Europe – Big air battle over Kursk: Russians claim 162 'kills' for loss of 30.
Sea War: Med. – Convoy of 129 ships, with 19 escorts, passes through Strs. of Gibraltar, *en route* for Oran, Algiers, Malta and Tripoli.

THURSDAY, JUNE 3

Occupied France – De Gaulle and Giraud reorganize French Committee of National Liberation under their joint presidency: other members inc. Gens. Catroux and Georges and MM. Jean Monnet, Massigli, Philip and Puaux. 300 t. of tyres burnt by French Resistance at Michelin works, Clermont-Ferrand.

FRIDAY, JUNE 4

Air War: Europe – Night raid on Gorki (Nishni Novgorod) – great tank-manufacturing centre on the Volga, E. of Moscow. First of series of strategic raids by *Luftwaffe* on industrial centres along the Volga during June. B-24s bomb Grossaglie airfield (S. Italy). Wellington night bombers attack Milo airfield (Sicily).
Neutrals: Argentina – Military coup topples Pres. Castillo.

SATURDAY, JUNE 5

Sea War: Atlantic – U-513 sinks 4 ships off Brazil.
Home Front: Japan – State funeral for Adm. Yamamoto in Tokyo.

SUNDAY, JUNE 6

Diplomacy – Spain proposes establishment of 'no-bombing zones'.

MONDAY, JUNE 7

Sea War: Atlantic – 8 U-boats simulate much larger 'wolf-pack' by transmitting frequent radio messages. *U-334* and *U-388* are sunk.

TUESDAY, JUNE 8

Sea War – Battleship *Mutsu* destroyed by magazine explosion in Hiroshima Bay.
Air War – Leaflets dropped on Pantellaria, calling for unconditional surrender of Italian garrison.

WEDNESDAY, JUNE 9

Air War – Since Pantellaria garrison still refuses to surrender, Allied Strategic and Tactical AFs redouble their bombardment.
Occupied Yugoslavia – Tito wounded in *Luftwaffe* raid.

THURSDAY, JUNE 10

Air War – 700 Russian night bombers (19 lost) raid airfields W. of Kursk.

FRIDAY, JUNE 11

Air War: Europe – 200 B-17s (8 lost) raid Wilhelmshaven. RAF night raid on Düsseldorf (2,000 t. bombs) and Münster. 43 bombers lost, inc. 5 shot down by 'ace' Maj. Streib, flying first purpose-built German night fighter, the He 219.
Sea War: Med. – Surrender of Pantellaria, Italian I. fortress.
Diplomacy – USA and Britain recognize new Provisional Govt. in Argentina. French Committee of National Liberation given official recognition by Uruguay (first nation to take this step). Saudi Arabia rejects idea of a Jewish state.

SATURDAY, JUNE 12

Air War: Europe – Devastating RAF night raid on Bochum in the Ruhr. Heavy night raid on Plymouth (repeated Aug. 11 and Nov. 15, 1943).
Italy – Sgt. Cohen, RAF, 'captures' Lampedusa I., near Sicily: Italian garrison surrenders when Cohen makes a forced landing.
Occupied North Africa – King George VI arrives in Morocco.

SUNDAY, JUNE 13

Air War: Britain – Night raid on Grimsby: many 'Butterfly' anti-personnel bombs and incendiaries dropped: 74 killed, 130 injured.

MONDAY, JUNE 14

Sea War – RAF Coastal Cmnd. (and attached Allied sqns.) begins systematic daily patrols to counter new U-boat tactics in Bay of Biscay (Ops. Musketry and Seaslug).
Air War – RAF Second Tactical Air Force formed.

TUESDAY, JUNE 15

Sea War – Disguised raider *Michel* sinks 2 Norwegian ships W. of Australia (June 15 and 17).
Air War – World's first jet bomber/reconnaissance aircraft – Arado Ar 234 – tested at Rheine, near Münster.

WEDNESDAY, JUNE 16

Air War: Pacific – 94 Japanese aircraft (93 lost) attack shipping off Guadalcanal.
Home Front: Canada – Mme. Chiang Kai-shek addresses Parliament.

THURSDAY, JUNE 17

Sea War – Force 'H' (inc. reconstructed *Valiant* and *Warspite*) transferred from Scapa Flow to Oran and Alexandria in preparation for Op. Husky (June 17-23).
Occupied Europe – BBC warns civilians to evacuate vicinity of factories working for Germany (similar warnings to Belgian, Dutch and Hungarian civilians broadcast later).

FRIDAY, JUNE 18

Home Front: India – F.M. Wavell appointed Viceroy of India.

SATURDAY, JUNE 19

Air War: Europe – RAF night raid on Schneider armament works at Le Creusot.
Home Front: Britain – Horse Racing. Dorothy Paget's 'Straight Deal' wins the Derby.
Sea War – Sub. *Barbarigo* sunk in Bay of Biscay.

SUNDAY, JUNE 20

Air War: Europe – FIRST ALLIED 'SHUTTLE' RAID. 60 RAF Lancasters bomb Zeppelin (radar) works at Friedrichshafen, then fly on to Algiers. After refuelling and rearming they return home, June 23-24 (bombing Spezia naval base *en route*).
Sea War – First of 5 troop convoys leaves the Clyde for Op. Husky. King George VI arrives at Malta aboard HMS *Aurora*. British naval anti-sub. 'Support' and 'Escort' grps. supplement Allied air offensive against U-boats in Bay of Biscay.

MONDAY, JUNE 21

Sea War: Pacific – Americans land on New Georgia (Solomons).
Air War: Europe – 705 RAF bombers (44 lost) despatched to Krefeld (Ruhr).

TUESDAY, JUNE 22

Neutrals: Eire – General Election: De Valera's *Fianna Fail* party loses overall majority, but he remains in office.

THE BATTLE OF THE ATLANTIC

Although Adolf Hitler's armies had failed to invade and conquer Britain after the Dunkirk Evacuation, the British Isles remained under a partial German blockade for most of the war. From their string of bases in Scandinavia, the Low Countries and France, German bombers, surface raiders, motor torpedo boats and especially submarines were able to pose a continual threat to vital trans-Atlantic and coastal shipping routes. Not only did these activities threaten the British civil population with eventual starvation; they also jeopardized the massive build-up of troops, equipment and fuel needed in Britain to launch a Second Front in Normandy.

After sinking 432 Allied and neutral merchant ships of 2,206,610 tonnes in 1941, the U-boats accounted for a staggering 1,027 victims of 6,326,145 tonnes during 1942. Stormy weather in the Atlantic early in 1943 temporarily reduced the carnage, but the March figure reached a new peak of 637,000 tonnes, including no fewer than 21 ships from two key convoys. Only one German submarine was detected and destroyed by the escorts of these two convoys – in a month when Admiral Dönitz had no fewer than 116 U-boats in the North Atlantic! Plainly, if this state of affairs had been allowed to continue unchecked over succeeding months, the British could indeed have been starving by Christmas (as claimed by Dr. Goebbels) and all hopes of a Second Front would have disappeared.

Fortunately for Britain and the oppressed, enslaved and tortured millions of Hitler's Europe, all the ingenious Allied counter-measures and tactical innovations which had long been under test – short-wave radar; powerful Torpex-filled depth charges, fired from multiple mortars; very-long-range patrol bombers; and specialized support groups of destroyers, corvettes and escort carriers – suddenly began to bring results. Instead of being left to their own devices in the notorious mid-Atlantic 'Gap', as formerly, convoys could now be provided with continuous, integrated air and surface escorts.

Fifteen U-boats were sunk in the North Atlantic during April at a cost of 249,000 tonnes of merchant shipping. But no fewer than 40 undersea raiders fell victim in May including 20 during wolf-pack attacks on five important convoys. Bereft of the leading aces of the early war years – Prien, Schepke and Kretschmer – and faced by dedicated, adept and aggressive U-boat hunters like Capt. Walker and Cdrs. Macintyre and Gretton, Dönitz's U-boat crews became increasingly demoralized and scored fewer and fewer successes. Between March and June 1943 sinkings of Allied merchant shipping in the North Atlantic fell dramatically – from 637,000 tonnes to a miniscule *18,000 tonnes.*

On May 24, 1943, Dönitz had tacitly admitted defeat by forbidding any further attacks on North Atlantic convoys until his battered U-boats could be re-equipped with Schnorkels as well as

new RCM (Radio Counter-measures) equipment and more potent torpedoes. While a 15-strong rearguard fanned out widely and kept the airwaves humming with misleading radio messages, the rump of the U-boat armada stealthily retired south-eastwards to the calmer latitudes of the Azores.

Although the U-boat war periodically blazed into life again during the latter stages of the war – particularly in British coastal waters – the gallant German submariners never again posed a serious threat to the Allied effort; 781 U-boats were lost during World War II, together with more than 32,000 officers and men. This was the terrible, inevitable price the losing side was bound to pay in this most merciless battle of the Total War.

Above right: U-243 sinks under attack from a Sunderland flying boat of 10 Squadron RAAF, Bay of Biscay July 8, 1944.

Below: A U-boat torpedoes a barrage-balloon equipped merchantman of Arctic convoy PQ.17, July 1942.

Below: A U-boat of 9th Flotilla (swordfish emblem).

SIKORSKI, Wladyslaw (1881-1943)
Polish: *General, CinC and Prime Minister*

Great Polish patriot; indefatigable champion of democracy during short years of Polish national independence (1918-39) and tireless leader of Polish resistance against Nazi terror, during most calamitous years of the war.

Born in Galicia (Russian Poland). Studied engineering at Cracow and Lwow universities. Head of war dept. of Polish 'Chief National Committee' (provisional govt.) during World War I. Imprisoned by Austrians, March-Nov. 1918. Held important field commands in Russo-Polish War, 1919-20: his 5th Polish Army largely responsible for defeating Red Army at gates of Warsaw, 1920. Chief of Staff, 1921; Prime Minister, 1922; founded Polish Navy and merchant marine and port of Gdynia. Minister of War, 1924-25. Condemned military dictatorship of Marshal Pilsudski (1926-35); in exile in Paris, 1928-38. Returned to Poland, 1938. Consistently warned complacent Polish govt. of grave threat posed by Germany.

Offered his services to Polish CinC, Smigly-Rydz on outbreak of war, but was refused a command. Escaped with other Polish officers to France. P.M. of Polish govt.-in-exile, Sept. 30, 1939. Appointed CinC of all Polish forces, Nov. 7, 1939. After Fall of France, set up his HQ in London. Polish armed forces re-established on British soil; Sikorski also organized creation of strong resistance movement within occupied Poland.

Visited Roosevelt and Stalin, 1941. Signed treaty of alliance with Russia, July 30, 1941. Strongly condemned Soviet 'massacre' of Polish officers at Katyn, April 1943, leading to breaking-off of diplomatic relations.

Killed when his Liberator aircraft mysteriously crashed into sea, shortly after taking off from Gibraltar (night July 3-4, 1943). Body returned to Britain aboard Polish destroyer and buried in Polish Forces' cemetery at Newark, Nottinghamshire.

WEDNESDAY, JUNE 23

Air War: Britain – First of 4 night raids on Hull during 1943 (2 raids totally unsuccessful).
Home Front: Australia – P.M. Curtin wins Vote of Confidence by 1 vote (Parliament dissolved June 24).

THURSDAY, JUNE 24

Air War: Europe – 9th AF Liberators bomb Sedes airfield (Greece) and drop pamphlets addressed to local population. Heavy RAF night raid on Elberfeld (Ruhr).

FRIDAY, JUNE 25

Russian Front – Hitler decides to launch the much-postponed Op. *Zitadelle* ('Citadel') on July 5: repeated delays largely due to problems with new tanks and the critical Italian situation.

SATURDAY, JUNE 26

Occupied Yugoslavia – New Yugoslav Cabinet under Trifunovich.
Occupied France – Brig. Claude Nicholson, heroic defender of Calais Citadel during Dunkirk Evacuation, dies in German PoW camp; aged 44.
Home Front: USA – Death of Dr Karl Landsteiner, discoverer of blood-groups; age 75.

SUNDAY, JUNE 27

Occupied France – French Resistance attacks *Ateliers des Fives* locomotive works at Lille.

MONDAY, JUNE 28

Air War – Japanese bomb Darwin. 8th USAAF bombs St Nazaire. 12th USAAF bombs Livorno.

TUESDAY, JUNE 29

Sea War: Med. – Greek sub. *Katsonis* torpedoes 3 ships in Aegean during June.

WEDNESDAY, JUNE 30

Sea War: Pacific – OP. CARTWHEEL: Americans begin series of ops. aimed at isolating Rabaul (main Japanese stronghold in SW. Pacific) with landings on Rendova I. and in Nassau Bay (New Guinea).
Sea War: Atlantic – Battleships *Alabama* and *South Dakota* arrive in Scapa Flow. Free French take over the Vichy warships at Martinique.
Air War: Pacific – US fighters (17 lost) break up break Japanese formations over Rendova. US transport *McCawley* bombed. Japanese bomb Darwin.
Air War – B-17s raid Palermo.

THURSDAY, JULY 1

Sea War – U-boat groups driven from Bay of Biscay (July 1-Aug. 2): 9 sunk, 20 damaged (and forced to return to base).
Air War – Allies bomb Sicily repeatedly (July 1-9).

FRIDAY, JULY 2

Air War – B-24s drop 200 t. bombs on 3 airfields in S. Italy; German aircraft make unsuccessful 'air-to-air' bombing runs over the US formations.

SATURDAY, JULY 3

Air War: Europe – RAF night raid on Cologne: Humboldt-Deutz works (U-boat accumulators) seriously damaged.

SUNDAY, JULY 4

Occupied Poland – GEN. SIKORSKI KILLED. Polish P.M. and CinC killed in air crash near Gibraltar (engine failure); aged 62. Mme Lesniowska, Sikorski's daughter, Maj.-Gen. Klimecki, Polish Chief of Staff and Col. Cazalet, M.P. (British Liaison Officer), also killed.

MONDAY, JULY 5

Russian Front – BATTLE OF KURSK (Op. *Zitadelle*: 'Citadel'): final German summer offensive; attempt to encircle and destroy 2 Russian army grps. in the Kursk Salient; Hitler declares, in Order of the Day, that the Op. will 'decide the war' and that giant new Tiger tanks will smash the Russian defences.

> **Kursk Forces**
> German: 900,000 men (37 divs., inc. 11 *Pz*); 2,500 tanks and assault guns, 10,000 guns; 1,830 planes. Soviet: 1,300,000 men (21 armies); 3,600 tanks, 20,000 guns; 2,500 planes.

Sea War: Pacific – Op. Toenails: US 43 Inf. Div. lands on New Georgia. Battle of Kula Gulf (night July 5-6): 7 Japanese destroyers (1 lost) attempt to land reinforcements on New Georgia; cruiser *Helena* sunk.
Sea War: Med. – U-593 sinks 2 US LSTs and 1 merchant ship off Algerian coast.
Air War – B-17s and Spitfires engage 100 German and Italian fighters over Gerbini airfield (Sicily): top Italian 'ace' Capt. Lucchini (26 victories) shot down and killed.
Secret War – Russian forces in Kursk Salient have long been preparing to meet German onslaught thanks to reports from 'Lucy' spy ring in Germany.

TUESDAY, JULY 6

Air War – Japanese bomb US troops on Rendova I.

WEDNESDAY, JULY 7

Sea War: Atlantic – U-185 sinks 3 ships in Brazilan convoy BT.18.
Air War – Top *Luftwaffe* 'ace' Lt. Erich Hartmann shoots down 4 Lagg fighters and 3 *Shturmoviks* near Kursk (Hartmann's final victory tally is 352). Japanese Ki-77 courier plane lost over Indian Ocean, *en route* to Berlin. RAF Vengeance dive-bombers attack Japanese HQ Thaungdara, N. of Rangoon.

THURSDAY, JULY 8

Sea War – British Home Fleet, USS *Alabama* and *South Dakota* carry out unsuccessful sortie along Norwegian coast, intended to divert German attention from Op. Husky.

FRIDAY, JULY 9

Air War – B-24s destroy Axis GHQ at Taormina (Sicily). British 1st Airborne Div. and US 82nd Airborne Div. land in Sicily (night July 9-10).

SATURDAY, JULY 10

Sea War: Med. – ALLIES INVADE

SICILY (Op. Husky): armada of 3,000 ships lands 12 divs. of 8th Army (Montgomery) and US 7th Army (Patton). Naval forces – 6 battleships, 2 carriers, 18 cruisers, 7 subs. and 210 other warships – escort invasion fleet and bombard coastal defences and communications.
Air War – 3,680 Allied planes participate in Op. Husky: prolonged series of raids on Sicilian airfields reaches devastating climax.
Russian Front – Hitler rejects his gens.' advice and decides to persevere with Kursk offensive.

SUNDAY, JULY 11

Sea War: Med. – Cruisers *Savannah* and

Boise with 8 destroyers halt *Pz* counter-attack near Gela. *King George V* and *Howe* bombard Favignana I., W. of Sicily. Italian coastal battery prevents Allied destroyers entering Augusta harbour. 7 German and Italian subs. sunk and Italian *Bronzo* captured around Sicily (July 11-30).

MONDAY, JULY 12

Russian Front – RUSSIAN COUNTER-OFFENSIVE AGAINST OREL SALIENT, N. of Kursk, begins; reaches climax in 'the greatest tank battle in history' (until 1973).
Sicily – Allies take Augusta and Ragusa.
Sea War: Pacific – BATTLE OF KOLOMBANGARA (night July 12-13): Japanese defeated near New Georgia, losing cruiser *Jintsu*; cruisers *Honolulu*, *St Louis* and *Leander* (British) torpedoed; US destroyer *Gwin* sunk.

TUESDAY, JULY 13

Russian Front – Battle of Kursk: Hitler reluctantly calls off the offensive.
Sea War: Atlantic – Planes from US escort carriers *Core*, *Santee*, *Bogue* and *Card* sink 12 U-boats and seriously disrupt German operations (July 13-Aug. 27).

WEDNESDAY, JULY 14

Sicily – Germans counter-attack at Augusta. British capture Primo Solo Bridge, S. of Catania. First issue of 'Eighth Army News' published in Syracuse; edited by Warwick Charlton.

THURSDAY, JULY 15

Russian Front – Russian spearheads have advanced 24-48 km in Orel sector.

FRIDAY, JULY 16

Sicily – British capture Lentini and descend on to Catanian Plain. Americans begin their assault on Agrigento.
New Guinea – Battle of Mt. Tambu (July 16-Aug. 19): Australians, advancing from Wau, capture Japanese stronghold near Salamaua.
Air War: Pacific – 100 Avengers and Dauntlesses bomb Munda airfield. Japanese night raid on Guadalcanal.
Sea War: Med. – Carrier *Indomitable* hit by Italian torpedo planes. Italian sub. *Dandolo* torpedoes cruiser *Cleopatra*. Night engagements off Sicily between German and British MTBs with Italian cruiser *Scipione Africano*: 5 German boats damaged and *MTB 305* sunk.

SATURDAY, JULY 17

Sicily – US Rangers capture Agrigento.
Occupied Sicily – AMGOT ('Allied Military Government of Occupied Territories') established in Sicily.

Soviet Offensives 1943–44

— Front line, end 1942
--- Front line, July 1943
— Front line, end 1943
--- Front line, end 1944
● Trapped German pockets
⇒ Soviet offensives, 1943
➡ Soviet offensives, 1944

miles
0   200
0   200
km

Air War: Pacific – 223 Allied planes attack shipping off Bougainville (1 destroyer sunk).
Sea War: Med. – *Warspite* bombards Catania.

SUNDAY, JULY 18

Sea War – Fight between USN 'Blimp' *K-74* and *U-134* N. of Cuba; former shot down.

MONDAY, JULY 19

Air War: Europe – **FIRST ALLIED RAIDS ON ROME.** 158 B-17s and 112 B-24s attack Lorenzo and Littorio marshalling yards. Marauders, Mitchells and Lightnings later hit Ciampino Airport. Only 5 planes lost.
Sea War: Atlantic – 4 U-boats sunk by US and Brazilian aircraft (July 19-31).
Sea War: Med. – German and Italian minelayers begin intensive operations around Italian coast.

TUESDAY, JULY 20

Sicily – Allies capture Enna, vital centre of communications.
Home Front: USSR – 'Free Germany National Committee' broadcasts Manifesto to German Army and people.
Sea War – 7 U-boats begin laying minefield S. of Novaya Zemlya in Arctic.

WEDNESDAY, JULY 21

Occupied Yugoslavia – Nazi authorities in Belgrade offer 2 rewards of 100,000 *Reichsmarks* for capture 'dead or alive' of Partisan leaders Tito and Mihailovich.

THURSDAY, JULY 22

Sicily – Palermo captured by US 7th Army.
Air War – B-24s raid Surabaya.

FRIDAY, JULY 23

Sicily – Americans capture Marsala.
Sea War: Med. – Cruiser *Newfoundland* torpedoed by *U-407*.

SATURDAY, JULY 24

Sicily – Americans capture Trapani, on W. coast.
Air War – **BATTLE OF HAMBURG** begins with raid by 700 RAF bombers (12 lost). Millions of metal-coated paper strips ('Window') dropped to blind German radar. Gloster Meteor jet fighter tested. 8th AF raids Trondheim.

SUNDAY, JULY 25

Home Front: Italy – **MUSSOLINI RESIGNS** and is arrested on the orders of King Victor Emmanuel.

Air War: Europe – Damaging raid on Hamburg docks and shipping by 68 US heavy bombers. Krupp works at Essen severely damaged by 368 RAF night bombers; fierce fires in the city.

MONDAY, JULY 26

Sea War: Atlantic – 4 British merchant ships bombed NW. of Lisbon (July 26 and 27).
Home Front: Italy – Fascist Party dissolved. Marshal Badoglio forms 'non-Fascist' Cabinet. Martial law in force throughout the country.
Air War: Europe – 53 B-17s bomb Neuhoff Power Station, Hamburg.

TUESDAY, JULY 27

Air War: Europe – **'FIRE STORM' ENGULFS HAMBURG**: numerous major fires started 3 nights earlier are stoked up by renewed bombing by 722 RAF bombers (17 lost) into single raging inferno.
Sea War: Pacific – 'Battle of the Pips': battleships *Mississippi* and *Idaho* engage imaginary 'Japanese battleships', spotted

on radar near Aleutians (the only Japanese vessels in the area are subs.).
Home Front: Britain – Churchill declares in the Commons that if new Italian Govt. does not surrender *'Italy will be seared and scarred and blackened from one end to the other'.*

WEDNESDAY, JULY 28

Sicily – Canadians capture Leonforte, NE. of Enna.
Sea War: Pacific – 5,200-strong Japanese garrison of Kiska secretly evacuated aboard 2 cruisers and 12 destroyers.
Air War: Europe – B-17s bomb Focke-Wulf works at Oschersleben.

THURSDAY, JULY 29

Air War: Europe – 726 RAF bombers raid Hamburg.

FRIDAY, JULY 30

Air War: Europe – 8th AF raids Fieseler aircraft works at Kassel. RAF night attack on Remscheid (Ruhr), centre of German machine-tool industry.

MUSSOLINI, Benito (1883-1945)
Italian: *Dictator;* Il Duce *('The Leader')*

Founder of the first fascist régime in Europe, after 'March on Rome' (1922). Crushed powerful Italian Communist Party, undertook great public works and brought temporary stability to domestic political scene. Dreamed of re-creating classical Roman Empire in the Med. region and Africa. Made disastrous miscalculation by entering World War II on side of Germany. Puppet ruler of German-occupied Italy, 1943-45. Notorious for his insatiable sexual appetites, but also a skilled aviator, a journalist and amateur violinist.
Born at Dovia near Forli (Romagna), son of a poor blacksmith. Socialist agitator in his youth; organized violent demonstrations and strikes; imprisoned 11 times. Edited Socialist newspaper, *Avanti*. Expelled from Socialist Party, 1914, for advocating Italian participation in World War I. Founded rabble-rousing daily newspaper at Milan, *Il Popolo d'Italia*. Fought in World War I as corporal of *Bersaglieri* ('Sharpshooters'). Inspired by fiery war hero and poet, Gabriele D'Annunzio, he founded Fascist Party at Milan, 1919 (named after the *fasces*, or bundles of rods which symbolized authority of ancient Roman

consuls). Terrorized Communists and Socialists with tacit approval of powerful land-owners and industrialists, heads of army and police. Installed as P.M. by King Victor Emmanuel and the Army, Oct. 1922. Assumed dictatorial powers, 1925; suppressed all opposition parties, 1926. Remodelled legal and educational systems on Fascist lines. Negotiated agreement with Pope Pius XI (Lateran Treaty, 1929). First meeting with Hitler at Venice, June 1934. Made armed preparations to resist possible Nazi seizure of Austria, July 1934.
Conquered Ethiopia and declared Victor Emmanuel 'Emperor', 1935-36. Sent 'volunteer' troops and airmen to assist Gen. Franco during Spanish Civil War (1936-39). Occupied Albania and deposed King Zog, April 1939. Joined Anti-Comintern Pact (Anti-Communist Pact) with Germany and Japan, Nov. 1937; 'Pact of Steel' (military alliance) with Germany, May 1939. Acted as 'honest broker' during Munich Conference of Sept. 1938. Issued declaration of neutrality in European War, Sept. 1939. Declared war on Britain and France, June 1940; USSR, June 1941; USA, Dec. 1941. Made premature arrangements for 'triumphal entry' into Cairo, July 1942. Met Hitler at Brenner Pass (March 1940), Munich (June 1940), Florence (Oct. 1940), and in Ukraine (Aug. 1941.)
Overthrown by Fascist Grand Council, July 1943. Imprisoned, July-Sept. 1943. Rescued by Germans, Sept. 1943. Denounced King Victor Emmanuel as traitor, disbanded Fascist Party and established 'Fascist-Republican State' in German-occupied N. Italy.
Congratulated Hitler on 'providential' escape from assassination at Rastenburg, July 20, 1944; their final meeting. Tried to flee to Switzerland with mistress, Clara Petacci, April 1945. Captured by Communist partisans near village of Dongo (Lake Como) and shot, April 28. Bodies displayed for amusement of the mob in Piazza Loretto, Milan (where 15 partisans had previously been shot). Corpses taken down at insistence of US Army, for burial in pauper's section of Cimitero Maggiore, Milan, May 1, 1945.

SATURDAY, JULY 31

Russian Front – Siege of Leningrad: 210 killed and 921 wounded by German shelling in July.
Sea War – Carrier-based Martlet (Wildcat) fighters shoot down 5 Bv 138 reconnaissance flying boats off Norway.
Home Front: Britain – Capt. Hedley Verity, Yorks. and England cricketer, dies in PoW camp in Italy; aged 38.

SUNDAY, AUGUST 1

Air War: Europe – 164 Liberators (56 lost) make low-level attack on Ploesti Oilfields, Rumania (Op. Tidal Wave). 25 German bombers cause heavy damage in Palermo.
Sea War: Pacific – *PT 109* – Lt. (later Pres.) John F. Kennedy – rammed and sunk by destroyer *Amagiri*, in Solomons.
Sea War – Op. *Wunderland II* ('Wonderland II'): planned combined anti-convoy op. by *Lützow* and 4 U-boats; only 2 ships sunk (Aug. 27 and 28).
Diplomacy – Nationalist China breaks off diplomatic relations with Vichy, in protest against hand-over of French Concession in Shanghai to 'Central Govt. of China'.
Occupied France – De Gaulle appointed Pres. of French Committee of National Defence and Giraud CinC.
Occupied Burma – Burmese puppet govt. formed by Ba Maw. Secret Burmese-Japanese military treaty. Burma declares war on Britain and USA.

MONDAY, AUGUST 2

Air War: Europe – 'Battle of Hamburg' ends with night raids by 425 RAF bombers (30 lost) in very bad weather.

Bombing of Hamburg (RAF raids)
2,752 planes (86 lost) dropped 8,621 t. of bombs. Civilians: *c.* 42,600 dead, 37,000 seriously injured; 580 factories, 170,000 t. of shipping and 3 U-boats lost.

Sicily – British and Canadians oust Germans from hill-top strongholds of Centuripe and Regalbuto; Gerbini airfield complex captured.
Diplomacy – Italian Ambassador in Lisbon contacts Allied representatives.
Home Front: China – Death of Pres. Lin Sen, aged 81; Chiang Kai-shek appointed Acting-Pres.

TUESDAY, AUGUST 3

Sicily – Canadians capture Agira.
Patton slaps hospitalized soldier (similar incident on Aug. 10); he later apologizes.
Sea War – 150 US merchant ships transferred to British Merchant Navy. Italian human torpedoes hit 3 ships at Gibraltar.

WEDNESDAY, AUGUST 4

Air War – B-17s bomb Naples harbour and factories; Cathedral and Royal Palace also hit. 150 killed, 228 injured.

THURSDAY, AUGUST 5

Russian Front – Orel and Belgorod taken by Russians.
Sicily – British take Catania.
Solomons – Americans capture Munda Airfield.
Home Front: USSR – 120-gun 'Victory Salute' fired in Moscow at midnight to celebrate liberation of Orel.
Diplomacy – Sweden revokes agreement permitting passage of German troops and munitions along her railways.

FRIDAY, AUGUST 6

Sicily – Troina, near Mt. Etna, falls to Americans after 5 days' heavy fighting.
Sea War: Pacific – Battle of Vella Gulf (night Aug. 6-7): US destroyer force springs devastating ambush on 4 Japanese troop-carrying destroyers, 3 destroyers explode from single salvo of torpedoes, killing most of 1,800 aboard.

SATURDAY, AUGUST 7

Russian Front – Russian 'West' and 'Bryansk Fronts' (army grps.) attack strong German defences E. of Smolensk. 2,133 members of Spanish *Division Azul* ('Blue Div.') killed since 1941.

SUNDAY, AUGUST 8

Sicily – Allies occupy 5 towns.
Home Front: Italy – Mussolini imprisoned.

MONDAY, AUGUST 9

Air War: Europe – RAF night raids on Mannheim and Ludwigshafen.

TUESDAY, AUGUST 10

Air War: Europe – First of 2 massive RAF night raids on Nuremburg in Aug.: total of 3,444 t. bombs dropped for the loss of 49 aircraft.
Occupied Yugoslavia – Buritch forms new Free Yugoslav Cabinet.

WEDNESDAY, AUGUST 11

Russian Front – German forces in Kharkov face threat of encirclement; Poltava-Kharkov railway cut in 3 places, W. of city.
Sea War: Med. – British sub. *Parthian* missing in Adriatic (mined?). 5 German MTBs hit by British fighter-bombers in English Channel.
Air War: Britain – 70-plane night raid on Plymouth; other bombers attack 'military installations' in Bournemouth.

THURSDAY, AUGUST 12

Air War: Europe – 330 heavy bombers of 8th AF (25 lost) despatched to the Ruhr and Bonn. Strong defences, thick cloud and smoke-screens hamper bombing. Capt. Clark Gable, the movie star, flies in leading B-17 of 351st BG. 656 RAF night bombers attack Milan (severe damage) and Turin.
Air War: Pacific – B-24s bomb Paramushiro and Shimushu in Kurile Is.
Neutral: Sweden – Sub. *Illern* accidentally sunk.

FRIDAY, AUGUST 13

Russian Front – Left wing of 'Kalinin Front' attack NE. of Smolensk.
Air War: Europe – B-24s from N. African bases carry out surprise attack on Messerschmitt works at Wiener Neustadt: first Allied attack on Austrian target.
Air War: Pacific – B-24s raid Balikpapan oil installations (Borneo).
Sicily – British capture Randazzo, vital road junction, SW. of Messina.
Sea War – U-boat grp. *Dachs* ('Badger') lays mines in Kara Sea. (*U-639* lost, Aug. 28.)
Sea War: Med. – Convoy MKS. 21 attacked by He 111 torpedo planes of KG 26: Germans claim devastating results, but only 2 ships actually damaged.

SATURDAY, AUGUST 14

Sicily – Allies capture Mt. Etna.
Diplomacy – **FIRST QUEBEC CONFERENCE** ('Quadrant'): Churchill and Roosevelt decide to launch cross-Channel invasion (Overlord), May 1, 1944 – employing artificial harbours ('Mulberries') off Normandy beachheads. (Conference ends Aug. 24.)
Home Front: Italy – Rome declared an 'open city'.

SUNDAY, AUGUST 15

Sicily – Allies capture Milazzo and Taormina and threaten Axis rearguard around Messina from W. and S.
Air War: Britain – 90-plane raid on Portsmouth.
Air War: Europe – First of series of B-17 raids on French airfields intended to deceive Germans into believing that Allies will land in Pas de Calais (Op. Starkey).
Sea War: Pacific – Farcical invasion of Kiska I. (Op. Cottage): following massive preparatory bombardment by 3 battleships, 2 cruisers, 7 destroyers and 168 aircraft, 35,000 US and Canadian troops land unopposed – unaware that Japanese have abandoned the I. 18 days previously. Americans land on Vella Lavella (Solomons). Battlecruiser *Alaska* launched at Camden, New Jersey.
Diplomacy – Castellano, representative

of Badoglio Govt., arrives in Madrid and informs British Ambassador Hoare that Italy wishes to join the Allies.

MONDAY, AUGUST 16

New Guinea – Australians and Americans encircle Mt. Tambu.
Home Front: Italy – Anti-Fascist parties issue joint demand for peace and release of political prisoners.

TUESDAY, AUGUST 17

Sicily — **END OF SICILIAN CAMPAIGN.** Americans and British enter Messina. Axis forces evacuated (Op. *Lehrgang*. 'Training course'): 39,569 German and 62,000 Italian troops, with all their equipment and supplies, transported across Strs. of Messina in small craft. Unprecedented flak 'umbrella' prevents Allied air forces from causing serious disruption during 14-day op.

Sicily Campaign Losses
German: 32,000, mainly PoWs.; 597 planes. Italian: 132,000, mainly PoWs; 144 planes. British and Canadian: 12,843. US: 9,968; 345 Allied planes.

Air War: Europe – **PEENEMÜNDE RAID.** 597 RAF night bombers (40 lost) attack V-weapons experimental establishment in NE. Germany, killing 732 and halting V-2 tests until Oct. 6.
FIRST SCHWEINFURT RAID: 230 8th USAAF B-17s bomb ball-bearing works at Schweinfurt and 146 B-17s bomb Regensburg; 60 planes lost.
Air War: Britain – 88 German bombers (11 lost) despatched to Lincoln; none find the target. Bombs scattered along E. Coast (night Aug. 17-18).
Air War: Pacific – US 5th AF carries out devastating series of raids on air bases in Wewak area of New Guinea (Aug. 17 and 18).
Home Front: Germany – Col.-Gen. Jeschonnek, *Luftwaffe* COS, commits suicide.

WEDNESDAY, AUGUST 18

Sea War: Med. — British submarine *Saracen* sunk by Italian corvette *Minerva* off Bastia.
Diplomacy – Anglo-Portuguese Agreement on establishment of air bases in Azores.

THURSDAY, AUGUST 19

Air War: Europe – B-17s, B-24s and Wellingtons attack Foggia marshalling yards by day and night.
New Guinea – Australians capture Mt. Tambu; Japanese retreat to R. Francisco (Aug. 19-26).

Italian Campaign
July 1943–May 1945
Allied advances and landings
miles 0 100
km 0 100

FRIDAY, AUGUST 20

Air War: Europe – US medium bombers raid Benevento marshalling yards, N. of Naples.
Home Front: Finland – Peace petition handed to P.M. Ryti.

SATURDAY, AUGUST 21

Home Front: Australia – General Election: Curtin's Labour Party wins decisive victory. Opposition Leader, Menzies, comments, 'the steam-roller has passed over us!'.
Home Front: USA – 100,000,000-volt X-ray machine announced by General Electric Co.
Diplomacy – Gromyko becomes Soviet Ambassador in Washington.

SUNDAY, AUGUST 22

Air War: Europe – B-26s and Wellingtons bomb Salerno railway yards.

MONDAY, AUGUST 23

Russian Front – **KHARKOV RECAPTURED BY RUSSIANS.**
Air War: Britain – Mosquito night fighters shoot down 4 Me 410 fighter bombers attacking E. Anglian airfields.
Air War: Europe – RAF Mitchells,

escorted by Spitfires, bomb St Omer marshalling yards; Wing -Cdr. J. E. Johnson scores his twenty-third victory.
Air War: China – Japanese bomb Chungking (first raid since 1941).
Home Front: USSR – Great crowds in Moscow celebrate liberation of Kharkov until 2 am: 224 guns fire 20 'victory salvoes'; fireworks display; all church bells rung.

TUESDAY, AUGUST 24

Home Front: Germany – Himmler appointed Minister of the Interior.
Occupied Denmark – Resistance blow up Forum Hall, Copenhagen.

WEDNESDAY, AUGUST 25

Burma – Mountbatten appointed Supreme Cdr. in SE. Asia.
Occupied Denmark – Shipyard workers on strike.
Solomons – End of Japanese resistance on New Georgia.

THURSDAY, AUGUST 26

Russian Front – Russians launch general offensive into E. Ukraine and across R. Dnieper using 4 'Fronts' and elements of 'Central Front'. Marshals Zhukov and Vasilevksy in overall cmnd.

Diplomacy – French Committee of National Liberation recognized by Britain, USA and Canada.

FRIDAY, AUGUST 27

Diplomacy – French Committee recognized by USSR and Nationalist China.

SATURDAY, AUGUST 28

Russian Front – Russian WF attacks main defence line E. of Smolensk.
Sea War: Atlantic – British sloop *Egret* sunk by Hs 293 glider-bombs, launched from Do 217s (first used on Aug. 25).
Occupied Denmark – 'Semi-collaborationist' Govt. rejects German ultimatum calling for draconian measures against 'saboteurs' and resigns. German CinC in Denmark takes over administration.
Home Front: Bulgaria – Assassination of pro-Axis Boris III, *Tsar* of Bulgaria, aged 49 by pro-Russian gunman. Succeeded by 6-year-old Simeon II, under 3 Regents (Prince Kyrill, Prof. Filov and Gen. Michov).

SUNDAY, AUGUST 29

Occupied Denmark – Martial law proclaimed. Army disarmed by German troops, but majority of Fleet scuttled to avoid capture, by order of V.-Adm. Vedel; Germans seize 5 small vessels (13 ships and small craft escape to Sweden).
Neutrals: Lebanon – General Election: Nationalists under Bechara el Khoury win big majority by pledging themselves to free the country from French rule.

MONDAY, AUGUST 30

Russian Front – Russian WF captures Yelnya; 50th Army transferred from Kirov to Yelnya to exploit breakthrough. Russians capture Taganrog.

TUESDAY, AUGUST 31

Sea War: Pacific – US 'Fast Carrier Task Force' (*Yorktown, Essex* and *Independence*) raids Marcus I.; Hellcat fighters in action.
Sea War: Atlantic – Japanese sub. *I-8* reaches Lorient after marathon voyage from Singapore (returns by Nov. 28).
Sea War: Med. – *Nelson* and *Rodney* shell Italian coast near Reggio di Calabria.
Air War: Europe – 45 RAF bombers shot down by German 'cat's eye' night fighters, aided by searchlights and flares, during 613-plane raid on Berlin.

WEDNESDAY, SEPTEMBER 1

Russian Front – Russian 5th Army (WF) captures Dorogobuzh.
Air War – 10th USAAF attacks Mandalay railway yards.
Air War: Europe – Oberstleutnant Dr.

Kupfer, *Stuka* 'ace', appointed first *Gen. der Schlachtflieger,* in cmnd. of all *Stuka* and ground attack units.
Home Front: Britain – Death of W. W. Jacobs, author; aged 79.
Occupied USSR – Second campaign by Russian Partisans against German rail communications: 193 grps. destroy 32,000 rails, from Crimea to Karelia (ends Nov. 1).

THURSDAY, SEPTEMBER 2

Sea War: Med. – *Valiant* and *Warspite* – refitted following damage sustained in 1941 – bombard Reggio di Calabria.

FRIDAY, SEPTEMBER 3

Sea War: Med. – INVASION OF CALABRIA (S. Italy): 13th Corps (8th Army) crosses from Sicily to Reggio di Calabria preceded by 900-gun barrage (Op. Baytown).
Air War: Europe – Lancaster force bombs Berlin (20 lost).
Home Front: Germany – One million women and children leave Berlin during or soon after the 3 big RAF raids of late Aug.- early Sept.
Diplomacy – Italian Armistice Terms: signed at Cassibile in Sicily (not made public till Sept. 8, *q.v.*).

SATURDAY, SEPTEMBER 4

Sea War – Australians land E. of Lae (New Guinea).

SUNDAY, SEPTEMBER 5

Russian Front – Russian 50th Army launches 2-pronged outflanking op. E. of Bryansk.
Air War – US paratroops land near Lae.

MONDAY, SEPTEMBER 6

Russian Front – Russian advance SE. of Smolensk temporarily halted by defence line from Yelnya to R. Desna.
Air War: Europe – 'Round-the-clock' bombing of airfields and communications around Naples.

TUESDAY, SEPTEMBER 7

Diplomacy – Correspondence published concerning US refusal to supply Lease-Lend aid to Argentina.

WEDNESDAY, SEPTEMBER 8

Diplomacy – SURRENDER OF ITALY. Eisenhower makes public announcement

in Algiers. Italian Armistice Terms: 13 points inc. immediate cessation of hostilities; Italy to deny all facilities to Germany; all PoWs to be handed over and none at any time sent to Germany. Immediate transfer of all warships and aircraft to designated points; merchant shipping to be requisitioned by Allies;

Allies to establish bases wherever they wish on Italian territory and Italian forces to protect bases until arrival of Allied forces. Italy to surrender Corsica.
Home Front: Italy – Op. Achse ('Axis'): GERMAN FORCES SEIZE ALL STRATEGIC POINTS IN ITALY and forcibly disarm Italian forces.
Occupied Yugoslavia – Tito's Partisans begin rounding up and disarming Italian divs.
Sea War: Med. – Surrender of Italian Fleet: 5 battleships, 8 cruisers and 11 destroyers leave their bases for Malta (Sept. 8-9).
Sea War – German 'invasion' of Spitzbergen: Gren. bn. lands from destroyers covered by *Scharnhorst,* to destroy colliery installations; *Tirpitz* shells Barentsburg town. Small Norwegian garrison offers stout resistance.

THURSDAY, SEPTEMBER 9

Sea War: Med. – ALLIES LAND AT SALERNO: US 5th Army (Lt.Gen. Mark Clark) and British 10th Corps land at Salerno, S. of Naples (Op. Avalanche). British 1st Airborne Div. lands, by sea, at Taranto (Op. Slapstick). Do 217 sinks battleship *Roma* with *Fritz X* radio-controlled missile (1,255 killed, inc. Adm. Bergamini). German MTBs *S.54* and *S.61* lay mines in Taranto harbour which sink HMS *Abdiel* (Sept. 10); then race to Venice, sinking Italian gunboat and destroyer and capturing troopship *Leopardi* en route and forcing Italian naval cdr. at Venice to surrender. King Victor Emmanuel and his Govt. proceed abroad cruiser *Scipione Africano* from Pescara to Brindisi.
Diplomacy – Iran declares war on Germany.

FRIDAY, SEPTEMBER 10

Italy – British capture Salerno. Germans occupy Rome and disarm Italian forces in the N.
Sea War: Med. – Huge crowds watch Italian Fleet enter Grand Harbour, Malta, led by *Warspite, Valiant* and *King George V*

(Italian ships fly black pennants). British land on 7 of the Dodecanese Is. (Sept. 10-17).

Sea War – 8,935 Russian Naval Inf. land from 129 small craft at Novorossisk.

Sea War: Med. – Evacuation of 25,000 German troops from Sardinia to Corsica (thence to Italy by air and sea).

SATURDAY, SEPTEMBER 11

Sea War: Med. – 7,139 French and US troops transported from Algiers to Corsica (Sept. 11-Oct. 1).

Italy – British 8th Army capture Brindisi. Italian garrison of Rhodes surrenders to Germans.

New Guinea – Allied force captures Salamaua, near Lae.

Air War – Do 217s of KG 100 (formerly KGr 100) commence series of attacks on Allied fleet off Salerno, using *Fritz X* and Hs 293 missiles: cruisers *Savannah* and *Uganda* and battleship *Warspite* seriously damaged; hospital ship *Newfoundland* and 1 transport sunk (Sept. 11-15).

SUNDAY, SEPTEMBER 12

Russian Front – Evacuation of German 17th Army from Kuban Bridgehead across Kerch Strs. to Crimea (Sept. 12-Oct. 9): 239,669 troops, 16,311 wounded, 27,456 civilians, 74,657 horses, 6,255 head of cattle, vast numbers of vehicles and quantities of supplies evacuated.

Sea War: Med. – U-boats commence ops. off Salerno bridgeheads: but sink only 3 ships during numerous attacks.

Secret War – **MUSSOLINI RESCUED** by Skorzeny and *SS* detachment from Gran Sasso in Abruzzi Mts. Ex-*Duce* flown out in *Storch* aircraft.

MONDAY, SEPTEMBER 13

Italy – *Pzs* counter-attack and seriously threaten Salerno bridgehead (Sept. 13-14). Allied naval and air forces bombard advancing Germans 'round-the-clock'.

Home Front: China – Chiang Kai-shek elected Pres.

TUESDAY, SEPTEMBER 14

Sea War: Med. – Greek sub. *Katsonis* sunk. British land on Kos (Dodecanese).

Sea War – U-boat grp. *Monsun* ('Monsoon') begins ops.: 6 ships sunk during Oct. All except *U-533* (lost) then go to Penang.

Russian Front – Yeremenko drives towards Smolensk from the N.

WEDNESDAY, SEPTEMBER 15

New Guinea – Lae captured by Allied forces.

Russian Front – Russians break through

Yelnya-Desna defence line.

Home Front: Italy – Mussolini re-establishes Fascist régime in N. Italy – along 'National Socialist' lines, as the 'Italian Social Republic' (*Repubblica Sociale Italiana,* or RSI).

Home Front: USA – US War Dept. states that the 'Bazooka' *'has penetrated the armour of any enemy tank encountered on any front'.*

THURSDAY, SEPTEMBER 16

Occupied Italy – Suicide of Marshal Cavallero, ex-Chief of Italian Gen. Staff.

Occupied Yugoslavia – Split occupied by Tito's Partisans (recaptured by Germans, Sept. 28).

FRIDAY, SEPTEMBER 17

Italy — Patrols of Allied 5th and 8th Armies link up near Agropoli, S. of Salerno.

Russian Front – **BRYANSK CAPTURED BY RUSSIANS.**

SATURDAY, SEPTEMBER 18

Sea War: Atlantic – **RESUMPTION OF 'WOLF-PACK' OPS. AGAINST CONVOYS** following re-equipment of U-boats with electronic monitoring equipment, 8x20-mm AA guns and acoustic torpedoes.

Sea War: Pacific – US carrier strike on Tarawa.

Italy – 5th Army captures Battipaglia. Germans retreat from Salerno bridge-head.

SUNDAY, SEPTEMBER 19

Sea War: Atlantic – 20 U-boats deployed against convoys ON. 202 and ONS. 18

(Sept. 19-23). Germans claim outstanding successes with acoustic torpedoes against escorting warships (12 sunk, 3 prob. sunk) but only 4 actually hit; 7 merchant ships sunk. 3 U-boats lost.

MONDAY, SEPTEMBER 20

Italy – British and US troops link up at Eboli.

Sea War – Italian sub. *Cagni* surrenders at Durban.

TUESDAY, SEPTEMBER 21

Sea War – *Tirpitz* disabled by 'X-Craft' (British midget subs.) in Alta Fjord, N. Norway. Australian commandos enter

Above: *Berliners walk to work after a Sept. RAF raid.*

Singapore Harbour in canoes and sink 2 Japanese transports (Op. Jaywick).

Italy – 8th Army captures Potenza – important road junction in central S. Italy.

Russian Front – Russians capture Chernigov.

Home Front: Britain – Churchill describes Salerno landings as *'the most daring amphibious operation we have yet undertaken'.*

WEDNESDAY, SEPTEMBER 22

Russian Front – **RUSSIAN 13TH ARMY CROSSES R. DNIEPER,** S. of Kiev – penetrating so-called 'Eastern Rampart' defences along right bank. Poltava captured by Koniev's forces.

THURSDAY, SEPTEMBER 23

Italy – 5th Army launches offensive N. of Salerno.

Sea War: Med. – Destroyer *Eclipse* sinks German torpedo boat and prison ship *Donizetti* carrying 1,576 Italians, S. of Rhodes.
Sea War: Pacific – Tanker convoy destroyed by US sub. *Trigger,* off Formosa.
Occupied Corsica – French occupy Bonifacio (Corsica).
Diplomacy – 'Pocket' republic of San Marino declares war on Germany in retaliation for capture and deportation of its 300-strong 'Army'.
Home Front: Britain – Death of Elinor Glyn, Anglo-Canadian author of 'scandalous' romances inc. 'Three Weeks' (1907); aged 78.

FRIDAY, SEPTEMBER 24

Sea War – Op. *Probestuck* ('Test Piece'): 29 German MTBs lay mines off Harwich.

SATURDAY, SEPTEMBER 25

Russian Front — RUSSIANS CAPTURE SMOLENSK.
Sea War: Pacific – Evacuation of Japanese garrison from Kolombangara (Solomons): 9,400 men taken off by landing craft and destroyers; US destroyers sink 40 boats; 1,000 Japanese drown (Sept. 25-26 to Oct. 3-4).

SUNDAY, SEPTEMBER 26

Sea War – British MGBs and Dutch MTBs attack German convoy in English Channel: 2 cargo ships and a patrol boat sunk (night Sept. 26-27).
Sea War: Med. – Destroyers *Intrepid* and *Vasilissa Olga* (Greek) sunk by Ju 88s at Leros.

MONDAY, SEPTEMBER 27

Italy – 8th Army captures Foggia, with vital airfields and marshalling yards.
Occupied Greece – Germans occupy Corfu.
Sea War: Atlantic – During series of attacks on 6 convoys (Sept. 27–Oct. 9) by 21 U-boats only 2 ships are sunk for the loss of 6 U-boats.

TUESDAY, SEPTEMBER 28

Occupied France – Gen. Legentilhomme appointed Free French Commissioner for National Defence.

WEDNESDAY, SEPTEMBER 29

Diplomacy – Offical signature of Italian Armistice by Eisenhower and Badoglio aboard HMS *Nelson* at Malta.
Italy – 5th Army captures Castellamare and Pompeii (ancient ruins slightly damaged). 8th Army enters Adriatic port of Manfredonia.
Russian Front – Russians capture Kremenchug.

THURSDAY, SEPTEMBER 30

Russian Front – Siege of Leningrad: 11,394 shells fall on city in Sept., killing 124 and wounding 468.
Home Front: Italy – Badoglio forms a new Cabinet, composed (with one exception) of top-ranking military and naval officers.
Occupied Denmark – Atomic physicist Niels Bohr escapes to Sweden.
Nazis begin rounding-up Danish Jews.

FRIDAY, OCTOBER 1

Italy – Allied 5th Army enters Naples.
Diplomacy – Harriman appointed US Ambassador in Moscow.

SATURDAY, OCTOBER 2

Italy – 5th Army captures Benevento, NE. of Naples.
Russian Front – Great Russian Smolensk offensive grinds to a stop, midway between that city and Vitebsk-Orsha.
Sea War: Med. – Royal Marine Commandos, supported by tanks, make surprise night landing at Termoli, N. of Manfredonia; cdr. of German garrison, Maj. Rou, captured in bed. T-5 acoustic torpedoes employed by U-boats off Algeria and Salerno: US destroyers *Bristol* and *Buck* sunk.
Sea War – German shipping in Baltic comes under increasing attack from Russian torpedo planes.
New Guinea – Australians capture Finschhafen.

SUNDAY, OCTOBER 3

Sea War: Med. – Op. *Eisbär* ('Polar bear'). Germans land on Kos, capturing 1,388 British and 3,145 Italians.
China – New Japanese drive in Central China.

MONDAY, OCTOBER 4

Sea War: Atlantic – Planes from US carrier *Card* sink 'U-tanker' *U-460 and U-422* and damage *U-264* near Azores. Passing convoy escapes attack.
Op. Leader: planes from USS *Ranger* hit 10 German ships at Bodo (N. Norway). British Home Fleet provides escort.
Cunningham appointed First Sea Lord.
Occupied Corsica – End of Corsican campaign.

TUESDAY, OCTOBER 5

Air War: Europe – *Stuka* units re-designated *Schlachtgeschwadern* and restricted to low-level night ground-attack duties over Russian Front.
Sea War: Atlantic – *U-389* sunk by RAF Hudson with rockets.
Sea War: Pacific – 6 carriers of TF 14 launch massive air strikes against Wake I. (26 aircraft lost).

WEDNESDAY, OCTOBER 6

Sea War – 3 Russian destroyers sunk by *Stukas* in Black Sea. Stalin imposes strict curbs on subsequent ops. by Black Sea Fleet.
Sea War: Pacific – Americans land on Kolombangara I. Battle of Vella Lavella (Oct. 6-7): Japanese win their last night victory in Solomons – torpedoing 2 US destroyers; Japanese destroyer *Yugumo* sunk. Meanwhile, small craft evacuate Japanese garrison from Vella Lavella.

THURSDAY, OCTOBER 7

Russian Front – Russians capture Nevel, W. of Velikie Luki.
Italy – 5th Army enters Capua, on R. Volturno, 32 km N. of Naples.
Sea War: Med – British cruisers *Penelope* and *Sirius,* with two destroyers, annihilate German troop convoy making for Kos I.
Secret War – Bohr flies to Scotland.

FRIDAY, OCTOBER 8

Sea War – 240 German barges, Siebel Ferries, etc. – used in Kuban evacuation – safely withdrawn from Kerch Strs. to Sebastopol.
Italy – 5th Army takes Caserta.
Home Front: Japan – Tojo assumes personal responsibility for war production.

SATURDAY, OCTOBER 9

Air War – 8th AF raids Gdynia.
Sea War: Med. – *Stukas* sink destroyer *Panther* and severely damage cruiser *Carlisle* in Scarpanto Str.

SUNDAY, OCTOBER 10

Occupied Russia – Hitler orders transfer of all Russian volunteers serving in the *Wehrmacht* to W. Europe.

MONDAY, OCTOBER 11

Air War – Japanese bomb Madras (India).

TUESDAY, OCTOBER 12

Air War – 350 Allied planes raid Rabaul.
Italy – BATTLE OF VOLTURNO RIVER (Oct. 12-19): Allied land attack followed by sea-borne op. (Oct. 13).

WEDNESDAY, OCTOBER 13

Diplomacy – ITALY (BADOGLIO GOVT.) DECLARES WAR ON GERMANY. She is not regarded as a full Ally and is classed as a 'Co-Belligerent'.

THURSDAY, OCTOBER 14

Russian Front – Russians recapture Zaporozhe.

Air War: Europe – **SECOND SCHWEINFURT RAID** ('Black Thursday'): 291 B-17s despatched; 228 drop 483 t. bombs on target. 60 planes lost. 8th AF temporarily abandons deep-penetration strategic raids.

FRIDAY, OCTOBER 15

Italy – 8th Army captures Campobasso and Vinchiaturo – important road junctions S. of Rome.

SATURDAY, OCTOBER 16

Russian Front – Fierce fighting in Melitopol.
Air War: Europe – *Luftwaffe* flies many hundreds of sorties against Dnieper bridgeheads.
Occupied Yugoslavia – Sixth German offensive against Tito's Partisans in Bosnia (ends inconclusively, mid-Jan. 1944).

SUNDAY, OCTOBER 17

Sea War: Pacific – German disguised raider *Michel* sunk off Yokohama by US sub. *Tarpon*. Exchange of Japanese and Allied civilian internees aboard liners *Teia Maru* and *Gripsholm* at Marmagao (Portuguese India).
Sea War – Allied destroyers land Norwegian troops on Spitzbergen.

MONDAY, OCTOBER 18

Home Front: Germany – Hitler confers with 2 Bulgarian Regents.

TUESDAY, OCTOBER 19

Air War – B-25s and Beaufighters attack convoys N. of Crete (Oct. 19 and 20): German prison ship *Sinfra* sunk (566 men rescued).
Diplomacy – London Protocol signed: Britain, USA and Canada to step up supplies to Russia. **SECOND MOSCOW CONFERENCE** (Oct. 19-Nov. 1): war criminals to be punished. Declaration on post-war status of Italy, Austria and China.

WEDNESDAY, OCTOBER 20

Russian Front – 4 Russian 'Fronts' (army grps.), previously known as 'Voronezh', 'Steppe', 'South-West' and 'South', redesignated '1st' to '4th' Ukrainian Fronts (UFs).
Sea War – *U-516* sinks 6 ships in Caribbean and escapes despite week-long hunt by Allied forces.
Sea War: Pacific – Op. *Ro*. 6 Japanese carriers ferry 173 planes from Truk to Rabaul in readiness for planned offensive in Solomons.
Air War: Britain – Attempted night raids on London and Hull fail abysmally.

Air War: Europe – RAF and RCAF Lancasters raid Leipzig in severe weather. Mosquitoes attack Berlin. 17 planes lost.
Diplomacy – Britain and USA agree to establish investigative War Crimes Commission.

THURSDAY, OCTOBER 21

Air War – American P-40 sqn. destroys *Stuka* formation about to attack Yugoslav Partisans.
Occupied Malaya – S. C. Bose forms provisional govt. of 'Free India' at Singapore.
Occupied Philippines – Japan grants 'independence' to Philippines.
Home Front: Britain – Death of First Sea Lord, Adm. Sir Dudley Pound; aged 66.

FRIDAY, OCTOBER 22

Sea War: Med. – 3 Allied destroyers mined in Aegean (Oct. 22-24).

SATURDAY, OCTOBER 23

Italy – 8th Army attacks across R. Trigno NW. of Termoli.
Sea War: Atlantic – Cruiser *Charybdis* sunk by German torpedo-boats off French coast. Destroyers *Duncan* and *Vidette* sink *U-274* using 'hedgehog' depthcharge patterns.
Russian Front – Russian 4th UF captures Melitopol.
Home Front: Britain – Maj.-Gen. Laycock appointed Chief of Combined Ops.; one of only 2 survivors from the 'Keyes Raid'. (*See* Nov. 17, 1941.)

SUNDAY, OCTOBER 24

Sea War – 32 German MTBs (2 lost) make

unsuccessful attack on convoy off Cromer (night Oct. 24-25).

MONDAY, OCTOBER 25

Russian Front – Russians recapture Dnepropetrovsk Dam.
Occupied Burma – Burma-Siam Railway ('Death Railway') completed by Allied PoWs and native coolies.

Death Railway
93,000 dead inc. 6,318 British, 2,815 Australians, 2,490 Dutch, 356 US.

TUESDAY, OCTOBER 26

Home Front: India – Wavell visits famine-stricken areas in Bengal; relief camps to be established.

WEDNESDAY, OCTOBER 27

Sea War: Pacific – NZ forces land in Treasury Is. (Solomons).
Home Front: Britain – Death of (Miss) Radclyffe Hall, notorious author of 'Well of Loneliness' (1928), dealing with lesbianism.

THURSDAY, OCTOBER 28

Home Front: USA – 530,000 coalminers on strike; Roosevelt commandeers mines, Nov. 1; strike ends Nov. 3.
Home Front: New Zealand – Butter rationed.

FRIDAY, OCTOBER 29

Italy – Port of Mondragone captured by 5th Army.

TITO (Josip Brozovich, or Broz) (1892-1980)
Yugoslav: *Marshal and President*

The last survivor of the great Allied leaders of World War II and the longest serving head of state in the world. Turned an army of 'partisans' into a Communist army of national liberation. His fierce campaign against the occupying forces tied down large numbers of Axis troops and, by 1944, won him Allied support.
  Born at Kumrovec, near Zagreb, in Austrian Croatia; worked as farm labourer.

Served in Austro-Hungarian Army. Captured by Russians, 1916 and joined Bolsheviks. Fought in Russian Civil War. Returned to Zagreb and arrested by Yugoslav authorities (1928-29). Spent two years at Lenin School in Moscow. Member of Politburo of Yugoslav Communist Party, 1934. Went to Paris, 1936, to organize supplies for Spanish Republicans. Gen. Sec. of Yugoslav Communist Party, 1937.
  Organized guerrilla army in the mountains after German *Blitzkreig* of April 1941 and maintained stubborn resistance despite seven punitive expeditions by German, Italian and 'puppet troops'. Narrowly escaped death, May 25, 1944, when German planes and airborne troops attacked his secret mountain HQ. Met Stalin, Sept. 1944, and agreed on entry of Red Army into Yugoslavia. Formed provisional govt., March 1945. Led his forces into Belgrade, May 1945.
  Expelled by the Cominform (predecessor of Warsaw Pact), in 1948, for deviating from strict Stalinist doctrine. Moscow called on Yugoslav people to overthrow Tito and imposed economic sanctions, but Tito rallied popular support and obtained aid from the West. Re-established relations with USSR after Stalin's death. Elected president, 1953 (re-elected 5 times, 1954-71); president for life from 1974.

SATURDAY, OCTOBER 30

Italy – Germans counter-attack 8th Army bridgehead over the Trigno.
Russian Front – Russians now control several bridgeheads on right bank of Lower Dnieper, together with entire left bank, except for the Nikopol Salient. Axis forces trapped in the Crimea.

SUNDAY, OCTOBER 31

Italy – 5th Army captures Teano, N. of Capua.
Home Front: USA – Death of Max Reinhardt, German-Jewish theatrical producer; aged 70.

MONDAY, NOVEMBER 1

Russian Front – Russians sever communications of German 17th Army in the Crimea.
Sea War: Atlantic – U-405 and American destroyer *Borie* fight epic duel; they collide and hand-to-hand fighting ensues; both sink.
Sea War: Pacific – Op. Cherry Blossom: **AMERICAN MARINES LAND ON BOUGAINVILLE**, largest Solomons I. Warships and carrier planes bombard Buka airfield. Battle of Empress Augusta Bay (night Nov. 1-2): Japanese make unsuccessful attempt to disrupt Bougainville landings, losing cruiser *Sendai* and a destroyer; US cruiser *Montpelier* later damaged by bombs.
Sea War – Russians land at Eltigen and Enikale in Kerch Pen. on Black Sea and establish bridgehead; 18th Army reinforcements land during following week, but German light naval craft establish blockade and sink 206 Russian craft. British convoy operations resumed in Arctic.

TUESDAY, NOVEMBER 2

Sea War – British blockade-runner *Master Standfast* – 1 of 5 fast boats plying between Hull and Lysekil (Sweden) – captured by German patrol boat in the Skagerrak. German MTBs sink 3 coasters in Convoy CW. 221 off Hastings (night Nov. 2-3): first torpedo attack in E. English Channel since 1941.

WEDNESDAY, NOVEMBER 3

Air War: Europe – 500 B-17s and 100 B-24s, heavily escorted by Lightnings and Thunderbolts, bomb Wilhelmshaven through dense cloud using H2X ('Mickey Mouse') radar.
Russian Front – Russian 2nd UF launches final assault on outnumbered and outgunned German garrison of Kiev.

THURSDAY, NOVEMBER 4

Italy – Americans cross upper Volturno R.

Above: *A Panzer IV and German infantry retreat north of the Pripet Marshes on the Russian Front, Nov.*

FRIDAY, NOVEMBER 5

Sea War: Pacific – 6 Japanese cruisers damaged by US carrier planes at Rabaul.
Sea War: Atlantic – Capt. Walker's 2nd Support Grp. saves Convoy HX. 264 and sinks 2 U-boats.
Air War: Pacific – Corsairs from Torokina airstrip, Bougainville, escort USAAF bombers to Rabaul.
Russian Front – Secret re-deployment of Russian 2nd Assault Army from Leningrad to nearby Oranienburg Salient commences: numerous small craft of Baltic Fleet transport 44,000 men, 600 guns and 200 tanks, Nov. 1943-Jan. 1944.
Occupied France – First 'Blackmail' op. by French Resistance: management of Peugeot factory (tanks, aircraft parts) at Montbéliard persuaded to sabotage machine tools. (Resistance then destroy replacement tools sent from Germany, Feb. 10 and March 15, 1944.)

SATURDAY, NOVEMBER 6

Russian Front – **RUSSIANS CAPTURE KIEV.**
Sea War: Pacific – Japanese reinforcements land on Bougainville.
Sea War: Med. – Troopships *Marnix van St Aldegonde* and *Santa Elena* and US destroyer *Beatty* sunk by Heinkel torpedo planes off Algeria.

SUNDAY, NOVEMBER 7

Italy – 8th Army reaches R. Sangro.

MONDAY, NOVEMBER 8

Home Front: Germany – Hitler speaks in Munich; promises retaliation for Allied 'terror' bombing.
Sea War: Atlantic – Abortive combined op. by U-boats and Condor aircraft W. of Portugal (night Nov. 8-9). RAF Fortress from Azores sinks *U-707*.
Neutrals: Lebanon – Chamber of Deputies votes to amend Constitution, in defiance of French Delegate General Helleu.

TUESDAY, NOVEMBER 9

Diplomacy – UNRRA Agreement: 44 Allied and Associated States establish United Nations Relief and Rehabilitation Administration.

WEDNESDAY, NOVEMBER 10

Home Front: USSR – 2 new military decorations created: 'Victory Order' (large ruby star inset with 91 diamonds) for senior officers; and 'Order of Glory' for lower ranks.
Russian Front – 'Battle of Cherkassy': Russian paratroops drop near Cherkassy, S. of Dnieper R.; and link up with partisans. Meanwhile 2nd Ukrainian Army closes in and ferries tanks on rafts and pontoons across R. Dnieper. German land and air forces subsequently launch violent counter-attacks. Battle ends Dec. 14 (*q.v.*).

THURSDAY, NOVEMBER 11

Sea War: Pacific – US carrier planes batter Japanese shipping, defences and airfields at Rabaul. 108 Japanese planes (33 lost) attack carrier TG 50.3 but without success.
Sea War: Med. – 4 ships sunk by German aircraft off Algeria.
Neutrals: Lebanon – French troops forcibly arrest Lebanese Govt. leaders

(martial law declared, Nov. 12). Bloody rioting in Beirut.

Diplomacy – Egypt, Iraq and Saudi Arabia issue vigorous protests against French actions in Lebanon (Nov. 11-15).

FRIDAY, NOVEMBER 12

Russian Front – Russians recapture Zhitomir, W. of Kiev, thereby cutting vital Leningrad-Odessa railway.
Sea War – British sub. *Taurus* sinks Japanese *I-34* off Penang. *U-220* lays mines off St. John's, Newfoundland (2 ships sunk).
Sea War: Med. – Op. Leopard: Germans land on Leros (Dodecanese); British-Italian garrison surrenders, Nov. 16, after fierce fighting.
Air War: Pacific – 50 surviving Japanese carrier planes withdrawn from Rabaul.

SATURDAY, NOVEMBER 13

Sea War: Med. – Germans land on Is. of Krk, Cres and Losinj off Yugoslav coast.
Occupied France – French Resistance attack SRO ball-bearing factory at Annecy.

SUNDAY, NOVEMBER 14

Sea War – *U-794*, world's first 'true sub.' enters service at Kiel; powered by the Walter hydrogen peroxide/fuel oil turbine. Unfortunately, the sub.'s phenomenal performance is marred by serious unsolved technical problems.

MONDAY, NOVEMBER 15

Sea War: Atlantic – DÖNITZ ABANDONS U-BOAT OPS. IN W. ATLANTIC following totally abortive forays against Convoys HX. 264 and SC. 146. German aircraft begin shadowing combined Convoy MKS. 30/SL. 139 N. of Gibraltar but all attempts to bring up U-boats are defeated. Eventually (Nov. 21) He 177 aircraft attack alone and hit 2 ships with Hs 293 missiles.

TUESDAY, NOVEMBER 16

Sea War: Med. – Germans gain control of Leros
Air War: Europe – B-17s and B-24s attack Knaben molybdenum mines and Norsk Hydro power station, Norway.
Neutrals: Lebanon – Gen. Catroux arrives in Beirut with full powers to settle constitutional crisis (French reinstate Pres. Khoury, and recall Gen. Helleu Nov. 22).

WEDNESDAY, NOVEMBER 17

New Guinea – Australians with Matilda tanks assault Sattelberg.

THURSDAY, NOVEMBER 18

Air War: Europe – BATTLE OF BERLIN. RAF launches 5-month-long

series of massive night raids, designed to 'wreck Berlin from end to end' (Air Marshal Harris). 50 diversionary raids on other cities. 25,000 t. bombs dropped in 16 major and 16 minor attacks, destroying 9 sq km of city.

Bombing of Berlin
25,000 t. of bombs dropped in 32 attacks destroying 9 sq km of city. 6,166 dead, 18,431 badly injured, 1,500,000 homeless; 325 factories damaged. RAF: 1,047 planes lost.

FRIDAY, NOVEMBER 19

Russian Front – Germans recapture Zhitomir.
Italy – BATTLE OF THE SANGRO (Nov. 19-24): British establish small bridgeheads over the swollen R.
China – Siege of Changteh: Chinese 57th Div. defends city against superior Japanese forces until Dec. 3. Only 300 Chinese survive.
Sea War: Pacific – 19 carriers of US TF 50 launch massive air strikes against Gilbert Is. and Nauru.

SATURDAY, NOVEMBER 20

Sea War: Pacific – US MARINES LAND ON TARAWA AND BETIO. 18,600 Americans engage 4,836 Japanese and Koreans until all organized resistance ends Nov. 23.
6,472 infantry land on Makin (Japanese

Tarawa Losses
Japanese and Korean: 4,690 dead, 146 PoWs (only 17 Japanese captured). US: 1,009 dead, 2,101 wounded.

Above: *Marines dash forward with satchels of TNT to destroy a Japanese bunker on heavily fortified Tarawa Island.*

resistance ends Nov. 23). Unsuccessful employment of 3 battleships at Betio prompts major revision of pre-invasion bombardment techniques in later ops.

SUNDAY, NOVEMBER 21

Italy – Kesselring made German CinC. Rommel leaves his cmnd. (*see* Dec. 12).
Occupied Norway – British and Norwegian Commandos destroy smelting works near Arendal (Norway).

MONDAY, NOVEMBER 22

Air War: Europe – First '2,000-ton' RAF night raid on Berlin.
Air War – Stukas attack Tigani on Samos; Allied garrison surrenders Nov. 23.
Diplomacy – FIRST CAIRO CONFERENCE (Churchill, Roosevelt and Chiang Kai-shek) begins. Meetings held up to Nov. 26.

TUESDAY, NOVEMBER 23

Russian Front – Gomel (Byelorussia) virtually encircled by Russians. Russians counter-attack near Kiev.

WEDNESDAY, NOVEMBER 24

Italy – 8th Army crosses Lower Sangro R. on 8-km front.
Air War: Europe – US bombers sink 4 ex-French warships at Toulon.
Sea War: Pacific – Escort carrier *Liscombe Bay* sunk by *I-175* off Makin.
Home Front: Germany – Goebbels issues proclamation to citizens of Berlin: 'Our will to win is unshakable.' He exhorts Berliners to defy RAF 'terror attacks'.

THURSDAY, NOVEMBER 25

Air War: Europe – US planes attack 2 airfields near St Omer. RAF light bombers and fighters attack numerous targets in N. France. Halifax night bombers raid Frankfurt and Offenbach; Goethe's house badly damaged (18 aircraft lost in all ops.).
Air War: Pacific – 14th AF destroy 42 Japanese planes on Schinchiku airfield (Formosa).
China – Japanese enter Changteh, Hunan Province (expel Chinese Dec. 3).
Sea War: Pacific – Battle of Cape St. George (night Nov. 25-26): US destroyers annihilate Japanese destroyer sqn. carrying reinforcements to Bougainville.

FRIDAY, NOVEMBER 26

Sea War: Med. – British troopship *Rohna* sunk by Hs 293 glider-bomb off Bougie, Algeria (1,115 killed).
New Guinea – Australians capture Sattelberg.
Russian Front – Russians capture Gomel.

SATURDAY, NOVEMBER 27

Russian Front – Russians close in from 3 directions on Zhlobin, vital rail junction NW. of Gomel.

SUNDAY, NOVEMBER 28

Italy – 8th Army drives N. from Sangro.
Diplomacy – CONFERENCE AT TEHERAN (ends Dec. 1). British and Americans give top priority to Op. Overlord. Soviet forces to fight Japan after defeat of Germany. Stalin receives ceremonial 'Sword of Stalingrad' – made in Sheffield, by order of King George VI.
Colombian Govt. proclaims 'state of belligerency' with Germany, following sinking of Colombian steamer, Nov. 27.

MONDAY, NOVEMBER 29

Russian Front – Fierce fighting in Kiev Salient; *SS Pzs* in action.
Occupied Yugoslavia – National Partisan Assembly appoints Tito to rank of Marshal.

TUESDAY, NOVEMBER 30

Russian Front – Russians now within 11 km of Zhlobin.

WEDNESDAY, DECEMBER 1

Air War: Europe – B-17s attack Solingen, E. of Dusseldorf, for second successive day.

THURSDAY, DECEMBER 2

Italy – 650-gun barrage heralds great 5th Army push in central Italy: line moves forward 3 km.

Air War – 88 German bombers carry out low level night raid on Bari in Italy (2 munition ships explode). 17 ships sunk, inc. SS *John Harvey* carrying mustard gas bombs. 1,000 plus killed, 800 injured. Thousands of civilians flee.
Home Front: Britain – Min. of Labour Bevin announces conscription to mines.

FRIDAY, DECEMBER 3

Air War: Europe – Göring orders Peltz – commanding German bomber forces in the W. – *To avenge the terror attacks of the enemy . . . by means of concentrated attacks on [British] cities. . . . '* (See Jan. 21, 1944.)
Occupied Norway – Capt. Nordahl Grieg, Norwegian airman, poet and playwright (relative of famous composer), killed in bomber over Berlin; aged 41.

SATURDAY, DECEMBER 4

Italy – 8th Army reaches R. Moro.
Russian Front – Germans crush Russian forces in Eltigen bridgehead: 10,000 killed, 2,827 taken prisoner.
Yugoslavia – Tito's Partisans establish Provisional Govt.
Sea War: Pacific – US Fast Carrier Task Force raids Kwajalein: 386 planes (5 lost) sink 6 transports and damage 2 cruisers. 55 Japanese planes destroyed. Torpedo planes hit USS *Lexington*. Carrier *Chuyo* sunk by US Sub. *Sailfish,* SE. of Tokyo.
Diplomacy – SECOND CAIRO CONFERENCE. Amphibious ops. in Bay of Bengal are cancelled. Timetable set for Pacific 'island hopping' campaign. Conference ends Dec. 7.
Bolivia declares war on all Axis States.

SUNDAY, DECEMBER 5

Air War – First Japanese daylight raid on Calcutta (350 killed).
Air War: Europe – Fighter-bombers of RAF, 2nd TAF, and US 9th AF attack V-1 launching sites in Pas de Calais.

MONDAY, DECEMBER 6

Italy – 8th Army crosses the Moro.

TUESDAY, DECEMBER 7

Home Front: USA – Battleship *Wisconsin* launched at Philadelphia Navy Yard.

WEDNESDAY, DECEMBER 8

Sea War: Pacific – US battleships and destroyers pound Nauru I.; destroyer *Boyd* damaged by Japanese batteries.

THURSDAY, DECEMBER 9

Italy – Important peaks, Monte Camino and Monte Maggiore, secured by 5th Army after 9 days' heavy fighting.
China – Chinese recapture Changteh.

FRIDAY, DECEMBER 10

Air War: Britain – Night raid on Chelmsford: 1 Mosquito destroys 3 Do 217s.

SATURDAY, DECEMBER 11

Air War: Europe – Heavy 8th AF raid on Emden U-boat yards (20 planes lost). Americans claim 138 German fighters shot down. Gen. Arnold, GC USAAF, declares that Allies are almost ready to launch a '24-hour 360-degree' bombing assault on Germany from N., S., E. and W. *'We are going to hit them every day and the RAF every night.'*

SUNDAY, DECEMBER 12

Home Front: Germany – ROMMEL APPOINTED CinC OF 'FORTRESS EUROPE'.
Diplomacy – Czechoslovak-Soviet Treaty of Friendship and Mutual Assistance.
Sea War: Med. – British destroyers *Tynedale* and *Holcombe* sunk by *U-593* (Dec. 12 and 13).

MONDAY, DECEMBER 13

Air War: Europe – Heavy US bomber raid on Kiel.
Air War: Pacific – US 5th AF drops 433 t. bombs on Arawe (New Britain).

TUESDAY, DECEMBER 14

Russian Front – Cherkassy captured by Russian 2nd UF after 5 days' house-to-house fighting. 6,000 Germans killed; Russians push on W. towards Smyela.

WEDNESDAY, DECEMBER 15

Russian Front – Bagramyovs' '1st Baltic Front' attacks S. of Nevel and quickly punches hole, 80 km wide and 30 deep, through strong defences (Dec. 15-19).
Occupied Russia – FIRST TRIAL OF NAZI 'WAR CRIMINALS' at Kharkov.
Sea War: Pacific – Americans land on Arawe Pen. (New Britain).

THURSDAY, DECEMBER 16

Russian Front – Novoseltsy, SE. of Cherkassy, captured by Russians.

FRIDAY, DECEMBER 17

Russian Front – Failure of German counter-attack in Kirovograd sector.
Italy – US assault troops capture shattered village of San Pietro, key to 'Mignano Gap', 13 km SE of Monte Cassino.

SATURDAY, DECEMBER 18

China – Stilwell to cmnd. Chinese troops in India and N. Burma.

SUNDAY, DECEMBER 19

Home Front: USSR – New National Anthem, composed by Alexandrov with lyrics by Mikhailov and Registan, replaces the 'Internationale'.

Occupied France – Rommel inspects 'Atlantic Wall' defences on French coast.

MONDAY, DECEMBER 20

Air War: Europe – 8th AF drops 1,200 t. bombs on Bremen and RAF delivers 2,000 t. to Frankfurt by night.

TUESDAY, DECEMBER 21

Sea War: Med. – Old German cruiser *Niobe* sunk by British MTBs (night Dec. 21-22).

WEDNESDAY, DECEMBER 22

Italy – Monte Cavallo taken by 5th Army.

Neutrals: Spain – Repatriation of 14,284 men of *Division Azul* from Russian Front officially completed; 3,000 volunteers fight on as the *Legion Azul*.

THURSDAY, DECEMBER 23

Air War: Europe – 200,000 t. bombs dropped on Germany to date.

FRIDAY, DECEMBER 24

Air War: Europe – 672 B-17s drop 1,400 t. bombs on 24 V-1 launching sites.

Russian Front – Russian 1st UF breaks out of Kiev bridgehead and begins reconquest of W. Ukraine.

Home Front: USA – **ROOSEVELT NAMES ALLIED COMMANDERS FOR INVASION OF EUROPE.** Gen. Eisenhower, Supreme Cdr; ACM Tedder, Deputy Supreme Cdr.; Adm. Ramsay, Naval CinC; Gen. Montgomery, CinC British armies (under Eisenhower).

Sea War – Op. *Bernau*: 6 German destroyers and 6 torpedo boats and Ju 88s escort blockade-runner *Osorno* into Gironde Estuary and repel Allied air attacks; but ship hits wreck and has to be beached.

SATURDAY, DECEMBER 25

Italy – Americans advance into mtns. NW. of San Pietro.

Sea War: Pacific – US carrier planes attack shipping at Kavieng (New Ireland).

New Britain – Japanese attack American beachhead at Arawe.

SUNDAY, DECEMBER 26

Sea War – **BATTLE OF NORTH CAPE.** Series of miscalculations by Adm. Bey of *Scharnhorst*, during sortie against a convoy leads him into British trap.

EISENHOWER, Dwight (David) (1890-1969)
American: *Supreme Commander Allied Forces in Europe; General of the Army;* 'Ike'

'Ike' saw himself as leader of multi-national crusade against ungodly Nazi tyranny. Realized that in modern war political and military strategy go together and require continual integration. Treated his famous associates — even the outspoken Montgomery and explosive Patton — with unfailing kindliness and courtesy, but could be a stern critic when the situation demanded. Possessed true hall-mark of good soldier — lucidity of mind.

Born at Denison, Texas; German ancestry. Graduated from West Point Military Academy, 1915. Instructor at US army camps during W.W.I. Sent to France to compile definitive survey of Western Front battlefields; work praised by Gen. Pershing. MacArthur's CoS at Manila, Philippines, 1935-39.

High staff appointments in Washington, 1940-42. Brigadier-Gen., 1941. Chief of War Plans Division, US General Staff, 1942. Commander of all US Forces in European Theatre of Ops., June 1942. Commander of Allied Forces in NW. Africa, Nov. 1942. Displayed considerable statesmanship in negotiating temporary 'arrangement' with former Vichy leader, Adm. Darlan, at Algiers. Took full responsibility for rash US invasion of Tunisia, leading to disastrous battle of Kasserine Pass, Feb. 1943. Commander of all Allied forces in North Africa, Feb. 6, 1943. Promoted to gen, Feb. 11, 1943; given overall command of Allied forces for Sicily invasion, July 1943. Directed covert negotiations with representatives of Italian armed forces leading to unconditional surrender of Italy, Sept. 8, 1943.

Appointed SAC of British and US expeditionary forces for the liberation of France, Dec. 24, 1943. Decided to launch invasion of Normandy despite doubtful weather forecast (June 5/6, 1944). Told German people in Sept. 1944 broadcast that, while his armies came as 'conquerors', they would not be oppressors. Commanded all Allied armies in the West from Oct. 1944. General of the Army, Dec. 15, 1944.

Official reception in Washington, June 1945. Military Govr. of US Zone of Germany, Sept. 1945. CoS, US Army, Nov. 1945. Pres. of Columbia Univ., 1948. NATO Supreme Commander Europe, 1950-52. Republican President of USA, 1953-61. Published 'Crusade in Europe' (1948), dedicated: 'To the Allied Soldier, Sailor and Airman of World War II'.

Scharnhorst attempts to escape in darkness but is torpedoed by 4 destroyers and crippled by battleship *Duke of York*. 36 survivors out of 1,970 crew. 2 British ships damaged.

Sea War: Atlantic – Op. *Trave*: German destroyer-torpedo boat force despatched to escort blockade-runner *Alsterufer,* but she is sunk before the rendezvous. The escorts then attack British cruisers *Enterprise* and *Glasgow*; British sink *Z-27* and 2 torpedo boats.

Sea War: Pacific – Americans land at Cape Gloucester (New Britain).

Home Front: Germany – Col. Count von Stauffenberg prepares to assassinate Hitler at staff conference, but the *Führer* changes his plans.

MONDAY, DECEMBER 27

New Guinea – Australians capture 'Pimple Hill' (Huon Pen.).

TUESDAY, DECEMBER 28

Italy – Canadians capture Ortona (Adriatic coast) after prolonged, savage, house-to-house fighting with German paratroops and *Pz Grens.*, supported by tanks concealed inside buildings.

Secret War – Abortive British Commando raid on Sark (Channel Is.).

WEDNESDAY, DECEMBER 29

Russian Front – New Russian offensive under way in Dnieper Bend, W. of Zaporozhe.

THURSDAY, DECEMBER 30

Sea War – *Queen Elizabeth, Valiant, Renown, Illustrious* and *Unicorn* leave Scapa Flow and the Clyde for Ceylon.

FRIDAY, DECEMBER 31

Russian Front – Russians storm Zhitomir – routing German garrison – and sweep westwards towards pre-war Polish frontier.

Home Front: USA – Death of Sergei Rachmaninoff, the composer; aged 69.

Italy – Montgomery leaves 8th Army.

Shipping Losses 1943
Allied and Neutral: 597 ships totalling 3,271,820 t. Axis: 237 U-boats, 24 Italian subs., 27 Japanese subs.

1944

SATURDAY, JANUARY 1

Russian Front – Russians capture Belokovorichi, only 43 km E. of old Polish frontier.
Air War: Europe – RAF raids Berlin on 6 nights in Jan.
Home Front: Britain – Death of Sir Edwin Lutyens, O.M., architect; aged 76.
Neutrals: Argentina – All political parties banned.

SUNDAY, JANUARY 2

Sea War: Pacific – Americans land at Saidor (New Guinea).
Air War: Pacific – First of 14 Allied bombing raids on airfields and shipping at Rabaul during the month.

MONDAY, JANUARY 3

Russian Front – Russians now 24 km from old Polish frontier.

TUESDAY, JANUARY 4

Italy – 5th Army begins crossing R. Peccia.
Russian Front – Russians cross Polish frontier near Olevsk; Byelaya Tserkov, 64 km SW. of Kiev, captured.
Occupied Greece – 3 quisling P.M.s deprived of nationality by exiled King.

WEDNESDAY, JANUARY 5

Russian Front – Russian 2nd UF drives salient into German lines at Kirovograd, S. of Kiev (Jan. 5-8).
Italy – Lt.-Gen. Leese appointed GOC 8th Army. 5th Army attacks 'Winter Line', E. of Cassino.
Sea War: Atlantic – Last German blockade-runner *(Burgenland)* scuttled, *en route* from the Far East.
Occupied Denmark – Pastor Kaj Munk, Danish cleric and author, murdered by Germans; aged 45.
Air War: Europe – RAF night raiders drop 1,100 t. bombs on Stettin.

THURSDAY, JANUARY 6

Russian Front – Rokitno (E. Poland) captured by Russians.
Air War – Joint RAF-USAAF statement discloses the hitherto secret development of jet aircraft in Britain and USA. Full details of the Whittle turbojet given to Gen. Arnold, USAAF, in July 1941.
Burma – Brig-Gen. Merrill to command volunteer unit ('Merrill's Marauders').

FRIDAY, JANUARY 7

Russian Front – Koniev's 2nd UF breaks through in Kirovograd sector – creating a 'bulge' 40 km deep by 97 km across.
Home Front: USA – Death of Mrs Lou Henry Hoover, wife of ex-Pres. Hoover; aged about 69.
Occupied France – Resistance sabotages electricity supply to *Arsénal National* at Tulle (first of many attacks).

SATURDAY, JANUARY 8

Russian Front – **KIROVOGRAD CAPTURED BY RUSSIANS.**
Occupied Italy – Ciano, Marshal de Bono and other anti-Mussolini 'conspirators' tried at Verona (executed Jan. 11).
Air War – First flight of Lockheed XP-80 Shooting Star jet fighter from Muroc Dry Lake. 5,000 ordered, but none operational before VJ-Day. ACM Sir Sholto Douglas appointed CinC Coastal Cmnd.

SUNDAY, JANUARY 9

Home Front: USA – Maj.-Gen. Bedell Smith appointed COS to Gen. Eisenhower. Antanas Smetona, ex-dictator of Lithuania, killed in fire at Cleveland, Ohio; aged 69.

MONDAY, JANUARY 10

Italy – 5th Army crosses R. Peccia.
Burma – British capture Maungdaw.

TUESDAY, JANUARY 11

Russian Front – Russian salient in E. Poland now 64 km across.
Sea War: Indian Ocean – Cruiser *Kuma* sunk by British sub. *Tally Ho.* U-boats of *Monsun* grp. sink 17 ships (Jan.-March), but British warships intercept 2 re-fuelling tankers (both scuttled).
Air War: Pacific – 43 Japanese landing barges sunk off C. Gloucester.
Home Front: USA – Death of John W. Christie, brilliant designer of armoured fighting vehicles; aged 87.

WEDNESDAY, JANUARY 12

Russian Front – Sarny rail junction (E. Poland) captured by Russians.
Italy – Gen. Juin's French Expeditionary Corps captures important German strongpoints near Monte Santa Croce, N. of Cassino (Jan. 12-14). 5th Army captures Cervara.

THURSDAY, JANUARY 13

Russian Front – Korets (Rovno sector) taken by Russians.

FRIDAY, JANUARY 14

Russian Front – **FINAL RUSSIAN**

COUNTER-OFFENSIVE AT LENINGRAD. 1,000 guns and 17 warships of Baltic Fleet pour 500,000 shells into Finnskoyo-Koirovo sector.
Russians capture 5 towns in Byelorussia.
Air War: Europe – Heavy night raid on Brunswick.

SATURDAY, JANUARY 15

Italy – 5th Army captures Monte Trocchio. Germans pull back over R. Rapido.
Neutrals: Argentina – Earthquake destroys city of San Juan (c. 1,600 killed).

SUNDAY, JANUARY 16

Air War: Europe – B-17s attack Messerschmitt factory at Klagenfurt (Austria).
New Britain – Americans defeat final Japanese counter-attack on New Britain.

MONDAY, JANUARY 17

Italy – British 10th Corps (5th Army) crosses R. Garigliano.
Home Front: USA – Lt.-Gen. Omar N. Bradley appointed to cmnd. US Army in the Field, under Eisenhower.

TUESDAY, JANUARY 18

Home Front: Britain – Churchill returns from N. Africa.

WEDNESDAY, JANUARY 19

Russian Front – **NOVGOROD CAPTURED BY RUSSIANS.**
Air War: Europe – Wing-Cdr. Lance Wade, American-born RAF fighter 'ace' (25 victories) killed in flying accident over Italy; aged 28.

THURSDAY, JANUARY 20

Italy – US forces reach R. Rapido.
Sea War – British cross-Channel guns sink blockade-runner *Münsterland* off Cap Gris Nez. German guns bombard Dover, Deal, Folkestone and Ramsgate.

FRIDAY, JANUARY 21

Russian Front – Shattering Russian artillery bombardment overwhelms German garrison of Mga, SE. of Leningrad.

Italy – US 36th (Texas) Div. heavily defeated during attempted crossing of R. Rapido.
Air War: Britain – 'LITTLE BLITZ' ON LONDON (Op. *Steinbock*: 'Ibex'): motley force of 447 aircraft (inc. He 177 heavy bombers) despatched, but only 32 t. bombs on target; 9 aircraft lost. 13 similar night raids Jan. 29-30 to April 18-19.
Air War: Europe – 648 RAF night bombers raid Magdeburg. 2 German night fighter 'aces' Wittgenstein (83 victories) and Meurer (65 victories) killed.
Secret War – German agents in Iceland report departure of British Convoy JW. 56A.

SATURDAY, JANUARY 22

Sea War: Med. – ANZIO LANDINGS. Allied 6th Corps lands near Anzio and Nettuno, S. of Rome (Op. *Shingle*) in bold attempt to outflank Germans at Cassino. Landing craft equipped with rocket launchers deluge the weak defences.

SUNDAY, JANUARY 23

Sea War: Pacific – RO 37 torpedoes tanker *Cache* – last success by a Japanese sub. in SW. Pacific.

MONDAY, JANUARY 24

Italy – French Expeditionary Corps attacks Monte Santa Croce. Hitler orders Germans to hold Gustav Line at all cost.

TUESDAY, JANUARY 25

Russian Front – Russian 1st and 2nd UFs launch pincer movement W. of Cherkassy and encircle 10 German divs. in the 'Korsun Pocket' (Jan. 25-28).
Sea War – 7 U-boats attack convoy JW. 56A near Bear I., sinking 3 ships.

Above: *A British 6-pounder anti-tank gun disembarks in Anzio.*

Occupied Norway – Death of Edvard Munch, Norwegian expressionist artist; aged 80.

WEDNESDAY, JANUARY 26

New Guinea – Elements of Japanese 18th Army, attempting to by-pass beachhead at Saidor and reach Madang, come under heavy bombardment from US warships.
Diplomacy – Liberia declares war on Germany and Japan. Argentina breaks off diplomatic relations with Germany and Japan.
Home Front: USSR – Soviet forensic medical commission on Katyn Massacre publishes report; blames Germans.

THURSDAY, JANUARY 27

Russian Front – SIEGE OF LENINGRAD ENDS after 872 days.

Siege of Leningrad Casualties
Soviet: *c.* 1,300,000-1,500,000 dead (of which 100,000-200,000 military).

Air War – Most concentrated night raid of the war on Berlin: RAF bombers drop 1,500 t. on target at rate of 75 per minute. Mediterranean Allied Air Forces established.
Occupied France – 39 aero engines destroyed in Resistance raid on Bronzavia plant, Lyons.

FRIDAY, JANUARY 28

Sea War: Atlantic – 2 'wolf-packs' (totalling 20 U-boats) totally prevented from interfering with Convoys OS. 66, KMS. 40 and ON. 221 by RAF Coastal Cmnd.
Air War: Pacific – 22 Corsair fighters and 6 pilots lost in severe storm while flying from Gilbert to Ellice Is.

SATURDAY, JANUARY 29

Sea War: Med. – British cruiser *Spartan* sunk by glider bomb off Anzio.
Sea War: Pacific – TF 58 attacks Marshall Is. (Jan. 29-Feb. 3): 6232 sorties (49 planes lost).

SUNDAY, JANUARY 30

Italy – 5th Army makes small breach in Gustav Line. Anzio: US Rangers advance to Cisterna and British 3rd Div. to Railway Station, N. of Aprilia.
Air War: Europe – US daylight raid on Brunswick. US Thunderbolt grp. shoots down 36 German and Italian fighters and formation of Ju 52s for the loss of 1 fighter.

MONDAY, JANUARY 31

Sea War: Pacific – AMERICANS LAND ON KWAJALEIN AND MAJURO ATOLLS (Marshall Is.).
Sea War – German MTBs attack Convoy CW. 243 (2 ships sunk).
Home Front: Australia – Commission established to investigate Japanese war crimes.
Occupied France – Resistance blows up Ratier aircraft propellor works at Figéac.

TUESDAY, FEBRUARY 1

Occupied Poland – Underground forces assassinate Gestapo Chief Kutschera.
Home Front: USA – Death of Piet Mondrian, Dutch painter; aged 71.

WEDNESDAY, FEBRUARY 2

Sea War: Pacific – Ships of TF 58 enter Majuro Atoll (soon to become a vital advanced base).

THURSDAY, FEBRUARY 3

Italy – Anzio: Germans counter-attack E. and W. of the Aprilia 'model farm' (the 'Factory').

FRIDAY, FEBRUARY 4

Burma – JAPANESE LAUNCH MAJOR OFFENSIVE IN THE ARAKAN (Op. *Ha-Go*).
Italy – Americans heavily engaged at Cassino.

SATURDAY, FEBRUARY 5

Russian Front – Russian 3rd and 4th UFs drive Germans from Nikopol Salient; then cross R. Dnieper to free Nikopol and its great manganese mines (Feb. 5-8).

SUNDAY, FEBRUARY 6

Russian Front – Russians clear Germans from E. bank of R. Narva.
Air War: Europe – 200 Russian planes attack Helsinki.

MONDAY, FEBRUARY 7

Italy – Anzio: renewed German onslaught on the 'Factory'.

Marshalls Campaign Losses
Japanese: 16,300 dead, 264 PoWs. US: 1,007 dead, 3,432 wounded.

Sea War – British sub. *Taku* sinks 3 ships in convoys off Stavanger (Feb. 7-13).

TUESDAY, FEBRUARY 8

Russian Front – Germans trapped in Korsun Pocket refuse surrender ultimatum and make unavailing efforts to link up with relief column under Manstein. *Luftwaffe* drops supplies to encircled troops.
Air War: Europe – 12,000-lb bombs dropped on Gnôme-et-Rhône aero-engine works at Limoges by RAF night raiders.

WEDNESDAY, FEBRUARY 9

Russian Front – Russians capture Oredezh, near Leningrad.
Home Front: Britain – Bishop of Chichester questions the wisdom of RAF 'area bombing' raids on German cities, during debate in House of Lords. Viscount Cranbourne, replying, concedes that, if necessary, British Govt. are prepared to *'bring the whole life of the German cities . . . to a standstill, in order to paralyse enemy production'.*

THURSDAY, FEBRUARY 10

Sea War – British tanker *El Grillo* bombed and sunk by FW 200.
Sea War: Pacific – Japanese Combined Fleet leaves Truk for Palau, near the Philippines.

FRIDAY, FEBRUARY 11

Air War: Europe – Russian heavy bomber sqn. makes night attack on *Tirpitz* in Alta Fjord (1 near miss).

SATURDAY, FEBRUARY 12

Italy – US 34th Div. attack halted only 274 m short of Cassino.
Sea War – British troopship *Khedive Ismail* sunk in Indian Ocean by *I-27* (c. 2,000 killed). Destroyers *Paladin* and

Petard sink the attacker after protracted struggle.
German MTBs lay mines off the Humber and near Gt. Yarmouth (nights Feb. 12-13, 13-14 and 14-15).

SUNDAY, FEBRUARY 13

Russian Front – Russians capture Luga (Leningrad Front).

MONDAY, FEBRUARY 14

Sea War: Pacific – American and NZ forces land on Green Is., between Bougainville and Rabaul.

TUESDAY, FEBRUARY 15

Air War: Europe – MONTE CASSINO BOMBARDED. Ancient Abbey of Monte Cassino shattered by Allied bombers and artillery fire. 135 B-17s and medium bombers drop 493 t. HE and IBs. 400 Italian women and children refugees killed inside Abbey – which is not occupied by Germans until *after* the bombardment.
Sea War: Pacific – Japanese convoy smashed by US bombers off New Hanover (near Rabaul).
Diplomacy – Polish Govt. in London rejects Soviet proposal that the Curzon Line (322 km W. of 1939 Russo-Polish frontier) should now be post-war frontier.

WEDNESDAY, FEBRUARY 16

Italy – Anzio: Germans drive deep salient into Allied line S. of the 'Factory'. Devastating artillery and air bombardment of entire Allied beachhead.

THURSDAY, FEBRUARY 17

Russian Front – Russians eliminate Korsun Salient: Germans have lost 55,000 killed, 18,000 taken prisoner.
Sea War: Pacific – THE TRUK RAID. 9

Above: *Kachin scouts, led by their US advisers, ford a stream in N. Burma.*

carriers of Adm. Mitscher's TF 58 launch massive air strikes (Feb. 17 and 18) against Truk – great Japanese naval/air base in Central Pacific. 30 ships sunk and 250 planes destroyed. Battleships *Iowa* and *New Jersey* (Adm. Spruance) sink cruiser *Katori* and 2 destroyers. Japanese torpedo planes damage carrier *Intrepid*.
Sea War – US warships bombard Rabaul and Kavieng (night Feb. 17-18).
HMS *Penelope* torpedoed by *U-410* off Anzio (second, fatal, attack Feb. 18).
Air War: Europe – Ceaseless Allied raids on German spearheads at Anzio.
Home Front: USA – Bomber crashes into USN barracks in San Diego, Calif. (34 casualties).

FRIDAY, FEBRUARY 18

Italy – Anzio: Allied situation becomes critical; Germans continue all-out efforts to capture 'Flyover Bridge' and reach the sea.
Air War: Europe – Amiens Prison Raid: 19 Mosquitoes (4 lost), led by Grp.-Capt. Pickard, breach walls and free 250 members of French Resistance.
Air War: Britain – 200-plane night raid on London: 139 t. bombs on target; considerable damage and numerous casualties. Raiders copy RAF Pathfinder tactics.

SATURDAY, FEBRUARY 19

Italy – Anzio: German onslaught wilts under ceaseless Allied air and artillery bombardment and they withdraw from 'Flyover'.
Sea War: Atlantic – First German sub. to be fitted with 'Schnorkel' equipment (*U-264*) sunk by sloops *Starling* and *Woodpecker*.
Air War: Europe – RAF loses 79 night bombers during ops. against Leipzig.

Occupied France – Resistance attacks *Arsénal National*, near Paris, crippling production of light artillery.

SUNDAY, FEBRUARY 20

Air War: Europe – 'BIG WEEK' (Op. Argument): heavy bombers (164 lost) of US 8th and 15th AFs fly 3,800 sorties with powerful fighter escort (28 lost): drop 10,000 t. bombs in attempt to knock out major fighter assembly and component plants in Germany and Austria. Americans claim 517 German fighters shot down.

MONDAY, FEBRUARY 21

Burma – 5th Indian Div. clears Japanese from commanding heights in the Arakan.
Diplomacy – US note to Eire requests expulsion of Axis diplomats (Irish rejection published March 10).
Home Front: Japan – Tojo becomes COAGS; Adm. Shimada, CONS.

TUESDAY, FEBRUARY 22

Russian Front – Krivoi Rog, iron-mining centre in Donbas, captured by 3rd UF. Stalin issues 2 Orders of the Day: first, concerning Krivoi Rog and second, announcing that three-quarters of Soviet territory has now been liberated; Red Army has advanced up to 1,642 km.
Sea War: Pacific – Japanese night bombers and torpedo planes attack TF 58.
Air War: Europe – In dense cloud and freezing conditions, a B-24 grp. bombs Nijmegen (Holland) by mistake, killing 200 civilians.
Occupied Greece – German troop train derailled in Tempe Valley by British-led guerrillas; c.400 killed. Athens-Salonika line blocked for 4 days.
Home Front: India – Death of wife of Mahatma Gandhi; aged about 74.

WEDNESDAY, FEBRUARY 23

Sea War: Pacific – TF 58 attacks air bases on Mariana Is.
Home Front: USA – Death of Dr Baekeland, Belgian-born inventor of 'bakelite'; aged 80.

THURSDAY, FEBRUARY 24

Russian Front – 2nd BF captures Dno junction, E. of Pskov. 1st BRF captures Rogachev.
Burma – British capture Nyakyedyauk Pass.
Air War: Britain – Ninth night raid on London since launching of 'Little Blitz': 129 bombers lost since Jan. 21.

FRIDAY, FEBRUARY 25

Air War: Europe – Climax of 'Big Week': 830 bombers of US 8th AF (30 lost) and 150 bombers of 15th AF (35 lost), with fighter

escorts (8 lost), attack Messerschmitt works at Regensburg and Augsburg (Bavaria). Americans claim 142 fighters shot down. 1,000 fighters are destroyed on assembly lines and 1,000 more lost due to temporary disruption of production. RAF drops bombs on Augsburg in 2-wave night attack.

SATURDAY, FEBRUARY 26

Air War: Europe – 600 Russian bombers (3 lost) raid Helsinki between 6 pm and 6 am, starting fires visible for 400 km.
Air War: Pacific – 200 Allied planes attack Rabaul, destroying munition dumps.
Home Front: British Guiana – Source of R. Orinoco discovered by crew of USAAF plane in mountainous gorge near Brazilian-Venezuelan border.
Occupied France – Resistance attack SOMUA armour plate works at Lyons (over 30 plastic explosive charges fail to explode).

SUNDAY, FEBRUARY 27

Russian Front – Russians capture Bezhakitsy W. of Chelm (Poland).
Home Front: Argentina – Perón appointed War Minister.

MONDAY, FEBRUARY 28

Italy – Renewed German onslaught at Anzio.

TUESDAY, FEBRUARY 29

Italy – German heavy artillery bombards Anzio beachhead.
Sea War: Pacific – Americans land on Los Negros (Admiralty Is.), N. of New Guinea. Gen. MacArthur inspects beachhead.
Air War: Britain – RAF Fighter Cmnd. temporarily redesignated 'Air Defence of Great Britain'.

WEDNESDAY, MARCH 1

Russian Front – Russians break German defences S. of Narva.
Home Front: Germany – *Jägerstab* (Fighter Staff) set up under Saür of Speer's Armaments Ministry to boost production of Me 109 and FW 190 to unprecedented levels. Many new assembly lines established in salt mines and tunnels; component stockpiles to be used up; plans for large-scale production of Me 262 abandoned.

THURSDAY, MARCH 2

Air War: Europe – Lancasters and Halifaxes attack aircraft factories at Meulan-les-Mureaux and Albert (France).

FRIDAY, MARCH 3

Air War: Europe – Lightnings carry out sweep over Berlin.
Italy – Germans cease bombardment of Anzio beachhead.
Occupied Greece – Resistance grps. EDES (Royalist) and ELAS (Communist) sign 'cease-fire' agreement and promise to co-operate against Germans.
Home Front: USA – Roosevelt announces that Italian Fleet is to be distributed equally between USA, Britain and USSR (in the event, Russia receives British and American ships in lieu).

SATURDAY, MARCH 4

Russian Front – Russian 1st and 2nd UFs capture Uman and Nouvoukrainka (March 4-10).
Air War: Europe – 30 B-17s bomb Berlin (first US raid).

SUNDAY, MARCH 5

Air War: Far East – SECOND CHINDIT OP. Allied planes transport

SLIM, William Joseph (1891-1970) British: *Field-Marshal, First Viscount Slim; 'Bill'*

First British gen. to dispel myth of Japanese Army's 'invincibility' in jungle warfare. Led 14th Army ('The Forgotten Army') to victory in Burma, Oct. 1943-Aug. 1945.

Worked as junior clerk, school teacher and foreman of testing gang in engineering works before W.W.I. Fought against Turks at Gallipoli (wounded) and in Mesopotamia. Served with Gurkhas between the wars. Fought with distinction in Eritrea (wounded), Syria, Iraq, Persia and the retreat from Burma (1941-42). GOC Fourteenth Army, Burma, Oct. 1943-Sept. 1945. Repulsed fanatical Japanese attacks at Imphal, Kohima and in the Arakan (April-June 1944); recaptured Mandalay (March 1945) and Rangoon (May 1945). Delivered coup de grâce in July 1945 when ragged and desperate Japanese 28th Army attempted to escape across Sittang R. to Thailand but were slaughtered in great numbers by British artillery and fighter-bombers.

Commandant, Imperial Defence College, 1946. CIGS, 1948-52. Gov.-Gen. of Australia, 1953-59. Talented journalist and auto-biographer, wrote 'Defeat into Victory' (1956), describing Burma Campaign.

9,000 men of Wingate's 'Long Range Penetration Grps.' to secretly prepared air strips ('Piccadilly') near Indaw, 161 km inside Japanese-controlled Burma (March 5-10).

MONDAY, MARCH 6

Air War: Europe – FIRST MAJOR ALLIED DAYLIGHT RAID ON BERLIN: 730 B-17s and B-24s of 8th AF (69 lost) bomb city and nearby Erkner ball-bearing works. 796 escorting P-38s, P-47s and P-51s (11 lost), plus 2 RAF Mustang sqns. US aircraft fight running battles with German interceptors from Dutch coast to Berlin; heavy flak over target. Halifaxes bomb Trappes marshalling yards on Paris-Brittany line.

TUESDAY, MARCH 7

Burma – JAPANESE LAUNCH MAJOR OFFENSIVE ACROSS R. CHINDWIN (Op. *U-Go*). Americans and Chinese surround 2,000 Japanese in Hukawng Valley.
Air War: Europe – Allied bombers attack marshalling yards in Florence and Rome.

WEDNESDAY, MARCH 8

Air War: Europe – 8th AF bombs Erkner ball-bearing factory, near Berlin.

THURSDAY, MARCH 9

Russian Front – Malinovsky (3rd UF) crosses R. Ingulets in the S.
Solomons – Japanese counter-offensive against Torokina Bridgehead (Bougainville): 5,469 Japanese and 263 Americans killed by March 24.
Neutrals: Argentina – Pres. Ramirez resigns following army coup.

FRIDAY, MARCH 10

Russian Front – 2nd UF has advanced up to 71 km in 5 days.

SATURDAY, MARCH 11

Air War – US bombers raid Toulon, Padua and Florence.
Home Front: Algeria – Pierre Pucheu, former Vichy Min. of Interior, sentenced to death by Algiers court.

SUNDAY, MARCH 12

Russian Front – Uman (Ukraine) captured by 2nd UF.
Occupied Czechoslovakia – Govt. in London broadcasts call to arms.

MONDAY, MARCH 13

Russian Front – Malinovsky captures Dnieper R. port of Kherson.
Sea War: Atlantic – *U-852* fires on

survivors of torpedoed Greek ship *Peleus* (32 of 35 killed).
Sea War: Pacific – Troopship convoy, *en route* to Mariana Is., destroyed by US sub. *Sandlance*.
Diplomacy – Italy and USSR establish diplomatic relations.

TUESDAY, MARCH 14

Russian Front – Malinovsky eliminates German pocket near Nikolayev (10,000 killed, 4,000 captured).
Occupied Italy – Virginio Gayda, retired editor of Fascist newspaper *Giornale d'Italia*, killed in air raid; aged 58.

WEDNESDAY, MARCH 15

Russian Front – 2nd UF reaches R. Bug near Uman.
Air War: Europe – Allied bombers obliterate Cassino town, dropping 1,107 t. bombs. 1,000 RAF 4-engined bombers raid Stuttgart, dropping 3,000 t. of bombs through dense cloud; many combats with night fighters. Diversionary raids on Munich, targets in NW. Germany and Amiens (40 bombers lost in all ops.).
Italy – Massive 5½-hour artillery barrage at Cassino. Indian and NZ infantry and tanks begin reoccupying shattered town; 'Castle Hill', near 'Monastery Hill' also captured.

Below: *Cassino town after 500 Allied bombers flattened it on March 15.*

THURSDAY, MARCH 16

Italy – Three-quarters of Cassino town now in Allied hands.
Occupied France – Déat appointed Vichy Min. of Labour.

FRIDAY, MARCH 17

Italy – NZ troops take Cassino railway station.
Sea War: Med. – *U-371* sinks US troopship *Dempo* (498 killed).
Diplomacy – Finns reject Russian armistice terms.

SATURDAY, MARCH 18

Italy – NZs repulsed with heavy losses at Cassino.
Sea War – 72 Allied prisoners (from MV *Behar*) beheaded aboard Japanese cruiser *Tone* in Indian Ocean.
Sea War: Pacific – US battleships bombard Mili Atoll; *Iowa* damaged by coastal battery.
Home Front: Italy – Eruptions from Mt. Vesuvius: 2 villages engulfed by lava; 26 killed (March 18-22).
Home Front: Hungary – Regent Horthy visits Hitler to request repatriation of Hungarian forces from Russian Front but the *Führer* declares his intention to occupy Hungary.
Air War: Europe – In heaviest raid of war to date, RAF bombers drop 3,000 t. bombs on Frankfurt (night 18-19).

SUNDAY, MARCH 19

Home Front: Hungary – GERMAN OCCUPATION OF HUNGARY (Op. *Panzerfaust*), to forestall Hungarian attempts to make separate peace with W. Allies; P. M. Kallay resigns; Sztojay, ambassador in Berlin, forms collaborationist Govt.
Russian Front – Russians reach R. Dniester on 97-km front.
Air War: Britain – Night raid on NE. coast of England (intended target, Hull); 9 planes lost.
Air War: Europe – Op. Strangle: MAAF begins 3-week all-out offensive against Italian railway system, designed to isolate German forces in Italy. Fighter-bombers and medium bombers attack bridges, viaducts, rail/road off-loading points; heavy bombers attack marshalling yards, repair shops and junctions in N. Italy; secondary targets inc. harbours and coastal shipping. 19,460 t. bombs dropped in March. In April-May, Op. Strangle merges into air phase of Op. Diadem (*see* May 11), when 51,500 t. bombs are dropped. Great damage done but bad weather and multiplicity of targets 'cheats' ambitious plan.

MONDAY, MARCH 20

Russian Front – First UF captures Vinnitsa on R. Bug.
Burma – Chinese and Americans secure Hukawng Valley.
Sea War: Pacific – 4 US battleships bombard Kavieng. Americans land on Emirau I. (Bismarck Archipelago).

Sea War – Cross-Channel guns sink German tanker *Rekum*.

TUESDAY, MARCH 21

Russian Front – Russians cut Cernauti-Balti railway.

WEDNESDAY, MARCH 22

Italy – Gen. Alexander abandons frontal attacks on Cassino.
Air War: Europe – 8th AF bombs Berlin. 816 RAF night bombers drop *c.* 3,000 t. on Frankfurt.

THURSDAY, MARCH 23

Air War: Europe – 8th AF attacks Hamm marshalling yards.

FRIDAY, MARCH 24

Russian Front – Russian 1st UF reaches R. Dniester.
Air War: Burma – Maj.-Gen. Orde Wingate, leader of the Chindits, killed in air crash in Burma; aged 41.
Air War: Europe – 1,000 bomber night raid on Berlin: heavy damage on target, but many bombers are blown off course and more than 50 shot down by flak; 73 lost in all ops. (inc. diversionary attack on Kiel). Flt.-Sgt. Alkemade jumps, *without parachute*, from blazing RAF Lancaster 5,486 m above W. Germany and lands safely in snow drift (night March 24-25).
Home Front: Germany – 'THE GREAT ESCAPE'. 76 Allied airmen escape from

Stalag Luft III near Sagan (night March 24-25); 50 recaptured and murdered.
Occupied Italy – Ardeatine Caves Massacre: Germans murder 336 Italian civilians (inc. Jews) near Rome as reprisal for Partisan activities.

SATURDAY, MARCH 25

Russian Front – Russians capture Proskurov, W. Ukraine.
Burma – US and Chinese forces capture Shaduzup in Mogaung Valley.

SUNDAY, MARCH 26

Russian Front – 2nd UF reaches R. Pruth (Soviet-Rumanian border) along 80-km front.
Sea War: Pacific – US sub. *Tullibee* sunk by one of her own (faulty) torpedoes near Palau Is.
Air War: Europe – 300 Marauders bomb E-boat pens at Ijmuiden (Holland).
Occupied France – Resistance blows up Philips radio factory at Brive-la-Gaillarde.
Occupied Greece – EAM (Greek Communist Party) establishes a provisional govt. in mtns. of N. Greece. Resignation of official Greek P.M., Tsouderos, follows on April 6.

MONDAY, MARCH 27

Air War: Europe – 8th AF attacks 9 airfields in central and SW. France.
Air War: Britain – Abortive night raid on Bristol (and on April 23-24).

TUESDAY, MARCH 28

Sea War – 24,145 German and Rumanian troops and wounded evacuated from Odessa (March 28 – April 10).
Home Front: Canada – Death of Prof. Stephen Leacock, economist and humorous writer; aged 73.

WEDNESDAY, MARCH 29

Russian Front – Russian 1st UF reaches Carpathian foothills.
Burma – SIEGE OF IMPHAL. Having crossed Burma-India border, Japanese 15th Army encircles 155,000 British-Indian troops on Imphal Plain and despite Allied air superiority, holds its positions until June 22 (q.v.).
Sea War: Pacific – Super-battleship *Musashi* torpedoed in the bows by US sub. *Tunny.*
Neutrals: Switzerland – Death of Dr Gina Lombroso Ferrero, Italian Sociologist and anti-Fascist; aged 73.

THURSDAY, MARCH 30

Air War: Europe – NUREMBURG RAID. German night fighters score their greatest victory, destroying 94 of 710 RAF bombers which approach the city by the most direct route in single huge stream without usual complex diversionary manoeuvre. British compelled to temporarily abandon deep-penetration raids on German cities.
Sea War: Pacific – US carrier planes raid shipping in Palau Is. (March 30 and 31) – Japanese Fleet has recently departed.

FRIDAY, MARCH 31

Air War: Pacific – Adm. Koga, CinC of Japanese Combined Fleet, disappears during flight from Palau to Mindanao (succeeded by Adm. Toyoda).

SATURDAY, APRIL 1

Russian Front – 1st UF reaches Jablonica Pass.

SUNDAY, APRIL 2

Russian Front – Russians enter E. Rumania.
Occupied Italy – Communist Party supports Badoglio Govt.
Neutrals: El Salvador – Attempted military coup (approx. 300 killed).

MONDAY, APRIL 3

Air War: Europe – 1,100 t. bombs dropped on Budapest rail targets and industrial sections by B-17s and B-24s of 15th AF;

Left: *A Sherman tank and US infantry mop up on Bougainville. Some Japanese held out till Sept. 8, 1945.*

strong fighter opposition. Follow-up night raid by RAF Liberators and Wellingtons. Attacks necessitate closure of all city's stations and large-scale evacuation of civilians, from April 7.
Sea War – Op. Tungsten: 41 FAA Fairey Barracudas (4 lost), escorted by 41 fighters, score 14 hits on *Tirpitz* in Alta Fjord (438 German casualties).
Home Front: USA – Supreme Court rules that Negroes have right to vote in Texas.

TUESDAY, APRIL 4

Air War: Europe – Bucharest marshalling yards 'blitzed' by heavily escorted 15th AF B-17s and B-24s (20 lost); fighters attack in strength. Civilian casualties: 2,942 killed, 2,126 injured.
Occupied France – De Gaulle appointed 'Head of Armed Forces'. Resistance halts production at Bronzavia aircraft components plant near Paris.
Occupied Greece – Greek brig. (in Egypt) mutinies; led by Communists. British troops blockade camp until April 24. Greeks kill 1 British officer.

WEDNESDAY, APRIL 5

Air War: Europe – Ploesti oil installations and rail sidings fired by 15th AF B-17s and B-24s, with strong fighter escort (12 lost). Heavy flak and determined opposition from German, Rumanian and Bulgarian fighters. Civilian casualties: 262 killed, 361 injured.
Home Front: USA – Wendell L. Willkie withdraws from Presidential Election Campaign.

THURSDAY, APRIL 6

Burma – SIEGE OF KOHIMA. Japanese besiege 3,500 British-Indian troops for 13 days; savage hand-to-hand fighting.
Air War: Europe – Spitfire fighter-bombers of DAF destroy many planes on Banja Luka airfield, Yugoslavia.
Home Front: USA – Death of Rose O'Neill, artist and creator of 'Kewpie Doll'; aged 68.
Occupied France – Resistance stop production at Timken ball-bearing factory, near Paris.
Russian Front – 1st Pz Army reaches German lines after 10-day fighting retreat.

FRIDAY, APRIL 7

Russian Front – German forces encircled near Tarnopol make desperate, but unavailing, attempts to break out.
Home Front: Germany – Goebbels appointed 'City President of Berlin', superseding *Oberburgmeister* (Lord Mayor).

SATURDAY, APRIL 8

Russian Front – Russian 4th UF launches Crimean offensive.
1st UF reaches Czech border.

SUNDAY, APRIL 9

Russian Front – Bukovina region completely occupied by Russians.
Occupied France – Giraud appointed Inspector-Gen. of French Army.

MONDAY, APRIL 10

Russian Front – ODESSA CAPTURED by Russian 3rd UF and Partisans.
Sea War: Atlantic – *U-515* and *U-68* sunk by US TG 21.12 (inc. carrier *Guadalcanal*).

TUESDAY, APRIL 11

Russian Front – Russians advance on Simferopol (Crimea).
Air War: Europe – 6 RAF Mosquitoes destroy Central Population Registry building in The Hague (containing Gestapo records).

WEDNESDAY, APRIL 12

Russian Front – 3rd UF captures Tirasapol, 97 km NW. of Odessa.
Occupied Italy – King Victor Emmanuel announces his plans to retire from office when Allies enter Rome, and to appoint Crown Prince Umberto of Piedmont 'Lieutenant of the Realm'.
Sea War – Evacuation of 61,600 German-Rumanian troops and Russian auxiliaries from Crimea to Constanta (April 12-16).

THURSDAY, APRIL 13

Home Front: Britain – Death of 5th Earl of Lonsdale, sportsman and donor of the 'Lonsdale Belts' awarded to champion boxers; aged 87.
Air War: Europe — US and British TAFs carry out heavy attacks on German coastal batteries in Normandy.

FRIDAY, APRIL 14

Russian Front – 1st and 2nd UFs capture Tarnopol (SE. of Lvov) and reach the Carpathians – driving massive wedge between German Army Grp. S. and Army Grp. A. (April 14-17).
Home Front: India – Fort Stikine Disaster: ship carrying explosives and cotton bales, catches fire and explodes in Bombay Docks: 27 ships wrecked; approx. 740 killed or missing; 476 servicemen and 1,000 Indians injured. 10,000 troops and Indians move 1 M.t. of rubble in 6 months. (See Sept. 10, 1944.)
Home Front: USSR – Death of Gen. Nikolai F. Vatutin, ex-cdr. of victorious 1st UF; shot in ambush by Ukrainian nationalists, Feb. 29, 1944.

SATURDAY, APRIL 15

Air War: Europe – 15th AF sends 500 sorties to Bucharest and Ploesti.

SUNDAY, APRIL 16

Russian Front – Yalta captured by Russian 'Indep. Maritime Army'. Germans launch fruitless counter-attack against 3rd BRF's bridge-heads over R. Niemen.

Air War: Europe – Russians bomb Galatz (Rumania).

Occupied Hungary – Eichmann begins systematic concentration of 800,000 Hungarian Jews in ghettoes prior to their deportation to Auschwitz. Concentration phase completed early July; deportation phase completed end July.

MONDAY, APRIL 17

Air War: Europe – B-17s and B-24s attack Belgrade and Sofia.

Sea War – 7,000 mines laid by RN and RAF Bomber Cmnd. in approaches to English Channel and as far north as Danish coast to prevent German interference with 'D-Day' invasion fleet (April 17-June 5); c. 100 light warships and other craft sink.

TUESDAY, APRIL 18

Russian Front – 4th UF besieges Sebastopol. *Pzs* and Hungarian troops, with air support, begin series of counter-attacks between Rs. Dniester and Pruth.

Air War: Britain – **LAST AIR RAID ON LONDON.** 'Little Blitz' ends with attack by 125 aircraft (14 lost); 53 t. bombs on target. Large hospital hit.

Little Blitz Losses
British civilians: 1,493 dead, 2,841 badly injured.

Air War: Europe – B-17s and B-24s bomb Heinkel works at Oranienburg and other targets near Berlin. RAF Bomber Cmnd. delivers record total of 4,000 t. against marshalling yards and railway workshops at Juvisy, Noisy-le-Sec, Rouen and Tergnier; Mosquitoes attack Berlin.

Home Front: Britain – Govt. makes incitement to strike punishable offence.

WEDNESDAY, APRIL 19

Sea War: Russians bombard Sebastopol. British Eastern Fleet planes attack Sabang harbour and airfields (Sumatra).

Air War: Europe – RAF drops mines in R. Danube.

Home Front: USA – Lease-Lend legislation extended by House of Representatives (Senate concurs May 8).

THURSDAY, APRIL 20

Burma – Allied garrison on Summer House Hill, Kohima, relieved by British 2nd Div.

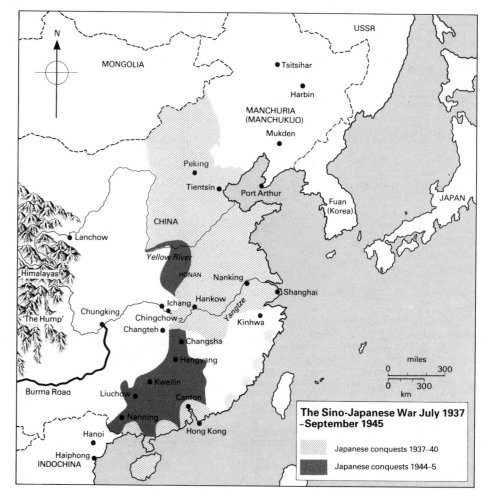

The Sino-Japanese War July 1937 –September 1945

Japanese conquests 1937–40

Japanese conquests 1944–5

Sea War: Med. – Germans use *Neger* ('Negro') human torpedoes against shipping off Anzio: 37 launched from beaches (24 lost) without result (night April 20-21). 6 Allied merchant ships hit by torpedo planes near Strs. of Gibraltar.

Air War: Britain – Abortive night raid on Hull.

FRIDAY, APRIL 21

Neutrals: Turkey – Exports of chrome to Germany cease.

Air War: Europe – 4.500 t. bombs dropped on 4 rail junctions: Cologne, La Chappelle (Paris), Lens and Ottignies (Brussels) by RAF night raiders.

Occupied Italy – Badoglio forms coalition govt.

SATURDAY, APRIL 22

Sea War: Pacific – **AMERICANS LAND AT HOLLANDIA** and Aitape, on N. coast of New Guinea: 52,000 troops in 113 ships, escorted by US 5th and 7th Fleets.

China – Japanese capture Chengchow (Honan).

SUNDAY, APRIL 23

Russian Front – Germans counter-attack SW. of Narva.

New Guinea – Hollandia fighting begins.

Occupied Greece – Communist-inspired mutiny aboard 5 Greek warships at Alexandria (Egypt) suppressed by loyal Greek forces; 50 casualties.

MONDAY, APRIL 24

Air War: Europe – 8th AF raids Friedrichshafen factories and airfields near Munich (55 planes lost, inc. 14 which land or crash in Switzerland). 250 Lancasters scatter 'Flying Meteor' methane-petrol IBs over Munich, devastating wide area between Central Station and R. Isar (night April 24-25). Italian 'Co-Belligerent Air Force' now operating regularly over the Adriatic.

TUESDAY, APRIL 25

Sea War – Cruiser *Black Prince* and 3 Canadian destroyers engage torpedo boats: *T.29* sunk (136 killed), *T.24* and *T.27* damaged (night April 25-26). In further engagements, 3 nights later, *T.24* sinks HMCS *Athabaskan*.

Air War: Britain – First of series of night raids on shipping at Portsmouth and Plymouth-Devonport (April 25-26 to May 29-30).

Home Front: Britain – Budget: Chancellor of Exchequer promises tax-relief for industry after the war.

WEDNESDAY, APRIL 26

New Guinea – Australians capture Alexishafen, W. of Madang.
Air War: Europe – RAF night raid on Schweinfurt.

THURSDAY, APRIL 27

New Guinea – US troops occupy main airstrip at Hollandia.
Air War: Europe – Russian night raid on Lvov.
Sea War – 3 American LSTs, carrying out invasion exercise, are torpedoed by MTBs in Lyme Bay; 638 killed (night April 27-28).

FRIDAY, APRIL 28

Air War: Europe – Lancasters bomb Kjeller aircraft factory, Oslo (night April 28-29).
Occupied France – Resistance damages 8 tanks and steals armd. car from Renault works, near Paris.
Home Front: USA – Death of Col. Knox, Sec. of Navy; aged 70. James V. Forrestal appointed, May 10.

SATURDAY, APRIL 29

Sea War: Pacific – TF 58 attacks Truk: 93 Japanese planes destroyed (26 US planes shot down).
Occupied France – Resistance cripples newly repaired (air-raid damage) Dunlop factory at Montluçon.

SUNDAY, APRIL 30

Air War: Europe – Lancasters blow up munition dump at Maintenon, SW. of Paris.
Home Front: Britain – ABSIE (American Broadcasting Station in Europe) on the air.
Home Front: USSR – Death of Alexei Novikov-Priboy, author of 'Tsushima'; aged 66.
Secret War – Gen. Kreipe captured in Crete and taken to Alexandria.

MONDAY, MAY 1

Russian Front – Zhukov and Vasilevsky begin detailed planning for decisive summer offensive against the 'Byelorussian Salient', lying between Smolensk and Minsk. Germans are to be misled into expecting the blow to fall in N. Ukraine, before a series of pincer movements trap their armies around Vitebsk, Mogilev, Bobruysk and Minsk.
Occupied Yugoslavia – Tito sends military mission to London.
Home Front: USSR – Stalin declares in Order of the Day: *The wounded German beast must be pursued and finished off in its lair.* Saluting batteries in Moscow and 8 other cities fire 20 salvoes.

Diplomacy – Commonwealth P.M.s' Conference in London.

TUESDAY, MAY 2

Diplomacy – Anglo-US-Spanish agreement on restriction of wolfram (tungsten ore) exports from Spain to Germany.
Occupied France – Management of Aubert and Duval steel works at Ancizes co-operates with Resistance in complete shut-down.

WEDNESDAY, MAY 3

Burma – 14th Army captures heights above Maungdaw-Buthidaung road (Arakan).
Air War: Europe – 49 RAF bombers lost during night raids on tank-truck park at Mailly, near Rheims; Montdidier aircraft stores; ammunition dump at Châteaudun; and Ludwigshafen.
Home Front: USA – Production of synthetic quinine (anti-malarial) by young Harvard scientists Woodward and Doering, announced at Cambridge, Mass.
Occupied France – 100,000 litres acetone burnt by Resistance in Lambiotte plant, Prémery.

THURSDAY, MAY 4

Air War: Europe – RAF night raid on Budapest rail installations.

FRIDAY, MAY 5

Air War: Europe – Torre Dam (Italy) dive-bombed and smashed by RAF Mustangs and Australian and S. African Warhawks.
Burma – Slim's 14th Army counterattacks near Imphal.

SATURDAY, MAY 6

Sea War: Pacific – Japanese troopship convoy destroyed by US sub. *Gurnard.*
Home Front: India – Gandhi released from imprisonment on medical grounds.
Home Front: Japan – First flight of Mitsubishi A7M (designed to replace the Zero). Technical problems and Allied bombing raids prevent mass production.

SUNDAY, MAY 7

Air War: Europe – 8th AF despatches 1,500 planes to Berlin. 9th AF Marauders and P-38s attack Mézières-Charleville railway yards. 15th AF and RAF bombers attack Bucharest railway yards by day and night, leaving target area in flames.

MONDAY, MAY 8

Western Front – Eisenhower selects June 5 as 'D-Day' for Normandy invasion.
Sea War – Second phase evacuation of Axis forces from Crimea (May 8-13);

Soviet forces sink 19 vessels (8,100 men drowned). Since April 12, 130,000 troops have left by sea and 21,457 by air.
Home Front: Britain – Death of Dame Ethel Smyth, composer and suffragette; aged 86.
Occupied Hungary – Eichmann offers to barter the lives of Hungarian Jews for 10,000 trucks, 2 M. cases of soap and other goods. This offer is transmitted to W. Allies by Joel Brand, member of *Vaadat Ezra v'Hazalah* (Jewish Assistance and Rescue Committee). Allies indignantly reject this outrageous proposal.
Home Front: USA – Senate extends Lend-Lease to June 1945.

TUESDAY, MAY 9

Air War: Europe – Allied AFs begin large scale raids on air bases in France in preparation for D-Day.
Russian Front – SEBASTOPOL CAPTURED BY RUSSIANS after 3 days' heavy fighting.

WEDNESDAY, MAY 10

France – FFI now total 175,000.
China – Chinese cross R. Salween, near Burmese border, on broad front.

THURSDAY, MAY 11

Italy – 5th AND 8th ARMIES ATTACK GUSTAV LINE (Op. Diadem) on 48-km front, supported by MAAF (2,750 sorties) and thousands of guns. During the previous 8 weeks 8th Army has been secretly transferred from the Adriatic sector to Cassino. 8th Army secures bridgeheads over R. Rapido and 5th Army over the Garigliano. Americans capture the much-contested Damiano Hill; French capture Monte Faito (777 m). Gen. Alexander issues Order of Day to Allied Armies: *'We are going to destroy the German armies in Italy . . . no armies have ever entered battle before with a more just and righteous cause.'*
Air War: Europe – Oberst Walter Oesau, fighter 'ace' (123 victories), shot down and killed over Eifel Mts. 9th AF begins series of raids on airfields round Caen. Lancaster 'S for Sugar', of RAF No. 467 Sqn., completes its 100th mission.
Sea War: Med. – Allied warships bombard German heavy batteries at Gaeta.

FRIDAY, MAY 12

Italy – Germans launch fierce counterattacks along Gustav Line.
Air War: Europe – 800 8th AF bombers (46 lost), with heavy fighter escort (10 lost), attack synthetic oil plants at Leuna-Merseburg, Böhlen, Zeitz, Lutzkendorf and Brüx (NW. of Prague). Americans claim 150 fighters shot down.
Home Front: Britain – Death of Sir Arthur Quiller-Couch ('Q'), novelist and

editor of 'The Oxford Book of English Verse'; aged 82.

SATURDAY, MAY 13

Russian Front – German and Axis forces completely ousted from the Crimea, leaving behind 78,000 dead or prisoners.
Italy – French Exp. Corps (5th Army) penetrates Gustav Line; captures Monte Majo (1,000 prisoners) and Castelforte.
Occupied France – Resistance attack halts production of SP guns at Lorraine-Dietrich works, Bagnères de Bigorre.

SUNDAY, MAY 14

Italy – French break through at Monti Aurunci, N. of Gaeta.
Air War – Night raid on Bristol and SW. England by 91 planes (15 lost).

MONDAY, MAY 15

Italy – Germans begin withdrawing from 'Gustav' Line to 'Adolf Hitler' ('Dora') Line, immediately S. of Rome.
Home Front: USSR – Death of Patriarch Sergei, Head of Govt.-approved Russian Orthodox Church; aged 77.

TUESDAY, MAY 16

Air War: Europe – Russians bomb Minsk railway junction.
Sea War: Atlantic – Coastal Cmnd. planes sink 5 U-boats off Norway; 3 others seriously damaged (May 16-31).
Diplomacy – Allies sign agreements with Belgium, Netherlands and Norway concerning their administration during the immediate post-liberation phase.

WEDNESDAY, MAY 17

Italy – Kesselring orders evacuation of Cassino garrison.
Sea War – Carriers HMS *Illustrious* and USS *Saratoga* launch combined 85-plane strike against Surabaya. 32 German MTBs lay mines off English S. and E. coasts; fight inconclusive engagements with both British patrols and a German convoy (night May 17-18). Americans land at Arare and Wadke I; W. of Hollandia (May 17-18).
Burma – Chinese and Americans capture Myitkyina airfield.
Home Front: Britain – Kathleen Ferrier takes part in performance of Handel's 'Messiah' at Westminster Abbey.
Occupied France – Resistance attack CAM ball-bearing factory at Ivry-sur-Seine.

THURSDAY, MAY 18

Italy – Poles occupy 'Monastery Hill' at Cassino.
Diplomacy – UK and USSR agree that Rumania will be in Soviet sphere of influence; Greece in British sphere.
Neutrals: Turkey – Martial law declared after fascist disturbances.

FRIDAY, MAY 19

Italy – British armour and infantry overrun Aquino airfield, in Liri Valley; German AT guns repulse attempted seizure of Aquino town. Americans capture Gaeta.
Sea War: Pacific – 6 Japanese subs. sunk by American destroyer escort *England* in SW. Pacific (May 19-31). US carrier planes raid Marcus and Wake Is. (May 19 and 23).

SATURDAY, MAY 20

Air War: Europe – Nearly 5,000 Allied planes operate against 12 rail targets and 9 airfields in France and Belgium.
Italy – Allies attack 'Dora' (or 'Adolf Hitler') Line, S. of Rome; Canadians break through, May 22.
Home Front: USA – Communist Party disbands.
Secret War – Experimental V-2 falls in R. Bug. Polish Underground drive cattle into river to hide intact rocket from German troops. After dismantling, vital components are flown to London in RAF Dakota (July 25).

SUNDAY, MAY 21

Home Front: USA – Explosion on landing craft in Pearl Harbor, Hawaii, kills 127, with 380 injured.

MONDAY, MAY 22

Occupied France – Resistance blows up hydroelectric station at Bussy.

TUESDAY, MAY 23

Italy – Allied 6th Corps breaks out of Anzio bridgehead (Op. Buffalo). 8th Army attacks 'Adolf Hitler' Line.

Anzio Losses
British: 9,203; 2 cruisers, 3 destroyers, 5 other ships. US: 23,860; 2 minesweepers, 2 Liberty and 6 landing ships. German: 10,306, (to March 3).

China – Chinese launch counter-offensive in Honan Prov.
Air War: Europe – Paris radio announces railway system in chaos (*see* May 20).

WEDNESDAY, MAY 24

Italy – Canadian 5th Armd. Div. establishes bridgehead over R. Melfa despite heavy fire.
Air War: Europe – RAF Spitfires shoot down 8 FW 190 fighter-bombers N. of Rome.

THURSDAY, MAY 25

Italy – Allied column, from Anzio meets US 2nd Corps (5th Army) near Latina (Pontine Marshes). 8th Army crosses R. Melfa in strength.
Occupied Yugoslavia – Tito narrowly escapes capture when German airborne force, supported by *Stukas*, attacks his secret HQ in Bosnian mtns.
Occupied France – Resistance raid halts production of artillery pieces at *Arsénal National*, Tarbes.

FRIDAY, MAY 26

Italy – Canadians reach R. Liri.
China – **MAJOR JAPANESE OFFENSIVE AGAINST US AIR BASES** in the SE. (Op. *Ichigo*): 620,000 troops, divided between 11th and 23rd Armies, drive from Hankow and Canton.
Sea War: Atlantic – U-541 stops Portuguese liner *Serpa Pinto*, carrying Jewish refugees to Canada. 2 US citizens taken off and 385 others aboard ordered into lifeboats; 9 hrs. later (after U-541 has radioed HQ) they are allowed back on board (3 die inc. 16-month old baby).
Occupied France – Resistance bombs hydroelectric station supplying Tulle Arsenal, guarded by 40 German soldiers.

SATURDAY, MAY 27

Italy – Germans repel 5th Army attacks on 'Adolf Hitler' Line at Valmontone and dig in.
Sea War: Pacific – Americans land on Biak I. (New Guinea).

SUNDAY, MAY 28

Air War: Europe – 8th AF attacks Leuna and Königsborn *Pz* depot (Magdeburg).

MONDAY, MAY 29

Air War: Europe – 8th AF attacks 5 Focke-Wulf and 2 Messerschmitt plants in E. Germany and Poland.
Sea War: Atlantic – US escort carrier *Block Island* sunk by U-549.
New Guinea – First tank battle in SW. Pacific fought on Biak I.

TUESDAY, MAY 30

Italy – 5th Army breaks through 'Adolf Hitler' Line at Valmontone.
Russian Front – Germans make tactical gains N. of Jassy (Rumania).
Occupied France – Resistance sabotages equipment at Decazeville Colliery (3 further attacks in June).

WEDNESDAY, MAY 31

Sea War: Pacific – Op. *Kon*: Japanese despatch 3 troop convoys to Biak, but only 1 lands troops (May 31 – June 12).

Secret War – Agents land on Ceylon coast from Japanese sub. *I-166.*

THURSDAY, JUNE 1

Italy – 8th Army captures Frosinone.
Air War: Europe – RAF night raid on Saumur railway junction. 'G Force Air HQ' formed at Bari, Italy (renamed Balkan AF, June 7).
Sea War: Med. – Last German supply convoy to Crete garrison: 3 heavily escorted cargo ships attacked by 70 Allied planes; 1 sunk, 1 badly damaged and third sunk by sub. *Vivid* during return voyage (June 9).

FRIDAY, JUNE 2

Italy – Americans capture Velletri and Valmontone – 2 German bastions S. of Rome. Nearby stronghold of Lanuvio is hammered by US artillery.
Air War: Europe – First 'shuttle' raid by 130 B-17s of 15th AF (Op. Frantic): Italian-based bombers attack Debrecen railway yard (Hungary), then fly on to Ukraine escorted by Marauders and Yak fighters. 8th AF attacks V-1 sites in Pas de Calais. RAF Typhoons attack Dieppe-Caudecote radar station. Night fighters (7 lost) shoot down 15 RAF bombers attacking Trappes marshalling yards, near Paris.
Home Front: Britain – Explosion on munition train wrecks Cambridgeshire station.

SATURDAY, JUNE 3

Italy – German forces evacuate Rome.
Burma – Japanese rearguard leaves Kohima.
Air War – Ju 290 lands in N. Greenland and rescues 26-man team of meteorologists (left by U-boat, Aug. 1943).

SUNDAY, JUNE 4

Italy – ALLIED 5th ARMY ENTERS ROME. MAAF fighter-bombers decimate German columns retreating N. along Highways 1, 2 and 3, destroying or damaging 1,000 vehicles; by night, Wellingtons and Liberators plaster Highways 3 and 4 with heavy bombs.

Cassino Losses
British: 5,500. US: 21,500. French: 10,500. Poles: 4,000. German: 10,000 dead and wounded, 20,000 PoWs.

MONDAY, JUNE 5

Air War: Europe – 'Transportation Plan': in preparation for D-Day, Allied AFs have flown 200,000 sorties delivering 200,000 t. bombs in only 2 months (200 planes lost). French railway system virtually im-

mobilized; all bridges over R. Seine, between Paris and the Channel, destroyed; coastal radar chain disrupted. Final strike is saturation bombing (5,267 t.) of 10 coastal batteries by 1,136 RAF heavy bombers (night June 5-6). Allied airborne invasion of Normandy (night June 5-6): US 82nd and 101st Airborne Divs. land in S. Cotentin Pen.; British 6th Airborne Div. lands near Caen.
Air War – Op. Taxable: 5 RAF Bomber Cmnd. sqns. and 18 naval vessels carry out diversionary ops. in Pas de Calais area.
Italy – King Victor Emmanuel cedes power: son Umberto is Lt-Gen. of Realm.

TUESDAY, JUNE 6

Sea War – 'D-DAY'. ALLIED IN-VASION OF NORMANDY (Op. Over-lord): Op. Neptune amphibious phase of Overlord. At dawn 50 convoys begin landing 5 divs. of AEF, US, British and Canadian troops on 'Utah', 'Omaha', 'Gold', 'Juno' and 'Sword' beaches.

D-Day Forces
Allied: 1,213 warships inc. 7 battleships, 23 cruisers, 105 destroyers, 4,126 landing ships and craft, 736 auxiliary ships; 864 merchantmen (195,701 sailors); 3,467 heavy bombers, 1,645 medium bombers, 5,409 fighters, 2,355 transports, 867 gliders (total 13,743 planes). Troops landed: 75,215 British and Canadians from sea, 7,900 airborne, 900 armoured vehicles, 600 guns; 57,500 Americans from sea, 15,500 airborne. German: *c.* 50,000 men (5 divs.), 100 tanks; 345 planes.

Below: *GIs of 1st US Division wade ashore onto 'Bloody Omaha' beach.*

3 escort carriers, 16 SGs and 2 destroyer sqns. scour W. Approaches to the Channel for U-boats.
Western Front – AEF meets slight resistance, except on 'Omaha Beach', where 1st US Inf. Div. suffers severe losses. 21st *Pz* Div. counter-attacks between 'Juno' and 'Sword' late in the day.
Air War: Europe – Allied AFs fly 14,674 sorties over Normandy up to midnight June 6-7 (*Luftwaffe* flies *c.* 100 sorties). RAF Coastal Cmnd. maintains continuous patrols over E. and W. approaches to English Channel. 250 gliders land reinforcements and supplies for 6th Airborne Div.
Sea War: Pacific – 3 destroyers sunk by US sub. *Harder* (June 6-8).
Occupied France – De Gaulle broadcasts to French people.
Home Front: Britain – The King broadcasts.
Home Front: Rumania – Death of Col. Josef Beck, ex-Polish Foreign Minister; aged 49.

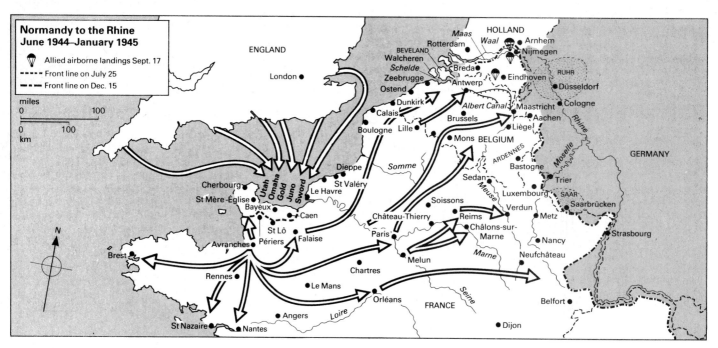

Normandy to the Rhine
June 1944–January 1945

Allied airborne landings Sept. 17
------- Front line on July 25
–·–·– Front line on Dec. 15

miles
0   100
0   100
km

D-Day Losses
British: 3,000 casualties. Canadian: 946. US: 6,603; 114 Allied planes. German: c. 6,500 casualties.

WEDNESDAY, JUNE 7

Western Front – Allied forces reach Bayeux and make contact with 6th Airborne Div. First Allied airstrip laid out at Asnelles, NE. of Bayeux.
Occupied Belgium – King Leopold deported to Germany.
Italy – 5th Army takes Civitavecchia, 56 km N. of Rome.
Sea War – German light naval forces and U-boats commence frequent sorties (mainly by night) against Allied invasion fleet, but suffer heavy losses – inc. 2 destroyers – and sink only small no. of transports and LC and 1 destroyer (RNN *Svenner*).

THURSDAY, JUNE 8

Western Front – British and Americans establish contact near Port-en-Bessin W. of Arromanches. British 7th Armd. Div. begins landing on 'Gold' beach.

FRIDAY, JUNE 9

Russian Front – **GREAT RUSSIAN OFFENSIVE ON FINNISH FRONT.** 21st and 23rd Armies attack with air support along 14-km-wide coastal sector of Karelian Isthmus. 3,000 guns obliterate Finnish advance positions, but Russian tanks make little progress by nightfall.
Western Front – Americans from 'Utah' beachhead capture Ste Mère-Eglise.
Home Front: Italy – Badoglio resigns as Premier to allow formation of new govt. (by Bonomi).

SATURDAY, JUNE 10

Russian Front – 3 Russian divs. annihilate 1 Finnish regt. (10th Div.) and advance 10 km in Karelian Isthmus.
Western Front – Montgomery establishes HQ in Normandy. US 2nd Armd. Div. begins landing at 'Omaha'.
Occupied France – **ORADOUR SUR GLANE MASSACRE:** Detachment of *SS Pz Div. Das Reich* murders 642 inhabitants of village near Limoges; 200 women and children burned to death in church.

SUNDAY, JUNE 11

Russian Front – Finnish 10th Div. retreats behind 'VT Line' (Vammelsuu-Taipale) across Karelian Isthmus.
Western Front – Americans from 'Utah' capture Carentan.
Sea War: Pacific – 15 carriers of TF 58 attack airfields on Mariana Is. and destroy 14-ship convoy (June 11-13).

MONDAY, JUNE 12

Russian Front – Finnish 4th Div. arrives in Karelian Isthmus from E. Karelia.
Western Front – By 'D + 6' (6 days after 'D-Day') 326,000 troops and 54,000 vehicles have been landed. 4 beachheads link up. Gens. Eisenhower, Marshall, Bradley, Arnold and Hodges and Adms. King, Starke, Kirk, Moon and Wilkes arrive aboard PT 71.

TUESDAY, JUNE 13

Sea War: Pacific – 7 US battleships bombard Saipan (Mariana Is.).
Air War: Britain – **FIRST V-1s LAUNCHED AGAINST LONDON** from Pas de Calais; only 4 of 10 reach fringe of target area – Gravesend,

Cuckfield, Bethnal Green (where 6 killed, 9 injured) and Sevenoaks.
Home Front: Britain – German cross-Channel guns hit Maidstone, Kent at record range of 81 km.
Secret War – Experimental V-2 crashes in Sweden. British Govt. purchases wreckage in exchange for radar equipment and flies it to Farnborough (July 31).
Western Front – Single Tiger tank, commanded by *Obersturmführer-SS* Wittmann, traps and totally destroys 25-vehicle column of 7th Armd. Div., in lane near Villers Bocage.

WEDNESDAY, JUNE 14

Russian Front – Russians break through 'VT Line' at village of Kuuterselka. Sole Finnish armd. div. counter-attacks (night June 14-15) and briefly recaptures heights near village, but Russians recapture them next morning.
Air War: Pacific – **FIRST B-29 SUPERFORTRESS RAID ON JAPAN.** 48 planes (4 lost) carry out ineffective night attack on Yawata iron and steel works from bases in China.
Air War: Europe – In heavy raids on Le Havre and Boulogne (nights June 14-15 and 15-16) 600 Lancasters sink 49 light naval craft; inc. 3 TBs and 14 MTBs.
Occupied France – De Gaulle appoints administrators for liberated areas.
Sea War: Pacific – 7 old US battleships bombard Saipan, which is then invaded by 5th Amphibious Corps (night June 14-15).

THURSDAY, JUNE 15

Western Front – Americans from 'Utah' capture Quineville.
Sea War: Pacific – **TWO USMC DIVS. LAND ON SAIPAN** (Op. Forager).
Occupied France – St Donat incident: Russo-Mongolian auxiliaries of German

Above: *Fuel-loaded US landing craft approach the burning town of Charan-Kanoa on the W. coast of Saipan.*

Army loot and destroy small S. of France town in first of series of reprisals for alleged Communist-led Resistance activities; 53 women and girls brutally violated and left for dead.
First of 2 Resistance attacks on *Air Liquide* liquid oxygen plant at Roubaix.

FRIDAY, JUNE 16

Air War: Britain – 244 V-1s launched against London since midday June 15.
Russian Front – Mannerheim orders Finnish forces, in the Isthmus, to retreat to 'VKT Line' (Viipuri-Kuparsaari-Taipale).
Western Front – King George VI tours battle area.
Italy – 8th Army threatens Perugia.

SATURDAY, JUNE 17

Sea War: Med. – French land on Elba from 37 PT boats which penetrate dense minefields (Germans surrender June 19).
Neutrals: Iceland – Independent republic founded with Sveinn Björnsonn as president after plebiscite (97% in favour). Union with Denmark ended.

SUNDAY, JUNE 18

Western Front – Americans capture Barneville and isolate Cotentin Penin and Cherbourg.
Italy – 8th Army captures Assisi, S. of Perugia.
Marianas – US Marines capture Aslito airfield, Saipan.
China – Japanese take key city of Changsha, 322 km. S. of Hankow.
Air War: Britain – V-1 destroys Guards Chapel, Wellington Barracks, London (119 killed, 102 injured).

MONDAY, JUNE 19

Sea War: Pacific – **BATTLE OF THE PHILIPPINE SEA** (June 19-20): V-Adm. Ozawa launches 372 carrier planes in 4 waves against US carrier force TF 58 at extreme range (480 km). 300 Hellcat fighters (29 lost) and proximity-fused AA shells shoot down 242 planes ('Marianas Turkey Shoot'). 1 bomb-hit on battleship *South Dakota*. US fighters shoot down or badly damage 49 Japanese attempting to land on Guam. Subs. *Albacore* and *Cavalla* cripple carriers *Taiho* and *Shokaku; Taiho* explodes 6 hours later.
Sea War: Atlantic – *U-505* captured (Secret code-books recovered). 4-day storm, commencing this day, wrecks American 'Mulberry' harbour off 'Omaha Beach' and seriously damages British 'Mulberry' off Arromanches. Many landing craft swamped.

TUESDAY, JUNE 20

Sea War: Pacific – Battle of Philippine Sea: V-Adm. Mitscher launches 216 planes at extreme range and surprises Ozawa's fleet refuelling. Carrier *Hiyo* sunk; carriers *Zuikaku, Chiyoda* and battleship *Haruna* damaged. 20 US planes shot down; 72 others lost during long return flight after dark.
Russian Front – Viipuri captured by Russians.
Russian 32nd Army attacks Finns N. of L. Onega.
Western Front – Americans besiege Cherbourg.
Occupied Byelorussia – Partisans in Byelorussia launch devastating 3-day campaign against rail communications of German Army Grp. Centre.
Italy – Perugia captured by 8th Army.

WEDNESDAY, JUNE 21

Russian Front – Russian 7th Army attacks across R. Svir, NE. of L. Ladoga.
Western Front – US ultimatum to Cherbourg garrison.
Sea War: Med. – British and Italian human torpedoes sink cruiser *Bolzano* at La Spezia.

THURSDAY, JUNE 22

Western Front – Saturation bombing attack heralds major US infantry assault on Cherbourg.
Air War: Europe – Poltava raid: *Luftwaffe* stages surprise night raid (60 planes) on 8th AF 'shuttle bombing' base in Ukraine. 44 Flying Fortresses destroyed; 26 men killed; 2,045,745 litres fuel burned. Shuttle raids subsequently abandoned.
Burma – Japanese siege of Imphal lifted.

> **Imphal-Kohima Losses**
> British and Indian: 16,700 plus 5,100 Chindits; 130 RAF and 40 USAAF planes. Japanese: 30,502 dead, 23,003 wounded; 120 tanks, c. 90 guns, 17,000 horses; c. 100 planes.

Diplomacy – Ribbentrop flies to Helsinki and brow-beats Finnish ministers into making public announcement that Finland will continue to support Germany (and not make a separate peace), in return for despatch of German troop reinforcements and arms.
Home Front: USA – GI 'Bill of Rights' promising generous benefits for returning US Servicemen, signed by Roosevelt.

FRIDAY, JUNE 23

Russian Front – **GREAT RUSSIAN OFFENSIVE IN BYELORUSSIA.**

> **Byelorussia-Opposing Forces**
> Soviet: 1,200,000 men (124 divs.); 31,000 guns and mortars, 5,200 tanks and assault guns; 6,000 planes. German: 63 divs.; 900 tanks and assault guns, 10,000 guns; 1,300 planes.

Russian Marines land behind Finnish lines N. of L. Ladoga. Col.-Gen. Dietl, cdr. of German forces on Arctic front, killed in air crash; aged 54.
Sea War – British MTBs virtually destroy convoy near Cherbourg.

SATURDAY, JUNE 24

Occupied France – Resistance blows up hydroelectric station, near Limoges.
Home Front: Britain – Sidney Keyes (war poet killed in Tunisia) posthumously awarded Hawthornden Prize.

D-DAY......
THE INVASION OF NORMANDY

'Soldiers, sailors and airmen of the Allied Expeditionary Force! You are about to embark upon the great crusade toward which we have striven these many months. The eyes of the world are upon you. The hopes and prayers of liberty-loving people everywhere march with you.' (From General Eisenhower's Order of the Day issued to each individual of the Allied Expeditionary Force, June 6, 1944.)

Adolf Hitler's failure to settle accounts with Britain in 1940 produced a most extraordinary strategic situation in Western Europe. While Britain remained unoccupied she posed an ever-present threat to Germany's far-flung continental empire. Not only might the British Army eventually return to France and Norway but Britain was also a base for the European Resistance movements and an unsinkable aircraft carrier from which most of Nazi-occupied Europe could be bombed.

So successful was the Allied bombing offensive by the summer of 1943 that Churchill and Roosevelt could claim that they had already partly satisfied Stalin's oft-repeated demands for a 'Second Front' in the West. This offensive paved the way for the greatest co-ordinated seaborne invasion in history – Operation Overlord; the Invasion of Normandy.

The Casablanca Conference of January 1943, however, gave priority to North Africa, followed, in July, by the invasion of Sicily. These decisions ruled out landings in France during 1943. But in May 1943 the Combined Chiefs of Staff at Washington set May 1, 1944 as the target date for Overlord. In August 1943, Lieutenant-General Morgan, Chief of Staff to the Supreme Allied Commander, submitted a draft plan that was approved by Allied leaders at Quebec. In December, Eisenhower was appointed Supreme Commander, Allied Expeditionary Force. Montgomery took command of the British 21st Army Group with operational control of all Allied land forces during the initial phase of Overlord.

A striking feature of Overlord was the small number of combat troops (only five seaborne and three airborne divisions and one division of special armour) to be landed on the first day (D-Day), compared with the 6,800-strong invasion fleet and the 13,000 planes

of the Allied air forces involved. Moreover, the troops landed would be self-sufficient in supplies for up to four weeks (i.e., until the capture and rehabilitation of Cherbourg harbour). Two completely pre-fabricated, reinforced concrete harbours (Mulberry A and Mulberry B) and numerous blockships were to be towed across the Channel and sunk off Normandy. Fuel was to be pumped by submarine pipeline from the Isle of Wight to Cherbourg, known by the mnemonic PLUTO ('Pipe-Line-Under-the-Ocean').

Although completely unaware of the scale and technological sophistication of Allied invasion plans, Hitler and his High Command saw the need for something more than ordinary defensive

Below: *A D-Day scene on the British beaches. Troops dig in beside their vehicles under German fire. The jeep is flanked by Bren-gun carriers and a Churchill tank.*

Right: *US tank landing ships (LSTs) disgorge the full panoply of Allied might onto the Normandy beaches.*

preparations. In November 1943, Field-Marshal Rommel was appointed to inspect German coastal defences (the *Westwall* or 'Atlantic Wall') from Denmark to the Bay of Biscay. Three months later he took command of 7th and 15th Armies, stationed from the Zuider Zee to Normandy.

Vainly demanding that the impending V-1 bombardment be targetted on the embarkation points in Southern England, Rommel initiated a crash programme to blanket the Normandy coast with 50,000,000 booby-trapped obstacles and mines, both above and below the water-line, plus many anti-glider obstacles inland and hundreds of new fortified batteries and pill-boxes. The 'Desert Fox' was convinced that Allied air supremacy would prevent large-scale movement of reserves to the threatened coastline. Maximum force must oppose the landings at the outset. *The first twenty-four hours will be decisive,'* he declared. *'We must stop the enemy in the water and destroy his equipment while it is afloat.'*

But Rommel's programme was opposed by the CinC West, von Rundstedt, and was seriously impeded by supply, transport and labour problems.

Hitler, who had earlier attempted to effect a compromise agreement on counter-invasion strategy between Rundstedt and Rommel, belatedly backed the former's outmoded concept of relying on powerful *Panzer* forces stationed well inland. The Führer also went back on his hunch that Normandy not the Pas-de-Calais was the Allied objective. This change of mind was assisted by an intricate deception operation, code-named Fortitude.

Although bad weather caused major problems for the Allied Supreme Commander during the final nerve-wracking hours before D-Day, a slightly more optimistic forecast for June 5, 1944, enabled Eisenhower to give the final go-ahead.

As Rommel had forecast, the ensuing three months were a time of unmitigated disaster for the German armies in France. After the 'brutal slugging battles' for Caen and Falaise, as Eisenhower described them, and the Allied invasion of Southern France in mid-August, the Germans were driven helter-skelter out of every corner of France, except Dunkirk and the beleagured former U-boat bases on the Atlantic coast. Rommel himself was almost killed by a low-flying Spitfire on July 17 and three days later a group of high-ranking German officers belatedly attempted to save the Army, and Germany herself, from utter destruction by planting a time-bomb in Hitler's HQ. Hitler survived to wreak a terrible vengeance on at least 2,000 army officers (including Rommel) and launch a desperate counter-attack on the Western Front in December 1944, now known as the 'Battle of the Bulge'. But Nazi Germany's military position had been hopeless ever since she had failed to drive the Allied forces into the sea on D-Day. The only question remaining in December 1944 was who would win the race to Berlin – the British, Americans and Canadians from the West, or the Russians from the East.

SUNDAY, JUNE 25

Russian Front – Russians trap 40,000 Germans W. of Vitebsk. Finns forced back 0.8 km at Tali, N. of Viipuri.
Sea War – Allied battleships and cruisers silence German coastal batteries near Cherbourg; USS *Texas* damaged.
Occupied France – Gen. Koenig to command Free French Forces of the Interior.

MONDAY, JUNE 26

Western Front – Americans capture Gen. Schlieben, Cherbourg fortress cdr. and R. Adm. Henneke, naval cdr. British 2nd Army attacks W. of Caen: meets fierce resistance (Op. Epsom).
China – Battle of Hengyang (June 26-Aug.8): Japanese 11th Army temporarily halted by Chinese 10th Army, near vital US air base. B-25s and P-47s make constant attacks on Japanese supply lines.
Italy – S. Africans of 8th Army occupy Chiusi, near L. Trasimene.
Sea War – HMS *Rodney* bombards German forces in Caen sector.

TUESDAY, JUNE 27

Sea War – German armed trawlers *M.4611* and *V.213* gallantly engage destroyers *Eskimo* and *Huron* off Jersey (night June 27-28).

WEDNESDAY, JUNE 28

Western Front – British 2nd Army crosses R. Odon, SW. of Caen.
Russian Front – 3rd BRF and supporting tank army, begin crossing R. Berezina. F. M. Busch dismissed from Army Grp. Centre; F. M. Model, C in C Army Grp. N. Ukraine, to command both Grps.
Occupied France – Philippe Henriot, Vichy Minister of Information and Propaganda, shot dead by the Resistance.
Home Front: USA – Republican convention nominates Dewey for president.

THURSDAY, JUNE 29

Russian Front – Russians encircle German forces at Bobruisk.
Western Front – **AMERICANS CAPTURE CHERBOURG.**
New Guinea – Australians reach R. Sepik.

FRIDAY, JUNE 30

Russian Front – 3rd BRF captures Borisov. Finns in the Isthmus, supported by reinforcements from other sectors, German AT units and *Stukas,* halt Russian onslaught.
Air War: Europe – 250 Lancasters drop 1,000 t. bombs on 2nd and 9th *SS Pz* Divs., as they pass through village of Villers Bocage, near Caen.

Diplomacy – USA breaks off diplomatic relations with Finland.
Sea War – Allied losses since 'D-Day': cruiser *Scylla* and 9 destroyers.

SATURDAY, JULY 1

Sea War: Pacific – US sub. *Cobia* sinks 6 ships in Japanese home waters during July; sub. *Ray* torpedoes 5 ships in Philippines–E. Indies area.
Home Front: USA – **BRETTON WOODS CONFERENCE** (UN Monetary Conference): establishes International Bank for Reconstruction and Development (World Bank).

SUNDAY, JULY 2

Sea War: Pacific – Americans land on Noemfoor I., W. of Biak.
Sea War – Japanese crew of *I-8* murders survivors of SS *Jean Nicolet*.
Home Front: Brazil – First contingent of Brazilian Expeditionary Force leaves Rio by sea to join Allied 5th Army in Italy.
Western Front – 'D+26': 929,000 troops and 177,000 vehicles have landed since 'D-Day'.

MONDAY, JULY 3

Russian Front – 100,000-strong German 4th Army encircled at Minsk.
Italy – Siena captured by French.
Sea War – U-boats equipped with schnorkels begin ops. off Normandy.

TUESDAY, JULY 4

Western Front – 2nd Army takes Carpiquet, W. of Caen.
Air War: Europe – V-1 storage depots in limestone caverns at St. Leu d'Osserat, NW. of Paris shattered by 12,000-lb bombs (second heavy raid 3 nights later).
Occupied France – Resistance destroy petrol stocks at Lievin refinery in Pas de Calais.

WEDNESDAY, JULY 5

Sea War – *Neger*-type U-boats begin operations off Normandy: in 3 night ops. they sink 4 light warships and cripple cruiser *Dragon* at cost of heavy losses.
Air War: Europe – 233 B-24s raid Toulon: 7 U-boats hit.

THURSDAY, JULY 6

Russian Front – Russian 1st BRF captures Kovel, in NW. Ukraine.
Air War: Pacific – First purpose-built US night fighter – Northrop P-61 Black Widow – destroys Japanese G4M bomber over Saipan.
Diplomacy – De Gaulle and Roosevelt confer in Washington; De Gaulle welcomed in New York City, July 10.

FRIDAY, JULY 7

Russian Front – N. of L. Ladoga, Finns complete retreat to the 'U' Line.
Air War: Europe – 450 Lancasters and Halifaxes saturate German defences near Caen with 2,300 t. bombs (night July 7-8).
Occupied Denmark – Danish mechanic with no pilot training steals He 111 and flies it to Sweden (shot down by Swedish flak).
Marianas – 3,000-strong rearguard of Saipan garrison storms US positions (night July 7-8) – before suffering annihilation.

Below: *US Marines blow up a Japanese dugout on the northern tip of Saipan.*

Gen. Saito and Adm. Nagumo commit *hara-kiri*.

SATURDAY, JULY 8

Western Front – 'Titanic' artillery barrage precedes major attack by British-Canadian 2nd Army NW. of Caen, which advances up to 5 km by nightfall against fierce opposition.
Air War: Britain – 1,750 barrage balloons in position S. of London to combat the V-1.
Home Front: Britain – Death of Capt. F. J. Walker, 'ace' U-boat hunter; aged 50.
Home Front: Argentina – Perón appointed Vice-Pres. by Pres. Farrell; from this moment Perón rapidly becomes virtual dictator.

SUNDAY, JULY 9

Russian Front – Russians cross R. Vuoksi in Karelian Isthmus.
Western Front – 2nd Army takes Caen.
Marianas – Americans in full control of Saipan.
Home Front: India – Gandhi concedes that Independent India must be partitioned between Hindus and Moslems.

MONDAY, JULY 10

Russian Front – Great Russian offensive into Baltic States: 2nd BF attacks NW. of Vitebsk (July 10); 3rd BF attacks near Pskov (July 17); 'Leningrad Front' attacks at Narva (July 26).
New Guinea – Japanese launch counter-offensive across R. Driniumor, in Aitape sector (night July 10-11).

TUESDAY, JULY 11

Russian Front – Elimination of trapped German 4th Army: 70,000 killed since late June; 35,000 captured.
New Guinea – 6,000 Japanese advancing W. of the Driniumor come under constant attack from Australian and US aircraft.

WEDNESDAY, JULY 12

Western Front – Brig.-Gen. Theodore Roosevelt, Jr., CGM, dies of heart attack.

THURSDAY, JULY 13

Russian Front – **RUSSIANS CAPTURE VILNA** (Lithuania).
New Guinea – Successful American counter-attacks on Japanese bridgehead W. of the Driniumor.
Secret War – Pilot of Ju 88G night fighter equipped with special radar and radio homing equipment lands by mistake at Woodbridge, Suffolk.

FRIDAY, JULY 14

Russian Front – Russians capture Pinsk.
Occupied France – Vichy announces

death of Georges Mandel, former Min. of Interior; murdered by the *Milice* (Vichy Secret Police).

SATURDAY, JULY 15

Russian Front – Russians halt in Karelian Isthmus.
Italy – 8th Army breaks through at Arezzo and reaches R. Arno (July 15-16). 5th Army approaches R. from SW. Italian Govt. returns to Rome.

SUNDAY, JULY 16

Russian Front – Germans launch fruitless counter-attack against 3rd BRF's. bridgeheads over R. Niemen.

MONDAY, JULY 17

Russian Front – 1st BRFr reaches 'Curzon Line'; 1st Guards Tank Army crosses R. Bug.
Western Front – **ROMMEL BADLY WOUNDED** by low-flying RAF fighters.
Italy – 8th Army crosses the Arno.
Air War – In bold move to protect London from V-1 bombardment 1,596 AA guns are moved to S. Coast (July 17-19). First use of napalm, by USAAF P-38s in raid on fuel depot at Coutances, Normandy.
Sea War – Abortive British carrier raid on *Tirpitz* in Kaa Fjord.
Home Front: Britain – 61,905 people unemployed (lowest wartime figure yet).
Home Front: USSR – 57,000 Germans, captured in Byelorussia, are paraded through streets of Moscow.

TUESDAY, JULY 18

Western Front – Americans capture St Lô, S. of Cotentin Penin. Op. Goodwood: 2nd Army attacks E. of Caen (July 18-21).
Italy – Polish troops of 8th Army take Ancona.
Home Front: Japan – **TOJO RESIGNS**, Gen. Koiso and Adm. Yonai appointed Co-Premiers, July 19; Gen. Umezu appointed COAGS.

WEDNESDAY, JULY 19

Italy – Leghorn captured by 5th Army.

THURSDAY, JULY 20

Home Front: Germany – **HITLER NARROWLY ESCAPES ASSASSINATION.** Col. Count von Stauffenberg leaves bomb in conference room at *Wolfsschanze* ('Wolf's Lair'), Rastenburg, E. Prussia. He then flies to Berlin to organize military coup, but this is badly bungled. Goebbels and Fromm, cdr. of Home Army, take vigorous counter-measures. Stauffenberg and other conspirators summarily executed. Col.-Gen. Beck commits suicide. Hitler broadcasts to German people condemning 'small clique of traitors'.

Occupied France – German military conspirators temporarily seize control of Paris and imprison local *SS* personnel but wait in vain to hear confirmation of Hitler's death from Berlin. *SS* regain control and release comrades after Hitler's broadcast.
Home Front: USA – Pres. Roosevelt renominated to run for 4th term by overwhelming vote of Democratic Convention at Chicago.

FRIDAY, JULY 21

Sea War: Pacific – **AMERICANS LAND ON GUAM** (Mariana Is.).
Home Front: Germany – Himmler appointed cdr. of Home Army; Guderian, COGS.
Von Stülpnagel, anti-Nazi cdr. in Paris, commits suicide.
Home Front: USSR – Moscow-based Union of Polish Patriots renamed Polish Committee of National Liberation (officially recognized as the 'legitimate' Polish Govt., Aug. 15).

SATURDAY, JULY 22

Occupied France – *SS* destroy village of St. Gingolph.

SUNDAY, JULY 23

Russian Front – 3rd BF captures Pskov. 1st BRF captures Lublin and Maidanek extermination camp.
Occupied France – Resistance sets fire to Engelbert tyre factory at Choisy-au-Bac.

MONDAY, JULY 24

Italy – Americans reach Pisa.
Sea War: Pacific – Americans land on Tinian (Mariana Is.).
Home Front: Germany – *Wehrmacht* ordered to use Nazi salute.

TUESDAY, JULY 25

Air War: Europe – 8th and 9th AFs drop 4,000 t. bombs on German defences in small area near St Lô.
Western Front – Op. Cobra: 7th Corps of US 1st Army attacks across Périers-St Lô road and advances up to 3 km. (Germans stunned by preliminary bombing.) Lt.-Gen. McNair, cdr. US 1st Army Grp., accident-

ally killed by American bomb; aged 61. Gen. Eisenhower visits Normandy. British-Canadian diversionary attack near Caen; 3 km advance despite strong resistance.
Sea War – British Eastern Fleet attacks shipping and airfields at Sabang (Sumatra); Dutch cruiser *Tromp* and 3 destroyers enter harbour and engage Japanese batteries at point-blank range (Op. Crimson).
Home Front: Germany – Goebbels appointed 'Reich Plenipotentiary for Total War Effort'.

WEDNESDAY, JULY 26

Marianas – Heavy artillery barrage heralds successful US attack on jungle-covered Orote Pen. Marines smash Japanese counter-attack on N. beachhead.
Home Front: USA – Roosevelt, MacArthur and Nimitz confer in Honolulu. MacArthur argues successfully for liberation of Philippines, against Formosa invasion.
Home Front: South Africa – Death of Riza Khan Pahlavi, exiled Shah of Iran; aged 67.

THURSDAY, JULY 27

Russian Front – 2nd BF captures Rezekne rail junction; 1st BF captures Daugavpils (Latvia).

FRIDAY, JULY 28

Russian Front – 1st BRF establishes 2 bridgeheads over R. Vistula, S. of Warsaw (July 28-Aug. 2). *Pzs* and *Luftwaffe* carry out repeated, furious counter-attacks, N. and S. of Warsaw, throughout Aug. Brest-Litovsk captured by 1st BRF.
New Guinea – Organized Japanese resistance ceases on Biak.
Western Front – US 1st Army takes Coutances, SW. of St Lô.
Sea War – German MTBs hit 5 cargo ships with *FAT* torpedoes in English Channel.

SATURDAY, JULY 29

Russian Front – 3rd BRF crosses R. Niemen.

SUNDAY, JULY 30

Sea War: Pacific – Op. Globe Trotter: Americans land at Sansapor, to complete occupation of New Guinea N. coastline.

MONDAY, JULY 31

Western Front – US 1st Army breaks through at Avranches.
Russian Front – Red Army 1st BRF reaches outskirts of Warsaw. 1st BF reaches Gulf of Riga, thereby cutting off German Army Grp. N. 2nd BRF reaches E. Prussian border.

Burma – 53,000 Japanese die during Imphal-Kohima battles and subsequent retreat to the Chindwin.
Marianas – Americans storm Japanese positions on Tinian.
Sea War: Pacific – Americans land at Sansapor, near NW. tip of New Guinea.
Home Front: Germany – Guderian to combine his existing duties, as Inspector-Gen. of Armd. Troops, with new position of COAGS.
Home Front: USA – Death of Marguerite A. Le Hand, personal sec. to Pres. Roosevelt; aged 46.

TUESDAY, AUGUST 1

Occupied Poland – **WARSAW RISING.** Polish 'Home Army' (*Armija Krajowa*) begins heroic 63-day struggle against German garrison.

Above: *An* SS *picture of the Warsaw Rising. The submachine-gunner has the support of a 75mm assault gun.*

Russian Front – 3rd BRF captures Kaunas (Lithuania).
Western Front – US 12th Army Grp. formed, under Bradley: inc. 1st Army (Hodges) and 3rd Army (Patton); 2 TACs of 9th AF under attachment.
Marianas – Americans secure Tinian.
Home Front: USA – Death of Manuel Quezon, Pres. of Filipino Govt.-in-Exile; aged 65. Sergio Osmena sworn-in.

WEDNESDAY, AUGUST 2

Western Front – Americans reach Vire, S. of Caumont.
Sea War – *Linse* ('Lentil') 'explosive boats' sink destroyer *Quorn* (night Aug 2-3)
Diplomacy – Turkey breaks off diplomatic and commercial relations with Germany.

THURSDAY, AUGUST 3

Western Front – US tanks reach Rennes (Brittany).
Burma – Chinese capture Myitkyina (NE. Burma).
Sea War: Pacific – US carrier planes attack shipping in Bonin Is. (Aug. 3 and 4).
Neutrals: Spain – Death of Gen. Count Jordana, the moderate Foreign Minister; Succeeded by Sr. Lequerica (Aug. 11).

FRIDAY, AUGUST 4

Western Front – British 2nd Army tanks reach Villers Bocage, for second time since 'D-Day'.
Italy – S. African units of 8th Army reach outskirts of Florence.
Home Front: Finland – Pres. Ryti resigns; Mannerheim takes over and forms 'peace' govt.
Home Front: USA – XP-47J experimental fighter aircraft attains 811 km/hour in level flight.
Air War – Gloster Meteor jet fighter in combat debut against V-1s.
Sea War – German MTBs fire T3D *Dackel* ('Dachshund') long-range torpedoes at shipping in Seine Bay (on 6 nights in Aug.); only 2 ships hit.

SATURDAY, AUGUST 5

Western Front – US armour reaches Redon (Brittany). British capture Villers Bocage.
Air War: Europe – RAF blast open U-boat pens at Brest, using 12,000-lb bombs.
Air War – Finnish ace, Maj. Luukkanen (54 victories) shoots down 20 Russian planes in his Me 109, June 14–Aug. 5.
Home Front: Australia – Japanese

PoWs attempt mass break-out from camp in NSW: 231 Japanese and 3 guards killed (Aug. 5-6).

SUNDAY, AUGUST 6

Western Front – Pzs counter-attack US forces in Mortain-Vire sector (begins night Aug. 6-7).
Air War: Pacific – B-24s bomb Davao (Philippines).

MONDAY, AUGUST 7

Western Front – Pzs counter-attacking E. of Avranches are decimated by Allied bombers and rocket-firing Typhoons; but Germans continue attacking. Canadian 1st Army (inc. Polish 1st Armd. Div.) attacks S. of Caen, supported by 1,000 RAF bombers. 9th Army encircles Brest, Lorient and St Nazaire (Aug. 7-13).
Occupied France – Resistance destroys 19 transport aircraft at SNCAC factory, Bourges.

TUESDAY, AUGUST 8

Western Front – Canadians push towards Falaise, supported by 600 US bombers.
Home Front: Germany – F.M. von Witzleben and 7 other 'July Plotters' executed by slow strangulation at Berlin's Plötzensee Prison, after being sentenced to death by 'People's Court'.
Home Front: Ceylon – Floating dock sinks at Trincomalee; HMS *Valiant* seriously damaged.

WEDNESDAY, AUGUST 9

Western Front – Americans capture Le Mans.
Air War – Capt. A. de Saint - Exupéry disappears during recce mission from Corsica over occupied France; aged 44.

THURSDAY, AUGUST 10

New Guinea – Japanese withdraw from Aitape sector towards Wewak.
Marianas – Americans secure Guam (small grps. of Japanese hide in the jungle; last man does not surrender until 1972).

Marianas Campaign Losses
Japanese: 40,000 dead, 2,030 PoWs. US: 4,596 dead, 19,323 wounded and missing.

Air War: Pacific – USAAF begins 7 month bombardment of Iwo Jima.

FRIDAY, AUGUST 11

Western Front – Americans capture Angers and Nantes.
Italy – German forces evacuate Florence.
Sea War – Germans scuttle 26 warships

BRADLEY, Omar Nelson (1893-)
American: *General of the Army;* 'the GI's general'

'A sound, painstaking and broadly-educated soldier', according to Eisenhower. 'He was a keen judge of men and their capabilities and was absolutely fair and just with them . . . he was emotionally stable and possessed a grasp of larger issues that clearly marked him for high office.' (*Crusade in Europe*, Dwight D. Eisenhower, Doubleday, New York 1948.)

Graduate of US Military Academy, West Point (1915), Infantry school (1925), Command and General Staff school (1929) and Army War College (1934). Chief of weapons section at the Inf. school, 1929-41. Commandant at West Point, 1935-38. Sec. of the General Staff in Washington, 1938-41. Commandant of the Inf. school, 1941-43.

Commanded US 2nd Corps in Tunisian and Sicilian campaigns, Feb.-Aug. 1943. Acting Lt-Gen., June 1943.

Appointed commanding Gen. of US ground forces (12th Army Group) for the invasion of Europe, Jan. 1944. His 1,300,000 combat troops were the largest number of US soldiers ever to serve under a single field commander. Major-Gen., Sept. 15, 1944. His army group temporarily transferred to Montgomery's command during 'Battle of the Bulge', Dec. 1944.

Administrator of Veterans' Affairs, 1945-47. Succeeded Eisenhower as US Army Chief of Staff, 1948-49. First permanent chairman of US Joint Chiefs of Staff, 1949-53. Retired 1953. Wrote 'A Soldier's Story' (1951).

and 28 merchant vessels at Nantes, Bordeaux and in Gironde and Seine estuaries (Aug. 11-25).
Sea War: Atlantic – 17 U-boats (1 lost) transferred from W. France to Norway in Aug. and Sept.
Secret War – First test launch of Ruhrstahl-Kramer X-4 rocket-propelled wire-guided missile, designed for use with Me 262.

SATURDAY, AUGUST 12

Western Front – German 7th Army withdrawing from Mortain-Vire sector towards Argentan and Falaise. PLUTO pipeline in operation between I. of Wight and Cherbourg.
Air War: Europe – Italian-based US bombers attack Bordeaux-Mérignac airfield, then fly on to Britain.
Diplomacy – Churchill meets Tito.

SUNDAY, AUGUST 13

Western Front – Americans reach Argentan.
Air War: Europe – 1,000 Allied heavy bombers attack roads leading to R. Seine, from Paris to the sea. Heavy raids on railway bridges in S. France.

MONDAY, AUGUST 14

Western Front – Canadians and Americans push towards Falaise, from N. and S., supported by RAF.

TUESDAY, AUGUST 15

Sea War/Air War – Op. Anvil/Dragoon: **ALLIED 7TH ARMY LANDS IN S. FRANCE** between Nice and Toulon; airborne forces land behind beachhead. 1,300 planes hammer weak German defences.

WEDNESDAY, AUGUST 16

Western Front – Allied seaborne and airborne forces link up in S. France.
Air War: Europe – Me 163 rocket fighters intercept B-17s near Leuna (Germany) for first time (no casualties).
Burma – All organized Japanese resistance ends along Burma-India border.
Diplomacy – In Note to Britain, Soviet Govt. condemns Warsaw Rising as 'a reckless, appalling adventure' and declares that Soviet High Cmnd. 'must dissociate itself' from same.
Occupied France – Resistance take control of large parts of central and S. France.

THURSDAY, AUGUST 17

Western Front – **FALAISE CAPTURED** by British-Canadian forces; Americans take Dreux, Chartres, Châteaudun and Orleans.
Russian Front – Russian guns bombard German territory – near Mariampole, E. Prussia.

FRIDAY, AUGUST 18

Western Front – Germans retreating through 'Falaise Gap' are decimated by Allied AFs.
Sea War: Pacific – Carrier *Taiyo* sunk by US sub. *Rasher* NW. of Philippines.

SATURDAY, AUGUST 19

Occupied France – **UPRISING IN PARIS** by FFI (Resistance). Vichy Govt. flees to Belfort. Pétain arrested and taken to Germany.
Home Front: Britain – Death of Sir Henry Wood, composer-conductor and founder of annual London 'Promenade Concerts'; aged 74.

SUNDAY, AUGUST 20

Russian Front – 2nd and 3rd UFs attack German-Rumanian Army Grp. S.; Rumanian 3rd Army broken.
Sea War – *Prinz Eugen* bombards Russian position on Gulf of Riga.
Western Front – Falaise Gap closed by Allied forces; British capture Argentan. Americans establish bridgehead over the Seine at Mantes-Gassicourt, NW. of Paris. De Gaulle lands at Cherbourg.
Air War: Europe – 142 Russian planes attack U-boats and shipping at Constanta.
Occupied France – Resistance forces capture Toulouse and set fire to Paix oil refinery at Douai.

MONDAY, AUGUST 21

Russian Front – Germans retreat towards R. Pruth in E. Rumania.
Western Front – Allied forces cross the Seine, N. and S. of Paris.
Diplomacy – DUMBARTON OAKS CONFERENCE at Washington DC; Allied representatives discuss post-war security and establishment of UN (ends Sept. 29).

TUESDAY, AUGUST 22

Western Front – Americans capture Sens, SE. of Paris.
Italy – Polish and Italian forces reach Metauro R., 48 km S. of Rimini.

Occupied France – FFI now control all public buildings in Paris.
Sea War – British escort carrier *Nabob* torpedoed by *U-354* off N. Norway. Her Avenger planes take off from sloping deck and prevent *U-354* from delivering *coup de grâce* (*Nabob* towed to safety).

WEDNESDAY, AUGUST 23

Western Front – Allied forces capture Evreux (Normandy), Melun (SE. of Paris) and Marseilles; Americans reach Grenoble. Eisenhower vetoes Montgomery's plan for bold drive through Low Countries into NW. Germany.
Sea War – Schnorkel U-boats operate around Scottish coast until early Oct.; only *U-482* (5 sinkings) achieves any success.
Air War: Britain – 211 people killed by V-1 at E. Barnet (London).
Home Front: Britain – Liberator bomber crashes on infants' school at Freckleton (Lancs): 57 killed.
Home Front: Rumania – King Michael dismisses and arrests the dictator, Antonescu, and sanctions formation of 'peace' govt. under Gen. Sanatescu. *Luftwaffe* bombs Bucharest.

THURSDAY, AUGUST 24

Western Front – French 2nd Armd. Div. enters Paris.
Allied forces take Cannes.

Home Front: Germany – All theatres, music-halls and cabarets to be closed from Sept. 1; all holidays suspended, students mobilized; all compassionate leave stopped for armed forces.
Home Front: Rumania – Rumanian Royal Guards defeat German attempts to occupy Bucharest. *Stukas* attack the Palace.
Air War – RAF Coastal Cmnd. attacks German evacuation ships off Le Havre.

FRIDAY, AUGUST 25

Western Front – DE GAULLE ENTERS PARIS. German garrison, Cdr.-Gen. von Choltilz, surrenders in left-luggage office of Montparnasse Station, after openly disobeying Hitler's orders to destroy city.
Russian Front – 3rd BF captures Tartu (Estonia).
Sea War – *Warspite* bombards Brest.
Diplomacy – RUMANIA DECLARES WAR ON GERMANY. FINNS BEGIN PEACE NEGOTIATIONS WITH RUSSIANS. Agreements signed between Britain, France and USA concerning civil administration of liberated territory.

SATURDAY, AUGUST 26

Western Front – Allied forces pour across the Seine at 4 points between Paris and the sea.
Air War: Europe – 110 killed and 719 injured during German night raids on Paris; numerous fires.
Occupied Greece – Withdrawal of German forces from mainland (ends Nov. 2).
Home Front: Bulgaria – Govt. announces its intention to withdraw from the war and begins disarming German garrisons.

SUNDAY, AUGUST 27

Western Front – Allied forces reach R. Marne. French capture Toulon.

MONDAY, AUGUST 28

Western Front – Americans reach Château-Thierry. British gain another bridgehead on lower Seine.
Air War: Britain – 90 out of 97 V-1s directed against London are destroyed by the defences.
Home Front: Germany – Death of Ernst Thaelmann, former leader of German Communist Party, at Buchenwald; aged 58.
Home Front: USA – Death of W. Franklin Knox, Sec. of the Navy since 1940; aged 70.

TUESDAY, AUGUST 29

Russian Front – German Army Grp. S. Ukraine ordered to hold Carpathian Mts. and Transylvanian Alps.

DE GAULLE, Charles André Joseph Marie (1890-1970)
French: General, President of French Committee of National Liberation, Supreme Commander of French Armed Forces

One of the most extraordinary and controversial figures of World War II. Although long mistrusted (even despised) by many Frenchmen after Fall of France and frequently in bitter conflict with his Anglo-American allies, he yet succeeded in building Free French movement into formidable force, which played significant role in latter, victorious, stages of the war. Became equally controversial Pres. of France after war.

Graduated from St. Cyr military college, 1914. Wounded three times during World War I. Captured at Verdun, 1916, but escaped and returned to duty on Western Front and in Macedonia. Advocated mechanization of French Army between the wars, but was cold-shouldered by conservative general staff.

Led 4th Armoured Div. in series of gallant, but ineffectual, counter-attacks against German salient in N. France, May 1940. Under-sec. for National Defence, June 1940. Escaped to England and formed 'French National Committee'. Adopted Cross of Lorraine – emblem of Joan of Arc – as his own. Sentenced to death *in absentia* for treason and desertion by Vichy military court, Aug. 1940.

Liberated most of the French colonial empire, 1940-42, despite defeat of British-Free French expedition to Dakar, W. Africa (Sept. 1940) and bitter fighting in Syria (May-June 1941), Morocco and Algeria (Nov. 1942). Reluctantly shared control of Free French movement with Gen. Giraud, Dec. 1942-Nov. 1943. Sole Pres. from latter date. Supreme commander of armed forces from April 1944. Entered Paris with Free French armoured units, Aug. 1944. Officially recognized as sole legal head of French govt., Oct. 1944.

Pres. of provisional govt., 1945-46. Formed and led his own right-wing party, *Rassemblement de la Peuple Française* ('Rally of the French People'), 1947-53. In retirement, 1953-58. Recalled to power during Algerian crisis of 1958. Student riots in Paris (May 1968) and defeat of de Gaulle in subsequent referendum led to his resignation, April 1969. Published 'The Army of the Future' (1934), 'War Memoirs' (1955-61).

Western Front – Americans capture Soissons, 89 km NE. of Paris. French advance from Nîmes towards Montpellier.
Burma – Allies capture Pinbaw.
Occupied Czechoslovakia – Germans move to occupy puppet state of Slovakia, sparking off long-planned Slovak national uprising. Slovaks hold central Slovakia throughout Sept. but *SS* units force them to retire into Low Tatra Mts. in Oct.
Occupied Hungary – Gen. Lakatos forms collaborationist govt.

WEDNESDAY, AUGUST 30

Russian Front – Russians occupy Ploesti.
Western Front – Canadians take Rouen; British take Beauvais, N. of Paris; Americans at Rheims and Châlons-sur-Marne.

THURSDAY, AUGUST 31

Russian Front – **RUSSIANS OCCUPY BUCHAREST** after advancing 56 km from Ploesti inside a day. Big crowds welcome the liberators.
Western Front – British cross the Somme and capture Amiens; Americans cross the Meuse, near Sedan.
Sea War: Pacific – 15 carriers of TF 38 carve swathe of destruction across Japanese-held Is. N. of New Guinea – attacking Iwo Jima, Chichi Jima, the Palaus, Mindanao, the Visayas and Luzon (Aug. 31-Sept. 24). 1,000 Japanese planes, 150 ships and craft destroyed, for loss of 72 US planes. Americans immediately decide to cancel step-by-step reconquest of the Philippines via Mindanao and to proceed directly to Leyte Gulf. (*See* Oct. 20, 1944.)
Occupied France – FFI liberate Bordeaux.

Normandy Campaign Losses
British and Canadian: 83,825 inc. 16,138 dead, 58,594 wounded; 2,036 RAF planes (8,178 aircrew). US: 125,847 inc. 20,838 dead, 94,881 wounded; 2,065 planes (8,536 aircrew). German: about 200,000 inc. 91,000 PoWs; 3,656 planes.

FRIDAY, SEPTEMBER 1

Western Front – Canadians occupy Dieppe (abandoned by Germans); British reach Arras; Americans capture Verdun. Montgomery promoted to F.M.
Italy – 8th Army captures Monte Gridolfo, a bastion of the Gothic Line.

SATURDAY, SEPTEMBER 2

Russian Front – Russians reach Bulgarian border.
Western Front – 51st (Highland) Div. captures St. Valéry-en-Caux. Allied forces reach Mons. US 3rd Army (Patton) temporarily immobilized through lack of fuel.

Above: *Belgian Resistance round up ex-German collaborators in the village of Peer, close to the Dutch frontier.*

Italy – 5th Army captures Pisa. 8th Army breaks through Gothic Line near Rimini.
Diplomacy – Finland breaks off diplomatic relations with Germany and accepts Russian peace terms.

SUNDAY, SEPTEMBER 3

Western Front – **BRUSSELS LIBERATED** by British forces after lightning dash of 362 km in 4 days. US and French troops enter Lyons.
Occupied Holland – Prince Bernhard appointed cdr. of underground forces.
Secret War – Retreating Germans abandon hundreds of thousands of intelligence dossiers at Brussels; these are subsequently discovered and examined by British investigators and found to contain street maps of *every* town and village in UK and Eire; maps of entire British and Irish coastlines and innumerable photographs, ranging from 1890s postcards to 1940 views of Battersea Power Station. All these data were to have been used during Op. Sea Lion.

MONDAY, SEPTEMBER 4

Russian Front – Cease-fire on Russo-Finnish front.
Western Front – **ALLIED FORCES CAPTURE ANTWERP.**
Diplomacy – British Govt. decides to forcibly repatriate captured Russian 'collaborators'.

TUESDAY, SEPTEMBER 5

Russian Front – Russians reach Turnu Severin, S. of Iron Gates gorge (R. Danube). Hungarian 2nd Army attacks Rumanian 4th Army.
Diplomacy – USSR declares war on Bulgaria. 5½ hours later (early on Sept. 6) Bulgaria requests armistice.

Secret War – Op. *Zeppelin*: KG 200 plane carrying saboteurs crashes near Moscow.

WEDNESDAY, SEPTEMBER 6

Western Front – Canadians besiege Calais.

THURSDAY, SEPTEMBER 7

Western Front – British cross Albert Canal (Belgium) and take Ypres. US 3rd Army secures 2 bridgeheads over R. Moselle.

FRIDAY, SEPTEMBER 8

Russian Front – Russians enter Bulgaria; port of Varna occupied (ops. suspended, Sept. 9).
Western Front – Allied forces capture Ostend, Liège, Le Creusot and Besançon.
Italy – 5th Army launches major attack on Gothic Line.
Diplomacy – Bulgaria declares war on Germany.
Air War: Britain – Explosion in Chiswick (3 killed) and supersonic boom heard all over London, announces **FIRST V-2 ROCKET ATTACK ON LONDON.**
Air War: Europe – Luxury liner *Rex* (51,062 t.) set on fire by RAF at Trieste.

SATURDAY, SEPTEMBER 9

Air War: Europe – US and British bombers batter cities along the Rhine – from Düsseldorf and München-Gladbach to Mannheim-Ludwigshafen.

SUNDAY, SEPTEMBER 10

Russian Front – 1st BRF attacks German forces in Praga, outside Warsaw (op. completed, Sept. 14).
Diplomacy – **RUSSO-FINNISH ARMISTICE** signed in Moscow.
Western Front – British attempt to storm Le Havre. Americans enter Luxemburg City.

Above: *A jeepload of wounded pass US troops crossing the Moselle, Sept. 12.*

Home Front: India – Commission of Inquiry into *Fort Stikine* disaster publishes findings: faulty loading of ship; capt.'s negligence; unco-ordinated emergency services.

MONDAY, SEPTEMBER 11

Western Front – US 1st ARMY CROSSES GERMAN BORDER N. of Trier. French capture Dijon.
Diplomacy – SECOND QUEBEC CONFERENCE ('Octagon'): CCS agree that Mountbatten should reconquer Burma as quickly as possible (by March 1945); agreement on occupation policy in Germany; Japan to be invaded Oct.-Dec. 1945 (ends Sept. 16).

TUESDAY, SEPTEMBER 12

Western Front – US 1st Army crosses Belgian-German border, near Eupen. Surrender of Le Havre.
Diplomacy – ALLIED-RUMANIAN ARMISTICE signed in Moscow: Rumania to supply 12 divs. to fight Germany and Hungary; Soviet-Rumanian frontier to follow line agreed June 28, 1940; Rumania to pay partial reparations for damage inflicted on Soviet territory; Vienna Award of Aug. 1940 cancelled and Transylvania to be returned to Rumania.

Southern France Campaign
German: 32,311 PoWs taken by US forces, 47,717 taken by French; 1,316 guns taken. US: 1,395 dead, 5,879 wounded and missing. French: 1,144 dead, 4,346 wounded.

WEDNESDAY, SEPTEMBER 13

Western Front – US 3rd Army captures Neufchâteau. French troops of 3rd and 7th Armies make contact at Chatillon-sur-Seine.
Sea War: Atlantic – 4 US warships and Liberty ship (previously torpedoed by *U-518*) lost in hurricane off Eastern Seaboard.
Home Front: Britain – Death of William Heath Robinson, eccentric cartoonist.

THURSDAY, SEPTEMBER 14

Western Front – US forces and Dutch Resistance capture Maastricht.

FRIDAY, SEPTEMBER 15

Russian Front – Polish 1st Army (of 1st BRF) begins crossing the Vistula, from Praga to Warsaw proper (night Sept. 15-16).
Italy – First inf. detachment of Brazilian Expeditionary Force joins 5th Army.
Sea War: Pacific – Americans land on Morotai (W. of New Guinea), Peleliu and Angaur (Palau Is.).
Western Front – Americans break through Siegfried Line, E. of Aachen. FFI and Americans capture Nancy.
Air War – Smoke screen saves *Tirpitz* during Lancaster raid on Alta Fjord, in Arctic.

SATURDAY, SEPTEMBER 16

Russian Front – Guderian counter-attacks near Gulf of Riga with troops brought from far S. of the Front, spearheaded by scratch *Pz* div. of Col.-Gen. Stachwitz. Contact re-established between Army Grps. Centre and N., by Sept. 26.

Sea War – Carrier *Unyo* sunk by US submarine *Barb*, in S. China Sea.
Occupied Holland – Hendrick Colijn, ex-P.M. of Holland, dies in German custody; aged 75.
Occupied Denmark – General strike (Sept. 16-21).
Air War: Europe – RAF bombs airfields in Holland and W. Germany.

SUNDAY, SEPTEMBER 17

Air War: Europe – BATTLE OF ARNHEM. 1st Allied Airborne Army (2 US and 1 British div. with Polish Para. Brig.) transported by 3,800 aircraft and 500 gliders lands in Arnhem-Nijmegen area in attempt to capture 3 bridges.

MONDAY, SEPTEMBER 18

Western Front – Armoured spearheads of British 2nd Army make contact with airborne forces in Holland.
Occupied Rumania – Antonescu arrested by Russians.

TUESDAY, SEPTEMBER 19

Western Front – Siege of Brest ends. Allies capture Eindhoven.
Air War: Europe – RAF night raids on Rheydt and München-Gladbach – key traffic centres behind Siefgried Line. Wing-Cdr. Guy Gibson, V.C., missing over Rheydt.
Sea War – Last 3 U-boats in Black Sea scuttled after running out of fuel and rejection of planned sale to Turkish Navy.
Diplomacy – ALLIED-FINNISH ARMISTICE signed in Moscow. 23 articles inc.: Finland to withdraw her troops behind 1940 frontier; to disarm all German forces still on her territory; Petsamo to be returned to USSR and Russian base to be established on Porkkala – Udd Pen., near Helsinki; Finland to pay $300 M. indemnity to USSR.

WEDNESDAY, SEPTEMBER 20

Western Front – Allied ground and airborne forces link up at Nijmegen. Polish Div. reaches R. Scheldt along 10-km front.

THURSDAY, SEPTEMBER 21

Russian Front – Polish 1st Army forced to withdraw from its bridgeheads in Warsaw.
Western Front – Inf. of British 2nd Army tries to break through to Arnhem.
Italy – Greek and Canadian units of 8th Army capture Rimini, eastern bastion of Gothic Line.

FRIDAY, SEPTEMBER 22

Russian Front – Russians capture Tallinn (Estonia).

Western Front – Germans surrender at Boulogne. Stolberg (E. of Aachen) captured.

SATURDAY, SEPTEMBER 23

Western Front – Successful German counter-attack N. of Eindhoven.
Air War: Europe – RAF night raids on Münster and Neuss (E. of Aachen). Lancasters breach Dortmund-Ems Canal.
Diplomacy – Tiny republic of San Marino (Italy) declares war on Germany, following capture of its 300-man army by German platoon.
Sea War: Pacific – Ulithi Atoll occupied by US forces, quickly transformed into great naval base, capable of sheltering 600 ships.

SUNDAY, SEPTEMBER 24

Western Front – Renewed efforts to save British airborne forces at Arnhem.
Sea War – Anti-sub. nets foil attempted U-boat attack on Russian battleship *Arkhangelsk* (ex-HMS *Royal Sovereign*).
Sea War: Med. – British Aegean Force (inc. 7 carriers) lands troops to reoccupy Aegean Is. and mainland Greece (Sept. 24-Oct. 31).

MONDAY, SEPTEMBER 25

Western Front – Remnants of British 1st Airborne Div. withdrawn over the Rhine, by night, after suffering 7,000 casualties.
Home Front: Germany – Allies exhort estimated 12 M. foreign workers and slave labourers in Germany to rise against their tormenters.
Hitler orders formation of *Volkssturm* ('People's Militia') to defend Germany.

TUESDAY, SEPTEMBER 26

Russian Front – The Central Front stabilizes along line of Rs. Narew and Vistula: Russians have advanced 604 km since June 23 and virtually annihilated the 25 divs. of German Army Grp. Centre.
Western Front – Allied salient around Eindhoven widened E. of R. Maas.
Italy – 8th Army begins crossing R. Uso (ancient Rubicon).
Home Front: Britain – German cross-Channel guns carry out furious bombardment of Dover; shell strikes hostel, killing 49.
Air War: Europe – 3,500 t. bombs dropped by RAF on Calais and Cap Gris Nez batteries.

WEDNESDAY, SEPTEMBER 27

Russian Front – 2nd and 3rd BFs make unsuccessful attempt to storm the 'Sigulda Line', NE. of Riga.
Western Front – British 2nd Army makes limited advances S. of Arnhem.
Air War: Europe – RAF bombers batter marshalling yards E. of the Rhine.
Home Front: USA – Death of Aimee Semple McPherson ('Sister Aimee'), charismatic and controversial evangelist; aged 53.
Neutrals: Sweden – Swedish ports closed to German shipping.

THURSDAY, SEPTEMBER 28

Western Front – Germans surrender Calais Citadel after further heavy bombing by RAF. German frogmen attempt to blow up bridge over R. Waal at Nijmegen (night Sept. 27-28).

Occupied Greece – All Greek Resistance groups and political factions agree to accept orders from Allied Supreme Cdr. in the Med. and from Lt.-Gen. Scobie, cdr. of Allied ops. in Greece.

FRIDAY, SEPTEMBER 29

Russian Front – Russian campaign by Leningrad Front and Baltic Fleet to recapture Moonsund Archipelago off Estonia (Sept. 29-Nov. 24): Russians land on Muhu I. (Sept. 29); Russians land on Himmaa (Oct. 5) – heavy fighting Oct. 5-10; Germans then retreat into Syrve Pen. and are not finally destroyed until Nov. 24.
Western Front – Canadians take Cap Gris Nez. Truce at Calais (where some Germans still hold out) to permit evacuation of civilians.

SATURDAY, SEPTEMBER 30

Air War: Europe – Renewed RAF onslaught on Rhineland marshalling yards.
Home Front: Britain – Great celebrations in Dover, following news that all German cross-Channel guns have been captured.

SUNDAY, OCTOBER 1

Western Front – Unsuccessful German counter-attack S. of Arnhem. Canadians secure Calais.
Russian Front – Finns begin ops. against German forces in N. Finland.

MONDAY, OCTOBER 2

Occupied Poland – **END OF WARSAW RISING.** Decimated Polish Home Army of Gen. Bor forced to surrender to Germans. 200,000 Poles killed.
Occupied Holland – Population of Dutch Is. in Scheldt Estuary warned that Allies intend to bomb dykes and create disastrous floods.
Western Front – US 1st Army attacks Siegfried Line, N. of Aachen.
Air War: Europe – Sqn.-Ldr. Berry, who has destroyed 60 V-1s, in his Tempest fighter, missing over Holland.

TUESDAY, OCTOBER 3

Western Front – Truce at Dunkirk; civilians evacuated. Americans attack Fort Driant near Metz.
Air War: Europe – Me 262 jet fighter becomes operational.
Lancasters breach dykes protecting Walcheren I.

WEDNESDAY, OCTOBER 4

Russian Front – Russians reach Pancevo, 16 km from Belgrade.
Air War: Europe – Heavy daylight raid on Bergen U-boat base by fighter-escorted Lancaster (1 lost) and Halifaxes.
Home Front: Japan – Death of Mitsuru Toyama, former leader of extreme right-wing terrorist organization, the 'Black Dragon Society'; aged 89.

THURSDAY, OCTOBER 5

Russian Front – 1st BF attacks E. of Memel; armoured spearhead reaches coast near Palanga, Oct 10; German Army Grp. N. isolated once again.
Western Front – Allied forces cross Belgian-Dutch border N. of Antwerp.
Air War: Europe – Lancasters fire-bomb Saarbrücken.
Home Front: Germany – 16-year-old youths to be conscripted for military service. All hospitals placed under military control. Nazi party and Hitler Youth activities 'cut to the bone'.
Sea War – 36 *Linsen* boats lost during attempted raid off R. Scheldt (night Oct. 5-6).

FRIDAY, OCTOBER 6

Western Front – Canadians cross Leopold Canal (Belgium).
Air War: Europe – Heavy day and night raids on Berlin.

SATURDAY, OCTOBER 7

Russian Front – Russian 14th Army attacks in N. Finland.
Western Front – US 1st Army penetrates Siegfried Line N. of Aachen. Germans counter-attack on Leopold Canal.

SUNDAY, OCTOBER 8

Western Front – US 1st Army attacks E. of Aachen; 3rd Army strikes between Metz and Nancy.
Sea War – British-Canadian troops of 1st Army land behind German lines, on S. bank of R. Scheldt (night Oct. 8-9).
Home Front: Britain – New ministries of Social Insurance and Aviation (Civil) established.
Home Front: USA – Death of Wendell L. Willkie; aged 52.

MONDAY, OCTOBER 9

Diplomacy – Third Moscow Conference: Allies discuss the Polish problem with Polish P.M. (ends Oct. 20).

TUESDAY, OCTOBER 10

Russian Front – Big tank battle at Debrecen, SE. Hungary: Germans are pushed back but then counter-attack and destroy 3 Russian corps. **BATTLE OF RIGA** (Oct. 10-13): city captured by 2nd and 3rd BFs.
Western Front – 24-hour ultimatum sent to German garrison of Aachen.
Air War – US Committee of Ops. Analysts backs saturation IB attacks on Tokyo and 5 other Japanese cities to cripple war production (*see* Feb. 4, March 9, 1945).

WEDNESDAY, OCTOBER 11

Western Front – Germans trapped at Aachen reject ultimatum.

THURSDAY, OCTOBER 12

Western Front – British capture Overloon (Holland).
Sea War: Pacific – **BATTLE OF FORMOSA** (Oct. 12-15): TF 38 launches massive strikes against the I. 400-strong Japanese 2nd Air Fleet (inc. fast new Ki-67 torpedo planes) launches repeated counter-strikes; cruisers *Canberra* and *Houston* torpedoed and carrier *Franklin* damaged by crashing raider. 2nd Air Fleet loses 321 planes; TF 38 loses 71.
Occupied Greece – Athens liberated by Resistance forces; British gliders land reinforcements.

FRIDAY, OCTOBER 13

Russian Front – Fall of Riga.
Western Front – US artillery and planes decimate *Pzs* counter-attacking near Aachen. V-weapon bombardment of Antwerp begins.

SATURDAY, OCTOBER 14

Air War: Europe – **2,000 RAF BOMBERS RAID DUISBURG.** 1,063 bombers (14 lost), escorted by 300 fighters, drop 5,000 t. bombs by day; 1,005

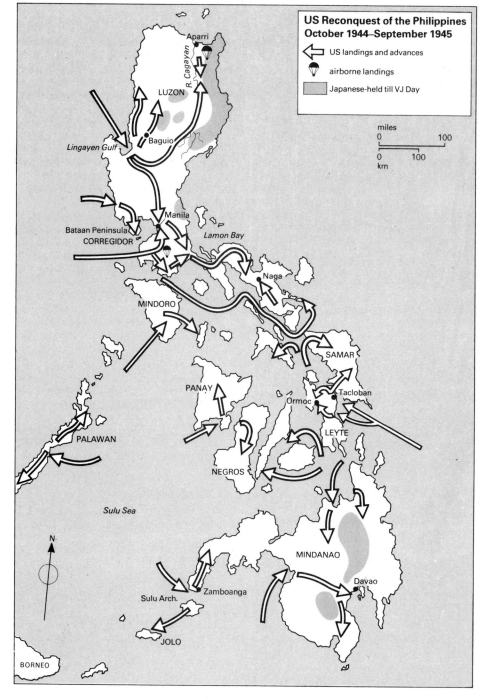

**US Reconquest of the Philippines
October 1944–September 1945**
⟵ US landings and advances
⛱ airborne landings
▨ Japanese-held till VJ Day

miles
0   100
0   100
km

(6 lost) drop 4,500 t. in 2 night attacks; 2,450 people killed. Diversionary ops. inc. destructive attack on Brunswick (561 killed). 8th AF sends 1,000 bombers, escorted by P-47s and P-51s, to Cologne.
Home Front: Germany – **ROMMEL COMMITS SUICIDE** following discovery of his indirect contacts with 'July Plotters'; aged 52. Goebbels announces (Oct. 15) he has 'died from wounds'.

SUNDAY, OCTOBER 15

Air War: Europe – Daylight raid on Sorpe Dam: Lancasters obtain direct hits on vast earthwork-concrete structure with 12,000-lb DA bombs.
Occupied Hungary – Skorzeny and *SS* men kidnap son of Regent Horthy; 24th *Pz*

Div. enters Budapest. Radio Budapest plans to broadcast statement by Horthy denouncing Hitler and appealing for immediate armistice with W. Powers. However, Veesenmayer, the German minister, confronts Horthy and threatens to shoot his son. Horthy and his P.M., Gen. Lakatos, meekly submit next day.

MONDAY, OCTOBER 16

Western Front – US forces close the ring around Aachen.
Occupied Hungary – Ferenc Szalasi, leader of fascist 'Arrow Cross' Party appointed acting-Regent and 'Royal Hungarian Premier'; his followers launch reign of terror against 160,000 Jews in the Budapest ghetto.

Home Front: Germany – Bread ration cut by 7 oz. (198 g.) per wk.

TUESDAY, OCTOBER 17

Air War: Europe – RAF makes 3,000 t. raids on German garrisons trapped at Boulogne and Calais (Oct. 17 and 20).
Sea War: Pacific – Adm. Toyoda activates Plan *Sho* ('Victory') in response to US invasion of Leyte.
Sea War – British Eastern Fleet attacks Nicobar Is. (Op. Millet) in unsuccessful attempt to divert Japanese from Leyte Gulf.

WEDNESDAY, OCTOBER 18

Russian Front – Russians now hold 5 Carpathian passes on E. borders of Czechoslovakia.
Burma – Lt.-Gen. 'Vinegar Joe' Stilwell, Deputy Allied S. Cdr., SE. Asia, recalled to Washington.
Home Front: Germany – *Deutscher Volkssturm* established (equivalent to British Home Guard). Himmler speaks at first parade and calls on every German to resist impending invasion by guerrilla tactics. They must fight *'like werewolves. . . . Every house, every ditch . . . every cluster of trees will have to be defended'.*
Greece – Govt. returns to Athens.

THURSDAY, OCTOBER 19

Burma – British capture Tiddim.

FRIDAY, OCTOBER 20

Sea War: Pacific – **US 6th ARMY LANDS IN LEYTE GULF (PHILIPPINES):** MacArthur wades ashore and declares: *'I have returned.'* He calls upon Filipinos to rise and strike blow after blow against Japanese.
Occupied Yugoslavia – Belgrade captured by Tito's Partisans and Russian forces.
Home Front: USA – Explosions at natural gas storage plant in Cleveland, Ohio, kill 121.

SATURDAY, OCTOBER 21

Western Front – Americans secure Aachen.
Sea War: Pacific – Cruisers *Honolulu* and *Australia* seriously damaged in Japanese air attack.

SUNDAY, OCTOBER 22

Western Front – Allied forces capture Breskens on Scheldt Estuary.
Italy – 8th Army crosses R. Savio, S. of Ravenna
Air War: Europe – Allied AFs bomb Hamm, Neuss, Hamburg and numerous targets across the *Reich* by day and night (losses nil).

MONDAY, OCTOBER 23

Russian Front – Russians now hold 137-km. front in E. Prussia.
Italy – 5th Army troops capture Monte Salvaro.
Air War: Europe – 955 RAF planes drop 4,538 t. bombs on Krupp's works, Essen; IBs start fires in vast slag heaps, which are still smouldering in late 1940s (night Oct. 23-24).
Sea War: Pacific – Japanese cruisers *Atago, Maya* and *Takao* torpedoed by US submarines *Dace* and *Darter,* off Palawan (Philippines); *Darter* runs aground.
Diplomacy – Britain, USA and USSR recognize de Gaulle's administration as Provisional Govt. of France.

TUESDAY, OCTOBER 24

Sea War: Pacific – **BATTLE OF LEYTE GULF** (Oct. 24-26): 2 Japanese fleets converge on Leyte in desperate bid to destroy US invasion fleet by surface bombardment; 4 carriers are to be sacrificed as decoys (due to lack of pilots and planes). The plan almost succeeds – but heroic resistance of US TF 77 (6 escort carriers, 7 destroyers) prevents Adm. Kurita's 1st Striking Force from entering the Gulf (Action off Samar). *Kamikaze* planes later hit 5 escort carriers. Seven Hellcat fighters from USS *Essex,* led by

Leyte Gulf Forces and Losses
Japanese: 6 carriers (4 lost), 7 battleships (3 lost), 16 cruisers (10 lost), 36 destroyers (11 lost), 11 subs. (0 lost), 916 planes (500 lost), 42,800 men (10,000 killed). US: 32 carriers (3 lost), 12 battleships (0 lost), 23 cruisers (0 lost), 100 destroyers (3 lost), 22 subs. (2 lost); over 200 planes lost; 143,668 men (2,803 killed).

Cdr. McCampbell, shoot down 14 Zeros and 9 bombers, N. of Philippines.
Battle of Surigao Strait (night Oct. 24-25): 6 old US battleships (rebuilt after Pearl Harbor raid) with cruisers, destroyers and PT boats destroy 2 Japanese battleships and heavy cruiser *Mogami* approaching Leyte Gulf from S. – last battleship-vs-battleship action of war.
Russian Front – Russians capture Augusto, near E. Prussia-Poland border.
Western Front – 2nd Army captures Hertogenbosch.
Burma/China – Stilwell's CBI cmnd. split into 'India-Burma Theatre' and 'China Theatre', under Gens. Sultan and Wedemeyer, resp.
Western Front – Hitler tells his gens. he intends to launch surprise counter-offensive against weakest point (the Ardennes) in Allied line (*see* Dec. 13).

MacARTHUR, Douglas (1880-1964)
American: *General of the Army*

Dubbed the 'American Caesar' by a recent biographer, MacArthur was legend in his own lifetime. After an early career of unsurpassed achievement he won undying fame by defeating the Japanese in World War II and then bringing them all the benefits of Western democracy. The invincible old warrior and peacemaker then succumbed to the temptation of total power and was forced to retire.

Born in Little Rock barracks, Arkansas, son of Lt-Gen. Arthur MacArthur. Graduated number one man of his class from US Military Academy, West Point and commissioned in Corps of Engineers, 1903. Went to Tokyo, 1905, as aide to his father, then US observer in Russo-Japanese War. Participated in US military expedition to Veracruz (Mexico), 1914; youngest divisional commander in American Expeditionary Force in France during World War I: decorated 13 times and cited 7 times for bravery. Promoted Brigadier, Aug. 1918. Youngest ever superintendent of West Point, 1919. Youngest Maj-Gen. in US Army, 1925. Commanded Philippines garrison, 1928-30. Chief of staff and full General, 1930: doubled enlisted personnel, expedited mechanization and enlarged Army Air Corps.

Military adviser to Philippines govt. 1935-42. Commanding gen. of US forces in Far East, Dec. 19, 1941. Directed campaign to delay Japanese occupation of Philippines, Dec. 1941-May 1942. Ordered to leave Corregidor I. by Pres. Roosevelt and re-establish HQ in Australia, (arrived March 17, 1942). Gave personal pledge to Filipino president and people 'I shall return'.

CinC Allied Forces in SW. Pacific Area, from March 1942, he masterminded defence and reconquest of New Guinea and liberation of the Philippines (Oct. 20 1944-July 5, 1945) after resisting all suggestions that Philippines should be 'by-passed' in favour of attack on Formosa. Gen. of the Army, 1944. Commander of all US Army forces in the Pacific, April 5, 1945. Supreme commander of Allied occupation forces in Japan, Aug. 14, 1945. Headed Allied delegation at surrender ceremonies aboard battleship *Missouri* in Tokyo Bay, Sept. 2, 1945.

Clashed with President and State Dept. over total number of US troops required for occupation purposes (Sept. 1945). He gave Japan new constitution, disbanded financial and industrial cliques (*Zaibatsu*) and carried out sweeping reforms, 1945-50. CinC of United Nations forces in South Korea, July 1950. Relieved of all his commands by Truman, April 11, 1951. In obscure retirement until his death, April 5, 1964. 'Reminiscences' published posthumously, 1965.

**HALSEY, William Frederick, Jr.
(1882-1959)
American:** *Fleet Admiral;* '**Bill' or 'Bull'**

Blunt, hard-driving, no-nonsense sailor of the 'old school'. One of the great pioneering practitioners of carrier warfare in W.W.II.

Graduated from US Naval Academy, Annapolis, 1904. Commanded destroyer squadron in World War I. Entered naval aviation branch after war. Conducted surprise carrier plane raids on Japanese-held Marshall and Gilbert Is., Wake I. and Tokyo itself (Jan.-April 1942). Commander of all US naval forces in S. Pacific, Oct. 24, 1942. Defeated Japanese in great series of battles in waters round Guadalcanal (Oct.-Nov. 1942).

Commanded US 3rd Fleet, including 15 fast carriers, from June 15, 1944. Virtually annihilated Japanese carrier fleet off Cape Engano, during Battle of Leyte Gulf (Oct. 1944). Made tireless efforts to repel repeated *Kamikaze* attacks on US invasion fleet during Okinawa invasion, April-June 1945. Paraded his fleet and attached British Pacific Fleet up and down Japanese E. Coast, June- Aug. 1945, destroying air bases, factories, naval bases and merchant shipping, by day and night. Entered

Tokyo Bay aboard battleship *Missouri* and attended surrender ceremonies, Sept. 2, 1945.

Returned to USA and relinquished command of 3rd Fleet, Nov. 1945. Made Fleet Admiral . Retired from Navy, 1947. Entered business. Died Aug. 1959

Home Front: France – Death of Louis Renault, automobile manufacturer; aged 62.

WEDNESDAY, OCTOBER 25

Air War: Europe – RAF daylight raids on Essen and Homburg oil refinery, near Duisburg. Further massive 8th AF attack on Hamm.
Sea War – Russians land near Petsamo (Finland) and Kirkenes (Norway); ops. suspended Oct. 29.
Western Front – Canadians take Fort Frederik Hendrik at Breskens, after 4 days' heavy fighting.

THURSDAY, OCTOBER 26

Western Front – British cross the Scheldt and land on S. Beveland (secured by Oct. 30).
Home Front: Britain – Death of Princess Beatrice, favourite daughter of Queen Victoria; aged 87. Death of influential and popular ecclesiastic William Temple, Archbishop of Canterbury; aged 63.

FRIDAY, OCTOBER 27

Western Front – British capture Tilburg; Canadians take Bergen-op-Zoom.
Air War: Pacific – Tacloban airstrip (Leyte) operational: 9th Fighter Sqn. flies first mission by Philippines-based US fighters since 1942.
Air War: Europe – F.M. von Richthofen, ex-cdr. of élite close-support force, *Fliegerkorps VIII* in France, Balkans and Russia, and cousin of the 'Red Baron', forced to retire from cmnd. of *Luftflotte 2* in Italy following brain surgery.
Neutrals: Spain – Army launches campaign against Republican invasion force in Pyrenees.

SATURDAY, OCTOBER 28

Air War: Europe – 700 RAF bombers raid Cologne. Lancasters attack U-boat pens at Bergen.
Diplomacy – **ALLIED-BULGARIAN ARMISTICE** signed in Moscow: Bulgaria to relinquish occupied areas of Greece and Yugoslavia; pay reparations and deliver foodstuffs to same.

SUNDAY, OCTOBER 29

Western Front – Polish Div. captures Breda (Holland).
Air War: Europe – Lancasters attempt to bomb *Tirpitz* at Tromsö.

MONDAY, OCTOBER 30

Occupied Greece – Govt.-in-Exile bans ELAS National Militia.

TUESDAY, OCTOBER 31

Russian Front – German Army Grp. N. trapped in Courland Pen. (Lithuania) where it remains until May 1945.
Air War: Europe – RAF daylight raid on Bottrop oil plant (Ruhr).

Gothic Line Campaign Losses
Allied: 14,000 British (to Sept. 21); 15,700 US, 465 tanks. German: 8,000 PoWs.

WEDNESDAY, NOVEMBER 1

Sea War – British inf. and Commandos land on Walcheren (Op. Infatuate): German garrison surrenders, Nov. 8.
Air War: Pacific – First of 9,000 paper balloons, carrying bombs, released near

Tokyo (small number reach N. America, but only 6 people killed). B-29 'Tokyo Rose' of 3rd PR Sqn. makes first reconnaissance over Tokyo since 1942.
Greece – British patrols reach Salonika.
Diplomacy – International Civil Aviation Conference at Chicago.

THURSDAY, NOVEMBER 2

Russian Front – 2nd *Pz* Army consolidates its position along R. Drina; W. of Belgrade.
Western Front – **LIBERATION OF BELGIUM** completed, Germans surrender at Zeebrugge, Knocke and Heyst.
Air War: Europe – Great air battle over Leuna synthetic oil plant at Merseburg: 8th AF claims 183 fighters (inc. 4 jets) for loss of 40 bombers and 28 fighters (inc. losses due to flak). By night, RAF despatches 992 bombers to Düsseldorf and small forces to other targets (20 planes lost in all ops.).
Home Front: USA – Roosevelt sends Donald M. Nelson, former chief of WPB, to reorganize Chinese war production.

FRIDAY, NOVEMBER 3

Western Front – Canadians cross from Beveland to join British on Walcheren. US 1st Army captures Schmidt, near Aachen (Germans recapture, Nov. 4).
Italy – Lt.-Gen. McCreery replaces Lt.-Gen. Leese as GOC 8th Army.

SATURDAY, NOVEMBER 4

Russian Front – Russian long-range guns bombard Budapest.
Western Front – Allies capture Flushing.
Balkans – **LIBERATION OF GREECE** completed.
Air War: Europe – 8th AF raids Gelsenkirchen oil plant. RAF night bombers make new breaches in Dortmund-Ems Canal.
Home Front: USA – Death of F.M. Sir John Dill, head of British Joint Mission in Washington; aged 63.

SUNDAY, NOVEMBER 5

Air War – B-29s attack Singapore.

MONDAY, NOVEMBER 6

Neutrals: Egypt – Lord Moyne, British Resident Minister in the Middle East, dies – shot by 'Stern Gang' (Zionist) terrorists, in Cairo.

TUESDAY, NOVEMBER 7

Home Front: USA – **ROOSEVELT RE-ELECTED.** Presidential Elections: Roosevelt (Democratic), 25,610,946; Dewey (Republican), 22,018,177; Roosevelt wins in 36 States and is re-elected for unprecedented fourth term. 'Fringe' candidates: 340,705.

WEDNESDAY, NOVEMBER 8

Western Front – US 3rd Army drives E. in Metz-Nancy sector.
Air War: Europe – Maj. Walter Nowotny, Austrian fighter ace (258 victories), dies in Me 262 crash over Achmer.

THURSDAY, NOVEMBER 9

Western Front – Polish Div. defeats German rearguard at Moerdijk (Holland); booty inc. ex-BEF AA guns, vintage 1940. US 3rd Army tanks plough through heavy rain and deep mud in Lorraine.
Air War: Europe – 8th AF heavy bombers and 9th AF fighter-bombers attack numerous targets ahead of advancing 3rd Army. RAF 2nd TAF attacks rail targets in Holland.

FRIDAY, NOVEMBER 10

Western Front – 3rd Army captures Château-Salins, NE. of Nancy.
Home Front: Japan – Death of Wang Ching-wei, Pres. of 'Central Govt. of China'; aged 59.

SATURDAY, NOVEMBER 11

China – Japanese capture Kweilin and Liuchow air bases; Americans have previously rendered Liuchow unusable.
Home Front: France – Churchill and Eden attend Armistice Day ceremonies in Paris.

SUNDAY, NOVEMBER 12

Air War – TIRPITZ SUNK at Tromsö (902 killed) by 21 Lancasters of Nos. 9 and 617 Sqns., RAF, carrying 12,000-lb. bombs. Allied bombers attack Brenner Pass railway.

MONDAY, NOVEMBER 13

Western Front – Churchill visits French troops in the Vosges.
Sea War – 3 Liberty ships torpedoed by *U-978* in English Channel.

TUESDAY, NOVEMBER 14

Western Front – British 2nd Army attacks German pocket W. of R. Maas.
Home Front: Britain – ACM Sir Trafford Leigh-Mallory, Allied Air CinC SE. Asia (designate), presumed killed in air crash (wreckage discovered in French Alps, June 4, 1945).

WEDNESDAY, NOVEMBER 15

Western Front – French 1st Army attacks in Jura Mtns.
Home Front: USA – Senior cdrs. of armed forces promoted *en masse* to new ranks of 'Gen. of the Army' and 'Adm. of the Fleet'; (each to be identified by '5-star' insignia).

THURSDAY, NOVEMBER 16

Air War: Europe – 10,000 t. bombs from 1,200 8th AF planes and 1,100 Lancasters and Halifaxes obliterate fortified towns of Düren, Julich and Heinsberg and defence line W. of Düren (E. of Aachen).
Western Front – US 1st and 9th Armies launch great attack into Roer Plain, E. of Aachen (Op. Queen).

FRIDAY, NOVEMBER 17

Western Front – 1st Army captures Gressenich, 16 km. E. of Aachen.
Sea War: Pacific – Carrier *Shinyo* sunk by US sub. *Spadefish*.

SATURDAY, NOVEMBER 18

Home Front: USA – Cost of living has risen 29% since Jan. 1941.

SUNDAY, NOVEMBER 19

Western Front – British and US troops capture Geilenkirchen, N. of Aachen.
Occupied Albania – Hodja's Partisans liberate Tirana.
Home Front: USA – Cost of the war now running at $250 M. per day.

MONDAY, NOVEMBER 20

Western Front – Tanks of French 1st Army drive through Belfort Gap and reach upper Rhine.
Sea War: Pacific – *Kaiten* 'suicide torpedo' sinks US naval tanker *Mississinewa* in Ulithi Atoll.
Home Front: China – Chiang Kai-shek appoints new Min. of War in attempt to mollify popular disenchantment with his régime.

TUESDAY, NOVEMBER 21

Air War: Europe – 247 RAF night bombers breach Dortmund-Ems and Mittelland canals (night Nov. 21-22).
Sea War: Pacific – Battleship *Kongo* sunk by US sub. *Sealion (II)*, near Formosa.

Home Front: France – Death of Maurice Paléologue, author and diplomat; aged 85.

WEDNESDAY, NOVEMBER 22

Western Front – Americans secure Metz. 1st and 9th Armies capture Eschweiler.

THURSDAY, NOVEMBER 23

Western Front – French and American forces enter Strasbourg.
Russian Front – Russians take Cop (Czechoslovakia).
Sea War: Pacific – British Eastern Fleet abolished: older ships plus escort carriers to form 'British East Indies Fleet'; modern ships detached for service as 'British Pacific Fleet'.

FRIDAY, NOVEMBER 24

Sea War: Atlantic – RCN corvette *Shawinigan* sunk by U-1228 in Cabot Str. (between C. Breton I. and Newfoundland). 91 killed; no survivors.
Air War: Pacific – FIRST B-29 RAID ON TOKYO. 111 planes (2 lost), led by 'Dauntless Dotty' despatched to Musashi aero-engine works. Bombers fly from NE. India via forward bases at Chengtu in China.

SATURDAY, NOVEMBER 25

Italy – 8th Army crosses R. Cosina.
Air War: Europe – Massive 8th AF raids on Leuna oil plant and Bingen marshalling yards.
Air War: Britain – V-2 hits crowded Woolworth dept. store in Deptford (E. London): 160 killed.

SUNDAY, NOVEMBER 26

Western Front – 1st Army captures Weisweiler, W. of Cologne.
Italy – Gen. Alexander promoted to F.M. and appointed SAC Mediterranean.
Air War: Europe – 8th AF attacks Misburg oil plant (Hanover), Hamm marshalling yards and Bielefeld railway viaduct; claims 138 fighters destroyed for loss of 36 bombers and 7 fighters. Spitfire fighter bombers attack 2 suspected V-2 sites in Holland.

MONDAY, NOVEMBER 27

Sea War – Prison ship *Rigel*, carrying 2,248 Russians, sunk by British carrier planes off Norway (415 survivors).
Air War: Europe – Very heavy day and night raids on marshalling yards in W. Germany. Freiburg severely damaged in night raid.
Air War: Pacific – Second B-29 raid on the Musashi plant, Tokyo. Japanese retaliatory strike against Saipan base. *Kamikazes* attack US battleships in Leyte Gulf.

Home Front: Britain – 4,000 t. bombs explode in underground dump at Hanbury, Burton-on-Trent, killing 70 people and hundreds of cattle.
Home Front: USA – Sec. of State, Cordell Hull, resigns because of ill-health; replaced by Edward Stettinius.

TUESDAY, NOVEMBER 28

Western Front – 3rd Army holds 42-km wide salient inside W. Germany. 9th Army patrols reach R. Roer.
Sea War – First Allied convoy (18 ships) arrives in Antwerp.

WEDNESDAY, NOVEMBER 29

Russian Front – Russian and Yugoslav forces capture Mohacs and Pecs, after crossing Danube S. of Budapest.
Sea War: Pacific – Giant carrier *Shinano* sunk by US sub. *Archerfish.*

THURSDAY, NOVEMBER 30

Air War: Europe – 8th AF encounters severe flak during raids on oil plants in Leipzig area (53 planes lost). RAF drops 2,000 t. bombs on Duisburg. RAF drops 14,312 t. bombs on German synthetic oil plants during Nov. 1944.
Sea War – 13 British subs sink 57 Japanese ships and small supply craft in Malacca Str.-Sumatra area during Nov.

FRIDAY, DECEMBER 1

Western Front – 3rd Army reaches R. Saar.
Occupied Crete – Germans on Crete abandon all areas except large towns.

SATURDAY, DECEMBER 2

Western Front – Americans enter Saarlautern.
Occupied Italy – Death of Filippo Marinetti, founder of 'Futurist' art movement (1909) and leading Fascist author; aged 67.

SUNDAY, DECEMBER 3

Western Front – 3rd Army captures main bridge over R. Saar at Saarlautern.

MONDAY, DECEMBER 4

Western Front – British 2nd Army eliminates last German bridgehead W. of the Maas. Americans bombard Saarbrücken.
Air War: Europe – Destructive night raid on Heilbronn, E. of Karlsruhe: numerous combats with night fighters.

TUESDAY, DECEMBER 5

Air War: Europe – 550 8th AF planes (12 lost) escorted by 800 fighters (9 lost)

attack Tegel tank works, Berlin and Münster marshalling yards; 91 German fighters shot down over Berlin. RAF makes day and night raids on Soest.
Philippines – Japanese paratroop suicide squads land on Burauen airfield, Leyte.
Balkans – British troops intervene in fighting between Greek Royalists and Communists.
Sea War: Med. – British and Greek warships bombard ELAS positions at Piraeus and Salamis.

WEDNESDAY, DECEMBER 6

Western Front – 3rd Army enters Sarreguemines (Moselle). 2nd Army held up SW. of Arnhem by German demolition of dykes and consequent flooding.
Air War: Europe – 'Round-the-clock' bombing of Leuna oil plant.
Home Front: Germany – He 162 *Volksjäger* ('People's Fighter') flight-tested over Vienna.

THURSDAY, DECEMBER 7

Western Front – 3rd Army penetrates Siegfried Line NW. of Saarlautern.
Sea War: Pacific – Americans land at Ormoc on W. coast of Leyte.
Home Front: Japan – Earthquake rocks Tokai area, disrupting rail communications and temporarily halting production at Mitsubishi aircraft works, Nagoya.

FRIDAY, DECEMBER 8

Western Front – Americans capture Fort Driant, near Metz.
Air War: Europe – RAF daylight raids on Duisburg.
Sea War: Pacific – US warships bombard Iwo Jima.

SATURDAY, DECEMBER 9

Western Front – 3rd Army repels German counter-attack at Saarlautern.
Air War: Europe – Stuttgart raided by the 8th AF.

SUNDAY, DECEMBER 10

Air War: Europe – Americans bomb rail targets at Coblenz and Bingen.
Diplomacy – Franco-Soviet 20-year Treaty of Alliance signed in Moscow.
Occupied Norway – Norwegian paratroops, flown from Britain, destroy hundreds of rails and the Koppang Bridge, to prevent withdrawal of German forces from N. Norway (Dec. 10, 1944-Jan. 5, 1945).

MONDAY, DECEMBER 11

Western Front – US 7th Army enters Haguenau (Alsace).
Air War: Europe – 2,000 bombers of 8th and 15th AFs attack rail targets in

Germany and oil plant and ordance depots near Vienna.
Sea War – *U-365* and torpedo planes attack Convoy RA. 62. Destroyer *Cassandra* damaged; U-boat sunk.

TUESDAY, DECEMBER 12

Western Front: – US 1st Army battles its way through the Hürtgen Forest to within 2 km of Düren.
Air War: Europe – Lancasters escorted by Mustangs bomb Witten, only 'virgin' target in the Ruhr.

WEDNESDAY, DECEMBER 13

Western Front – Allied forces capture Fort Jeanne d'Arc – last German stronghold at Metz.
Air War: Pacific – B-29s seriously damage Mitsubishi works at Nagoya.

THURSDAY, DECEMBER 14

Western Front – Germans counter-attack at Colmar (Alsace).
Sea War: Pacific – TF 38 raids airfields on Luzon, destroying 170 Japanese aircraft for the loss of 65 US planes.

FRIDAY, DECEMBER 15

Western Front – 7th Army enters Germany from Alsace.
Burma – Chinese capture Bhamo.
Air War: Europe – Lancasters escorted by Spitfires drop 12,000-lb. bombs on E-boat pens at Ijmuiden.
Sea War: Pacific – Americans land on Mindoro (Philippines).

SATURDAY, DECEMBER 16

Western Front – BATTLE OF THE BULGE. Rundstedt and Model, under Hitler's direct cmnd., launch surprise counter-offensive into the Ardennes on weakest sector of Allied line, held by 8th Corps, US 1st Army. Germans employ 5th *Pz* Army, 6th *SS Pz* Army and 7th Army with 20 divs. inc. 7 *Pz.* Appalling weather virtually grounds Allied AFs and the weight of the German onslaught ensures rapid progress. Paratroops and *SS* men disguised as American MPs add to the confusion.
Air War: Europe – Main weight of the V-weapon offensive switched from London to Antwerp: V-2 kills 271 in Rex Cinema.

SUNDAY, DECEMBER 17

Western Front – Germans capture 9,000 Americans at Echternach, on extreme left flank of the 'Bulge'. THE MALMÉDY MASSACRE: *SS* murder at least 71 captured American soldiers.
Air War: Europe – RAF starts big fires at Ulm (first major night raid).

PATTON, George Smith, Jr. (1885-1945)
American: *General;* 'Old Blood and Guts'

Most successful commander of armoured forces in history of US Army. Equally renowned for outspokenness and short temper. 'Accidental' death in Dec. 1945 has also become subject of controversy, following suggestions that his jeep was deliberately rammed by driver of army truck, under instructions of jealous subordinate officers.

Born at San Gabriel, California. Graduated from West Point Military Academy, 1909. Cavalry Lt., 1913. Aide-de-camp to Gen. Pershing in Mexico, 1916-17, and London, 1917. Attended course at French tank school. Organized American Tank Centre in France. Commanded American tank brigade in St. Mihiel and Meuse-Argonne battles, Sept.-Nov. 1918.

Tank brigade commander, July 1940. Maj.-Gen. and commander of 2nd Armored Div., April 1941. Corps commander (1st and 2nd Armd. Divs.) and commander of desert training centre at Indio, California, Dec. 1941. Commanding gen. of western task force during 'Op. Torch'; carried out successful landing in Morocco despite Vichy French resistance. Made Lt.-Gen. during Tunisian campaign, March 1943. Temporarily relieved of command during invasion of Sicily, after striking shell-shocked American soldier. Reprimanded by Eisenhower and obliged to make public apology to unit concerned.

Commander of 3rd Army, April 1944, prior to Normandy invasion. His armour smashed through German defences in Aug., by-passed Brittany peninsula, then wheeled eastward and swept on to Paris, German border and Siegfried Line. During 'Battle of the Bulge', Patton skilfully disengaged his armour from the battle of the Saar and wheeled N. to strike 97 km over icy roads against German flank and siege ring around US garrison of Bastogne. Played major role in advance to the Rhine. Sent his armour over the river at Frankfurt into central Germany and Czechoslovakia.

Four-star Gen., April 1945, and military gov. of Bavaria, May 1945. Dismissed from command of 3rd Army and his gubernatorial duties, Oct. 7, 1945, for ridiculing official 'denazification' programme, designed to 'rehabilitate' former Party members. Given command of non-operational 15th Army staff, who were compiling tactical history of World War II. Seriously injured in road accident near Mannheim, Dec. 9, 1945; died at US military hospital in Heidelberg, Dec. 21, 1945. Memoirs, 'War as I knew it' (1947).

MONDAY, DECEMBER 18

Air War: Europe – RAF night bombers sink *Schleswig-Holstein* and 8 other ships at Gotenhafen (Gdynia).
Air War: Pacific – B-29s bomb Mitsubishi aircraft assembly works at Nagoya. 84 B-29s and 200 14th AF planes destroy Japanese supply base at Hankow, China (fires burn for 3 days).
Sea War: Pacific – Typhoon plays havoc with TF 38: 7 carriers damaged, 3 destroyers sunk.

TUESDAY, DECEMBER 19

Western Front – Montgomery to command all Allied forces N. of the 'Bulge', inc. US 1st and 9th Armies; Bradley to command 3rd Army and other forces to the S. *Pzs* reach Bastogne and Houffalize.
Sea War: Pacific – Carrier *Unryu* sunk by US sub. *Redfish*.

WEDNESDAY, DECEMBER 20

Western Front – *Pzs* reach Noville, N. of Bastogne and Stavelot, N. of St. Vith.

THURSDAY, DECEMBER 21

Western Front – BASTOGNE BESIEGED. US 101st Abn. Div. and 10th Armd. Div. have to be supplied by air.
Sea War – German convoy runs into minefield laid off Norway by FF submarine

Rubis bringing her total no. of sinkings to 23.
Neutrals: Switzerland – Death of Abbas Hilmi Pasha, last *Khedive* (Turkish Viceroy) of Egypt, 1892-1914; aged 70.

FRIDAY, DECEMBER 22

Western Front – Germans make final effort to reach the Meuse and break through to Antwerp. Gen. McAuliffe, cdr. US 101st abn. div. at Bastogne, replies 'NUTS!' to German surrender ultimatum.
Occupied Hungary – Provisional Hungarian Govt. established in Soviet-held territory.
Home Front: USA – Death of Harry Langdon, silent movie star; aged 60.

SATURDAY, DECEMBER 23

Air War: Europe – Allied TAFs fly 900 sorties against German armour and MT in the 'Bulge'. 26 V-2s explode in Antwerp.
Home Front: USA – All horse-racing banned to save labour.

SUNDAY, DECEMBER 24

Russian Front – RUSSIAN TANKS ENTER BUDAPEST.
Air War: Europe – Allied TAFs fly 600 sorties over the Ardennes; 260 planes drop supplies on Bastogne.
Air War: Britain – 50 He 111s, modified to carry and launch V-1s in flight, attack

Manchester area; 1 missile on target, 17 fall near; 37 killed, 67 injured. Steps immediately taken to strengthen AA defences, but there are no more attacks.
Sea War – Transport *Leopoldville* sunk by *U-486* (819 drowned) in English Channel.
Home Front: Britain – Maj. Glenn Miller, director of USAAF band, reported missing over Channel in light plane (took off Dec. 15); aged 35.

MONDAY, DECEMBER 25

Western Front – *Pzs* halted by US armour at Celles, 6 km E. of the Meuse, having advanced 80 km since mid-Dec.
Philippines – Americans secure Leyte I.
Occupied Greece – Churchill and Eden fly to Athens to mediate in civil war.

TUESDAY, DECEMBER 26

Western Front – 3rd Army tanks (4th Armd. Div.) break through to Bastogne and relieve the garrison.
Air War: Europe – RAF Bomber Cmnd. makes devastating daylight attack on German MT and troop concentrations at St Vith.

WEDNESDAY, DECEMBER 27

Russian Front – SIEGE OF BUDAPEST begins.
Western Front – 3rd Army establishes 'safe' corridor to Bastogne.
Air War: Europe – 8th AF bombs rail targets at Coblenz, Bonn and Kaiserslautern. RAF night raids on München-Gladbach and Bonn.

THURSDAY, DECEMBER 28

Western Front – Eisenhower meets with Montgomery at Hasselt (Belgium) to concert Ardennes counter-offensive.

FRIDAY, DECEMBER 29

Air War: Europe – Lancasters and Halifaxes drop pattern of 12,000-lb bombs on E-boat pens at Rotterdam.

SATURDAY, DECEMBER 30

Western Front – Fierce fighting in Houffalize-Bastogne sector.
Occupied Greece – Archbishop Damaskinos appointed Regent.

SUNDAY, DECEMBER 31

Air War: Europe – RAF attacks Solingen marshalling yards.

Shipping Losses 1944
Allied and Neutral: 205 ships totalling 1,062,411 t. Axis: 239 U-boats, 54 Japanese subs.

1945

MONDAY, JANUARY 1

Western Front – German offensive (Op. *Nordwind*) towards Strasbourg, halted 21 km away, Jan. 12.
Air War: Europe – 800 German fighters carry out massed low-level raids on Allied airfields in Belgium and Holland (Op. *Bodenplatte/Hermann*): British 2nd TAF loses 144 planes and US 9th TAF 75 planes. Many inexperienced German pilots crash (188 fighters lost). 4 Mosquito sqns. toss 4,000-lb DA bombs into railway tunnels E. of the Ardennes. Mosquitoes of 'Light Night Striking Force' carry out first of 67 raids on Berlin during Jan.-April 1945: only 14 planes lost; 1,459 4,000-lb bombs on target.

TUESDAY, JANUARY 2

Air War: Europe – 1,000 US bombers hammer troop concentrations and communications in W. Germany. 1,000 RAF bombers attack Nuremburg and Ludwigshafen.
Home Front: Britain – Adm. Sir Bertram Ramsay, Naval CinC AEF and organizer of Dunkirk Evacuation, killed in air crash.

WEDNESDAY, JANUARY 3

Burma – Allied forces land on Akyab I.
Sea War – British sub. *Shakespeare* depth-charged by Japanese patrol boats.

THURSDAY, JANUARY 4

Air War: Pacific – Americans bomb Clark Field, Manila.

FRIDAY, JANUARY 5

Air War: Europe – 8th AF despatches

1,000 planes with 500 escorts to bomb and strafe rail targets across W. Germany.

SATURDAY, JANUARY 6

Diplomacy – Churchill informs Stalin that position on W. Front is very grave and asks: *'Can we count on a major Russian offensive on the Vistula front . . .?'*
Air War: Pacific – *Kamikaze* planes damage battleships USS *California*, *New Mexico* and 14 other warships; minesweeper sunk (608 casualties).
Sea War: Indian Ocean – 6 remaining U-boats begin returning home.

SUNDAY, JANUARY 7

Diplomacy – Stalin informs Churchill that, although bad weather is forecast, which will deprive Red Army of air cover, preparations for a great offensive are to be completed *'at a forced pace . . . disregarding the weather'* in the interests of *'our allies on the Western Front'*.
Sea War – German Navy begins regular convoy ops. between G. of Danzig/W. Baltic and trapped Army Grp. Courland in Latvia: 8 divs. evacuated by late March.

MONDAY, JANUARY 8

Western Front – Allied forces eliminate German position on W. bank of the Maas.

TUESDAY, JANUARY 9

Sea War: Pacific – **AMERICANS LAND IN LINGAYEN GULF** 172 km from Manila (Op. Mike I). 70 Japanese *Shinyo* suicide boats attack invasion fleet (night Jan. 9-10).
Sea War: Irish Sea – *U-1055* sinks 4 ships.

WEDNESDAY, JANUARY 10

Western Front – Bure and Samree (Ardennes) captured by Allied forces.

Below: *A US M5 Stuart light tank passes a ditched M10 tank destroyer on the N. side of the 'Bulge'.*

THURSDAY, JANUARY 11

Sea War – British sqn. inflicts heavy damage on convoy off S. Norway.
Sea War: Pacific – Op. *Kongo*: 6 Japanese submarines launch *Kaiten* torpedoes against Allied naval bases in Central Pacific (1 LC sunk, munition ship damaged).

FRIDAY, JANUARY 12

Russian Front – **LAST SOVIET WINTER OFFENSIVE:** 1st UF (Konev) launches offensive from Sandomierz bridgehead on W. bank of R. Vistula.

SATURDAY, JANUARY 13

Russian Front – Konev advances 40 km on a 64-km front.

SUNDAY, JANUARY 14

Russian Front – 1st BRF (Zhukov) attacks from 3 bridgeheads N. and S. of Warsaw. Zhukov and Konev have total of 163 divs. with 32,143 guns, 6,460 tanks and SP guns and 4,772 aircraft. Germans are outnumbered 5 to 1 and their 1,100 tanks are virtually immobilized by fuel shortages.
Air War: Europe – 8th AF resumes large-scale strategic ops. after a month-long interval, caused by 'Battle of the Bulge': 600 B-17s and B-24s attack oil targets in Germany, meeting heavy fighter opposition.
Sea War – 6 German MTB flotillas operate in estuaries of the Scheldt, Thames and Humber (night Jan. 14-15).

MONDAY, JANUARY 15

Sea War – Escort carrier *Thane* torpedoed by *U-482* off the Clyde.
Neutrals: Spain – Italian naval sqn. interned in Port Mahon (Minorca) since Sept. 8, 1943, leaves for Malta.

TUESDAY, JANUARY 16

Western Front – US 1st and 3rd Armies link up at Houffalize in the Ardennes.

Battle of the Bulge Losses
German: 120,000 dead, wounded and PoWs; 600 tanks. US: 8,607 dead, 47,139 wounded, 21,144 missing; 733 tanks. British: 1,400 casualties.

Sea War: Indian Ocean – Op. Meridian: British Pacific Fleet (TF 63) leaves Ceylon for the Pacific.

WEDNESDAY, JANUARY 17

Russian Front – **ZHUKOV CAPTURES WARSAW.**

THURSDAY, JANUARY 18

Russian Front – 2nd BRF (Rokossovsky) captures Modlin.

FRIDAY, JANUARY 19

Russian Front – Konev takes Cracow.
Air War: Europe – Soviet AF flies 30,000 sorties against communications and airfields.
Air War: Pacific – B-29s destroy Kawasaki aircraft factory near Kobe.
Secret War – Ultra reads Dönitz's orders for 5% Navy manpower cut to release men for Army.

SATURDAY, JANUARY 20

Russian Front – 3rd BRF (Cherniakhovsky) captures Tilsit, E. Prussia.
Diplomacy – Armistice between Provisional National Govt. of Hungary and the Allies: war declared on Germany and $300 M. to be paid in reparations.

SUNDAY, JANUARY 21

Russian Front – Rokossovsky captures Tannenberg.

MONDAY, JANUARY 22

Sea War – German MTBs attack convoy N. of Dunkirk; 8th MTB Flotilla penetrates into Thames Estuary.

TUESDAY, JANUARY 23

Russian Front – Konev's forces reach R. Oder on 64-km front. Zhukov captures Bromberg. Himmler takes personal cmnd. of 'Army Grp. Vistula'.
Home Front: France – Charles Maurras, editor of Royalist and anti-Semitic *Action Française*, on trial at Lyons for collaboration (life imprisonment, Jan. 27).
Home Front: Germany – Execution of Count Helmuth von Moltke-Kreisau, leader of 'Kreisau Circle' (pacifist organization).

WEDNESDAY, JANUARY 24

Sea War – British Pacific Fleet carriers attack Pladjoe and Soengi-Gerong oil refineries at Palembang, Sumatra (Jan. 24 and 29): Pladjoe plant severely damaged and 132 Japanese aircraft destroyed. British lose 48.

THURSDAY, JANUARY 25

Sea War: Baltic – **GREATEST EVACUATION IN HISTORY** 1,500,000-2,000,000 German troops and civilians rescued by May 8 from Prussia, Pomerania and Courland in operations involving surface warships and 36 merchantmen.

FRIDAY, JANUARY 26

Russian Front – Rokossovsky breaks through to G. of Danzig, virtually isolating German forces in E. Prussia.
Western Front – Lt. Audie Murphy, most decorated US soldier of W.W.II, single-handedly repels repeated *Pz* and inf. attacks on his position, near Colmar; awarded Medal of Honor.
China – Imperial GHQ orders Japanese forces to withdraw to the coast.

Above: *A Japanese train in Burma under attack by RAF Beaufighters.*

Air War: Europe – Op. Thunderclap: British COAS decides that RAF Bomber Cmnd. should launch *'one big attack on Berlin and Dresden . . . where a severe blitz will not only cause confusion in the evacuation from the East but will also hamper the movement of troops . . .'*

SATURDAY, JANUARY 27

Russian Front – Zhukov's forces now only 161 km from Berlin; Memel falls.
Sea War: Atlantic – 5 ships sunk by *U-1232* off Halifax during Jan.

SUNDAY, JANUARY 28

Western Front – US 1st Army attacks E. of St Vith.
Air War: Europe – 1,000 bombers of 8th AF attack Ruhr oil plants and bridges over the Rhine.
China – First supply convoy reaches China via Ledo Rd.

MONDAY, JANUARY 29

Russian Front – Zhukov encircles large German garrison in Poznan.

Sea War – *Prinz Eugen* and destroyers bombard advancing Russian forces on E. Prussian coast.

TUESDAY, JANUARY 30

Western Front – Allied forces capture Gambsheim, German bridgehead over the Rhine, N. of Strasbourg
Home Front: Germany – Hitler's last broadcast: *'German workers, work! German soldiers, fight! German women, be as fanatical as ever! No nation can do more.'*
Sea War: Baltic – **WORST SEA DISASTER IN HISTORY.** 7,000 refugees drown when Russian submarine *S-13* sinks liner *Wilhelm Gustloff.*

WEDNESDAY, JANUARY 31

Russian Front – Zhukov's forces invade prov. of Brandenburg.
Western Front – Elements of US 1st Army cross German border E. of St Vith.
Air War – B-29s sink giant floating dock at Singapore.
Home Front: USA – 16 war workers' children killed by fire in nursery at Auburn, Maine.
Home Front: Germany – Gollob (150 victories) succeeds Galland as *Gen. der Jagdflieger.*

THURSDAY, FEBRUARY 1

Russian Front – Rokossovsky captures Torun after 6-day siege.
Western Front – US 7th Army crosses R. Moder in Alsace.

FRIDAY, FEBRUARY 2

Western Front – French and Americans enter Colmar (Alsace).

SATURDAY, FEBRUARY 3

Philippines – US 1st Cavalry Div. reaches outskirts of Manila.
Air War: Europe – 1,000 B-17s, escorted by 900 fighters (24 planes lost), **RAID BERLIN** setting fire to 5 sq km in central districts; Tempelhof marshalling yards and Airport seriously damaged; 1,000 killed, inc. Judge Roland Freisler, fanatical head of 'People's Court'.

SUNDAY, FEBRUARY 4

Diplomacy – **YALTA CONFERENCE** ('Magneto'): Churchill, Roosevelt and Stalin meet in Crimea. Latter succeeds in winning big concessions from ailing US Pres., inc. free hand in E. Europe; territorial gains in Far East, in return for declaration of war on Japan within 2 months of defeat of Germany; Germany to pay reparations in kind; Germany to be divided into 4 zones of occupation; Polish and Yugoslav Govts. to encompass all shades of opinion (ends Feb. 11).

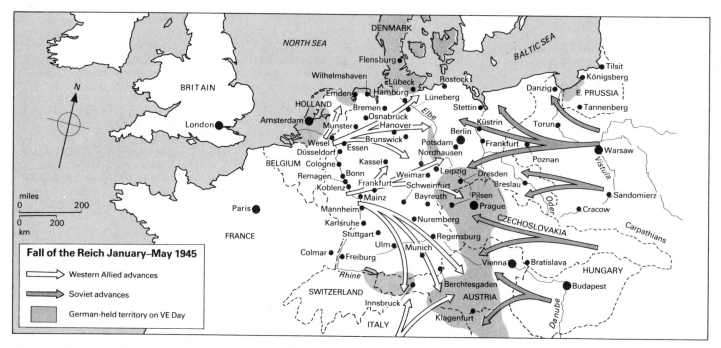

Fall of the Reich January–May 1945

→ Western Allied advances

→ Soviet advances

▓ German-held territory on VE Day

Western Front – Liberation of Belgium completed: Americans expel last remnants of German forces.
Russian Front – KONEV'S TANKS BEGIN CROSSING R. ODER, near Breslau.

MONDAY, FEBRUARY 5

Western Front – Colmar Pocket cut in two as US and French troops link up.
Air War: Europe – Death of Capt. Marcel Doret, leader of FF *Groupe de Chasse* 'Doret' and former test pilot; aged 48.

TUESDAY, FEBRUARY 6

Russian Front – Konev crosses the Oder and lays siege to Breslau: hundreds of thousands of panic-stricken German civilians flee westwards, many into 'safe' city of Dresden.

WEDNESDAY, FEBRUARY 7

Air War: Europe – RAF night attack on German forces at Kleve and Goch.

THURSDAY, FEBRUARY 8

Western Front – Canadians advance into Reichswald SE. of Nijmegen, between Maas and Rhine (Op. Veritable).

FRIDAY, FEBRUARY 9

Western Front – BRITISH AND CANADIANS REACH THE RHINE in strength. US 3rd Army crosses R. Prum.
Russian Front – Königsberg now virtually encircled by 2nd and 3rd BRFs.
Air War: Europe – Halifaxes bomb Wanne-Eickel oil plant (Ruhr); B-17s attack Lützkendorf plant.
Diplomacy – Ecuador and Paraguay declare war on Germany and Japan.

SATURDAY, FEBRUARY 10

Russian Front – Rokossovsky captures Elbing and Preussisch-Eylau.
Western Front – Germans open flood gates of Schwammenauel Dam on R. Roer, in attempt to halt advancing US forces.

SUNDAY, FEBRUARY 11

Western Front – British enter Kleve.
Home Front: Germany – Entire gold reserves (c. 100 t.) transported from Berlin to salt mine near Eisenach. Americans capture Merkers, April 4.

MONDAY, FEBRUARY 12

Diplomacy – Peru declares war on Germany and Japan.

TUESDAY, FEBRUARY 13

Western Front – British secure the Reichswald.
Russian Front – SIEGE OF BUDAPEST ENDS after 6 weeks of savage house-to-house fighting.
Air War: Europe – DESTRUCTION OF DRESDEN. 773 Lancasters (5 lost) and 311 B-17s deliver 'triple blow' against this virtually undefended city near Russian Front, dropping 3,370 t. bombs, inc. c. 700,000 IBs. 'Fire storm' rages over 6.5 sq km killing between 135,000 and 250,000 civilians, refugees and Allied prisoners; city burns for 7 days and 8 nights (68,650 corpses burnt on vast communal pyres).
Sea War: Pacific – 3 Japanese subs. sunk by US sub. *Batfish* over 4-day period (Feb. 10-13).

WEDNESDAY, FEBRUARY 14

Russian Front – Zhukov captures Schneidemuhl.

Western Front – Canadians repel 4 counter-attacks in Reichswald sector.
Air War: Europe – 8th AF completes Allied 'triple blow' against Dresden; also bombs Chemnitz, Magdeburg, Prague (in error) and Wesel Bridge over R. Rhine. Total no. of bombers and escorts 1,440 (13 lost). Severe RAF night raid on Chemnitz.
Diplomacy – Chile declares war on Germany and Japan.

THURSDAY, FEBRUARY 15

Western Front – Canadians now hold 16-km front along W. bank of the Rhine.
Air War: Europe – Dresden, Magdeburg and Cottbus attacked by 1,000 bombers of 8th AF.

Below: *The centre of Dresden as it still looked from the town hall in 1949, four years after the bombing.*

FRIDAY, FEBRUARY 16

Sea War: Pacific – 1,000 US carrier planes of TF 58 raid Tokyo and Yokohama (repeated Feb. 17).
Air War: Pacific – US PARATROOPS TAKE CORREGIDOR.
Diplomacy – Venezuela declares war on Germany and Japan.

SATURDAY, FEBRUARY 17

Home Front: Britain – World Trades Union Conference in London.

SUNDAY, FEBRUARY 18

Russian Front – Gen. Ivan D. Chernyakhovsky, cdr. of 3rd BRF, fatally wounded near Königsberg; aged 40. Marshal Vassilevsky takes cmnd. of 3rd BRF.
Western Front – US 3rd Army breaks through Siegfried Line, NW. of Echternach (Ardennes).

MONDAY, FEBRUARY 19

Sea War: Pacific – AMERICANS LAND ON IWO JIMA (Op. Detachment): 4th and 5th Marine Divs. employed. Sgt. John Basilone, first enlisted US marine to receive Medal of Honor (1943), killed on Iwo; aged 26.
Russian Front – German garrison of Königsberg launches desperate counter-attack.
Western Front – Scottish troops of Canadian 1st Army enter Goch.

TUESDAY, FEBRUARY 20

Air War: Europe – 900 B-17s blast passenger station and marshalling yards at Nuremburg. 700 escorts (23 lost) strafe locomotives, rolling stock and parked aircraft.

WEDNESDAY, FEBRUARY 21

Western Front – US 3rd Army attacks Saar-Moselle 'triangle'.
Sea War: Pacific – Escort carrier *Bismarck Sea* sunk by *Kamikaze* planes off Iwo Jima.

THURSDAY, FEBRUARY 22

Air War: Europe – OP. CLARION. 9,000 Allied bombers and fighters from bases in England, France, Belgium, Holland and Italy attack rail and road targets over 647,497 sq km of the *Reich*. 8th AF alone attacks 30 targets, inc. Lüneberg, Halberstadt, Ludwigslust and Göttingen.
Home Front: Germany – Fugitive Vichy leader Jacques Doriot, killed in air raid; aged 56.
Diplomacy – Turkey declares war on Germany and Japan. Uruguay declares war on Germany and Japan.

FRIDAY, FEBRUARY 23

Iwo Jima – Marines take Mt. Suribachi. Hoisting of US flag captured in classic photograph by Joe Rosenthal.
Russian Front – Siege of Poznan ends: Zhukov takes 23,000 prisoners.
Western Front – US 1st and 9th armies attack across R. Roer (Op. Lumberjack).
Air War: Europe – Pforzheim (Rhineland) devastated by 369 RAF bombers (12 lost, inc. the 'Master Bomber's' plane).
Sea War: Arctic – SS *Henry Bacon* sunk by Ju 88 torpedo planes – last Allied ship sunk by German aircraft in W.W.II.

SATURDAY, FEBRUARY 24

Philippines – Americans crush desperate Japanese resistance in the Intramuros – old walled quarter of Manila.
Air War: Europe – Col. Ivan Kojedub, top-scoring Russian (and Allied) fighter 'ace' (62 victories), shoots down Me 262 over Berlin.

SUNDAY, FEBRUARY 25

Western Front – 1st and 9th Armies break German defences W. of Cologne, capturing Düren and Jülich.

MONDAY, FEBRUARY 26

Air War: Europe – 8th AF carries out 3,000 t. raid on Berlin; ½ M. incendiaries dropped. Main targets: 3 railway stations (15 bombers and 7 escorts lost). RAF Mosquitoes bomb Berlin by night, guided by fires started by Americans.
Diplomacy – Egypt and Syria declare war on Germany and Japan.

TUESDAY, FEBRUARY 27

Russian Front – Rokossovsky drives into Pomerania.
Diplomacy – Lebanon declares war on Germany and Japan.

WEDNESDAY, FEBRUARY 28

Western Front – US 1st Army crosses R. Erth, 10 km from Cologne.
Diplomacy – Iran declares war on Japan. Saudi Arabia declares war on Germany and Japan.
Sea War: Pacific – Americans land on Palawan (Philippines).

THURSDAY, MARCH 1

Western Front – München-Gladbach captured by US 9th Army.

FRIDAY, MARCH 2

Western Front – 9th Army takes Krefeld, Venlo and Roermond.
Air War: Europe – 2 RAF daylight raids on Cologne.

SATURDAY, MARCH 3

Western Front – Canadians and Americans link up between Maas and Rhine.
Philippines – Japanese resistance in Manila ends.
Air War: Britain – 100 German night intruders attack more than 20 airfields from Northumberland to Oxon. 20 RAF bombers destroyed for loss of 6 intruders.
Diplomacy – Act of Chapultepec: 20 American states, meeting in Mexico City, pledge themselves to protect each other's territorial and political integrity.

SUNDAY, MARCH 4

Western Front – US tanks (1st Army) reach the Rhine N. of Cologne.
Burma – British 14th Army captures Meiktila, S. of Mandalay.
Air War: Pacific – First damaged B-29 uses landing field on Iwo Jima.
Diplomacy – Finland declares war on Germany (unofficial state of hostilities having existed since Sept. 1944).

MONDAY, MARCH 5

Western Front – Americans enter suburbs of Cologne.
Air War: Europe – RAF daylight raid on Gelsenkirchen oil plant.

TUESDAY, MARCH 6

Russian Front – Rokossovsky captures encircled fortress of Grudziadz. Op. *Frühlingserwachen* ('Spring Awakening'): 6th SS *Pz* Army attacks N. of L. Balaton in attempt to recapture Budapest and gains 32 km by March 8.
Western Front – Cologne taken by US 1st Army.

WEDNESDAY, MARCH 7

Western Front – LUDENDORFF BRIDGE CAPTURED INTACT. Bridge at Remagen over the Rhine near Bonn captured intact by US 1st Army, which immediately pours across.
Burma – Chinese capture Lashio on 'Burma Road'.
Occupied Yugoslavia – Tito forms provisional Govt.

THURSDAY, MARCH 8

Western Front – British 2nd Army captures Xanten: Allied armies now stand along the Rhine from Nijmegen to Koblenz.
Burma – Indian tanks enter Mandalay.
Air War: Britain – V-2 kills 110 and seriously injures 123 at Farringdon Market, London.
Sea War – Granville Harbour (Normandy) raided by German assault troops from Channel Is. who sink 4 coasters and free 67 prisoners (night March 8-9).

FRIDAY, MARCH 9

Air War: Pacific – 'MARCH FIRE BLITZ' ON TOKYO. 279 low-flying Superfortresses drop 1,667 t. napalm and oil bombs on Tokyo (night March 9-10); 'fire-storm' devastates 26 sq km of built-up area, killing 84,000; 102,000 injured, a million rendered homeless. Similar raids on Nagoya, Osaka, and Kobe. Inadequate Japanese defences and ARP services are unable to cope.
Occupied Indo-China – Japanese depose Vichyite administration, forcibly disarm French garrisons, and establish puppet 'Empire of Annam'.
Western Front – Patton and Hodges (1st and 9th Armies) join forces near Remagen.

SATURDAY, MARCH 10

Western Front – Canadians eliminate the Wesel Pocket opposite Xanten. Kesselring takes over command from von Rundstedt, sacked on March 7, and jokes to his staff *'I am the new V-3.'*
Diplomacy – Roosevelt informs Spain she can expect no US aid while Franco dictatorship continues.

SUNDAY, MARCH 11

Air War: Europe – RAF drops 4,700 t. bombs on rail targets at Essen; all production stops at Krupp's Works. 1,000 US bombers attack U-boat yards in NW. Germany.
Air War: Pacific – Op. *Tan*: 24 *Ginga* fast 2-engined bombers carry out night *Kamikaze* raid on Ulithi Atoll; carrier *Randolph* hit.
Home Front: Britain – 70 Germans stage mass escape from PoW camp at Bridgend, Glamorgan (S. Wales); all recaptured by March 17.
Secret War – Ultra gives warning of jet attacks on the Remagen Bridge.

MONDAY, MARCH 12

Russian Front – Zhukov takes Küstrin on the Oder. Rokossovsky captures Tczew and reaches G. of Danzig, S. of Gdynia.
Air War: Europe – RAF drops 4,851 t. bombs on rail targets at Dortmund.

TUESDAY, MARCH 13

Burma – British capture Maymyo, cutting rail communications of Japanese garrison in Mandalay.

WEDNESDAY, MARCH 14

Russian Front – Russians capture Zvolen, in Carpathians, N. of Budapest.
Air War: Europe – Bielefeld Viaduct smashed by 22,000-lb bomb ('Grand Slam'), thereby preventing movement from the Ruhr to Remagen.

THURSDAY, MARCH 15

Air War: Europe – *Wehrmacht* GHQ at Zossen, S. of Berlin, pounded by 8th AF.
Burma – Japanese counter-attack at Meiktila (they retreat March 28).

FRIDAY, MARCH 16

Air War: Europe – Heavy RAF raids on Nuremburg and Wurzburg. Clear skies assist night fighters; 30 bombers lost.
Russian Front – Tolbukhin's 3rd UF launches major counter-attack against 6th *SS Pz* Army and 3rd Hungarian Army (latter collapses).

SATURDAY, MARCH 17

Western Front – Ludendorff Bridge collapses following repeated raids by Ar 234 jet bombers; many US engineers killed. 3rd Army enters Koblenz.

SUNDAY, MARCH 18

Air War: Europe – 1,300 US bombers (25 lost) and 700 escorts (5 lost) drop 3,000 t. bombs on Berlin despite heavy flak and numerous jet fighters. Typhoons of RAF 2nd TAF attack HQs of Gens. Blaskowitz and Christiansen in Holland with bombs and rockets.
Western Front – US tanks enter Bad Kreuznach and Bingen.
Russian Front – Polish 1st Army takes Kolberg after 75,000 Germans evacuated.
Sea War: Pacific – TF 58 attacks Kure Naval Base and airfields in S. Japan: Americans land on Panay (Philippines).

MONDAY, MARCH 19

Air War: Pacific – Carriers *Wasp* and *Franklin* severely damaged by Japanese bombers (825 killed).
Sea War – U-boats withdrawn from E. Baltic.
Home Front: Germany – Hitler orders total scorched earth policy.

TUESDAY, MARCH 20

Burma – BRITISH CAPTURE MANDALAY.
Russian Front – Russians eliminate German bridgehead on lower Oder at Altdamm.
Home Front: Britain – Death of Lord Alfred Douglas, poet and much-maligned friend of Oscar Wilde; aged 75.

WEDNESDAY, MARCH 21

Western Front – Ludwigshafen captured by Americans.
Air War: Europe – Mosquitoes destroy *Gestapo* HQ in Copenhagen; bombs accidentally dropped on nearby school kill 86 pupils and 17 teachers. 8th AF attacks Me 262 bases in W. Germany.

Advance to the Rhine Losses
Allies: 20,000. German: 60,000 dead and wounded, 250,000 PoWs.

THURSDAY, MARCH 22

Western Front – US 3rd Army crosses the Rhine, W. of Mainz.
Russian Front – In Silesia, Konev's forces break through W. and S. of Oppeln.
Neutrals: Spain – Don Juan, the Pretender, demands resignation of Franco and restoration of the Monarchy.

FRIDAY, MARCH 23

Western Front – MONTGOMERY'S 21st ARMY GROUP CROSSES THE RHINE AT WESEL (Op. Plunder): attack takes place in bright moonlight under cover of dense smoke screen and shattering artillery bombardment. Montgomery issues Order of the Day: *'21st Army Grp. will now cross the Rhine. The enemy possibly thinks he is safe behind this great river obstacle . . . we will show him he is far from safe behind it.'* Monty also issues 'no fraternization' order to his troops.
Air War: Europe – RAF bombers virtually obliterate Wesel. 6,000 Allied planes participate in ops. connected with Rhine crossings.
Home Front: Britain – Death of jockey 'Steve' Donoghue, 6-times winner of the Derby; aged 61.
Sea War: Pacific – TF 58 attacks Okinawa.

SATURDAY, MARCH 24

Russian Front – Russians capture Zoppot, between Danzig and Gdynia. Tolbukhin's forces sweep forward to Szekesfehervar (Stuhlweissenburg), 58 km SW. of Budapest.
Western Front – British Commandos occupy Wesel. Montgomery's forces link up with airborne detachments.
Air War: Europe – Allied 18th Airborne Corps lands E. of Wesel.
Sea War: Pacific – TF 58 annihilates Japanese convoy S. of Kyushu.

SUNDAY, MARCH 25

Russian Front – Malinovsky breaks through W. of Budapest, crossing R. Hron and capturing Esztergom.
Western Front – Montgomery's 4 bridgeheads over the Rhine merge into 48-km -wide salient. 3rd Army captures Darmstadt.
Air War: Pacific – 5th AF Liberators destroy hydro-electric power station on Formosa. First *Kamikaze* attack on US warships near Okinawa.
Air War: Europe – 8th AF B-24s bomb underground oil stores at Hamburg.
Home Front: Japan – Imperial GHQ

initiates Op. *Tengo* for defence of Okinawa and Kyushu. V.-Adm. Ugaki commands *Kamikaze* force '5th Air Fleet'.

MONDAY, MARCH 26

Pacific – AMERICANS SECURE IWO JIMA.

Iwo Jima Campaign Losses
Japanese: 20,703 dead, 216 PoWs. US: 19,939 inc. 4,630 dead.

Western Front – Patton's tanks cross Bavarian border. British troops capture Rees, near Wesel.
Sea War: Pacific – British Pacific Fleet (TF 57) launches first of many air strikes against airfields on Sakishima Gunto Is. between Okinawa and Formosa.
Sea War: Indian Ocean – British destroyers and Liberator bombers annihilate Japanese convoy.
Home Front: Britain – Death of David Lloyd-George (Earl Lloyd-George of Dwyfor); aged 83.
Home Front: USSR – Marshal Boris M. Shaposhnikov, former personal military adviser to Stalin and Red Army's greatest strategist, dies after protracted illness; aged 62.

TUESDAY, MARCH 27

Russian Front – Russians launch final attacks on Danzig and Gdynia.
Western Front – Americans reach Limburg.
Sea War: Baltic – 3 German MTBs attack 9 Russian 'torpedo cutters' (MTBs); 3 of latter sunk.
Air War: Pacific – B-29s carry out first of series of mine-laying ops. in Japanese waters.
Air War: Europe – Lancasters drop 'Grand Slam' bombs on U-boat shelters at Vegesack (Bremen). Second formation attacks Paderborn junction, E. of Hamm.
Diplomacy – Argentina declares war on Germany and Japan.
Air War: Britain – V-2 destroys block of flats in Hughes Mansions, Stepney, killing 131 and seriously injuring 49. 9½ hours later, last V-2 to reach Britain lands at Orpington, Kent.

WEDNESDAY, MARCH 28

Russian Front – Rokossovsky captures Gdynia. Malinovsky takes Gyor (Hungary). Guderian replaced by Krebs as COS after row with Hitler.

THURSDAY, MARCH 29

Western Front – Tanks of 21st Army Grp break out of Wesel bridgehead. US 7th Army captures Mannheim and Heidelberg.
Air War: Britain – 2,419th (and last) V-1 reaches Greater London.

V-Weapon Casualties
From V-1s: 6,184 dead, 17,918 badly injured. From V-2s: 2,754 dead, 6,523 badly injured.

FRIDAY, MARCH 30

Russian Front – Danzig stormed by Rokossovksy's 2nd BRF. Tolbukhin enters Austria.

Below: *US B-25s bomb a Japanese escort off Vietnam. Two were sunk on March 29.*

Air War: Europe – 8th AF attacks Wilhelmshaven, Hamburg and Bremen, sinking cruiser *Köln*, 14 U-boats and 11 other vessels.
Western Front – Patton issues Order of the Day to US 3rd Army: claims that in 7 weeks it has occupied 14,484 sq km of Germany, taken 3,072 inhabited places, killed or wounded 99,000, taken 140,000 prisoners and eliminated 2 German armies.

SATURDAY, MARCH 31

Western Front – French start crossing the Rhine near Speyer.
Russian Front – Russians take Ratibor on Upper Oder.

SUNDAY, APRIL 1

Sea War: Pacific – US 10th ARMY LANDS ON OKINAWA (Op. Glacier); captures Kadena and Yontan airfields.
Russian Front – Russians take Sopron, SE. of Vienna. Koniev captures fortress of Glogow on the Oder.
Western Front – German Army Grp. B (21 divs.) trapped in the Ruhr Focket by link-up of Allied 1st and 9th Armies near Lippstadt.

MONDAY, APRIL 2

Western Front – Montgomery's forces capture Rheine jet fighter base and Münster.

TUESDAY, APRIL 3

Russian Front – Tolbukhin captures Wiener Neustadt.
Okinawa – US Artillery spotter planes begin operating from Kadena airfield.

WEDNESDAY, APRIL 4

Russian Front – Bratislava captured by Malinovsky.
Western Front – Allied forces at Kassel, Gotha, Karlsruhe and Aschaffenburg.

THURSDAY, APRIL 5

Western Front – Allied forces cross R. Weser. 18 US divs. begin clearance of Ruhr Pocket.
Okinawa – US forces, pushing S., encounter first line of Japanese defences.
Home Front: Japan – Koiso Cabinet falls; Adm. Suzuki forms new administration.
Diplomacy – Russo-Japanese Non-Aggression Pact denounced by USSR a year in advance of agreed expiry date.
Sea War: Pacific – Op. *Tengo*: last operational Japanese battleship – *Yamato* – is to be sacrificed in suicidal attempt to reach Okinawa, where she will be deliberately run aground.

FRIDAY, APRIL 6

Sea War: Pacific – Op. *Kikusui* ('Floating Chrysanthemum'): first of 10 massed *Kamikaze* attacks on US invasion fleet off Okinawa (April 6-7 to June 21-22).
Russian Front – Russians enter suburbs of Vienna and launch final assault on Königsberg.
Western Front – Americans enter Hamm.
Occupied Yugoslavia – Sarajevo liberated.

SATURDAY, APRIL 7

Sea War: Pacific – BATTLE OF EAST CHINA SEA. *Yamato* (2,498 killed), cruiser *Yahagi* and 4 destroyers sunk by TF 58 (10 planes lost).
Air War: Pacific – 107 Iwo-based Mustangs escort B-29s to Tokyo.
Air War: Europe – First Mosquito raid on Berlin from continental base. French paratroops dropped N. of Zuider Zee. US bombers make wide-ranging attacks on German airfields and railways.

SUNDAY, APRIL 8

Russian Front – Col-Gen. Schörner becomes the last *Wehrmacht* field marshal.
Western Front – Americans enter Schweinfurt; French capture Pforzheim.
Air War – RAF Bomber Command sinks 6 U-boats in Hamburg.
Occupied Denmark – Danish Resistance grp. steals 21 boats and escapes to Sweden.

MONDAY, APRIL 9

Russian Front – FALL OF KÖNIGSBERG after 59-day siege. Tolbukhin's troops smash their way into centre of Vienna.
Western Front – Americans occupy Krupp's Works at Essen.

TRUMAN, Harry Shippe (1884-1972)
American: *President*

Often described as a 'mild-mannered, self-effacing little man', Truman was faced with the greatest strategic and moral decision of the war – whether to drop the atomic bomb on Japan – only 3½ months after his sudden elevation from comparative obscurity to the world's most powerful presidency. His calm, rational judgement in this, as in many later crisis, confounded his many critics and assured Truman of an honoured place among America's greatest war leaders.

Born at Lamar, near Kansas City, Missouri. Worked in and around Kansas City and on family farm at Independence, Missouri, 1901-16. Joined National Guard, 1905; made First Lt. by 1917. Served in France, April-Nov. 1918 in battles of St Mihiel and Meuse-Argonne. Ran clothing store in Kansas City, 1919-22, but went bankrupt. Spent nearly 15 years paying off debts – necessitating frugal life style.

Elected Senator 1934, under auspices of Tom Prendergast, an unscrupulous Democratic 'boss'; Truman came under suspicion but emerged without stain. Head of committee of Senators entrusted with task of investigating expenditure of public money on national defence programme.

Elected Vice-Pres., Nov. 1944. Automatically became President on sudden death of Roosevelt, April 12, 1945. Met Churchill and Stalin at Potsdam (Berlin), July 1945. Ordered dropping of atomic bombs on Japanese cities after Japanese rejection of 'Potsdam Declaration'. Described his appalling dilemma in 'Year of Decisions' (1955). Defeated Governor Dewey in 1948 presidential election; 'one of the greatest political surprises in US history'. Survived assassination attempt by Puerto Rican gunmen, Nov. 1950. Retired from presidency, 1952. Died Dec. 26, 1972.

Italy – 8th Army crosses R. Senio, W. of L. Comacchio, under massive air cover.
Home Front: Germany – Pastor Dietrich Bonhoeffer, Adm. Canaris, former chief of the Abwehr, and Maj.-Gen. Oster hanged at Flossenburg Concentration Camp.
Home Front: Italy – Liberty ship loaded with aircraft bombs blows up in Bari harbour: 360 killed, 1,730 injured.
Air War: Europe – RAF night raid on Kiel: *Admiral Scheer* capsizes; *Admiral Hipper* badly damaged. 8th AF attacks jet fighter bases in Munich and Berlin areas (April 9 and 10): 367 German fighters destroyed on the ground.

TUESDAY, APRIL 10

Western Front – Americans capture Hanover.
Okinawa – After massive preparatory barrage, US 96th Div. seizes part of Kakazu Ridge.
Air War – Last enemy sortie over Britain: by *Luftwaffe* Ar 234 recce jet.

WEDNESDAY, APRIL 11

Russian Front – Russians cross Danube Canal in Vienna.
Western Front – US 9th Army reaches R. Elbe, near Magdeburg. Canadians cross R. Ijssel.
Italy – Op. Impact: British 6th Armd. Brig. crosses L. Comacchio (second attack, April 13).
Sea War: Pacific – British Pac. Fleet attacks airfields in N. Formosa.
Secret War – *Mittelwerke* underground V-2 factory at Nordhausen captured by US 3rd Army.

THURSDAY, APRIL 12

Western Front – US 9th Army crosses R. Elbe, SE. of Magdeburg. 3rd Army takes Weimar.
Okinawa – Japanese counter-attack near Kakazu Ridge.
Home Front: USA – DEATH OF PRESIDENT ROOSEVELT at Warm Springs, Georgia; aged 63. Vice-Pres. Truman takes oath of office. Goebbels comments 'This is the turning point'.
Diplomacy – Spain breaks off diplomatic relations with Japan.
Sea War: Pacific – US destroyer *Mannert L. Abele* destroyed by *Baka* rocket-propelled piloted missile, near Okinawa.

FRIDAY, APRIL 13

Western Front – Patton captures Jena.
Air War: Pacific – 327 Superfortresses destroy arms manufacturing district of Tokyo with 2,139 t. IBs (night April 13-14).
Russian Front – VIENNA CAPTURED by Tolbukhin's 3rd UF.
Italy – NZ troops capture Massa Lombarda, SW. of L. Comacchio.
Diplomacy – Chile declares war on Japan.

SATURDAY, APRIL 14

Western Front – ARNHEM CAPTURED BY BRITISH FORCES. Germans offer fierce resistance and demolish bridge before retreating. Patton captures Bayreuth.
Okinawa – Americans attack strong Japanese defences in hilly Motobu Pen. (N. Okinawa).
Sea War: Atlantic – Op. Teardrop: 2

carrier TGs carry out urgent search for *Seewolf* U-boat grp. suspected of transporting V-2 rockets to be launched against New York.
Home Front: Germany – Himmler orders that no prisoners at Dachau *'shall be allowed to fall into the hands of the enemy alive'.*

SUNDAY, APRIL 15

Western Front – US 1st Army captures Leuna. 2nd Armd. Div. (9th Army) forced to withdraw from bridgehead over R. Elbe near Magdeburg, after destruction of pontoon bridge. Colditz liberated.
Air War: Pacific – Fast Ki-84 fighters strafe US air bases on Okinawa. 303 Superfortresses drop 1,930 t. IBs on Tokyo Bay conurbation (night April 15-16).
Occupied France – Op. *Vénérable*: after heavy napalm bomb attacks by 8th AF and shelling by battleship *Lorraine*, French and US forces attack Royan 'Pocket' (Gironde); all resistance ends, April 20.

MONDAY, APRIL 16

Russian Front – ZHUKOV OPENS OFFENSIVE ON BERLIN.
Western Front – Canadians take Gröningen; Americans enter Nuremburg.
Okinawa – Americans land on Ie Shima I.
Air War: Europe – Lancasters cripple *Lützow* at Swinemunde.
Sea War: Baltic – 6,220 refugees drown when German transport *Goya* is sunk by Soviet sub. *L-3* (night April 16-17).

TUESDAY, APRIL 17

Air War: Europe – Mosquitoes bomb *Gestapo* HQ at Odense, Denmark.
Air War: Pacific – B-29s carry out first of series of raids on 17 *Kamikaze* bases in S. Japan (April 17-May 11).
Okinawa – Americans capture Yae-Taki Hills in Motobu Pen.
Sea War: Pacific – Americans land at Illana Bay, Mindanao (Philippines).

WEDNESDAY, APRIL 18

Western Front – 370,000-strong Army Grp. B. surrenders in Ruhr 'Pocket'; F.M. Model commits suicide. Royal Engineers begin constructing Bailey Bridge over the Rhine, near Rees. Canadians reach Zuider Zee. Patton crosses Czech border.
Air War: Europe – RAF drop 5,000 t. bombs on Heligoland. *Oberst* Steinhoff (176 victories) suffers hideous burns when his Me 262 crashes near Munich; he recovers to become CinC of post-war W. German *Luftwaffe*.
Okinawa – Ernie Pyle, Pulitzer Prize-winning war correspondent, killed on Ie Shima; aged 45.
Italy – 8th Army capture Argenta, key to the 'Argenta Gap'.

THURSDAY, APRIL 19

Russian Front – Russians secure bridge-head across R. Neisse and push towards Dresden.
Western Front – US 1st Army captures Leipzig. 7th Army troops break through medieval walls of Nuremburg and eliminate fanatical *SS* garrison.
Okinawa – 24th Corps, 10th Army, launches general assault on outer defences of 'Shuri Line', in the S., after preparatory bombardment by 139 planes, 18 warships and 324 artillery pieces. Bombardment has little effect on elaborate underground defences; 96th Div. makes limited progress in the centre.
Sea War: Med. – Carrier *Aquila* sunk by Italian human torpedoes at Genoa.

FRIDAY, APRIL 20

Western Front – 'Stars and Stripes' raised over rostrum of Nuremburg Stadium – scene of Nazi Party rallies. Lattre de Tassigny's French 1st Army execute rapid advance along Neckar Valley, trapping German forces in Black Forest.

SATURDAY, APRIL 21

Russian Front – BATTLE OF BERLIN. ZHUKOV'S TROOPS ENTER SUBURBS. Konev attacks N. of Dresden.
Western Front – French occupy Stuttgart.
Italy – ALLIES CAPTURE BOLOGNA. Gen. Mark Clark issues Order of the Day: *['We] now stand inside the gateway to the Po Plain, poised to destroy the Germans who continue to enslave and exploit Northern Italy'.*
Okinawa – Americans secure Ie Shima after 6-day battle. Casualties: 4,706

Japanese; 1,100 Americans.
Diplomacy – USSR and Polish 'Lublin' Govt. (Communist) sign 20-year mutual assistance pact.

SUNDAY, APRIL 22

Russian Front – Battle of Berlin: Russians capture Weissensee district. Hitler decides to remain in Berlin.
Italy – 5th Army reaches R. Po at Ostiglia.
Western Front – US 7th Army captures bridge over Danube at Dillingen. Patton drives towards Regensburg.
Okinawa – TF Bradford (Brig.-Gen. Bradford) formed to eliminate strong Japanese force on Kakasu Ridge.
Diplomacy – Himmler meets Bernadotte of Swedish Red Cross and requests him to initiate armistice negotiations with Britain and USA (offer rejected April 27).

MONDAY, APRIL 23

Russian Front – Frankfurt-on-Oder captured by Zhukov.
Occupied Czechoslovakia – Govt.-in-Exile calls for final national uprising.
Home Front: Britain – Black-out restrictions cancelled.
Italy – 8th Army captures Ferrara and reaches R. Po at Pontelagoscuro and N. of Bondeno.
Okinawa – Japanese withdraw from outer defences of Shuri, except at 'Item Pocket'.
Sea War – 5 German merchant ships hit in Baltic by RAF Coastal Cmnd.

TUESDAY, APRIL 24

Russian Front – Battle of Berlin: Konev's and Zhukov's troops link up in S. suburbs.
Western Front – British reach Bremen.

ZHUKOV, Georgi Konstantinovich (1896-1974)
Russian: *Marshal*

'The general who never lost a battle' was born in extreme poverty in village of Stretkovka near Moscow. Conscript into Novgorod Dragoons in World War I. Wounded by land-mine, Rumanian front, Oct. 1916. Joined Red Army, 1918; Communist Party, March 1919, and was devoted member. Cavalry commander on Siberian and Southern fronts during Russian Civil War, 1919-1920; wounded by hand-grenade near Tsaritsyn (Stalingrad), 1919. Attended Red Cavalry Commanders' courses, 1920 (student sgt-major); cavalry sqn. commander, 1922-23. Commanded 39th/40th Buzuluk Cavalry Regt., 1923-30. Assistant Cavalry Inspector of Red Army, 1930. Cavalry divisional and corps commander, 1930-38, including 6th Cossack Corps. Deputy Commander of Byelorussian military district, 1938-39. CinC of Russian forces Manchurian-Mongolian border, summer 1939: defeated Japanese offensive across R. Khalkhin Gol by masterly use of tanks and air power. Chief of Red Army General Staff, Dec. 1940.

Appointed personal military adviser at Stalin's HQ, Oct. 1941. Masterminded defence of Leningrad and Moscow, Sept.-Dec. 1941 and phenomenally successful counter-offensives of 1942-45, which drove Hitler's armies 3,000 km westwards, from Stalingrad to Berlin.

His unprecedented prestige in the Red Army excited Stalin's jealousy in 1946, but Zhukov regained his position in 1953. Dismissed from high political office in autumn 1957; restored to official favour after fall of Khrushchev. Awarded 'Star of Hero of Soviet Union' four times (unique honour). Memoirs, 'Reminiscences and Reflections', published 1969.

Italy – La Spezia naval base captured by 5th Army. Germans abandon Genoa, scuttling 40 warships and many merchant ships in harbour.

Home Front: Britain – Budget: Chanc. reveals that total war expenditure up to March 31, 1945, is £27,400 M.: announces Double-Taxation Treaty with USA (business enterprises not to be taxed simultaneously in both Britain and USA).

WEDNESDAY, APRIL 25

Russian Front – Battle of Berlin: Zhukov and Konev forces near Potsdam to complete their 'iron ring' around the city.

Air War: Europe – RAF bomb Berchtesgaden; Americans raid Skoda Works at Pilsen. RAF bomb coastal batteries at Wangerooge (Frisian Is.).

Diplomacy – SAN FRANCISCO CONFERENCE text of UN Charter completed by June 23; signed June 26.

THURSDAY, APRIL 26

Russian/Western Front – RUSSIAN AND AMERICAN FORCES LINK UP at Torgau on the Elbe.

Western Front – Patton crosses Danube in Regensburg sector. Battle of Berlin: Dahlem and Siemensstadt districts captured. Port of Stettin falls.

Italy – Verona captured by 5th Army.

Home Front: Germany – GÖRING DISMISSED for proposing separate peace 'deal' with W. Powers. Von Greim appointed last CinC of *Luftwaffe*.

Okinawa – US 24th Corps attacks Maeda Escarpment (Shuri Line); tanks reach reverse slope.

Burma – 14th Army tanks, racing S. from Meiktila to Rangoon, capture Toungoo.

FRIDAY, APRIL 27

Russian Front – Battle of Berlin: Russians capture suburbs of Potsdam, Spandau and Rathenow; central districts of Neukölln and Tempelhof.

Western Front – Bremen captured by British forces.

Italy – Allies enter Genoa.

Okinawa – Item Pocket eliminated. Japanese defy US tanks and armd. flame-throwers in Maeda sector.

Sea War – 26th Indian Div. embarks at Akyab and Kyaukpyu for Op. Dracula (assault on Rangoon). E. Indies Fleet leaves Trincomalee to carry out neutralizing attacks on Japanese bases in Andaman and Nicobar Is.

Home Front: Britain – Mrs. Tate and Parliamentary delegation publish horrific description of Buchenwald.

SATURDAY, APRIL 28

Occupied Italy – MUSSOLINI AND HIS MISTRESS, CLARA PETACCI, CAPTURED AND SHOT by Communist

DÖNITZ, Karl (1892-)
German: *Grand Admiral, CinC of German Navy, Führer of Germany*

Masterminded devastating U-boat operations during Battle of the Atlantic. Although Hitler did not permit building of U-boats in the great numbers proposed until 1942, when tide was beginning to turn, Dönitz showed great skill and ingenuity in using available subs. to best advantage. Despite catastrophic losses, Dönitz continued ops. until war's end; he was then unexpectedly nominated to succeed Hitler as *Führer*.

Entered Imperial German Navy, 1910. Captained *U-63* in Med. Taken prisoner, Oct. 1918, and taken to Malta. Feigned insanity to avoid being sent to PoW camp. Committed to mental asylum in England. Staged lightning 'recovery' and was repatriated, 1919. Served in small coastal defence navy of German Republic between the wars. Engaged in clandestine building and testing of subs. in Finland and Turkey.

Officer Commanding Submarines, 1935-43 (Rear-Admiral, 1939-40; Admiral 1942-43). Grand-Admiral and CinC, Jan. 1943-May 1945. Temporarily suspended U-boat operations in N. Atlantic, May 1943, while feverishly working on measures to counter Allied air and naval superiority. Despite all efforts, new types of U-boat needed to turn the tide did not enter service in time. Exercised nominal authority as *Führer* and CinC of Armed Forces, at Flensburg (NW. Germany), May 1-23, 1945. Ordered German Army to surrender to Western Allies only and to continue operations against Red Army (May 5, 1945).

Tried for war crimes at Nuremberg, 1945-46. Denied responsibility for isolated atrocities committed by U-boat captains. Sentenced to 10 years' imprisonment in Spandau Gaol, Berlin; released 1955. 'Memoirs' published, 1958.

Partisan leader 'Col. Valerio' (Walter Audisio) at Dongo (L. Como). Bodies then taken in removal van to be publically exhibited and mutilated by the mob in a Milan square (April 28-29).

Western Front – US troops liberate the Stauffenberg family at Niederdorf, S. Tyrol.

Okinawa – US tanks enter Kuhazu village.

Home Front: Germany – 200 pro-Allied German troops stage attempted coup in Munich, under Maj. Braun, and seize radio station; try to seize Gauleiter Geisler, but *SS* bodyguard stamp out uprising.

SUNDAY, APRIL 29

Italy – SURRENDER OF 1 MILLION GERMAN TROOPS IN N. ITALY AND AUSTRIA, signed at Caserta, near Naples (effective May 2).

Western Front – British capture Lauenburg, trapping German forces in Denmark.

Russian Front – Battle of Berlin: Hitler marries Eva Braun and dictates 'Political Testament'; Russians capture Moabit power station and Anhalter railway terminal.

Sea War: Arctic – Last battle between U-boat 'wolf-pack' and Allied convoy escorts. 2 U-boats sunk; *U-427* miraculously survives prolonged attacks with 678 depth charges; frigate *Goodall* sunk.

MONDAY, APRIL 30

Russian Front – Hitler and Eva Braun commit suicide in *Führerbunker* beneath Reichs Chancellery, Berlin, at 3.30 pm. Cremated with burning petrol in Chancellery Garden. Russian artillery bombards Chancellery; advancing infantry now only 2 blocks away.

Western Front – Munich captured by US 7th Army.

Italy – Tito's Partisans occupy Trieste.

Sea War – Japanese convoy annihilated by British destroyers in Indian Ocean.

Occupied Holland – Seyss-Inquart meets Allied representatives to discuss prevention of starvation amongst civil population.

TUESDAY, MAY 1

Russian Front – Battle of Berlin: Goebbels and wife Magda poison their 6 children before committing suicide. Russians capture Charlottenburg and Schoeneburg districts.

Home Front: Germany – DÖNITZ ANNOUNCES DEATH OF HITLER ('fighting in Berlin'); becomes second *Führer* of the *Reich*.

PINK EDITION · DAILY NEWS · 2¢

NAZI RADIO ANNOUNCES:

HITLER DEAD

'FELL IN COMMAND POST'

ADM. DOENITZ NAMED HEAD OF REICH, ARMY

Sea War: Pacific – Australians land at Tarakan (Op. Oboe I).

Air War – Mexican Expeditionary Air Force (equipped with P-47s) arrives at Manila.

Burma – Gurkha paratroops seize coastal battery at Elephant Point, near Rangoon.

Okinawa – US inf. bn. scales precipitous E. face of Maeda Escarpment, but is thrown off after nightfall.

WEDNESDAY, MAY 2

Russian Front/Western Front – STALIN ANNOUNCES FALL OF BERLIN in Order of the Day No. 359: *'Troops of the 1st Byelorussian Front, commanded by Marshal Zhukov ... have today May 2 completely captured Berlin ... hotbed of German aggression.'* The Order mentions 131 gens. and confers on their units honorary designation of 'Berlin' divs. Battle of Berlin ends with surrender or annihilation of last pockets of resistance; 2,600 captured in shattered Reichstag. Russians capture ports of Rostock and Warnemünde. British 6th Airborne Div. links up with tanks of 70th Russian Armd. Div. at Wismar.

Burma – 14th Army reaches Pegu, 58 km N. of Rangoon. Scratch force of 7,000 Japanese offers fanatical resistance.

Sea War – Indians land S. of Rangoon. 23 out of 60 U-boats sunk by RAF while attempting to escape from NW. Germany to Norway (May 2-6).

Okinawa – Marines suffer heavy casualties near R. Asa.

Neutrals: Spain – Pierre Laval interned at disposition of the Allies.

Secret War – Dr Wernher von Braun, Gen. Dornberger and other rocket experts surrender to US 44th Inf. Div. near Reutte (Austrian Tyrol).

THURSDAY, MAY 3

Burma – INDIANS CAPTURE RANGOON.

Western Front – British capture Hamburg. 59 merchant ships and 600 small craft scuttled. Patton takes Branau (Hitler's birthplace). German surrender envoys meet Montgomery on Lüneburg Heath.

Sea War – At least 5,000 former concentration camp inmates, of many nationalities, drowned when RAF fighter-bombers sink liner *Cap Arkona* and SS *Thielbek* off Lübeck.

Okinawa – Major Japanese counteroffensive, involving tanks, inf., heavy artillery, 800 seaborne assault troops and 125 *Kamikaze* planes, which hit 17 ships (May 3-5).

Philippines – Davao, cap. of Mindanao, captured by Americans.

Neutrals – Eire P.M. De Valera calls at German Legation to offer his condolences on death of Adolf Hitler. Salazar orders day's mourning in Portugal.

Occupied Holland – Return of the Queen and Princess Juliana.

FRIDAY, MAY 4

Western Front – SURRENDER OF ALL GERMAN FORCES IN NW. GERMANY, HOLLAND AND DENMARK to F.M. Montgomery at ceremony on Lüneberg Heath (surrender effective from 8 am, May 5).

Sea War: Pacific – British carrier *Formidable* hit by *Kamikaze* plane off Sakishima Gunto.

Okinawa – A Japanese column penetrates more than 1.5 km behind US lines before being destroyed. Renewed Japanese assault after dark is also repelled, bringing Japanese casualties to c. 5,000.

SATURDAY, MAY 5

Occupied Czechoslovakia – The Prague Rising: Resistance attack on radio station sparks off general uprising, directed by Czech National Committee.

Sea War: Atlantic – Last U-boat success off America. *U-853* sinks SS *Black Point*, and is then sunk by USS *Atherton*.

Okinawa – US 77th Div. gains secure foothold on Maeda Escarpment.

SUNDAY, MAY 6

Western Front – Patton occupies Skoda Works.

Burma – 14th Army links up with 'Dracula' forces, N. of Rangoon.

Occupied Czechoslovakia – 3 SS divs. ordered to crush Prague uprising.

Diplomacy – Portugal severs diplomatic relations with Dönitz Govt.

MONDAY, MAY 7

Diplomacy – UNCONDITIONAL SURRENDER OF GERMANY. Gen. Jodl signs instrument of surrender at 2.41 am in schoolroom at Rheims.

Western Front – Allied forces occupy Emden and Wilhelmshaven and move into E. Holland and Denmark. Hungarian P.M., Szalasi, captured by US 7th Army near Salzburg. Hungarian Crown Jewels found in railway carriage.

Russian Front – Siege of Breslau ends after 82 days. 40,000 Germans captured.

Sea War – *U-2336* claims last U-boat victims in W.W.II – coasters *Avondale Park* and *Sneland*, off Firth of Forth. *U-320* sunk by RAF Catalina off Bergen; last U-boat sunk by Allied forces in W.W.II.

TUESDAY, MAY 8

Home Fronts – VE-DAY ('Victory in Europe'): great celebrations.

Diplomacy – In Berlin, F.M. Keitel, Marshal Zhukov and A.M. Tedder ratify Rheims surrender document.

Russian Front – Dresden occupied by Russian forces.

Sea War – Liberty ship *Horace Binney* mined off Flushing and almost broken in two, but remarkable salvage op. saves ship and cargo. Final German evacuation convoys from Courland (Latvia); 126 small craft. 1,420,000 people evacuated from Pomerania and E. Prussia since Jan. 25.

Occupied Norway – Crown Prince Olaf lands at Oslo from British warship and proclaims surrender of German occupying forces.

Czechoslovakia – Capitulation of German garrison in Prague.

WEDNESDAY, MAY 9

Russian Front – German Army Grp. *Kurland* begins surrendering to Russians. 133,000 surrender (May 9-11).

Occupied France – Surrender of German garrisons at La Rochelle, St Nazaire, Lorient and Channel Is.: V.-Adm. Huffmeier, Cdr. of Channel Is. garrison, surrenders aboard destroyer *Bulldog*.

Occupied Austria – Göring and Kesselring captured by Americans.

Occupied Norway – *Reichskommissar* Terboven commits suicide; aged 46. Quisling arrested by Resistance.

Occupied Greece – 20,000 German troops on Crete, Rhodes and other Is. surrender to Allied troops.

Home Front: Britain – Many Defence Regulations revoked.

Home Front: USSR – Victory celebrations in Moscow: 2 M. people watch spectacular fireworks display.

Okinawa – Americans take Hill 60 and Kochi Ridge.

THURSDAY, MAY 10

Okinawa – Marines establish bridgehead over R. Asa.

Russian Front – Russians occupy Prague.

FRIDAY, MAY 11

Russian Front – Russians launch final assault on German forces still holding out in Bohemia.

Okinawa – 10th Army launches coordinated attacks on both flanks of Shuri Line.

New Guinea – BATTLE OF WEWAK. Australians launch final attack on last Japanese stronghold on N. coast. Despite fanatical resistance, tanks and seaborne inf. link up on May 23 and compel Japanese 18th Army to retreat into the forbidding Prince Alexander Mts.

Sea War: Pacific – Carrier *Bunker Hill* (TF 58) hit by 3 *Kamikaze* planes off Okinawa; 392 killed, 264 wounded.

Occupied France – German garrison of Dunkirk surrenders to Czech troops.

SATURDAY, MAY 12

Occupied Czechoslovakia – Gen. Vlasov, cdr. of anti-communist ROA and KONR, reluctantly handed over by Americans to Russian troops (executed Aug. 1946).

Occupied Germany – US 7th Army captures Japanese ambassador Gen. Oshima and 130 staff.

Okinawa – Marines repulsed with heavy loss at Sugar Loaf Hill, key point of Shuri Line.

Sea War – Last Arctic convoys JW. 67 (eastbound) and RA. 67 (westbound); on May 16 convoy escort accepts surrender of 14 U-boats and escorts them to Loch Eriboll.

SUNDAY, MAY 13

Occupied Germany – Scots Gds. occupy Heligoland.

Home Front: Britain – Thanksgiving Service in St. Paul's Cathedral, attended by Royal Family.

Okinawa – Americans take Conical Hill at E. end of Shuri Line.

MONDAY, MAY 14

Okinawa – 20 US Marines reach summit of Sugar Loaf Hill (forced to withdraw, May 15).

Air War: Pacific – **DAYLIGHT FIRE RAID ON NAGOYA.** In order to further undermine Japanese morale and industrial output, following severe psychological blow of the German collapse, 21st BC, US 20th AF, launches daylight saturation bombing attacks on 4 cities – Nagoya, Yokohama, Osaka and Kobe – between May 14 and June 15. In total of 4,700 sorties (77 B-29s lost) 16,647 t. of napalm and oil bombs wipe out 36 sq km of built-up area.

TUESDAY, MAY 15

Sea War – Japanese cruiser *Haguro* trapped and torpedoed by 5 British destroyers in Malacca Str. (night May 15-16).

Occupied Yugoslavia – Surrender of last pocket of German resistance.

WEDNESDAY, MAY 16

Occupied Channel Is. – British forces liberate Alderney.

Okinawa – US 6th Marine Div. suffers heavy casualties.

THURSDAY, MAY 17

Okinawa – Lt.-Gen. Simon Bolivar Buckner, Jr., CG 10th Army, takes personal cmnd. of ops. Marines reach crest of Sugar Loaf Hill, but run short of ammunition and have to withdraw.

FRIDAY, MAY 18

Okinawa – Sugar Loaf Hill captured by US Marines.

Home Front: Britain – Avro Lancaster 'Aries' flies over N. Magnetic Pole for first time in history during series of trans-Polar proving flights.

SATURDAY, MAY 19

Sea War: Pacific – British submarine *Terrapin* depth-charged.

SUNDAY, MAY 20

Okinawa – Chocolate Drop Hill secured by US inf. after savage fighting around maze of interconnected tunnels. Japanese counter-attack on 'The Horseshoe' (200 killed).

MONDAY, MAY 21

Okinawa – Americans capture Sugar Hill – exposing right flank of Shuri Line. Japanese decide to withdraw farther S.

Occupied Germany – Himmler arrested by British troops at Bremervoerde, disguised as commercial traveller.

Above: *British 14th Army troops mop up in Pegu, last town before Rangoon.*

Home Front: Japan – 2 million students mobilized in 'Student Defence Corps'.

Home Front: USA – Humphrey Bogart marries Lauren Bacall.

TUESDAY, MAY 22

Okinawa – Persistent heavy rain until early June seriously reduces mobility of US armour and gives Japanese respite, during which they evacuate wounded and equipment from Shuri Line. Marines cross R. Asato.

Occupied Germany – Montgomery appointed CinC of British Forces of Occupation.

Home Front: Britain – Rationing: new cuts affecting fats, bacon, meat and soap.

WEDNESDAY, MAY 23

Home Front: Britain – Churchill resigns and forms 'Caretaker' administration of Conservatives, Nat. Libs. and Indeps. (former Lab. ministers refuse to serve).

Occupied Germany – Members of Dönitz Govt., German High Cmnd. and Gen. Staff, taken into custody and interned aboard liner *Patria* in Flensburg harbour. Adm. von Friedeburg commits suicide. Himmler commits suicide; buried on Lüneburg Heath.

Air War: Pacific – 1,000 B-29s (30 lost) participate in 2 climactic night raids on Tokyo; determined fighter opposition and heavy flak (nights May 23-24 and 25-26). These attacks bring total burned-out area to 90 sq km.

THURSDAY, MAY 24

Okinawa – 9 Japanese bomber/transports approach the I. (8 lost); survivor crash-lands 12-man suicide squad on Yontan airfield, which destroys 7 planes, petrol and ammunition dumps before being over-whelmed. Japanese counter-attack on Oboe Hill.

New Guinea – Australians encircle Wewak, last Japanese coastal stronghold.

Occupied Austria – Suicide of F.M. von Greim, last CinC of *Luftwaffe;* aged 50 in hospital at Salzburg.

FRIDAY, MAY 25

Secret War – Allied European Commands

asked not to reveal Ultra Secret.
Home Front: USA – Over 60 casualties in blast at Edgewood Arsenal, Maryland.

SATURDAY, MAY 26

Okinawa – US guns and bombers pound Japanese troops withdrawing from Shuri Line.
Occupied Germany – SHAEF HQ transferred from Rheims to Frankfurt-am-Main.

SUNDAY, MAY 27

Sea War: Pacific – Japanese submarine pack makes unsuccessful attacks on US convoys on Leyte-Okinawa and Guam-Okinawa routes (May 27-June 28).

MONDAY, MAY 28

Occupied Germany – 'Lord Haw-Haw' (William Joyce) captured by British troops.
Sea War – British Admiralty ends Atlantic convoy system. In Pacific, US TF 58 transferred from 5th Fleet to 3rd Fleet and redesignated 'TF 38'.
Okinawa – Marines advance to Naha Harbour and Kokuba Estuary.
Home Front: USA – Truman proposes to increase Federal unemployment insurance to $25 a week.

TUESDAY, MAY 29

Okinawa – Marines capture Shuri Castle, former Japanese HQ, and Shuri town (both are in total ruins).
Syria – Fighting between French forces and Syrian Nationalists in Damascus. British arrange cease fire, May 31.
Air War: Pacific – 101 Mustangs – escorting B-29 formations over Yokohama – shoot down 26 of 150 defending Zeros and other JNAF interceptors, for loss of 3.
Home Front: Japan – V.-Adm. Ozawa succeeds Adm. Toyoda as CinC Combined Fleet.

WEDNESDAY, MAY 30

Occupied Germany – Zhukov appointed Soviet representative on Allied Control Commission.
Iran – Foreign Min. demands withdrawal of all British, US and Russian forces.
Home Front: France – 100,000 German PoWs to be used to clear 100 M. mines.
Okinawa – US forces occupy abandoned strongpoints of Shuri Line.

THURSDAY, MAY 31

Okinawa – 6th Marine Div. runs into strong Japanese rearguard near Hill 46.

FRIDAY, JUNE 1

Okinawa – Americans pursue retreating Japanese towards S. Coast.
Burma – British 12th Army joins 14th Army.
Air War: Pacific – 27 P-51s collide during thunderstorm *en route* to Osaka.
Occupied Austria – **THE PEGGETZ 'MASSACRE'.** British troops begin forcible repatriation of Cossack Corps to Judenborg in Russian zone of Austria. Pitched battle occurs; *c.* 700 Cossacks trampled or commit suicide.

SATURDAY, JUNE 2

Air War: Pacific – TF 38 raids *Kamikaze* bases in S. Japan: this, and other raids, compel Japanese to continue ops. from bases farther N.
Diplomacy – At San Francisco, Russian delegates demand right of veto in proposed UN Security Council.

SUNDAY, JUNE 3

Okinawa – Japanese forces trapped in Oroku and Chinen Pens.
Occupied Europe – Captured maps of German minefields distributed by SHAEF to all Allied govts. in Europe (selected from 4 t. of these maps seized by US 7th Army in Bavaria).
Syria – French forces, escorted by British troops, leave Damascus.

MONDAY, JUNE 4

Okinawa – Marines land behind Japanese lines in Oroku Penin.
Occupied Germany – Paul Ferdonnet – the 'Radio Traitor' of Stuttgart – arrested by French troops in Bavaria; executed Aug. 5.

TUESDAY, JUNE 5

Diplomacy – **ALLIED AGREEMENT ON PARTITION OF GERMANY AND CITY OF BERLIN** signed by Eisenhower, Montgomery, Lattre de Tassigny and Zhukov.
Okinawa – Naha airfield captured by US forces.
Sea War: Pacific – Cruiser *Pittsburg* loses 32 m of her bows in typhoon off Okinawa but eventually reaches Guam (1,448 km S.).

WEDNESDAY, JUNE 6

Diplomacy – Brazil declares war on Japan.
Secret War – Detention of 4 agents landed on Orissa coast (India) by Japanese sub. (March 1944): 2 Bengalis and 2 Punjabis.

THURSDAY, JUNE 7

Home Front: Britain – King and Queen visit Channel Is. First performance of Britten's opera 'Peter Grimes' at Sadler's Wells Theatre, London.

Above: 'A' Company, 5th Marines, 3km north of Naha, Okinawa's capital.

Norway – King Haakon returns to Oslo.

FRIDAY, JUNE 8

Sea War – Cruiser *Ashigara* sunk by British sub. *Trenchant* off Sumatra.

SATURDAY, JUNE 9

Occupied Germany – Montgomery takes salute at last parade of Gds. Armd. Div.
Diplomacy – Anglo-British-Yugoslav Agreement on future status of Trieste.
Home Front: Britain – Horse Racing: Derby won by 'Dante', from 'Midas' and 'Court Martial'.

SUNDAY, JUNE 10

Home Front: Japan – P.M. Suzuki granted dictatorial powers by Imperial Diet (Parliament).
Occupied Germany – Zhukov decorates Eisenhower and Montgomery with Order of Victory.
Okinawa – 24th Corps launches all-out attack on Yaeju-Dake Line, in extreme S. Marines compress Japanese pocket in Oroku sector.
Sea War: Pacific – Op. Oboe VI: Australians land at Brunei.

MONDAY, JUNE 11

Okinawa – Japanese pocket in Oroku sector now only 914 metres square.

TUESDAY, JUNE 12

Okinawa – Japanese marines in Oroku sector request cease-fire, which will permit them to commit *hara-kiri;* hundreds jump off cliffs or disembowel themselves with grenades.
Home Front: Britain – Eisenhower receives Order of Merit and Freedom of City of London.

WEDNESDAY, JUNE 13

Okinawa – End of organized Japanese resistance in Oroku sector. Farther S., heavy Japanese gunfire forces Americans to use tanks for all normal MT duties in Kunishi Ridge sector.

THURSDAY, JUNE 14

Okinawa – US inf. capture Yaeju-Dake peak.
Sea War: Pacific – British TG raids Truk (June 14 and 15).
Occupied Germany – Von Ribbentrop arrested by British military police.

FRIDAY, JUNE 15

Burma – Mountbatten addresses Victory Parade in Rangoon.
Home Front: Britain – Parliament dissolved in anticipation of first General Election since 1935.

SATURDAY, JUNE 16

Okinawa – Yuza-Dake peak captured by US inf.

SUNDAY, JUNE 17

Air War: Pacific – B-29s of 21st BC, 20th AF, carry out first of series of complex night incendiary raids on 58 of the smaller industrial cities in Japan. 3 or 4 cities are raided simultaneously, at 2- to 3-day intervals. Targets are virtually undefended and only 1 bomber is shot down and 66 damaged (June 17-18 to Aug. 14-15, 1945).

MONDAY, JUNE 18

Okinawa – Lt.-Gen. Buckner fatally wounded by artillery shell at forward observation post; aged 58.
Occupied Germany – Col.-Gen. Berzarin, outspoken Soviet military cdr. in Berlin, killed in road accident; aged 40.

TUESDAY, JUNE 19

Home Front: USA – 4 million people give Eisenhower 'ticker-tape' welcome in New York City.

WEDNESDAY, JUNE 20

Okinawa – Americans reach Hill 89, location of Japanese emergency HQ.
Philippines – US forces reach Aparri, having advanced 322 km N. along Cagayan Valley in 28 days against determined resistance.
Diplomacy – Anglo-Yugoslav Agreement on zones of occupation in Trieste.

THURSDAY, JUNE 21

Okinawa – Americans capture Hill 89.

FRIDAY, JUNE 22

Okinawa – **AMERICANS SECURE OKINAWA.**
New Guinea – Australians drive Japanese 18th Army from Mts. Tazaki and Shiburangu (June 22 and 27).

> **Okinawa Campaign Losses**
> Japanese: 129,700 dead, 10,755 PoWs, 42,000 civilians; 7,830 planes; 6 major warships. US: 12,520 dead, 36,631 wounded; 763 planes; 22 destroyers, 18 other warships sunk.

SATURDAY, JUNE 23

Diplomacy – Agreement in Moscow between Polish administrations in London and Lublin on formation of Provisional Govt.

SUNDAY, JUNE 24

Home Front: USSR – Victory Parade in Moscow: captured Nazi banners are ceremonially dragged across Red Square.

MONDAY, JUNE 25

Sea War: Pacific – TF 92 – cruisers *Richmond* and *Concord* with 4 destroyers – leaves Attu for Sea of Okhotsk; scatters Japanese convoy, June 26.
Occupied Austria – Allies announce their 4 zones of occupation.

TUESDAY, JUNE 26

Air War: Pacific – Radar-equipped B-29s bomb Utsube Oil Refinery at Yokkaichi, near Nagoya: first of 15 heavy night raids on Japanese oil targets in June-Aug.
Diplomacy – **UN CHARTER** (World Security Charter) **SIGNED** by representatives of 50 nations at San Francisco. Truman pleads with signatories to translate 'lofty words' of the Charter into 'worthy deeds'. Allied lawyers discuss War Crimes Trial procedure in London.

WEDNESDAY, JUNE 27

Home Front: USSR – Stalin appointed to new rank of 'Generalissimo'.
Home Front: Czechoslovakia – Former puppet-Pres. of 'Bohemia-Moravia Protectorate', Dr Emil Hacha, dies in Prague prison hospital, aged 73, while awaiting trial.

THURSDAY, JUNE 28

Air War: Pacific – B-29s drop nearly 3,000 t. IBs on Sasebo naval base.

FRIDAY, JUNE 29

Air War: Pacific – Allied bombers raid Balikpapan oil installations for 9th consecutive day.

SATURDAY, JUNE 30

Okinawa – Americans complete 'mopping up' ops.: 8,975 Japanese killed and 2,902 captured, June 23-30.

Sea War: Pacific – 9 US subs. which have penetrated heavily mined Tsushima Strs., sink 31 ships in Sea of Japan during June.

SUNDAY, JULY 1

Sea War: Pacific – Australians land at Balikpapan (Op. Oboe II).

MONDAY, JULY 2

Sea War: Pacific – Rockets fired at Kaihyo I. (N. Japan) by US sub. *Barb*.

TUESDAY, JULY 3

Occupied Germany – First US occupation troops arrive in Berlin; British contingent arrives, July 4.

Above: *US infantry of 38th Div. blast Japanese positions with explosive charges, north of Santa Fe, Luzon.*

WEDNESDAY, JULY 4

Philippines – MacArthur announces liberation of Philippines.

THURSDAY, JULY 5

Home Front: Britain – **LABOUR WINS BRITISH GENERAL ELECTION.** Labour, 394; Cons., 188; Lib., 14; Nat. Lib., 13; Ulster Unionists, 9; Communists, 2; Others, 20. Results announced July 26.
Home Front: Australia – Death of John Curtin, P.M. since 1941; aged 60. Mr Chifley takes over, July 13.
Diplomacy – Britain and USA recognize Polish Provisional Govt.
Sea War – Op. Collie: E. Indies Fleet clears mines from W. coast of Malaya, prior to Op. Zipper (see Sept. 9) and bombards Japanese bases in Nicobar Is. and Sumatra (July 5-11).

FRIDAY, JULY 6

Diplomacy – Nicaragua becomes first nation to ratify UN Charter.

SATURDAY, JULY 7

Sea War: Pacific – Many small Japanese vessels sunk or damaged by USN Privateer patrol bombers (modified B-24s) in Yellow Sea and off S. Japan.

SUNDAY, JULY 8

Air War – Sgt. Simon Eden, RAF (aged 20), son of British Foreign Sec., missing in action over Burma.

MONDAY, JULY 9

Sea War: Atlantic – Brazilian cruiser *Bahia* sunk by mysterious explosion (294 killed).

TUESDAY, JULY 10

Sea War: Pacific – 1,022 planes of TF 38 raid 70 air bases in Tokyo area destroying 173 aircraft: only resistance, light flak.

WEDNESDAY, JULY 11

Air War – Redeployment of 2,118 4-engined bombers of 8th AF from Britain to USA (*en route* for Pacific) completed within 51 days.
Home Front: Canada – General Election: Liberals, 119 seats; Progressive Cons., 65; C.C.F., 28; Others, 33. Lib. P.M. Mackenzie King defeated at Prince Albert (Saskatchewan); he is re-elected at by-election Aug. 6, 1945.

THURSDAY, JULY 12

Diplomacy – Hirohito appoints former P.M. Prince Konoye as secret peace emissary in Moscow. Russians refuse to receive him.

FRIDAY, JULY 13

Sea War: Pacific – US Govt. admits responsibility for sinking, in error, of Japanese relief ship *Awa Maru*.

SATURDAY, JULY 14

Sea War: Pacific – TF 38 launches devastating attack on ferry traffic between Honshu and Hokkaido (N. Japan): 37 steamers and 6 warships sunk (July 14 and 15). Battleships *South Dakota*, *Indiana* and *Massachusetts* bombard Kamaishi steel works, N. of Tokyo.
Occupied Germany – Ban on troop fraternization with Germans lifted in US and British zones of Germany and Austria. SHAEF dissolved.

SUNDAY, JULY 15

Diplomacy – Italy declares war on Japan.

MONDAY, JULY 16

Secret War – **FIRST ATOMIC BOMB TESTED** at Alamogordo in New Mexico desert (Op. Trinity).

Occupied Germany – Churchill tours Berlin; during inspection of Hitler's Bunker, he declares: *'I have tracked the Nazi beast to his lair!'*

Below: *A B-29 Superfortress showers incendiaries on Japan, July 16.*

TUESDAY, JULY 17

Sea War: Pacific – First joint US-British carrier strike on Tokyo area (repeated July 18). By night, *King George V* and 5 US battleships bombard Hitachi.
Diplomacy – **POTSDAM CONFERENCE** ('Terminal') opens: Churchill, Attlee, Truman and Stalin confer near Berlin.
Home Front: Britain – Death of F.M. Busch, former cdr. of German Army Grp. Centre in Russia, at military hospital in Notts.; aged 60. King, Queen and Princess Elizabeth visit Ulster.

WEDNESDAY, JULY 18

Air War: China – 200 B-24s and B-25s of FEAF from Okinawa bomb Kiangwan airfield, Shanghai.
Home Front: Italy – Captured German mines explode, destroying American Red Cross club (36 killed).
Home Front: Brazil – Brazilian Expeditionary Force parades through Rio de Janeiro, on its return from Italy.
Home Front: Canada – Explosions in RCN Magazine rock Halifax (NS): firemen narrowly avert cataclysmic detonation of main magazine, containing 6,000 t. ammunition, vast numbers of depth charges and mines (15 casualties).

THURSDAY, JULY 19

Air War: China – FEAF bombs 4 air bases in Shanghai area.

FRIDAY, JULY 20

Home Front: USA – Congress votes to increase Export-Import Banks lending ceiling from $700 M. to $3,500 M. and passes Bretton Woods Bill. Passed 61-16 in Senate.

SATURDAY, JULY 21

Sea War: Pacific – US Navy planes attack shipping in Tsushima Str. and off Fusan (Korea).

SUNDAY, JULY 22

Air War: China – 300 planes of FEAF (inc. new Invader fast bombers) again hit air bases and shipping in Shanghai area.
Sea War: Pacific – 9 US destroyers penetrate Tokyo Bay under cover of a storm and attack convoy (night July 22-23). Allied task forces resupplied at sea in greatest such op. of the war. TF 92 bombards Paramushiro in the Kuriles.

MONDAY, JULY 23

Home Front: France – Trial of Pétain opens at Palais de Justice, Paris.

TUESDAY, JULY 24

Sea War: Pacific – Immobilized Japanese battle fleet virtually annihilated at Kure in 2 massive ops. by US and British carrier planes (July 24 and 28). Battleships *Haruna*, *Ise* and *Hyuga* and carrier *Amagi* sunk.

WEDNESDAY, JULY 25

Sea War: Pacific – Cruisers *Pasadena*, *Springfield*, *Wilkes-Barre* and *Astoria* bombard air bases in S. Honshu.

THURSDAY, JULY 26

Diplomacy – POTSDAM DECLARATION: Allied leaders demand immediate and unconditional surrender of Japan; threaten 'prompt and utter destruction' of Japanese homeland.
Home Front: Britain – CHURCHILL RESIGNS AFTER MASSIVE LABOUR VICTORY IN BRITISH GENERAL ELECTION. Attlee forms first Lab. Govt. with working majority. Lab. Cabinet appointments: P.M. and Min. of Defence, Attlee; Foreign Sec., Ernest Bevin; Chancellor of Exch., Hugh Dalton; Pres. of Board of Trade, Sir Stafford Cripps; Lord Pres., Herbert Morrison; Lord Chanc., W. Jowitt.
Sea War – First *Kamikaze* attack on British E. Indies Fleet: escort carrier *Ameer* damaged; minesweeper *Vestal* sunk off Malaya.

FRIDAY, JULY 27

Air War: Pacific – B-29s drop 660,000 leaflets by night over 11 Japanese cities, warning inhabitants to flee before selected targets are destroyed. By Aug. 5, 35 cities have been subjected to this novel, and highly effective, form of psychological warfare (16 actually bombed).

SATURDAY, JULY 28

Burma – Japanese 28th Army attempts to escape across R. Sittang; suffers catastrophic losses – over 13,000 killed or drowned.
Diplomacy – Attlee and Bevin arrive at Potsdam for further consultations.
Home Front: USA – B-25 bomber lost in fog, collides with Empire State Building, New York City (19 killed). Senate ratifies UN Charter by 89 votes to 2.

SUNDAY, JULY 29

Home Front: Britain – 8th Army disbanded.
Sea War: Pacific – Cruiser *Indianapolis*, sailing unescorted after delivering atomic bomb components to Tinian I, is sunk by sub. *I-58*. Ship not missed for several days and only 316 out of 1,196 are rescued by Aug. 8. US battleships and *King George V* bombard Hamamatsu, S. of Tokyo.

MONDAY, JULY 30

New Guinea – Japanese 18th Army makes last stand at village of Numbogua; Gen. Adachi orders his troops 'to die in honourable defeat'.
Sea War: Pacific – TF 37/TF 38 planes sink 11 ships in Kobe, Nagoya and Maizuru harbours.

TUESDAY, JULY 31

Sea War – Cruiser *Takao* sunk by British frogmen with limpet mines at Singapore.

Occupied Austria – Laval arrives by air from Spain and is handed over to French authorities.
Home Front: Canada – F.M. Alexander appointed Gov.-Gen.

WEDNESDAY, AUGUST 1

Air War: Pacific – 820 Superfortresses drop record total of 6,632 t. bombs on cities of Hachioji, Nagaoka, Mito and Toyama (latter target obliterated).

THURSDAY, AUGUST 2

Diplomacy – Attlee, Truman and Stalin agree at Potsdam to place sharp curbs on German industrial power; USSR to annex E. Prussia and Poland to take over large segment of E. Germany.
Home Front: Italy – Death of Pietro Mascagni, composer of *Cavalleria Rusticana*, aged 81.
Home Front: Britain – King George VI receives Pres. Truman aboard HMS *Renown* at Plymouth.

FRIDAY, AUGUST 3

Home Front: France – Battlecruiser *Strasbourg* refloated at Toulon.

SATURDAY, AUGUST 4

Home Front: Britain – Govt. appointments: Min. of Health, Aneurin Bevan; Min. of Fuel and Power, Emmanuel Shinwell.

SUNDAY, AUGUST 5

Air War: Pacific – 325 planes of US 5th and 7th AFs, based on Okinawa, raid Tarumizu, S. Japan.
Occupied Austria – Death of Emil von Reznicek, composer; aged 85.

MONDAY, AUGUST 6

Air War: Pacific – DESTRUCTION OF HIROSHIMA. B-29 'Enola Gay' of 393rd Bomb. Sqn., 509th Composite Grp., 20th AF, commanded by Col. Tibbets, drops 20-kilotonne atomic bomb ('Little Boy')

from altitude of 9,449 m; device explodes 18 secs. after 8.16 am (local time) 564 m. above city. 12 sq km of built-up area obliterated.
Home Front: USA – Maj. Richard I. Bong, top American fighter 'ace' of W.W.II (40 victories), killed testing jet fighter; aged 24.

TUESDAY, AUGUST 7

Home Front: Japan – First flight of Nakajima *Kikka* ('Orange Blossom'), jet-propelled attack bomber (copy of Me 262).

WEDNESDAY, AUGUST 8

Diplomacy – USSR DECLARES WAR ON JAPAN (as from Aug. 9).
Home Front: Yugoslavia – King Peter gives wide-ranging powers to Tito.

THURSDAY, AUGUST 9

Air War: Pacific – DESTRUCTION OF NAGASAKI. B-29 'Bock's Car' drops 20-kilotonne atomic bomb ('Fat Man'). Area of 4 sq km destroyed.

Atomic Bomb Losses
Hiroshima: perhaps 80,000 dead inc. 6,769 military personnel, *c.* 80,000 injured; radiation sickness still affects *c.* 4,000 survivors (as of 1979).
Nagasaki: *c.* 40,000 dead, *c.* 60,000 injured.

Above: *The 6,000-m high mushroom cloud over Nagasaki, 3 minutes after the second atomic bomb was dropped.*

Russo-Japanese War – RUSSIANS INVADE MANCHUKUO (Manchuria) on 1,609 km front.
Home Front: Britain – Death of Sir Bernard Partridge, political cartoonist of 'Punch' magazine; aged 83.

Manchurian Campaign
Soviet: 1,158,000 men (76 divs.); 5,500 tanks and assault guns, 26,000 guns and mortars; 3,900 planes. Japanese: 663,000 men plus 117,000 Manchukuo troops (25 divs.); 1,155 tanks, 6,260 guns; 1,000 planes.
Losses – Soviet: 8,219 dead, 22,264 wounded. Japanese: 21,389 dead, 594,000 PoWs.

FRIDAY, AUGUST 10

Home Front: Japan – Radio Tokyo announces that Japan is willing to surrender provided future status of the Emperor can be assured.

SATURDAY, AUGUST 11

Diplomacy – Allies reject Japanese pre-conditions on surrender question.
Home Front: Britain – *Queen Mary* docks at Southampton.

SUNDAY, AUGUST 12

Korea – Russians invade N. Korea by land and sea.
Sea War: Pacific – Battleship USS *Pennsylvania* damaged by torpedo plane, off Okinawa.

MONDAY, AUGUST 13

Air War: Pacific – Sub.-Lt. Saburo Sakai, one-eyed Zero 'ace' (64 victories), shoots down B-29 near Tokyo (night Aug. 13-14).
Occupied Germany – French troops deployed in W. Berlin.
Diplomacy – Mongolia declares war on Japan.

TUESDAY, AUGUST 14

Diplomacy – Japan accepts Allied demand for Unconditional Surrender.

WEDNESDAY, AUGUST 15

Home Front: Britain/USA – VJ-DAY ('Victory over Japan'). National holiday in Britain. King opens new British Parliament.
Home Front: Japan – EMPEROR HIROHITO BROADCASTS to Japanese people news of surrender which has been necessitated by the fact that 'the war situation has developed not necessarily to Japan's advantage'. MacArthur orders Japan to cease hostilities and sends representatives to Manila.
Sea War: Pacific – TF 38 launches massive air strikes on Tokyo area, which lead to numerous encounters with Japanese fighters; but strike planes are precipitately withdrawn upon receipt of surrender announcement.
Air War: Pacific – V.-Adm. Ugaki, cdr. of

Kamikaze ops., leads final *Kamikaze* mission, but his 7 dive-bombers are shot down by US fighters off Tokyo before they can reach Okinawa.
Diplomacy – Treaty of Friendship between Nationalist China and USSR.

THURSDAY, AUGUST 16

Home Front: Japan – Emperor issues Imperial Rescript (decree) at 4pm Tokyo time ordering all Japanese forces to cease fire. Cabinet resigns; Prince Higashikuni forms 'caretaker' administration.
Manchuria – Vassilevsky calls on Japanese Kwantung Army in Manchuria to surrender by Aug. 20.

FRIDAY, AUGUST 17

Home Front: Japan – P.M. Higashikuni orders Army to obey Emperor's call and lay down their arms.
Occupied Dutch E. Indies – Sukarno proclaims 'Provisional Indonesian Republic Govt.' on Java.
Home Front: France – De Gaulle commutes death sentence on Pétain to life imprisonment.
Argentina – *U-977* arrives at Mar del Plata and surrenders, having left Kiel on April 13 and sunk a Soviet ship in the Arctic.

SATURDAY, AUGUST 18

Air War: Pacific – 2 F-7 reconnaissance planes (converted B-24s) attacked by 10 fighters and flak over Tokyo. Both damaged (1 man killed); 2 fighters destroyed.

SUNDAY, AUGUST 19

Diplomacy – Japanese representatives arrive in Manila.
Manchuria – 2nd FEF captures Tsitsihar in Manchurian Plain; TBF tanks race towards the town from the W., despite pockets of fanatical Japanese troops.
China – Chiang Kai-shek forbids Japanese forces to surrender to Red Chinese and orders latter to hold its positions (Mao disregards this).
Home Front: India – Subhas Chandra Bose fatally injured in plane crash on Formosa; aged 48.

MONDAY, AUGUST 20

Burma – Mountbatten broadcasts surrender instructions to Japanese forces.
Home Front: Norway – TRIAL OF QUISLING FOR HIGH TREASON OPENS at Oslo: claimed to be 'saviour' of Norway (sentenced to death, Sept. 10; executed by firing squad, Oct. 24).
Home Front: USA – War production Board lifts restrictions on production of consumer goods.
Manchuria – Russians capture Harbin and Mukden.

TUESDAY, AUGUST 21

Home Front: USA – All outstanding Lease-Lend contracts cancelled.

WEDNESDAY, AUGUST 22

Manchuria – KWANTUNG ARMY SURRENDERS AT HARBIN. Russian airborne forces land at Port Arthur. 'Emperor Kang Teh' of Manchukuo – Japanese puppet ruler in China – captured by Russians on Mukden airfield.
Sea War: Pacific – At ceremony aboard US destroyer escort *Levy*, cdr. of Mili Atoll garrison (Marshall Is.) surrenders. This is first voluntary handover of a Japanese-occupied I.
Home Front: Japan – 'People's Volunteer Corps' (Home Guard) is disbanded.

THURSDAY, AUGUST 23

Occupied Austria – British, American and French troops enter Vienna.
Home Front: Britain – Both Houses of Parliament ratify UN Charter.

FRIDAY, AUGUST 24

Home Front: Britain – Attlee complains that abrupt ending of US Lease-Lend programme has left Britain in a 'very serious financial position'. Bevin says 700,000 London homes need repair.

SATURDAY, AUGUST 25

Occupied Germany – British forces in W. Europe redesignated 'British Army of the Rhine' (BAOR).
Home Front: USA – V.-Adm. Willis A. Lee Jr. ('Ching' Lee) dies of heart attack; aged 56.

SUNDAY, AUGUST 26

Occupied Japan – Russians begin occupying Kurile Is.

MONDAY, AUGUST 27

Sea War: Pacific – Allied 3rd Fleet – inc. US, British, Commonwealth and Dutch warships – anchors in Sagami Bay, within sight of Mt. Fujiyama.

TUESDAY, AUGUST 28

Occupied Japan – Advance guard of 150 US soldiers lands at Atsugi airfield.

WEDNESDAY, AUGUST 29

Home Front: USA – Secret Army and Navy reports of official enquiries into Pearl Harbor Raid are made public, placing blame on lack of preparedness, confusion and breakdown of interservice co-ordination. Gen. Marshall criticized.
Occupied Germany – Göring, Ribbentrop

and 22 other Nazi leaders indicted as war criminals.

THURSDAY, AUGUST 30

Home Front: Japan – American and British forces land in Tokyo area. MacArthur flies in from Manila.
Diplomacy – Mexico recognises Spanish Republican Govt. as legitimate govt. of Spain.

FRIDAY, AUGUST 31

Occupied Germany – Arrest of F.M.s von Brauchitsch and von Manstein.
Diplomacy – USA re-establishes diplomatic relations with Finland.

SATURDAY, SEPTEMBER 1

Home Front: Italy – Polish cemetery at Monte Cassino dedicated.

SUNDAY, SEPTEMBER 2

Diplomacy – **SURRENDER DOCUMENT SIGNED BY JAPANESE AND ALLIED LEADERS** (headed by MacArthur and Foreign Min. Shigemitsu) aboard battleship *Missouri* in Tokyo Bay.

Above: *Japanese Foreign Minister Shigemitsu about to sign the surrender aboard USS* Missouri.

Occupied Japan – Op. Blacklist: US 6th and 8th Armies begin landing.
Home Front: USA – VJ-Day celebrations.
Indo-China – Ho Chi Minh proclaims Democratic Republic of Vietnam in Hanoi.

Shipping Losses 1945
Allied and Neutral: 105 ships totalling 445,864 t.

MONDAY, SEPTEMBER 3

Philippines – Surrender of Japanese forces, under Gen. Yamashita.

MOUNTBATTEN, Louis (Francis Albert Victor Nicholas) (1900-1979)
British: *Admiral of the Fleet, Earl Mountbatten of Burma, Marquis of Milford Haven*

Great war hero and statesman. Heroic exploits as commander of destroyer HMS *Kelly* inspired celebrated Noel Coward/David Lean movie, 'In Which We Serve' (1942). As Supreme Allied Commander, SE. Asia, his diplomatic skill, tact, charm and obvious concern for troops' morale and general welfare, paid rich dividends.

Born at Windsor, June 25, 1900, son of Admiral Prince Louis of Battenberg (known as Mountbatten from 1917); great-grandson of Queen Victoria and related to most of royal families of Europe. Educated at Royal Naval College, Dartmouth. Midshipman aboard battlecruiser HMS *Lion* and battleship HMS *Queen Elizabeth*, 1916-17; Sub-Lt. in HM subs. *K.6* and *P.31* (1918); became Lt., 1920. Aboard HMS *Renown* and *Repulse* during Prince of Wales' tours to Australasia and the Far East, 1920-21. Signals officer and instructor with Home and Med. fleets, 1926-33; promoted to Cdr. 1932.

In command of destroyer HMS *Daring* (1934) and 10 destroyers of 5th Flotilla, 1939-41 (flagship HMS *Kelly* sunk by *Stukas* in Med. off Crete May 1941); twice mentioned in despatches. Commanded aircraft carrier HMS *Illustrious*, 1941; awarded D.S.O. Commodore Combined Operations, 1941-42; Chief of Combined Ops. 1942-43; attached to British Chiefs of Staff; involved in early planning of amphibious invasion of France. SAC, SE. Asia, 1943-46. Accepted Japanese surrender in Singapore, Sept. 12, 1945.

Last Viceroy of India, March-Aug. 1947; first Gov-Gen. of India, Aug. 1947-June 1948. Knight Commander of the Bath, 1945 and Knight of the Garter; Viscount, 1946; Earl Mountbatten of Burma and Baron Romsey, 1947. Personal aide-de-camp to Queen Elizabeth II, 1953-79. First Sea Lord, 1955-59. Chief of UK Defence Staff and Chairman of Chiefs of Staff Committee, 1959-65. Assassinated by Provisional IRA bomb aboard private motor cruiser, *Shadow V*, at Mullaghmore, Donegal Bay, Irish Republic, Aug. 27, 1979. State funeral in Westminster Abbey; buried at Romsey Abbey, Hampshire.

Philippines Losses
Japanese: 450,000. US: 62,143 inc. 13,700 dead.

TUESDAY, SEPTEMBER 4

Occupied Singapore – **BRITISH-INDIAN FORCES RETURN TO SINGAPORE.**
Diplomacy – Allies inform Spain that they intend to re-establish international zone of Tangier.

WEDNESDAY, SEPTEMBER 5

Home Front: USA – State Dept. alleges that Japanese Govt. ignored 19 US protests against atrocities committed against American troops.

THURSDAY, SEPTEMBER 6

Diplomacy – Unconditional surrender of strong Japanese forces in SW. Pacific signed aboard British carrier *Glory* off Rabaul.
Occupied Germany – Eisenhower lifts Press censorship.
Home Front: USA – Vice-Adm. John S. McCain, ex-cdr. of US Navy's TF 58, dies of heart attack; aged 61.

FRIDAY, SEPTEMBER 7

Occupied Germany – Allied Victory Parade in Berlin.

SATURDAY, SEPTEMBER 8

Occupied Japan – 1st US Cavalry Div. enters Tokyo.
Occupied Korea – Americans land at Inchon.

SUNDAY, SEPTEMBER 9

China – **MILLION-STRONG JAPANESE FORCES IN CHINA, FORMOSA AND N. VIETNAM SURRENDER** at Nanking, thus ending conflict which has killed at least 10,400,000 since July 7, 1937.
Manchuria – 594,000 Japanese troops, inc. 148 generals, now in Russian hands.
Occupied Korea – Japanese forces surrender at Seoul. Japanese administrators to remain in office.
Sea War – Op. Zipper: Indian forces land on W. coast of Malaya (Sept. 9-12).
Home Front: Canada – Meat rationing reintroduced to assure adequate exports to UK and Europe.
Home Front: USA – **OP. MAGIC CARPET.** 1,307,859 US servicemen return home from Pacific aboard fleet that eventually totals 369 warships (ends March 1946). First day of the op. is marred by typhoon 'Louisa', which batters Okinawa area.

MONDAY, SEPTEMBER 10

Occupied Japan – MacArthur orders dissolution of Imperial GHQ and imposes censorship.

TUESDAY, SEPTEMBER 11

Occupied Japan – Former P.M. Tojo attempts suicide in attempt to escape arrest on war crimes charges.

WEDNESDAY, SEPTEMBER 12

Diplomacy – **SURRENDER OF JAPANESE FORCES IN SE. ASIA** at Singapore.
Occupied Japan – Suicide of F.M. Sugiyama, CinC Japanese Home Army.

THURSDAY, SEPTEMBER 13

Burma – Surrender of Japanese forces at Rangoon (CinC Gen. Kimura surrenders Oct. 24, 1945).
New Guinea – Lt.-Gen. Adachi of Japanese 18th Army surrenders on Wom airfield, near Wewak.
Occupied Germany – British military authorities publish captured *Gestapo* 'deathlist' of 2,300 British and Allied notables, ranging from Churchill and the Chief Rabbi to Jacob Epstein, Noël Coward and leaders of French, Polish and Czech govts.-in-exile.

FRIDAY, SEPTEMBER 14

Occupied Dutch E. Indies – Japanese garrison of Celebes surrenders at Menado.

SATURDAY, SEPTEMBER 15

Home Front: USA – Hurricane ravages S. Florida and Bahamas; 366 planes and 25 blimps destroyed at Richmond Naval Air Station, Fla.

SUNDAY, SEPTEMBER 16

Occupied Hong Kong – Surrender of Japanese forces at Hong Kong.

MONDAY, SEPTEMBER 17

China – Nationalist Chinese occupy Peking.
Occupied Germany – Josef Kramer and 44 other *SS* officers stand trial at Lüneburg on charges of conspiracy to commit mass murder at Auschwitz and Belsen.

TUESDAY, SEPTEMBER 18

Home Front: USA – Henry L. Stimson resigns as Sec. for War; succeeded by R.B. Patterson.

WEDNESDAY, SEPTEMBER 19

Occupied Indo-China – British and French forces suppress Vietnamese nationalist insurgents at Saigon.
Home Front: Britain – 'Lord Haw-Haw' sentenced to death at the Old Bailey, London.

THURSDAY, SEPTEMBER 20

Sea War: Pacific – British and US warships arrive at Shanghai.

FRIDAY, SEPTEMBER 21

Home Front: India – Congress Party demands that SE. Asia be freed from 'Imperialist domination'.

SATURDAY, SEPTEMBER 22

Home Front: Britain – Aircraft carrier *Hercules* launched on the Tyne (joins RIN in 1961, as *Vikrant)*.

SUNDAY, SEPTEMBER 23

Diplomacy – Egypt demands British withdrawal from the Sudan prior to its incorporation with Egypt.

MONDAY, SEPTEMBER 24

Home Front: USA – Elevator operators of 2,000 sky-scrapers and other buildings in Manhattan on strike.

TUESDAY, SEPTEMBER 25

Occupied Germany – Nazi Party and all German armed forces declared illegal.

WEDNESDAY, SEPTEMBER 26

Indian Ocean – Japanese on Andaman Is. surrender to RIN sloop *Narbada*.
Argentina – State of siege declared.

THURSDAY, SEPTEMBER 27

Occupied Japan – Emperor Hirohito visits Gen. MacArthur in Tokyo.

FRIDAY, SEPTEMBER 28

Occupied Germany – Patton ridicules 'de-nazification' programme in Bavaria.

SATURDAY, SEPTEMBER 29

Occupied Dutch E. Indies – British troops land in Java to combat rebellious Nationalists.
Argentina – 500,000 demonstrate against Perón in Buenos Aires.

SUNDAY, SEPTEMBER 30

Home Front: Britain – Bourne End (Hemel Hempstead) rail disaster: 44 killed, 88 injured.
Home Front: China – US Marines land at Tientsin.

TUESDAY, NOVEMBER 20

Nuremburg Trials ('Trial of German Major War Criminals') begin in Palace of Justice at Nuremburg (end Oct. 1, 1946).

1946

FRIDAY, MAY 3

Tokyo War Crimes Trial (ends Nov. 12, 1948).

MONDAY, JULY 29

Paris Peace Conference draws up peace treaties between the Allies and Italy, Hungary, Rumania, Bulgaria and Finland (ends Oct. 14).

TUESDAY, OCTOBER 1

Nuremburg Trials end: Bormann, Frank, Frick, Göring, Jodl, Kaltenbrunner, Keitel, Ribbentrop, Rosenberg, Sauckel, Streicher and Seyss-Inquart sentenced to death by hanging; Funk, Hess, Raeder, von Schirach, Speer, von Neurath and Dönitz receive prison terms of 10 years to life. Schacht, von Papen and Fritsche acquitted.

TUESDAY, DECEMBER 31

Pres. Truman terminates 'State of Hostilities' between USA and former Axis Powers.

1947

MONDAY, FEBRUARY 10

Signature of Peace Treaties drawn up at Paris Conference.

1948

WEDNESDAY, NOVEMBER 12

Tokyo War Crimes Trial ends. Tojo and 7 others sentenced to death; 17 defendants receive prison sentences.

1951

MONDAY, JULY 2

State of War between Britain and Germany officially terminated.

SATURDAY, SEPTEMBER 8

Treaty of San Francisco ends state of war between Japan and USA and 48 other non-Communist states.

THE COST OF WAR

JEWISH DEAD

Baltic States (Estonia, Latvia, Lithuania)	200,000
Belgium and Luxemburg	75,000
Bulgaria	30,000
Czechoslovakia	310,000
France	120,000
Germany (1933-1945)	330,000
Greece	60,000
Hungary	400,000
Italy	12,000
Netherlands	117,000
Norway and Denmark	1,000
Poland	3,000,000†
Rumania	230,000
USSR	700,000
Yugoslavia	60,000
Grand Total	5,645,000

All figures are estimates

† includes 1,950,000 killed at Auschwitz and other camps; 550,000 killed, starved or died of disease in Warsaw and other ghettoes; and 500,000 killed by mobile extermination squads.

WARTIME EXPENDITURE

Great Britain	£30,000,000,000
Belgium	£812,500,000
Canada	£3,920,000,000
China	†
Czechoslovakia	over £200,000,000
France	£3,750,000,000
Germany	£67,500,000,000
Greece	over £55,000,000
Italy	£23,500,000,000
Japan	£14,000,000,000
Latin American countries	£250,000,000
Netherlands	£231,250,000
Poland	£387,500,000
USSR	£48,000,000,000
USA	£85,372,750,000
Yugoslavia	over £50,000,000

All figures are estimates in 1946 pounds (£) sterling.
£1 (1946) = approx. US $4 (1946) = approx. £8 (1980).
† no reliable data; at least equal to figure for USSR.

AIRCRAFT LOST IN ACTION

Germany	c. 28,000
Great Britain	15,992
Italy	5,272
Japan	over 31,500
USSR	56,000
USA	22,948

MILITARY AND CIVILIAN CASUALTIES

	Killed in action, or died of wounds	Wounded	Captured or missing	Civilian deaths†
ALLIED POWERS				
British Empire and Commonwealth total	373,372	475,047	251,724	93,423
Great Britain	264,443	277,077	213,919	92,673††
Australia	23,365	39,803	32,393	c.250
Canada	37,476	53,174	10,888	–
India	24,338	64,354	91,243	c.500
New Zealand	10,033	19,314	10,582	–
South Africa	6,840	14,363	16,430	–
British Colonies	6,877	6,972	22,323	–
Belgium	7,760	–	–	76,000
Brazil	943	4,222	–	c.100
China	c.2,200,000	c.1,800,000	–	c.20,000,000
Czechoslovakia	10,000	–	–	215,000
Denmark	1,800	–	–	c.2,000
France	210,671	400,000	–	350,000
Greece	73,700	–	–	325,000
Netherlands	6,238	c.2,860	–	200,000
Norway	1,000	–	–	7,000
Philippines	27,000	–	–	91,000
Poland	c.123,178	c.236,606	c.1,000,000	c.5,675,000
USSR	c.7,500,000†††	–	c.6,000,000	c.7,000,000
USA	292,131	671,801	139,709	6,000
Yugoslavia	410,000	425,000	–	1,200,000
ALLIED TOTALS	11,237,793	4,015,536	7,391,433	35,240,523
AXIS POWERS				
Germany	c.3,500,000	c.5,000,000	c.3,400,000	c.780,000
Italy	242,232	c.66,000	c.350,000	c.152,941
Japan	c.1,219,000	c.4,000,000	c.810,000	c.672,000
Bulgaria	10,000	–	–	10,000
Finland	82,000	50,000	–	2,000
Hungary	140,000	–	170,000	290,000
Rumania	300,000	–	100,000	465,000
AXIS TOTALS	5,493,232	9,116,000	4,830,000	2,371,941
GRAND TOTALS	16,731,025	13,131,536	12,221,433	37,612,464

† estimates including Jews and merchant marine casualties.
†† includes 60,447 killed by aerial bombardment, 148 by cross-Channel guns, 30,248 in Merchant Navy, 1,206 in Home Guard and 624 in Women's Auxiliary.
††† estimates vary hugely from 6,000,000 to 7,500,000 in official Soviet figures to 13,600,000 (including 2,600,000 PoW deaths), giving a widely-quoted total of over 20,000,000 Soviet military and civilian deaths.

WARSHIP LOSSES

	Battleships and battlecruisers	Aircraft carriers†	Heavy cruisers	Light cruisers	Destroyers	Submarines
Great Britain and British Commonwealth	5	10	4	33	165	79
France	4	1	4	6	58††	58
Germany	7†††	1	2	4	28	998††††
Italy	3	2	9	12	56	112
Japan	11	29	17	24	134	130
Netherlands	—	—	—	3	11	16
USSR	2	—	1	—	20	108
USA	2†††††	11	7	3	70	52

† includes escort carriers (ex-mercantile) and seaplane carriers.
†† includes 26 *contre-torpilleurs* ('super-destroyers').
††† includes pocket-battleships.
†††† includes 217 scuttled in 1945.
††††† only 2 of the 5 battleships sunk at Pearl Harbor were total losses.

GLOSSARY

AA Anti-aircraft (guns or gunfire)
AAF Army Air Force
Abn. div. Airborne division
Abwehr Espionage, counter-espionage and sabotage service of German High Command (OKW)
ACM Air Chief Marshal (RAF)
Adm. Admiral
AEF Allied Expeditionary Force
AF Air Force
Afrika Korps see DAK
AFV Armoured fighting vehicle
AMC Armed merchant cruiser
AOCinC Air Officer Commanding-in-Chief (RAF)
AP Armour-piecing
Ar Arado, such as Ar 234 twin-engine jet bomber
Armd. Armoured
Armd. div. Armoured division. British: 290 tanks and 14,964 men (1943-45). US: 263 tanks and 10,937 men (1943-45). Soviet tank corps: 189 tanks and 10,500 men. German: *see Panzer* div.
Armée de l'Air French Air Force
ARP Air Raid Precautions
A/S Anti-submarine
ATS Auxiliary Territorial Service (British)
AVG American Volunteer Group
B Bomber, such as B-17 Boeing Fortress four-engine heavy bomber.
BBC British Broadcasting Corporation
BEF British Expeditionary Force
BF Baltic Front: Soviet army group operating on northern part of the Russian Front.
Blitz The British nickname for German night bombing offensive against London and other cities, Sept. 1940-May 1941.
Blitzkrieg ('Lightning War') Allied-coined word for German concept of swift and decisive military victory (1939-42).
Bn. Battalion, unit of 600-1,000 infantry, 20-60 tanks, 12-48 guns.
Bomb. Sqn. Bombardment Squadron (USAAF)
BRF Byelorussian Front: Soviet army group operating on central part of the Russian Front.
Brig. Brigade, unit of usually 3 bns. or 3 regts. (1,500-4,000 men if infantry, 60-226 tanks if armour).
Brig.-Gen. Brigadier-General (US rank)
c. circa, approximately
C Cargo, such as C-47 Douglas Dakota DC-3 twin-engine transport.
CAM Catapult Armed Merchantman, ship equipped with Hurricane fighter launched by catapult.
Capt. Captain
CBI China-Burma-India (theatre of war)
CCS Combined Chiefs of Staff
Cdr. Commander, rank and position
Cdre. Commodore
CG Commanding General
CGM Conspicious Gallantry Medal

Cmnd. Command
CMG Congressional Medal of Honor: highest US military decoration
CO Commanding Officer
COAGS Chief of Army General Staff
COGS Chief of General Staff
Col. Colonel
Commissar Senior Communist Party official in the Soviet Union
Comp. Company
CONS Chief of Naval Staff
Cons. Conservative (political party)
Corps Several divisions operating in concert
COS Chief of Staff
Cpl. Corporal
CW. British westbound Channel coastal convoy
DA Delayed Action
DAF Desert Air Force
DAK Deutsches Afrika Korps ('German Africa Corps'): the German motorized part of Rommel's forces, 1941-43.
Div. Division
Division, Infantry German: 17,200 men and 74 guns (1939-44); 12,352 men and 72 guns (1944). French: 16,500 men and 60 guns (1939-40). British: 13,600 men and 72 guns (1939-40); 18,347 men and 72 guns (1943-45). Soviet: 17,500 men and 78 guns (1939-40); 14,500 and 78 guns (1941-42); 9,200 men and 54 guns (1943-45). US: 15,289 men and 66 guns (1943-45). Japanese: 20,000 men and 66 guns.
Do Dornier, such as Do 17 twin-engine bomber, nicknamed the 'Flying Pencil.'
Duce, Il Leader (Italian)
EAM Greek National Liberation Front (Communist), formed Sept. 27, 1941.
E-boat Allied term for German motor torpedo boat, more correctly designated 'S-boat' (*q.v.*)
EDES Greek National Democratic Army
Einsatzgruppe Special duty (motorized) battalion of *SS* for operating in Occupied Eastern Europe, especially for the liquidation of Jews, partisans and other 'dangerous elements'.
ELAS Greek People's National Army of Liberation (Communist), created Dec.1942
Enigma German cipher machine
ENSA Entertainments National Service Association (British)
Erpr. Grp. Erprobungsgruppe ('experimental group'), *Luftwaffe* unit
Escort carrier Allied auxiliary aircraft carrier from 1941; usually a converted oil tanker or cargo ship.
FAA Fleet Air Arm (British)
FAT *Feder Apparat Torpedo:* German torpedo pre-set to approach target on circuitous course ('pattern running').
FBI Federal Bureau of Investigation (US)
FEAF Far East Air Force (US)
FEF Far East Front: Soviet army group

operating on Manchurian front, Aug. 1945.
FF Free French (supporters of Gen. de Gaulle)
FFI Free French Forces of the Interior
Flt. Lt. Flight Lieutenant
Flt. Sgt. Flight Sergeant
Force de raide Fast Striking Force, French Navy, 1939-40
F.M. Field-Marshal
FW Focke-Wulf, such as FW 190 single-engine fighter and FW 200 four-engine maritime recce bomber (Condor).
Gauleiter Chief Nazi official in a *Gau* (territorial division of the Reich)
Gds Guards
Gestapo *Geheime Staatspolizei* ('Secret State Police')
GHQ General Headquarters
GOC General Officer Commanding
GOCinC General Officer Commanding-in-Chief
Grp. group or *gruppe* (German)
Grp. Capt. Group Captain
HE High Explosive
He Heinkel, such as He 111 twin-engine medium bomber and He 115 twin-engine torpedo/recce seaplane.
HG. Gibraltar-Britain convoy
HMAS His Majesty's Australian Ship
HMCS His Majesty's Canadian Ship
HMIS His Majesty's Indian Ship
HMNZS His Majesty's New Zealand Ship
HMS His Majesty's Ship
HM Sub. His Majesty's Submarine
Hptm. Hauptmann (Captain); German
Hs Henschel, such as Hs 129 twin-engine ground attack plane.
HX. Halifax (Canada) or New York-Britain convoy
I Japanese 'cruiser'-type submarine
IB Incendiary bomb
Inf. Infantry
Inf. div. Infantry division
JAAF Japanese Army Air Force
JCS Joint Chiefs of Staff (US)
JG Jagdgeschwader, Luftwaffe fighter wing
JNAF Japanese Naval Air Force
Ju Junkers, such as Ju 52 three-engine transport, Ju 87 (*see Stuka*) and Ju 88 twin-engine multi-role aircraft.
JW. Britain-N. Russia convoys from Dec. 1942
Katyusha Multiple rocket-launchers of the Red Army; nickname from contemporary popular song 'Little Kate'.
K. fl. Gr. Küstenfliegergruppe, Luftwaffe coastal air group
KG Kampfgeschwader, Luftwaffe bomber wing
K. Gr. Kampfgruppe, Luftwaffe bomber group
Ki *Katai* (airframe): each JAAF aircraft type was designated by letters Ki, followed by a number (e.g. Ki-43 fighter).

KONR Committee for the Liberation of the Peoples of Russia; pro-Nazi Russian organization

Lab. Labour (political party)

LC Landing Craft

Lib. Liberal (political party)

'Little Blitz' British nickname for German night bombing raids on London, Jan.-April 1944 (also known as the 'Baby Blitz').

LST Landing Ship Tank

Lt. Lieutenant

Lt.-Cdr. Lieutenant-Commander

Lt.-Col. Lieutenant-Colonel

Lt.-Gen. Lieutenant-General

Luftflotte German Air Fleet: comprised several *Fliegerkorps* (Air Corps) each consisting of 4-6 *geschwadern* (wings).

Luftwaffe German Air Force (literally, 'Air Weapon')

M. Million

Maginot Line French belt of fortifications along German border from Switzerland to Luxembourg, built 1927-35.

Maj.-Gen. Major-General

Me Messerschmitt, such as Me 109 single-engine fighter.

MGB Motor Gun Boat

Min. Minister

Molotov Cocktail Crude home-made petrol bomb developed in the Spanish Civil War. Often consisting of a bottle filled with inflammable liquid with a strip of cloth inserted in the neck. The weapon got its name from Finnish ridicule of the Soviet Foreign Minister during the Winter War.

MP Military Police

M.P. Member of Parliament

MT Motor Transport

MTB Motor Torpedo Boat

MV Motor Vessel (diesel-engine merchant ship)

Nazi *Nationalsozialistiche Deutsche Arbeiterpartei* ('National Socialist German Workers' Party')

NKVD *Narodny Komisariat Vnutrennykh Del* ('People's Commissariat for Internal Affairs'), the Stalinist secret police

OB. Outwardbound convoy, Liverpool-Western Approaches

Obergruppenführer *SS* Lieutenant-General (German)

Oberleutnant Lieutenant (German)

Oberst Colonel (German)

Obersturmführer *SS* 1st Lieutenant (German)

OC Officer Commanding

OG. Britain-Gibraltar convoy

OKH *Oberkommando des Heeres,* High Command of the German Army

OKW *Oberkommando der Wehrmacht,* High Command of the German Armed Forces

ON. Britain-N. America convoy

Op., ops. Operation, operations

P Pursuit, letter designating USAAF fighters such as twin-engine P-38 Lockheed Lightning.

PAA *Panzer Armee Afrika:* designation of Rommel's Axis forces in N. Africa from Jan. 30, 1942.

Pac. Pacific

Panzer **division** 328 tanks and 11,790 men (1939); 276 tanks and 3,000 vehicles (1940); 165 tanks and 15,600 men (1941); 103 tanks, 2,685 vehicles and 13,725 men (1944).

Pen. Peninsula

'Phoney War' US newspaper term for the stalemate on the Western Front, Sept. 3, 1939-May 10, 1940. Nicknamed the 'Twilight War' (Churchill); *Drôle de Guerre* (French Army); *Sitzkrieg* (German Army).

Pocket battleships Three hybrid warships (6 x 11 inch guns and diesel engines) built by Germany (1931-34) to circumvent the Versailles Treaty restrictions.

PoW Prisoner of War

PQ. Britain-N. Russia Arctic Convoy, Sept. 1941-Sept. 1942.

Pte. Private

PR Photo-reconnaissance

PT Patrol Torpedo Boat (US Navy Motor Torpedo Boat)

Pz *Panzer* (armour), abbreviation for *Panzerkampfwagen* (armoured fighting vehicle or tank) normally abbreviated to *PzKpfw* or *PzKw.*

QP. N. Russia-Britain Arctic Convoy, Aug. 1941-Nov. 1942

Quisling Vidkun Quisling, leader of small Norwegian Nazi party and head of collaborationist 'puppet' government in Norway during World War II. Term 'quisling' consequently applied (with contempt) to any collaborationist organization or individual in other countries.

q.v. quod vide, which see

RA. N. Russia-Britain convoys from Dec. 1942

RAAF Royal Australian Air Force

RAF Royal Air Force (British)

RCAF Royal Canadian Air Force

RCN Royal Canadian Navy

Rear-Adm. Rear-Admiral

Regt. Regiment, unit of 3 bns. (2,000-3,500 men or 24-54 guns or 70-100 tanks)

Reichskommissar Senior Nazi administrator of occupied territory

RIN Royal Indian Navy

RM Royal Marines (British)

R.Neths.N Royal Netherlands Navy

RNN Royal Norwegian Navy

RNZAF Royal New Zealand Air Force

ROA Russian Army of Liberation; pro-Nazi organization

RO Small Japanese coastal submarine

S Schnellboot ('Fast Boat'): German motor torpedo boat or E-boat *(q.v.)*

SAC Supreme Allied Command(er)

SC. Slow Convoy

SD *Sicherheitsdienst,* Nazi Party security service

SEAC South-East Asia Command

SG. Support Group (Allied naval escorts)

SHAEF Supreme Headquarters Allied Expeditionary Force

Siegfried Line German system of fortifications built opposite the Maginot Line, 1938-40 under direction of Dr Todt.

SL. Sierra Leone (W. Africa)-Britain convoy

SOE Special Operations Executive, British intelligence organization for resistance and sabotage in occupied countries.

SP Self-propelled gun. German *Sturmgeschütz* (assault gun).

Sqn. Ldr. Squadron Leader

SS Steamship

SS *Schutz Staffeln* ('Protection Detachments'). Nazi 'elite corps, which carried out special police duties'.

St.G. *Stukageschwader, Luftwaffe* dive-bomber wing

Stalag German camp for Prisoners of War

Stavka GHQ of the Soviet High Command

Stuka *Sturzkampfflugzeug* ('dive-bomber'): German term applied to all dive-bombers, but which quickly became synonymous with the notorious Junkers Ju 87 as used here.

Sub-Lt. Sub-Lieutenant

T *Torpedoboot:* German torpedo boat, equivalent of a small destroyer

t. tonne

T-34 Soviet medium tank.

TAF Tactical Air Force

TBF Trans-Baikal Front: Soviet army group operating on the Manchurian front, Aug. 1945

TF Task Force (naval)

TG Task Group (naval)

U, U-boat *Unterseeboot:* submarine (German)

UF Ukrainian Front: Soviet army group operating on southern part of the front.

Ultra British security classification for the intelligence from reading German Enigma cipher messages.

USAAC United States Army Air Corps, till June 20, 1941

USAAF United States Army Air Force, from June 20, 1941

USMC United States Marine Corps

USN United States Navy

USS United States Ship

V-1 *Vergeltungswaffe Ein* ('Revenge Weapon Number 1'). German propaganda designation of *Fieseler FzG 76* jet-propelled flying bomb.

V-2 *Vergeltungswaffe Zwei* ('Revenge Weapon Number 2'). German propaganda designation of A-4 long-range supersonic missile.

V.-Adm. Vice-Admiral

V.C. Victoria Cross, highest British award for gallantry

Vichy French Supporters of semi-independent French government established by Marshal Pétain at Vichy in unoccupied France.

Volkssturm 'People's Storm': German equivalent of British Home Guard

Waffen-SS Armed Protection Detachments, military wing of Himmler's *SS* from June 1940

Wehrmacht German armed forces

WPB War Production Board (US)

WS. Code-letters for Allied Atlantic troop convoy (taken from Churchill's first two initials)

Zero Mitsubishi A6M, Type O Japanese Navy fighter. Allied code-name 'Zeke'.

INDEX

NOTE: numbers in *italics* refer to illustrations

Pictures supplied by:
Associated Press: 190
Barnaby's Picture Library: 81T, 136
Bildarchiv Preussischer Kulturbesitz: 4, 37, 44, 59, 101, 108, 120/1, 143, 178, 184T
Bundesarchiv Koblenz: 10, 36/7, 68, 69, 107, 123T
Fox Photos: 7, 9, 18, 19, 23, 28, 30/1, 34, 43, 46, 49, 72, 75, 87, 93, 134, 146T, 165, 171, 172, 182, 192T
Imperial War Museum: 29, 114, 118, 130, 133T, 140
Jennifer Moore Personality Picture Library: 71T, 78T, 85T, 127B, 166
Keystone: 13, 16, 17, 21, 40/1, 42B, 50B, 51, 56B, 60, 61, 62, 73, 77, 88, 98, 102, 105, 106, 127T, 142T, 148, 149, 151, 160, 162, 176, 183, 185, 186, 188, 192B
Military Archive and Research Service (MARS, London): 56T, 78B, 80/1, 81B, 91, 92, 96/7, 97, 100, 103, 104/5, 112/3, 124, 128, 132/3, 152, 160/1, 181, 187, 189
Novosti: 123B
Popperfoto: 38, 47, 65, 86R, 110, 111, 116/7, 150, 177
Süddeutscher Verlag: 1, 11, 67, 74, 109, 122/3
US Army: 168
US Coastguard: 157

Maps by Illustra Design
Newspaper Headlines supplied by John Frost, Marshall Cavendish and the British Library Newspaper Library, Colindale.

Principal Sources
Bekker, Cajus *The Luftwaffe War Diaries* (Macdonald and Janes, London 1969).
Britannica Books of the Year 1942-1947 (Encyclopædia Britannica, London).
Chronology of the Second World War (Royal Institute of International Affairs, London 1947).
Churchill, Winston S. *The Second World War,* 6 vols (Cassell, London 1948-54).
Hammerton, Sir John (ed) *The Second Great War,* 9 vols (Amalgamated Press, London 1940-47).
Hinsley, F. H. *British Intelligence in the Second World War,* vol 1 (HMSO, London 1979).
Irving, David *Hitler's War* (Hodder, London 1977).
Keesing's Contemporary Archives (Bath 1937-46).
Rohwer, Jürgen and Hummelchen, G. *Chronology of the War at Sea 1939-1945,* 2 vols (Ian Allan, London 1972-74).
Thompson, Lawrence *1940: Year of History, Year of Legend* (Collins, London 1968).
Trevor-Roper, Hugh *Hitler's War Directives 1939-1945* (Sidgwick, London 1954).
Williams, Mary H. *US Army Chronology 1941-1945* (Department of the Army, Washington D.C. 1960).

Acknowledgements
We are grateful to the following publishers for their kind permission to quote from the books listed below:
Clarkson N. Potter Inc.; *The Great Sea War,* E. B. Potter and Admiral Chester W. Nimitz (Bramhall House, 1960)
Doubleday & Company Inc.; *Crusade in Europe,* Dwight D. Eisenhower (Doubleday, New York 1948)
Granada Publishing Ltd.; *The Beginning of the Road,* Marshal Vasili I. Chuikov (MacGibbon and Kee, London 1963)